Los Angeles Times

1984 OLYMPIC SPORTS PAGES
INTRODUCTION BY BILL DWYRE, SPORTS EDITOR, *LOS ANGELES TIMES*

HARRY N. ABRAMS, INC., PUBLISHERS, NEW YORK

Editor: Robert Morton
Designers: Bob McKee and Carolyn Carpenter

Library of Congress Catalog Card Number: 84-70472
ISBN 0-8109-1286-4
Copyright © 1984 *Los Angeles Times*

Published in 1984 by Harry N. Abrams, Incorporated, New York
All rights reserved. No part of the contents of this book may be
reproduced without the written consent of the publishers

Printed and bound in the United States of America

The publishers wish to thank the following persons for their invalu-
able help in the preparation of this book: John L. Snyder, Judith
Wilson, Max Westphalen, Nancy Kennedy, and Gary May.

INTRODUCTION

At 10:03 P.M. on Monday, August 13, Thomas Morphew of the *Los Angeles Times* pasted down the last correction of the last page of the last section of OLYMPICS '84, the special sports supplement we had published since July 22. Page 24 of the forty-page section of August 14 was headed for the presses, leaving behind a small group of people who suddenly felt as if someone had just found the key to the prison door.

Newspaper people are, by necessity, unemotional and unsentimental. But this was a moment unlike any ever experienced by the people in that room—and the collective years of newspaper experience on hand at that moment probably exceeded 150 years. So we applauded, feeling a little silly while we did it, but feeling the need to do so nonetheless.

And one by one, I shook their hands: Dave Moylan, the *Times*'s associate sports editor and the main editorial production supervisor throughout the twenty-four-day run of OLYMPICS '84; Jim Rhode and Rick Jaffe, two of the brightest young makeup men (people who design how pages look) in the business; Bob Lochner, John Cherwa, Reid Grosky, and Paul Gelormino, the news editors in charge of running the copy desk and getting the type down to the makeup men in correct and usable form; and John Foley, the *Times*'s deputy managing editor, who, along with Mike Chaplin from business news and Terry Redknapp from the feature department, had spearheaded our color photo production, an unprecedented undertaking by the *Times*.

And so, after three years of planning and four weeks of virtually nonstop work, perhaps the largest project ever for an American sports department had come to an end.

It hadn't been easy, it hadn't really been fun. But the creation and production of OLYMPICS '84 had been rewarding. Also, it had exceeded by miles our wildest expectations of success.

Circulation figures rose by nearly 100,000 during the 24 days that OLYMPICS '84 was published. Television stations interviewed members of the staff; *Newsweek* magazine did a highly favorable article about the project; and hundreds of letters from readers praised what had been done—a reader response almost unheard of in the newspaper business, where people write in only if they are angry with your product.

OLYMPICS '84 ran from July 22 through August 14. The Los Angeles Olympic Games ran from July 28 through August 12. Both went much more smoothly than anticipated.

How this rare newspaper extravaganza came to pass, and why, involve many years and hundreds of people. I will try to condense the story as best I can.

When Los Angeles was awarded the 1984 Olympics in 1978, the *Times* had the foresight to put somebody on the story immediately. That somebody was Ken Reich, a veteran political reporter, who took on the assignment with the same energy that he took on corruption in politics.

Before long Reich had become an internationally known expert on the inner workings of the Olympics, and he traveled the world to attend scores of International Olympic Committee meetings. For years the joke in the newsroom was that the *Times*'s budget for Reich's coverage of the Olympics was higher than Peter Ueberroth's budget for putting them on.

While Reich wrote about the Olympics, others began planning how the paper would handle the actual coverage of the event.

Bill Shirley was sports editor of the *Times* from the mid-1960s until June of 1981, when he was named national sports correspondent. As one of his first duties, Shirley was assigned to write a memo about how the *Times* might cover the '84 Olympics. He completed his Olympic project in about a month, and the memo that was turned in to editor Bill Thomas became the starting point for OLYMPICS '84.

As Shirley's replacement in the sports editor's office, I became responsible for the actual execution of the project. And so, from late summer 1981 until the time that last page was sent to press on August 13, the Los Angeles Olympics and its projected coverage by one of the largest papers in the world became a little cloud that was always right there, a few feet over my head.

The various stages of the project included a definition of whether it would be separate from a daily sports section, how much involvement the metropolitan news department (known to us as Metro) would have in its production, how large a section it could be and still attract sufficient advertising support to make it profitable, and how much use would be made of color advertising and color news photos.

Procrastination was not allowed. So many segments of the company were involved with the Olympics and so many people realized what vast marketing and journalistic potential an Olympic Games provided for a newspaper of the *Times*'s size and stature that the project moved ahead continually. There was very little patience with anyone who said that there was plenty of time, so no need to hurry.

I set the publication schedule for the section, which was to run on twenty-four consecutive days. I felt that a full week's head start on the competition, and a full week's chance to become habit reading, would take us into the Games well established as *the* newspaper of the Olympics. I also felt, having attended the Olympics in Montreal and having felt the wave of emotion and sentimentality as the Games closed, that an extra day at the end would capture for the readers more of those feelings.

I received little resistance to that. Actually, I received little resistance to anything I wanted to do. I never felt that upper management was fighting me on anything. Mostly, they seemed anxious to help with ideas, manpower, and even money. In the newspaper business that is a rare situation, especially in reference to the latter two things.

Metro's involvement was hard to pin down at first. But there was very little power brokering, and in the end a Metro Olympic staff headed by Frank Sotomayor and Craig Turner worked well with the sports staff while coordinating coverage of the nonsports news of the Olympics. The expectations—correct as they turned out—were that the Olympics would be, for the sixteen days of competition, 99% a sports story. So the OLYMPICS '84 section was designed to be 99% a sports section. And that's what it turned out to be.

The size of the section was determined at first by hit and miss. The advertising department needed a prototype to show advertisers what this thing might look like. So, to that end, I sat down with a tentative Olympic schedule for one of the projected busiest days of the Games and made up dummy headlines and stories for a section that covered all the sports of that day. I included other features such as a picture page, a forum page for letters, a giant map page showing all the venues of the Olympic sports, and three full pages for results and schedules near the back of the section. I asked for a 50–50 division between advertising space and news content, an unusual ratio at the *Times*, where ads normally take a bigger chunk. Then, from those rough drafts, Tom Trapnell and Ken Bruns of the *Times* art department polished the section and gave it consistency and structure, front to back.

The completed prototype was a thirty-two-page broadsheet section with full-color photography on the front page and a full-color ad on the back. The concept struck enough of a chord with the advertising department to have them quickly talking about making it a forty-four-page section each day. I felt that filling a section was never as much of a problem as not having enough space to print the stories in hand, so I agreed to the forty-four pages. Also, advertising okayed a ratio close to the 50–50 proposal, a pleasant shock to me.

As soon as word got out in my sports department that I had committed us to a forty-four-page section for twenty-four days, with a 50–50 ad ratio, the status of my sanity became widely questioned. Once I had time to sit and think about it myself, the questions suddenly seemed quite valid. But I somehow remained confident that it could be achieved, even though the rallying cry around the sports desk was: "It'll never work!"

Once we had the prototype in our hands, the next steps were taken quickly and logically. One reporter was assigned to each Olympic sport, several of them to the major events such as track and field and swimming. Helping determine the assignments was George Kiseda of our sports department, who was named co-Olympic coordinator and who worked directly with me on the project. Reporters were assigned in February of 1983, after a memo had been circulated to the entire newsroom testing the interest of writers from outside the sports department. The assignments were made a year and a half ahead of the Games to give the reporters time to become experts in their individual sports. That idea, like so many of those that made OLYMPICS '84 work, was Kiseda's.

Making that many assignments that early was a gamble because we had no guarantee that the *Times* would be able to acquire the large number of Olympic press passes (called credentials) needed to allow each reporter to cover his or her event. But after much negotiating Richard Perleman of the Los Angeles Olympic Organizing Committee (LAOOC) awarded the *Times* forty-eight credentials from his local allotment, less than our request but a reasonable and workable number.

Soon reporters with Olympic assignments were coming up with story ideas on their beats, and we were sending them off to national and international events to increase their expertise. As Kiseda had hoped when he devised the plan, we had a staff of experts when the Games began on July 28.

In 1983, the *Times* sent twelve different reporters out of the country to cover international events related to the Olympics. In 1984, the *Times* covered every U.S. Olympic trial held, with the exception of rhythmic gymnastics, which was missed because of a schedule conflict.

As the Games got closer and closer, two problems knocked us off track for a while.

The first was our plan to run color photos on the front page of each OLYMPICS '84 section. To that end, we had begun to run color sports-action photos in the sports section each Monday morning.

It worked well at first, but the quality began to decrease as we got closer to the Games. We had new presses in each of our three plants, dedicated to producing the Olympic section each night, but the million-plus papers we sold daily meant that the presses were forced to run at a very high speed, making it difficult to maintain the quality of the color. Also, we had never produced color under strict time restraints, and the late-night events of the Olympics were certain to put us under deadline pressure with color production.

The sentiment in my department and in most of the newsroom was to drop the color and just give the readers the best black-and-white product possible. The sentiment in upper management, however, was that a commitment had been made to advertisers and to the general public, and we were going to stay with that color commitment. And so we did, mostly with success, thanks to Mike Feasy's color lab crew, Jim Wilson's photo crew, and Chuck Ryan's proud pressroom crews.

On the last day of the section, we ran twenty color photos, ten on the front page and ten more in a double-page ad in the middle of the section thanking all those involved in the Olympic movement. If somebody had suggested a month earlier that we would pull off twenty color photos in one section, we all would have laughed hysterically.

The second problem was out of our control. Well out.

On the morning of May 8, 1984, in Reston, Virginia, I led a discussion at the American Press Institute on the Olympics and the problems of covering such an event. The last question raised at that session of fellow sports editors was: "Do you think the Russians will come to the '84 Games?"

My answer was the same as it had been for many months: "Of course they'll come to L.A. They have too much at stake not to."

About forty-five minutes later, while I was eating lunch with other members of the panel, someone came in with the stunning news that the Russians had decided to boycott the Los Angeles Games.

For the next few weeks, the *Times* Olympic staff suffered from much the same malady that afflicted everyone connected with the Olympics. It was a form of depression, brought on by facing up to the reality that although your project may be huge—the biggest thing you have ever been involved with—it just wasn't going to be quite as big as you had hoped, nor quite as meaningful. We acted like a newspaper, dutifully reporting the significance the Soviet-bloc losses held for the overall athletic quality of the Games. But there was a general depression nevertheless.

Time seemed to heal that: time, and the press of business ahead. If there were still to be an Olympics, as it was obvious there would be, then we still had to give it our best shot. So we did.

I had moved out of the sports editor's office and into a special Olympic office with Kiseda in mid-April. Kiseda quickly labeled it the War Room. Every minute of ABC's telecast was taped in the War Room, and the room became a center for writers to double-check events or just plain hang out.

From this battlefront, we processed copy assigned long ago and targeted to run in the first week of the section. It was mainly feature material about past Olympians but also included pieces on likely medal winners in the '84 Games. A high percentage of story ideas came from Kiseda, a former writer and veteran newspaperman who knew more about the Olympics than many members of the LAOOC.

Friday, July 20, began the real endurance test. We started production of the first section, due out on Sunday, July 22. About a dozen staffers had moved into downtown hotels, and when the Games began a week later another two dozen or so joined them in hotels. Many Olympic writers also stayed in hotels near their venues in an attempt to avoid making long work days even longer with commuting time home and back.

Once the sections began hitting the streets, and once we began to have confidence in the color reproduction, adrenaline flowed freely and time passed fairly quickly.

As part of our considerable logistical support, the *Times* had installed telephones at each venue. But we also asked for a system of electronic paging beepers for instant contact with each writer. Neither Kiseda nor I had ever worked with this kind of system, but we quickly found out how valuable it was and ended up driving many writers crazy with our constant contacts and queries. One writer, Mike Penner, had a silent, vibrating "beeper" that once vibrated right off his bedside table and hit him on the head in the middle of a nap.

As the Games progressed, "being beeped" became kind of a status thing. Those reporters who weren't being beeped as often as others began to feel unloved and taken for granted. We cured some of that by beeping them at 1:00 A.M.

The first real crisis in the production of OLYMPICS '84 occurred on the night of July 31, the night the U.S. men's gymnastics team shocked everybody by upsetting China for the team gold medal. By the time that result was final, we had already committed to a nice, but somewhat ordinary color picture of a U.S. gymnast during a floor exercise. When the magnitude of the news story hit me, I knew that the reader, having seen the event on television and sharing the great emotion of the victorious team, would want an Olympic section the next morning that would reflect that emotion. And all we had was somebody doing a floor exercise.

All the celebration had taken place well past the time when we could shoot a color picture and get it back to the *Times*, processed, and ready to print. All I could hope for was a great black-and-white picture from our photographers who had stayed on the scene after the color film had been sent in. What I got was good, but not great, so the general feeling was to simply stay with the color, since dropping it and going to black-and-white would cause problems in the press room.

But at the last second, a great Associated Press black-and-white photo came through, showing the American team celebrating its great moment. And so, despite the hassle of dropping the color, we went to black-and-white. The next day the phones rang off the hook at the *Times*. People who hadn't seen color in the *Times* for fifty years had been spoiled by it in just over a week; they missed it.

We never went without a color photo on the front page for the rest of OLYMPICS '84. But had a similar news situation arisen, we would have dropped it again. I was determined that the news, not pretty color pictures, would dictate our choices.

Dave Moylan was the hero of that night of July 31, remaking the front page for the switch to black-and-white in less than ten minutes. He was also the hero a few nights later, when, well past deadline for color production and near the deadline for the front page to be off the floor, photographers Jayne Kamin and Joe Kennedy came rushing in with prize-winning photos of basketball player Pam McGee, a member of the United States's gold-medal team, hugging her twin sister Paula and putting her medal around Paula's neck. Pam and Paula had both been stars at USC, but only Pam had made the Olympic team, her twin left behind to watch and agonize. It was a poignant moment, captured beautifully on film. This time, Moylan remade the page while working around the color photo already there. And once again, the edition somehow went off on time.

Perhaps the most rewarding night of all for me also involved Kamin and Kennedy. It was the night Zola Budd and Mary Decker tangled and Decker fell to the track infield, injured and out of the race she had been aiming at for a lifetime. The fall occurred at a place on the coliseum track away from most credentialed photographers. Kamin was about thirty yards away from the incident and she knew she didn't have the shot. So she quickly turned and scanned the crowd to see if she could find somebody who had.

She saw Hiram Clawson of Santa Barbara, sitting in the stands exactly opposite the spot where Decker fell and well-outfitted with quality camera equipment. She quickly got to him and with help from Kennedy convinced him to sell his film to the *Times*. The result was a prize-winning color shot of the biggest news event of the Games.

I watched the closing ceremonies on a little black-and-white television set near the back of the *Times* sports department. I felt relieved that this ordeal was almost over, but I also felt sad that this ordeal was almost over. My feelings didn't make sense, and yet they did.

I was surrounded by an inside staff who had performed so incredibly well. I regretted that I had not been present at any of the events so that I could have observed the writers at work also performing so admirably.

But most of all, as I sat there, I felt overwhelmed that the L.A. Olympics had gone as well as they had and that our coverage of the Games, portions of which are reproduced in this book, went almost as smoothly as the Games themselves. When we had finished, we had written and processed nearly 2.4 million words in 24 days, and put those words on 960 pages. A staff of about 125 writers, deskmen, and photographers had worked an average of 14 hours a day during the period, often with only two days off.

And the funny thing was, when we shook the exhaustion out of our heads and reflected on the project for a few days, we all came to the same conclusion: OLYMPICS '84 was well worth it.

OLYMPICS '84

6 DAYS TO GAMES

Jim Murray

Remember Munich? IOC Won't

On Sept. 5, 1972, at the Olympic Games in Munich, West Germany—while Teofilo Stevenson, the mastodonic Cuban, was systematically dismantling the American, Duane Bobick, while fencers fenced and basketballers took free throws and the children of sport enjoyed the camaraderie of the Olympic Village malt shops and jukebox—nine Jewish athletes lay slumped in a room at 31 Connollysstrasse, bound hand and foot and blindfolded, with Kalashnikov machine guns held at their heads by eight heavily armed Arabs. Two comrades lay dead on the floor. None of the nine would see sunrise.

It was, and is, a shocking intrusion of deadly world politics into the toyland of sports.

And the International Olympic Committee has never forgiven the Jews for it.

At least, so it would seem. Consider what has been done by the Olympic movement to commemorate that terrible day.

First of all, on the day of the attack, it was business as usual. The Games went on. The government of West Germany sealed off the Olympic Village—24 hours too late—and, having let armed guerrillas in at 4 a.m., then attempted to keep accredited journalists out in broad daylight. Some of us managed to elude the secret cops, but what we saw in the village was indifference bordering on callousness. Irritation, even.

□

It was not until nightfall that IOC President Avery Brundage's stubborn fiat that the Games must go on was overruled.

A 24-hour suspension of the sports was ordained, no more and no less. A memorial service was permitted. Beethoven was played. Speeches were made. The Russians and Arabs boycotted the service. So, to tell the truth, did a lot of Americans. Brundage seized the occasion to equate the issue with another "savage attack" on the Olympic Games, the threat of African neighbors to boycott if white Rhodesia were admitted.

Governments had fought to save the lives of the hostages. Sadat of Egypt was pleaded with to intervene. German lives were sacrificed. German officials offered to substitute themselves for the Israeli Olympians.

Books were written about it.
Please see MURRAY, page 7

Carl Lewis, who says, "Nobody finishes better than I do," backs up what he says.

Lewis thinks he can go as far as Bob Beamon . . .

A THRILLER

First Carl Lewis Will Take Care of Jesse Owens; After That? Well, How About Michael Jackson?

By MIKE LITTWIN, Times Staff Writer

Rectangular, white-framed sunglasses. *Tres chic.* Sleeveless, turquoise T-shirt slit down the sides. Oversized white shorts, highlighted by a gold belt buckle. All that was missing was the white glove.

Introducing the World's Greatest Athlete and, perhaps, the World's Greatest Wardrobe.

Michael Jackson would die. Other athletes would laugh. Some do, behind the World's Greatest's back.

But give the man this: He has style. And he can make an entrance.

On this day, Carl Lewis was meeting the press, a group almost certain to be unimpressed by high fashion. The reporters were more concerned that Lewis was a half hour late. Lewis is always late, dependably so.

But Lewis knows about making an impression. He has looked up at us from the cover of Esquire, from the cover of Gentlemen's Quarterly. The 6-2 175-pounder can wear clothes you and I would look ridiculous in.

Carl Lewis looks like a cover boy, a celebrity, in them.

As Lewis makes clear, he is a celebrity and entitled to all the trappings.

Jesse Owens, Lewis' boyhood idol and a man whose achievements Lewis seems destined to equal, raced horses to put food on his table. What would he think?

What do you think?

□

Lewis is standing behind the starting blocks. Dressed in skin-tight warmups, purple on black, he is readily distinguishable from his competitors—even before the race begins. He's no mere runner and jumper, remember. He has plans to transcend this business of track and field.

Running for himself, for America, for glory, Carl Lewis is shaking the tension from his arms, his legs. Then he is standing, hands on hips, staring down the track toward the finish line. There's something remarkable about his face, its regal bearing suggesting he owns all that lies before him. The finish line is at the burning end of his concentrated stare.

When he is introduced, there are cheers, but Lewis acknowledges them only briefly. He peels off the warmups and resumes his staring. And as the racers get into the blocks, one by one, most eyes stay on Lewis. His stay straight ahead. Confident. Sure.

But wait: Something is wrong. Lewis doesn't get a good start out of the blocks, and Ron Brown, who does, streaks ahead and reaches the tape before America's Greatest Athlete can catch him.

Lewis has lost in the Olympic Games.

A dream is shattered.
Please see LEWIS, page 7

. . . The question is: Can he go as far as Michael Jackson?

Photos: JAYNE KAMIN
Los Angeles Times

Tully Vaults 19-1 for a U.S. Mark; Zhu Wins, Too

By RANDY HARVEY, Times Staff Writer

EUGENE, Ore.—For the third time this year, Mike Tully broke the American record in the pole vault Saturday night at the Prefontaine Classic.

His goal now?

"I just want to make sure I can get to the Olympics without a cast on my leg," he said.

Tully, 27, jumped 19-1, then missed three attempts at 19-2¾.

He set the previous record of 19-0¾ a month ago at the Olympic trials.

Only four men have ever gone higher than Tully's jump Saturday night, but he chose not to challenge the world record of 19-4¼ held by the Soviet Union's Sergei Bubka.

Instead, after clearing 19-1¼, he asked another pole vaulter, Earl Bell, for the height that would make him the second-best performer ever in the event.

Bell told Tully that another Soviet, Konstantin Volkov, had jumped 5.85 meters (19-2¼) this year.

"Raise the bar to 86 (5.86)," Tully told the officials at Hayward Field.

Tully was close at 19-2¾ only on his second jump. He bent the bar on his way down, but it stayed in place just long enough for the crowd of 13,680 to think it was secure.
Please see TULLY, page 7

Jesse Owens Loved by All

The Best in Sports; Also in Kindness, Generosity

By EARL GUSTKEY, Times Staff Writer

If you knew him, you loved him. That's how he's best remembered, by the men who knew him best.

When he competed, Jesse Owens was the world's fastest human. But he had a lot more than that going for him, said his old teammates and other friends. A lot more.

Marty Glickman, Owens' teammate on the 1936 U.S. Olympic team, said Owens had a certain effect on people.
Please see OWENS, page 9

Michigan Athletic Department

Top performance ever? Jesse Owens set long jump world record at Ann Arbor May 25, 1935; also set two others and tied third.

MURRAY

Continued from page 6

Movies were made of it. Songs were sung, poems read.

But the Olympian response of the IOC was to sweep it under the rug. It's never mentioned in polite circles at cocktail parties around Lausanne, Switzerland, home of the IOC. The monocles focus on more chic subjects. It was as if it had all been just another breach of protocol which the IOC, like the Sun King of France, is big on.

The IOC is also big on the past, given to ancestor worship. Statues of Discobolous abound. So do Grecian urns, or amphora. Founder Baron de Coubertin's picture and utterances are everywhere.

But that one day in 1972 seems to have been dropped from the Olympic calendar.

It can't be that the IOC is trying to forget the terrorists. Several of them were even released from prison, if you can believe it. No, it must be the Israelis. They must have committed some monumental gaffe, some unforgivable breach of etiquette.

Because, since that day, the government of Israel has been interested in obtaining some recognition of the sacrifices of their athletes and coaches, slaughtered in a shootout, unprotected, unrescued, unremembered.

Sports commemorates everything. Statues of deceased sluggers dot major-league outfields, plaques recall where a golfer sank a "courageous" two-wood shot, streets are named for football players. But, would you even know who Yosef Gutfreund, Moshe Weinberg, Yaacov Springer, Amitzur Shapira, Joseph Romano, David Berger, Mark Slavin, Eliezer Halfin, Zeev Friedman, Kehat Schorr and Andre Spitzer were? This may be the only place you'll read their names during this Olympics.

Joseph Shane, a Los Angeles businessman; the Southern California Olympians, an organization of ex-Olympic athletes here, headed by Andrew Strenk, and the Israeli consul general in Los Angeles, Gen. Jacob Even of Entebbe fame, have petitioned the IOC for a simple moment of silence in honor of the martyred Israeli athletes at the opening ceremonies of the Los Angeles Games here this week.

It seems a reasonable request. But the IOC reacts as if it were recalling a bad dream. Spokesmen privately point out that the IOC severely curtails all opening-ceremony rites to weed out any "political or national statements." The head of state, be he Hitler or Emperor Hirohito or Ronald Reagan, is restricted to 16 words of opening statement, for example. The IOC not only wants not to honor the 11 dead athletes, it wants to forget them.

Why? They should be on the conscience not only of the Olympic leaders but of society. It isn't as if they were killed in a head-on on the Santa Monica Freeway. They are an ineradicable part of the fabric of the Games forever.

As Gen. Even says, "To forget is to condone—and we must never forget we are in a struggle with terrorism every day of our lives."

If its victims are forgotten, so will be its crimes.

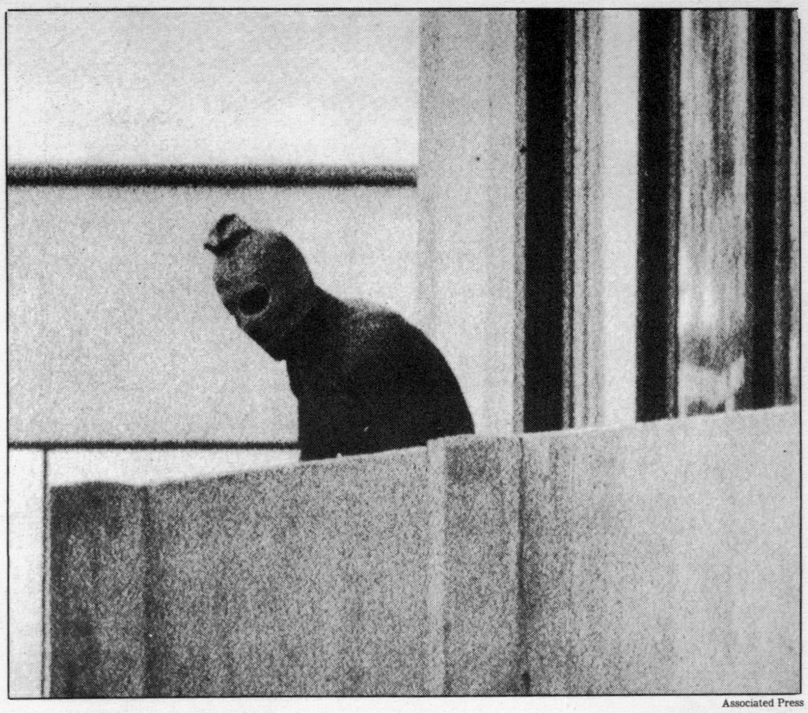

Associated Press

When masked terrorists killed 11 Jews in Munich in 1972, the IOC let the Games go on.

TULLY

Continued from page 6

Then the bar fell. Everyone breathed again.

But Tully, the former UCLA vaulter whose best official jump before this year was an 18-8¼ left over from 1978, said he was satisfied.

"I'm jumping so high now, I feel I can flop over anything," he said. "That's basically what the Russian (Bubka) is doing."

Until Tully's performance, the highlight of the meet had been the first appearance in the United States of China's world record-holder in the high jump, Zhu Jianhua.

Jimmy Howard, who made the U.S. Olympic team in 1980, matched Zhu jump for jump through 7-6½. But neither was able in three attempts to clear 7-7¾.

To decide the winner, they were given a fourth chance. Howard failed, but Zhu did not.

Zhu was not available to interviews afterward.

"He's the best jumper I've ever jumped against in my life," said Howard, who was impressed by the ease with which Zhu clears the bar. His world record is 7-10.

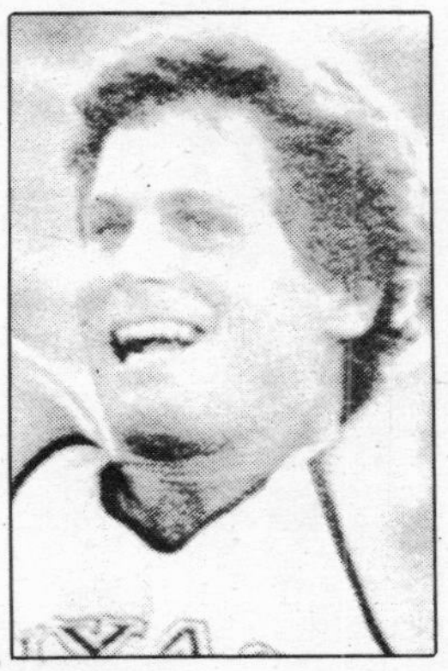

Mike Tully

"But I don't think he's unbeatable."

In his record-setting performance, Tully said he benefitted from a strong tailwind. But most of the other athletes here had nothing kind to say about the stiff breeze that toyed with them in the field events and provided a barrier in the running events.

"It was like running into a brick wall," said Steve Scott, who is still chasing Jim Ryun's 3:51.1 in the mile, the best ever run on American soil.

For the second straight week, he thought he was prepared to challenge the record. But he was disappointed again, even though his 3:54.44 was good enough to win.

"Knowing you can do something and doing it are two different things," said Scott, who will run the 1,500 at the Olympics.

Another middle-distance runner who won Saturday, but was not particularly satisfied with his time, was New Zealand's John Walker, who ran a 13:43.32 in the 5,000 meters.

Walker said last week he would make a decision following the Prefontaine Classic whether he will run the 1,500 or the 5,000 in the Olympics. He won the 1,500 in the 1976 Olympics.

But he said Saturday that he will delay his decision for at least another week.

Even though he has made it no secret that he prefers the 1,500, he said, "I've got to run the one I think I have the best chance of winning."

About the only runner who did not appear affected by the wind was Brazil's Joaquim Cruz, a local favorite, since he attends the University of Oregon.

Running the 1,000 meters, a non-Olympic event, he won easily over Jim Spivey, who will run the 1,500 at the Olympics, in 2:14.54, the fastest time ever run on American soil. Only three men have ever run faster anywhere.

Like Walker, Cruz is having a difficult time deciding his schedule for the Olympics. He prefers to run both the 800 and the 1,500, but his coach is attempting to persuade him to run only the 800.

"He's a certain winner in the 800," Walker said.

Another favorite with the crowd, Alberto Salazar, did not fare so well in the 10,000 meters, finishing third in 27:58.25 behind American Mark Nenow (27:57.49) and Kenyan Simeon Kigen (27:57.68).

Salazar, who lives in Eugene, will run the marathon in the Olympics.

Another Eugene resident, Mary Decker, withdrew from the 1,500 because of a strained right Achilles tendon that has hampered her training since the trials.

There were a number of minor upsets.

Brian Diemer, second in the trials, beat the trials champion, Henry Marsh, in the steeplechase.

Michael Carter, third in the shot-put in the trials, and Dave Laut, first in the trials, both had 68-11¾ Saturday, but Carter was awarded the victory on the basis of a better second-best throw.

No one was more disappointed than Tom Petranoff, whose world record in the javelin of 327-2 was shattered Friday by East German Uwe Hohn's throw of 343-10.

Petranoff could manage a best of only 263-7 in this meet to finish fifth.

"I was trying not to press, yet I was pressing," Petranoff said. "I was trying to throw it out the end of the stadium. I fell on my face."

LEWIS

Continued from page 6

America is minus one hero.

Could it happen? Sure. Even as Lewis heads toward a possible four gold medals, be assured that he is beatable. Many of the great ones before him have lost. Jim Ryun. Mark Spitz. Ron Brown did beat Lewis twice in races this winter at a meet in San Diego. Of course, they were indoors and only 50 or 60 meters long and Lewis wasn't thinking about peaking in January.

He hasn't been beaten outdoors in anything this year. And after his nonpareil performance at the Olympic trials, no one of sane mind would pick against him come August.

But put aside the speculation for now. Assume he wins the four golds. Assume that he streaks to wins in the 100 and 200 meters. Assume he continues to own the long jump. Assume he gets a final gold medal in the 400-meter relay.

Even assume—and this may take some doing—that Lewis' four golds make him as big a celebrity as his manager, Joe Douglas, says it will. That he will take on Michael Jackson-like proportions. That America will open its heart and pocketbook to Lewis.

If you assume all that, you must also wonder about that night in San Diego. Not the losing. What made the evening remarkable was the reaction of the other athletes on the track, those who took time from what they were doing to applaud.

Applauding Lewis' defeat.

It was just as Larry Myricks had prophesied the year before, saying, "There's going to be some serious celebrating when Carl Lewis gets beat."

Maybe Carl Lewis, America's Greatest Athlete, does stand alone.

□

Everybody sees me as getting it all and they think that they can get it all, too. And they don't understand why they don't. The only reason I do is because what I do is unique and I have a ball doing it.

—CARL LEWIS

Lewis' defenders—and in the narrow world of track and field, he needs defenders—have it that the World's Greatest is the victim of jealousy, of a sensational press, of vicious rumors.

Lewis, they say, is a shy young man who would just as soon duck the limelight.

For sure, he takes the limelight only as he wants it. Said one track promoter: "When you talk to him, you feel like you have to bow to the East." Another promoter had to pay Lewis $1,000 to attend a press conference.

Of course, he is crushed by media requests. He handles it on his terms. And measured by his success, by his popularity, you must say he handles it in his best interest.

And once he begins to talk, be prepared for speech in double time. Lewis may also be the world's fastest talker. He speaks often these days of his love for America, how he feels honored to run for his country. "When I go to Europe," he says, "I can't wait to get back. This is the greatest country in the world." Wrap him in a flag.

He is asked to talk about himself. It's a favored subject.

Come the Olympics, he will probably pass up the post-event press conferences until he has completed the 100 meters, the long jump and the 200 meters. He used a similar formula at the U.S. trials and at the world championships in Helsinki, Finland, the year before, and it worked. The idea is to maintain concentration.

After the 200 meters, when he is expected to have won his third of four gold medals, Lewis will talk gladly of his triumph.

On a recent day, he talked of triumphs to come.

He talked about his finish: "Nobody finishes better than I do."

He talked about the 200 meters: "The way I'm running the curve, no one can beat me in the 200."

He talked about his competitors: "They need to concentrate more on what they're doing and less on what Carl Lewis is doing."

He talked about Jesse Owens: "When people started comparing me to Jesse Owens, it was flattering. That was two years ago. Now I'm doing my own thing. He did some things I don't do. I do some things he didn't do."

This is all spoken with a certain equanimity. What he says he does with the certainty that it will be accepted and believed. When he says he could be All-Pro for the Dallas Cowboys, though he has never played football, we are supposed to believe that, too. You don't tug on Superman's cape.

It takes some probing to get beyond that, but not much. We learn about the song he's releasing, "Going for the Gold." And about the writer following him around all year for the book. It's all planned, all programmed. All Lewis has to do is come through. As far as Lewis is concerned, that's the easy part.

"There's no reason to think I can't do it," he said.

And, indeed, there isn't. He's proven what he can do several times—dominate a world-class track meet. Now, he has only to prove that he can do it again in the world's foremost track meet.

In a press conference situation, he is in complete control, taking the tough questions in stride, fielding the easy ones with grace.

Alone with a reporter, he talks animatedly, but evenly. He can get excited about his white Samoyed dog, Tasha, for whom he has parental feelings. He talks calmly about his religion, the Lay Witnesses for Christ.

But the passion in his voice is most notable when he's talking about track, about the intricacies of the long jump, about leaning into the curve in the 200, about his stride in the 100.

On the 200: "When you stay low through the curve and come out like a rocket . . . getting faster, faster, faster . . ."

His eyes light up. Winning gold medals is one thing, running and jumping as only he can run and jump is another. Of course, he also enjoys what it all brings him.

No track athlete can command more money, more attention. He does command it, too. There are always rules for athletes and rules for Carl Lewis. He doesn't want to stay in the Olympic Village with the other athletes. At a track meet, he gets a police escort to a place where he can hide from the fans. Lewis is special and he knows it.

His life style befits that of a once-in-a-lifetime athlete. He lives in a Victorian house in Houston he bought at age 20 for $175,000. There's a Persian rug as the centerpiece of his living room, the Baccarat crystal and Chrisofle silver in the dining room, jacuzzi off the bedroom, arcade games in the game room, a BMW parked out front. Carl Lewis is what amateur athletics has come to.

But the flashy dresser who talks fast and lives well is not the whole of Carl Lewis. He is a track star first and foremost.

He has other interests. He loves cars, drives them at extraordinary speeds.

"Once, 150 miles an hour," he confesses. "I love speed."

He likes fast boats. In fact, running faster than anyone else in the world is about as slow as he ever moves.

"I feel like I'm running almost in slow motion," he said. "When I finish the 100, I feel I can run another 30 or 40 yards at the same speed, just running and running and running. Relaxed."

Lewis likes money, too. When he first came to the University of Houston, he told his coach, Tom Tellez, "I plan to become a millionaire."

He didn't know then he could do that as an amateur athlete. He figured he wouldn't have to.

"I'm not limited to sports," he said. "I can do different things. If I didn't win the four gold medals, that doesn't mean I have nowhere else to go. I can act, I could make a TV series. There are other ways to be a success."

Fortunately for Lewis, he can be a success on the track and make all the money he needs. Everything else is cream.

'It's a scam," says Joe Douglas, Lewis' manager, of amateurism. "It doesn't exist now, if it ever existed."

Edwin Moses has shown how he can make nearly a half-million dollars a year as an amateur. Lewis, who is looking for the big grab later, makes much less, but still more than six figures. And the money he does make is supposed to go into a trust fund—that is, money above expenses.

An expensive home and car, they're expenses. Expensive clothes, more expenses.

Raised in a middle-class environment, he has moved easily into the upper class, but with the old respect for how difficult money can be to come by.

As teen-agers, Lewis and a boyhood friend, Thomas Mayfield, were inveterate window shoppers and bargain hunters.

"We found bargains women didn't because it was fun," Lewis said. "It's fun to buy and bargain instead of just buying . . . and that's changed now. Still, even though I've acquired more money, I say to myself, 'No way am I going to pay $60 for a belt.' I still get stingy, but it's fun because half the fun of shopping isn't getting it, it's the finding."

He found a bargain on the crystal two years ago in France and became an amateur collector.

"The bargain got me interested," he says.

Mayfield remembers the early days. "We didn't have much, but we had fun. Carl was kind of in a shell except when he was with friends. I think he's come out of the shell now, which is good."

Recently, Mayfield went to Houston to visit Lewis and came home wide-eyed.

"It's got a den on the second floor," Mayfield said. "A big-screen TV. A wet bar upstairs you won't see at home in New Jersey. He's in love with water beds. There's one in his room, one in the guest room . . . The

Please see LEWIS, page 8

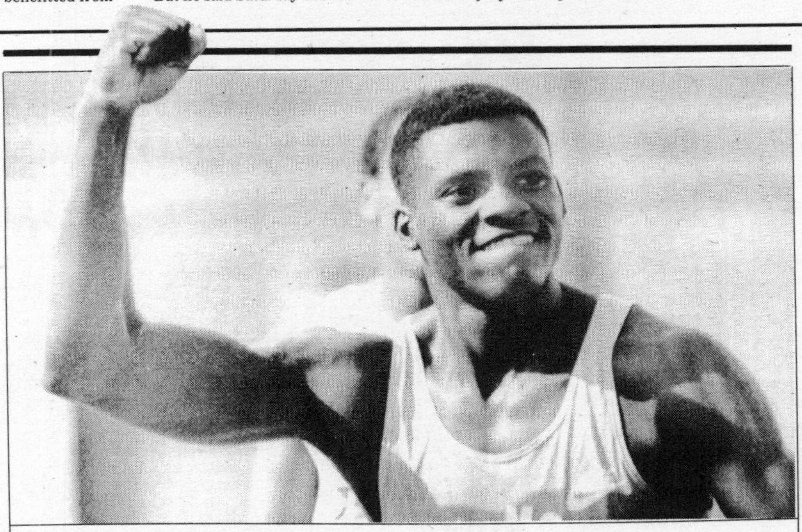

THE TALKER

'I'm not limited to sports. I can do different things. If I didn't win the four gold medals, that doesn't mean I have nowhere else to go. I can act, I could make a TV series. There are other ways to be a success.'

—CARL LEWIS

LEWIS

Continued from page 7

living room is sunken in when you walk in the door. His room, my mother fell in love with. Walk-in bathroom, closets. In the corner a little table, a breakfast table. Stereo system runs all through the house. Video machines . . . movies, big arcade games."

A Newsweek story said its interviewer was greeted at the Lewis house by a uniformed servant. Lewis lives well, so well that he doesn't allow the press into his home anymore. Perhaps that is because the house doesn't seem to match the image of a macho athlete. But Lewis makes no pretense about being macho. Purple tights are not macho.

His tastes are not simple, but neither is Lewis some party animal.

"Eating, I love," he says. "Shopping. Sitting around with friends. I don't need to be going out to a party every night. That's not me. Just a few friends over at the house."

And a lot of friends, he says, "I've had to ax. They know why."

Said Mark McNeil, a close friend and competitor: "Carl is always in control. Nobody takes advantage of him. He lives his life the way he wants no. Nobody can tell him different."

It is his life. And he lives it well.

With no regrets.

□

Carl Lewis is in part a natural, in part a creation.

"Everyone thinks that the earth opened and out popped Carl Lewis," says Carl Lewis. "I've been competing since I was 8 years old. I didn't just arrive." The story is by now familiar.

Born of athletic parents, Lewis grew up with two older brothers and a younger sister, Carol the Olympic long jumper, in Willingboro, N.J., a suburb of Philadelphia. Theirs was not a normal childhood. The parents were track coaches, year-round track coaches, and the children grew up literally building sand castles in the long-jump pit. It was a rushed childhood, with time split among school and track and music lessons and swimming and gymnastics and whatever direction young minds could travel in. It was a childhood that any child would love.

"We were lucky," Carl said. "We could come home to our parents and talk to them about things they cared about, too. There was no mystery conversation over the dinner table. We were in it together."

Carol developed quickly, Carl less so. He was small for his age and was a strong competitor but no champion in age group.

"He was just another competitor, another guy your coach said you had to beat," remembers Jason Grimes, who competed against Lewis as a teen-ager.

But by the time Lewis was a senior in high school, people were starting to take notice. He went to Houston on a scholarship, and Coach Tom Tellez turned him into the best long jumper in the world.

"What really bothered me was the way it happened," Myricks said. "One day he wasn't there and the next day he was all over the place."

Said Lewis: "I wanted to be No. 1 in the world, so Myricks had to go."

He jumped 28 feet, started jumping it consistently. Myricks went. But Lewis was not satisfied. That was almost too easy.

So, Carl took up the 100 seriously. Then the 200. And a couple of years ago, the dream began to take focus.

"I would run a great 200 and nobody could believe it," Lewis said. "It was fun. I loved the way they looked at me, like, 'What is he trying to do?' "

Here, Lewis rolls his eyes. He talks with his entire body, his eyes, sometimes his hands.

"They say it looks easy, too easy. It's supposed to be easy. You're supposed to run relaxed, and right now I'm running more relaxed than I ever have in my life."

Lewis has run 200 meters in 19.75 seconds, a record for sea level. He has run the 100 in 9.97 seconds, also a sea-level record. His long jump of 28-10¼ is the best at sea level. You've got to climb mountains to beat Carl Lewis.

What can't Lewis do? He talks about running the 400 in 44 seconds. He talks about what a great 110-meter hurdler he could be. And he'd like to do them just for the shock value if nothing else. Recently, he's been talking about what a great wide receiver he could be. All-Pro.

What can't he do?

He can act. His acting coach, Warren Robertson, says Lewis "has the temperment of an artist with the type of intelligence where the mind is still in touch with the feeling." He compares Lewis unabashedly to Montgomery Clift or Sidney Poitier.

Lewis is an excellent communicator, and when he's not too busy running, he works for a TV station in Houston. Even though he was once scholastically ineligible at Houston, he's a good student, with a sharp mind.

Lewis has money, fame, maybe a little too much attention to suit him. And he's on the verge of a breakthrough—four possible Olympic golds.

Still, life isn't perfect. The fans love him, his colleagues don't. Many don't even like him. They talk behind his back, some obviously jealous. Some even talk aloud to reporters. Lewis is the subject of constant rumors, some of which he says cause him great pain. There are a lot of people after Carl Lewis. If they can't catch him one way, they'll try another.

Is it all jealousy?

The back-biting became serious when Lewis threw up his arms in victory before reaching the finish line in the 200 meters at the The Athletics Congress meet last summer in Indianapolis. The gesture probably cost Lewis a world record. Certainly, it cost him some friends.

"I wasn't trying to show anyone up," Lewis said. "I was just expressing my own joy, my own feelings of the moment at what I had accomplished."

But he's aware of the backlash. "Sure it hurts when people you think are your friends are sticking the knife in," Lewis said. "I thought, 'What's going on? It's not that they want to win. They want me to lose.'

"Sometimes I think, 'Screw the yo-yos, screw the athletes; win for yourself, win for America.' "

His sister, Carol, sees the problem as simple jealousy.

"I can't believe some of the things they say about us," Carol said. "It makes me sick. Look at Jason. We've known him since we were kids."

Look at Grimes. He says that whatever he said to offend Lewis he did not mean it.

"I think it's mostly jealousy," Grimes said. "There are some people who just can't accept Carl's success."

Of course, he says things that anger other athletes. He raises his hands in victory. He takes a victory lap.

"People try to tear down anyone who's on top," said Joe Douglas. "Carl is not the kind to sit around in the lobby and shoot the bull. They didn't say these things about him when he wasn't famous and he acts the same way now as he did then. It would be a shame to destroy the real Carl Lewis.

"He's a sensitive person. He collects nice crystal, very beautiful stuff. He's not a guy who goes to a new city and spends his time hustling girls. He's not a party person. He's a private person. That's no crime."

Surely, no crime. But some of the biggest names in track have taken it upon themselves to bring Lewis up short.

Among them were Edwin Moses and Willie Banks, brilliant performers and among track and field's most respected people.

"Winning is one thing, but you should do it without any big hype or marketing," Moses once said of Lewis. "There's a lot of negative vibrations surrounding the guy."

Retorts Lewis: "Everyone knows Edwin wants publicity and he feels if he shoots me down it shoots him up . . . Edwin runs the 400-meter hurdles. There's only so far you're going to go with that. He's made a lot of money. He's fairly famous. But they want it all. They want it all.

"And you know, I think a lot of them were happy with where they were going until they saw somebody else do things they never thought possible. Go places they never dreamed of.

"Willie (Banks) wants more attention. He talked about how none of the athletes like me and how it's going to be sad if I win four gold medals because none of the athletes will congratulate me.

"What can I say to that, except I don't believe it."

He is sensitive about the subject. And say those who know him, sensitive period.

"He doesn't have the protective armor of most athletes," said Robertson, the acting coach. "An actor needs subtext and Carl has that. The parts seem to commune in a balanced way. In a critical moment, the sum total of Carl kind of gathers and he has forceful moments."

On a stage—theatrical or athletic.

Is the pressure getting to him? You judge. He breezed through the trials with that pressure. If anyone suffered, it was the competition.

Lewis gleefully agrees.

"I think all the pressure people try to put on me goes right back to them," Lewis said. "It's always Carl Lewis this or Carl Lewis that and on and on and on. Now they have to beat me to prove they can beat me. Every race we go in and every race I win makes me a more convincing No. 1 and that much harder for them to believe they can beat me.

"After a while, it's like, 'Gosh, I can't believe we can beat this guy.' Who do you think the pressure is on then?"

□

Take a step back and look at what Carl Lewis is attempting to do and you gain a better appreciation of the athlete and, perhaps, the man.

His coach, Tom Tellez, told him he was crazy last year when he first tried to put all three individual events together at the national championships in Indianapolis. He bowed to Tellez's judgment and passed up the 200 in Helsinki at the world championships.

"I should have been out there," Lewis said. "Why do I want all those medals? People ask me if I'm greedy. I don't think so. I just do what I want to do. I think that's why athletes don't like me, but people do. I smile. They think I'm real. They can see I'm not fabricated.

"I have the God-given talent to be the best."

All along, he has known he can do it. All along he has said that when he is right, no one can beat him.

Now, we shall see.

The schedule is incredibly demanding, one that would try a lesser athlete. Carl Lewis is not a lesser athlete as he will show beginning Friday, Aug. 3.

The Lewis schedule:

—Friday: Two morning heats in the 100 meters.
—Saturday: The 100 semifinals and 100 final.
—Sunday: Long jump qualifying.
—Monday: Two heats of the 200 meters in the morning, the long jump final in the afternoon.
—Tuesday: An off day.
—Wednesday: The 200 semifinals and 200 final.
—Thursday: An off day.
—Friday: One heat of the 400-meter relay.
—Saturday: Semifinals and final of 400-meter relay.

Eleven races and two days of long jumping. Tough for some. Tough for Lewis?

"He's a special athlete," says Tellez, who has made a career of coaching special athletes. "He doesn't accept the same limitations other athletes do. He made up his mind that he could be at his best in each event, avoid injury and perform at the highest level . . . It looks like he was right."

Lewis' only coach in the long jump before college had been his mother, and still he was jumping 26-8 by his senior year. So when Tellez got hold of him, he had an idea Lewis was going to be world class, though he had seen him jump only once before signing Lewis to a scholarship.

The first thing Tellez did was break down the way Lewis jumped and change it completely.

"Most people don't realize that Carl was injured when he came here," Tellez said. "Because of the way he was jumping, Carl was putting undue pressure on the patella tendon and the kneecap. We had to change his technique. With a lot of athletes, you get resistance when you talk about change. But Carl is very open-minded. He wants to be the best and he's willing to listen and learn.

"You don't have to tell Carl the same thing over and over. You push the button and he responds."

The maddening thing is that it is easy for him. No, he didn't pop out of the earth one day, but practice takes only a few hours of his time. He listens to what Tellez tells him, absorbs it, works on it and, there you have it, world-class performance.

Tellez moved his approach in the long jump from 150 feet to what is now 171 feet as Lewis plans his assault on Bob Beamon's record. Together they changed his style of jumping to the double-hitch kick where the legs and arms pedal for 1.5 seconds of grace and strength and speed that routinely carries him 28 feet in the air. One day, he says, it will carry him 30. Technically no one is better. Bob Beamon says as much.

The long jump is his favorite event, his first love. But it wasn't enough. For the last three years, he has been ranked No. 1 in the world in the 100. This year, thanks to an improved start, he has been invincible. In the 200, he has no equal. He spent much of the offseason working on running the curve and talks a lot about setting a record.

"Maybe someone can beat him in the 100," said Calvin Smith, who is second to Lewis among the world's sprinters. "Ron Brown could do it. But the way he's running the 200, I don't know."

Smith smiled.

"It's hard to see him losing."

No one has more problems seeing that possibility than Lewis himself. Remember, "If I'm right . . ." He has a few theories on his near invincibility. The first, although not necessarily the most important, is technical.

But at least as important is psychology. Lewis has changed the face of his three events and has altered the careers of his challengers, not the least of them Larry Myricks, once the best long jumper in the world.

When Lewis eclipsed him, Myricks wasn't sure how to take it. He redoubled his efforts, but that wasn't enough. He started saying what a lot of athletes were beginning to think about Lewis, but that didn't help him any either. He tried the 200 and was beginning to do very well there—until Lewis followed him to the 200 and, of course, began to beat him.

Last year, Myricks didn't even qualify for the long jump at the world championships. He did make it in the 200, an event that Lewis passed. This year, he made the Olympic team in the long jump, but not in the 200.

THE PERSON

"Sure it hurts when people you think are your friends are sticking the knife in. I thought, 'What's going on? It's not that they want to win. They want me to lose.' Sometimes I think, 'Screw the yo-yos, screw the athletes; win for yourself, win for America.' "

—CARL LEWIS

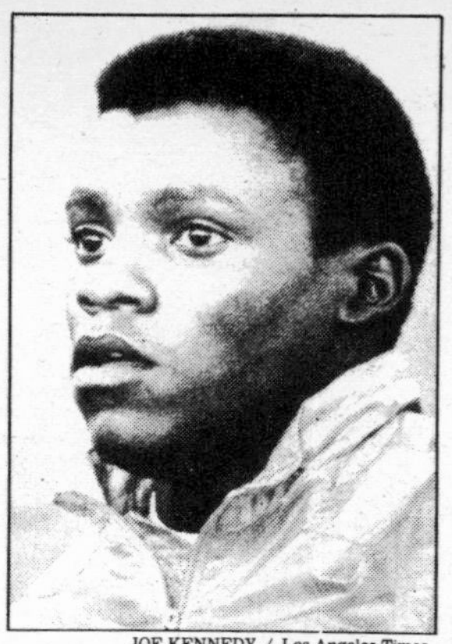

JOE KENNEDY / Los Angeles Times

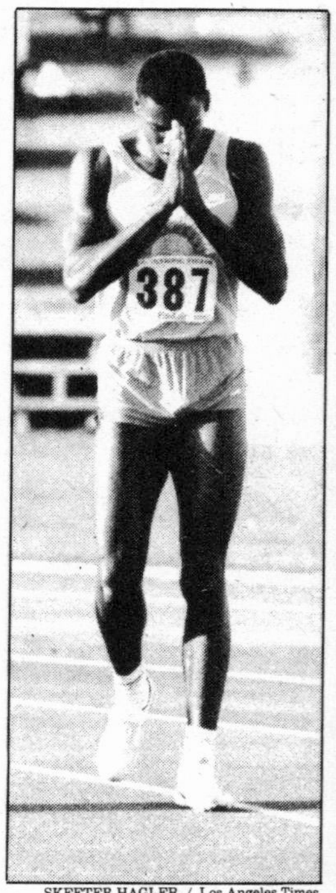

SKEETER HAGLER / Los Angeles Times

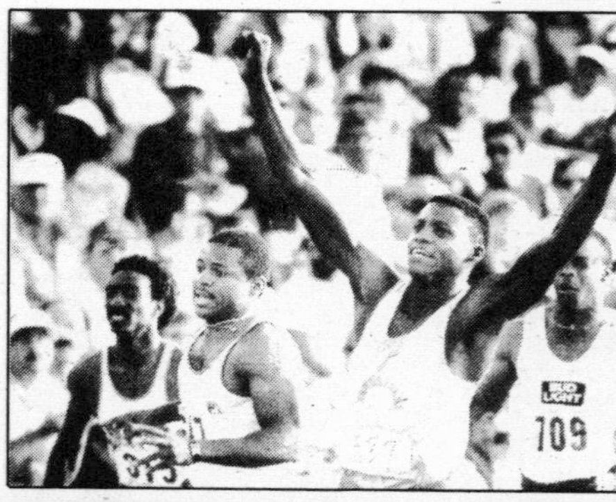

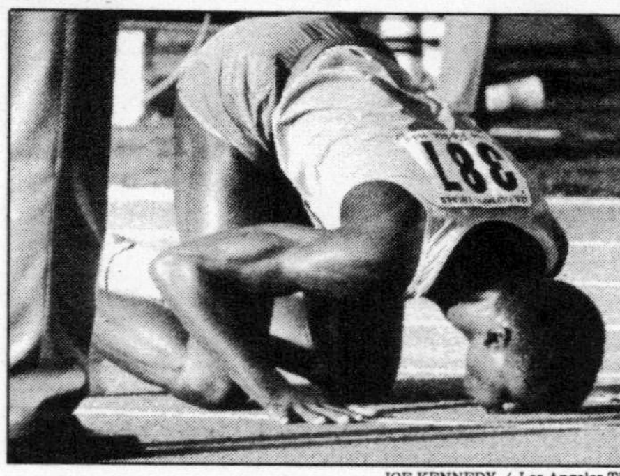

JOE KENNEDY / Los Angeles Times

"Larry just went crazy," Lewis said. "I'm not sure he knew what he was saying . . . (But) every minute he thinks about me and what I'm doing is a minute he's not thinking about himself and what he's doing. He's the one with the problem, not me. He can do what he wants. He's a grown man. What hurts is that we were friends, that there was a time when he wanted to help me."

Lewis looked truly hurt. It isn't his favorite subject. "We have sort of a truce now," Lewis said.

And now Myricks says he doesn't talk about Lewis anymore.

Sam Graddy likes to say he can beat Lewis. Ron Brown points to his victories in the 60 meters. Mel Lattany, a Lewis critic who Lewis calls an "evil person," runs great times—when Lewis isn't running against him.

When Lewis is on the track, they all change. Even the great Calvin Smith was spending all his winter trying to remodel his start in the vain hope that he could catch Carl. Instead, Smith got hurt and will be running only the relays in the Olympics. For the others, though they often deny it, there is fear.

"Running against Carl Lewis, you're in awe of him," said Roy Martin, the brash youngster who had predicted he would beat Lewis in the 200 at the Olympics trials but who finished fourth instead.

"You can see the fear in their eyes," Lewis said. "They just don't run the same way."

He doesn't just beat them, of course. He raises his hands in victory as he crosses the finish line. He takes a victory lap, playing to the crowd.

The losers, they stew.

Even Brown, a friend, says he "wouldn't raise my hands like that. It's just not my style."

But style, of course, is much of what Lewis is all about.

"The fans love it," Lewis said. "Why should I care what the athletes think?"

□

Joe Douglas is in a hurry. Always. He jumps into his expensive sports car and races to his next meeting.

When Carl Lewis calls, Joe Douglas jumps.

When Carl Lewis doesn't call, say a reporter or a promoter he was supposed to meet, Joe Douglas jumps.

"Carl got tied up," Douglas explains.

Douglas does a lot of Lewis' explaining, but that's only a small part of what Douglas does for Lewis. Douglas is coach of the Santa Monica Track Club, a job designed to keep anyone's life complete. And that was before Lewis joined up.

Now, the club is a part-time gig. Lewis is Joe Douglas' all-day, every-day, full-time job.

With help, of course, he negotiates Lewis' endorsement contracts, poster contracts, appearance money. He helps set up Lewis' schedule. He is the middle man between Lewis and the incredible media crush. Heady work for a former high school math teacher.

"I never had any idea it would get this big," said Douglas. "It never stops."

So it's no wonder that, like the white rabbit, Douglas never has enough time. Because when he has nothing else to do, Douglas is planning, scheming. All for the good of Carl Lewis.

"Carl goes way beyond track and field," said Douglas, while driving the car that Carl Lewis gave him. "He is not just an athlete. He is a personality. Who are your biggest stars? Michael Jackson? Well, there's no reason why Carl Lewis won't be as valuable as Michael Jackson or anyone else.

"He's bright, good looking and he has star quality. We're not going to underestimate ourselves."

There's no danger there. Joe Douglas, a little man, thinks big. And while some in the field say that Douglas is in over his head, he has the full support of the man who counts most—Carl Lewis.

"Joe has always done the best he can for me," Lewis said. "He has never tried to promote himself. He has looked out for my interests, and he has taken some grief for it."

Well, he can be demanding. At track meets, he insists on top dollar for his athlete. Sometimes, according to promoters, Douglas will settle for a certain sum and then come back and renegotiate, concerned that he didn't get enough. Foremost in Douglas' mind is that someone out there is trying to take advantage of them, of him.

"You wouldn't believe what we get offered," Douglas said. "They think we don't know what we're doing."

What they've done is mount a strategy, giving what time they have to the major media markets of Los Angeles and New York and concentrating on the upscale, nonsport magazines such as Esquire and Gentlemen's Quarterly. They've also committed to few endorsements, preferring to wait for the big moment, the four golds, when they can really cash in.

Like Michael Jackson?

Lewis laughs brightly at the comparison, without dismissing it entirely. He enjoys this business of superstar comparisons—it's still that new. But it's not so new that he is immune to the crush of the crowd, to the invasion of his privacy, to the hostility that is the modern companion to celebrity.

After running or jumping at a meet, the real work begins. The crowds gather around him and, while all the time moving, Lewis pulls out pre-signed postcards. It's all planned. Except that he usually runs out and now he starts looking around nervously, hoping Joe Douglas will rescue him.

It was not so long ago that there was another Carl Lewis, a simpler Carl Lewis.

"I look at him sometimes and I can't believe he's the same person," says his mother, Evelyn.

"When I was younger, I was extremely shy," Lewis says. "I couldn't talk in front of a crowd—not at all. Now I've been able to adjust, to be more relaxed, more comfortable. I feel like I'm in control now."

Carl has reached the land of Oz, somewhere far over that rainbow. And, with the Olympics yet to come, he's still climbing.

"I don't know how it can get much bigger, more hectic," Lewis says.

Just wait.

□

One more big meet. Lewis must dream of those four golds, but says he doesn't dream at all. Maybe not. He acts on dreams and they all come true.

Four golds.

If he doesn't get them, he'll be branded a failure.

"In their minds," Lewis says. "Not in my mind. If I'm prepared and I've done all I can, how can I fail?"

Oh, he can fail. He can lose millions of dollars by losing.

But how do you bet against him?

"He's doing some very special things right now," Calvin Smith says.

And it's going to get even more special, come those gold medals.

The poster rights are already sold. There will be only one picture of the four golds swinging from his neck. He'll take that picture with him after the Games for a triumphant tour of Europe.

Then he'll return, maybe finish school, maybe try acting, certainly do a little more running and jumping.

He'll make millions.

He'll buy more crystal, more silver, more clothes.

Maybe he'll be what Mark Spitz never could. Maybe he'll eclipse Bruce Jenner. Maybe he will be the next Michael Jackson.

And make millions.

The competition will get even more jealous.

And you can read about it all in the book.

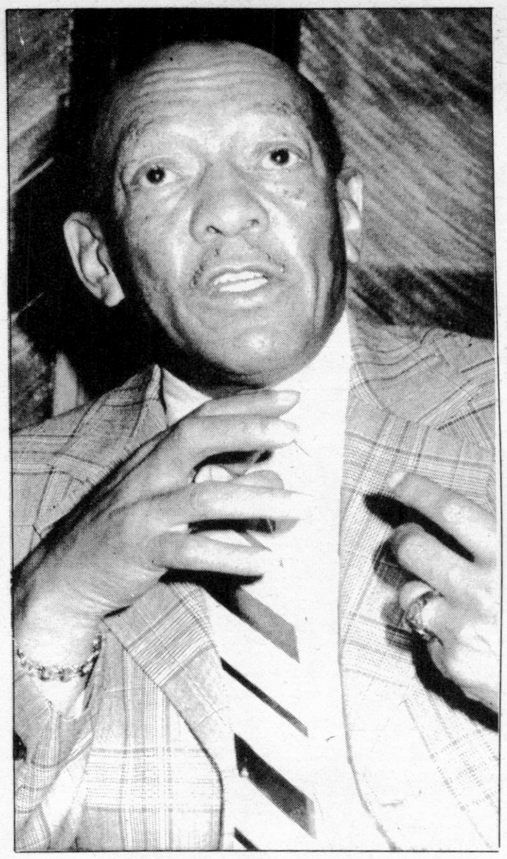

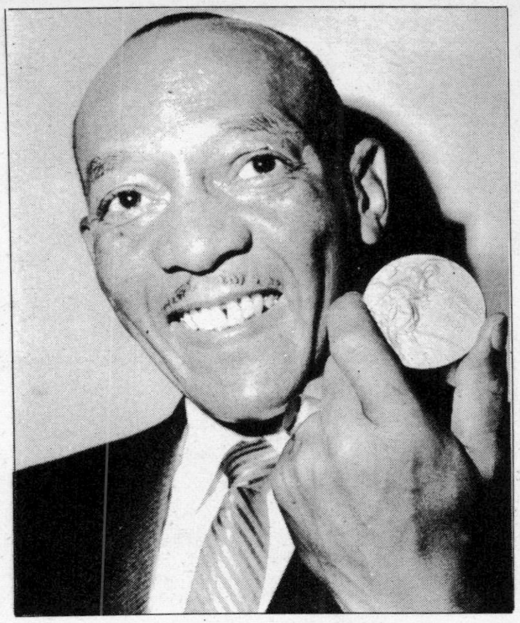

'How people loved him! I'll never forget walking into a restaurant in New York about 10 years ago with him. One person recognized him, stood up and started clapping, and by the time we got to our table, everyone in the restaurant was standing and clapping.'

—HERB DOUGLAS on Jesse Owens

OWENS

Continued from page 6

"He was a warm, beautiful man, in every sense," he said. "He knew how good he was, but he handled himself in a way . . . well, it was impossible not to like him.

"I competed against him maybe a dozen times. I'm proud to say I never beat him."

Forty-eight summers have passed since Jesse Owens held the Olympic Games in the palm of his hand, in Berlin. For 15 August days in 1936, he was The Olympian.

He won four gold medals, in the 100- and 200-meter dashes, the long jump and the 400-meter relay.

Then, of course, there was Hitler. And Goering, and Goebbels, and Frick, and Himmler. They were all there, the Nazi lords, in Hitler's box. Legend has it Owens was snubbed by Hitler, but the legend falls short of being accurate.

A teammate of Owens, Mel Walker, said the media had distorted the story.

"That was blown all out of proportion," he said. "There was nothing to that. We didn't even know there was a controversy until we got home."

Does it really matter?

To a man, his old teammates dismiss the old, tiresome controversy as media-created, even though Owens himself helped perpetuate the myth. They say it was insignificant when stacked against what Owens achieved, how in those two weeks he affected the lives of black athletes who followed him.

Remember, it was 1936. Joe Louis had not yet won the heavyweight championship. Jackie Robinson was 11 years away from breaking major league baseball's color barrier. Black athletes at Ohio State, Owens' school, weren't allowed to live on campus.

So, in this Olympic year, they remember The Olympian, the way he was.

In the summer of 1936, they were young and strong. Today, they're in their late 60s, early 70s. They still remember.

Mel Walker remembers Owens, in 1935, giving him a $5 bill so he could buy a $20 suit. He also remembers Owens 46 years later, on his deathbed, trying to help him in a business deal. John Woodruff remembers a man "who'd do anything for you." Dave Albritton treasures his friendship with Owens to this day, and resents those falsely claiming to have known him. Louis Zamperini remembers quiet words of advice from Owens in Berlin. Herb Douglas remembers him signing an autograph for a youngster when it seemed Owens was dying.

□

Herb Douglas, 61, is vice president of Schieffelin & Co. in New York, importers of liquor products. He was a long jump bronze medalist in 1948. He never competed against Owens, but says meeting him as a boy turned his life around. In 1980, the year of Owens' death, Douglas organized the Jesse Owens International Amateur Athlete Award, presented to the world's best amateur athlete each year. Winners so far: Eric Heiden, Sebastian Coe, Mary Decker and Edwin Moses.

"After the '36 Olympics, Jesse was campaigning for Alf Landon. He came to Pittsburgh, where I lived, and my mother took me to see him. She pushed me in front of him and introduced me. I was 13. I told him what I'd done in track in junior high. He said to me:

" 'Say, that's terrific. You're way ahead of me at your age, you'll probably do well in sports—but make sure you work harder at your education, promise?'

"More than any one event in my life, I think that brief conversation with Jesse Owens that day had a more positive influence in my life than anything else.

"I got a degree later at the University of Pittsburgh, and later a master's.

"Jesse was one of the all-time nice guys. No athlete was ever more cooperative . . . I never heard him say a bad word about another person.

"He was in Tampa in 1971 with me, appearing in a commercial I was in charge of. He had lung trouble even then, and went into a bad coughing fit. It was really bad. He couldn't come out of it, and we called an ambulance. We rode to the hospital with him, and they wheeled him into emergency.

"Some kid runs up as they wheel him in and says: 'Mr. Owens, I know this isn't a good time, but would you sign your autograph for me?'

"And he signed it, coughing terribly, turning blue. We thought we were going to lose him, right there, and he's signing an autograph for this kid.

"How people loved him! I'll never forget walking into a restaurant in New York about 10 years ago with him. One person recognized him, stood up and started clapping, and by the time we got to our table, everyone in the restaurant was standing and clapping.

"He had a way of doing something nice for you, even a little thing . . . and you never forget the little things. One time I introduced him to my mother—40 years after she introduced me to him—just before the 1976 Olympics. And he told her he'd send her something from Montreal. Well, he sent her a box of 1976 Olympic glasses. She never forgot that."

□

Mel Walker, 70, lives in Chicago. He was an Ohio State teammate of Owens. He failed to make the 1936 Olympic team, but in 1937 broke the world indoor and outdoor records in the high jump, jumping 6-9¾ and 6-10¾.

He remembers the last time he saw Owens, in 1980.

"Jesse and I talked off and on over the last 10 years of his life about starting a chain of sporting goods stores in the Chicago area. Just before he found out he had lung cancer, he'd almost put a deal together with a franchiser.

"Then I found out he was in the hospital, with cancer, and I went to see him. We both knew how sick he was.

"He motioned me to his bed, and said quietly to me: 'I made that contact . . . I told him about you . . . You follow through on this deal, Mel. This guy's waiting for your call.'

"That was two months before he died. Here's a guy dying, with nothing else on his mind but trying to do me a favor. He was the most unselfish man I ever knew.

"I'll always remember a day in 1935—the year he set four world records in one meet—when we came upon each other in the street in Columbus. I needed a suit, found one for $20, and told him I only had $15. Well, he was making 40 cents an hour working in the state office building, just like me. We were both broke most of the time. He reached in his pocket and handed me $5.

"He was a guy who'd give you the shirt off his back, if he thought it'd make you happy.

"Jesse ran the freight elevator in the state building, I was on the janitorial crew. We worked from 5 p.m. to 10 p.m., Monday through Friday, all through our Ohio State years.

"I never heard him say a negative thing about anyone, even during the trouble at the Mexico City Olympics, when some rough things were said about him. (Harry Edwards, an organizer of the black American boycott that year, reportedly called Owens "a boot-licking Uncle Tom.")

"Jesse did not like controversy. He'd do anything to avoid it. We all thought of him as sort of a pacifist. But near the end of his life, he became a bit more militant. I went with him to a gathering in Columbus in the mid-1970s, where he gave a speech.

"He talked about the tough days at Ohio State, when we couldn't live on campus and couldn't buy a meal at any restaurant near the campus. He summed it all up by saying: 'We paid our dues, we paid our dues.'

"You know, we actually lived in the stadium at Ohio State when we trained for the 1936 Olympic trials. Jesse, Dave Albritton, Charlie Beetham and I had four cots in the stadium. We trained until dark, then studied and slept in the stadium. Our Negro rooming house was quite a ways from the campus.

"I'll tell you something funny about his four world-record day at Ann Arbor in 1935. He'd fallen down the steps of his rooming house a few days before the meet and hurt his back.

"At Ann Arbor, it wasn't much better. I got him in a hot tub and rubbed down his back the night before. Over all the years, I teased him about it, for never giving me any credit for just one of those world records."

□

Marty Glickman, 66, was a Syracuse University sprinter who made the 1936 Olympic team in the 400-meter relay.

He was a sportscaster for many years, and is now retired, living in New York City.

"Jesse Owens was class, all the way. Let me tell you what he tried to do for me in Berlin, at the Olympics. He'd won three gold medals and we were at the end of the Olympics.

"The 400 relay was coming up. Sam Stoller and I had made the relay team, with Foy Draper and Frank Wykoff.

"Then the head coach, Lawson Robertson, and his assistant, Dean Cromwell, called a meeting of all the sprinters the day before the relay trials were to start.

"Robertson started talking about rumors that the Germans had some great sprinters under wraps, to surprise us in the relay. So he said he was pulling Sam and I off the relay and putting Jesse and Ralph Metcalfe on the team.

"My heart sank. I mean, it was a real blow. Jesse stood up and said:

'Coach, let Marty and Sam run. Ralph and I have won our medals. They deserve to run . . .'

"Cromwell cut him off by pointing a finger at him and saying, 'You'll do as you're told.'

"Well, of course there were no secret German sprinters. We won the relay final by 15 yards. My opinion then and now is that Avery Brundage (U.S. Olympic Committee president then, later president of the IOC) didn't want to embarrass the Germans further by having two Jews win medals, in addition to all the American black athletes who'd already won medals. It was well known then that Brundage was sympathetic to the Nazis.

"As far as I know, in the history of the Olympics, Sam and I are the only physically fit athletes to have qualified to compete in the Olympic Games, and then not been permitted to compete.

"Jesse and I became good friends and stayed close over the years. I never saw him angry. I saw him somber and serious, like the time he and his wife, Ruth, and my wife and I had lunch one day in 1979, in New York.

"He started talking about the old days, before the Berlin Olympics, when he competed for Ohio State. He told me when he came to Madison Square Garden for an indoor meet, he was allowed to stay at the Hotel Paramount, but only on the second floor and he had to ride the freight elevator.

"He talked about Columbus, after the Olympics. He told us about his ticker-tape parade up Broadway, in New York, when the Olympic team came home, about riding in the lead car with Mayor (Fiorello) La Guardia . . . then two weeks later being told he had to ride in the back of a city bus, in Cleveland.

"He wasn't bitter, he was matter-of-fact about it, and seemed just grateful those days were behind him.

"My gosh, what an athlete he was! He was far and away the greatest athlete at the Olympics, and so well liked by all the rest of us on the team. And he was such a beautiful-looking athlete, the perfect build. He had the second-most beautiful pair of legs I ever saw, next to my wife's.

"He was a very confident athlete, he knew how good he was. But he always handled it so well.

"As a sprinter—and I know this from having run against him maybe a dozen times in competition—the best part of his race was his midrace acceleration. From 20 to 80 yards, he was the fastest man in the world. Ralph Metcalfe was a great closer. Ralph could close on Jesse, but couldn't stay with him in the middle of the race, nobody could."

□

Louis Zamperini, 67, set a national high school mile record of 4:21.3 at Torrance High School in the spring of 1934. Much to his surprise, he made the Olympic team the next year, as a 5,000-meter runner.

He's still at his running weight, 147 pounds, still lives in Torrance, still runs, and is youth counselor at Hollywood First Presbyterian Church.

"So much was made over the Hitler business at the Olympics that year, that people forget how enamored the German people were of Owens. Gosh, the mobs of people who wanted his autograph.

"After the Olympics, the Germans had a sculptor engrave in the stone walls of the Olympic Stadium Owens' name and the records he set there. Yet all anyone remembers is Hitler.

"I first met him at the Olympic trials, at Randalls Island, and kept in touch over the years. I was thrilled just to be on the Olympic team, let alone meeting and becoming a friend of Jesse Owens.

"I was 18, the youngest runner on the team. My Olympics were to have been the 1940 Games (canceled because of World War II).

"I got into a little scrape with some German policemen in Berlin. After my event (he finished eighth in the 5,000), I went out for a walk and found myself out in front of the German Chancellery building.

"All these flagpoles were around, with Nazi flags. I figured one would make a great souvenir. So when the guards weren't looking, I untied the cord on one and ran it down the flagpole. I'd taken it off, when one of the guards spotted me.

"He yelled at me in German, and I started to run off with the flag. He yelled some more, but I kept running. When he fired a shot in the air, I stopped.

"They knew I was an American Olympic athlete, but they hauled me inside and into the office of a guy named Frick (Wilhelm Frick, Hitler's interior minister). He said to me: 'Why did you take that flag?'

" 'To remind me of the wonderful time I've had in Berlin,' I said.

" 'Let him have the flag,' " he said, and waved me away.

"There was a lot of commotion about the incident and back at the village, Jesse took me aside and said: 'Look, I know you meant no harm, that it was a harmless prank. But remember, you could get in serious trouble over here. Be careful.'

"What a beautiful runner he was. You know, he was so smooth he looked like he was working out when he ran hard. Now Metcalfe, he was a pounder . . . You could hear him coming. Jesse sort of floated.

"Jesse had a wonderful temperament, he always made you feel good. But I did see him angry, and that was right after the Olympics, when they (U.S. Olympic officials) booked him to run in meets all over Europe without consulting him. He was tired and homesick and wanted to go home.

"He refused to run anymore that summer, and the AAU threatened to bar him from amateur competition. He called them on it, and despite the fact he was only a junior at Ohio State, he never competed again."

□

John Woodruff, 68, was the 1936 gold medalist at 800 meters. He was a social worker most of his working life and is now retired and lives in East Windsor, N.J.

He plans to attend the Los Angeles Olympics, saying he'll park his trailer on the front lawn of Mack Robinson's Pasadena home.

"He had a big heart, one of the nicest people I've ever known. He'd do almost anything to help you out.

"I remember five years ago he'd agreed to appear at a youth sports awards banquet I'd put together. He called one night from St. Louis to tell me he couldn't, that his doctor was putting him in the hospital for a checkup. He talked like he'd let me down. That's the kind of guy he was. He made it so easy to be his friend.

"Well, he went in the hospital and found out he had cancer.

"In 1936, we all knew he'd do well in Berlin. He was the star of the Olympic team, we all knew that. He was so much better than everyone else.

"That Hitler snub stuff . . . there was nothing to that. One day, Jesse waved at Hitler and Hitler waved back. I saw it.

"But Jesse became a professional speech-maker, you know, and it made such a good story, Jesse kept telling it the way people wanted to hear it.

"In Berlin, we didn't even know there was a controversy going on. We didn't know about it until we got home."

□

Dave Albritton, 73, was the silver medalist in a 1-2-3 U.S. high jump sweep in 1936. He lives in Dayton, Ohio. He declined to be interviewed at first, saying he felt uncomfortable being interviewed over the telephone. Then he consented to talk briefly about Owens.

"I resent all these people who've appeared over the years, claiming to have known Jesse for years. It happened all the time when he was alive and now that he's gone, it happens even more.

"It bothers me because I knew him longer than anyone, longer even than Ruth (Owens' wife). Our families lived near each other in Alabama, we were boyhood friends, although I was two or three years older. Our fathers were friends.

"I'm godfather to his kids, he was godfather to mine.

"We roomed together on the Olympic team. The man had no enemies, ever. He was a warm, friendly man, and that's how I'll always remember him. He had a contagious personality. He could make you feel good even in tough times, and don't let anyone kid you, we went through tough times together. I mean, we were kicked out of places."

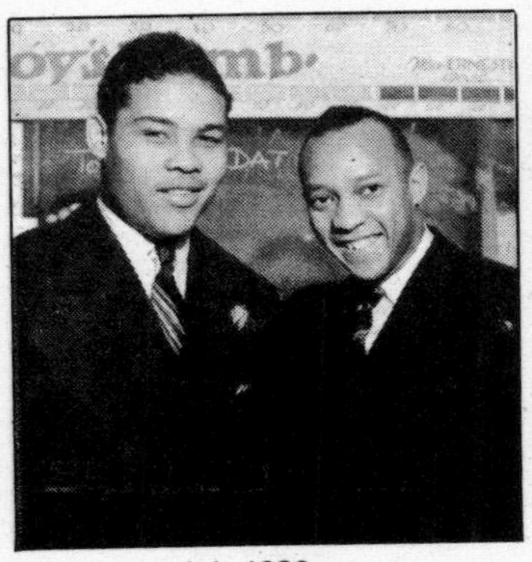

With Joe Louis in 1936.

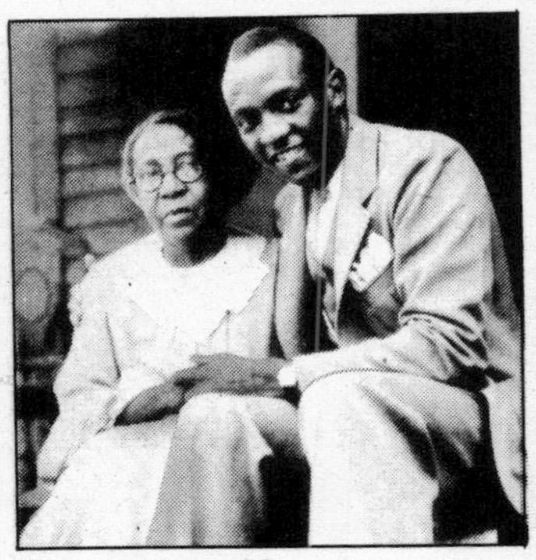

With mom in the '30s.

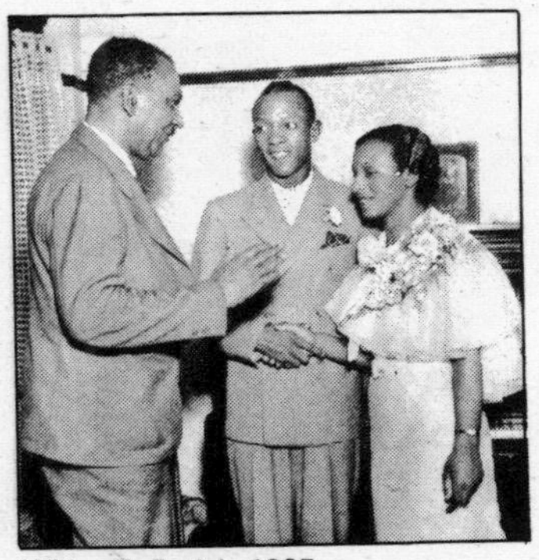

With wife Ruth in 1935.

OLYMPICS '84

5 DAYS TO GAMES

Coming Soon on the High Bar, the Utterly Amazing Gaylord II

Just When You Thought It Was Safe to Watch Gymnasts Again, a UCLA Athlete Tests the Limits of Ability and Good Sense

By RICHARD HOFFER, *Times Staff Writer*

Mitch Gaylord, who has grinned back at us from everything from Esquire ("Man at his Best") to Super Teen ("He's a super athlete with movie star looks!"), suddenly grimaces.

"Oh, *that* story," he says, reminded of the kind of tale that would make any athlete squirm. The one where he used to make himself unavailable whenever his gymnastics coach was instructing in the daring opportunities of the high bar. "The one," he offers finally, "where I used to conveniently hide in the bathroom."

Be fair. Who wouldn't? The high bar is, well, high. Getting on presupposes getting off, and gymnasts are supposed to do the latter with some kind of dangerous flair. And in between those two acts, a lot of really hairy stuff goes on. Giant circles, *one-handed* giant circles, blind release moves, somersaults over the bar, you name it. It looks plenty scary from the stands, where you're safely anchored on a bleacher seat. What do you think it looks like to the athlete who is momentarily suspended in midair,

coming out of a release move, looking for the bar and hoping he can catch it with something handier than his forehead?

It looks scary, of course. And it's a wonder whole teams of gymnasts aren't found loitering in the bathroom, pacing back and forth, hoping their coach doesn't think to peer into a stall. Waiting for somebody to dismantle that damn high bar and put it in a safe place.

Mitch Gaylord, 23, one of this country's brightest hopes for a medal, has, you might have guessed, long since reappeared, come out of that Northridge water closet so to speak, and attacked that high bar to international wonderment. What this Valley Boy does on that same high bar nine years later is so breathtakingly extraordinary, so unnecessarily risky that it is almost impossible to believe any story in which he might have shown fear.

The story is important to keep in mind, though, as we watch him throw that great, frenzied Gaylord II over the unforgiving high bar, filling that dangerous airspace with somersaults and twists. To know

that he once knew fear at least proves he's human. Or was once.

□

Men's gymnastics is a strange and demanding enterprise. To perform it well requires attention to detail as well as to the more appealing flair of flight. A triple fly away somersault off the rings counts for little if, during one of his stationary strength moves, the gymnast allows the wires to sway. A "full-in, full-out"—a double twist, double somersault—may be discounted during floor exercises if the gymnast fails to point his toes, or if he steps out of bounds.

Any single routine is made up of thousands of alignments, subtle positionings of the body that lead smoothly from one movement to the next. Sometimes this prized continuity is broken and a miscalculation can be compounded by another to the point where a gymnast may simply halt, dead in the air, so out of synch and position he may be unable to complete his routine at all, much less poorly.

More often these tiny miscalcu-

Please see GAYLORD, page 12

GARY FRIEDMAN / Los Angeles Times
Mitch Gaylord, 23, is one of this country's brightest hopes to win a medal in gymnastics.

GARY FRIEDMAN / Los Angeles Times
Mary Lou Retton, at age 16, is rated the best and most popular gymnast in the United States.

Wait Until TV Catches This Act

Everything Points to 4-9 Mary Lou Retton Emerging as a Star

By RICHARD HOFFER, *Times Staff Writer*

Mary Lou Retton, who is not above gushing over teen idol Matt Dillon (at 4-9, she can not be considered above much of anything), is on the verge of becoming a teen idol herself. As it is now, little girls routinely unfurl banners with her name from the upper levels of stadiums. They gather in post-meet hordes and squeal for her autograph. Once, following a public haircut, girls stooped to collect her shorn locks.

When these Olympics are over, however, it is possible this little fireplug of a girl will be much more than a gym club pinup, a picture on somebody's bedroom wall. Matt Dillon will look like small potatoes indeed if things go right.

If things go right, she will vault into global fame, her televised smile—it stretches from here to there—becoming a part of history. Ever after, she will beam down from that small constellation of

stars, athletes who have leapt into public consciousness on the strength of a smile or a tear, athletes who have transcended their sport. There was Olga, there was Nadia. There could be, if things go right, Mary Lou shining down from the heavens, the twinkle in her eye all the star power she needs.

She is without doubt both the best and most popular gymnast in this country. That is a small thing normally. But the Olympics have a way of turning these little tumblers into full-blown heroines. The camera's eye, fixed on this bundle of grace and charm and energy, seems always to find theater, to find drama on the large mats, to find grown-up stars in a giggling gaggle of junior high girls.

Olga Korbut took us all by surprise in 1972. In 1976, our last Olympics, it was the steely perfection of 14-year-old Nadia Comane-

ci that drew us to the screen, transfixed by her youthful achievement. It hardly mattered that we couldn't do a Tsukahara vault ourselves. It hardly mattered that we didn't know when they were doing one. Gymnastics was as inaccessible as ever, a cult sport if ever there was one. What mattered was our exhilaration in the presence of such on-screen and unspoken personality, charm articulated wholly by movement.

If you accept the time-tested premise that a child shall lead them, be prepared to accept Mary Lou Retton, a 16-year-old who is almost painfully normal in street clothes, but superhuman in leotards. If things go right, if she wins a medal, America's first ever in this sport, the name Mary Lou will become as Olga and Nadia before her. A lot more enduring than, for example, Matt Dillon.

Please see RETTON, page 11

Agony Joined in the Ecstasy of Victory for Japan's Shun Fujimoto

By BILL SHIRLEY, *Times Staff Writer*

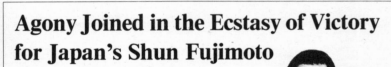

TOKYO—The Olympic Games are a splendid stage for high drama. The world will long remember the marvelous skills and gold-medal performances of Jim Thorpe, Babe Didrikson, Paavo Nurmi, Jesse Owens, Bob Mathias, Emil Zatopek, Olga Korbut, Nadia Comaneci, Mark Spitz and all the other virtuosos of their sport?

The world should also long remember Shun Fujimoto. He won a gold medal, too, but it is unlikely that many people remember the little Japanese fellow or even what sport he played.

The noun "courage" and the adjective "courageous" are often misused by sportswriters, who in their zeal to overdramatize games, rhapsodize over injured athletes as if they are heroes.

But what Shun Fujimoto did one night in July, 1976, in the Olympic Games at Montreal was, even in the little world of sports, an act of courage.

"It was the most incredible thing we saw happen here," ABC's Frank Gifford said in a televised review of the dramatic events of those Games.

Fujimoto was on the rings in the Forum on the last day of the men's team gymnastic competition. The Japanese were losing to the Russians at the time but still had a good shot at the gold medal. Fujimoto knew that, of course; that's why he had not told his coach or teammates about his injury. He feared they would worry and be distracted.

His performance on the rings went well and then came the moment when he had to dismount. He hurled himself off the rings with a flourish, twisting and flipping his 136-pound body high into the air, and headed for a landing. There was no water, no foam rubber pit to cushion his fall.

It was over in a fraction of a second. He landed hard, as he knew he would.

His right leg buckled slightly and he raised it, almost imperceptibly, to ease the pressure on his knee.

Please see FUJIMOTO, page 11

Associated Press
Gymnast Shun Fujimoto displays his gold medal and a cast on his broken leg at Montreal in 1976.

RETTON

Continued from page 10

Mary Lou Retton, b. Jan. 24, 1968, in Fairmont, W. Va. . . . Father Ron was a 5-7 guard at West Virginia University, co-captain with Jerry West, later a shortstop in Yankees' farm system. "Competitive guy," remembers West . . . Collects stuffed animals . . . Weighs 94 pounds (sometimes 92, sometimes 95), wears size 3 shoe . . . Energy was finally channeled into gymnastics when mother Lois decided that far too may lamps had been overturned and broken . . . Older sister Shari (who also broke lamps) was an All-American gymnast at West Virginia as a freshman . . . Trained by hometown coach Gary Rafaloski until early 1983, when Bela Karolyi, Nadia's old coach, "recruited" her Rafaloski stopped speaking with the Retton family . . . A top junior gymnast, she burst onto the elite scene last year by winning the prestigious American Cup as a walk-on. She replaced her injured Houston teammate Dianne Durham in the meet. Durham, briefly the top-ranked gymnast, later left the club and returned. She failed to make the Olympic team . . . Retton has won the all-around in every meet this year, including U.S. Championships and Olympic trials . . . Inspired, of course, by Nadia . . . Performed during halftime of West Virginia basketball games at 9, has dim memory of experience . . . Was always shaped like a block, with broad shoulders and massive thighs. Family used to tease her by calling her Miss Grace or Miss Flexibility . . . Has been known to show fear; sweated out one bad moment while sharing a Twinkie under the table with Durham while Marta Karolyi was on patrol . . . Asked whether she worries about growing she answers in wide-eyed surprise: "I hope I grow."

□

Bela Karolyi, the enormously likable megalomaniac, has hardly ever spared a moment in the creation and nurturing of his own legend. Since defecting from Romania in 1981, he has told yarn after yarn, most so good you are afraid to check them out. One example: Things were so bad when he first came to the United States, he tells you, that he had to supplement his income from a small gymnastics club in Oklahoma with money from a paper route.

You don't dare check this one out but you happen to run into Paul Ziert, who has been a top coach of both women and men for a long time. Ziert was the man who first befriended Karolyi, gave him that first menial job. Well, not so menial. "We were paying him, altogether, nearly $50,000 when he first got here," says Ziert. "I want to make it clear that I'm not saying he was lying in that paper route story. He may well have thrown the paper. But he surely was the best-paid paper boy in history."

TONY BARNARD / Los Angeles Times

The timing is perfect for gymnastics phenom Mary Lou Retton, 16, who is ready to bend over backward to win a medal in the L.A. Olympic Games.

Ziert remains a fan of Karolyi, even though he had to fire him from his club when Karolyi began recruiting for his own club on the sly. Does the word entrepreneur apply to Karolyi? Ziert raises his eyebrows about nine feet. Manipulative? Eyebrows are in another stratosphere now.

But if Karolyi is interested in his own legend (one more example, to the possible surprise of the U.S. Olympic Committee: Outside his Houston club is a sign that says U.S. Olympic Gymnastics Center, he is also making his gymnasts legends. It makes good sense. Not only do parents want to send their youngsters to the man who crafted Nadia, but the youngsters themselves are willing to listen to such a formidable name in gymnastics. He did it for Nadia, he'll do it for me. The man with the magic wand.

"Of course, five years from now, the way this sport changes," says Ziert, "you'll say Nadia to these kids and they'll look at you like this." By that time, it is suggested, he may have another name to bandy about. "Right, Mary Lou Retton."

Karolyi learned excellent English within two years but nevertheless seems always to be doing an impersonation of Dan Aykroyd and Steve Martin in their old Saturday Night Live "Two Wild and Crazy Guys" routine. His manic, open face is a hilarious feature at meets, especially when he runs out to embrace his gymnasts. It's as if he's this big innocent lug who has never seen anything so wonderful in all his life.

But, if he at times seems a comic figure, be advised that he is shrewd and serious about the development of Retton, who is both his gymnast and his ticket. This may sound overly cynical but in this game a coach is only as good as his latest prodigy. A coach only has power in relation to the rankings of his gymnasts. Right now he is powerful and intends to remain so.

However, in the creation of the Retton legend, Karolyi has not had to do much. Just respond to the obligatory comparisons to Nadia and Olga—"Mary Lou is a combination between the two. Mary Lou is very aggressive but also has concentration and a very open and pleasant style. She can represent herself beautifully." By that he means, Mary Lou has the ability of Nadia, the outgoing personality of Korbut.

Occasionally Karolyi does get caught up in his own enthusiasm. "Mary Lou cannot be stopped," he will say. "She will win many medals. For sure, she will win the vault."

Just a manipulative entrepreneur talking? Not at all. Retton's Olympic coach, Don Peters, has to agree with Karolyi. He even gives Mary Lou a good chance to win the all-around, no small thing even during a boycotted Olympics. The Soviets may be missing but the Romanians will be here, making women's gymnastics nearly as competitive as before. Moreover, to lend some objectivity to Karolyi's effusive predictions, Peters gives her a chance to become this Olympics' star. "Didn't she get your heart?" he asked after a recent competition. "She got mine."

That she smiles naturally and playfully is part of her gift to the sport. With some gymnasts, any show of joy is forced. Julianne McNamara, a Houston teammate who had been the reigning gymnast in this country until Retton burst onto the scene, will smile occasionally. However, it looks like she is just remembering to do so, as if somebody from the stands reminded her to. Retton, meanwhile, plays the crowd like a lounge singer. "I like to use the crowd to my advantage," she says, shrugging. In one of her moves on the uneven bars, she shoots to the top bar where, miraculously, she lands right on her seat. She throws her hands up—"Look Ma!"—in an almost shameless display of a playful self-confidence. When she completes any of her three tumbling passes on the floor exercise, she smiles right up into the crowd, communicating her sheer pleasure at achieving perfection.

If that is rare, it is not all she has going for her. Besides her own perky personality, besides having the legend-maker behind her, she is also an extraordinary, albeit unusual gymnast. Traditionally this has been a sport of elegance, with wispy bags of bones posturing from here to there. And then comes Retton, who (this isn't meant unkindly) seems to waddle onto the mat like a power lifter. No pretty posing for her. Brute strength all the way. On her vaults, she occasionally gets lost in the lights—"I see her now, here she comes!" On the floor exercise her three tumbling passes are of such difficulty that even somebody who doesn't know double-layout from a double-cheese can recognize that something is going on.

"There is no secret to her gymnastics," says Karolyi, for once demystifying an issue. "It is strength." Even Retton fesses up. "I'm not the traditional gymnast," she says, "with a skinny body and a ponytail. I'm the opposite, muscular built with short hair. It's my natural body type and I use it to my advantage."

When she first exploded onto the scene—and that word is not used carelessly—there were detractors. Many of the traditionalists (a traditionalist: any coach who doesn't have Retton) considered her a freak, a bouncing phenomenon whose initial shock value would wear off and yield once more to pretty gymnastics. The novelty of her tumbling wouldn't last. International judges would tear her apart.

As Retton has never competed in a big-time international meet, there could yet be something to this. At the world championships, for example, which she did not compete in, Natalia Yurchenko of the Soviet Union, a throwback to a more elegant era in the sport, won the all-around championship. However, Peters doubts Retton will suffer. In fact, he thinks her limited exposure will work to her advantage. "The first time you see her, you're most impressed," he says. "She just knocks your socks off." The wow value, in other words, may cloud a judge's eyes to any deficiencies.

As Retton has continued to win whatever meets she enters, her detractors have fallen by the wayside. Gymnastics is above all a sport of change and coaches and athletes who resist it get left behind. Who knows that better than Karolyi, who has been willing to change everything (countries even) to keep in the forefront? What of the style popular in 1976, with nice fluid movements? "That time is over, we already have had Nadia," he says. "That happened eight years ago. We have to provide a new style to win. We have to do something very different."

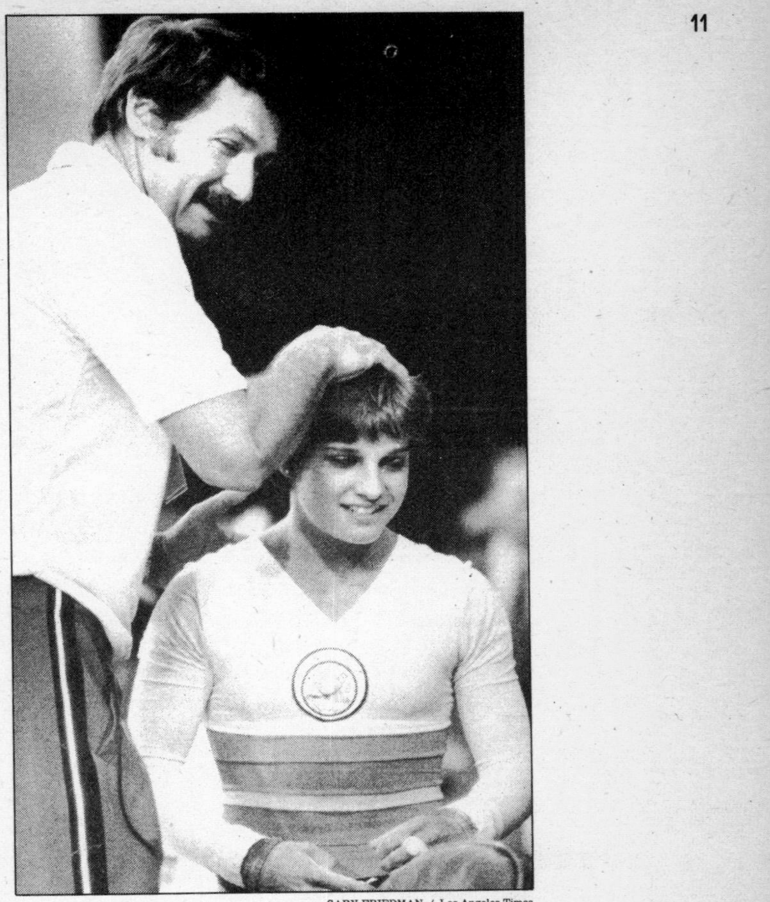

GARY FRIEDMAN / Los Angeles Times

The coach is Bela Karolyi of Romania; the smile is vintage Retton.

Karolyi implies that the cutting edge in women's gymnastics is now power. You may not doubt this when you see Retton perform three double-backs on floor, one of them a layout with a full twist (nobody does so much in midair). However, Karolyi didn't create a trend, only recognized it. He was smart enough to see what he had in Retton, smart enough to package it. On those same floor exercises, for example, Karolyi has not just created a showcase of brute strength. He has also gotten Geza Poszar to create a dramatic dance routine for her. Poszar is the man who choreographed Nadia's routine. Nice touch.

Probably anybody who doubts that this will be rewarded by judges is, as Karolyi suggests, living in another age. Gymnastics celebrates the new, history teaches us that. Korbut, who wasn't even the best gymnast on her 1972 Olympic team, is the name that comes to mind simply because she was a daring enough gymnast to compete in an innovative way. Judges will probably fall in love with Mary Lou, too.

If that happens—if judges are compelled at all by a display that is equal parts raw strength, determined perfection and what can only be called happiness in flight—then Retton will surely win a medal, many maybe. For sure, this bouncing 16-year-old with the size 3 feet and size 10 grin, this girl who hopes only to win Matt Dillon's heart, will win yours.

FUJIMOTO

Continued from page 10

In the ABC film, Fujimoto grits his teeth in pain as he lands. More pain is evident as he holds his position steadily for a moment then straightens and raises his arms in the traditional pose of the gymnast who has concluded his routine. He limped off the mat, favoring his right leg noticeably, into the arms of his coach.

Routine was it? Shun Fujimoto had performed on the rings knowing he would have to come down on a broken leg.

The story, which went virtually unnoticed during the Games, even in the Japanese press, ended happily. Fujimoto was awarded a score of 9.7 on the rings, points that helped Japan win the gold medal.

Recently, Fujimoto sat with a reporter in the stands of the Metropolitan Gymnasium here, the site of the gymnastics competition in the 1964 Olympic Games, and talked about the incident.

Today at 33, he retains the slight, muscular build of a gymnast. He is, in fact, the same size he was at Montreal: a wiry 5-4, 136 pounds. He was nattily attired in a double-breasted navy blue blazer and gray slacks, the uniform of a judge in the Japanese Olympic gymnastic trials which were in progress. He was judging the rings. He does not speak English; the interview was conducted through an interpreter.

Fujimoto broke his right leg on the second day of the competition while performing in the floor exercise. It broke at the knee, he said, as he flipped at the end of his routine and tried to keep his body stable as he landed.

He knew when it broke. "It happened at my knee. It was so strange because it felt as though there was air in my knee. It became numb, and although I felt pain, I didn't feel anything at my knee."

Fujimoto blames the softness of the Forum surface for his injury. "Japanese floors are much harder," he said, "so it is much easier to stop. When I tried to stop with all my might, this reflex came back to me and it was very hard to keep my body stable at the time of landing."

The sidehorse was next. He knew he was hurt. What were his thoughts?

" When I broke my leg," he said, "I was more concerned with the next routine that I was to perform than the breaking of my leg.

"Up to that point the Soviet Union was beating Japan, so I felt I could not fail on the sidehorse. It is the hardest event, the easiest one in which to make mistakes. So I was completely occupied by the thought that I could not afford to make any mistakes."

But what about he pain?

"Of course, my leg was hurting me, but I really could not afford to care about this injury. So I didn't even think about my knee before I tried the sidehorse. I just concentrated on that because I had to do it successfully."

He was successful enough to get a 9.5 and was relieved that the sidehorse was behind him. "But soon I had to think of the rings," he said, "and I realized I had to do some taping of my knee because with the rings the landing is very hard and is a tremendous shock on the knees." He stood up and flexed his knees to show the reporter how the landing goes.

He didn't get the knee taped, however. Why?

"I must tell you I didn't really care about the injury," he replied. "I was so preoccupied with winning that I did the rings without taping my knee."

At the moment he landed off the rings, he compounded the agony of a broken knee by dislocating it. "I finished with the rings," he said, "and at the time of landing, fortunately my body stopped. At that moment the joint of my knee was dislocated. If my body was not stable at that time it could have been really serious and I could have been handicapped. I was lucky to be able to avoid that."

How badly did it hurt when he landed?

"I can only describe it as . . . well, it hurt as much as my whole blood was boiling at my stomach."

Why didn't he tell anybody that his leg was broken?

"I tried not to show it (the injury) to them because I did not want to cause any trouble for my teammates and my coach. If I had done that it would have caused some fear, so I didn't say anything."

After finishing his routine on the rings, however, Fujimoto knew he had to do something about his leg.

"After the rings there was supposed to be the long horse, which requires running and jumping and a lot of exercise using the legs and feet," he said."So I went to talk to a Japanese doctor to see if he would give me a shot to kill the pain."

Told that the shot would not be subject to a drug check, Fujimoto went to the Olympic medical center to get it. The Canadian doctors took one look at his leg, however, and suggested he quit the competition.

He missed three individual events as well as the final team routine. Remarkably, his scores, after his leg was broken, were satisfactory for him, he said.

After his withdrawal, his teammates joked with him and said "they were awakened and felt pressed that they had to do better to make up for his absence. They later told me they all turned pale."

The injury ended Fujimoto's gymnastic career. In the first year after the accident, he concentrated on healing his leg. He tried to compete the next year but his right knee no longer could support him. He had lost the ligaments in it. "So I had to give it up," he said.

He is often reminded of the accident today because the knee still collapses on him. He lives in a small town with his wife and young son about a two-hour train ride from here. He is a physical education instructor at a teachers' college and owns a small gym where he trains young gymnasts, ages 9 to 15.

Is his sport getting too dangerous?

"It's not basically dangerous," he said as he watched his country's finest gymnasts do their hazardous stunts in the arena where he had often performed. "Skills are improving because safety measures are better today. But carelessness causes accidents; I'm more afraid of traffic accidents than accidents in gymnasiums."

Judge Fujimoto had to get back to the rings again. He was asked one more question before he left: "Would you do it again, knowing about the pain?'

The reply was emphatic. "No," he said, "I would not do it again."

He bowed to the reporter and went back to work.

Runners in a 100-meter qualifying race at the 1896 Olympic Games in Athens line up for the start. Second from left is American Thomas Curtis, the only runner starting from a full crouched position.

GAYLORD

Continued from page 10

lations are simply logged by judges, people trained to notice such flaws, any indication that the athlete has lost control. A wondrous, crowd-pleasing routine may show up as a 9.5. The crowd may be baffled but gymnast and judge know something was wrong, some alignment of body was not achieved, some position not maintained.

To that extent, gymnastics is a tedious game, the winning routines products of mind-numbing repetitions. The gymnast spends hours a week traveling the length of a pommel horse, up and down, putting his hands just so every time. Or doing the same vault, timing his spring from the handstand into a somersault just so.

For all that, nobody wins without what is known as ROV—risk, originality and virtuosity. Nobody wins without that veneer of spectacle, without the big trick, the killer move that leaves even judges open-mouthed. Gymnastics may be a strict and unyielding organization of body mechanics on the one hand, on the other it's an outrageous flouting of physics, a mockery of all its laws. *Hey, let's try a triple somersault on floor. Who will ever notice. Gravity?*

Gymnasts hate any analogy to the circus but, in truth, some of their moves belong more under the big tent than on any platform. Their fundamental mastery achieved—toes pointed, rings motionless—they move quickly into the business of creating awe, in us, each other and judges. It's a competition, of course, with each gymnast trying to outdo the other, childlike almost. *You do three, I'll do four somersaults.* It creates a momentum of escalating difficulty that surprises us every Olympics.

We should not be surprised. In between these public exposures, these parades of gymnastics' military hardware, these gymnasts are busy crafting knock-your-socks off routines, drafting whole new movements, inventing new moves, enlarging the parameters of motion. In short, engaging in an acrobatic one-upmanship, pushing back the edge of the envelope.

Somewhere out there is a "10," or else the biggest, most spectacular, midair flameout seen this side of the FAA. "Crash and burn," you should know, is a descriptive phrase that turns up as much in talk of gymnastics as aviation.

□

All the gymnasts you will see in these Olympics have the Right Stuff, that combination of ambition, courage and good sense that make safe landings at least thinkable along with their increasingly daring routines. Each of the U.S. gymnasts has long since worked up his element of amazement, the stunner that forces a judge to care about his performance, in a sudden and personal kind of way.

All these gymnasts have developed some move or some moves that are original in combination to anticipate the incoming surprises of the gymnastics powers. In the past, U.S. athletes lagged in this regard, staying far from the cutting edge. But now they all have their tricks. For Gaylord, who was once afraid of the high bar, it is the Gaylord II. We'll be looking at that trick, as much to understand Gaylord as the scarifying evolution of men's gymnastics.

'You do need something—either this or consecutive releases—to set you apart. You have to do something so that the judges almost want you to win it. . . . You have to do something where they'll reward you even if you are sloppy doing it. If I catch that, they definitely overlook things.'

—MITCH GAYLORD

In gymnastics, it is possible to achieve immortality by performing an original trick in international competition. A Hecht reverse or a Stalder shoot, for example, are moves named after their creators. In time, Hecht has come to stand more for a move than a gymnast. Which is good. Because a gymnast will lose his flexibility and his usefulness long before his move does. Should anyone be so foolish as to take up the Gaylord II, Gaylord's legacy also will be extended.

How to describe it? "It's a fly away with a half twist, one-and-a-half over the bar," Gaylord explains, removing as much of gymnastics' jargon as possible. But that doesn't really describe it, either, does it. Let's try again. Somehow, Gaylord achieves enough speed on the bar during a giant circle that, when he lets go near the top of his arc, he has the time and distance to perform a one-and-a-half somersault in midair, with a half twist thrown in. When it works, he will catch the bar out of his tumble and go on with his routine, the remainder of which hardly anybody is in a state to notice.

Nobody else does it or should be made to. Some gymnasts, even at the Olympic level, will not use releases of any kind. There are two things that can happen and one is bad. Some will do simple, basic recatches, if blind faith in your own trajectory can be called basic. Others use more fanciful combinations. Gaylord's teammate, Peter Vidmar, does two recatches in breathless succession, remarkable in that they are consecutive.

Nobody does anything like Gaylord, though. It's too hard. Here's one way to think about it. Until 1974, maybe one or two gymnasts were doing something as routine as a one-handed giant swing (when we say routine, be advised that all things are relative). And suddenly there's a man tumbling in the dead zone above the bar, having to twist out of his own private aerial circus at the last minute just to see that awful looming piece of aluminum, either his salvation or his damnation.

There are things that can go wrong, and have. The Gaylord Flip, the precursor, is a similar trick but without the twist. It went wrong often enough that Gaylord had to abandon it altogether. He would miss the bar and crash to the mat. It happens enough with Gaylord II, for that matter, to keep him sensitive to the demands of gravity. In the Olympic trials, he came out of his spin too late and crashed on his elbow. He had performed it flawlessly all week and he had no reason to believe he couldn't wrestle that bar to submission in competition.

There are worse things that can happen, though. As it happens, Gaylord is not the originator of this trick, only the first one to throw it—and catch it—in international competition. The inventor is UCLA and Olympic teammate Tim Daggett, who came up with the trick when he was far too young to envision its consequences. The precocious Daggett was in high school when, in the constant evolution of movement, he came up with the idea for this trick. "You're always looking for something bigger and better," he says, articulating every gymnast's credo. Ah, youth.

Daggett was doing it a little differently than Gaylord does it now. Believing that in gymnastics everything must come out of a handstand, Daggett was catching the bar out of his somersault while coming down on it, instead of going away from it. "One time I got into a poor situation," he said, sounding a little bit like Chuck Yeager describing a flameout at Mach II, "and landed really bad." He missed his grip and his arms slid straight down until his neck came to rest on the bar. "It didn't collapse my windpipe," he says, "but it did compress it a little."

Daggett tried to get back to the trick but hardly any gymnast recovers from disaster to

Please see GAYLORD, below

THE GAYLORD II

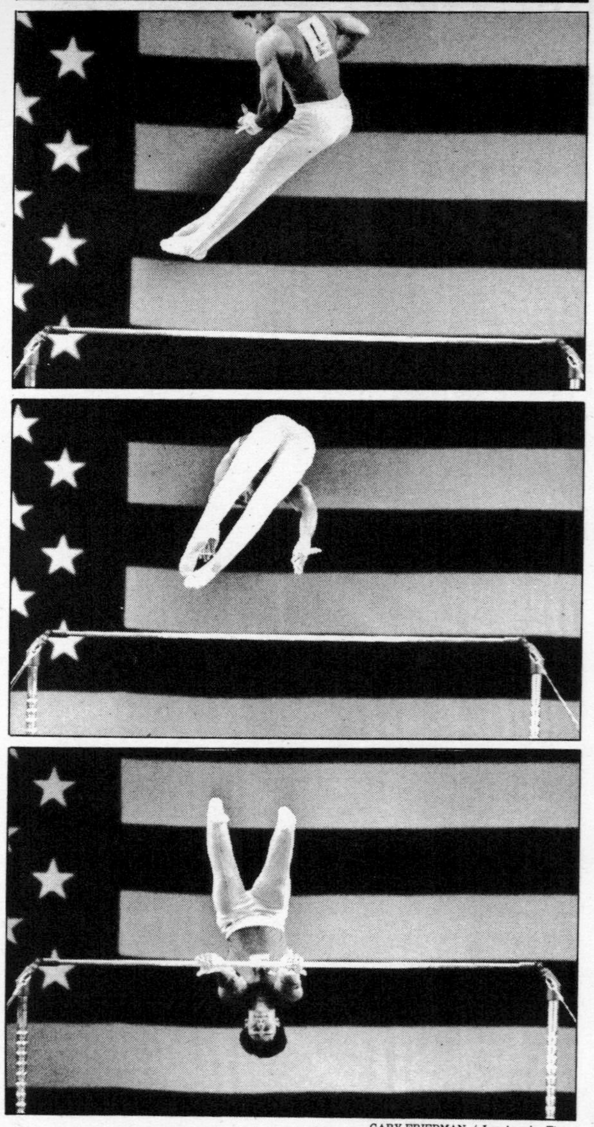

GARY FRIEDMAN / Los Angeles Times

Mitch Gaylord is in the middle (top photo) of both his forward somersault and half twist as he soars above the bar, in the new release move called Gaylord II. The somersault and twist completed (middle), he grabs the bar with an under-grip and then finishes (bottom) the giant swing.

GAYLORD

Continued from above

perform the same trick with confidence. "I tried to relearn it," he said, "but it was too traumatic. It was making me hate the sport. It was fear. You need fear with that trick but I had a kind of fear that made that trick impossible. I'm certain I could learn that trick again but . . ."

But he has learned others instead and now courts disaster and perfect scores in other, no less amazing ways. But leave that particular trick to somebody else.

□

"I saw Tim doing it about five years ago," Gaylord said. "It's a wild trick if you think about it. But he's a wild guy. I'm sure if I had seen him hit his neck on that bar, though, I wouldn't be doing it now."

It's no use to ask Gaylord why he's doing it at all. He admits it's not necessary. He was scoring well without it, winning the U.S. championships two years running. "All last year, when I wasn't using either (I or II), using a really conservative routine, I was scoring a 9.9 when I hit. But I've always been considered a high-bar guy. I thought I always used to be exciting."

So he put in Daggett's trick, Gaylord I. That was adventuresome enough but then it got too adventuresome. "That was the most frustrating trick," he said. "It's what brought me into the high ranking, what brought me a lot of attention. I used to hit it all the time but then I developed too much strength." Something was amiss, thrown off, and suddenly he rarely ever hit it.

'That was the most frustrating trick (the Gaylord I). It's what brought me into the high ranking, what brought me a lot of attention. I used to hit it all the time but then I developed too much strength.'

—MITCH GAYLORD

So he modified it, adding a half twist in February. The half twist adds both an element of danger and safety. It's one more movement to complete in the air, when his agenda is already pretty full. On the other hand, it allows him to glimpse the bar a little sooner. Actually this wasn't his idea either. In practice he noticed UCLA teammate Tony Pineda, who will be competing on Mexico's Olympic team, "playing around with it in the belt (a suspension device)." He said, "That's the trick for me."

It's still not what you'd call sure fire. Whenever Gaylord misses the bar, he's cashing in a half-point deduction, not to mention his good looks. And he never knows when he'll miss. Before the trials, he was hitting it 80% of the time. He missed it. Before the U.S.-China meet he was missing it. He caught the trick in the meet. "No real theme to it," he said. "It's nothing to keep stats on, you just throw it."

It's possible he won't throw it in Olympic competition because there are team considerations. A safe 9.9 might look better in the final standings than a spectacular, crash-landed 9.2. On the other hand, Gaylord knows there is no way to win a medal in an event without throwing some death-defying stunt at the judges. "No way I can medal without it."

Gaylord says, "You do need something—either this or consecutive releases—to set you apart. You have to do something so that the judges almost want you to win it. They have to be saying to themselves, 'This is awesome, he's doing something nobody else is doing. If he nails it, he has to win.' You have to do something where they'll reward you even if you are sloppy doing it. If I catch that, they definitely overlook things."

Missing it destroys a lot of good will but catching it, well, there's nothing like it to create instant empathy, to have judges actually rooting for you. To help create it, Gaylord has put his big trick right in the beginning of his routine. The wow factor of the trick is such that it might be hard to remember any flaws to follow. The other thing is that Gaylord likes to get the trick out of the way, when he's strong and confident, before anything can disturb his momentum. "If I catch it," he says, "the routine's over."

Of course it's not over, not really. A difficult dismount—either a triple somersault or a twisting layout, depending on what everybody else is doing—must follow eventually, the icing on the cake. And judges will only overlook so much, big tricks notwithstanding. "In the China meet," Gaylord admits, "I made it but I didn't come out of it smoothly and I only got a 9.85. I didn't even win."

Muses Gaylord, his winning smile back, his education in this difficult sport finally complete, "They want everything." Not delivering everything is all that scares him these days.

Legendary Trivia

Playing Dress-Up Hurt Athletes in 1900

The first U.S. woman to win a gold medal in the Olympic Games was Margaret Abbott. In the 1900 Games at Paris, Abbott won the women's golf, shooting 47 for nine holes.

Abbott, 5-foot-11, was a 22-year-old Chicago socialite who traveled to Paris in 1899 with her mother, literary editor and novelist Mary Ives Abbott, so she could study art.

Abbott later told relatives that she won the tournament "because all the French girls apparently misunderstood the nature of the game scheduled for that day and turned up to play in high heels and tight skirts."

□

Golf was dropped as an Olympic sport after the 1904 Games at St. Louis. The men's champion that year was Canada's George Lyon, an eccentric who didn't pick up a golf club until he was 38 years old. Before that, he had competed successfully in baseball, tennis and cricket. Once, he even set a Canadian record in the pole vault.

Lyon was 46 when he won the Olympics. On the course, he was an endless source of cheerful energy, singing, telling jokes and even doing handstands. In the match play final, he beat 23-year-old Chandler Egan of the United States, 3 and 2. He was awarded a $1,500 sterling silver trophy, which he accepted after walking down the path to the ceremony on his hands.

□

Randy Williams was a USC freshman when he won the Olympic long jump in 1972. Incredibly, he never won the event in a dual meet against UCLA. More amazing, he lost to four different Bruins. In order, they were Finn Bendixen, Jerry Herndon, James McAlister and Willie Banks.

Banks was a freshman when he beat Williams, a senior, in the 1975 USC-UCLA meet. And later in the same meet, Banks was a hero in the triple jump. USC was leading the meet with one round left in the final event, the triple jump. Banks was third behind two Trojans when, on his final attempt, he went 55-1½, almost two feet better than his previous best, to win the event and give UCLA the victory.

□

In the first modern Olympics at Athens in 1896, the winner of the marathon was Spiridon Louis of Greece. When Louis appeared at the marble entrance to the stadium, Prince George and Crown Prince Constantine of Greece rushed down to greet him. Then they escorted him the rest of the way to the finish line where Louis summoned enough energy to bow to the delighted King George.

Leading the event with only four miles left was Australia's Edwin Flack, who only hours earlier had won the 800 meters. Fatigue finally overtook Flack, who began to stagger. A Greek fan tried to help him, but Flack, thinking he was being attacked, smashed the helpful Greek with his fist and knocked him down. Flack was loaded into a carriage and driven to the dressing room at the stadium, where he was attended to by Prince Nicholas himself and revived with a drink of egg and brandy.

□

After Ethiopia's Abebe Bikila won his second gold medal in the marathon in the 1964 Games at Tokyo, he entertained the crowd by doing stretching and bicycling exercises and generally looking like he was sorry the race had been so short. At the medal ceremony, none of the Japanese officials knew the Ethiopian national anthem, so the band took the opportunity to play the Japanese national anthem instead.

In the 1920 marathon at Antwerp, Valerio Arri of Italy celebrated his bronze medal by performing three cartwheels as soon as he crossed the finish line.

1960, 1964

THE MAKING OF A LEGEND

HOW ABEBE BIKILA WON TWO GOLD MEDALS IN MARATHON

1960 / ROME		
1. Bikila	Ethiopia	2:15:17*
2. Rhadi	Morocco	2:15:42
3. Magee	New Zealand	2:17:19
1964 / TOKYO		
1. Bikila	Ethiopia	2:12:12**
2. Heatley	Britain	2:16:20
3. Tsuburaya	Japan	2:16:23

* indicates Olympic record
** indicates world record

Much of this material is taken from "The Complete Book of the Olympics" by David Wallechinsky.

Mary T. Meagher

Swimming's Old Lady Not Finished After All

By JOHN WEYLER, Times Staff Writer

Kareem Abdul-Jabbar spent his youth on the asphalt courts of New York, imagining himself a professional superstar. Dan Fouts played catch, as a ball boy, on the sidelines of San Francisco 49ers games, envisioning the day when he would be throwing touchdowns in the NFL. Steve Garvey rode along when his father drove the Dodgers' bus, fantasizing about a future in Dodger blue.

Mary T. Meagher grew up swimming in a pool near her home in Louisville and never once thought about being a world record-holder. Not until she was 14, anyway, and then she *was* a world record-holder.

It wasn't that Meagher (pronounced MAH-HER) was a late bloomer. At 5, she was setting 6-and-under age-group records.

Since then, she has lost a butterfly race about as often as Martina Navratilova has lost a tennis match. She has held the 200-meter world record for four years and the 100-meter mark for more than three, breaking her own records seven times since.

This Madame Butterfly has turned in six of the seven fastest performances ever in the 100 and the five top 200 times in history.

But there was never any grand scheme. She joined the River Road Country Club swim team because her father was a charter member and her brother and some of her nine sisters swam there. Her middle initial (the T. stands for Terstigge, her mother's maiden name) is the legacy of a large family. She has an older sister named Mary . . .

Please see MEAGHER, page 14

CON KEYES / Los Angeles Times

Mary T. Meagher doesn't swim as fast as she used to, but she still has to be considered one of the favorites in the L.A. Games.

Jim Murray

The Real Star in Los Angeles Is the Weather

A lot of people are worried about the Olympic weather in Los Angeles. Not me. It'll be just fine.

I'm not a meteorologist, but you might say I'm a student of nature. Usually, human nature. But in this case, I can tell you that L.A. weather has much of the character of its inhabitants. Or, maybe it's the other way round. You be the judge.

The L.A. weather is not the best in the world all the time — although it's in the hunt. It's way ahead of Duluth and Calcutta, any way you look at it.

But, it's a vain old bawd, a pure show-biz type, a ham actor, if you will.

If you come from another part of the country or the world, when is the last time you looked up on the television screen and saw the weather here without its makeup? I can tell you: never.

Turn on the Rose Bowl game on New Year's Day. What do you see? Flowers blooming in the sunlight. Air so light you can see into the future. People sitting stripped to the waist in January getting a sun tan. You can make book on it.

□

Now, I hate to tell you this, but L.A. has smog, fires, fog, rain, wind and, as you all know, earthquakes.

But not on New Year's Day. New Year's Day, it turns into Eden West. Year after year after year.

Do you know the last time it rained on the Rose Bowl game? 1955. Do you know the time before that? 1935.

The weather is a wholly owned subsidiary of the Chamber of Commerce. It has a nonbreakable clause in its contract. It might rain in Los Angeles Christmas Day. It often does. It might rain one week steady. Streets might be flooded. Houses might be floating down Pacific Coast Highway. The sea might be pulverizing shore-front property. Lightning might be playing around the mountains. Mud slides might be coming down the canyons.

But not on January 1. Whatever onslaughts of weather besiege the city that week or that month will stop at midnight December 31. It's in the fine print. Look it up.

Years ago, on the eve of the Dodgers' move to Los Angeles from Brooklyn, I was in an eatery in Vero Beach with some of the Dodger brass of that era—Buzzie Bavasi, Al Campanis, Fresco Thompson and an official from the Montreal farm club. They were querying me about L.A. weather. The club was going to open there for the first time in a week or 10

Please see MURRAY, page 14

John Moffet, world record-holder in the 100 breaststroke, has been more than diligent in his training for the Olympics.

CON KEYES / Los Angeles Times

Perfect Swimmer in Perfect Body

John Moffet Enters the Games as the World Record-Holder in the 100 Breaststroke and Seems to Have It All Going for Him

By TRACY DODDS, *Times Staff Writer*

There must be a chink in that silver-plated armor. Maybe a scratch or a dent. At least a spot of rust.

But where?

The image of John Moffet, member of the 1984 Olympic swimming team, new world record-holder in the 100-meter breaststroke, is just too, too perfect.

Nobody can be that good-looking, that well-built, that smart, that talented and a cordial, heck of a nice guy on top of it all.

Hey, this is a newspaper, not a book of bedtime fairy tales.

Even Moffet, himself, is beginning to chip away at the emerging hero using his name.

"I get these articles written about me where they try to portray me as an All-American nice guy, good student, all that," Moffet said.

"But it's not that simple. Things go wrong for anybody. They make it sound like everything goes my way all the time, and it's easy. It's just not like that."

Being an only child born to affluent parents doesn't come with a lifetime guarantee for happiness.

Which brings us to the real point of this happy story that seems to get happier and happier long before we reach the ever-after point:

"People look at me and they look at my life and they say, 'That guy's had everything handed to him on a silver platter,'" Moffet said. "But nobody hands you a world record on a silver platter.

"They haven't been the one spending the last eight, nine years in the pool."

Please see MOFFETT, page 15

He May Be Best Diver Ever and His Moment Is at Hand
Louganis Should Turn Strength and Grace Into Two Gold Medals

By SEYMOUR BEUBIS, *Times Staff Writer*

Like any other tourist in town, Chinese assistant diving coach Xu Yiming, 42, visited Disneyland. But the real attraction during his week-long stay last March wasn't the Magic Kingdom; it was the magical diving skill of Mission Viejo's Greg Louganis.

Everywhere Louganis went during the two-day invitational diving meet at the Olympic Stadium, Xu's eyes followed. He watched Louganis walk, talk and finally dive.

There was an obvious reason for Xu's fixation. He and his divers had come to the meet to learn. And who better to learn from than the man they call the Baryshnikov of diving. Many feel he is the greatest diver in the history of the sport.

That's lofty praise for a man who has never won an Olympic gold medal. Only an Olympic boycott by the United States in 1980 prevented him from possibly winning two gold medals in Moscow.

Barring a cruel twist of fate, that will all be remedied by Aug. 12. Louganis, 24, will have two Olympic golds in his pocket then, one in the men's 3-meter springboard and the other in the 10-meter platform, to go with a silver he won in Montreal when he finished slightly behind the all-time Olympic great, Italy's Klaus Dibiasi.

"I've been around diving for 52 years and there's no comparison between Greg and all the others," said Dr. Sammy Lee, himself a two-time Olympic gold medalist from the platform in 1948 and 1952.

Please see LOUGANIS, page 15

CON KEYES / Los Angeles Times

Greg Louganis' optional dives are usually more difficult than those of his opposition. They usually bring frowns from opponents and smiles from Greg.

MEAGHER

Continued from page 13

her parents obviously liked the name.

"My mom used to drop me off at the pool and the lifeguards and my sisters were my babysitters," Meagher said. "It was a fun place to play in the summer."

That's all it was at the time . . . fun.

"She had no goals," her mother, Floy, said. "She never talked about being in the Olympics or anything. She was just having a good time. There was nothing else she'd rather do."

Meagher looks back at it now and giggles. "We were *so* naive," she said. "We didn't shave, we didn't wear skin suits, we didn't wear caps . . . none of that. My parents didn't know anything about swimming. *I* didn't even know about junior nationals or nationals for a long time.

"When I did make qualifying times for junior nationals I told my Mom I went 25 in the 200 (yard) fly. She said, 'You went four laps of the pool in 25 seconds?' I said, 'No Mom, two minutes and 25 seconds.' We were really naive."

Still, there were indications of things to come.

"We had a small gathering of friends over one Sunday night," Floy said. "I guess Mary T. was about 11 or so. She came home from this meet with trophies spilling out of her towel and one of our guests wondered why they would make a little girl custodian of all the trophies for a meet."

Mary T. nonchalantly explained *she* had won them all that day.

"That kid's gonna be in the Olympics some day," the guest remarked.

□

If that day had come in 1980, Mary T. Meagher might be tanning herself by a pool right now instead of working out in one. She almost certainly would have been a double gold medal-winner in Moscow if it hadn't been for the boycott.

In a sport in which first and second place are often decided by hundredths of a second, Meagher was so far ahead of her competition four years ago that she would cling to the wall after finishing the 200-meter butterfly and watch the rest of the field battle for second.

She was the only American woman favored to win a gold medal in Moscow. And favored is hardly a strong enough word.

The letdown was predictable, and, at 15 years old, Meagher decided to quit swimming. But then again, so did almost everyone else. Retirements—most of which proved to be short-lived—were definitely chic in the summer of 1980.

In Meagher's case, however, the boycott was little more than a convenient excuse.

"Swimming and winning had come so naturally for me," Meagher explained. "I was swimming because I had always been so successful on the level I was competing and the Olympics were just the natural progression of things.

"So when the boycott came, it was disappointing but a lot of it was just because everyone else was so upset and I just sort of joined in. The funny thing is that I had already pretty much decided to quit and go back to playing basketball and field hockey and all the things I enjoyed before."

Don Gambril, the 1984 Olympic team coach, has an explanation for what seems a rather casual dismissal of a promising athletic career. Few people are far and away the best in the world at what they do. Most who are that gifted, cherish it.

"You've got to remember we're talking about a kid here, a young kid," Gambril said. "You've seen it before. They just don't appreciate what they've accomplished and how much it's worth. The success comes so fast and easy at that age. It always takes years before they really appreciate it."

It wasn't the advice of a coach, however, that brought Meagher back into the world of six-mile workouts at dawn and a fleeting moment on the top level of the victory stand for the very lucky. It was a 16-year-old veteran who had been the same route, experienced the same early successes . . . and some of the emotional valleys.

CON KEYES / Los Angeles Times

Mary T. Meagher has held the 200-meter world record for four years and the 100-meter mark for more than three.

Cynthia (Sippy) Woodhead didn't force Meagher to appreciate her accomplishments as much as she helped her to accept them, strive to better them and somehow still have fun at the same time. There were no lectures, either. Just a lot of late-night talks between two of swimming's youngest, and most-celebrated world record-holders.

Meagher and Woodhead were members of the 1980 Olympic team that traveled to China (they didn't have any other pressing engagements). Meagher spent most of her time complaining about the food and the heat and discussing her intentions to pursue athletic glory on the hockey fields of Sacred Hearts Academy in Louisville.

Her roommate, Woodhead, couldn't understand Meagher's admittedly vague reasons for quitting, though.

"Sippy kept telling me that swimming could be fun again and the more we talked the more I realized that I was taking the decision too lightly," Meagher recalled. "Most of the time when I told people I was quitting, I'd be laughing about it."

Woodhead, who is again Meagher's roommate during training camp for this year's Olympics, still rejects the idea that she alone is responsible for Meagher's change of heart.

"I never take credit for it," Woodhead said. "If you heard a world record-holder was going to quit at so young an age, you'd be shocked too. I was still excited about swimming and I was surprised to see her willing to throw so much fun down the tubes.

"So we talked about going to college and getting a full ride (scholarship) and traveling. I'd been on every national team and made every trip I could since 1977 and we talked a lot about that.

"We were in China for three weeks so we had a lot of time to talk. I guess it came up almost every night. I tried to tell her she didn't have to set the world on fire every time she got in the pool.

"But she's given me too much credit . . . all we did is talk."

Less than a year later, Woodhead was beginning to experience difficulties of her own. It was the beginning of a three-year period of personal turbulence during which Woodhead bounced from one swim team to another and during which a host of swimmers she had once left in her wake bounced her out of final heats and into also-ran status.

"I remember the first time I beat Sippy," Meagher said. "It was in the 200 free at the nationals in '81 and we got down to the last 50 meters and I knew I was going to beat her. She was starting to fade and I remember thinking, 'Oh God, should I be doing this?'

"The year before she had talked me back into swimming and now I was beating her. It was eerie."

□

The mystery during that U.S. Nationals in 1981 was "How can Mary T. swim so fast?" She had bettered both butterfly world records within a couple of days and trimmed an incredible 1.33 seconds off her mark in the 100-meter event.

The experts were flabbergasted.

"If anyone knows what she can do it's me," Bill Peak, then Meagher's coach at Louisville's Lakeside Swim Club, said after the race, "but I looked up at the clock and thought it was a men's heat."

Now, however, the big question is: "Why can't Mary T. go that fast anymore?"

In the Olympic trials last month, Meagher was upset in the 100-meter butterfly by 16-year-old Jenna Johnson, but she finished second and made the U.S. team in the event. She came back to win the 200 going away, but she was still more than a second and a half off her world record.

"I don't know what the problem is," she told the press after winning the 200 at the trials, "If I knew, I'd probably do something about it."

Meagher, always the easy-going extrovert, was still smiling. But it was obvious she was frustrated.

Please see MEAGHER, below

MEAGHER

Continued from above

That's as close to sarcasm as she gets.

Walking away from the press conference, Meagher turned to a reporter and faked a short cry. She had trained more than she ever had in her life, her family was in attendance en masse (all wearing their "This Is a Mary T.-Shirt" shirts) and she very much wanted to break her record and stifle the premature reports of her decline.

"I guess I raised my expectations a little too much," she said. "But I've never been in better shape and I have confidence in Mark's (Schubert, her coach at Mission Viejo) taper. Everybody says I was doing this or that differently in 1981 . . . I just don't know. But every time I get in the water, I feel like there are a hundred eyes in the underwater windows trying to figure out what I'm doing wrong.

"I don't know, maybe my body's just different."

Bingo.

Mary T., the 14-year-old little girl sweetheart of American swimming, is now Mary T., the 19-year-old woman sweetheart of American swimming. She's undergone the natural physical changes and it hasresulted in changes in her stroke. She's probably just not as efficient in the water.

"It's maturity," Gambril said, smiling. "There are some girls who are great at 14 and 15 and can barely swim at all at 17 or 18. That's the difference. She still has an absolutely classic stroke."

Meagher likes to say that the butterfly chose her, not the other way around. She was seven when she saw a senior swimmer at her neighborhood club doing the butterfly and was intrigued.

"I started doing it and I guess I did it right because she did it right," Meagher said. "Anyway, I was winning 10-and-under butterfly races at seven and I never got any actual instruction except when my brother showed me how to make a legal, two-handed turn."

Naivete aside, her parents finally realized that their No. 9 daughter was destined for big things.

"We knew very little about swimming even though all our children swam some," said Meagher's father, Jim, chairman of the board of a hardware distribution firm. "We didn't realize what we had in T until about 1978 and then her mother and I decided to make every possible sacrifice for her."

Meagher began training at Lakeside and eventually came under the tutelage of Peak, her coach for five years before she moved to Mission Viejo to train with the Nadadores last fall.

"Mary T. loves to race," Peak said. "And she's a great workout swimmer. She swims these all-butterfly workouts that are impossible for most swimmers. And she must have a high pain threshold because she pushes herself to limits that most athletes just will not do.

"But after the disappointment of 1980, we decided to have her work out once a day and do some of the other things she wanted to do. I thought the break would be beneficial."

The relaxed training schedule paid off. Meagher had her best year ever, a year she's still trying to recapture.

"I can't imagine not swimming my fastest times in the Olympics," she says, shaking her head.

Merely a couple of gold medals (and likely three if she wins the 100 and competes on the sure-bet U.S. medley relay team) would not be good enough, obviously.

"I definitely feel she's in the shape to do her best times," Schubert said. "And for this season to be a success, she's going to have to do just that. That's the way she looks at it. I don't think there's anything drastically wrong with her stroke, either. Quite frankly, I think she's pressing. I just think she needs to relax."

□

Meagher tried relaxation. Well, maybe she overdid it a little. Last year, her first year at Cal, was a growing experience in a lot of ways. She graduated from an all-girl parochial school in Louisville and a couple months later was living in a co-ed dorm in California.

Her social life expanded and her times went up. So did her dress size.

"Berkeley is a blast," Meagher said. "I was never a partyer in high school and think it was a good experience for me, making my own decisions for a change. I wasn't doing things just to please my parents anymore."

Meagher, who has been known to sneak into a press trailer, grab a piece of pizza or a candy bar and hide from her coach to eat it, wasn't burning the calories in workouts like she was used to.

"I didn't train as much as I needed to and I gained a lot of weight. And I didn't do enough weight training, either, so I wasn't just fat, I was weak, too. For the first time in my life I was way out of shape. I didn't want to accept it, but I found out what it takes."

Meagher returned to Lakeside and became painfully aware of "what it takes."

"I did the best coaching job I ever did with her last summer," Peak said. "She was 15 pounds overweight and in the worst shape of her life . . . I mean *awful.* I kept her in the pool for an extra 45 minutes of butterfly workouts every day.

"She was crying and begging to get out. She hated my guts then."

Meagher had finally come to appreciate her accomplishments and her determination to better them was redoubled.

Together, Peak and Meagher decided she should drop out of college for a year and move to Mission Viejo where the competition in the pool during training is legendary.

"All the people at Lakeside went back to college, and competition in workouts is very important for me," Meagher said. "After the NCAAs last year, I started to really evaluate where I was going and it occurred to me that even though I'd swum a lot of laps and all, I wasn't sure if the extra effort and the mental concentration that I needed was there.

"I had started thinking more about social occasions than swimming . . . which is healthy, of course," she said, adding her infectious giggle as an exclamation point. "But I decided I needed to be somewhere where my life would be centered around swimming."

Schubert, who has been called the Patton of the pool deck, had just the place and was more than willing to add a world record-holder to his flock.

"Swimming is a business at Mission," Meagher said, "and Mark runs a strict show. There's some complaining because people feel like it's the coach who makes you come to workouts, but I felt like that was what I needed. If you give Mark 100% effort and concentration, he'll do everything in his power to see that you get the attention and everything else you need."

□

Well, maybe not everything. The maturation of Mary T. Meagher is evident in more than just a womanly figure and an understanding of what it takes to stay on top.

She never really dated much until her freshman year at college and now she talks often about getting married and raising a family—even before she finishes college. "I see myself getting married young and having a big family . . . five kids maybe, not 11 like my mom."

Meagher has never had any trouble reconciling her athleticism with her femininity. "The only time I wish I didn't have big shoulders is when I go shopping," she said, smiling. "You know, the look today is so petite.

"This is the way I am and I never wished to be any other way. People make fun of the East Germans but I think most of the U.S. girls have managed to maintain their femininity."

It's certainly never been a problem for Mary T. Her All-American good-looks and all-world athletic prowess have long made her a crowd favorite. She still receives ovations that are longer and louder than the cheers for anyone else.

She's a favorite with her peers as well, giving advice when it's requested and pep talks on a regular basis. She's almost always in a good mood and is quick to offer her expertise—which extends to a number of subjects beyond swimming.

A photographer was getting ready to take a picture of a young female teammate and Meagher rushed over.

"Turn your shoulders just a little this way," she whispered. "It'll make 'em look smaller."

Somehow, Meagher has handled the frustration of falling short of her time goals at the Olympic trials with typical good-natured charm. Always the optimist, she's still convinced that she will return to the form of 1981 . . . even if her figure will never again be like it was when she was 15.

"I've never been to an Olympics before and I'm really excited," she said. "In a lot of ways I feel like the Old Lady of Swimming, but I've never experienced an Olympics so I'm young in that sense.

"Hopefully, the Olympic atmosphere will do the trick and I'll swim out of my head just once more."

'I've never been to an Olympics before and I'm really excited. In a lot of ways I feel like the Old Lady of Swimming, but I've never experienced an Olympics so I'm young in that sense.'

—MARY T. MEAGHER

WOMEN'S 100 AND 200 BUTTERFLY

100

All-Time List

Mark	Name		Country	Year
57.93	Mary Meagher		United States	1981
59.08	Jenna Johnson		United States	1984
59.46	Andrea Pollack		East Germany	1978
59.54	Laurie Lehner		United States	1983
59.78	Christiane Knacks		East Germany	1977
59.88	Ines Geissler		East Germany	1984
59.98	Tracy Caulkins		United States	1980
1:00.13	Kornelia Ender		East Germany	1976
1:00.20	Joan Pennington		East Germany	1978
1:00.34	Jill Sterkel	(10)	United States	1980
1:00.40	Ute Geweniger		East Germany	1981
1:00.40	Melanie Buddemeyer		United States	1982
1:00.42	Caren Metaschuck		East Germany	1980
1:00.47	Nancy Hogshead		United States	1984
1:00.59	Lisa Buese		United States	1980
1:00.60	Tatiana Kurnikova		USSR	1984
1:00.70	Patty King		United States	1983
1:00.75	Maud Lauckner		East Germany	1982
1:00.83	Cornelia Polit		East Germany	1983
1:00.89	Takemi Ise	(20)	Japan	1981

Other Americans:

1:00.97	Diane Johanningman	1980

World Record Progression

Mark	Name	Country	Year
1:05.1	Ada Kok	Netherlands	1964
1:04.7	Sharon Stouder	United States	1964
1:04.5	Ada Kok	Netherlands	1965
1:04.1	Alice Jones	United States	1970
1:03.9	Mayumi Aoki	Japan	1972
1:03.80	Andrea Gyarmati	Hungary	1972
1:03.34	Mayumi Aoki	Japan	1972
1:02.35	Kornelia Ender	East Germany	1973
1:02.31	Kornelia Ender	East Germany	1973
1:02.09	Rosemarie Kother	East Germany	1974
1:01.99	Rosemarie Kother	East Germany	1974
1:01.88	Rosemarie Kother	East Germany	1974
1:01.33	Kornelia Ender	East Germany	1975
1:01.24	Kornelia Ender	East Germany	1975
1:00.13	Kornelia Ender	East Germany	1976
1:00.13	Kornelia Ender	East Germany	1976
59.78	Christiane Knacke	East Germany	1977
59.46	Andrea Pollack	East Germany	1978
59.26	Mary Meagher	United States	1980
57.93	Mary Meagher	United States	1981

200

All-Time List

Mark	Name		Country	Year
2:05.96	Mary Meagher		United States	1981
2:07.82	Cornelia Polit		East Germany	1983
2:08.03	Ines Geissler		East Germany	1983
2:09.59	Heike Dahne		East Germany	1981
2:09.87	Andrea Pollack		East Germany	1978
2:10.09	Kathleen Nord		East Germany	1983
2:10.45	Sybille Schonrock		East Germany	1980
2:10.55	Jaqueline Alex		East Germany	1984
2:11.07	Nancy Hogshead		United States	1980
2:11.22	Rosemarie Gabriel	(10)	East Germany	1976
2:11.29	Michelle Ford		Australia	1978
2:11.31	Tatiana Kurnikova		USSR	1984
2:11.57	Kim Linehan		United States	1980
2:11.70	Linda Thompson		United States	1980
2:11.74	Mayumi Yokoyama		United States	1980
2:11.96	Naoko Kume		Japan	1980
2:12.12	Linda Hanel		Australia	1980
2:12.15	Wendy Quirk		Canada	1980
2:12.16	Anett Kalatz		East Germany	1981
2:12.20	Petra Zindler	(20)	West Germany	1983

Other Americans:

2:12.48	Diane Johannigman	1984

World Record Progression

Mark	Name	Country	Year
2:26.3	Kendis Moore	United States	1965
2:25.8	Ada Kok	Netherlands	1965
2:25.3	Ada Kok	Netherlands	1965
2:22.5	Ada Kok	Netherlands	1967
2:21.0	Ada Kok	Netherlands	1967
2:20.7	Karen Moe	United States	1970
2:19.3	Alice Jones	United States	1970
2:18.6	Karen Moe	United States	1971
2:18.4	Ellie Daniel	United States	1971
2:16.62	Karen Moe	United States	1972
2:15.57	Karen Moe	United States	1972
2:15.45	Rosemarie Kother	East Germany	1973
2:13.76	Rosemarie Kother	East Germany	1973
2:13.60	Rosemarie Gabriel	East Germany	1976
2:12.84	Rosemarie Gabriel	East Germany	1976
2:11.22	Rosemarie Gabriel	East Germany	1976
2:09.87	Andrea Pollack	East Germany	1978
2:09.87	Tracy Caulkins	United States	1978
2:07.01	Mary Meagher	United States	1979
2:06.37	Mary Meagher	United States	1980
2:05.96	Mary Meagher	United States	1981

MURRAY

Continued from page 13

days. "What about rainouts?" Bavasi asked. "It doesn't rain in L.A. from March till October or even December," I told them.

Well, the hoots were deafening. Get a load of this Chamber of Commerce type!

It so happened that early April of that year was "unusual." Inches of rain fell in a day. A whole cliff slid down on the Coast Highway in Pacific Palisades. Buzzie was derisive.

"I thought it never rained in April," he mocked.

"Listen!" I told him. "I know that old broad. Your opening game is going to be sunny, 85 degrees, not a cloud in the sky or mud on your shoes. You're going to have the only ballclub in the majors that doesn't need six starting pitchers. Because you'll never get a home doubleheader caused by a makeup game for a rainout."

Well, never is a long time. But the Dodgers set the major league record for number of games—no, number of *years*—without a rainout.

"What about San Francisco?" Buzzie demanded. The Dodgers opened there first.

"That's different," I told him. "San Francisco weather has no pride."

L.A. weather is like a grand old trouper who believes the show must go on. No matter what's going on before the curtain goes up, the play's the thing. It's like a family that is having this terrible fight—screaming, hair-pulling, punching—and then the doorbell rings. Immediately, all activity ceases, chairs are put back in their original upright positions, pillows are picked up, the bleeding is stopped—and they open the front door with pasted-on smiles as if they had all just been saying vespers.

Lord knows Los Angeles has had other performers like that. Actors have given screen caresses to actress wives they broke up with violently the week before. I can remember the great Spencer Tracy going through a rehearsal scene for a director, mumbling, coughing, blowing his line, shambling. Then, it's a "take," and Tracy comes on camera and glows. Bing Crosby could be dour, aloof, disinterested—and then the mikes were turned on for the Kraft Music Hall and he was the soul of wit and charm and bonhomie.

That's the way L.A. weather is when the country's looking on. It puts on its best finery and doesn't let you see the frayed gloves, the holes in the shoes. It gets like a guy who picks up the tab even if he has to hock the car.

It doesn't matter what the event is—the U.S. Open or PGA at Riviera, Rose Bowl, Super Bowl, World Series. Los Angeles never lets you see backstage. When the lights come up, you'll never be able to notice that the curtains are dusty, the costumes have been repaired.

L.A. weather knows it's a Star. And Stars don't let down. Other cities go on camera with their hair in rollers, their reading glasses on, their makeup off. Boston weighs in with an auditorium that lacks air conditioning. Green Bay weighs in with sleet and temperatures 20 below.

Los Angeles knows that's not box office. When we have a winter golf tournament, football game, Rose Parade or even an auto race, 40-million people in snow up to their hips in Duluth or Fond du Lac look up on that screen and say: "What are we doing here with this snow shovel? Mama, put the mattress on the Toyota, and get out the suntan oil, we're heading for lotus land."

We used to have an organization, the Society For Los Angeles to Come On Like Pittsburgh in the Rain When the Cameras Come On. We did everything but hold rain dances. But, no dice. The old girl's position was, "Carmen was announced, Carmen will be sung."

The summer poses a bit more of a challenge. It's a tough part. Like King Lear. But Los Angeles can do it. The day after the Olympics are over,, two smog alerts may move in with air quality unhealthful for sensitive people, insensitive people and all in between.

But, during the Games, or at least that portion of them on worldwide television, I'm betting on the old bawd to put on her act and sashay down the old runway like Miss Universe of 1984. As usual.

MOFFET

Continued from page 13

"I've been working my butt off. I don't care what anybody says. A lot of sacrifices go along with it."

Not even his incredible physique, which Moffet swears was gene-produced, not Nautilus-induced, would let him swim 100 meters of breaststroke in 1 minute 2.13 seconds without the nine years of training.

He had the talent, tools and advantages to start with, but nobody else could use them for him. He had to do it himself.

Even his drive, his motivation, his discipline have been his own.

He didn't have pushy, overbearing parents standing over him with a whip and a stopwatch.

He didn't even have an ambitious super-coach standing over him with a whip and a stopwatch.

Moffet started swimming in Claremont, in a recreation league, when he was 11. The coach was the same one who had flunked him in his swimming course a couple of years earlier because he couldn't swim the breaststroke. His parents didn't want him to waste away his summer, so they gave him a choice: summer school or competitive swimming.

A star was born.

He came up through age-group swimming, first with Tom Grall in Claremont, then with Ann Simmons at the Beach Swim Club, and later with a small group called the Southern California Swim Club. He's still affiliated with the Southern California club, but now he trains, mostly, with his college coach, Skip Kenney of Stanford.

Worthy of note is what he didn't do. Even after his parents moved near the ocean, to Costa Mesa, and he was living 25 minutes from Mission Viejo, Moffet never even considered joining the prestigious club there, the Nadadores.

"I just don't agree with that philosophy of swimming," Moffet said. "I just think they take out a lot of the fun. I'm not condemning it. It's just too rigorous for me.

"A guy on that team can't even be on a girls' floor. You can't even converse with the girls in the hotel. You can't miss workouts, other than being sick.

"I'd feel like a robot. I don't like that total intenseness. I gain my intensity from inside myself. The last thing I need is being bombarded from the outside, too.

"Not too many people work the way I do . . .

"I knew most of the people on the team and I knew that team just wasn't for me."

Which may suggest that he wanted to be where he could goof off, go his own way, chase the girls.

Not so, said Kenney, his college coach.

"The guy loves to have a good time, but he knows how to handle it," Kenney said. "We tease him that we have a team goal to have a dual meet in a city where John doesn't have a girlfriend. The girls at school are waiting in line to go out with him."

That, however, doesn't detract from his goals.

Kenney said, "Absolutely, he is self-motivated. He's very disciplined. He started out this year, an Olympic year, he didn't miss a practice. He didn't miss a morning workout. He was there. He was doing everything right.

"He was motivated. Self-motivated. His freshman year he had a bad alarm clock. But this year there was no problem.

"There are a lot of guys who have that physical talent who try to ride off of that. He doesn't.

"He's one of the most coachable kids I've ever had. He came in as a freshman, and he already had been on the 1980 Olympic team. He'd been great for a long time. But every time I talked to him he was listening, there was eye contract, and he'd try it, whatever I said. It wasn't like he had all the answers. He was trying to be better.

"He's worked his tail off and he's studied the stroke. He has put it all together."

He also brought it all together at just the right time. When he broke Steve Lundquist's world record at the Olympic trials in Indianapolis a few weeks ago, it was his first world record.

"That was just when I wanted to do it, in the trials," Moffet said. "That was the time. In trials you just swim as fast as you can. My philosophy is not to look at other people. As soon as you look at someone else, you put a limit on yourself. You don't break a world record looking at somebody or plotting yourself against somebody else."

It was also the first time he had ever beaten Lundquist.

"I'm glad I did it now," he said. "I really would have had second thoughts about it if I had done it last summer. I was really close last summer."

Now, the schedule calls for him to swim even faster at the Olympics. He doesn't like to go on too much about what he can or will do, but he did say, "I'm expecting a better swim at the Olympics than I had (at Indianapolis). When Richard Schroeder beat me in the 200 (meter breaststroke) I didn't feel good at all."

Kenney agreed that Moffet is on schedule.

"His whole history is that he's faster on his second shave," Kenney said. "His muscles are amazing. They take a lot of rest. Most coaches, most programs, tend to under-rest a little for fear of over-resting. But John has always gone faster on his second shave because those big muscles need rest."

Moffet doesn't have an incredible hulk of a body. He's 6-1 and weights 186 pounds. But he does have plenty of muscles, perfectly proportioned, and with the kind of definition body builders look for.

"He really didn't build that with weights," Kenney said. "He came to Stanford with that body with no weight program.

"What he doesn't need is more bulk. He has plenty of bulk. What we've tried to do is condition the muscles that he has."

It's easy to believe what Moffet says about the body type being in the genes after seeing him with his father, Cliff. The senior Moffet, who was a high school swimmer and football player, has the same muscular legs, the same muscle definition.

According to Kenney, there is more to Moffet than being a strong swimmer. "He also has a history of handling the pressure of a meet better than anybody," he said.

"Of course, that's what it takes. That's what separates No. 1 from No. 3. He's had the Pan Ams and the NCAA championships. So he's been there before.

"What you have to remember is that there aren't going to be very many swimmers who have any more Olympic experience than he has. A lot of the swimmers in Los Angeles didn't get to go in '80.

"He'll be on the same level with everybody else, and he can handle it."

Some who missed the Olympics in 1980 missed the peak of their development. For Moffet, not getting to compete in 1980 was a disappointment, but it really didn't shake him from his long-term schedule.

He was just 16 then. Now he is 20 and has all of that international experience. These are the Games he has been peaking for. He has been on a steady course toward these Olympic Games since he was 11.

At 12 he held national age-group records. At 13 he made the national junior Olympics. At 14 he won one event and was second in the other in the junior Olympics, then went on to the U.S. national meet and made the consolation finals in both events.

At 15 he went to nationals again and placed second in the 200-meter breaststroke and sixth in the 100.

At 16 he was on the Olympic team.

Never, as he blazed this trail, did he experience the burnout so many swimmers talk about. Never did he take a year off, or consider quitting.

"There have been times when I wasn't happy swimming," he admitted. "Midseason, it's real easy to lose sight of your goals. There are six months there when you're training hard, really hard. It's no fun. It's raining, it's cold. You have morning workout at six every morning and then on to school. Then you're back at three or so for another two or two and a half hours.

"But it's funny. You get up, you go to workout, you hate it. You go to meets and you hate it. You're so nervous, you're scared to death, you don't want to swim. But overall, you're having fun.

"When I look back on it, I've always loved it . . .

"I can't picture myself having any more fun than I'm having right now, or being happier than I have been for the last eight or nine years. Even though it is a bunch of work and it's year 'round and it's crappy sometimes, the friends I've made, the places I've been, the things I've had opportunity to do make it all worth it.

"I've been to China. I've been to Europe three times. I've been to Russia, to South America, all over the United States.

"And I keep meeting neat people.

"For example, right before I swam the 200 at the Olympic trials, Glenn Mills came up to me and said, 'No matter what happens in this race—best friends.' "

Mills is a 23-year-old breaststroker who was also on the 1980 Olympic team but who did not make the 1984 team.

"Glenn Mills and I have been friends for years, and it's hard . . . to keep the friendship and camaraderie when you've been so competitive for so many years," Moffet said. "It's hard to keep the competition in the pool and when you're out not have it.

"Glenn and I have been able to fight through that. I can't tell you how much a friendship like that means."

Moffet is known for his positive approach and reasonable perspective to just about everything:

—On why he picked Stanford. "Stanford was the best place to get the combination of swimming and academics. It's so hard to get in that place, that once you're accepted, how can you turn it down? I know a lot of 4.0 students who didn't get in. It doesn't make sense to turn it down . . .

"They have a good group of guys there. All of them get along together. There are no real jerks on the team—out of 30 guys! We're swimming together an average of four hours a day with no arguments. One-upmanship is nonexistent.

"Everybody on the team is special."

—On swimmers who purposely try to psych others out with an overtly aggressive style. "People who are nasty and mean find that works for them. If it's successful for them, they stay with it. I totally disagree with that attitude. It has to affect them in some way, too. You get what you ask for."

—On the fear-of-failure motivation that many athletes use. "I can't stand any of that sports psychiatrist stuff. They try to drag me to those lectures, and I won't have any part of it. It's just too negative for me.

"The older you get, the more sensitive or aware you are to all the negative things that are always going on. You start to realize that you are fallible, for one thing. It's hard to combat if you think about it too much.

"That's why it's so easy for age groupers to drop five seconds every time they swim. Sure, they're getting stronger all the time, but the biggest advantage they have is that they don't have any mental blocks. They're not thinking too much.

"A problem for a lot of swimmers is that they are very intelligent. They know what the stakes are and what they're doing. What you have to learn to do is not let your mind work on it too much."

—On constantly running into the attitude many hard-core sports fans seem to have toward the stereotype of the country-club swimmer. "A lot of swimmers were brought up in a more affluent atmosphere. That doesn't make them any less tough. They still work as hard as any other athletes. Boxing may be more of a brutal sport, or whatever adjective you want to use for it. But still, the work is there for a swimmer. The dedication has to be there.

"A swimmer has to be as mentally tough as any other athlete. It's all the same when it gets down to the nitty-gritty."

MEN'S 100 BREASTSTROKE

World Record Progression

Mark	Name	Country	Year
1:12.7	Viteslav Svozil	Czechoslovakia	1957
1:11.6	Chi Lieh Yung	China	1957
1:11.5	Vladimir Miashkin	USSR	1957
1:11.4	Leonid Kolenikov	USSR	1961
1:10.8	Gunter Tittes	East Germany	1961
1:10.7	Chet Jastremski	United States	1961
1:10.0	Chet Jastremski	United States	1961
1:09.5	Chet Jastremski	United States	1961
1:07.8	Chet Jastremski	United States	1961
1:07.5	Chet Jastremski	United States	1961
1:07.4	Georgy Prokopenko	USSR	1964
1:06.9	Georgy Prokopenko	USSR	1964
1:06.7	Vladamir Kosinsky	USSR	1967
1:06.4	Jose Fiolo	Brazil	1968
1:06.2	Nicoli Pankin	USSR	1968
1:05.8	Nicoli Pankin	USSR	1969
1:05.68	John Hencken	United States	1972
1:05.13	Nobutaka Taguchi	Japan	1972
1:04.94	Nobutaka Taguchi	Japan	1972
1:04.35	John Hencken	United States	1973
1:04.02	John Hencken	United States	1973
1:03.88	John Hencken	United States	1974
1:03.88	John Hencken	United States	1976
1:03.62	John Hencken	United States	1976
1:03.11	John Hencken	United States	1976
1:02.86	Gerald Morken	West Germany	1977
1:02.62	Steve Lundquist	United States	1982
1:02.53	Steve Lundquist	United States	1982
1:02.34	Steve Lundquist	United States	1983
1:02.28	Steve Lundquist	United States	1983
1:02.13	John Moffet	United States	1984

All-Time List

Mark	Name		Country	Year
1:02.13	John Moffet		United States	1984
1:02.16	Steve Lundquist		United States	1984
1:02.36	John Moffet		United States	1983
1:02.81	Dmitriy Volkov		USSR	1984
1:02.82	Victor Davis		Canada	1982
1:02.86	Gerald Morken		West Germany	1977
1:02.93	Bill Barrett		United States	1980
1:02.93	Adrian Moorhouse		Britain	1982
1:03.03	Richard Schroeder		United States	1984
1:03.11	John Hencken	(10)	United States	1976
1:03.20	Rickie Gill		United States	1981
1:03.26	Peter Evans		Australia	1981
1:03.31	Duncan Goodhew		Britain	1980
1:03.32	Robertas Zhulpa		USSR	1983
1:03.33	Aleksandr Fedorovsky		USSR	1978
1:03.43	David Wilkie		Britain	1976
1:03.44	Yuriy Kis		USSR	1981
1:03.50	Peter Evans		Australia	1984
1:03.56	Walter Kusch		West Germany	1978
1:03.58	Peter Lang	(20)	West Germany	1981

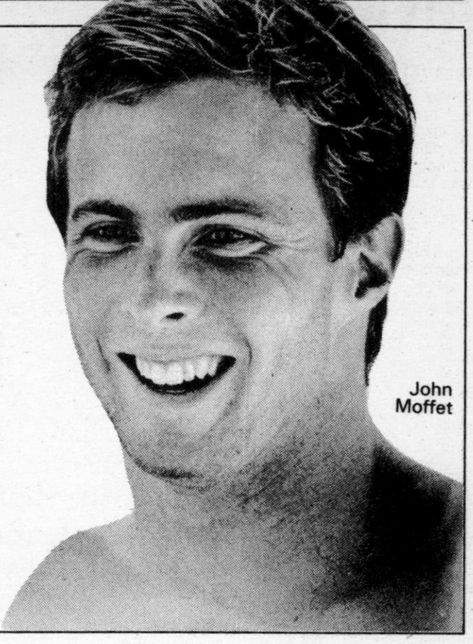

John Moffet

LOUGANIS

Continued from page 13

"He has had more 10s (perfect scores) than anyone in history. In my prime, I would have been lucky to be within 100 points of him."

Ron O'Brien, who coaches Louganis at Mission Viejo and will serve as an Olympic coach along with Dick Kimball of the Kimball Divers of Ann Arbor, Mich., said others have won more Olympic medals than Louganis, but no one has performed better.

"If someone else scores a 10, it's unusual," O'Brien said. "If he (Greg) goes *without* 10s at a competition, that's unusual."

Kimball, whose son, Bruce, 21, is one of Louganis' foremost challengers on the platform, calls Louganis "the best diver of all time. Klaus (Dibiasi) was a great, great diver, but Greg is much better."

Even on his bad days, and there are some, Louganis can usually outscore his opposition by 50 points.

OK, it's been established beyond question that Louganis is great. But what is it that makes him that way? What puts him alone at the top?

For openers, former diving greats start with Louganis' body, which they claim is a perfect diver's physique. It is a combination of strength and grace, the strength inherited (he does almost no weight training) and the grace coming from long hours in dance studios.

He is 5-9, a solid 160 pounds, with a 28-inch waist, a 44-inch chest and a vertical leap of 33 inches. The soaring ability comes from legs that are almost too muscular for a diver—more like those of a football player.

"His strength and dance background are the two factors that make Greg so special," O'Brien said. "When he dives, it's like he is dancing—he's so fluid. And his strength allows him to leap higher than most others. That gives him more margin for error, to make adjustments while he is in the air."

"He has the quickness, the desire, body strength, complete coordination and an uncanny sense of where the water is," Lee said.

"He does the simple dives as well as anyone, and when he gets to the tougher dives, he's even better.

"He never telegraphs his punches on a dive. He approaches all his dives the same way. You can't tell whether he's about to perform a 1.5 degree-of-difficulty dive (one of the lowest) or a 3.4 (the toughest)," Lee said.

Phil Boggs, the last American to win an Olympic gold medal (1976 from the springboard), calls Louganis "the consummate diver."

"He has the greatest physical talent of anyone ever. He has the strength, quickness, grace, catlike awareness and mental toughness—all the elements," Boggs said.

Boggs, president of U.S. Diving, the governing body of the sport, said there are divers who spin faster than Louganis, or who enter the water with less splash, "but no diver does all the things as well as Greg. He's just so graceful and explosive. There just is no one like him."

DAVE GATLEY / Los Angeles Times

Greg Louganis does a reverse dive during the recent U.S. Olympic trials in Indianapolis.

Cynthia Potter, who has won more U.S. titles than anyone (28; Louganis has won 26), adds still another explanation for the Louganis success.

"He just looks like a Greek god up there. He's wonderful to look at. You just expect him to be dazzling."

Potter called Louganis "a great diver" but stopped short of classifying him as the best ever.

"It's difficult to compare divers from different eras," Potter said. "Sammy Lee was great for his time. Everything has changed so much. The facilities are better now and so is the coaching. The list of dives has changed, too—they're much more difficult, and so the potential for much higher scores is there.

"But there's no question that Greg is in a class by himself. He has gymnastic ability, rhythmic movements and great strength. He has the perfect body for diving. There are so many variables, but he has it all."

"Did you see the movie, 'The Natural?' " asked Steve McFarland, the diving coach at the University of Miami, in answer to the question of how he rates Louganis on the list of all-time diving greats.

"That's what Greg is, the natural," said McFarland, who coached Louganis at Miami for two years before Louganis transferred to UC Irvine.

"He's the perfect blending of strength and grace. Usually, the graceful divers lack strength and the stronger ones lack grace. But he has them both. I don't know if that can be acquired.

"Greg is the most dominant figure in the history of the sport. He's the Kareem (Abdul-Jabbar) of diving. He's head and shoulders above the rest. He should dominate the Olympic Games."

Louganis also has one additional ace in the hole: a list of exciting dives, unparalleled in degree of difficulty. This enables him to outscore opponents handily even if they receive the same scores from judges that he does. (Diving points are accumulated by multiplying the scores received on a dive by the degree of difficulty.)

With all his strengths, Louganis, like all others, does have some weaknesses.

"Every once in a while he loses his concentration," Lee said.

"On forward entries, spinning to the water, he ducks his head and goes through vertical every now and then," O'Brien said. "There are also times on optional dives from the platform when Greg doesn't get into the water cleanly."

McFarland said the one area of concern to him is that Louganis, like most everyone, is not immune to pressure.

"He sometimes struggles in competition when the pressure is on—when the diver in front of him or directly behind is hitting on all of their dives." McFarland said.

Kimball said Louganis is not always as consistent as he should be. "In recent years Bruce (Kimball's son) has been able to beat him by riding with him and keeping the pressure on."

Kimball doesn't beat him often, though. Nobody beats him often.

GREG LOUGANIS

How He Placed

Year	Event	1*	3**	P***
1978	U.S. Indoors	1	x	1
	U.S. Outdoors	1	3	1
1979	U.S. Indoors	1	1	2
	U.S. Outdoors	1	1	1
1980	U.S. Indoors	1	1	3
	U.S. Outdoors	1	1	1
1981	U.S. Indoors	1	1	2
	U.S. Outdoors	1	1	2
1982	U.S. Outdoors	1	1	2
1983	U.S. Indoors	1	1	2
	U.S. Outdoors	2	1	1
1984	U.S. Indoors	1	1	2

Louganis has won 26 U.S. championships.
*1 meter; **3 meters; ***platform.

OLYMPICS '84

3 DAYS TO GAMES

THE LEGENDS

Sports Illustrated

With All Those Gold Medals, Mark Spitz Became the Winner the World Loved to Hate

THE SURVIVOR

By MIKE LITTWIN, Times Staff Writer

He looks much the same as we remember him. The ruddy good looks, the familiar mustache, the bronze tan, the blinding smile.

Mark Spitz electrified a nation for one week in 1972 by winning seven Olympic gold medals. He then bored the same nation for some few months as a much-hyped, would-be celebrity who never quite made it. We've never decided just how to grade Spitz—whether as failure or success—and finally we relegated him to that never-never land reserved for great athletes who have had their day and won't have another.

Spitz resurfaces occasionally, especially at this time every four years, as an expert commentator in swimming. When he does, he assures us that he is happy in his relative anonymity. He is wealthy and healthy and, he says, satisfied.

Oh, but what days those were. Those days of his magnificent obsession. Those days of abject failure in 1968 when he boldly predicted he would win six gold medals and won two. Those days of unprecedented success four years later.

"Surprisingly, people tend to think that I'm four years younger than I am because there has been only one Olympics televised since I last swam," said Spitz, the successful businessman who swims, he says, maybe once a week. "A lot of people wonder if I'm still swimming. I'm 34 years old. I've been retired for 12 years."

But the name doesn't disappear. He is still far better known than any current swimmer, and he is still resented by many in the swimming world who say he took from the sport but never gave back.

That was all part of his public life, the affection and the disaffection.

Please see SPITZ, page 17

NEIL LEIFER / Sports Illustrated

Mark Spitz is elated with his first gold medal in Munich.

NEIL LEIFER / Sports Illustrated

Mark Spitz won both the 100- and 200-meter freestyle events on his way to seven gold medals at the 1972 Games at Munich.

1972

THE MAKING OF A LEGEND

HOW MARK SPITZ WON SEVEN GOLD MEDALS AT MUNICH

100-Meter Freestyle

1. Spitz	United States	51.22*
2. Heidenreich	United States	51.65
3. Bure	Soviet Union	51.77
4. Murphy	United States	52.08
5. Wenden	Australia	52.41

200-Meter Freestyle

1. Spitz	United States	1:52.78*
2. Genter	United States	1:53.73
3. Lampe	West Germany	1:53.99
4. Wenden	Australia	1:54.40
5. Tyler	United States	1:54.96

100-Meter Butterfly

1. Spitz	United States	54.27*
2. Robertson	Canada	55.56
3. Heidenreich	United States	55.74
4. Matthes	East Germany	55.87
5. Edgar	United States	56.11

200-Meter Butterfly

1. Spitz	United States	2:00.70*
2. Hall	United States	2:02.86
3. Backhaus	United States	2:03.23
4. Delgado	Ecuador	2:04.60
5. (t) Fassnacht / Hargitay	West Germany / Hungary	2:04.69

400-Meter Freestyle Relay

1. United States (Edgar, Murphy, Heidenreich, Spitz)		3:26.42*
2. Soviet Union		3:29.72
3. East Germany		3:32.42
4. Brazil		3:33.14
5. Canada		3:33.20

800-Meter Freestyle Relay

1. United States (Kinsella, Tyler, Genter, Spitz)		7:35.78*
2. West Germany		7:41.69
3. Soviet Union		7:45.76
4. Sweden		7:47.37
5. Australia		7:48.66

400-Meter Medley Relay

1. United States (Stamm, Bruce, Spitz, Heidenreich)		3:48.16*
2. East Germany		3:52.12
3. Canada		3:52.26
4. USSR		3:53.26
5. Brazil		3:57.89

* indicates world record.

Scott Ostler

Wyomia Tightened Up to Loosen Up for Gold

Who was the last American woman to win an Olympic medal—gold, silver or bronze—in the sprints?

For that one, we take you back 16 years to Mexico City. It had been raining all afternoon. It was drizzling steadily as the finalists in the women's 100 meters were called to the starting line.

Wyomia Tyus, the surprise winner four years earlier in Tokyo, at the age of 19, felt good.

No athlete, man or woman, had ever won back-to-back Olympic sprint gold medals, but Tyus was a slight favorite in this race.

She was four years more mature, a college graduate, well-trained, healthy and fast as the wind through the woods back home in Griffin, Ga. This was no time to tighten up, with the gold medal a minute away.

"I felt real good in '68," said Tyus, looking back. "I just felt that '68 was my year. I had said that in '64 (that '68 would be her year), and I felt I had to make that come true. . . .

"I wanted it so bad, and I was in great shape. I felt very confident. I didn't go around saying anything, but deep down inside I felt that was *my* race and no one was going to take it from me."

The eight women approached the starting line and began to peel off their warm-ups. What was Tyus thinking? Was she worried about getting a bad start, or pulling a muscle?

"I *always* had a bad start," she said with a laugh. "And I was never injured my whole career. . . . I was completely loose that day. It was all positive, I never thought of anything negative. It (the gold medal) was just there for me. It was there for everybody, but I thought it was mine. I felt I had rights to it."

Waiting for the starter's signal to take marks, what was left for her to do, then, but to dance? The night before, Wyomia had jokingly told friends she would loosen up at the starting line by doing the Tighten Up, a popular dance.

"Up in the stands, the athletes from Jamaica and Trinidad were playing tambourines and bongos. You could hear all that going on. I got into the enthusiasm of the crowd."

As amazed competitors stole

Please see OSTLER, page 18

Associated Press

In 1976 in Montreal, Nadia Comaneci (left) suddenly stood head and shoulders above the 1972 queen of gymnastics, Olga Korbut.

OLGA AND NADIA

These Gymnasts Took What Was Considered a Minor Sport and Transformed It Into a Nielsen Bonanza

By RICHARD HOFFER, Times Staff Writer

Until 1972, gymnastics was essentially a cult sport, something that could inspire fierce enthusiasm among the knowledgeable but which otherwise failed to stir the masses. As far as most people in this country were concerned, gymnastics was something the neighbor girl did, more or less as preparation for the cheerleading tryouts that would come later.

But then came Olga and, a little later, Nadia. The first combined a new style of circus acrobatics with the calculated public presence of a politician on the make. She was almost as much actress as athlete. The second, while the better gymnast, seemed indisposed to capitalizing on her talent. Her indifference to public acclaim was so pronounced she might just as well have been performing in an empty room.

They had their strange and different appeals and together their impact on this sport was near total. They reworked the game, changed all the old rules. And somehow inspired a following among both the fanatics and the casual observer that has never abated.

It has been reported that in the 10 years after Olga, this country's talent pool of 15,000 gymnasts grew to 150,000. And if they all weren't Olga-inspired, with their trademark pigtails, then some of them were certainly Nadia-inspired, wearing her trademark leotards, the racing stripes up the sides.

So pervasive has been their influence, in fact, that almost everything that will happen in the women's gymnastics competition this year will derive from their legends. The sport as we know it is their legacy. Their routines may be outdated by now, but the trend Olga began and Nadia sustained, a move toward a more theatric and athletic sport and a move away from a kind of stoic Olympic ballet, are intact.

More than that, though, keep in mind that, but for Olga and Nadia, much of

Please see GYMNASTS, page 18

SPITZ

Continued from page 16

And while Mark Spitz is off the roller coaster now, he doesn't object to describing the ride.

□

"Hey, Jewboy, you're not going to win any golds."

—American swimmer to Mark Spitz at '68 pre-Olympic camp

The lasting image of Mark Spitz is not that of the swimmer in a pool but of the Olympic champion in the poster with his seven gold medals. They meant everything to him. They meant the reassembling of a shattered dream, the end of a chase for glory.

But perhaps he conjures up another picture of those 1972 Olympics in Munich, one nearly as important to him.

It would be this:

After Spitz won that seventh gold, his teammates picked him up on their shoulders and carried him around the pool. Four years earlier, they might have thrown him in. He had won. He had been accepted.

He could retire happily.

"I had taken everything I could from the sport and I have given everything I could," he says. "I had eaten, lived and breathed the sport for 14 years. I swam some 26-odd thousand miles. I put in probably 10,000 hours for a chance to swim for less than 60 seconds.

"I had been to two Olympic Games. I had set 35 world records. I won everything I swam and set a world record doing it. I went out on top and I called it a day."

Yes, there were some disappointments to come in his post-Olympic career when he proved that good looks and athletic ability bear little relation to theatrical talent. But those disappointments couldn't match what he went through at the 1968 Olympics in Mexico City, the Games that were nearly his undoing.

There was no fun in these Games for Spitz. In fact, the brash young man who was sure he would set the swimming world afire hadn't had any fun for weeks prior to the Games. He was locked away instead with hostile Olympic teammates for six weeks at a training camp in Colorado Springs, Colo., that more closely resembled an armed camp.

"Mark was beaten before he ever got to Mexico City," said Gary Hall, perhaps the best swimmer never to win a gold medal and, eventually, a close friend to Spitz. "The older guys were all over Mark all the time, especially Doug Russell. But it wasn't just one guy. And they didn't just pick on Mark. It was an ugly, hostile place that I'll never forget."

The swimmers stayed in a ski lodge, four to a room. Soon after the camp began, Spitz was kicked out of his room and sent to a smaller room in the back with Ronnie Mills, who was called Ronnie Sue because he had been a cheerleader in high school.

"Ronnie was the most immature guy I had ever met and even he couldn't put up with Mark," Russell said.

Says Hall: "There were guys on the team who didn't dislike Mark. But nobody liked him."

Spitz, by his own admission, was immature. He was also 18. A year removed from winning five gold medals at the Pan American Games, Spitz unabashedly predicted he would win six golds in Mexico City. Some teammates were not amused. Also Spitz was, in Russell's words, "a borderline hypochondriac."

Says Russell: "He'd get up and say, 'I think I had a heart attack last night.' And he'd be serious. Guys would start falling out of their chairs with heart attacks all around him. He was just immature."

Hall says that Spitz, because of assorted ailments, didn't swim at all the first two weeks of camp.

"No one could believe it," Hall said.

They would make fun of him and they'd call him names. "Yeah, they said Jewboy," Hall said.

And one man, Doug Russell, stalked him.

Russell swam the 100-meter butterfly and swam it faster than anyone in the world—except Mark Spitz, the world record-holder. They had faced each other nine times and Spitz had won nine times.

"Swimming Mark in the 100 butterfly was a passion with me," said Russell, who now works for the L.A. Olympic Organizing Committee raising funds for youth groups. "All I wanted to do was beat him. I really felt like Mark had no respect for me as an athlete in terms of being a challenge.

"He had beaten me nine times but never by more than five-tenths of a second, three times by one-tenth of a second. I was right there."

And right there he stayed, where Spitz could see him every time he looked over his shoulder. Russell determined that he was going to make Spitz's life at the training camp, uh, difficult.

"Whenever Mark got in the pool, I was there, swimming right next to him," Russell said. "I would always get in the lane next to Mark. If he went first, I went first, in the next lane. If he went second, I went second. I was ready to punch anyone who challenged me. I raced him every lap of practice. I raced him in warmups."

The psych was on.

Why did he object to Spitz so much? No mystery there. One story, as told by both Russell and Hall, sums it all up.

Spitz and Russell were showering next to each other after practice one day when Spitz, trying to break the ice between them, began a conversation.

Spitz: "Doug, what are you going to do after the 100 butterfly?"

Russell: "Why Mark, I'm going to rest up so I can swim in the medley relay at the end of the week. That's what I'm going to do."

There you have it. The winner of the butterfly swims in the relay. Spitz, making innocent conversation, had shown not only that Spitz expected to win the 100 butterfly, but that he assumed Russell also expected Spitz to win the race. Spitz just had trouble seeing from any viewpoint that was not his own.

"His problem is that he used the word 'I' so much," says George Haines, who coached Spitz through his formative years. "Mark was immature and had this tendency of putting his foot in his mouth. If he had learned not to say too much, he would have been OK . . . Mark wants people to like him, but he sometimes says and does stupid things."

And sometimes he just showed people up. Haines tells this story of the time when Spitz, as a high school senior, had won the 100-yard and 200-yard butterfly races at the nationals. A teammate, Fred Haywood, won the 100-yard backstroke.

Haines: "The day we returned home, Mark talked me into timing him in the 100-yard backstroke. I should never have done it. I knew what Mark was trying to do. He wanted to get under Haywood's skin. Mark swam the 100 back with no one in the pool and beat Haywood's time. And the worst part was Haywood showed up while he was doing it."

Spitz never learned anything, Haines says, about humility. But at this training camp, Spitz learned all there was to learn about humiliation.

"It was a shame what they did to him," Haines says. "It was a damn shame."

That was camp.

□

Gary Hall knew Spitz was in trouble. It had nothing to do with his swimming, everything to do with his head.

"Mark was one of the most suggestible people that I ever knew," said Hall, who is now an ophthalmologist in Phoenix. "He didn't have a lot of self-esteem, self confidence. If anyone pulled the rug out from under him, Mark would crumble.

"He was an easy person to psych out. And when people tried, they could do it."

In Mexico City, they tried and they did do it.

Spitz began his Mexico City Olympics by finishing third in the 100-meter freestyle, an event he only recently had begun to swim seriously.

"It was like a gift," Spitz said. "I had very little experience swimming the 100. That bronze medal was very important to me. It was kind of a cornerstone in building my confidence."

That same confidence was soon destroyed. And now, older and wiser, Spitz wonders if he should have attempted the 100 freestyle at all. He wouldn't have swum the 100 and 200 freestyles except that he needed to swim them in the trials to qualify for a relay team.

"I did so well, I figured I'd try it," Spitz said. "Now I think I probably should have stuck to my original program."

Spitz's next event was the 100 butterfly. Here the psyching really began.

Every time Russell and Spitz had met, Russell had gone out fast and Spitz had caught him.

"I was a drop-dead sprinter," Russell said. "I'd get a big lead and then I'd die at the end. This time it would be different."

Finally, Russell adopted another strategy.

"I decided to go out much slower than usual," Russell said. "When Mark would get to the other end, he'd be ahead for the first time and I knew he'd be thinking, 'I'm ahead of Russell. I really must be going out hard.' And that's just what happened. My plan was to be even with him at 75 meters. I knew that he would look at me in the middle of the pool, and he did.

"When he put his head down, I kicked. I beat him by five-tenths of a second, as bad as he ever beat me. At any point I could have taken him. The longer we were into the race, the cockier I felt."

When Russell touched, he put a finger in the air, signifying that he, at last, was No. 1. He then clambered out of the pool, got on his knees and, in his words, "thanked the good Lord above."

It was just one race, but it was the Olympics as far as Spitz was concerned. Russell took his place on the 400-meter medley relay team, costing Spitz a sure gold medal.

"It screwed me up for the rest of the Games," Spitz said. "I really don't know what happened. I rushed it a little bit in the first 50. That's all I can remember. I know it cost me two gold medals."

Even now, Spitz either doesn't know he was had—or won't admit it.

Hall knows. "Mark was just psyched out," he said. "He was destroyed, psychologically destroyed, for the rest of the time he was there. He almost cost the team a gold medal in the 800 (freestyle) relay. He swam a 2:01. His best time was 1:55.

"Then he finished last in the 200 butterfly. He was just hanging on by then."

He had swum the 200 butterfly in a trial that morning and had swum a time fast enough to win it in the evening.

"By the time I swam it," he says now, "I could have given a darn. I was just ready to go home."

He held the 200-butterfly record for 10 years.

He lost the 100 butterfly once in his lifetime.

"Just before the '72 Olympics," Spitz said, "I was thinking that if I never go to another Olympics, I could still say 30 years from now 'Well I got two golds, a silver and a bronze. I didn't win any individual events, but I held 35 world records. Well, it isn't all that bad.'

"That's what I kept telling myself, anyway."

Said Russell at the time: "It could have happened to a nicer guy."

A postscript:

Russell and Spitz met next in the 1969 NCAA championships. You can guess what happened.

"He kicked my butt," said Russell, laughing. "I was cocky by then. I swam the old sort of race. That shows you how smart I am."

Associated Press

His seventh gold medal in Munich Olympics earned Mark Spitz ride on shoulder of teammate Mike Stamm of San Diego. Also helping was teammate Jerry Heidenreich of Dallas.

□

Spitz was 18 years old when life crumbled briefly in 1968. He spent the next four years putting it back together.

In 1972, he was ready.

"I was bigger, stronger, more mature, more experienced," Spitz said. "I felt like I was in complete control."

Hall roomed with him in the 1972 training camp, and Spitz got along with everyone.

"He was a leader, somebody the others guys looked to," Hall said. "The Indiana guys (his college teammates) got along well with Mark. He was more like one of the guys this time."

Says Jerry Heidenreich, a Spitz rival in 1972: "Mark stayed to himself a lot, but he didn't have problems with anyone. Some people thought he was arrogant. That may have been jealousy. Basically, he got along."

There were few distractions—and one obsession.

His name was Don Schollander. He had won four gold medals in the 1964 Olympics and those four golds hounded Spitz, particularly after his failure in 1968.

"If I would have broken five times as many records as Don Schollander and if I didn't win four gold medals, equaling what he did, I basically would have felt I was just another name in swimming . . . I felt it when I swam. I always felt that no matter what I did, I just wasn't as good as Don Schollander. Even if the time was faster or the competition was better, to me, it didn't mean a darn thing. He had the gold medals.

"You can't imagine how that haunted me . . . I lived, ate and breathed that thing until it finally came. One of the happiest days of my life was the day I won the fifth gold medal in Munich. Now I became the record-holder. I finished my career with the seven golds and I think it haunts a lot of people, deep down inside."

Everything was better in 1972, even the order of the events. In Munich, Spitz could open with his longer races.

"It was a perfect program," Spitz says now.

And as he had unraveled in training camp in 1968, he had come together in the U.S. trials four years later.

"The trials were what spurred him on," Hall said. "With Mark, it was often the tone of the first event that kind of set him up. He was swimming well. In the 200 (butter) fly, for example, the year before . . . he swam a 2:03.9 or 2:03.8 and he just touched me out in the nationals. And just one year later he swam 2:00.7 and he said, 'I could have gone under two minutes if somebody had pushed me.'

"And he probably could have. The point with Mark was that he never swam up to his potential in 1972, and then all of a sudden he realized the timing was right."

He opened his 1972 Olympics with the 200 butterfly, the same event in which he had bombed out four years before, and he won it going away.

"Why should I have been worried?" Spitz said. "I was three or four seconds faster than anyone in the race."

That was easy. His next individual race, the 200-meter freestyle, looked as if it might be a little tougher. The only person on the team with whom Spitz had problems was Steve Genter, and it was Genter who would be Spitz's principal competitor.

Genter was always looking for a way to psych someone. He was one of the first swimmers to shave his head, and that wasn't the strangest thing he did.

"He tried to stare down his opponents," Halls says of Genter. "He'd get up on the (starting) block and do a little Indian war dance while everyone else was shaking his arms. Mark considered it a psych-out routine that was pointed at him and he said so. Mark started referring to Steve as Genitilia instead of Genter."

Eventually, the two had to be separated during workouts.

A few days before the 200, Genter suffered a collapsed lung. When he came back the day before the race, Spitz advised Genter not to swim.

"Steve resented it," Hall says. "And he swam like it and almost beat Mark."

Spitz trailed Genter with 50 meters remaining, but he came back to beat him by nearly a second, setting a world record as he did in all of his individual races. Spitz had won his third gold medal, including a relay, in two days. The Games were on.

The only question remaining at that point was whether Spitz would go for six gold medals or seven. What he did not want to do was lose, and he thought it was possible he could lose in the 100 freestyle to Heidenreich.

"I could have swum six gold medals and a silver and it wouldn't have had the same effect," Spitz said. "I almost didn't do the 100. I started believing what the press was writing. But the event I didn't want to swim was the event I had to swim. I could have won 15 gold medals, but if I didn't win the 100 freestyle I would not have been considered the fastest in the world.

"In every sport, there's an event that signifies the pinnacle, the best, the fastest, the strongest. In swimming, it's the 100-meters freestyle."

The press got wind that he might not swim, and Spitz says he played along. Spitz says that by this time in his career, he was the master of the psych. He talks about sitting in the warmup room when his coach, Sherm Chavoor, would come by and say, "Mark, how's the shoulder?"

Says Spitz: "My shoulder was never sore, but I'd say, 'Gee, that rubdown wasn't long enough.' And I'd start going through these crazy calisthenics. Whether you want to act cool or not, it was definitely heard and it probably affected some people."

So Spitz let Heidenreich think he might not swim. But Heidenreich says he never believed it.

"I knew he'd swim," he said. "I never thought that he wouldn't."

Heidenreich had swum a faster time than Spitz in the freestyle relay and felt confident going into the race, so confident that he didn't attempt to psych out Spitz. That, he says, was his mistake.

"When I look back on it," said Heidenreich, who owns a computer company in Dallas, "I could have talked to him more. He was nervous. I had a way to talking to the other swimmers, but I didn't work on Mark. If I did, it might have screwed up his whole Olympics."

But nothing was screwing Spitz up this go-round. He won his sixth gold, his fourth individual gold and set his fourth world record in the process.

"During that Olympics, everyone became a spectator to the spectacle I was creating," Spitz said. "I think they felt the pressure, the pressure to mess up my winning streak. Jerry Heidenreich, who could have beaten me, the only man who could have beaten me, I think he felt the additional amount of pressure."

Heidenreich can laugh about it now. "The first time I faced Mark in the nationals, he finished first and I finished last," he said. "The last time, he finished first and I finished second. Who improved the most?"

Spitz had improved enough. He made everyone forget about Don Schollander. And he made sure no one would ever forget about Mark Spitz.

□

Mark Spitz was a genuine American hero. Offers to endorse products started rolling in, guaranteed to make him a rich hero. Hollywood beckoned. He was good-looking and he was going to dental school, so maybe he was smart, too.

But things started going wrong before they even had a chance to go right.

The day after Spitz won his seventh gold medal, terrorists attacked the compound where Israeli athletes were living and killed nine of them. Spitz, as a Jew, was asked for his reaction, and he didn't quite know what to say.

What he did say—"I think it's tragic—no comment"—came out badly.

Then, when he started appearing on television on variety shows, he came out badly again. Time had called him a "Jewish Omar Sharif," but that was before he had been seen anywhere outside of a swimming pool. The critics would come to ravage him. He was wooden, they said. He had no sex appeal. He just sort of stood there.

There was no reason to think that he could act, of course. Spitz wonders now why people didn't see that.

"I wasn't an actor and I wasn't an entertainer," Spitz said. "I was on variety shows doing little skits designed to make a mockery of yourself, to kind of have fun. The worse you acted, the more fun you had. The better the ratings, the more effective the piece was. For that I was successful, doing just that, getting rating points for those shows.

"But it certainly wasn't helping my career. But I didn't want that career anyway. I had movie offers and I turned them down. I had no ability to act. The only lure would have been to make money, but I can make money in other ways. I'm not such a total egomaniac."

Isn't he?

"My name is recognized all over the world," Spitz said. "Far more than any movie actor's. You go to the middle of India and they know who Mark Spitz is. I doubt they know who Tom Selleck is."

So, he turned away from Hollywood, or maybe more accurately, Hollywood turned away from him.

"I knew he wouldn't do well on television," Hall said. "He does not communicate well in crowds. We'd do clinics together and he wouldn't even look up at the audience."

Spitz now represents a brand of swimwear and he sells real estate and has an office in Beverly Hills and another office in Germany. He travels a lot. He owns a big house and a fast car and sails competitively. Occasionally, he works for ABC-TV, as he will during the Olympics. He has been married for 11 years, has a young son and says he is living happily ever after.

As he was sitting in a hotel lobby in Indianapolis, the site of the U.S. swim trials, Spitz seemed content, seemed unconcerned with how the world views him.

"This hotel is really interesting," Spitz was saying. "I could just sit here for hours and look."

In other words, he's saying the slow lane suits him fine.

But while he says he doesn't like to talk about how much money he makes, he recently told an interviewer that he had turned down a $1.2 million deal because it wasn't big enough to interest him.

It sounds to some like bragging. And that perception continues to put off a lot of people in the world of swimming. One prominent swim coach, when asked to talk about Spitz, said: "Why would you be doing a story on him? It's ridiculous."

Says Russell: "Most of us thought he was just trying to use those gold medals to grab all he could."

Whenever he shows his face around swimmers, the old criticisms begin. But there is no one to say that Mark Spitz wasn't the best of them all.

"I went out gracefully," Spitz said. "How many athletes ever do that? I can look back on that with a lot of satisfaction."

Success or failure? Gary Hall has an idea.

"People look at Mark as a failure," Hall said. "But maybe he really got what he wants. He wanted the fame and fortune, but I don't think he really wanted the limelight, the crowds of people. He wants privacy. It's pretty hard to have your cake and eat it, too, but that's kind of what happened. I think he got what he wanted.

"I think it's a happy ending."

Staff writers Seymour Beubis and Tracy Dodds also contributed to this story.

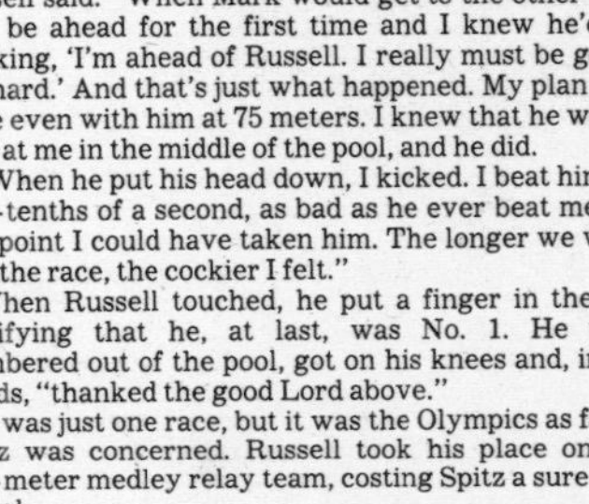

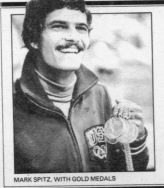

MARK SPITZ, WITH GOLD MEDALS

'If I would have broken five times as many records as Don Schollander and if I didn't win four goal medals, equaling what he did, I basically would have felt I was just another name in swimming . . . You can't imagine how that haunted me . . . I lived, ate and breathed that thing until it finally came.'

—MARK SPITZ

GYMNASTS

Continued from page 16

the talent you will see prancing and twisting and flying through the air would never have been inspired to stretch on a pair of leotards in the first place.

The popularity of the sport is their gift. Even as the years distance them from new generations of sprites, it is difficult to find a young gymnast who has not somehow found her way into the sport through Olga or Nadia. Olga and Nadia were the force behind this enthusiasm and in their wake an estimated 10,000 clubs sprang up across the country. In addition, they had made it a spectacular sport, with an appeal to masses as well.

It has proven to be a happy story for gymnastics, which is now a superstar sport, a sure sellout, a sure ratings fix. But for these two superstars, the story did not unfold nearly so happily. Their gifts to the sport have gone largely and surprisingly unrewarded. While their heirs have danced happily, they, meanwhile, have settled into various stages of exile, from which periodically would issue strange and tragic reports of nervous breakdowns and even an attempted suicide.

So strange, isn't it, that these wonderful young women, who seemed to live suspended in midair, tumbling in that rare ether of achievement, would crash to the earth so soon, so heavily. But they were human, it turned out, subject to the same unhappiness that afflicts others, dragged down by life's true gravity. On the other hand, as we continue to see, their legacy has known no such bounds.

□

Little Olga Korbut, the 84-pound Elf from Grodno. She was not, first of all, pretty, what there was of her. Her physical makeup seemed to consist entirely of pigtails and teeth. Emotionally, she was capable of wide shifts of mood, waving jubilantly from the platform one time, weeping openly another. And technically, aesthetically, however you wanted to look at it, she was not the best gymnast of her time.

Who would have predicted this was the gymnast to overhaul this sleepy sport, to turn it into a spectacle, to capture a world-wide audience in the process? Not even her own country. The Soviet Union thought so little of her that it didn't even include her biography in the team's publicity material at those 1972 Games. She was an alternate on the Soviet team and wasn't expected to turn so much as a somersault, much less our heads.

Gordon Maddux, the man ABC calls in to make sense of this very difficult sport every four years, certainly wouldn't have predicted it. He was probably the first man to notice Olga and as such the originator of Olgamania. But, as he points out, he was in no way prepared for her. Her subsequent buildup can hardly be considered calculated when you know going into the Games that Maddux had never heard of her.

Who had? Korbut, it should be remembered, had arrived in Munich as just one more little tumbler out of weird Renald Knysh's stable in Grodno. Knysh, who used to keep a card file on all the young married couples in Grodno with an eye toward those who might produce future gymnasts, was decidedly out of the mainstream. For one thing, he encouraged more athletic and daring routines among his gymnasts than were generally acceptable. What Knysh was doing went against tradition, which rewarded the more static posing then popular.

But here came Olga, making the team on a fellow gymnast's injury. And there went tradition.

It took some luck. Remember that Maddux, and therefore the rest of our little world, was unaware of Olga.

"I wasn't even aware she was there," he said.

Know, too, that ABC had planned to de-emphasize its coverage of Soviet gymnastics, beginning with the team finals. The feeling was that ABC had done enough with them. Besides, there was a nice little dogfight for third place shaping up with Hungary, Czechoslovakia and, yes, the United States.

Then, while the athletes were doing their two-minute warmups, Maddux happened to look over to where the Soviets were working on the uneven bars.

"I just happened to glance over Jim McKay's head and I see this ugly kid with pigtails, doing a back somersault recatch on the uneven bars. We re-wrote the script right there."

Korbut's little piece of daring on the bars was just the beginning of Olgamania. McKay asked the astonished Maddux if that move had ever been performed before. "That's when I made this real stupid comment," remembers Maddux, "I said, 'not by any human.'"

Don Peters, now the U.S. women's coach, remembers her appeal less in a gymnastics sense than a human sense.

"I think what she did in 1972, and what kind of made her so interesting, was that gymnastics had long been so militaristic, a calisthenic-type thing which started in Europe way back at the turn of the century," he said. "Everything was very stoic. You marched and saluted, a lot of things we still do. No one showed any emotion. No way in 1956 did you do a high five after the pommel horse.

"That's what made Olga so interesting. She did a very unique bars routine that was very spectacular, very exciting and the crowd went bonkers. And Olga went back on the platform. Everyone in gymnastics was shocked."

But this toothsome cheerfulness, this playing to the crowd, alone did not secure her popularity. It wasn't enough that her pouty peasant looks transformed her

Olga Korbut

into a special kind of beauty as she flew through the air. She had to cry, too.

It happened in the all-around finals. Korbut, whose theatrics on the platform had overly influenced the judges (the revisionist historians insist), was somehow in the lead going into the final day. But then disaster struck.

"The whole world was watching," says Maddux. "Here was this alternate, leading the whole thing. Then she got to bars. She stubbed her toe on the mat. Then she slipped off the bars. She did it again. She totally bombs out and she cries. Then some old lady climbs over the barrier and handed her a bouquet. By then, some 15,000 were crying in the arena."

And millions more at home. If the TV audience hadn't already taken this 17-year-old into its hearts, endorsing a never-before-seen cheerfulness, they certainly did at the sprite's sorrow. "When she cried," Peters recalls, "you just wanted to hug her."

The next day, ABC had its script etched in stone; there would be no rewriting this time. Olga, Olga, Olga. Their attention was rewarded as Korbut, who had placed seventh in the all-around, came back to win gold medals on beam and in floor exercises.

And so Korbut emerged as the greatest gymnast of all time in public opinion, although she wasn't even the best on her team. This, you should know, was a puzzling phenomenon back in the Soviet Union. On the one hand, the Soviets were eager to capitalize on the propaganda possibilities of her success. On the other hand, they flat out hated the leverage this seventh-place gymnast, this little prima donna, was able and all too eager to wield.

Some first-class bickering emerged from this, confirming that cattiness is a world-wide phenomenon. Ludmilla Turischeva, the all-around winner from those Olympics, was certainly shocked to find herself supplanted by this middling gymnast. And in 1973, Turischeva's coach, Larisa Latynina, came out with, "The real leader of the Soviet gymnastics team is Ludmilla Turischeva. A leader should be able to win in any situation and for that, one must be a complete person in every respect—in relation to the sport, to yourself, to your own triumph and the triumph of others. An Olga Korbut does not yet have enough of these qualities."

Even Pravda seemed to agree. In 1974, Knysh acknowledged that Korbut had her knuckles rapped "for lack of proper attitude" following her Olympic triumph.

But what did experts or government officials know? The public wanted Olga. And the Soviets knew better than to blow this opportunity to gain some attention.

So it was that Korbut was the star of the Soviet team that toured the United States in 1976, playing to the crowd, as calculating an actress as ever lived, able to stretch the party line to its breaking point.

Maddux, who was the pubic address announcer on this tour, says "the Russians, deep down, hated it." People in the know were very much aware of this little pixie's shrewd use of her own charisma. Bela Karolyi, who coached Comaneci before defecting here, said this manipulative style was probably necessary for her to even stay in gymnastics, she had so little else going for her.

"There was something about her that was spectacular," Karolyi admits. "She came on very strongly because of the personal manner, the smile on her face which was actually impressing the people more than the judges. It was a happy style."

But, adds Karolyi, it was a calculating style. "Korbut was the type of person who could sell, and was doing everything in the world to sell. That happens when your product is not very valuable."

Maddux wasn't about to confuse her for the greatest gymnast of all time, either. But for a saleswoman, he had to admit, she was right up there. He recalls one of the stops on the Soviets' tour, coming late in the tour when officials, especially the KGB who accompanied the athletes, had relaxed a bit.

"Olga had a chance to go to this mall in St. Louis," he said, "and she managed to break away from the crowd and she found her way to this J.C. Penny's. There she got the attention of the store manager and got the message through to him that she wanted to buy a wedding gown."

Of course, Olga could deliver, too. Maddux recalls one stop in Philadelphia, which was announced as Olga's swan song. She performed a fairly routine floor exercise—"watered down, skill-wise"—but performed it theatrically enough to pull everyone from their seats.

"She got a standing ovation. Her pianist motioned her back for an encore, starting in the middle of the performance. She went on for about five minutes. Then she tells me to announce that 'This one I dedicate to the Sparrow,' meaning her idol, Edith Piaf. She vamped for about five more minutes. I cried."

The Soviets, meanwhile, were shedding tears of frustration. What to do with this imp? When she demanded to be allowed shopping sprees to bring home gifts to her family, they were forced to concede. When the 1976 Olympics rolled around, they were forced to make her team captain, even though Turischeva and newcomer Nelli Kim ranked above her. Turischeva, who had toed the party line all those years, was reported to have felt shock and betrayal at being removed as team captain.

It hardly mattered for that was the year of Nadia. Anyway, how long can somebody stay in the air, so high. Gravity calling. At the Montreal Olympics, Jim McKay seemed to signal her exit when he reported: "Now after seasons of endless tours and dieting, she seemed generations removed from Nadia, a weary old lady of the gymnasium trying to dredge up the magic that once came instinctively."

When the public removed support, Olga came crashing down. She announced her retirement after those Games and went into a sort of exile. Turischeva, meanwhile, rose to a surprisingly quick prominence. She married Olympic sprint champion Valery Borzov, a high-ranking sports official, and herself gained high rank on the gymnastics technical committee, rising to that position in an unheard-of two years. Whether she exacted any revenge on her rival is hard to say. In any event, Olga virtually disappeared.

By 1983, she was almost impossible to locate. Soviet officials, their power over her returned, refused to cooperate with journalists hoping to contact her. Local reporters said her "head had been turned" by her success and that she was a victim of "star disease."

Reports would surface from time to time. Nervous breakdowns were reported. Another report, published earlier this year, described her living modestly in a third-floor walkup in Minsk, 450 miles from Moscow. She lives there with her husband (yes, she finally did marry), who is a former rock star who is now an aspiring film-maker, and their five-year-old son. Still other reports have her dreaming of yet another Olympics, but as an equestrienne. It is certain, however, that the glory of her gymnastics remains central to her life. One entire room of her apartment is set aside for her gymnastics mementoes.

"Every day, every night she thinks about gymnastics," her husband has been quoted as saying. "She even cries."

□

And then came Nadia. Nadia Comaneci, the ice princess from Romania. She was just 14, but as impenetrable as Olga was accessible. She was aloof, mysterious, untouchable. She was, in short, the opposite of Olga. She was, in her way, just as unlikely a choice to popularize gymnastics.

Nobody remembers loving Nadia the way they loved Olga, the clown princess of her sport. Comaneci, by far the better and more consistent gymnast, was robotic in comparison, not at all endearing. But her steely perfection was somehow able to arouse yet another wave of appreciation for gymnastics.

How? Olga smiled and wept, but Nadia never twitched a single muscle in pursuit of public attention. Did she, like Garbo, want only to be alone? Well, during those 1976 Games, when asked what her greatest wish was, she replied, "I want to go home."

Sheer excellence has its rewards, too, and that was exactly what was being rewarded in Montreal. "Nadia was extremely stoic," recalls Don Peters, the U.S. women's coach. "She was like a robot. But she was in a class by herself. She won the all-around, won two of the four events and placed second in another. She was heads and shoulders above the rest and for that she was appreciated."

She was the first gymnast ever to receive a perfect score of 10 and she did it seven times in those Olympics. At times, she, too, may have been overscored. But, as with Olga, the judges could hardly deny the enthusiasm of the crowds. She was perfect. You didn't need to know the difference between a Stalder Shoot and a Moon Shot to see that.

Maddux says Nadia had nowhere near the charisma of an Olga and this was proven when Nadia failed to turn on the crowds during her own subsequent tour. But she was just so good. How to deny that?

"In 1976," Maddux said, "Nadia was the best athlete in the world, all sports included. If you consider weight to strength, she was stronger than Russia's Vassily Alexeyev."

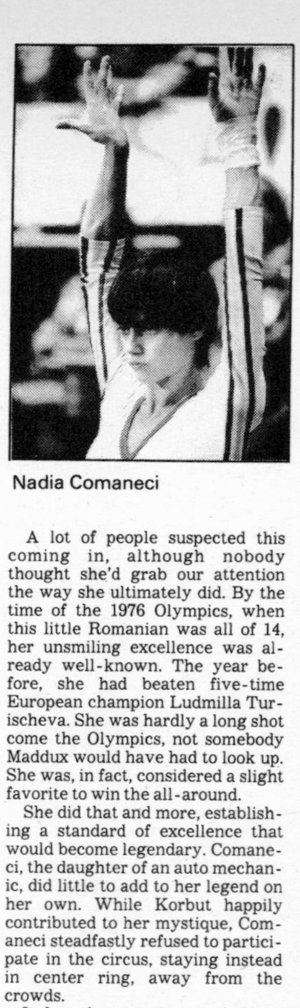

Nadia Comaneci

A lot of people suspected this coming in, although nobody thought she'd grab our attention the way she ultimately did. By the time of the 1976 Olympics, when this little Romanian was all of 14, her unsmiling excellence was already well-known. The year before, she had beaten five-time European champion Ludmilla Turischeva. She was hardly a long shot come the Olympics, not somebody Maddux would have had to look up. She was, in fact, considered a slight favorite to win the all-around.

She did that and more, establishing a standard of excellence that would become legendary. Comaneci, the daughter of an auto mechanic, did little to add to her legend on her own. While Korbut happily contributed to her mystique, Comaneci steadfastly refused to participate in the circus, staying instead in center ring, away from the crowds.

In fact, the attention puzzled her. The questions, always the questions. "How long will you compete, when will you retire?" What to make of this? Little Nadia pursed her lips. "I'm 14 years old."

Her coach, however, was all too happy to do what Nadia either could not or would not do. Create a legend. Bela Karolyi, who has since come to Houston where he continues to develop Olympic-quality gymnasts, made up a whole past for her during those Olympics. According to him, he was a junior coach, very much on the make, combing kindergartens in his isolated turf of Transylvania, looking for the one gymnast to bring his program to prominence.

According to the lore, he spotted two 6-year-old girls playing in a courtyard during recess.

"They were running and jumping and pretending to be gymnasts," he said. "Then the bell rang and they ran into the building and I lost them."

Frantic—did he sense his destiny so immediately—he went from room to room to find them. He went into each room three times. "A third time I went and asked 'Who likes gymnastics?' In one of the two classrooms, two girls sprang up."

One of them was Nadia, a cheerless perfectionist, so dedicated to this new game that Karolyi found he actually had to chase her out of the gym. It was this determination that impressed Karolyi the most. "This little kid had on her mind, I want to be a winner. With that wish, she became an unbelievable competitor."

She was a competitor, all right. The 1976 Olympics were billed as a kind of duel between the faded Olga and the fresh Nadia. Nadia blew her away, cooly and dispassionately. A little too coolly for some.

Even Karolyi had hoped to inspire some charm in her, to combine her athletic perfection with a little theatrics.

"We tried to encourage her," he says. "We were working hard on that part. But she wasn't the person that could have played the so-called game. She was aggressive, concentrated, very self-confident but not to gain attention. We tried to improve her representation, to make her style more understandable for younger kids. We decided it wouldn't be a good idea to change her personality.

"In Nadia's case, it just wasn't necessary to add to her from the selling standpoint."

Hardly. She needn't have said a word to secure her stardom. Moves that a gymnastic critic later wrote were "hardly conceivable from a biomechanic viewpoint," that a gymnastics official judged so dangerous that he asked they be banned, garnered all the attention she would require.

And just maybe she didn't need any of that attention in the first place. In any event, her instincts were right not to contribute to the hysteria that surrounded her, in which politics somehow replaced gymnastics in her life. After those 1976 Olympics, in which everything was perfect, she found herself sufficiently flawed that, according to reports filtering out of Romania, she attempted suicide, drinking bleach.

To this day, that attempted suicide has not been officially confirmed. A nervous breakdown, perhaps. Some time in the sanitarium. But other reports, so many of them, confirm this awful thing. Nadia's former pianist told Maddux it is so. A documentary film that was viewed in Cannes says it is so. Karolyi says it must be so.

"We have heard that," he said, wearily. "Yes, she did it."

Maddux says, "She was a desperately unhappy girl. Her life was in a gym, in an airplane, in an arena. Her body was in a survival mode . . . It was around '77 that the Romanians reported a nervous breakdown and sent her off to a sanitarium. Her pianist says that wasn't so. She tried to kill herself."

Karolyi says everything would have been fine if the government hadn't exploited her. With this fantastic global success on its hands, the Romanian government simply couldn't help itself. They dragged her across the country, squeezing as much propaganda out of that 85-pound body as Nadia used to squeeze strength.

Karolyi, who felt strongly enough about such intervention that he eventually defected ("I could not give up my system for something that is like candlelight, here now and then extinguished"), says it began when the government moved his entire team from Deva to Bucharest to better exploit its fame. "She then gained a lot of weight, going from party to party, where she was being shown off. They got her away from her usual program, from gymnastics, which was her priority. It was a desperate situation. She looked like a monster and she felt there was only one way out."

The suicide attempt was well concealed, but her career failure was not. By 1978, news of her weight and a few defeats here and there was so widespread that People magazine, hardly the journal of the cognoscenti, carried a picture and this caption: "Is Her Career Bottoming Out?"

Had she become "just another gymnast," the cruel words she once used to describe Olga? Briefly she had. But then she commenced a miraculous comeback, paring off the weight, rededicating herself to gymnastics. By 1979, she was all the way back, taking an early lead in the world championships held that year in Fort Worth. Only a hand injury, which knocked her out of the event, prevented her from regaining the old glory.

She was still there for the Moscow Games in 1980. Taller, but no less athletic or silent, she nearly made a 1976-like run, failing to win the all-around only on the last event when political considerations intervened. For 28 minutes after her beam routine, which most felt gave her victory over the Soviet Union's Yelena Davydova, the judges argued. She needed a 9.90 to tie. Finally the score, a 9.85. Poland and Soviet judges had each given her a 9.8.

The next day she won gold medals on the beam and in floor exercise, but they were the last golds for her.

Like Olga, she returned to the muffling silence of her Communist homeland. As with Olga, unofficial reports of her baffling career would make the rounds. She was coming back; she was retiring; she was going to school; she was coaching; she was judging; she had appendicitis; she was exhausted. None of the reports struck so tragic a chord as in 1977, though.

Briefly she did consider coming back for the 1984 Games. A reporter found her back in Deva earlier this year, training with the national coach. She seemed to have that old enthusiasm, though it had apparently taken a turn for refined sugar. When a Pepsi-Cola truck pulled in at the camp, bringing a beverage that is rare and much sought-after, she jumped for joy. "Look," she said, "they have brought us Pepsi!"

But the comeback came to nothing and the country that she glorified with her fabulous tumbling eventually held a retirement party for her, dignifying her achievements with a political stamp of approval.

And just recently, it was announced that she will, indeed, be in attendance at the L.A. Games, coming here as a guest of the L.A. Organizing Committee.

Haralambie Alexa, the Romanian sports minister, says she is now coaching in a junior program. "The big ones and the little ones look up to Nadia," he said.

Everybody else will just remember her, like Olga, for a long time after she finally returned to earth.

OSTLER

Continued from page 16

glances, Wyomia danced.

"And it (the Tighten Up) really did relax me."

Eight women lowered themselves into their starting blocks. Four of them had equaled the world record during the preliminary races.

Barbara Ferrell of the United States false-started, then Tyus false-started. The drizzle was picking up in tempo, the clouds rolling over the stadium were dark and heavy.

"I can see it just like it was yesterday," Tyus said. "We came out of the blocks, I could hear the crowd cheering and all that, but basically all I thought of was 'stay relaxed and lean at the tape.'. . .

"It's amazing all the things that can go through your mind in 11 seconds. I had time to say to myself: 'Gosh, you got a good start. You gotta go, you gotta go. Now stay relaxed, keep your knees up.'

"I was also thinking, 'Don't tighten up at 90, 80 yards. (Poland's Irena) Szewinska's gonna be there, she's always coming at the last, this has got to be the strongest part of your race.'

"All this went through my mind."

Tyus leaned into the tape in 11.0, still the Olympic record. Ferrell was second and Szewinska third.

The American 400-meter relay team, Wyomia anchoring, won the gold medal. That was her third gold. She also helped win a relay silver in 1964, the Americans finishing behind a Polish team later stripped of its world record time when one runner became the first athlete to fail a sex test.

Today Wyomia lives in Los Angeles with her husband, Duane Tillman, 12-year-old daughter Simone and 5-year-old son Tyus.

Her Olympic feats are not forgotten. She is in demand for public public speaking and PR work. She gives clinics. She tries to encourage young women runners, remembering how her father, Willie, encouraged her to run in spite of the social stigma of that time against women with muscles and medals.

She had four older brothers and they always included Wyomia when they played football or baseball. Willie's orders.

A couple years ago Wyomia dug her two 100-meter gold medals out of a bedroom drawer, framed them and hung them on a wall in the living room. Most people, she says with a laugh, walk in and don't even notice them.

"I'm no superstar at home," she said. "It's like when I was growing up. I still had to go home after '64 and clean the house, clean the toilets. . . .

"I was special because I was their daughter, and that's as far as it goes. I really can appreciate that. It makes you a better person. You don't start thinking that you're better than anyone else."

But on two occasions, in 1964 and 1968, Wyomia Tyus *was* better than anyone else.

In 1968, moments after she crossed the finish line, the Mexico City skies opened up. Wyomia Tyus received her gold medal in a downpour, standing drenched and proud as the American flag was raised toward the clouds.

OLYMPICS '84

2 DAYS TO GAMES

Jim Murray

Saudi Prince Strikes Oil in Soccer

One of the great fringe benefits of covering an Olympic Games is that you get to meet royalty. I mean the real McCoy, not the raggedy doormen in fur hats outside Soviet tea rooms or the exiles parking cars along the Cote d'Azur or plotting a restoration while reading palms at Coney Island.

So I couldn't wait when my friend, publicist Chuck Panama, asked: "How'd you like to meet a real live prince of the realm who's here from Saudi Arabia with his soccer team?"

"Saudi Arabia's got a soccer team?" I marveled. "How do you play that in a bedsheet and burnoose?"

"Be serious, will you?" scolded Panama. "They play it in shorts and cleats like everyone else. They play it damn well. They're one of 16 teams to make the Olympics. Beat all the Asian countries and New Zealand to get here. Match that around New York."

"Wait a minute. What does the prince have to do with this?" I asked suspiciously.

"He built this team. From scratch." shouted Chuck. "He's a regular Knute Rockne. Lombardi. It's a Cinderella story."

□

I held my ears. "Just a minute," I told him coldly. "By last count there were 1,115 'Cinderella' stories in this Olympics. Cinderella makes page 21 in these Games. Is this prince legit? He's not just here running a tour to Disneyland or something?"

"Legit?" roared Panama. "Listen, dummy, if you were in Riyadh he could get you thrown out of the Middle East. You'd need a letter from the White House just to look at him. They'd make you bring incense and back out of the room. I'm talking ruling family here, not Mike Romanoff."

"Could he make me fight a lion?" I asked.

"Be serious," hissed Panama. "Yes."

"Will I have to take off my shoes?" I asked, contrite. "If so, I better change my socks. Do you bow or curtsy?"

"Both," Panama advised. "And, for heaven's sake, don't clap him on the back and ask him if he heard the one about the two Jews and the traveling salesman."

"What if he gives me a bag of jewels?" I asked. "We're not allowed to keep gifts over two dollars."

Please see MURRAY, page 20

'Did you know that the greatest fear of my life, and that includes the Olympics and everything else, was having to read in front of the class as a young kid?'
— BRUCE JENNER

Associated Press

With a dad like Bruce, Brandon Jenner, 3, knows that winning feeling, too. And he doesn't even need to win Olympic decathlon. Dad took care of that.

CON KEYES / Los Angeles Times

THE NOW JENNERATION

The American Ideal Lives On In a Style, Personified by the '76 Hero, Bruce Jenner

By GERALD SCOTT, Times Staff Writer

There stands the World's Greatest Athlete, 1976 edition, lord and master of all he surveys. What he surveys is a life that is, by most any measure, a dream, American or otherwise.

Now eight years and 3,000 miles removed from his victory at the Montreal Olympics, he still seems capable of turning in an 8,000-point decathlon at a moment's notice.

The chest isn't as massive as the one that strained his USA jersey en route to Olympic gold and immortality soon thereafter, but he still has, as his agent George Wallach once remarked, "the face of Robert Redford and the body of Tarzan."

He is, of course, the Unsinkable Bruce Jenner, the same Jenner who burst across the finish line in Montreal and embraced, in order, his wife, an audience of millions and the American consciousness, all in a made-for-TV moment of spontaneity.

Never mind that he finished second in that particular race. The point is that he scored enough points in the overall decathlon competition to set a world record and win the gold medal in the Bicentennial Year and, perhaps most important, had the good sense to do it all in prime time.

For most athletes, an experience like that would be the ultimate. When you're glib, handsome and photogenic, however, as Jenner surely is, it is only the beginning. Jenner's greatest leap was not one he made on the track, but across that perilous chasm that so many lesser lights have fallen short of—from athlete to businessman.

True to form, Jenner did them all one better. He not only made that leap but went even farther. He is not just Bruce Jenner, entrepreneur. He is now Bruce Jenner, growth industry.

Jenner, who goes through life as if he were 90 points behind the leader with two events to go, apparently has found the same balance in living that he once had on the track.

"Bruce Jenner may not be the world's greatest actor, sportscaster or pilot, but he is very good at all those things," noted his agent, Wallach. "In many ways, his life has paralleled the decathlon."

Now, however, instead of the 100 meters, pole vault, javelin and all the rest, it is his wife, children, sportscasting, flying, auto racing and his business life, which includes television and movie projects and commercial endorsements of varying kinds, that are his passion.

It is all centered here, at Jenner's secluded Malibu estate, tucked away at the base of some foothills not far from Pepperdine University.

Even by Malibu's upscale standards, Jenner has done well. The chalet-style home looks as if it dropped off a Swiss postcard. There are tennis courts, a guest house that most people would be proud to call their first, and a creek running by the property.

Then there are the toys: his and her Porsches, motorcycles, sailboards, a Jeep, an ultra-light hang-glider, all of which belong to the biggest kid of the lot, Bruce.

The children even have their own fort to go along with smaller scale versions of Bruce's toys.

In the center of this Fantasyland we find Jenner mugging for a family portrait with his wife, Linda, and sons, Brandon, 3, and Brody, 9 months. They are posing in front of the family pool.

Jenner and family are smiling, for these are the good years. The battle has long since been won. Yet this idyll did not come without a price to pay for the man behind it. The portrait may readily be titled, "The Education of Bruce Jenner."

Please see JENNER, page 21

ROBERT LACHMAN / Los Angeles Times

Mark Breland is a 6-3 stringbean welterweight who moves in the ring like a big cat.

104 AND 1

Near Perfect, Stringbean Mark Breland Packs Heavyweight Right-Hand Punch

By EARL GUSTKEY, Times Staff Writer

First, the record. It's so brilliant it looks like a typographical error.

In amateur boxing, everyone loses once in a while. That's exactly how often Mark Breland has lost.

Once.

He's 104-1.

Even Teofilo Stevenson, Cuba's legendary triple-gold medal winner, has lost a dozen or 15 times in his long career. Amateur boxing historians believe Breland has the best record in the history of the sport.

A record of 104-1—achieved in a sport where international judges are often swayed by nationalism and where nearly anyone can get taken out by a lucky punch now and then—simply doesn't happen. Breland, a phenomenal 147-pound athlete from Brooklyn, made it happen.

By winning an Olympic championship, he would cap possibly the greatest career in the history of amateur boxing

. . . and possibly emerge as the star of the Games.

Big numbers, 104-1.

Said Col. Don Hull, 71, president of the International Amateur Boxing Federation and a witness to every Olympic boxing tournament since 1932, about Breland:

"No one in the history of the sport ever had a record like that. And what makes it more impressive is that today the level of talent around the world is at an all-time high. He's put that record together against world-class athletes.

"Sugar Ray Robinson, Lazslo Papp, Floyd Patterson, Cassius Clay . . . none of those people had a record like that as amateurs."

In 1981, at the U.S. nationals at Concord, Calif., Breland lost a 3-2 decision to Darryl Anthony, now a pro. Breland is still sore about that. He

Please see BRELAND, page 20

BRELAND

Continued from page 19

wants Anthony for his pro debut, tentatively scheduled for Madison Square Garden in November.

For now, though, the 6-3 stringbean welterweight, who moves around like a big cat and hits like a heavyweight, wants to be the knockout of the Olympics.

Will he be the one? Will he emerge as the star?

He has formidable competition: Carl Lewis, the U.S. sprinter-long jumper; Mary Lou Retton, the U.S. gymnast; Greg Louganis, the U.S. diver; Daley Thompson, the British decathlete. Of course, there are others.

Few, though, seem to dominate their specialties as Breland dominates his.

Talking to him, you almost get the idea that it's a joke.

Reporter: "Mark, who would you say is the second best welterweight in the Olympic tournament?"

Breland: "A guy named Bum."

Reporter: "Excuse me?"

Breland: "Bum. A guy named Bum."

At that, Breland can no longer keep the laughter inside and breaks up. He says he is referring to a South Korean boxer, Yong-Beom (pronounced Bum, according to Breland) Chung.

There are four outstanding welterweights in international amateur boxing—Breland, Louis Howard of St. Louis, Serik Konakbaev of the Soviet Union, and Candelario Duvergel of Cuba. Breland has beaten each of them, decisively.

Most students of amateur boxing agree that the only thing that could keep Breland from his long-awaited gold medal is a broken hand, and even at that, some crack, he'd win the silver.

Actually, he does worry about a hand injury. He has had surgery on his right hand, to repair a tendon injury caused by the impact of his punches on opponents' heads.

You watch him move around a ring so easily, so smoothly, and you grope for faults, for a missing link. He just *can't* be as good as the buildup. No one is.

Ha! There it is. He holds his left hand too low! Look, he's vulnerable to an overhand right to the head.

Emanuel Steward, the Detroit Kronk Gym trainer who will manage Breland after the Olympics, dismisses the low left with a wave of the hand the day after Breland has clinched his berth on the Olympic team.

"A lot of tall, long-armed boxers do that," he said. "Gene Tunney did it. Cassius Clay did it. They didn't get hit with rights very often. Mark is an extremely alert boxer in the ring; it's not the problem some people think it is."

Steward trains some of the best of our time—Thomas Hearns, World Boxing Council super-welterweight champion; Milton McCrory, WBC welterweight champion, and former champions Aaron Pryor and Hilmer Kenty.

In preparing for the Olympic trials, Breland held his own in four- and five-round sparring sessions with Hearns. He decked McCrory in another sparring session.

Says Steward, "Mark's the most talented boxer I've ever worked with."

□

You look at Breland's long, lean body at 21 and figure he's a cinch to grow into the heavyweight division some day, but Steward doesn't think so.

"Mark's got an unusual metabolism," he said.

"He eats more than my heavyweight, Tony Tucker, and he was the biggest eater we had until Mark joined us. He just burns it off. I think he'll be a pro welterweight longer than a lot of people think, and I think the biggest he'll go is a junior middleweight (154 pounds), some day.

"He's a very unusual talent in that he does everything so effortlessly and naturally," Steward said. "He has that instinctive ability to know the precise instant when to strike out, to see an opening coming before it's there and then—bang—to deliver the blow at the right instant.

"Mark often lands scoring blows, even knockdown blows, while he's backing up."

Steward walks into an adjacent room, where Breland and his closest friend on the Olympic team, lightweight Pernell Whitaker, are watching a video tape of the Olympic trials tournament. They are scrutinizing Breland's 41-second, one-punch knockout of Mylon Watkins.

Watkins is pressing the attack when Breland, in retreat, almost casually rocks back on his right foot and delivers a perfect punch, a straight right that explodes on the tip of Watkins' chin. Watkins crashes onto his back and can't even rise to his knees.

Steward studies the punch again, and says, "Mark, that's one of the most beautiful knockout punches I ever saw."

Breland nods, says nothing, backs the tape up and watches it once more.

Steward is asked if this is the perfect boxer. What can he be taught?

"Mark will have to learn how to throw a left hook," he said. "He's dominated amateur boxing with the right, so he's had little incentive to use a left hook. And he needs to get more body weight behind his punches. He lands an amazing percentage of the punches he throws, but many of them are while he's backing up or moving.

"He knows he has some things to learn. You don't have to push him. He's realistic about the work involved in becoming a world-class pro."

□

It began with a man named Goat.

"He was a retired Navy man, who lived in my building when I was a little kid," Breland said.

"He was in his 50s, about 5-foot-6. I never called him anything but Goat. When I was 9, he took me to a gym to show me how to box. He also took me to see the Ali-Frazier fight, at Madison Square Garden.

"We sat up in the rafters and all I can remember is looking way down there and how smoothly Ali moved around the ring."

Breland is the son of Herbert and Luemisher Breland, both of whom grew up in rural South Carolina. One brother is a lawyer. Another is an Army sergeant stationed in Germany.

His first coach, and for many years his only coach, was George Washington, an old sparring partner of Joe Louis. Washington fought on the undercard of both Louis-Walcott fights. At Brooklyn's Bedford Stuyvesant Boxing Assn. Gym, he applied order and polish to Breland's obvious but undisciplined skills.

Breland gained prominence by winning a New York Golden Gloves championship.

Then he won another. And another. Altogether, he won five of them in a row, a feat he's as proud of as his world championship.

In April of 1983, while he was with the U.S. national team in Cuba, he talked in a Havana hotel lobby about what the Golden Gloves mean to a kid from Brooklyn.

"I guess if I win a gold medal in the Olympics, it'll top it," he said. "But when I imagine myself winning championships in the pros and looking back . . . I'm going to be awfully proud of those five Golden Gloves."

In 1980, Breland met Shelley Finkel, who promotes rock concerts in the East. They struck up a friendship. Finkel will manage his affairs as a pro, as well as those of three other Olympic team boxers (lightweight Whitaker, light-welterweight Jerry Page and super-heavyweight Tyrell Biggs).

After he had won a couple of Golden Gloves titles, offers to turn pro began. Only Finkel advised him to remain an amateur, to wait until after the Olympics, Breland said.

In 1982, he made the American team that went to Munich for the world championships, and became a world champion.

He stopped a Swede in the second round, stopped a Romanian in the first round, won two 5-0 decisions and wound up in the final against a Soviet, Serik Konakbaev, thought to be too experienced and too skilled for the 19-year-old with the skinny legs.

Breland won a 5-0 decision.

Recalled Mal Kennedy, a U.S. amateur boxing official who was at ringside that night, "It was a slaughter. The referee was close to stopping it in every round."

After that, there were more offers to turn pro. The numbers were much bigger, too. Breland said one would have earned him $500,000. Wait, Finkel advised.

In 1983, Breland injured his hand twice in consecutive long tournaments, the New York Golden Gloves and the U.S. nationals in Colorado Springs. In the first, he had surgery to repair a damaged tendon in his right-index knuckle. The second injury was less serious, but it still required Breland to wear a cast for a few weeks.

After that, he competed sparingly, choosing to save his hands for major international events, and the long, arduous Olympic trials.

He earned $30,000 for appearing in a movie, "The Lords of Discipline," portraying a persecuted black cadet at a southern military school. A casting director saw his picture in a newspaper and invited him to take a screen test for the part.

After the Olympics, he is tentatively scheduled to play a football player in a film about a woman coach.

At the Fort Worth Olympic trials earlier this summer, Breland proved to be a crowd pleaser out of the ring, as well as in.

Each morning during that five-day tournament, boxers were brought to the press room for news conferences.

At one session, before about 20 reporters, Breland began talking about his boyhood in Brooklyn, of street combat, of years of dreaming.

He spoke of flings with other sports. He talked of a long-ago basketball game in which he was whistled for one too many fouls by a referee.

"I got into a fight with him," Breland dead-panned. "Well, it wasn't really a fight . . . it was just one punch." His audience cracked up.

Breland grinned broadly, and went on to football. "I was a wide receiver. I was supposed to go out to the defensive back, pivot, and go around him for a pass. That seemed like a lot of wasted motion to me, so I decked him with a short right, and then went out for the pass."

Breland has a soft, low-pitched delivery and he is genuinely funny. Pleased at the laughs he was generating, he went on for nearly an hour.

At one point, he said: "My time isn't up yet, is it? I'm on a roll, now."

Finkel was in the room, and was pleased. It was as if a blinking neon sign was spelling out: "TV Talk Shows."

"It was a side to Mark I hadn't seen, not before a group of people," he said. "He's growing."

Breland at the trials, and later at the Las Vegas boxoff, demonstrated how easily he dominates the welterweight class. Some believe that Howard of St. Louis, a 5-9 boxer-puncher, would win the gold medal at the Olympics were Breland in another weight class.

Howard never had a chance of getting there, though. Breland has a 79-inch reach. Sonny Liston's was 82. But Breland uses his great arm length to greater advantage than most, almost always maintaining punching distance between himself and always-shorter opponents.

They fought twice and neither bout was ever in doubt. Howard was battered. He proved only that he could take a punch. The judges voted 5-0 for Breland both times, against an opponent superior to any Breland is likely to encounter in the Olympic tournament.

Defensively, Breland is like a column of smoke.

Watch his feet. He's a dancer. He glides and pivots in seemingly effortless fashion, yet he's moving faster than he appears. You play back the tapes of his bouts and you're surprised at the number of times a boxer throws a punch at Breland, only to find him simply not there.

He's a tempting target, with the left hand low, the head unprotected. But he slips punches like Ali used to, leaning back or to the side at the last second, then counters with that right hand.

The right. The most feared right this side of Teofilo Stevenson.

Said Rolly Schwartz, chief of officials for the USA Amateur Boxing Federation: "He's got one of the great straight rights in the history of amateur boxing, and I include Stevenson in that statement. A lot of guys, you nail them cleanly with a straight right, they go down, and bounce right back up.

"When Breland gets you with that right, the lights go out. He's so much taller than everyone he boxes, he's got two things going for him: great leverage from those long arms and the fact he's coming down on you with the punch.

"The negative side of that is that the impact of his punch is so great, he'll have to be careful in the Olympics. He'll have to pick his spots, to use that jab a lot and not try to knock everybody out."

Said Bob Surkein, USA/ABF board member: "He's the best amateur boxer in the world. I can't imagine him not winning the gold medal. He's got that God-given characteristic where his punches explode at impact on his opponents. He's got tremendous leverage with those long arms.

"He's light-boned. I don't think he'll ever grow into a heavyweight. I'm not even sure he'll grow into a middleweight. He's intelligent, trains hard, takes care of himself. Anything you want in a boxing prospect, it's all there."

It's all there.

So here are the Olympics.

And here is Breland.

MURRAY

Continued from page 19

"Give it to me," Panama said.

Prince Fahd bin Sultan turned out to be living in a leased Beverly Hills mansion surrounded by Mercedes and polite guards in black suits and with no visible sidearms.

"Who's going to interpret?" I whispered to Panama.

"Interpret?" he scoffed. "He went to school in Santa Barbara."

"In that case, he may need an interpreter to understand us," I whispered.

I almost gave my coat and hat to a smiling young man in a blue coat and tie standing by the door, but he stuck his hand out and Panama said quickly, "Your Highness, I would like to present Mr. Murray of The Times."

It was too late to bow. This guy looked more like he was ready to give me a high five. He beamed as we were introduced. "Wait a minute," I growled at Panama. "How come he's not wearing a veil?"

"You're lucky he's not in tennis clothes," Panama whispered. "What do you think this is, a Thousand and One Arabian Nights? Song of Scheherazade? An opera by Rimsky-Korsakov? Saudi Arabia's in the 21st Century, man."

The prince was kindly, bemused. "I am," I began awkwardly, "a little nonplused. I mean, we don't ordinarily think of Saudi Arabia as a world power in soccer."

"You are familiar with my country?" he asked.

I thought to myself, when this guy says "my," he means it. "Oh, sure," I contemplated saying. "I saw 'Lives of a Bengal Lancer,' 'Lawrence of Arabia' twice, Valentino in 'The Sheik,' and I know all the words to 'One Alone' from 'The Desert Song' by Romberg. One of my favorite Bedouin characters is The Red Shadow. Next to Muhammad Ali, of course."

Instead, I said, "How did that soccer team get that good that fast?"

"Well," the prince began, "we have always had a great interest in sports in my country. The West thinks of us as a people on camelback riding through shifting sands over a pool of oil, but we have some 256 sport centers. We brought in an English coach 16 years ago and he installed the British system of football. Then, we brought in a Brazilian coach. The system, while admirable, proved not suited."

"What did you do?" I asked.

"I brought in a Saudi coach," the prince answered. "When we lost to Iraq, 4-0, I called Khalil Zayyani in the middle of the night and told him to report at 7:30 a.m. to take over the team."

"You're George Steinbrenner." I exclaimed. "Did you fire him, too?"

"The team hasn't lost since," he said.

The new coach, he added, was familiar not only with the language but with the fasting and prayer requirements of the Moslem religion. "That's very important," he noted.

"I know," I told him. "I saw 'The Spirit of Notre Dame' three times and 'Knute Rockne, All-American'' twice. Not to mention 'Navy Blue And Gold' with Tom Brown." Panama groaned in the background.

"The team," the prince went on, "played a game more suited to our character, based on speed, surprise of attack and agility."

"'Not big but quick,' Lombardi and Red Sanders used to call it," I told him.

"When we played New Zealand (in the Asian Olympic playoffs at Singapore), the press said we would get run over. They were bigger, stronger, more experienced. We won, 4-1. Against South Korea in the critical game, we were down 2-0 early."

"Did you get angry? Want to make a change? Get nervous?"

The prince shook his head. "You have patience," he explained. So much for George Steinbrenner.

The capital city went wild. But the purists point out that the Saudis are in tough at the Olympics, where professionals from the national teams of other countries are permitted to play.

The prince smiled and shrugged as we said goodby. "It is an honor just to be here," he said. "In 1988, at Seoul, we will have an even larger team."

We walked out. "Do you think this team can win a medal?" someone in the party asked. "If they do," I advised, "look around for this big guy with a towel around his head coming out of a lamp."

I turned to Panama. "He invited me to visit him if I'm ever in Riyadh," I boasted.

"Bring incense," he suggested.

JENNER

Continued from page 19

Heredity or environment?

Even the most dedicated sociologist might have trouble determining which was more important in the development of the gold medal-winning Jenner.

Said his father, Bill, 62, a retired tree surgeon, "Why, he's a chip off the old block, of course."

The elder Jenner makes more than just a friendly boast. Bruce Jenner's grandfather, Hugh, ran in several Boston Marathons and was a contemporary of Tom Longboat, winner of that race in 1907.

Bill Jenner, himself, ran in the U.S. Army Olympics at Nuremberg after World War II, competing in the 100-yard dash, 440 relay and pole vault. He was a member of the 5th Ranger Battalion that landed at Ste.-Mere-Eglise near Utah Beach during the Allied invasion of Normandy.

Bruce Jenner found enough competition growing up in a typical middle-class family, first in New York and later in Connecticut. "There were always some kind of games going on, but it was fun, never life or death," he said.

One thing that was life and death for Jenner as a youngster was the classroom. He was dyslexic, but it wasn't diagnosed until high school. Dyslexia is a developmental disorder affecting a child's ability to read.

It's not surprising to find, then, that Jenner would take to athletics so enthusiastically as a youngster.

Said Jenner: "Here's the same kid sitting in the classroom getting an A on a test, while I was getting Cs or Ds, but I could go out on the athletic field and hold my own against them. The reason I think I grasped on to athletics and took off is because it's important for any young kid to get that pat on the back.

"I was not a very good student and, not knowing I was dyslexic, my image of myself while growing up was really of this 'slow kid' in school. Sports changed all that."

Through high school, Jenner involved himself in a variety of sports. He was good at all of them, but not great at any one thing. As a football player at Tarrytown (N.Y.) High, Jenner had his picture in the New York Times when Tarrytown edged arch-rival Ossining in a battle of unbeaten teams.

By his senior year, after the family had moved to Newtown, Conn., he was brought to the attention of L.D. Weldon, the track coach at Graceland College, a private school of 1,200 students in Lamoni, Iowa.

Said Weldon, who had coached Jack Parker to a bronze medal in the decathlon at the 1936 Games and could smell a good decathlete half a continent away: "A coach in Connecticut had called me and told me about this boy who could high jump 6-2, throw the javelin 185 feet and pole vault 13-6. I figured he had possibilities."

Jenner did not go to Graceland with the decathlon in mind, however. He went there largely because Graceland was the only school that wanted him. His grades discouraged widespread interest.

Despite Weldon's long-range plans, the decathlon discovered Jenner, not vice versa.

At the Drake Relays in 1970, during Jenner's sophomore year, he saw his first decathlon. It was the one he was competing in. Without ever having previously competed in five of the 10 events, Jenner scored 6,991 points. The school record was 6,915.

"With the variety of sports involved, I knew that I'd never get bored with it," Jenner said. "After it was over that first time, I said to myself, if there was ever any sport that had my name on it, this was it."

□

That Bruce Jenner would win the Olympic gold medal in the decathlon six years later was anything but a fluke. The exorbitant acclaim that surrounded his feat, however, probably was.

Or, as Jenner himself sums up the experience: "Well, it just goes to show you the power of television, doesn't it?"

Jenner's gold was the result of cold, logical planning on Jenner's part. First, he made the Olympic standard for 1972 (7,600 points). Then he came in third at the U.S. trials, went to Munich, where he finished 10th in only his 10th decathlon. By 1975, two years after moving to San Jose, where he could train year-round, he had set the world record with 8,524 points.

The hype that surrounded Jenner's winning the gold, however, was a made-for-TV, and made-by-TV, event. One can imagine the scene in the ABC studios at the Olympic Stadium in Montreal the night of the decathlon.

Cosell? Roone here. Loved the boxer, what's his name—Leonard?—just loved him! Nice touch, that picture of his girlfriend taped to his shoe. They're weeping from coast to coast. Fine job, Howie—take a fresh toupee out of petty cash.

Click.

McKay! How many times do I have to tell you—ease off the Greco-Roman wrestling already. I've got six advertisers on the horn from New York threatening to pull unless things pick up. This is the Olympics and that means track and field. Find me a hero in five minutes or you're fired!

Click.

So the cameras pan the track. Edwin Moses in the hurdles? Naw. Great name, but when was the last time you saw a 400-meter hurdler hawking orange juice on TV? The 800 meters? No chance. The Cuban's got it in the bag. High jump? There's Stones, but we did him at Munich.

Hello, who's this? Hmmm, an American 35 points behind the leaders in the decathlon with five events to go. What's he look like? Face like Redford? Body like Tarzan?

I like it, I like it. Tell me more.

Well, let's see here. Beautiful wife—blonde, too. Brought his own cheering section with him . . . Still figures to edge the Russian for first place. Twenty-six years old. Confident. Handsome. Went to college in the Midwest.

That's him! But one more question—what's his name? I don't care if he scores 9,000 points, if it's Rodney Danks or Leo Farnsworth, it'll never sell.

Jenner. Bruce Jenner.

Why, that would fit just perfect on a box of Wheaties. Fine job, McKay. I think I've got my gold and you've got a new contract. Quiet on the set!

Jenner was about to become a hero. He had come into the meet as the world record-holder and was the logical choice to topple the Soviet Union's Nikolai Avilov, the defending Olympic champion.

In fact, decathletes are so tuned in to their event, its scoring tables, personal bests and so on that they often know who the winner will be after only two or three events. It's not unlike the master chess players who can project the probable winner after a handful of moves.

Said Jenner, "After the first event (100 meters), once I'd finished with my fastest electric timing ever, and compared to what the competition ran, I said to myself, 'You've just won the Games right there.' Even with nine events to go—as long as I didn't make a stupid mistake—I knew it was mine."

To ABC, however, it was: *Can Jenner Catch the Russian and Win the Gold?* (And take his time doing it to keep the ratings up?)

The answer? Well, sure he could, silly. Jenner was only the best second-day decathlete in history, and while he'd hoped to be about 200 points back after the first day, here he was only 35 off the pace.

Anybody who knew anything about the decathlon knew it was all but over, so that excluded, of course, the audience of millions. Their eyes were the cameras and between the lens and the player was tendered this unwritten pact:

If you whip the Russian and win the gold, next week at this time your people will be doing lunch with our people at the Polo Lounge and you'll have more fame and fortune than you ever dreamed possible. Anything less and it's back to Iowa to sell insurance with Ralph Branca and Jim Ryun. Forever.

So how about it, kid? This is the biggest moment of your life. Can you handle the pressure?

Pressure, what pressure? Through Jenner's veins coursed the blood of a man who'd battled Hitler's toughest SS Panzer Divisions—and won. And have you ever tried to live on peanuts for six years, training 12 hours a day, all the while keeping the wife happy?

You want pressure? This is pressure: "Did you know that the greatest fear of my life, and that includes the Olympics and everything else, was having to read in front of the class as a young kid?

"That absolutely terrorized me. Not only because I was dyslexic, but I'd be sitting there watching them go around the class—you know how each kid reads a paragraph?—breaking out in a cold sweat because of the anxiety that I was going to have to read out loud."

But this was the track. Jenner's office, Jenner's turf. Was there ever really any doubt? When he crossed the finish line of the last event, the 1,500 meters, Jenner's now-famous triumphant pose was as much for the end of his long training ordeal as it was for the gold.

Zoom back, camera three. Make sure you get the crowd cheering in the background there.

Yet Roone Arledge's cameras saw much more: the World's Greatest Athlete was being crowned; this was the Bicentennial and there were 8,618 points, a world record, and the gold medal; the warrior's son, in a USA jersey, waving the flag; hugging his wife; the exultation, the sweet exuberance of youth. Quick, somebody, get a Kleenex.

All of which helps to explain why Jenner can live like a king today. The cameras caught not necessarily the man, but rather what we wanted him to be. He had become the living embodiment of the hero of an untitled poem by Dag Hammarskjold, secretary-general of the United Nations during the '50s:

"Smiling, sincere, incorruptible—His body disciplined and limber. A man who had become what he could, And was what he was—Ready at any moment to gather everything into one simple sacrifice."

That's a wrap. Fade to black. Roll the Wheaties commercial.

□

The power of television is great, but it is not the omniscient eye that it is often thought to be.

A case in point would be Jenner again, but not the one crossing the finish line in Montreal. Rather, the one who pushes the cereal and orange juice, does sportscasting for NBC, and appears occasionally in TV series or movies.

To some, that Jenner comes across as confident to the point of being smug. Unfortunately for Jenner, what hasn't really emerged in his TV appearances is his surprising sense of humor.

There is a closet loon struggling to get out.

While training for the Olympics, Jenner kept a hurdle in his living room for practice. He'd sleep with his discus so it wasn't "unfamiliar" to him on the field. Before the technique was banned, he somersaulted during the long jump to improve his distance.

His son by his first marriage, Burton, then 2 years old, was Jenner's best man at his wedding to Linda Thompson in 1981. He once dressed in drag at a benefit for multiple sclerosis, appearing with Bob Hope and Merlin Olsen in a spoof of the Mandrell Sisters, crooning "Take This Job and Shove It."

Maybe that's mild compared to somebody like John Belushi, but it lays waste to his stiffer image. The difference would be that while Jenner sees the humor in both himself and the world, he has never been self destructive about it.

Jenner revels in telling the story about the late Belushi, who did a hilarious takeoff of Jenner on "Saturday Night Live," which featured the pot-bellied comedian jogging around a track in a USA jersey, waving a flag and crediting his success to chocolate-covered doughnuts instead of cereal.

Jenner was so taken with the bit that when a friend in the cycle business once went to deliver a three-wheeler to Belushi, Jenner went along as one of the delivery men, catching a dumbfounded Belushi completely by surprise.

The point is that by most accounts, Jenner has long managed not to take himself or his celebrity status seriously, in spite of coming off as somewhat cocksure to his critics.

□

In any given interview, the reporter's notebook will often serve as an inhibitor, with the subject saying what he thinks the public should know, which is not always necessarily the whole truth.

Bruce Jenner proved more open than most, talking freely about subjects ranging from his fame and fortune, to the divorce, to his All-American image—"Hey, I happen to like ice cream and apple pie—it's great stuff."

But, then, maybe it's difficult to put on airs when Brandon is chasing the dog through the living room, the vacuum cleaner is running, Brody is spitting up his food, the cat is pawing at your ankles, the dog is now chasing Brandon, and, honey, can you get the phone and tell them that I'll call them right back?

Incidentally, Jenner's wife, the former Linda Thompson, was once Elvis Presley's girlfriend. Linda, a striking blonde who had been a dancer on the "Hee Haw" show, went from the King of Graceland Mansion to the King of Graceland College.

From the outside, Jenner appears to have lived the perfect life—great guy wins gold medal, cashes in and lives happily ever after. Yet he has experienced more than his share of tragedy and bad fortune, another part of Jenner's life that remains largely unknown.

At the 1972 Games, Jenner witnessed the effects that the Israeli massacre had on the world in general and the Olympic community in particular.

Jenner's roommate and close friend at those Games, distance runner Steve Prefontaine, who was being touted as the Olympic hero that Jenner would eventually become, died in an auto accident in 1975.

Three months after winning the gold medal, Jenner's brother Burton, then 18, died in an auto accident.

And, of course, there was his publicized divorce from his first wife, Chrystie, whom he'd met at college. They were considered to be America's Couple after the acclaim of the Olympics.

By Jenner's own account, the same tunnel vision that allowed him to focus on the gold medal also prevented him from seeing the obvious—that the relationship was in need of attention, long before the medal. "I had a lot of growing up to do," Jenner said.

Both Bruce and Chrystie agree that it wasn't the gold medal that led to their split, but rather what happened after. Each politely says that "redefining the relationship" after the Olympics was the cause. "It seemed to work best when it was my job to score points," Bruce noted.

Said Chrystie, who has since married lawyer Richard Scott and lives not far from Jenner in Malibu: "The training and the Olympics and the medal were all the fun part. In retrospect, I can't tell you how much I hated the rest. The pressure of the public life didn't allow us to mend (our differences)."

Said Bruce, "I don't think it would have worked out anyway over a long period of time. I really don't. It's just that people grow up and change. And we grew up and changed, both of us. Drastically. The relationship just didn't work."

They forget to mention that they helped contribute greatly to the overwhelming limelight that they blame their troubles on—Chrystie running past press row in a "Go Jenner Go" T-shirt, into Bruce's arms after he won the gold is kind of hard to miss—but by now it is, perhaps, a moot point.

Both seem happier now that they have found other mates and they seem glad it is all behind them.

The divorce was messy, with plenty of lawyers and name-calling, so they are not what would be characterized as good friends, but Bruce has no problems visiting their children, Burton, 5, and Cassandra, 4.

□

The most telling comment from Jenner was uttered not during two days of interviews but when a photographer asked Bruce an idle question about his auto racing interests.

After answering it, Jenner characterized racing: "It's fun, but you're not in control of your own destiny there. Too many variables."

Jenner was just cruising through life until the decathlon found him; he has been the principal architect of his own destiny ever since. And unlike many ex-jocks, he has managed to control the variables in his business life as well.

Even so, Jenner remains athletic. A physical person, he hugs his children . . . wrestles the dog . . . can't sit still while posing for pictures on his motorcycle. Exertion and movement are his natural states.

Once he released that energy on the track. Now he now does it flying his biplane or hang-gliding off the Malibu cliffs, something his life style affords plenty of time to do.

While Jenner bristles at the notion that he ran at Montreal for anything but his place in decathlon history, the gold in his life obviously did not end on the victory stand.

He has a lovely wife, handsome children, an oceanside estate, his toys, fame and financial security. He is his own boss; he punches no time card. With a lifetime still ahead at 34, he has life on his own terms.

He bet six years of his life on his ability as an athlete to come up with his personal best when it counted the most. He rolled the dice, the numbers came up 8,618, and he's been collecting the payoff ever since.

□

A footnote: Jenner was recently involved in filming a video that required him to pole vault, something he hadn't done since Montreal. In fact, he had even left his poles there after winning the medal.

"Because of the (camera) angle," Jenner said, getting a little excited as he explained, "I could take only a limited number of steps before jumping. Cleared 13-6 without a problem, though."

Could Jenner secretly be seeking to recapture his glorious past? Not a chance. Who needs wind sprints at 6 a.m. when you can hang out in the Jacuzzi with Linda and the kids all day?

"The *form* was there," Jenner said, laughing and absent-mindedly rubbing his shoulder, "but I was sore for a week."

Los Angeles Times (above); Associated Press (right)

Jenner's license plate shows his gold-medal point total at Montreal.

'After the first event (100 meters), once I'd finished with my fastest electric timing ever . . . I said to myself, you've just won the Games right there.'

IOC Decides to Tackle Boycott Problem

But It Says L.A.'s Not the Place to Hold 1st Extraordinary Session

By KENNETH REICH, *Times Staff Writer*

The International Olympic Committee decided Wednesday to hold the first extraordinary general membership session in its history—probably in Lausanne, Switzerland—in November to discuss what to do to stem boycotts of future Olympic Games.

IOC leaders, who announced plans for the session, said that in the meantime it had decided not to take up any divisive political matters pertaining to the Soviet-led boycott or any previous ones at the organization's L.A. meeting.

That decision also shelves an earlier proposal by the IOC executive board that would make attendance by national Olympic committees at future Olympics compulsory and possibly set up a system of suspensions from subsequent Games for national committees that joined any boycotts.

IOC Executive Director Monique Berlioux said that 26 of the 83 IOC members present Wednesday morning, including both Eastern Bloc and Western members, had supported the idea of the extraordinary session.

"All felt our attention here should be focused on the Los Angeles Games," Berlioux said. "After Los Angeles is the time to discuss other matters."

She said that between now and November each IOC member is being asked to submit ideas to IOC President Juan Antonio Samaranch on what to do to discourage boycotts.

Berlioux was at pains to announce that the decision to hold the 1988 Games in Seoul will not be reversed.

An IOC board member who also discussed the decision with reporters, Richard Pound of Canada, said there had been a strong desire at the meeting to take up the boycott question on neutral ground. The next IOC general membership session has been scheduled for East Berlin next June.

Pound said it is conceivable that the meeting could be held in Mexico City during a gathering of the worldwide Assn. of National Olympic Committees. But Berlioux said a site in or close to Lausanne is much more likely.

Berlioux said that the Commission on the Olympic Movement will also participate in the session. This group, in addition to nine IOC members, also includes nine leading international sports federation figures as well as nine leaders of various national Olympic meetings. It last met May 18 in Lausanne and deplored the Soviet boycott.

Bringing in this group indicates that the IOC may consider a proposal that has recently been advanced by the Soviets and other Eastern Bloc Olympic officials: To give a more important role to national Olympic committees and the sports federations in the selection of Olympic host cities.

The Soviets have not gone so far as to suggest a veto power for the various blocs over future cities. But it has long been clear that one key contributing factor to both the Moscow and Los Angeles boycotts was the placement of the Olympics in countries that are in the mainstream of world power politics.

Today, Amsterdam is scheduled to formally announce its candidacy for the 1992 Summer Games, and Amsterdam officials who were interviewed this week said that one of their biggest selling points will be that the Netherlands, although aligned with the West, is still far enough removed from power politics to be prone to a boycott.

Samaranch seemed pleased with the decision to hold the special session and put off possibly heated debate until after Los Angeles. On Tuesday night, the IOC president had sharply watered down certain remarks critical of the Soviet boycott that he had been scheduled to deliver at the opening ceremonies of the IOC session.

Los Angeles Times

1 DAY TO GAMES OLYMPICS '84

ROSEMARY KAUL / Los Angeles Times

USC's talented Cheryl Miller looms as the leader of the U.S. women's team.

Basketball, USA Style

The Talented Troops of the Crusading Knight Figure to Be the Class of the Games, Easily

By MARK HEISLER, *Times Staff Writer*

At last, Bob Knight gets to take on the whole world, formally, with the world a distinct underdog. U.S. men's basketball teams have scattered challengers with more modest squads than he has, playing in far more hostile surroundings than his will, so what does everyone have to look forward to?

As they said in "Bad News Bears," bad news for the world.

Knight is drilling his players furiously. Errors are called to their attention, posthaste. He sat down Pat Ewing for 35 of 40 minutes in an exhibition game in Iowa City. He raged at a referee in Milwaukee, during the game and afterward in the press conference.

His team toured the nation in triumph. It went 9-0 against various combinations of NBA stars. If the summer fell short of everything he could

A PREVIEW
MEN'S BASKETBALL

have asked for, it didn't miss by much. In his pageant in the Hoosierdome, a flag-waving crowd of almost 70,000 booed President Reagan's videotaped address, if gently, just after Knight had given a little speech about pride and America.

Meanwhile, the world awaits its turn, tittering uneasily.

"I read in the paper that they were having trouble with their outside shooting," said Canadian Coach Jack Donohue at breakfast during a recent tournament in Ontario. "I was going to

Please see PREVIEW:
Men's Basketball, page 23

ROSEMARY KAUL / Los Angeles Times

Opponents of the U.S. men's team will have to deal with Patrick Ewing.

USOC Is Losing to Drugs

Cracks Surface in the Crackdown

By JULIE CART
and RANDY HARVEY,
Times Staff Writers

Eventually, we might remember the Pan American Games last summer in Caracas, Venezuela, as the beginning of the end of drug use by American athletes.

There might come a day when those American athletes who are depending on drugs to make them faster, higher, stronger will rely more on their natural abilities than on their pharmacists.

But that day is not tomorrow, when the Summer Olympics officially open, or the next day or even next year.

In the U.S. Olympic Committee's war on drugs, the drugs are still winning.

The drug bust at the Pan American Games was supposed to have at least signaled a shift in momentum. But even that appears at this point to have been an illusion.

It might have been different if the USOC's actions had been as swift and decisive as its rhetoric.

When the final urinalysis had been completed in Caracas, 19 athletes from 10 countries, two from the United States, had been disqualified for using substances banned by the International Olympic Committee. In all but four cases, the offending drug was an anabolic steroid.

Anabolic steroids, derivatives of the male hormone testosterone, are believed by some to enhance performance by building muscle. There are concerns not only about the ethics of athletes who use them but also about the safety of the drugs.

Confronting those issues, F. Don Miller, executive director of the USOC, said in Caracas last summer that doping control at the Pan American Games had spurred the USOC to begin an all-out offensive against drug use by athletes. For this purpose, $250,000 was added to the USOC budget.

In announcing random drug tests of American athletes at selected national championships during the months before the Summer Olympics, Miller said, "This is the only way we can meet this problem head-on. We've waited around too long. Too many people have acted like ostriches, with their heads in the sand.

"Doctors, coaches, trainers and athletes have been in collusion on the use of banned substances. The USOC is assuming the leadership

Please see DRUGS, page 24

It's Miller Time Again as U.S. Team Maps Out New Dynasty

By CHRIS COBBS,
Times Staff Writer

The moment has arrived for Cheryl Miller to exercise her birthright as the greatest player in women's basketball—and for the United States to begin a new era as the dominant power in the sport.

Such are the expectations of competitors and analysts alike. One dynasty has defaulted and a new one seems ready to emerge at the 1984 Olympics.

Although the Soviet Union won

A PREVIEW
WOMEN'S BASKETBALL

the gold medal in 1976 and 1980, the only years in which women's basketball appeared on the Olympic agenda, many believe that the Soviet reign would have been in jeopardy even if there had been no boycott this year.

The reason? It's Miller time.

If the 6-3 forward from Riverside is not already the No. 1 player in the world, she's so near that

comparisons are moot. That is the view of Don McCrae, coach of the Canadian team, one of six in the Olympic round-robin tournament with Australia, South Korea, Yugoslavia, China and the United States.

Because of Miller's presence, and the deepest array of talent in the Games, the United States all but has a lock on the gold medal, according to McCrae and other

observers.

"The U.S. has all the ingredients," McCrae said. "It would have been a classic confrontation with the Soviet Union and, I believe, it would have been the last chance for the Soviets to win the gold. From now on, the U.S. will be the dominant team."

Ann Meyers, a star on the 1976 silver medal team and now a TV analyst, said the United States would have been the gold-medal favorite even if the Soviets had participated this year.

"Our players believe they will

win, and that is so important," she said. "In '76 we had a couple of girls who doubted we could beat the Russians, and that attitude hurt us."

There are no such doubts among U.S. players this year. "The Russians knew they were beatable in '84," said Cindy Noble, a center with seven years' international experience.

"We beat the Russians in (foreign tournaments) in '79, '82 and '83. They were weary of us."

Please see PREVIEW:
Women's Basketball, page 23

Jim Murray

The Agony of Olympic Victory

A great many Olympic athletes know the agony of defeat—the hurdle crashed into, the height missed, the bar not cleared, the baton not hung on to, the concentration lapsed. Still others, though fewer, know the thrill of victory.

But only a few know the agony of victory . . .

Jim Thorpe was the most celebrated of cases, a tragic figure of Olympic history.

And next was Rick DeMont . . .

Rick DeMont, like Thorpe, was one of America's premier athletes when he showed up for his Olympic Games in Munich in 1972. He was the world record holder in the 1500-meter swim. He was favored to win at least two, and maybe three, gold medals in the German swimhalle. While this was sub-Mark Spitz that year, it was still something to hand down to your grandchildren one day.

Rick was only 16. But what was really remarkable was that he was not really a well child. He became a world champion swimmer while afflicted with chronic allergenic bronchial asthma.

This is a fairly crippling disorder for a person working in a library. For one who spends his life in a chlorine pool trying to outrace human dolphins at distances up to a mile, it can be torturous. It was hardly an environment you might choose for clogged lungs, obstructed air passages. Even a shark might head for shore when his breath came in restrictive rattles.

Two days before his first Olympic event, the 400-meter freestyle, Rick DeMont felt the old

familiar symptoms. The lung tissue became waterlogged, the mucous buildup became crippling, the lips turned blue. Rick DeMont began to fight for air: "I was coughing, wheezing, lightheaded." It was an all-out attack.

The athletic world is insular. It deals with infirmity only if it is the macho kind. It can understand shin splints, charley horses, bone chips, ligament damage, knee swelling. Ingrown toe nails they can fix. But, respiratory ailments afflict the 97-pound weaklings of the world, the bookworms, the timid, the underachievers, the indoorsmen. They certainly have nothing to do with world-class athletes and especially gold medalists.

□

Rick DeMont had thought he had covered his eventualities by making a full disclosure of all medications he needed, not to compete, but to live. Asthma is controllable, not curable.

The international governing bodies that regulate Olympics and world track and field games are in a posture of fighting a constant desperate rear guard action against the chemists of our time. No Olympics goes by without rumors floating through the venues about blood-doping, miracle steroids, chromosome alterations. When a man breaks a world record now, the first thing the track federation worries about is whether he is a real person or a product of a laboratory in Transylvania. When a woman wins, they check to see if she isn't Frank Merriwell in drag.

Please see MURRAY, page 24

TRAVEL GUIDE

Above are downtown Los Angeles area bus routes along which traffic during the 1984 Olympic Games is expected to be heavy.

Today's Tip: Leave Driving to the Buses

By TED VOLLMER,
Times Staff Writer

If you've just arrived for the Olympics, have taken one final nervous glance at your dog-eared Auto Club map and are now summoning the courage to drive to one of the 23 venues, the local freeway system—Southern California's answer to a tortoise race—is awaiting you.

If, on the other hand, you call Southern California home and are under the illusion that, so far as commuting is concerned, you've experienced it all—forget it.

It may be small consolation if you're inching along the Santa Monica, Hollywood, Pasadena or Harbor Freeways toward the Coliseum or other Olympic sites, but for nearly two years, scores of transportation planners have been working to avoid traffic gridlock.

(For those of you unfamiliar with the term gridlock, imagine for a moment a 600-mile-long parking lot with off-ramps.)

But then again, for longer than most Olympic traffic planners care

Please see TRAFFIC, page 24

PREVIEW: MEN'S BASKETBALL

Continued from page 22

call Bobby up and ask if he wants three or four of our guys."

And yet . . .

Not all hearts are light.

On the banks of the Volga, Coach Alexander Gomelsky of the Soviet Union cries into his vodka, as should anyone who is hoping for real competition in the competition. It isn't that the Soviets would necessarily have won, but they'd have made it so much more interesting.

U.S.-USSR is the big matchup, offering even a bigger clash of cultures than Lakers-Celtics, but they haven't met since 1972—when the U.S. lost at Munich.

The Soviets may or may not be as good as the Americans, but they're a lot bigger, which would have counted for something. They can start a front line that goes 7-4, 7-1, 6-11, with a 6-11 and a 6-10 in reserve. They shoot the ball as well as anyone in the world. In the European qualifying tournament at Paris, they made 82% of their free throws, which was better than any NBA team did last season.

The Soviets went 9-0 in Paris, with an average margin of 26 points. Even before it started, Gomelsky, no blushing comrade, ventured the following observations:

"Bobby Knight, no problem now. Russians not come. He win."

And:

"I know Bobby Knight prepare for my team press defense. But I have countergame for press."

And:

"I have three very nice pivots. Three very big and very good players . . . Bobby Knight doesn't have big center."

"He has Patrick Ewing," someone said.

"How big, seven?" Gomelsky asked. "Seven feet."

"That not 7-4," said Gomelsky.

And, says Dan Peterson, an American coaching in Italy:

"It would have been a tossup, even on American soil. The Russians have 12 guys who can *play*."

Since the boycott, Knight has maintained a stony silence, although it's a safe bet he's not enchanted about it. He has called this assignment perhaps the only important thing in his career. And then to lose his Big Red foil? It's like Don Quixote watching a wrecking ball demolish his windmill.

Anyway, what remains is a heavily favored U.S. team.

From Coach Alessandro Gamba of Italy:

"I'm telling everybody we have to give the gold to the United States right away. No play. They can stay home."

And Donohue:

"I just think the United States is head and shoulders over everyone."

So they're a little bashful. Nevertheless it doesn't figure to be like 1960, when the United States won its games by an average of 42 points, or '56 when it won by 55. Foreign players are no longer one-handed, mechanical or awestruck. By 1976, Dean Smith's team was down to 14 and he was one point away from being knocked off in the preliminary round by Butch Lee and his fellow Puerto Ricans.

The world has closed a lot of ground. Just how much, the next two weeks will tell.

Here is how it shapes up:

Behind the U.S., at whatever distance, are Yugoslavia and Italy. Both have size, experience and they're bruisers.

Behind them are Spain, Brazil and Canada. They're good teams, not as bruising, but capable of the Big Upset.

Two more teams will make the second round. Say, Uruguay and Australia.

After that come the endangered species, France and West Germany. Some of their beatings won't be pretty.

Followed by the cannon fodder, China and Egypt. Most of their beatings won't be pretty.

WHAT OTHERS ARE SAYING ABOUT THE U.S. TEAM

'It would have been a tossup, even on American soil. The Russians have 12 guys who can *play*.'

—DAN PETERSON, American coaching in Italy

'Bobby Knight, no problem now. Russians not come. He win.'

—ALEXANDER GOMELSKY, Soviets' coach

CANADIAN COACH JACK DONOHUE

'I'm telling everybody we have to give the gold to the United States right away. No play. They can stay home.'

—ALESSANDRO GAMBA, Italian coach

'I just think the United States is head and shoulders over everyone.'

—JACK DONOHUE, Canadian coach

UNITED STATES

In public, Knight is studiously low-key about his team. What he's told his players, according to center Jon Koncak, is that they have a chance to go down as the greatest team in the history of amateur basketball.

But they're going to have to do it his way. Ewing and Wayman Tisdale, used to posting up and having the ball pounded into them, struggled with Knight's motion offense. Knight's defense doesn't put the same premium on shot-blocking that Georgetown's does, so Ewing had to make another adjustment. After the first seven exhibitions, Tisdale and Ewing were Nos. 8 and 9 on the squad in minutes played, respectively. With Charles Barkley cut, this team hasn't been as physical as it once looked.

Knight bristled at questions about his lineup and he probably will start several. Nevertheless, he seemed to like Ewing at center, Sam Perkins and Michael Jordan at forward, Vern Fleming and Alvin Robertson at guard, and Chris Mullin as sixth man.

International teams still have trouble guarding quick players or great jumpers, so good luck with Jordan, who is both and figures to make them realize all their worst fears. Most of them will forsake pursuit and fall back into zone defenses, which could make Mullin, the outside shooter, a star.

There was some grumbling about Knight's selection of his own player, Steve Alford, but he and Mullin are the team's best outside shooters. If there is a problem on this team, it's that there aren't enough outside shooters, given the number of zones it is likely to see.

What will make this team is what makes all Knight teams: It will play tough man-to-man defense, it will execute on offense and, prohibitive favorite or not, it will play hard.

Knight is the coach whose team is least likely to let down against a weak opponent. Any Knight team's chief worry is surviving *him*.

YUGOSLAVIA

The mystery men, capable of anything. They won the silver at Montreal, where they beat the Soviets, and the gold at Moscow, where they beat the Soviets and the Italians.

Then they fell apart. Several of their best players got old, or disenchanted, or both. They finished seventh in Europe last year, which a Yugoslav, writing for International Basketball Magazine, called a "fiasco."

Yugoslav coaches had been tied up by local politics, but the federation finally went back to Mirko Novosel, the coach at Moscow and Montreal. He's an unimposing-looking man with a bald head and a habit of pulling it down into his shoulder and glaring out at his players, like an angry turtle.

Appearances notwithstanding, he is rated a top coach and he has put the Yugoslavs back together. Before leaving home, they beat the Russians by 20 points in an exhibition in Budapest. In Ontario last week, they beat Italy by 18.

Novosel retains veteran small forward Drazen Dalipagic (pronounced Dolly-PAH-zhitz) and has broken in two brothers at guard, 20-year-old Drazen Petrovic (PET-ro-vich), and his older brother, Aleksandar, at the point.

Drazen is described, somewhat enthusiastically, by a Spanish writer, Victor de la Serna, as "Pete Maravich with a better outside shot." He is certainly very talented and still fairly hot-headed. Last summer he spat at a referee in the World University Games in Edmonton, Alberta. He was considering attending Notre Dame this fall, but reportedly has changed his mind and signed with a Yugoslav team.

The front line goes 6-10, 6-10, 6-6 and doesn't jump badly either. For undiscovered reasons, Yugoslavia is the Rucker Playground of Europe. Yugoslavs love to break out their playground stuff. "Most Yugoslavs are a little wild," says de la Serna, "including Pete Maravich."

ITALY

This may already be the greatest of the Italian teams. They were silver medalists in Moscow in 1980, and now they're defending European champions.

If not overwhelming, they're big and beefy, with a roster full of European all-stars: Dino Meneghin, 6-8, 240-pound center; Renato Villata, 6-8, 220-pound forward who was the leading scorer and rebounder at Moscow in 1980; Romeo Sachetti, a 6-5, 230-pound small forward, and Antonello Riva, a 6-5, 210-pound guard who may be their best player. Riva is the youngest of the four, at 22, which makes him as old as any U.S. player.

Italy's Coach Sandro Gamba, a friend of Knight, plays a hard-nosed man-to-man defense that Knight would love to play at Indiana, if only the NCAA refs would let him.

Italy, however, has trouble guarding quick players, especially up front. Canada's Tony Simms, a fast 6-5 forward, burned them for 30 points in Ontario and ran by everyone Gamba sent at him. And, for whatever reason, perhaps jet lag, Italy didn't play well last week in Ontario.

SPAIN

The Spaniards stunned the Soviets by a point in the '83 European semifinals, a loss the Russians avenged this summer, winning twice in exhibitions in Spain, and by 27 points in Paris.

Nevertheless, this is a very good team and an exciting one. The Spaniards are good athletes and they're very well coached by another friend of Knight, Antonio Diaz-Miguel.

They run the Continent's best fast break behind the real Dr. J, Juan-Antonio Corbolan, a short, balding 29-year-old resident in cardiology, generally considered the best point guard in Europe.

Forwards Fernando Martin and Juan San Epifanio are very strong. The latter, "Eppy," was a guard until another forward, Chicho Sibilio, dropped off the team to earn more money in his native Dominican Republic shortly after almost personally burying the Russians in '83.

Without him, the Spaniards are very thin. In some games in Paris, Diaz-Miguel used his first five players for the game's first 30 minutes.

Nevertheless, Diaz-Miguel doesn't seem to be aching for Sibilio's return. Asked if he might get him back, he said, smiling, "No, thank you."

Diaz-Miguel seems to like his small lineup more than his big one. He has a seven-foot center, Fernando Romay, but plays him only against other seven-footers.

The Spaniards are in Group B with the U.S. They figure to be 4-0 when they meet the Americans.

BRAZIL

Good size, good athletes and good shooters. The host team for the American qualifying tournament in Sao Paulo, they went 9-0.

The leading scorer is Oscar Schmidt, a 6-7 forward who was among the leading scorers in Italy last season. He's a long-range shooter who can take the ball inside. Says Canada's Donohue: "He can play with anybody in the world."

The front line will go about 6-10, 6-8, 6-7. In Sao Paulo, Brazil was without another high scorer, Marcel DeSouza, who was injured but is expected back.

CANADA

Animal House comes to the L.A. Games.

The day after losing to Italy in an Ontario exhibition tournament, members of the squad engaged in a food fight, after which they won their last three games and beat Yugoslavia twice.

Not much had been expected of them. Canada knocked off a U.S. team, not its best but still with Charles Barkley on it, in last summer's World University Games, touching off a national celebration. Then it finished fourth in the Pan-American games.

The Canadians have good size with 6-11 Greg Wiltjer, briefly of Oregon State, and 7-0 Bill Wennington of St. John's, and they're battlers. Guard Jay Triano, returning to the Forum after twice being cut by the Lakers, is the team's high scorer. Point guard Eli Pascuale just survived the Seattle SuperSonics' first cut.

They seemed to be missing one scorer, but in Ontario, they were led by small forward Tony Simms, a greyhound who played at Boston U., and who'd always reported too late to be a starter. This year, he's right on time.

URUGUAY

This was supposed to be Cuba, Puerto Rico, Mexico, or Argentina, but, surprise . . . In the upset of the American qualifying tournament, the Uruguayans went 7-2, including a victory over Canada, and finished second.

They don't have great size, but they shot the ball well in Sao Paulo and had two of the tournament's top scorers, 6-6 forward Horacio Lopez and 6-2 guard Wilfredo Ruiz.

AUSTRALIA

Another team without much size. It has a terrific player, Ian Davies, another 6-6 forward who likes to bomb from the outside. He has a great release, a la Rick Barry. You know it's coming, you just can't do anything about it. Italy's Gamba sent two of his bruisers, Sachetti and Marco Bonamico, at him in platoons with orders to deny him, and still he scored.

Too much of Australia's offense comes from outside, though. The Aussies are tenacious and very physical. Yugoslavia beat them by 17, but in the last two minutes, Aussies were still hurling themselves across the floor for loose balls.

Otherwise, they'd have been beaten by 30.

"We're playing near the top of the arc," said Coach Lindsay Gaze.

WEST GERMANY

Size they've got.

Detlef Schrempf and 6-11 Christian Welp are back on the West Coast where they led Washington to a Pacific 10 title last season. The 7-4 Gunther Behnke, newly signed for Kentucky, dropped off the team, but the Germans still have 7-2 Uwe Blab of Indiana and 6-11 Ingo Mendel, once of USC.

Their game in Paris against the Russians might have been the tallest matchup ever, with six players 6-11 or taller.

But the Germans are slow and they aren't very aggressive. In Paris, the smaller, quicker Spaniards routed them and even out-rebounded them by 12. The British, a bunch of second-echelon U.S. college players who were smaller than the Spaniards, tied the Germans on the backboards and were barely beaten. The German guards aren't considered strong. Against presses, they used Schrempf to bring the ball up.

The German coach is Ralph Klein, who grew up in Berlin, was forced to flee the Holocaust with his family and emigrated to Israel, before returning to Germany, a controversial move in Israel.

One reason his team qualified, however, is that Europe went six deep. Yugoslavia and Italy had already qualified for the Games by winning the gold and silver at Moscow. Then the Soviets boycotted, making the Germans' 6-3 record in Paris good enough.

They're in Group A. Italy, Yugoslavia and Brazil figure to make it out easily. The Germans could be the fourth team, if they can make their size count against the Australians.

FRANCE

A surprise qualifier in Paris, where they went 7-2, although they didn't threaten the Soviets or Spaniards.

They played Spain the day after clinching their Olympic berth and partying in the hotel bar. By halftime, they were down 19 points, when they posed on the court for a team picture.

The next day the French sports daily, L'Equipe ran a headline that included the word, "*L'Humiliation.*" French Coach Jean Luent, noting that he'd used his reserves, as had Spain, told the writers they were always negative.

In France, of course, this is nothing. When tennis star Yannick Noah stopped talking to the papers who had idolized and pursued him, his last words were, "To speak with them is to feed marmalade to pigs."

The French have some ability. Their stars are center Philip Szanyiel, forward Eric Beugnot, and Herve Dubuisson, who was recently signed by the New Jersey Nets. Dubuisson has range halfway back to the mid-court line and is a great jumper, capable at 6-4 of cradle-dunking while flying past the basket, a la Jordan.

The French don't play real well together, though, and they give up a lot of points.

They're in Group B, where the U.S. and Spain are expected to dominate. France has to knock off either Canada or Uruguay to survive.

CHINA

Champions of the Asian qualifying tournament, played in Hong Kong. Most of what is generally known about them comes from their U.S. tours, but they haven't toured lately.

They have a huge, useful center, Mu Tieh-chu, also known as Mister Mu and they're said to be very well drilled.

Said Donohue, "The Chinese have come a long way. And don't get carried away with how small they're going to be. They got two billion people hanging around to choose from.

"They still play an Oriental-type game, where they throw the ball back out for a 25-foot jumper. They wouldn't get embarrassed by a U.S. college team, but they're not going to win. And they might get embarrassed if their shots don't fall."

They play the U.S. first.

EGYPT

Even less is expected of the Egyptians than of the Chinese.

They toured the U.S. last winter and lost to Hofstra, New York Tech, Monmouth, the State University of New York at Stony Brook and to Concordia College of Bronxville (N.Y.) which beat them by 27 points.

However, the experience was a good one. The Egyptians went home and, in a surprise, won the African qualifying tournament at Alexandria.

This is something for them to remember, because they've got a lot more experience on tap.

PREVIEW: WOMEN'S BASKETBALL

CHERYL MILLER WITH U.S. COACH PAT HEAD SUMMITT

'It's a realistic goal, but we're not a sure winner . . . We may not have a set lineup as such. With all our talent, we don't want to get locked into one combination. We may do a lot of platooning.'

—PAT HEAD SUMMITT

Continued from page 22

Even so, Miller believes that the absence of the Soviets will put more pressure on the United States.

"Everybody will be shooting for us," she said. "We'll be the team to beat. I won't say we are a shoo-in for the gold, but I feel pretty good about our chances."

She deflected McCrae's flattering judgment of her place at the top of the women's game, but accepted his view that the United States hereafter will be the power in the sport.

Meyers pretty much agreed with McCrae's assessment of Miller. "Cheryl plays like a man," she said, perhaps the ultimate compliment from a woman who once tried out for a man's professional team.

It's hard to find weaknesses, either in Miller or the U.S. team as a whole.

Miller's only real flaw, a tendency to lose control of her emotions, may keep her from becoming a genuine leader, but the presence of more mature players such as Lynette Woodard and Denise Curry should more than fill any leadership vacuum.

Coach Pat Head Summitt, one of the leaders of the '76 team, has been criticized for being too demanding, the female equivalent of men's coach Bob Knight.

The point, if it was ever valid, is no longer applicable, according to Meyers.

"Pat's mellowed out," she said. "She's in her 30s now, and she doesn't feel as much tension as she did when she first started coaching our international teams. She understands when to soften up."

The U.S. players know better than to expect a soft Summitt in Los Angeles.

With no clearly defined challenger—China and Canada are seen as the probable silver- and bronze-medal contenders—the Americans know they should win. Summitt has made it quite clear she will employ every player at her disposal if she detects less than maximum effort from the starters.

"She can dig deep into her bench," McCrae said. "She has 12 players she can win with."

Summitt is too conservative to publicly predict a gold medal. "It's a realistic goal, but we're not a sure winner," she said.

She won't hesitate to substitute liberally, however, to chase away creeping complacency. "We may not have a set lineup as such," she said. "With all our talent, we don't want to get locked into one combination. We may do a lot of platooning."

If the Soviets had been present, the U.S. players certainly would have been pointing for a showdown, and in so doing, might have tended to let down against lesser opposition.

Summitt once harbored that particular fear, but no more. "Our players most definitely were looking forward to a showdown with the Soviets, but we have accepted (the boycott)," she said.

"A gold medal is a gold medal, and our players want it. It won't dampen our spirits.

"Sometimes, there are surprise teams in tournaments, like the NCAAs this year. My team (Tennessee) wasn't supposed to be there, but we made it anyway, and I don't think that took away from USC's feeling at winning."

The five players who line up for the first jump ball likely will come from a group that includes Miller, Woodard, Anne Donovan, Janice Lawrence, Curry and Lea Henry.

Among the strategic weapons at their disposal are a pressure defense that relies on quickness and the finest group of jump shooters in the field.

"They're just the class of the tournament," McCrae said.

Maybe so, but the United States can't afford to take lightly either Canada or China.

The Canadian team is led by two players familiar to West Coast fans. Center Allison Lang and forward Bev Smith were teammates at Oregon and have sufficient talent and savvy to pose a mild threat to the United States.

The Canadians are lacking in height—only the South Koreans have less overall team size—but Summitt isn't writing them off.

"They are very familiar with our style and they always give us a good game (in international tournaments)," Summitt said.

Smith, a 6-2 forward, was runner-up for the 1982 Wade Cup, the highest honor in women's collegiate basketball.

"She's our Larry Bird," McCrae said, meaning she's not flashy, but a solid, versatile player. "She doesn't have Cheryl Miller's quickness, but she's a better shooter."

Lang is a mobile 6-3 center who will receive rebounding support from 6-2 power forward Sylvia Sweeney, a veteran of 10 years on the Canadian national team with so much aggressiveness she's often in foul trouble.

The Canadians have rehearsed lots of alternative strategies with the goal of making them adaptable enough to adjust to nearly any opponent. In this patchwork tournament, where nearly every style of play will be in evidence, that multi-faceted approach may be just the ticket to produce a silver medal.

That is, if the Canadians can find a way to corral 6-9 Shen Yuefang of China.

Next to 7-1 Uliana Semenova of the Soviet Union, the Chinese star is regarded as perhaps the most dominant inside player in women's basketball.

Recent progress in her game has made the Chinese the most improved team in the world over the last year, according to Summitt.

"They're scary," she said.

Other top players are Zheng Haixia, Xian Liqing and Son Xiabo.

The Chinese have excellent quickness among their guards, according to McCrae. They have defeated the Canadians in four of five exhibition games in recent years, and so rank as the favorite for the silver medal.

Less threatening, by a few centimeters, is Yugoslavia, headed by center Polona Dornik and forward Jasmina Perazic, an all-star at the University of Maryland last season.

The Yugoslavs run a deliberate 1-4 offense and can trouble any team with their 2-3 zone.

Similarly physical in style is Australia, a regimented team that runs a UCLA-style high-post offense.

A sharp departure in style is offered by South Korea, which provides a throwback to the 1950s with a weave offense that affords long set shots. The Koreans are very quick and have a good fast break. They're small, though, and thus can be beaten inside.

Their best player is forward Kwa Soon Kim. Guard Ae Young Choi augments the running game.

Will the competition be tarnished by the absense of the Soviets?

"We've all come in through the front door (through qualifying tournaments)," McCrae said. "We all believe we have a chance for a medal.

"The competition no longer will be so much a matter of an upper tier, represented by the U.S. and the Soviets, and a bottom tier, composed of the rest of us. It's going to be more exciting this way."

MURRAY

Continued from page 22

It's demeaning, degrading and almost demonic.

Rick DeMont sensibly took medication for his asthma attack. It was either that or turn blue. Fighting for oxygen can tear the lungs and cause scar tissue as the victim stretches the alveoli without pharmaceutical help. DeMont even went to the doctors to report he had taken the medication and why. The doctors were not in. "I guess," recalls Rick now, "they were out to lunch. For two days."

Rick won his race. But, not, as it turned out, his gold medal. Three days later, the committee at the Games notified him he was barred from further competition and his 400-meter win was nullified. De Mont was practically on the starting platform for the 1500 meters at the time. Traces of ephedrine had been found in his urine. Minute amounts but any amount was too much.

It was, of course, an historic injustice. Antihistamines can hardly be thought to be a performance-enhancer but the International Olympic Committee is so hysterical about the drug menace that Coca Cola may be a banned substance any day now and traces of aspirin may get a decathlete barred for life.

What really tore Rick DeMont up was not entirely the rubout of his 400-meter win but the disqualification from the upcoming 1500. "I had had no asthma attack before that race. I had no ephedrine in my system. I had set the world record in the trials. I had qualified fastest. Then, ten minutes before the race they come in and tell me to get dressed."

DeMont was not permitted to keep his gold medal. When he returned with it to California, he was pursued by correspondence from the international swim federation that he would be banned from competitions unless he returned his gold medal forthwith. He did so.

"They tell me that Brad Cooper, of Australia, who moved up to the gold when I was disqualified, refused to accept it and keeps his silver medal only."

DeMont is now a painter, a water-colorist, not the kind that does houses or rolls walls. "What has my life been like?" he rejoins. "Well, I'm the 'gold medal loser.' You know, 'the guy who lost the Olympics in a bottle.' It isn't as if I ran the wrong way or drowned in the pool or fainted in the home-stretch. I live with it. The drug I took was 'Marax.' I have no idea whether it's legal or not now. Why not?"

If it's not, others are. A footnote to the DeMont story deals with the other ill-starred Olympian of those Games, Jim Ryun. Also bedevilled by allergies, Ryun had been taking antihistaminic medicine at Munich—until the DeMont episode. His doctor took him off the regiment. Well in advance of his competition.

It didn't matter. Ryun's allergy turned out to be an overeager Ghanaian who crashed into him in the first heat of the 1500 meter run and tumbled him, and his gold medal hopes to the turf.

Ironically, Jim Ryun is at the Olympics campaigning for the Glaxo pharmaceuticals, Kentolin, Beclovent and Beconase, safe and approved substances for asthma medication at the Olympics. "Because of the air quality, problems are sure to occur," predicts Jim Ryun.

Nobody in Los Angeles will be asked to return his medals. Jim Thorpe and Rick DeMont will be able still to stand alone in Olympic annals. However, if the IOC runs true to form, Rick, like Jim, will one day get his medals back, and his name put back in the record book. If they run true to form it will be long after he is any longer able to read them or it.

DRUGS

Continued from page 22

role to see that it stops."

When asked whether national governing bodies of each sport would cooperate with the USOC's random testing program—the pop quizzes—Miller said they had no choice.

"We will assume the leadership by the Amateur Sports Act of 1978," he said. "We have the responsibility for amateur athletics as they pertain to international competitions. We have the authority to impose this."

In the ensuing 11 months, the USOC has done everything it possibly can to establish a fair and effective program of testing except for the one thing that is absolutely necessary to make it work, the one thing which Miller insisted it would do. It has not imposed the program on all of the national governing bodies.

The USOC has allowed officials from each national governing body to determine their own course. Some have chosen a more littered highway than others.

Naturally, there were no objections from any of the officials to the USOC's informal testing, which allowed athletes to be tested without fear of sanctions.

That practice was controversial because it enabled athletes who are using anabolic steroids to project when it was safe to take the drugs without fear of detection. But it also was a safeguard for innocent athletes who were taking a legitimate medication that they were not aware was on the banned list.

Some officials, particularly those involved in sports in which drugs are not believed to be prevalent, even volunteered for formal testing, which could have resulted in suspensions for athletes who were discovered to have used illegal substances.

But in the spirit of cooperation, however misguided, the USOC did not require any of the national governing bodies to submit their athletes to formal, punitive drug testing until the Olympic trials, where testing was mandatory for all sports.

In track and field, where drug use reportedly is widespread, world class athletes went a year or longer before they were tested. There were none of the random tests that Miller said would strike fear into the cheating hearts of athletes.

The Athletics Congress (TAC), the national governing body for track and field, required formal testing only at the national cross-country championships and the national indoor championships.

At the indoor nationals last winter, only those few athletes who wished to participate in a dual meet in England the following week were forced to undergo testing.

Carl Lewis, who wanted to clear his name after rumors were published that he tested positive last summer at the world championships, had to volunteer for a formal test at the indoor nationals.

"At the present time, TAC does not have a war on drugs policy," said Scott Irving, assistant track coach at the University of Florida, in a letter last November to Dr. Evie Dennis, an official of TAC and the USOC.

So even though Miller was able to announce last week that no one among the 597 members of the U.S. Olympic team tested positive at the trials, he has no assurances that American athletes who were using drugs last summer are no longer using them.

To the contrary, all evidence points in the other direction.

That is not to imply that UCLA's $1.6-million testing facilities are unreliable. Employed for the trials, the UCLA laboratory also will be used during the Olympics.

In fact, the chances for dependable tests at UCLA are considerably better than in Caracas, where electrical malfunctions, improper testing procedures, sloppy handling of some samples and inconsistent recording practices have cast doubts on the accuracy of those positive results at the Pan American Games last summer.

Following a three-day examination by Dr. Arnold Beckett of the IOC Medical Commission last winter, the UCLA laboratory was awarded a 100% rating and became one of only seven drug-testing facilities throughout the world to earn IOC accreditation.

"If any athletes are taking something that's on the banned list, we'll find it," said the Los Angeles Olympic Organizing Committee's medical director, Dr. Anthony Daly, during a press conference this week. He said approximately 1,500 samples will be tested during the Olympics.

But even the best of labs have their limitations. During the height of the Pan American Games drug bust, there were reports that the equipment there, basically the same as can be found at UCLA, could detect illegal substances up to a year after they had been ingested.

Dr. Manfred Donike, a member of the IOC Medical Commission from West Germany and the coordinator of the laboratory in Caracas, called that an exaggeration.

"It depends on several factors," he said during an interview in his Cologne office with Times reporter Earl Gustkey. "However, as a rule, we can test up to 14 days when the drugs are ingested orally and up to three or four months when they are injected."

One U.S. Olympian, who did not want to be identified, said he became concerned about the testing during the USOC's informal program. He said he submitted a sample after being off anabolic steroids for 21 days and was notified several weeks later that he had tested positive.

Having resumed his steroid use following the informal test, he feared he also would test positive following his participation in the Olympic trials 21 days later. That would result in disqualification. But he was found to be clean in the test at the trials.

Another U.S. Olympian, who also did not want to be identified, said he quit using drugs four days before one informal test, got the word that he was clean and gave little thought afterward to the laboratory's capabilities. He also tested negative at the trials.

Dr. Kenneth Clarke, director of the USOC's sports medicine program in Colorado Springs, called that kind of thinking "Russian Roulette."

But a large number of athletes have been willing to play.

Despite reports of more stringent testing, and despite recent reports of potentially serious liver, kidney and heart ailments caused by anabolic steroids, doctors who prescribe the drugs to athletes report no decrease in their number of patients.

Following the Pan American Games, Dr. Robert Kerr, a San Gabriel sports medicine specialist who said he treats Olympians from 19 countries, was easily accessible to speak with reporters about prescribing anabolic steroids for athletes.

But he began rejecting some interview requests in the spring. His receptionist explained that Kerr would be too busy treating athletes until after the Olympics.

Asked during an interview last October whether his patients are frightened by the drug testing, Kerr said, "All this B.S. about not taking anabolic steroids goes in one ear and out the other, and these athletes laugh about it. I don't know of any athlete who's been influenced by it."

If anything, the reports of stringent drug testing have caused athletes either to search for more creative methods of beating the tests or switch to a drug that is not on the IOC's banned list.

The IOC Medical Commission's Beckett said in November that some track and field athletes were discovered to have used human growth hormone (STH) before last summer's world championships in Helsinki. There is no reliable test for the drug, believed by some athletes to be more effective than synthetic anabolic steroids.

Despite the high price of STH, Kerr said, "This is the elite drug. The really elite athletes are taking STH. Period."

More recently, Dr. Paul Ward, the coordinator of the USOC's Elite Athlete Project for shotputters and discus, hammer and javelin throwers, said he gave some athletes drug information. The information could conceivably have been used by athletes to beat drug tests.

USOC officials responded indignantly, disavowing knowledge of Ward's activities and announcing that he will not be associated with the Elite Athlete Project when it resumes following the Olympics.

A week later, Sports Illustrated reported that four members of the USOC's drug-control task force had known that Kerr appeared before Ward's athletes in late 1982 to give his views on the benefits of anabolic steroids and human growth hormone.

Officials from other countries no doubt have watched the USOC's attempts to exorcise drugs from its athletes with equal parts amusement and incredulity.

But at least, they say, the Americans finally are addressing the issue. They say that, before Caracas, the Americans were more resistant to drug testing than the Eastern Bloc.

"We are very pleased the Americans are beginning to move," Beckett said. "They've been the biggest stumbling block internationally. Their national governing bodies have been so hypocritical. Any step to try to get them into line with everyone else will certainly meet with my approval."

When Miller was informed of Beckett's comments, the USOC director's response was that the British are not as diligent in drug testing as they would have everyone believe.

But it is not fair to say we are back where we started before Caracas.

In two progressive actions, the International Amateur Athletic Federation, which governs track and field, announced this year it will not certify world records unless the athlete is tested for drugs following the performance and that it will institute random, unannounced tests in international meets, perhaps as early as 1985.

Olympic Notes

Women's 10,000 Meters Added to Games by the IOC, But Not Until '88

From Times Staff Writers, Wire Services

The International Olympic Committee officially added the women's 10,000-meter run to the program of the 1988 Seoul Olympics Thursday, thus meeting a key demand of women's athletic groups who had sought its inclusion in the Los Angeles Games.

IOC Executive Director Monique Berlioux said the decision was taken for the Seoul Games only and the IOC will examine how the competition goes there before deciding whether to make the race a permanent part of Olympic competition.

Berlioux said the IOC general membership session had also decided to add a women's 470 class dinghy event to the 1988 yachting competition.

But she said several other women's events that had been proposed for the Seoul Games—including modern pentathlon competition, seven weight categories in judo and a sprint cycling event—had been rejected.

In another step, the IOC agreed to add four major events to the Calgary Winter Games schedule in 1988, including nordic combined skiing, team jumping, alpine combined and supergiant slalom. As with the 10,000 meter run for women in the Summer Games, these events were added on a provisional basis only for the Calgary Games, pending further review.

—KEN REICH

□

The Australian men's and women's field hockey teams have been dealt blows via injury as they near weekend games.

The men's team, top-seeded in the field of 12, will decide today whether longtime star Jim Irvine will play. Irvine, one of the team's top shooters, has been nursing an Achilles tendon injury.

The women, who weren't considered a gold medal contender, have lost their top player, Elspeth Clement, with a badly broken thumb suffered in practice. Clement has been the team's top scorer in international competition.

Irvine worked out with the team at the East Los Angeles College Olympic site Thursday and appeared mobile. Coach Richard Hedges said he would decide today whether to replace Irvine, who is on his third Olympic squad, with 21-year-old newcomer John Bestall.

—ALAN DROOZ

□

The L.A. Olympic Committee held a dress rehearsal for Saturday's Opening Ceremonies, and word apparently got out. Some 42,000 of the committee's closest friends and acquaintances showed up, according to wire service estimates.

□

Heike Daute of East Germany leaped 24 feet, 3½ inches to set an East German women's long jumping record Thursday in a meet in Dresden, East Germany. Her leap fell just 1¼ inches short of the world mark of 24-4½ established by Romanian Anisoara Cusmir in June.

The 19-year-old Daute improved her old national record by 2¼ inches in her fifth attempt, as a two-day East German track and field meet opened.

Daute set her old national record of 24-1 on May 19 at the same Heinz-Steyer stadium.

Helga Radtke placed second in the long jump with 23-8.

In other events, Marlies Gohr won the women's 100 meters in 10.87 seconds, the 18th time in her career she has clocked under 11 seconds.

Gohr held the world record of 10.81 until July 3, 1983, when American Evelyn Ashford clocked 10.79 at Colorado Springs, Colo.

Uwe Hohn won the javelin competition with a throw of 299-4, well below his world record of 344-10 set in East Berlin last Friday. Hohn fouled four times on throws. World champion Detlev Michel was second with 297-10.

Petra Felke won the women's javelin with a throw of 230-11½.

World record-holder Uwe Beyer won the shotput Beyer's world record is 72-10¾. The meet continues Friday.

□

Puma USA Inc., has sued four members of the U.S. Olympic team for $3.5 million, claiming the athletes agreed to wear Puma footwear, but then trod on their contracts with adidas shoes.

The Los Angeles Superior Court civil suit filed Wednesday accuses Kim Gallagher, Jodi Anderson, Pam Spencer and Pamela Page of breaking one-year contracts with Puma to switch to adidas.

The suit also accuses coach Charles Debus and Three Stripe Promotions of persuading the athletes to repudiate their contracts to sign up with Three Stripe.

In exchange for agreeing to wear Puma footwear, the athletes became members of the Puma and Energizer Track and Field Club, the suit claims. The group was formed by Puma and Union Carbide Corp. to aid amateur athletes with training and living expenses.

Each of the athletes sent Puma a "notice of termination" on July 13, and made a new agreement with Three Stripe Promotions to wear Adidas shoes. Puma claims the termination notices were invalid.

The suit seeks $1 million in compensatory damages and $2.5 million in punitive damages.

□

American basketball officials are crying foul over an Olympic schedule that calls for the U.S. women to play two early morning games within 24 hours.

The American squad, 25-1 in exhibitions and the gold medal favorite in the Los Angeles Olympic tournament, opening Sunday, plays at 9 a.m. Monday and Tuesday.

The U.S. women take on another medal contender, Yugoslavia, in their opener Monday in the Forum. They play Australia Tuesday.

"They (Olympic officials) don't think about the athletes," said Bill Wall, executive director of the Amateur Basketball Association of the USA. "The game is not sport, it's money and television.

Wall contends the Los Angeles Olympic Organizing Committee "stuck us in the 9 o'clock time frame just because of ticket sales. Nine o'clock is not when you want to watch a basketball game, especially when you're the host."

The Olympic basketball tournament draw was conducted in Munich three weeks ago. "We had no say in the schedule," Wall said.

To cope with the scheduling problem, U.S. Coach Pat Head Summitt has ordered her players out of bed at 6 a.m. for the last three weeks so they could work out at 9.

"She's been trying to get the women's bodies in tune after we learned of the horrendous schedule we're stuck with," Wall said.

□

U.S. Olympic officials failed Thursday in an attempt to prevent officials from four boycotting nations from judging or refereeing fights involving American boxers.

The United States dropped the request after the International Amateur Boxing Association's executive committee indicated it would not alter its existing rules to exclude the three referee-judges and one jury member, according to Col. Don Hull, president of [illegible] association.

"We made the decision to follow the norm[illegible] procedures," said Hull.

Loring Baker, head of the USA Amateur Boxi[illegible] Federation, said the effort to remove the officials ca[illegible] about because of concerns over reaction to th[illegible] decisions in close bouts.

"We based it on the fact that if it was a cl[illegible] decision, it would put the referee or judge in a no-w[illegible] situation," said Baker. "Either way he would r[illegible] would be questioned.

The three referee-judges are from Poland, Bulga[illegible] and Cuba. The jury member is from the Soviet Union[illegible]

Under the judging rules used during the Olympi[illegible] the five-member jury is called into action if the f[illegible] ringside judges split 3-2 on a decision. The jury m[illegible] vote at least 4-1 to overturn a decision.

Baker said the United States request was not ma[illegible] because of any doubts of the competency of t[illegible] officials, but because of the way their decisions mig[illegible] be interpreted due to the boycott.

Hull said the committee decided not to change t[illegible] rules partly because it felt the possibility of t[illegible] referee-judges being used in fights involving the American boxers was remote.

"As was pointed out before the committee, t[illegible] theory of probability might be one in a thousand th[illegible] they judge a U.S. fighter," said Hull.

Sources close to the U.S. team indicated they nev[illegible] expected the protest to be successful. The sources, w[illegible] asked that their names not be used, said the U.S. tea[illegible] wanted to raise the issue so officials from boycotti[illegible] officials would be extra careful in any decisio[illegible] involving American fighters.

JAYNE KAMIN / Los Angeles Time[illegible]

The United States' Gary Newton, No. 10, and Andrew Stone try to get the ball past Holland's goalie Lex Bos in a field hockey exhibition match. The Netherlands won the game, 2-0[illegible]

TRAFFIC

Continued from page 22

to admit, they have been warning that during the period of the Summer Games you should be rumbling along on the bus, not grumbling along in your car.

If those warnings have not quite persuaded you that taking the bus to work or to one of the 23 Olympic venues is a good idea, maybe the following arguments put forth by transportation officials will:

—The Southern California Rapid Transit District will dispatch a fleet of 550 buses, dedicated to Olympic spectators, for all of the major venues and a number of the smaller ones. The RTD service, in the form of express, park and ride and shuttle buses, will complement the district's regular bus lines, which run to 18 of the 23 venues.

—The regular lines, while less expensive than the Olympic service, also are expected to take longer because they make more frequent stops. And an RTD spokesman said that the regular lines may be a little more crowded, with up to 300,000 more riders per day

—Numerous downtown-area streets and local freeway off-ramps will either be closed or set aside exclusively for buses, particularly near the Exposition Park/Coliseum area. (See accompanying chart.) And, on-ramp meters, normally calibrated for weekday rush-hour use, will be operating longer and even on some weekend days and nights, particularly near the venues.

—Downtown traffic has been altered somewhat since mid-May with normal two-way traffic now one-way from 11th to 38th Streets southbound on Figueroa Street and northbound on Flower Street.

—Traffic during the Summer Games is supposed to be 7% to 10% higher than normal if the estimated 650,000 extra visitors to the region appear, and if 60% of the spectators take the bus. And *if* a higher than usual number of commuters form car pools. And *if* a large number of residents jockey their work or vacation schedules. And *if*. . . .

It may be clear to you now why transportation planners have been preparing for almost any contingency.

DAY 1 OLYMPICS '84

THE GAMES OF THE XXIII OLYMPIAD

LOS ANGELES 1984

All Systems Are Go—for Gold

By RANDY HARVEY, *Times Staff Writer*

There no doubt were countless times when even the most stout and hearty of the Los Angeles Olympic Organizing Committee figured that if they could pull this one off, then this really must be the City of Angels.

The International Olympic Committee officially awarded Los Angeles the Games of the XXIII Olympiad in 1979. In the five years since, the LAOOC has worked hundreds of millions of hours, spent hundreds of millions of dollars and suffered hundreds of millions of headaches.

Those headaches have ranged from the minor—the death earlier this week of Bomber the bald eagle during training for the opening ceremonies—to the migraine—the Soviet-led boycott by 14 nations.

As if the LAOOC did not have its hands full taking care of things that it can control, it also has been asked to make the impossible possible—clean the air, create a cool breeze, reduce the traffic and make sure there is plenty of parking for everyone. Welcome to L.A.

It also has been forced to think, and plan for, the unthinkable, a terrorist attack such as the one that resulted in the murder of 11 Israelis in the athletes, village during the 1972 Munich Olympics.

And, somehow, the LAOOC is expected to put a happy face on it all for a worldwide television audience of 2.5 billion people. ABC, which paid $225 million for the exclusive rights, will be on the air for 180 hours.

The organizers of the 1932 L.A. Olympics had their own problems, including a depression. But it is not likely that they would want to trade places with the planners of a modern Olympics.

The LAOOC has a budget of a mere $525 million for its no-frills Olympics. Although this is unverifiable, it is estimated that Moscow spent $9 billion for the 1980 Games. Montreal still has a deficit of $559.6 million as part of the price it paid for the 1976 Games. Brother, can you spare a dime?

Carrying on its shoulders the burdens of outrageous costs, political interference and the threat of terrorism, the Olympic movement is beginning to resemble the dinosaur.

Upon the announcement of the Soviet boycott, a tit for Jimmy Carter's tat in 1980, there was speculation that this might be the final Olympics, or at least the final Olympics in some country other than Greece or Switzerland.

But IOC President Juan Antonio Samar-anch has insisted that the Games will go on, and that they will go on as planned, which means he believes Seoul, South Korea, will hold them in 1988. Even though South Korea's government is not recognized by several IOC member nations, including the Soviet Union, Samaranch remains a Seoul man.

Today, however, it is time to get on with the pomp and forget the circumstances.

The opening ceremonies, a David Wolper production, begin at 4:30 p.m. in the Coliseum. They are guaranteed to bewitch, bewilder and bedazzle.

There will be the usual speeches, including one of 27 words by President Reagan to officially open the Games. But mostly it is show business—involving 12,000 people, 4,000 pigeons and 85 pianos. "There is nothing as big as this, except maybe

D-Day," Wolper said.

Be respectful. Bomber the eagle gave his life for this show, and it must go on. He would have wanted it that way.

Amid all of the concerns, real and imagined, and the hype, all real, it is difficult sometimes to remember that the Olympics are, first and foremost, a sporting event.

More worldly than the Super Bowl, more spectacular than the World Cup of soccer, the Olympics still are just games, even if they are more majestically referred to as the Games.

As of today, the stars of this show no longer are Samaranch or LAOOC President Peter V. Ueberroth but the 7,800 athletes from a record 140 countries.

Please see OLYMPICS, page 26

Dime Store Wrestlers? Not Schultz Brothers

By DAVE DISTEL, *Times Staff Writer*

Far from the wrestling meccas of Iowa and Oklahoma, Dave and Mark Schultz live in the same big yellow house in Palo Alto and work daily in what might be called shared solitude.

They emerged long enough to earn positions on the U.S. Olympic wrestling team—and show the world that a couple of Californians can do things their way and get the job done.

Their way entails brotherly head knocking with an occasional slip into outright mayhem. Indeed, the Schultzes have had to survive each another to get to the L.A. Olympics.

A mere two weeks before Olympic qualifying was to begin, Dave's wife Nancy arrived at the Stanford wrestling room to retrieve the brothers after a workout.

"When I got there, there was

blood all over the mat and Mark was in the hospital," she said. "Dave was slumped in a corner."

She sighed. She had seen it all before.

"I got three stitches in the top of my head, and Dave had to get his nose realigned," Mark said. .

Still, no one ever said wrestling was supposed to be easy. It's better than being shot at, though, and that happened to Dave in Iran. And a little commingling of blood was more fun than a three-day train ride out of Mongolia, a "holiday" they enjoyed together. After all, it cannot all be a life of glamour.

Dave, 25, is the more renowned of the brothers, an internationally successful wrestler while still in high school and currently the world champion at 163 pounds.

Mark, 24, got off to a late start

Please see SCHULTZ, page 26

VINCE COMPAGNONE / Los Angeles Times

These two sets of brothers will look more ferocious when they wrestle for the United States in the Olympics. They are Mark Schultz (top), Lou (left) and Ed Banach, and Dave Schultz.

There's Twin Success for Wrestling Banachs

By DAVE DISTEL, *Times Staff Writer*

Lou Banach was upset, and maybe a little concerned. That meant that Ed Banach was upset, and maybe a little concerned.

That is the way it is when twin brothers have twin goals.

Lou Banach had been only a few seconds away from qualifying for the U.S. Olympic freestyle wrestling team at 220 pounds, but a two-point move by Dan Severn had beaten him and forced a third and deciding match in the final trials.

Lou stalked out of the arena at Grand Valley State College in Allendale, Mich. He wandered in the dark for an hour and a half, swatting pesky mosquitoes and trying to align reality with his dreams.

Finally, Ed went in search of his younger—by five minutes—brother.

"That was ridiculous," Lou fumed. "It was the referee's fault."

"No, it wasn't," Ed said. "It was your fault. You got tilted. Block it out. Forget it. You've got another match."

Lou Banach won the rubber match from Severn and earned a spot on the Olympic team. Ed Banach did his thing three nights later, making the freestyle team at 198 pounds.

Thus, they will be together at the ultimate competition in the one aspect of their lives that they seem to share in their 24th year.

These are definitely not twins who live in the same town, wear the same clothes, eat the same food, listen to the same music, enjoy the same hobbies and share the same ideas. They both wrestle. Period.

Appropriately, they are fraternal, not identical, twins.

Ed is the twin who lives in Iowa City, Iowa. He rides motorcycles, and hunts and fishes with a bow and arrow. Lou lives in West Point, N.Y. He writes poetry, paints and works crossword puzzles.

Indeed, they cannot even agree on which is the extrovert and which is the introvert.

Please see BANACH, page 27

SCHULTZ

Continued from page 25

because he had taken a fling at gymnastics in high school. He caught up, however, in time to qualify for the Olympic team at 180.5 pounds and join his brother in Los Angeles.

Neither went to Stanford—"You've gotta have a 4.0 and a 1,200 on the SAT," Dave said—but they still are Palo Alto guys, despite all but the years they spent away in college.

Dave went to Oklahoma State, UCLA and Oklahoma. Mark went to UCLA and Oklahoma. The emphasis was on Oklahoma, where they competed together for two years.

They have lived in the big yellow house with the jungle-like yard, though, since they were brought home from the Stanford hospital.

It is much too big for them, but they fill up the empty space with boarders from the nearby university. To pay for the avocado and onion sandwiches, and fruit juices they consume, they work as assistant wrestling coaches at Stanford.

"Stanford kids are different than we were," Dave mused. "I worked summers in Oklahoma flipping burgers or in construction, and Mark sand-blasted. These guys spend their summers designing computer software."

On a recent afternoon, the Schultzes sat on the one sunny patch of grass in the midst of the greenery and went through bottle after bottle of whatever juice they could find in an outdoor refrigerator.

Dave looked around, frowned and said: "This place is beginning to look like a graveyard for plastic bottles."

Dave Schultz has sleepy eyes, thinning dark hair and an ambling, bowlegged gait that makes him look as if he is always about to wade into an opponent. Mark, with thick, wavy blond hair, has more the preppy look of the young men who will come to fill the extra rooms in the fall.

Naturally, folks wonder what the scraps are like when they wrestle together.

"Who wins?" asked Nancy. "What's it like? Boring. Nobody ever scores."

Said Dave, "We've gone whole days and scored a total of three points. Of course, I score all three."

Dave has a whimsical nature. Mark is more cautious, or maybe just quieter.

Both, however, love to talk about their first mutual international experience, the Mongolian trip in 1979.

"That was the all-time most brutal," Dave said. "We use it to compare all other trips. Like, how does it rate with Mongolia?"

Mongolia, it would seem, was a bit primitive, television being a rather recently discovered phenomenon at the time. The officiating, they felt, left a little bit to be desired and U.S. coaches were imposing 10 miles of running a day as part of the training.

"The referees were like a band of hoodlums with no cops," Dave said. "There were 20 communist countries and three free-world countries, and each one had one referee. Mark watched one of my matches and thought I'd won, 10-3. I lost, 11-10. I found out later that I had to lose so the match judge's brother would win the tournament. I tried the old protest trick, but the videotapes had been erased."

The 10-mile runs were definitely alien to the Schultzes' method of training. They run intervals, and maybe stadium steps, but not distances. They and what they call the Iowa clan differ in their training methods.

"The differences would be minor to outsiders," Dave said. "I guess it would be easiest to explain that they have a mentor, Dan Gable, and a structured program year-round."

"Besides," Mark said, "we don't like people telling us what to do."

Said Dave, "I guess that cuts through the baloney."

Of course, 10-mile runs were nothing compared to the three-day train ride *out* of Mongolia.

"We stopped every 20 minutes," said Dave. "Then we got to Moscow and had to spend a half-day in the airport. We were dirty and smelly because there hadn't been any showers, so people were moving away from us in airport lines."

Obviously, a wrestler has to make sacrifices. And maybe be a little crazy.

Dave, for example, has taken as much as a month away from wrestling only once since he got into it in the seventh grade.

"I've been blessed with a natural attraction to the sport," he said. "I try to take a couple of days off, but I'm always back at it by the end of the second day."

'Dan Gable talks about team championships, but his approach to winning team championships is the same as our approach to individual championships. His approach is to get 10 individuals as ready as they can be.'

—DAVE SCHULTZ

In high school, Mark was drawn to gymnastics for a couple of years.

"It was fun learning the tricks but I got out of it because I couldn't get into pointing my toes and stuff like that," he said.

"Gymnastics did him good," Dave said. "Most guys are strong when they're in the proper (wrestling) position, but Mark's strong when he's out of position. He's able to do weird things I don't think I could do."

Mark got into wrestling as a high school junior and had a rather undistinguished 4-6 record. However, he was 30-2 as a senior and won the state championship.

By the time Dave was a high school senior, he was already competing against the best in the nation and world.

"When Dave was a senior in high school he pinned Chuck Yagla, who was a senior in college and a two-time NCAA champion," Mark said. "Dave was fourth in the Tbilisi tournament in Russia, and Tbilisi is tougher than the Olympics or the world championships."

Added Dave, "I got kind of a lucky draw at Tbilisi. I got through a few guys and then hit some of the meat of the tournament and got slaughtered twice. An East German pinned me and a Russian beat me up so bad the refs threw me out to save my life."

It was still not bad for a high school kid, and put him in demand among collegiate recruiters.

"Recruiting was a positive experience for a while, but it ended up being a pretty negative experience," he said. "It was neat having all those people telling me I was great, but I didn't enjoy telling them I wasn't coming to their schools. And I got so I didn't have that great a perspective on myself. I lost sight of how important I was and how important wrestling was. I think I got conceited."

Mark did not have the same recruiting experience, because he simply did not have the wrestling experience. He had the good senior year, which spoke well of his potential.

"I was only a state champion and that's nothing like the No. 1 guy in the country," he said. "Nobody knew me."

Mark ended up at UCLA, and Dave joined him. Dave had transferred from Oklahoma State after one year that he cares not to discuss. They stayed one year at UCLA and went on together to Oklahoma, where Dave won an NCAA title in the two years of eligibility he had remaining. Mark wrestled for three years, winning three NCAA championships.

Dave said, "I was never that much interested in the college style but I always wanted to do well."

International style is different from college style, and the Schultzes were getting a taste of both. They were both in Iran in 1979, when Dave found out how fast and how far he could do something as distasteful as running.

"I was up on a hill and I heard this whir go by," he said. "I thought maybe it was a big dragon fly, but it sounded awful loud for a bug. I turned around and saw a puff of smoke. I'd been so sick I didn't think I could run, but I found out I wasn't that sick. I don't know if they were trying to hit us, but I didn't want to stay around for target practice."

Nor, for that matter, did he want to stay around for wrestling.

"We hid out in the interpreter's apartment for two days waiting for a flight," he said. "It was shaky."

Both tried out for the 1980 Olympic team, but neither made it.

"Mark was a sleeper back then, but he had John Peterson (a two-time Olympic medalist) beaten with about 10 seconds to go and they cautioned him out," Dave said.

Dave caught Lee Kemp, a three-time world champion, in his prime and Kemp won the Olympic berth at 163 pounds. Their rivalry was to become one of the best in American wrestling, and Schultz beat Kemp this year to make the team.

In fact, the Schultz-Kemp finale was inaccurately perceived as a grudge match.

"I like Lee," Dave said. "After the trials, I invited him to come out to visit. I think he's a classy guy. I actually felt bad for him. He had such a great career. He was our most accomplished wrestler ever in international wrestling. It was sad he had to lose, but I'm glad he didn't win at my expense."

But weren't Schultz and Kemp pacing at opposite corners of the arena at the trials? Didn't it seem like they were avoiding each other?

"Before a competition, it's hard to feel comfortable around a guy," Dave said.

Indeed, there seems to be a particularly strong camaraderie among wrestlers. Wrestling rooms all seem to be open to anybody with a singlet and shoes who happens to be wandering through town.

"Wrestlers are a great group of guys," Dave said. "You hardly ever find a jerk in wrestling. I can't think of a wrestler I dislike."

There are times, though, when it is even hard to be comfortable around a brother.

"Mark's very serious before he wrestles," Dave said. "You can't talk to him for three days. It's like he's off in an ozone."

"Dave's the one who's real grouchy," said Mark.

Dave's wife agreed.

"No fair," Dave laughed. "Really, it's when I'm competing that I'm having a blast."

A serious blast, to be sure. Dave, particularly, is considered to be a very serious student of the sport of wrestling. It is often said that he is the best technician in the United States, and maybe as good as any in the world.

"I'm honored when people say that, but I wonder if people look at my body and figure I have to be a good technician," he said. "Really, I've been lucky. I've been involved with quality people from a young age. It's like I've been able to get a doctorate and others haven't had a chance to start college as far as wrestling education is concerned."

Exactly what *is* a technician?

"Wrestling is a very technical sport," he said. "For example, there are 100 different ways to grab a leg. If you had a playbook of wrestling moves, it would be *thick.*"

All wrestlers, thus, are technicians in the sense that they employ techniques.

"You don't use everything," Dave said. "Certain things are open with certain people and other things are open with other people. Every move is an option play. It's a dynamic sport, kinda scary. You never know what's going to happen."

Wrestling has, at times, been described as a physical chess match. It *is* very much a one-on-one endeavor.

"Dan Gable talks about team championships, but his approach to winning team championships is the same as our approach to individual championships," Dave said. "His approach is to get 10 individuals as ready as they can be."

In Palo Alto, the Schultzes work to get two individuals as ready as they can be.

"We're always being kidded about what new tricks we are developing in the Stanford labs," Dave said.

"I was only a state champion and that's nothing like the No. 1 guy in the country. Nobody knew me.'

—MARK SCHULTZ

When one of the Schultzes is wrestling, the other is likely to be in the corner—but the corner may as well be in Mongolia.

Mark said, "If something's lacking, I'll say something. I never really have to say anything to Dave but 'go.' "

Dave said he was not quite as reserved. "I know how good Mark is. It irritates me when he gets into a close match with someone he shouldn't have any trouble with. Especially when he won't let me score in practice."

Their practice matches, of course, are less than quiet exercises wrestled in quiet gyms, away from the roar of the crowds.

"When we let our egos get involved it can get kinda hairy," Mark said.

Their most enjoyable moments are when they are coming up consecutively in the wrestling order, first Dave at 163 and then Mark at 180.5.

"Once in a while, in a big meet, we'd start at the same time," Dave said. "I used to try to beat my guy before Mark could beat his guy."

Their starts and finishes will be staggered in the Olympics.

"I start a day before Mark and finish a day earlier," Dave Schultz said. "It would be nice to win it—and then watch him win it."

Regardless of what happens in the Olympics, both Schultzes intend to continue wrestling—and not necessarily with 1988 in mind.

"People seem to think in terms of four-year spans," Dave said. "Everyone talks about '88 as though there isn't any '85. The world championships are a big deal, even if they don't attract the national press like the Olympics."

In spite of their success, they must contend with self-doubt. Even champions are not immune to such emotion.

"You can't let fear paralyze you," said Mark. "It's not like real fear, but more like the fear of losing."

Dave shrugged.

"You have to deal with self-doubts," he said. "It's hard for me to believe I'm good. It's hard for me to believe I'm the world champion and it would be hard for me to believe if I won the Olympics. It doesn't seem like it should be me. It would be too good to be true."

Especially if the big yellow house were decorated with *two* gold medals.

OLYMPICS

Continued from page 25

That does not include 19 countries that, for one reason or another, declined invitations.

Thirteen of them joined the Soviet Union's boycott, which was prompted by concerns over security and, perhaps, just plain spite. The United States led a 60-nation boycott of the Moscow Summer Olympics.

As the boycott unfurled, the attention was focused on the athletes who will not be here. Pole vaulter Sergei Bubka and swimmer Vladimir Salnikov of the Soviet Union, runner Jarmila Kratochvilova of Czechoslavakia, sprinters Marlies Gohr and Marita Koch and swimmers Astrid Strauss and Kristin Otto of East Germany and boxer Teofilo Stevenson of Cuba are only a few of the marvelous athletes we will not see in Los Angeles.

But today, at the opening ceremonies, all eyes will be on the athletes who march into the Coliseum for the inspirational parade of nations.

As required by tradition, Greece will be first. The ancient Olympics began there in 776 BC and were reborn in Athens in 1896.

The United States, as the host country, will be last. It has a contingent of 597 athletes, the largest.

Bangladesh, Burma and Tonga will be represented by one athlete each.

Somewhere in between is China, participating in the Olympics for the first time since 1948. There are 353 Chinese athletes here, including their remarkably acrobatic gymnasts and divers and the man-child who has cleared 7-10 in the high jump, Zhu Jianhua.

Romania also sent a team, the only Soviet Bloc country to do so.

Nadia Comaneci, the Romanian gymnast who was identified with the perfect 10 long before Bo Derek, has returned to the Olympics as an official. But she has more imitators than Michael Jackson.

The Romanians have a couple in Ecaterina Szabo and Lavinia Agache, while the U.S. counters with its own Nadia, 16-year-old Mary Lou Retton. She is even coached by Comaneci's former coach, Romanian defector Bela Karolyi.

Romania also is blessed with several outstanding track and field athletes, but the country's greatest successes may come from its women's kayakers and rowers.

Many Americans not only will be introduced to them but possibly will be sold. They may also learn from the New Zealand men's rowers, the Dutch field hockey teams, the South Korean women archers and the Italian fencers. For proficiency in their particular calling, the Dodgers have nothing on any of them.

But the anthem that will be heard most often as the athletes collect their medals will be "The Star Spangled Banner."

Carl Lewis has a song of his own called "Go for the Gold." The most talented track and field athlete since Jesse Owens, King Carl could go for four golds.

The question is not whether anyone can beat him. He has proved time after time that he is the world's best in his individual events, the 100 and 200 meters and the long jump. He will also anchor the 400-relay team here. The question is whether he will allow himself to be beaten.

Also in charge of their own destinies are such favorites as intermediate hurdler Edwin Moses, seeking his 90th straight victory in a final, diver Greg Louganis, boxer Mark Breland, swimmers Rick Carey, Tracy Caulkins and Tiffany Cohen, and synchronized swimmers Tracy Ruiz and Candy Costie, sort of an aquatic version of Torvill and Dean.

If Retton does not capture the hearts of ABC's Jim McKay and millions of other Americans watching on television, Ruiz and Costie will. The quiet one of the two, Ruiz is also expected to win a solo gold.

The United States' two most acclaimed women track and field athletes, middle-distance runner Mary Decker and sprinter Evelyn Ashford, might also be prohibitive favorites if not for injuries that have interrupted their training.

Ashford appears almost completely recovered from a hamstring injury, but Decker has not competed since the Olympic trials because of a sore right Achilles tendon.

If she is not healthy, she will have all she can handle in the 3,000 meters against Romania's Maricica Puica and shoeless South African Zola Budd.

As a result of the IOC's ban against South Africans because of its government's apartheid policies, Budd, 18, became a citizen of Britain last spring and, thus, is eligible to participate in the Games.

But even without Budd, the British have no scarcity of track and field stars. Daley Thompson will attempt to become the only man other than American Bob Mathias to win back-to-back decathlon championships. His primary competition will come from West Germany's Jurgen Hingsen, the world record-holder.

After more than a year of not facing each other, Sebastian Coe and Steve Ovett will meet in the 800 and 1,500 meters. Coe won the 1,500 in Moscow, while Ovett won the 800.

If security for the more than 10,000 athletes and coaches housed in the villages becomes a problem, the great American shot-blocker, Patrick Ewing, can be called upon to protect the middle.

Olympic organizers surely hope on Aug. 13, the day following the closing ceremonies, that jokes can still be made about the massive security measures they have taken.

Enlisted for the effort are approximately 17,000 law enforcement officers and 8,000 unarmed guards, as well as Secret Service agents here to protect the President, Great Britain's Prince Philip and as many as 12 other heads of state who may attend. It is believed to be the largest peacetime security operation west of Moscow.

Following a visit to Los Angeles last week, University of California sociology professor Harry Edwards said he did not blame the Soviets for boycotting if concern for their safety was the reason.

"Go down and take a look," he said after giving a speech on Violence and Aggression in Sports at a conference in Eugene, Ore. "There's double barbed-wire cyclone fences with dogs and cops on every corner.

"You can tell it's not going to be a love festival. The closest thing I've seen to it is the Berlin Wall."

No one can protect the athletes from Los Angeles' most villianous enemy, the smog. Headlines in Moscow proclaimed the L.A. Olympics, "The Games in Gas Masks." The city has had its smoggiest July in six years, but observers of that sort of thing expect air quality to improve in August.

Just in case, the British brought oxygen masks—not for their athletes but for their horses in the equestrian competition.

As for the human contestants, Salazar, the marathon runner from cool, clear Eugene, said last winter he had arrived upon the perfect method of training for the smog. "I'll start the car in the garage and run in there," he said.

But most athletes, particularly the runners, have voiced more concern about the heat than the smog.

"We're surprised to find it hotter here than where we just left," said Mohammed Redwan Khari, an Egyptian coach.

Searching for more comfortable living accommodations than provided by the USC dorms, several U.S. athletes have said they will stay outside the village, but U.S. Olympic Committee officials prefer that their athletes stay in the village. One reason is so they will not be trapped in traffic while their competition is taking place. It has been estimated that traffic in Los Angeles will increase by 10% over the next 16 days.

One reason U.S. Olympic Committee officials prefer that their athletes stay in the village is so they will not be trapped in traffic while their competition is taking place. It has been estimated that traffic in Los Angeles will increase by 10% over the next 16 days.

You can run, but you can't hide. The Southern California portion of the Games, not including the soccer competitions in Cambridge, Annapolis and Palo Alto, covers 4,500 miles of Greater Los Angeles, touching five counties and 80 communities.

The organizers have attempted to make the traffic jams as pleasant as possible, placing 8,000 colorful banners along 120 miles of streets and highways.

The primary color is described as hot magenta. Whatever that is. The organizers say the magenta and the other hot colors and playful patterns of proportional bands and rows of stars combine to create a look they call "Festive Federalism." Whatever that is.

But they have been somewhat more creative than the Muscovites in 1980. They painted the town red. Perhaps they called it Festive Communism, if there can be such a thing in Moscow.

BANACH

Continued from page 25

"Eddie's more introverted and I'm more extroverted," Lou said. "He's a shy person, except around his wife and close friends."

"Louie said *that?*" Ed asked. "I think it's the other way around. At least, it was. I haven't changed. I'm my same old self. I've always been outgoing. I like meeting people. Louie's changed. He's changed so much maybe he makes me look like an introvert."

It can probably be said that both are extroverts, although not in a life-of-the-party sense. Lou is more philosophical and talks at greater length. If Ed is considered less extroverted, it is likely because he is more intense.

Lou's self-described "artsy-philosophical" bent, which manifested itself when the brothers were freshman at the University of Iowa, probably was the cause of their drift from the sameness of their boyhoods in Port Jervis, N.Y.

"We started growing apart because we discovered that we had different lives to lead," Lou said.

They certainly had much in common in their boyhoods, beyond the fact that they came into this world five minutes apart on Feb. 6, 1960.

Two years later, there was a family-shattering tragedy they were too young to remember—yet will never forget.

"We were originally from a family of 14 but our home burned down when we were 2," Lou said. "Our mom had a nervous breakdown and our dad took off. We all ended up in foster homes."

Ed and Lou Banach were passed from foster home to foster home for two years. In the summer of 1964, their brother, Steve, was taken in by Alan and Stephanie Tooley in Port Jervis. The twins joined Steve for what was supposed to have been a two-week visit around Thanksgiving of the same year.

"The Tooleys really wanted little babies," said Ed. "Steve was 5 and Louie and I were 4. When the agency called to take us back, Mom said, 'You can't take 'em so soon.' "

As it turned out, no one ever came to take the Banach boys from the Tooleys. When they talk now of mom and dad, except during their vague recollections of the fire's aftermath, they are talking of Alan and Stephanie Tooley.

"They are my parents," Lou said. "We were so young that we never understood we had another mom and dad."

The Banachs' biological mother is still in a nursing home, but their father died a few years ago.

"I know I was supposed to feel sorrow and anguish," said Ed. "But I couldn't. The feelings I have toward parents are toward the Tooleys."

Lou could not get away from Iowa for the funeral.

"A lot of my brothers and sisters were hurt, but, really, Eddie and I didn't know him," he said.

The Tooleys raised the three boys in Port Jervis, described by Lou as a railroad and trucking town of about 5,000 residents that hugs the New York border where Pennsylvania and New Jersey intersect.

"It was nice," Ed said. "Kind of out in the country. We had a big backyard. We were out of the house from 8 o'clock in the morning until 8 o'clock at night."

They were not necessarily angels. Three rambunctious youngsters never are.

"Mom and Dad couldn't have raised us any better," Ed said. "The things we did." He laughed and shook his head. "Mom's nickname was Sarge."

Ed remembered one occasion when Lou did something wrong for the fourth or fifth time and incurred the Sarge's wrath. It was the last straw, and their father was sent to dispense a whipping.

"Dad didn't like to hit us, so he went into Louie's bedroom and took off his belt and started slapping the dresser," Ed said. "He told Louie to cry out each time he hit the dresser. After 12 or 13 belts, Mom was afraid he was killing poor Louie so she went in to tell him to stop. Louie was laughing and Dad was laughing and Mom was furious. I did all I could to stifle a laugh. Man, was she hot."

Port Jervis happened to be a town in love with football, and the Tooley household had three of the best football players in the state. Lou played on the offensive line and Ed and Steve were linebackers. All three were all-state. All three also were outstanding wrestlers, Lou and Ed winning state championships.

"We got into wrestling in the seventh grade mainly to stay out of trouble," Lou said. "Our friends were into the partying scene and into drugs. Wrestling kept us away from adversity."

Said Ed, "Mom was always telling us to stop fighting. We found out we could wrestle without getting yelled at."

They did so well that Dan Gable, the Olympic legend and the coach at Iowa, found his way to Port Jervis. Steve had already gone to Clemson, and a number of Eastern universities were trying to get the twins to stay much closer to home than Iowa City.

Gable and J Robinson, his assistant, made their presentation and set up housekeeping at a local inn.

"J and Dan never talked badly about the other programs," Lou said. "All the other programs talked badly about Iowa. They said Iowa was like a machine and I would be turned into a robot. It kinda scared me."

Ed said, "We listed the good things and tried to decide what place would give us the most of the good things."

"There was no decision to make," Lou said. "Iowa was the place."

And so the twins packed their bags. They would go from a little town in New York to a sprawling state university in the Midwest. And Steve would join them.

"I remember kissing Mom goodby," Ed said. "It hurt to leave her and I remember crying. It was a cry of sorrow and a cry of happiness. It was a release from all the old things and a start on another part of our lives."

The adjustment, however, was difficult, especially for Lou. It was the fall of 1978, and the next part of his life would be different from the next part of Ed's life.

"I roomed with Ed," Lou said. "It might have been easier if I had roomed with someone else. We were so close, but we weren't feeling the same pains. Eddie kind of reinforced my anxieties. I started living the role everyone had painted for me and I got so I started to feel like a robot. I thought I had to take control of my life. A year later, I quit wrestling."

A fellow simply does not quit wrestling at Iowa without taking some heat.

"A lot of people were disgruntled," Lou said. "I was called a quitter and a loser. It sliced me hard and cut me deep. I heard that I had tarnished Dan Gable's image. I heard that my life was ruined. How could my life be ruined? I was 19 years old."

Lou Banach had decided to travel his own path through life. It eventually led him back to the Hawkeyes' wrestling room, but he had lost his scholarship. He worked his way through school as a dormitory resident adviser.

Ed, meanwhile, was adapting quite nicely to the Hawkeyes' regimen. He did not need a different drummer. He had Gable, and he liked the beat.

"You can see the desire in the hearts of Hawkeye wrestlers and desire manifests itself in hard work," he said. "Nothing is impossible. The impossible just takes longer."

Nothing seemed impossible to Ed Banach at Iowa, where he won four Big Ten and three NCAA championships. He had an overall record of 141-9-1 with an Iowa-record 73 pins.

Lou's career was less spectacular. He won two NCAA championships and two Big Ten titles, and had a record of 93-14-8 with 48 pins. His record was outstanding on its own merits, but his accomplishments were always to be compared to Ed's.

'We got into wrestling in the seventh grade, mainly to stay out of trouble. Our friends were into the partying scene and into drugs. Wrestling kept us away from adversity.'

—LOU BANACH

People simply could not understand that twins could be different, that maybe Lou was not quite as gung-ho as his brother.

"Our differences surfaced in college," Ed said. "The things I wanted to do, he didn't. Louie established his own life style, and what was right for him wasn't right for me. He broke out of the pattern."

Lou's most satisfying year, he said, was his junior year, even though he had to settle for third in the NCAA meet.

"It was most satisfying because that was the year I grew close to Dan Gable," he said. "Even then, I didn't think I wanted to wrestle after my junior year. I thought I had given everything I had to give. I talked to Dan and he said to relax and see how I felt later."

Lou came back and the twins finished their collegiate careers in 1983 with NCAA championships, Ed at 190 pounds and Lou at heavyweight.

Ed Banach expounds the Gable gospel as part of his job now. He is coach of the Hawkeye Wrestling Club, a post-graduate off-shoot of the varsity program that prepares wrestlers for international competitions. The adopted son of the Tooleys of Port Jervis has adopted Iowa City as his home.

"It's a nice little town," he said. "It's large enough to have entertainment pleasing to me and small enough to be comfortable."

Ed is married and settled down and comfortable. Lou is single and lives in West Point, N.Y., where he is a second lieutenant in the Army.

Steve is in the Army, too, the 82nd Airborne, stationed at Fort Bragg, N.C. He tried out for the Olympic team at 198 pounds, but lost early in the trials.

"I think Lou and Steve are so comfortable with the Army life style because they were used to the Sarge's authority," Ed mused.

Most of Lou's time in the service is spent either coaching or wrestling, reinforcing that common thread with his twin. Both Banachs had to make the transition from college style wrestling to international freestyle rather rapidly.

Lou was reluctant to continue wrestling, but decided to give it a try. He went to the Soviet Union to wrestle in the Tbilisi tournament last winter, and did not fare well. He decided to retire in March, because he did not feel the motivation was there.

Ed also made a Soviet trip, to the world championships in Kiev, and also came away unfulfilled.

"I just didn't know if I had enough time to get ready for wrestling freestyle in the Olympics," Ed said. "But the trips were a learning process for me. I was a good college wrestler, one of the best, but I was a pup at freestyle. I took my lumps, but I had the desire to get better."

Ed Banach said he reached his turning point during the World Cup competition in Toledo, Ohio, in March. He was matched against the Soviet Union's Sanasar Oganasyan, the 1980 Olympic gold medalist, for the championship at 198 pounds, and came away a loser, 14-3.

"When I've watched videos I've always watched myself," he said. "But I was embarrassed by Oganasyan, darn near 12-pointed. I had figured I was further along. I decided maybe I was wasting my time watching myself. I thought, 'He scored 14 points and you scored 3. Maybe you can learn more by watching *him.*' "

Banach, thus, became a clone of sorts of the man he figured he would have to beat to win an Olympic gold medal. However, because of the Soviet boycott, Ed Banach—*and* his twin brother—are among the favorites at their weights.

Brother Lou had to overcome his own recalcitrance, as well as a ruptured disc in his back and resultant spasms. He came back from the Soviet Union, rested awhile and did a lot of reading.

"It was back to the drawing board," he said. "I was anxious to get wrestling. The rest had brought me around."

However, when it was time for the all-service wrestling championships, Banach's back was bothering him again. He wanted to skip the tournament, but the Army coach, Floyd Winter, talked him into wrestling. He won.

'Our differences surfaced in college. The things I wanted to do, he didn't. Louie established his own life style, and what was right for him wasn't right for me.'

—ED BANACH

"I realized I could wrestle with an injury," he said. "I had learned to deal with it."

It all came down to the match with Severn in the final U.S. trials. He had rallied from a 5-0 deficit to win the first match on a pin, then lost the second match when Severn turned him in the final seconds. He had to go to a third and deciding match, which he won, 7-5.

"There was a ton of pressure on Louie," Ed said. "He didn't waver one bit. He was strong as steel."

Said Lou, "I cried afterwards. Words couldn't describe my feelings. I'd gone through so much to get there."

Of course, Ed Banach still had to win a match against Mitch Hull a few nights later to get the brother act to Los Angeles.

"I was confident," Ed said. "Louie has more fears that maybe he hasn't done enough to get ready. I *knew* I was ready."

And Ed, too, was choked with a bit of the emotion of the moment.

In the aftermath of his win over Hull, he said: "I've been through so much with my brother. I've practiced with my brother. I watched him defeat Severn, and I was high in the clouds. I was anxious to do my stuff. Now we're on the Olympic team. Together."

Even Without Cuba, This Is Big

By EARL GUSTKEY, *Times Staff Writer*

It was to have been a boxing tournament for the history books, the biggest amateur tournament in history. And two of the powerhouse boxing countries represented, the United States and Cuba, were to have suited up possibly their best teams ever.

And, it was to have been the grand finale, the final curtain call, for one of the sport's legendary figures, Cuba's Teofilo Stevenson.

It's something less than that now, of course. The Soviet-led boycott has removed one team, Cuba, which, seemingly had a chance of winning up to half a dozen gold medals, just as it did in Moscow. And the Soviet Union might have won a couple of golds.

It's still the biggest tournament ever held—more than 400 boxers from 84 countries are expected—but it shapes up as an All-American show.

The 1952 and 1976 Olympic teams each won five Olympic championships. This time, if five or less is the number, there will be some long faces at the U.S.A. Amateur Boxing Federation's Colorado Springs headquarters.

Said U.S.A./ABF President Loring Baker: "We have one weight class where we have very little experience, another where we're simply weak. But I give us a shot at a medal in every one of the other 10."

The head coach of the American Olympic team, Pat Nappi, is loath to make medal predictions. He does say, though, that the 1984 team is "deeper" than the 1976 team he coached.

Col. Don Hull, president of the International Amateur Boxing Assn. (AIBA), sees the U.S. winning something like half the gold medals in what he says could turn out to be a tournament where no one misses the Cubans.

"In all fairness to the great 1952 and '76 U.S. squads, I really think this is the best U.S. Olympic team ever," he said recently.

"There are a lot of world-class guys on this (U.S.) team that 10 years ago would have turned pro before the Olympics. I'm talking about guys like (Pernell) Whitaker, (Mark) Breland and (Tyrell) Biggs. An Olympic gold medal enhances their value on the pro market by so much, they've remained amateurs to compete in the Olympics."

Baker won't make predictions because he will serve on the scoring jury during some tournament bouts.

"Predictions for the Olympic boxing tournament are meaningless," he said. "It's all based on the luck of the draw. You could have the best guy in one weight class eliminating the second best guy in the preliminaries. So instead of winning the silver medal, he gets no medal."

Baker, like other U.S.A./ABF officials, is tired of talking about the missing Cubans.

"To me," he said, "It's a question not of how Cuba hurts the tournament by not being here, but how much they would have added to it. We've got countries coming to this tournament with the best Olympic teams they've ever had—Puerto Rico, Kenya, Canada, Italy—so we'll have the finest boxing competition in the history of the Olympics, I'm sure."

Here's a look at the Olympic boxing tournament, the top contenders in the 12 weight classes.

106

Paul Gonzales, East Los Angeles, probably has more experience, more boxing skills and more height (he's over 5-9) than anyone else in the weight class. But he also has a bad right hand, which he plans to put in a cast after the Olympics. He's also in one of the two deepest weight classes. If he's unlucky in the draw, he might have to box world class light-flyweights in every apperance, like South Korea's Kwang Sun Kim, Puerto Rico's Rafael Ramos and the Dominican Republic's Hector Diaz. Don't miss Ramos' act. He's barely five feet tall, weighed exactly 100 pounds when he boxed Gonzales last summer at the Pan Am Games, and bounces around the ring pogo-stick style. Gonzales lost a disputed decision to Ramos at Caracas and avenged it in Los Angeles last February. Both bouts were close.

Prediction: Gonazales, but it's a tough call in a tough class.

112

Steve McCrory, Detroit, lost his world championship in Los Angeles last April to Cuba's Pedro Reyes. He also lost to Laurenzo Ramirez of the Dominican Republic at the Pan American Games. Another contender: Yung Mo Huh of South Korea. McCrory, a left-hander with great hand speed, is the younger brother of pro welterweight champion Milton McCrory.

Prediction: McCrory, if he can avoid chronic spells of inconsistency.

119

Robert Shannon, Edmonds, Wash., is a pure puncher who finds himself in possibly the deepest, talented weight class in the tournament. He boxes out of an effectively awkward stance, a trait that might cause him difficulty with East European referees. Shannon's punches tend to sometimes land a touch sideways, a no-no in amateur boxing. The contenders: Maurizio Stecca (Italy), Manuel Vilchez (Venezuela), Sangram Terapo (Thailand) and Pedro Nolasco (Dominican Republic). Stecca is ranked No. 1 in the world by AIBA and Vilchez, rated 2nd, was voted outstanding boxer at the Pan Am Games.

Prediction: Stecca, on the strength of outclassing a strong field at the World Cup in Rome last October.

ROBERT LACHMAN / Los Angeles Times

Shawn O'Sullivan, left, connects to the chin of Frank Tate.

125

Meldrick Taylor, Philadelphia, is a phenomenal young talent who just keeps winning. At 17, he's the youngest on the U.S. team. In 1982, two weeks past his 16th birthday, he won a national championship with a 5-0 decision over Shannon, when both were in the 112 pound class. Taylor is the most effective body puncher on the U.S. team.

Prediction: In a division where six of the top ranked 10 are staying home because of the boycott, Taylor looks like an easy choice.

132

Pernell Whitaker, Norfolk, Va., is the national and world champion and ranked No. 1 in the world. He's a master counterpuncher and looks to be too strong and too good for anyone in the class. Three of the top five-rated boxers in the 132s won't be here.

Prediction: Easy, Whitaker.

139

Jerry Page, Columbus, Ohio, is a sound, fundamental boxer who rarely seems to be in trouble. He's occasionally bothered by a left knee that's been operated on twice since 1980. He has shown that he is good enough to compete with the best, since he lost a narrow 3-2 to Cuba's Carlos Garcia at the 1983 World Championships. Top contenders: Dong Kil Kim (South Korea), Shadrach Odhiambo (Sweden) and Tawee Umphomana (Thailand).

Prediction: Page.

147

Mark Breland, New York, is not only the class of this weight class and this Olympics, but some say he may be the greatest talent in the history of the sport. The No. 2 ranked amateur welterweight in the world is Italy's Luciano Bruno, and Breland easily decisioned him here last April, 5-0. Pencil in the South Korean, Yong Beom Chung, for a medal, along with Bruno.

Prediction: Breland.

156

Frank Tate, Detroit, must rate as a boxer's chance in a weight class where the favorite, Canada's Shawn O'Sullivan, is a hard-hitter who leads with his face. Tate has shown that he can win internationally. In 1983, e defeated Soviet Alexander Koshkin, the 1982 world champion, in his second international bout. He's a boxer who possesses an effective jab and he moves well. Like super-heavyweight Tyrell Biggs, he wins most of the time but never brings a crowd to its feet with blazing combinations, like Shannon, Breland or Whitaker. He's 1-1 with O'Sullivan, losing 3-2 in Houston last September and beating him, 5-0, to gain the world championship here last April, when O'Sullivan was recovering from the flu. Contenders: Romoso Casamonica (Italy), Hae Jung Lee (South Korea), Hector Ortiz (Puerto Rico).

Prediction: O'Sullivan, but if they meet, the Canadian will need his best to beat Tate.

165

Virgil Hill, Williston, N.D., is a superb athlete who would probably be the favorite in this class were he from a big boxing city like Detroit or Philadelphia. But because there are few sparring partners worthy of the name in Williston, Hill suffers from a lack of tough gym combat. With Cuba's Bernardo Comas absent, the favorite is Joon Sup Shin (South Korea), who won the World Cup title with a 4-1 over Italy's Noe Cruciano. Another contender is a Dutch boxer who lives and trains in Los Angeles, Pedro Van Raamsdonk.

Prediction: Shin.

178

Evander Holyfield, Atlanta, is on top of his game. He was extremely impressive at the Las Vegas Olympic team box-off, beating rugged Ricky Womack twice in 18 hours to make the team. Holyfield never brings the crowd to it feet, either. He's a technician, and he wins. He throws short, hard punches, tucks his chin away inside his shoulder like Ezzard Charles used to, and makes few errors. Contenders: Ki Ho Hong (South Korea), Carlos Salazar (Venezuela).

Prediction: Holyfield.

201

Henry Tillman, Los Angeles, is 0-2 against the favorite, Canadian strongboy Willie DeWit. But Tillman, the least experienced (he is 33-7 as an amateur) boxer on the U.S. team, on his best night could give DeWit a difficult time. Tillman is a natural boxer with an excellent jab and ring movement. He's cool under fire, and he will need it if he draws DeWit. The Canadian is the hardest hitter in the tournament, perhaps in all of boxing. DeWit already has won a major Olympic victory—when the AIBA rules committee voted last April to make headgear mandatory in the Olympics. DeWit is a bleeder. Without headgear he might have been even money to be put out of the tournament on a cut. Contenders: Angelo Musone (Italy), Virgilio Frias (Dominican Republic).

Prediction: DeWit.

201+

Tyrell Biggs, Philadelphia, and Francesco Damiani, Italy, look like the only real contenders in a weight class decimated by the boycott. In addition to Stevenson, the boycott removes five other super-heavyweights ranked in the top 10 worldwide. Biggs is a stand-up boxer with an excellent jab. Damiani hasn't figured him out in two tries. Biggs beat him at the 1982 World Championships in Munich and again last April in Los Angeles, both on 4-1 decisions. Damiani is a brawler-slugger who looks like Gerry Cooney. He likes to lean on his opponents and work the body, with an occasional surprise uppercut in search of a chin.

Prediction: Biggs.

Soviets Say U.S. Forced Boycott to Avoid Defeat

By ROBERT GILLETTE, *Times Staff Writer*

MOSCOW—The boycotting Soviet Union is heralding the opening of the Los Angeles Olympic Games with fresh volleys of bitter criticism, alleging that the United States forced Communist countries to withdraw in order to prevent a demoralizing defeat of American athletes.

State-controlled newspapers said Friday that the absence of so many top athletes means the Games will lack the excitement of past Olympics and will prove to be a commercial flop.

"It is a pity that the Olympics will not be such a thrilling performance as usual, that the spectators will not see in Los Angeles over half of the current world champions," the nationwide daily Sovietskaya Rossiya (Soviet Russia) said.

The newspaper insisted that the Soviet-led pullout of most Communist countries on grounds of inadequate security was fully justified. But it put a new twist on the boycott by contending that the United States had forced Moscow's hand so as to spare the American public the sight of its team going down to defeat.

The "bosses of big business," the newspaper said, realized that "a defeat in important sports competitions produces the same impact as the loss of a big battle."

"This," it went on, "is why the U.S. authorities, seeing that the U.S. would not defeat athletes from the USSR and other socialist countries in an honest sports struggle, went out of their way to actually bar them from participation in the Los Angeles Olympics. U.S. politicians who sacrificed the Olympic Charter and the traditions of the Games for the sake of furthering their hegemonistic aims are fully responsible."

The newspaper dismissed as absurd suggestions in the West that the Soviet Union itself feared an embarrassing loss in the medal count to the United States and its own ally, East Germany. It claimed that Soviet athletes were favored in 62 events, East Germans in 44 and Americans in only 28.

Soviet press reports have not made it clear that several Communist countries are in fact sending teams to Los Angeles, including China, Yugoslavia and Moscow's Warsaw Pact ally Romania.

Nearly every major Soviet newspaper joined state television and the government news agency Tass Friday in carrying harsh criticism of the Olympics. The youth newspaper Komsomolskaya Pravda decorated its commentary with a cartoon showing a hooded Ku Klux Klansman leering at the Olympic symbol of five rings—portrayed as hangman's nooses.

Friday's issue of Soviet newspapers assailed the Games as an economic failure. A Tass report from San Francisco said that because so many world-class athletes will be absent, attendance will be down by two-thirds from the expected level.

"It seems that a 'bold experiment' of holding the Olympic Games on a commercial basis is about to become a flop," Tass said in its English-language service.

OLYMPICS '84

DAY 2

Now, That Was a Party! Glad You Could Join Us

Well, it's here, and it's happened.

The Olympic Games they said would never take place are taking place.

The Olympics they said couldn't be held are being held.

The Olympics they said would drown in politics, strangle in traffic are floating and breathing.

The Olympics they said would tap the taxpayers out of billions are paying their way.

The Olympics everyone said they were going out of town to escape are doing nicely without them.

The Olympics the Soviets tried to strangle in their crib are crawling and walking and talking.

The Olympics they said were too commercial are being done with as much taste as a High Mass.

The Olympics they said would be the "Wall Street Olympics" turn out to be more democratic than the Wehrmacht Olympics (1936), the Red Army Olympics (1980) or anything put on by the

Jim Murray

Emperor of Japan, the king of Sweden or the royal family of Greece.

The Olympics every two-bit politician with an election coming up tried to block now find these same politicians standing with their hats over their hearts, tears in their eyes, wishing they could take credit.

The Olympics they said would be the

"Mickey Mouse Olympics" have more countries (140) than ever and more world records.

The Olympics this town gave when it was small, broke, unknown but brave and daring are now being given by a town that's big, rich, famous but grown timid and frightened and almost afraid to give a lousy party for itself, and the world—for which it has furnished dreams for over half a century.

The Olympics that war-torn London was able tp give on tracks made of blitz rubble, the Olympics that plucky little

Finland gave, heroic Mexico, daring Melbourne, penitential Munich, glorious Rome, gallant Montreal and mighty Moscow are finally being given by the country once known as the most hospitable on earth—and it's about time.

The Olympics no one wanted have a city festooned with flags, flowers on lamp posts, banners on buses, singing in the streets, and music in the heart, a city awash with the costumes and customs of every culture on the planet

Please see MURRAY, page 29

Old Glory Stars in a Parade

92,655 Cheer All, Roar for U.S.

By RANDY HARVEY,
Times Staff Writer

The rumble began even before the U.S. Olympic team, 589 strong, emerged from the tunnel Saturday at the west end of the Coliseum.

Zimbabwe was announced, leaving only the host country to come in the 140-nation parade of athletes at the Opening Ceremony of the XXIII Olympiad.

Then came the roar, almost drowning out "Stars and Stripes Forever."

By the time Ed Burke, 44, the U.S. flag bearer from Los Gatos, Calif., was in clear view, most of the 92,655 spectators were on their feet.

President Reagan and his wife, Nancy, watching from the press box, leaned forward for a closer look.

It was the Fourth of July, only more so. This was more spontaneous.

Caught up in the euphoria, some of the U.S. athletes literally were jumping for joy. Some were giving each other high-fives. Others were blowing kisses to the crowd.

Burke marched straight ahead, his eyes unaverted, holding the flag firmly in his right hand.

He was at the pinnacle of an athletic career that has carried him to two previous Olympics, 1964 in Tokyo and 1968 in Mexico City.

Following the 1968 Games, he retired from competitive athletics, becoming a political science professor before opening his own health clubs.

It was while watching the 1979 World Cup of track and field on television that Burke's young daughters became interested in seeing their father throw the hammer.

For old time's sake, Burke took them to a local athletic field and showed them his Olympic form. He was more surprised than they were to find he still had it.

When he walked off the field after several throws, he smiled at his wife, she smiled at him, and he was on his way back to the Olympics.

On the morning of the hammer throw competition at the U.S. track and field trials, in which Burke finished third to earn his berth on the team, his daughters gave him a musical card that played "Rocky."

Burke's story is a good one, but it is just one of 589 on the U.S. team. Boxer Henry Tillman never participated in his sport until he was sentenced to the California Youth Authority. Cyclist Nelson Vails learned his sport as a bicycle messenger in New York City. Kayaker Greg Barton is a pig farmer from Homer, Mich. Cyclist Andrew Weaver is a 4.0 student at MIT.

Shotputter Michael Carter weighs 290 pounds, gymnast Julianne McNamara 88. Basketball player Jon Koncak is 7 feet tall, gymnast Mary Lou Retton 4-9¾. Yachter Bill Buchan is 49 years old, swimmer Michelle Richardson 15.

Basketball player Patrick Ewing was born in Jamaica, marathoner Alberto Salazar in Cuba. Diver Greg Louganis was an orphan, adopted by a Greek father and a Samoan mother. And on and on.

Please see GAMES, page 29

Games of the XXIII Olympiad open Saturday with the spelling of "Welcome" in Coliseum scene of balloons, music, happy athletes. **Photo:** KEN HIVELY, Los Angeles Times

GARY FRIEDMAN / Los Angeles Times

The man of the day in 1984 Olympics Saturday is final torch-bearer Rafer Johnson, the former decathlon gold medalist, who climbed the steps of the Coliseum to light the flame.

MURRAY

Continued from page 28

and the envy of every capital on it.

The Olympics they said were going to be the Hollywood Olympics turned out to be the American Olympics. Hollywood is America, and vice versa.

The Olympics they mocked, jeered, and tried to throw out the window have showed up shining and gay and smiling, anyway.

The Olympics they said would be too hot, too smoggy, too unhealthful, too crowded, too inconvenient are a gas instead.

The Olympics they said would overcrowd the inns have suites for sale.

We're having a party; what's wrong with that? It's our turn, so grab a flag, trade a button, hoist a toast. We only get one of these things once to a lifetime, every 52 years; so we better get with it. The party-poopers will be out in force in 2036, too. Next time, they may win.

The world paraded before our doors in the Opening Ceremony, proud rows of the fittest people on this earth. Our youth. Our hope. The world's real wealth. Specimens we would all like to be, should be. Joyous in their youth, gladdened in their strength.

Who could look at an Olympic Opening Ceremony and grouse about traffic? Gripe about cost? Are an Olympics a celebration for a Scrooge, a Swiss banker, a warlord, a misanthrope, a cynic, a miser, a hermit? The Olympics are a vision. They sing to the old of what might have been, to the young of what can be. That's their promise. They make the world a family for a fortnight. They're a teacher. They show us what we ought to be, could be.

An Opening Ceremony is not the start of the Olympics, it's the culmination. It makes the Olympic statement. It's a valentine to tomorrow. Tomorrow will be all right. Tomorrow is in good hands.

RICK MEYER / Los Angeles Times

Gina Hemphill, granddaughter of the late Olympic great Jesse Owens, carries torch around the Coliseum track before handing it off to Rafer Johnson, who lit Coliseum flame.

The Olympics are the politics of joy. Or should be. The Olympics are the legacy of a gallant old Frenchman, a baron by birth but a common man by choice who wanted to bring the world brotherhood, to replace the comradery of war with the bonds of friendly competition. He kept bouncing into hard-headed councils of selfish politics, too. But his dream persevered. There are always men who believe in it, and may history salute them, too.

De Coubertin would have rejoiced Saturday, a fete to gladden a Gallic soul.

An Opening Ceremony is more than just 84 pianos or 76 trombones, more than Busby Berkeley, George M. Cohan, Irving Berlin, or even Beethoven or John Philip Sousa. It's not a show, it's not Abie's Irish Rose or Gilbert and Sullivan or even Aida. It's a rite as ancient as Greece. It's also a 10-handkerchief production, as emotional as an aria, as sentimental as a wedding cake.

The athletes are the star of this extravaganza. They're the plot, the lyrics, the marquee value, the lump in the throat. No playwright, librettist could hoke up the moment when 92,655 throats roared salute to countries that have been our enemy too long, like China, and countries that are our friends in the camp of the enemy, like Romania, which defied the disapproval of the masters of the Kremlin to march here, and the Yugoslavs, who march to their own drummer, too. An Olympic parade is a lesson not only in geography but history.

So, welcome, world and especially China, Romania and our pals the Yugos. Let the Games begin, the revels start. Let our world play together for a change. If it's costly, wrong, difficult—well, so was the Boston Tea Party.

GAMES

Continued from page 28

They were never more unified, or appreciated, than on Saturday, when, dressed in red, white and blue Levi's uniforms, they marched into the stadium as America's Team.

Then, it was the President's turn. For security reasons, he gave his proclamation from the press box. But the crowd could view the President on the giant screen at the east end of the Coliseum.

Perhaps looking ahead to the election, he asked for more than 16 words. But the IOC, no doubt like some of the directors Reagan once worked for in Hollywood, told him to stick to the script.

But he could not resist the temptation to ad-lib. Instead of the traditional "I declare open the Olympic Games of 1984 celebrating the twenty-third Olympiad of the modern era," he turned it around and said, "Celebrating the twenty-third Olympiad of the modern era, I declare open the Olympic Games of Los Angeles."

Reagan was able to speak as long as he desired in an appearance before the U.S. team Saturday morning at the USC village. Recalling his former movie role as Notre Dame football legend George Gipp, the President exhorted the athletes to "do it for the Gipper."

Following Reagan's proclamation, nine former U.S. Olympic medalists were among the 11 persons who carried the Olympic flag into the Coliseum.

The medalists were decathlete Bruce Jenner, sprinter Wyomia Tyus, shotputter Parry O'Brien, discus thrower Al Oerter, swimmer John Naber, diver Sammy Lee, 200-meter runner Mack Robinson, 10,000-meter runner Billy Mills and diver Patricia McCormick, whose daughter, Kelly, is a member of the 1984 U.S. team as a diver.

The two non-medalists who carried the Olympic flag were Richard Sandoval, a boxer on the 1980 U.S. team that did not participate in the Games because of the boycott, and Bill Thorpe Jr., grandson of Jim Thorpe.

Besides the inclusion of Sandoval among the group that presented the flag, there was one other prominent reminder of the 1980 boycott.

Anita DeFrantz, a 1976 bronze medalist in rowing who, on behalf of the athletes, sued the USOC over its decision not to attend the Moscow Games, was the last person to carry the torch Saturday before it entered the Coliseum.

Moments later, the suspense over the identity of the final torch-bearers ended when Gina Hemphill, granddaughter of Jesse Owens, emerged from the tunnel at the west end of the Coliseum with the torch, ran one lap around the track and delivered it to Rafer Johnson.

Now there is a story. Johnson, who won the decathlon gold medal at the 1960 Rome Olympics, moved when he was 11 from Hillsboro, Tex., to Kingsburg, Calif., where he and his family lived in a boxcar until times got better.

Impressed with Johnson's athletic potential, his high school track coach took him to Tulare, 25 miles away, to see Bob Mathias train. Mathias is the only two-time winner of the Olympic decathlon. Inspired, Johnson became a decathlete and won the gold medal at the 1960 Olympics in Rome.

Twenty-four years later, Johnson was honored with the most meaningful duty of the Opening Ceremony.

As a silver staircase rose out of the east end of the Coliseum, Johnson ascended with the torch to light the flame that will continue to glow until the Closing Ceremony 15 days from now.

Thus ended a torch run that began 82 days ago in New York City and evoked charges from the Greeks, the keepers of the eternal flame, that the Los Angeles Olympic Organizing Committee was guilty of crass commercialism. Those who carried the torch during the trek across the United States each paid $3,000, the proceeds going to charity.

But on Saturday, LAOOC President Peter V. Ueberroth was King for a Day. International Olympic Committee President Juan Antonio Samaranch's remarks were interrupted for several seconds by applause after he paid gratitude to Ueberroth.

Samaranch, who is from Spain, ended his portion of the program by saying: "God Bless America."

Most of the speeches were brief.

U.S. 400-meter intermediate hurdler Edwin Moses, the son of a high school principal from Dayton, Ohio, and an outspoken advocate of athletes' rights, was chosen by the Unite States Olympic Committee and the LAOOC to read the Athletes' Oath for the 7,800 competitors.

Moses, 28, won a gold medal in the 1976 Montreal Olympics and has lost only one race since.

He said: "In the name of all the competitors, I promise that we shall take part in these Olympic Games, respecting and abiding by the rules which govern them, in the true spirit of sportsmanship, for the glory of the sport and for the honor of our teams."

He twice repeated "in the true spirit of sportsmanship," presumably because the teleprompter he was reading from malfunctioned.

The oath for officials and judges was read by U.S. gymnastics judge Sharon Weber of the United States. She said: "In the name of all judges and officials, I promise that we shall officiate in the Olympic Games with complete impartiality, respecting and abiding by the rules which govern them in the true spirit of sportsmanship."

The Opening Ceremony began with a show that could only have been produced by Hollywood, costing $5 million and featuring a cast of thousands, 12,000 to be exact, 2,500 pigeons, 1,065 balloons and 84 baby grand pianos. They were used for a performance of George Gershwin's "Rhapsody in Blue."

There also was music from George M. Cohan, Irving Berlin, Duke Ellington, Glenn Miller, Count Basie, Leonard Bernstein, Stephen Sondheim, Marvin Hamlisch and, of course, Michael Jackson.

Producer David Wolper said he wanted the Opening Ceremony to be "majestic and inspirational,

KEN HIVELY / Los Angeles Times

Rafer Johnson is a tiny figure on top of the ladder, setting afire the flame that will burn in the Coliseum for the '84 Olympics.

evocative and emotional."

They were all of that, especially during the parade of athletes.

As the home of the ancient Olympics and the first site of the Modern Olympics in 1896, Greece led the nations into the Coliseum.

Except for the United States, which—as the host country—marched into the Coliseum last, the other countries followed in alphabetical order.

There were an Olympic-record 140 nations represented, Libya having withdrawn on the eve of the Games because of the IOC's refusal to accredit three journalists from the country.

Nineteen other countries stayed away, 15 in sympathy with the Soviet Union's decision not to attend. The United States led a 60-nation boycott of the 1980 Summer Games at Moscow.

Romania is the only Soviet Bloc nation that accepted an invitation to the 1984 Summer Games, a point that was not lost on the crowd as the 129-member Romanian delegation received a louder ovation than any of the other foreign athletes.

Not far behind on the applause meter were athletes from two other Communist countries, Yugoslavia and the People's Republic of China. Others greeted with noticeably favorable crowd reaction were Canada, the Federal Republic of Germany, Great Britain, Ireland, Israel, Italy, Mexico, Puerto Rico, Sweden and Switzerland.

Many of the athletes dressed in traditional costumes of their countries, the Australians in bush hats, the Indians in red turbans, the Bahrainians in the robes and headdress of sheiks. The Swiss were the most colorful, their athletes dressed in either red, green, black or yellow blouses.

Athletes from several countries broke rank to pose with show business personalities Brooke Shields, Kirk Douglas and Linda Evans, who were watching from the second row of the Coliseum.

As they reached their appointed places on the field, dyed green for this occasion, the Brazilians took pictures among themselves. The Israelis and Italians took pictures of each other. Before they were through, the Opening Ceremony had turned into a giant love-in.

At the end, while Nick Ashford and Valerie Simpson sang "Reach Out and Touch Somebody's Hand," athletes from all the nations joined hands and swayed to the music. The crowd of 92,655 did the same.

Only minutes before, they had all heard Ueberroth say: "Through sport, we can take an important step toward peace and understanding."

Opening: Fun and Emotion

L.A. Start More Enjoyable Than Moscow Precision

By BILL SHIRLEY,
Times Staff Writer

The temptation is to say, if you've seen one you've seen them all. After a while, ceremonies opening Olympic Games do start to look alike.

Still, it's hard to knock one. They all have memorable moments along with the corn and schlock. It's sort of like listening to Beethoven's 5th Symphony. No matter how many times you hear it, it still sounds pretty good.

The little 200-minute, $5-million show staged in the Coliseum on Saturday evening was not much different than the ones held in Montreal, Lake Placid and Moscow. It was corny, dazzling, spectacular, stirring and emotional. It was part Hollywood, part Las Vegas. In places it looked like an MGM or Warner Brothers musical. It was also pure Americana. And the 92,655 spectators present loved it.

Thousands waved American flags and cheered loudly for the nations who defied the Kremlin and came to Los Angeles' party. The Romanians wouldn't have been more popular in Bucharest.

Give David L. Wolper's production four stars, which gets it a tie with Montreal's Opening Ceremony in 1976. But it was not as good as Moscow's five-star production in 1980. Still, it was a lot more fun to watch.

The "explicitly American" (Wolper's words) show was livelier than the Soviets' militaristic precision and gymnastic stunts. Wolper's just wasn't choreographed as well. But then Wolper didn't have help from the Bolshoi ballet and the Red Army and all those rubles from the Kremlin.

Moscow used music from Shostakovich and Tchaikovsky; Wolper had Aaron Copeland, John Williams, George Gershwin, Irving Berlin, Duke Ellington and Leonard Bernstein. No contest; score one for Wolper. Everybody uses Beethoven; his "Ode to Joy" from his 9th Symphony shows up at every Olympics. Also, Wolper used live music; the Soviets took no chances and put theirs on tape.

The United States finally caught up with the rest of the world and sent its President to open the Games. While kings and queens, presidents and premiers, opened the Olympic Games in other nations, the United States sent its vice presidents—Charles Curtis to L. A. in 1932, Richard M. Nixon to Squaw Valley in 1960 and Walter F. Mondale to Lake Placid in 1980.

However, President Ronald Reagan delivered his 16-word address virtually hidden from most of the crowd from a booth in the press box, much as President Leonid I. Brezhnev did in Moscow. At Montreal, Queen Elizabeth II of Great Britain stood for more than an hour in the Royal Box to salute the athletes as they marched into Stade Olympique. She was dressed regally in pink from head to toe.

International Olympic Committee rules have given Opening Ceremonies everywhere a similar look. Athletes march into stadiums either precisely, as Japan did Saturday, or sloppily, as did most of the other nations. Someone takes the oath for the athletes, some politican or head of state officially opens the Games and the Olympic torch is lit. Only their production numbers and the manner in which they light the torch separate one from another.

At Montreal, the Canadians added a nice touch to the traditional torch ceremony when they had two teen-agers, a boy and a girl, carry the flame into the stadium and light the torch. As they circled the track, the girl rested her hand on the boy's arm.

At Moscow, basketball star Sergei Belov raced spectacularly to the top of Lenin Stadium on a platform laid on the backs of some of the 3,500 Red Army soldiers who made up the card-stunt section to do the honor. L.A.'s trick of raising stairs in the Coliseum's peristyle tower for Rafer Johnson to climb to send the flame shooting through the five circles of the Olympic symbol was almost as good.

The Opening Ceremony is held to introduce the athletes, not showcase singers, dancers or even Presidents. L.A.'s did that as well as anybody's. In fact, the athletes seemed to be having so much fun it appeared at the end they didn't want to leave. They danced in the infield and took pictures and cheered each other.

It was such a good show, it was easy to forget that something after all was not right about it. Some major teams were not there. The Romanians and Yugoslavians were welcomed noisily. The Soviets, East Germans, Poles, Bulgarians, Cubans, and Hungarians probably would have been, too, had they not stayed home.

This was the third straight Opening Ceremony that had gaping holes in the traditional March of the Athletes, although a record 140 nations marched in Saturday's parade. At Montreal, nobody knew how many countries would march; reporters had to keep score—as they did at Moscow. As the nations marched at Montreal, 600 African athletes packed their bags at the nearby Olympic Village.

They were going home. The boycott had become an Olympic event.

Only 3,700 athletes from 81 nations marched before 103,000 spectators at Moscow half a year after Soviet troops invaded Afghanistan. The United States wasn't there; neither were Japan, West Germany, China and about 40 other countries. Ten nations did not allow their athletes to march and six others marched but carried no national flags.

When athletes march to stirring music behind flags of their nations as they did Saturday, the intrusion of politics and other problems affecting the Olympic Games today is easily forgotten. Pageantry and pride, youthful enthusiasm and stirring music have a way of erasing acrimony.

But as the troubled history of the Olympic Games has shown, it is only a temporary interruption.

Mike Littwin

Ceremony Is Much More Than a Show

We saw America at its best at the Coliseum Saturday afternoon. The America we all believe in. The America we're so proud of. The America we love.

The Opening Ceremonies were guaranteed to produced several large lumps in the throats of anyone breathing. No one who saw it will soon forget the reception given the U.S. team, Ed Burke proudly carrying the flag with one strong arm. Or Gina Hemphill, the grand-daughter of Jesse Owens—the man who helped teach America that a black man can be a hero—carrying the Olympic torch around the Coliseum track. Or Rafer Johnson, 24 years ago the Olympic-champion decathlete, who as a child once lived in a boxcar in the San Joaquin Valley, lighting the Olympic flame.

The show was vintage Hollywood, an old-fashioned, flag-waving musical tribute to America as we want it to be. In one part of the show, there was an old-west town, straight from a studio backlot, constructed on the Coliseum floor, recalling pioneer days, invoking the American spirit that made this country great.

It was an enjoyable afternoon, a moving afternoon, a cry for international peace as athletes from around the world joined in hand and in spirit. It almost made you believe that peace could be achieved as easily as the releasing of so many pigeons.

Just as the Olympic spirit has been torn by consecutive boycotts, however—first America's, then the Soviet Union's—the American spirit may also be in need of some repair.

In the Munich Olympics 12 years ago, 11 Israelis were murdered and the world was shocked by the senseless carnage.

In Westwood on the night before the Opening Ceremonies, a man drove his car onto a crowded sidewalk, killing one person and wounding scores.

In San Ysidro only days earlier, a man, after telling his wife he was going out to hunt humans, massacred 21 men, women and children, using a pistol, a rifle and a semi-automatic weapon.

□

I wonder what our thousands of foreign visitors must think of this country where such random violence is all too common.

Those acts were the work of madmen, isolated incidents, we tell them. They don't represent America, we tell them.

Of course they don't represent America. But what of the story of Paul Gonzales, an Olympic boxer out of Aliso Village in East Los Angeles, 10 minutes from downtown? In a recent interview, He recalled that as a youngster he was involved in a gang fight in which somebody might have been killed; he couldn't be sure. He told of young people in the barrio, young people not yet teen-agers, who carry guns and knives.

Which is the real America?

We are the richest, the freest, the most powerful and arguably the best country in the world. But in the swell of patriotism that swept the Coliseum and the nation Saturday, we should remember, too, the other America.

Some of our best athletes have seen firsthand the underside of this great land. Some of our best athletes have escaped the drug-filled, crime-ridden ghettos where survival is considered success.

□

Often, we hear these Olympic athletes called our nation's best hope. They persevered, they overcame, they proved the value of hard work, they proved that anyone in America can climb to the top.

I was touched by the sight of Jesse Owens' granddaughter carrying the torch, glad that he was remembered. But I have read that Jesse Owens once had to race horses to put food on his table.

I was touched by Rafer Johnson. My memory of the great athlete is not of him on the athletic field, however, but at the Ambassador Hotel alongside Robert Kennedy on the night the presidential candidate was assassinated.

President Reagan said in an interview after the ceremonies that if international problems were given to the young people on the Coliseum floor, the problems would be solved by the next day. Reagan, who was once shot by a would-be assassin, spoke those words from behind a bullet-proof window high above the Coliseum floor.

Watching the ceremonies, it is easy to get caught up in them, in their splendor, in their breathless patriotism. I recall my own good fortune—living in a land where I can earn an excellent living, where I can vote and speak freely, where I can write this column without fear, saying that America, while often great, is not perfect.

I have a 10-year-old daughter who lives in comfort and safety, whose room is lined with cuddly stuffed animals, who has Michael Jackson's latest album and a stereo to play it on, who has never faced any danger greater than crossing the street or taking a math test.

She watched the Olympic celebration at home on television, along with hundreds of millions around the world, and believed with all her young heart that what she saw is America.

I want to believe it, too.

Associated Press

Hammer thrower Ed Burke, at 44 the old man of the U.S. track and field team, carried the American Flag into the Coliseum Saturday—with one arm—leading in his teammates.

Critic's View / Dan Sullivan

Hollywood Just Showing Off a Bit

Open-air extravaganzas on the scale of the one Saturday at the Coliseum are not really in the American tradition. Circus parades and flashy half-time ceremonies in October—these we can relate to. But three hours of marching bands, balloons, bells, flags, young women parading synchronously in gym suits, doves of peace, pledges of allegiance and sacred torches feel vaguely totalitarian to us.

Therefore a layer or three of Hollywood glitz isn't at all out of place when such a spectacle is mounted in America, especially in the city that so many people take for Hollywood.

It would have been positively disappointing if David L. Wolper's opening ceremonies for the 1984 Olympics hadn't included 84 pianists in blue suits playing, (or, playing at playing) "Rhapsody in Blue." Or if John Williams hadn't conducted an original "Olympics Theme" that sounded just like every other John Williams theme. Or if Ray Agayhan's bandsmen costumes hadn't suggested that little Shirley Temple was just about to tap dance through the Coliseum arches, saluting.

These touches were Hollywood's way of showing the flag, so to speak. If Moscow in 1980 could present a field full of dancing bears (pure Disneyland), why couldn't Los Angeles salute the hardy pioneers who won the west for MGM? Who invented tinsel anyway?

The kitsch was so well kept in bounds that one was inclined to think of it, rather, as wit. As theater, this show didn't forget that its reason for being was to celebrate, not show-biz, but a gathering of nations. It was particularly pleasing, sitting in the Coliseum, to see that the entering parade of athletes hadn't been chopped and channeled for television. Here they all were, from Greece to Zimbabwe, for as long as it took them to march around the track.

If the marching bands had looked best in longshot, and if the Fred and Ginger routine had looked best on the Coliseum's enormous TV screen, here you were glad you had binoculars to train on the individual faces—on the woman athlete from Kenya displaying a yellow toy lion, for instance, doubtless in violation of the dress code. A show so smartly routined needs a little eccentricity.

Live theater is participation. It was intriguing (because none of us knew what was coming) to hold up one's plastic color-coded card and find one's self in the middle of a national flag—a whole garden of flags instantly blooming up and down the stadium and then disappearing at the count of ten.

TV could catch that. What it couldn't convey was the shock of joy that ran around the Coliseum—tingle is too mild a word for it—when the U.S. team ran out of the tunnel, in their controversial sweatsuits, to "The Stars And Stripes Forever."

Whether one calls this emotion jingoism, patriotism or team spirit, it has the kick of a double bourbon on an empty stomach. If the Olympics were devised to elevate us beyond this sort of primal nationalism, I am afraid they don't.

Another blast was Rafer Johnson's spectacular ladder-climb to light the Olympic torch, via the five-ring Olympic logo, one of the show's best uses of state-of-the-art technology. (The state-of-the-art in stadium acoustics is not very high.) The music here was a new piece by Philip Glass that could well become a part of all future Olympic games, a simple theme that somehow kept expanding beyond its notes, like a post-modern "Bolero."

The reach-out-and-touch-your-neighbor number and the cascade of fireworks also pushed the right buttons—a good release for the crowd at the end of a long sit.

RICK MEYER / Los Angeles Times

A dazzling show of balloons, ribbons and performers in colorful costumes was all part of the Opening Ceremony of the Games of the XXIII Olympiad at the Coliseum Saturday.

TV / Howard Rosenberg

This Hollywood Production Was Not Made for TV

I sat down in front of my TV set wearing my official Olympics T-shirt and my official Olympics cap, drinking coffee from my official Olympics mug.

What a way to watch Saturday's opening ceremonies for the 1984 Summer Games. No traffic. No smog. No heat. No noise. No crowds to fight at the Los Angeles Memorial Coliseum.

No fun.

Not much in the beginning, anyway. The joys of watching at home included hearing my wife and daughter bicker about the volume on the set, hearing the phone ring half a dozen times and hearing the commercials on ABC and the promos for its new Fall shows.

The commercials should have had "bumpers" to separate them from the televised ceremonies. Going directly from 8,000 joyous athletes on the floor of the Coliseum—snap!—to an electrifying promo for "Paper Dolls" was to sharp a curve to maneuver.

Beyond that, you have the limits of the TV screen itself, which is too small for spectacles. TV shows us an event in sections, only what the director wants us to see. It mutes the impact.

David Wolper's production for the Los Angeles Olympic Organizing Committee was an extraordinarily ambitious undertaking that must have blown away the Coliseum crowd. But much of that was lost on on TV. It was like seeing the world through the wrong end of a telescope.

On TV, those 84 pianos sounded like two.

And it didn't help that ABC's Peter Jennings and especially Jim McKay—he was getting to be Jim McPain—blabbed on and on through some of the most exciting material.

"When the Saints Come Marchin In:" Singing by Etta James. Talking by Jim McKay and Peter Jennings. During that number, for example, McKay said, "Soon, will appear 84 grand pianos." And Jennings said, "Here they are." And McKay said, "An actual gasp from the crowd." And I said to myself, "Will someone please tape their mouths."

But. . . .

The card display of national flags, some of the photography and those soaring pigeons—whose freedom flight was captured so perfectly by director Terry Jastrow's cameras—were exhilarating even on the small screen.

When it comes to Opening Ceremonies for any Summer Olympics, however, the athletes' parade of nations is in a universe all its own. And it was glorious Saturday, perhaps the truest expression of internationalism and the continuity of the Games.

This *was* the time to talk, and Jennings, the ABC News anchorman and former foreign correspondent, added a rare dimension and was the perfect complement to McKay's sports talk. You just don't expect to hear political analysis amid such an emotional crescendo. There was the Chilean team, for example.

McKay: "They have a good soccer team."

Jennings: "They are waiting in Chile, of course, for democracy."

Not only that, but Jennings may have been the only person covering the Games who knew that prices had gone up in Nepal.

The arrival of the Unites States team—captured from the front by a ground-level camera—was a lump-in-the-throat high, transforming ABC's stumbling start and some technical problems into a distant memory. The euphoric reception in the Coliseum was "deafening," Jennings said.

Well, if you couldn't hear the "deafening," you could feel the emotion, and feel it and feel it, and the swelling suspense accompanying the Olympic torch's final journey.

The carrying of the torch by Jesse Owens granddaughter and then former gold medalist Rafer Johnson—the identities of the final torch bearers were not known beforehand—was one of TV's greatest moments, when the small screen seemed to expand ten-fold and become 3-D.

Bravo for ABC's sense of history and for its decision to stay with the event a few minutes longer than its scheduled three and a half hours, enabling it to capture the spontaneous dancing by athletes in the center of the Coliseum.

This display of athletic solidarity won't change the world, which will be as messed up after these Games as it was when they began. But it was a wonderful sight to watch.

This a city that has spawned many big TV shows, yet never one as special and emotional as this. To light the Olympic flame, Rafer Johnson had to climb a flight of steps so steep that you wondered how he could do it without falling. "How will he get down?" my wife asked. "He'll do it somehow," I replied.

After all, this is Hollywood.

THEY CARRIED THE OLYMPIC TORCH

1936—Fritz Schilgen (Germany)
1948—John Mark (Britain)
1952—Paavo Nurmi (Finland)
1956—Ron Clarke (Australia)
1960—Giancarlo Peris (Italy)
1964—Yoshinori Sakai (Japan)
1968—Enriquetta Basilio (Mexico)
1972—Gunter Zahn (West Germany)
1976—Sandra Henderson-Stephen Prefontaine (Canada)
1980—Sergei Belov (USSR)
1984—Rafer Johnson (United States)

NOTE: Torch relay from Olympia, Greece instituted in 1936.

American athletes enter the Coliseum Saturday during opening ceremonies of the XXIII Olympiad.

JAYNE KAMIN / Los Angeles Times

JOSE GALVEZ / Los Angeles Times

American team members.

The Grand Entrance

The Canadian team.

Athletes from Ghana in formal gowns.

Los Angeles Times

ANACLETO RAPPING / Los Angeles Times

New Zealand team members.

ANACLETO RAPPING / Los Angeles Times

New Zealand archer Neroli Fairhall.

The Chinese delegation.

Los Angeles Times

JOSE GALVEZ / Los Angeles Times

Kenyan woman and friend.

American hammerthrower Ed Burke.

JOSE GALVEZ / Los Angeles Times

TONY BARNARD / Los Angeles Times

DAY 3 OLYMPICS '84

CON KEYES / Los Angeles Times

Steve Lundquist, after breaking John Moffet's world record in the 100-meter breaststroke, reaches down to console Moffet, who swam the final injured.

Lundquist Takes the Record Away From Moffet

By SEYMOUR BEUBIS, *Times Staff Writer*

Outside of a few James Bond movies, about the most exciting water chases in recent years have involved breaststrokers Steve Lundquist and John Moffet.

A classic duel between the two was anticipated Sunday at the Olympic Games.

But it never really materialized.

While setting an Olympic record and posting the fastest time in the qualifying heats for the 100-meter breaststroke (1:02.16, just slightly over his world record of 1:02.13), Moffet, 20, of Costa Mesa and Stanford University, reinjured the inner thigh muscle on his right leg.

"Before we went out to swim the final, John and I shook hands," Lundquist said. "He told me that if something went haywire with his leg . . . to win the gold for the U.S."

That's exactly what Lundquist, 23, of Jonesboro, Ga., did.

The man they call Lunk, one of the free spirits of swimming, exploded off the blocks like a rocket. He

■ West Germany's Michael Gross wins the 200-meter freestyle event in world-record time of 1:47.44.

wanted the world record he had lost to Moffet in the Olympic trials at Indianapolis, and he got it—becoming the first man in history to break 1:02. His time was a blazing 1:01.65.

Lundquist needed just that type of a performance to hold off Victor Davis, 20, of Canada, the world record-holder in the 200-meter breaststroke who also went under the old world record in the 100 breaststroke with a time of 1:01.99. Peter Evans of Australia took the bronze in 1:02.97. Moffet gave it the old college try but could finish no better than fifth with a 1:03.29.

In the preliminaries, Lundquist qualified fifth but said he really didn't push himself. "I wanted to save something for the finals."

Lundquist, who fought through the disappointment of not being able to swim in the 1980 Olympic Games because of the U.S. boycott, said "I feel like the Grinch that stole Christmas. My heart's so big right now. I couldn't be happier."

"I can't express the feeling in words. I wanted this so much. I set my goals to make the Olympic team and to win a gold medal, and reaching both with a world record, it's great."

Davis was disappointed with his second-place finish. "I came here to win two gold medals. I wanted to swim a 1:01.9, and I did, but Steve was better. He got away. I had him. I had him. I had him."

Moffet, speaking barely above a whisper, said that "to say I am terribly disappointed would be an understatement. I'm pretty numb."

He said that he reinjured the thigh he had hurt two weeks earlier in training camp on the second 50 meters of his preliminary race.

Please see LUNDQUIST, page 33

U.S. Women Get 2 Golds in One Event

Steinseifer and Hogshead Share a Historic Moment

By JOHN WEYLER, *Times Staff Writer*

Nancy Hogshead and Carrie Steinseifer spent Sunday morning together in their room at the Olympic Village, lying on their beds watching a Three Stooges movie. A few hours later, they were together again, but this time they were standing and sharing the highest level of the victory stand before a crowd of 10,690 at the Olympic pool.

Together, they had combined to get the United States off to its fastest start ever in Olympic swimming competition.

After the first race of the 1984 Games, the United States already had *two* gold medals.

Veteran Hogshead, 22, and newcomer Steinseifer, 16, tied in the 100-meter freestyle as both caught and then passed the Netherlands' Annemarie Verstappen before hitting the wall simultaneously in 55.92 seconds. Verstappen, who finished in 56.08, got the bronze.

It was the first time in Olympic history that two gold medals were awarded in the same swimming event.

In the 1972 Olympics at Munich, Sweden's Gunnar Larsson and the United States' Tim McKee tied in the 400-meter individual medley. The Swiss Timing device connected to the touch pads on the wall at the finish does record 1,000ths of a second, and based on that time, Larsson was awarded the gold and McKee the silver.

The decision was upheld, but the International Olympic Committee later decided that 1,000th of a second was actually no difference at all, especially considering that a dimple in the plaster on the wall could account for that much of a time difference.

In 1956, before electric touch pads were used, Judith Grinham of Great Britain and Carin Cone of the United States had the same time in the women's 100-meter backstroke, and Grinham was judged the winner.

Steinseifer probably hit the wall first because the computer-operated scoreboard listed her as No. 1 and Hogshead as No. 2. IOC officials said the results (carried out to 1,000ths of a second) would not be disclosed, though. The official tape will be turned over to FINA (the international ruling body of swimming) and will never be made public, they said.

Without paying attention to the times, Steinseifer began to celebrate. She threw her arms in the air and hung on to the lane line, waving to the crowd. Then Hogshead swam over, and the two embraced.

Please see SWIMMING, page 33

Grewal's Journey Was Uphill, but He Pedaled Home a Gold for U.S.

By DAVE DISTEL, *Times Staff Writer*

Alexi Grewal's front wheel wobbled, his body seemed drained from exhaustion, and it looked as though that uphill on Vista del Lago would be the end of this cyclist's troubled Olympic dream.

But the controversial Grewal, from Aspen, Colo., pulled himself together and beat Canadian Steve Bauer by one length and less than a second to give the United States a sweep of Sunday's road racing gold medals at Mission Viejo.

Grewal, 23, covered the 120 miles in 4 hours 59 minutes 57.9 seconds.

The men did not quite match the 1-2 finish of Connie Carpenter-Phinney and Rebecca Twigg in the morning, but the United States certainly did itself proud for a country that had not won a road racing medal since 1912.

Behind Grewal's gold, Bauer's silver and Norwegian Dag Otto Lauritzen's bronze, the U.S. took fifth, sixth and ninth. Davis Phinney, hoping to join his wife on the victory stand, finished fifth. Thurlow Rogers was sixth, and Ron Kiefel was ninth.

But this race—a journey through oppressive heat but buoying cheers—belonged to Grewal and Bauer from the time Grewal figuratively hit the wall on Vista del Lago on the 12th and last lap.

Bauer, the Canadian national champion for the last two years, quickly erased a 24-second lead that Grewal held after 11 laps.

"I saw Steve coming," Grewal said, "and I knew I couldn't stay out in front alone. I was dying. It was a matter of survival."

It had been a seven-man race from the eighth lap. There were Grewal, Phinney and Rogers, the Americans; Lauritzen and Morten Saether of Norway, and Bauer and Colombia's Nestor Mora, both flying solo.

Grewal broke two-thirds of the way through the 11th lap, and Bauer broke away shortly after the bell rang for the last lap.

"A lot of other guys stopped for bottles (of water)," Bauer said, "but I kept going."

And it appeared that Bauer would be fresher once he caught Grewal.

"My teammates," he said, "were very instrumental in keeping me fresh."

Through the early stages of the race, Bauer's Canadian teammates, Alain Masson and Pierre Harvey, covered the breakaways and forced the pace. Bauer sat back in the pack and did not emerge as a contender until the eighth lap.

Meanwhile, Grewal, more often than not, was the American forcing the pace.

When he made his run through the last part of the 11th lap into the uphill at Vista del Lago, it appeared that he would not have anything left.

But he obviously is not a man who surrenders easily. Indeed, he only "made" the Olympic team last Monday when an appeals jury overturned a ruling that a banned substance in a recent urine test was sufficient to disqualify him.

"That," Grewal said, "was a long

Please see GREWAL, page 34

JAYNE KAMIN / Los Angeles Times

U.S. cycling gold medalist Connie Carpenter-Phinney is flanked by silver medalist Rebecca Twigg (left) and West German bronze medalist Sandra Schumacher.

Carpenter Wins Gold, Twigg the Silver in Cycling

By SHAV GLICK, *Times Staff Writer*

All Connie Carpenter-Phinney and Rebecca Twigg wanted was for the two of them to be in the lead pack for the final sprint.

That's right where they were, and when the historic first Olympic women's cycling road race ended Sunday, the veteran Carpenter-Phinney and the youthful Twigg were together, less than half a wheel-length apart, after racing 49 miles under a blazing sun in Mission Viejo.

When they flashed across the finish line, Carpenter-Phinney with the gold medal and Twigg with the silver, the two once-bitter rivals reached up and clasped hands—dissolving their old animosity in a sea of Stars and Stripes.

The estimated 200,000 fans—at least those of whom were clustered on the hills and sidewalks around the finish line at O'Neill Road and Marguerite Parkway—let loose a roaring cheer that was probably heard all around the 9.85-mile course, and maybe even all the way back to the gold medalist's home in Boulder, Colo.

It was a historic moment—not only for the women who were making their cycling debut in the Olympics, but also for American cycling. Carpenter-Phinney, whose husband, Davis Phinney, finished fifth in the men's race later in the day, became the first American medal winner in cycling since 1912. And in another moment of history of sorts, it was her first ride as Connie Carpenter-Phinney after being married 10 months.

Sandra Schumacher, 17, from Stuttgart, West Germany, was third, followed by surprising Unni Larsen of Norway and Maria Canins, 36, of Italy. Those five, along with Jeannie Longo of France, had broken away from the rest of the 45 starters midway through the 2-hour 11-minute 14-second race and turned the event into a six-rider showdown.

For the last 25 miles, first one and then another would make a false break, jumping into a short lead only to settle back in position when caught by the others. It wasn't until the final 500 yards when Canins, better known as a climber than a sprinter,

Please see CARPENTER, page 33

Associated Press

Carrie Steinseifer (left) and Nancy Hogshead share the top rung on the victory stand—and tears of joy—after they tied for first in the 100 freestyle.

MARK BOSTER / Los Angeles Times

Jubilant road-race winner Connie Carpenter-Phinney (left) hugs runner-up Rebecca Twigg as they cross the finish line Sunday.

SWIMMING

Continued from page 32

"That's when Nancy told me we tied," Steinseifer, a junior at Saratoga (Calif.) High School, said. "I knew we were close, but not *that* close."

Hogshead: "She was hooting and hollering, and then I told her we tied, so we cheered together."

After the announcement of the tie, the already wildly cheering crowd broke into a rousing ovation that lasted until both swimmers had left the pool. They broke into a chant of "USA . . . USA . . . USA" as IOC President Juan Antonio Samaranch placed the medals around the two Americans' necks.

Hogshead, a member of the 1980 Olympic team who quit swimming for almost two years before returning to the pool in 1983, and Steinseifer, who burst on the national scene when she won the gold medal in the 100-meter freestyle during the Pan Am Games last year, have become close friends in the past year.

How did they feel about the tie?

"Great," Steinseifer said.

"Ditto," Hogshead said. "This is better than winning the gold alone. It's the neatest experience of my life."

They met last winter in a national team training camp in Hawaii and have been close ever since, despite the age difference. They even shared a two-level bunk in their room at the Olympic Village.

"She (Hogshead) had the top bunk, and she's been stepping on me all week," Steinseifer said, laughing.

For about 90 meters Sunday, it looked like the two U.S. women would be sharing the lower levels of the victory stand. Verstappen turned first, with Hogshead close behind and Steinseifer third. Hogshead, who took a year off from her pre-law studies at Duke University to train in Concord, Calif., caught Verstappen with about 20 meters to go, and then Steinseifer surged and came over with an excellent touch.

CON KEYES / Los Angeles Times

Nancy Hogshead (left) embraces Carrie Steinseifer as each wins gold medal in 100 freestyle.

Hogshead had a preliminary time of 55.85. Hogshead's and Steinseifer's 55.92 in the final was well off East German Barbara Krause's world record of 54.79, set in the 1980 Olympics at Moscow, but that didn't dim the glitter of the gold on this day.

"We were lying there watching TV, and Carrie looked over to me and said, 'Nancy, let's go 1-2 today,' " Hogshead said. "I said, 'All right.' "

She paused and smiled. "Instead, we went 1-1."

Swimming Notes

The fastest American in the Olympic 100-meter freestyle swims the freestyle leg for the U.S. 400-meter medley relay team (the women's event is scheduled Friday). Since **Nancy Hogshead** and **Carrie Steinseifer** tied in the 100 Sunday and both will compete in Tuesday's 400-meter freestyle relay, the one who turns in the fastest leg Tuesday will represent the United States in the medley relay and very likely take home another gold medal. "What we'll have is a swim-off for a gold medal in front of 18,000 people," Olympic Coach **Don Gambril** said. "It should be exciting." Gambril may be overestimating the crowd, if not the the drama. Only 10,690 paying spectators were on hand Sunday (12,500 tickets were available). A total of about 14,000, including press and athletes, were in attendance.

CARPENTER

Continued from page 32

decided to go for broke. As quickly as if it had been choreographed, a line—Schumacher, Twigg, Carpenter-Phinney and Larsen—formed on her rear wheel.

When Longo, a former world champion, tried to move with them, her chain broke loose, and in the brief moments it took to engage it, her Olympic medal hopes were dashed. She finished a distant sixth.

Canins was overtaken by Schumacher with 200 yards to, with Twigg and Carpenter-Phinney launching an all-out attack. As the three reached the short incline 80 yards from the finish line, Twigg was on one side of Schumacher and Carpenter-Phinney on the other.

Twigg caught Schumacher and in turn was overhauled by Carpenter-Phinney, whose margin may have come from a tactic taught her by her husband.

"In races as close as this, and most of the ones Rebecca and I ride are that close, the difference can be inches," said Carpenter-Phinney. "Davis taught me how to 'throw my bike' at the finish line. I don't know how much it helps, maybe a foot or two, but sometimes that's the difference."

Twigg, who came out of Seattle a few years ago as a precocious teen-ager to challenge Carpenter-Phinney's dominance as the Grand Dame of American women riders, made the day's only solo break. On the third lap, when the women were being handed food and water bottles, Twigg, in a characterisitic tactic, jumped the field as the riders headed up the 12.5% grade on Vista del Lago—the one the women called Suicide Hill. Her widest margin was 15 seconds, but when they reached the long, punishing uphill grind on La Paz Road, Canins reeled her in.

"As long as Maria (Canins) was with the lead pack, no one was going to make a solo break," analyzed Carpenter-Phinney. "She is so strong she goes out and gets you. Having her with us (the six leaders) set the race up for Rebecca and myself. She pushed the pace, and when we looked around at who was with us, we were pretty sure it would finish the way it did."

The other two American riders, who did not figure to be in the lead pack in the final few miles, finished as expected. Both Janelle Parks, of Dayton, Ohio, and Inge Thompson, of Reno, finished with the main pack. Park was 10th, and Thompson, who never rode in a bicycle race before last March, was 21st.

Twigg seemed pleased with the American 1-2 finish, even if she was the one with the silver.

"My initial thought (at the finish) was I was overjoyed at seeing it was Connie, and not one of the other women, who was there at the end," she said. "This was the first event of the Olympics, and we set a precedent for the men, a 1-2 finish. A little later, I felt a little disappointed, but I won a silver last year (in the world championships), too, and it wasn't too bad."

The two Americans were favored to win on their home course, but just before the start, Carpenter-Phinney reminded Twigg what it really meant.

"Connie leaned over to me and said, 'If we don't bring home some medals and one of us isn't the winner, we'll have to crawl home.'"

Carpenter-Phinney, who started her athletic career in Madison, Wis., was a speed skater on the 1972 Winter Olympic team before a skating injury caused her to take up cycling. She was a member of the University of California's four-oar national champion crew.

"This is it," said Carpenter-Phinney, 26. "This is my last race. I came out of retirement (in 1981) when I heard there would be a women's Olympic race. I thought it would be a great way to go out. After 12 years in international sports, I still can't believe I won. Personally, I feel proud. I was a pioneer in women's cycling, and I worked very hard for this day. I think it may mean more to me than it might to some others."

THE MEDALISTS

WOMEN'S

Cycling

ROAD RACE

1. Connie Carpenter (U.S.)
2. Rebecca Twigg (U.S.)
3. Sandra Schumacher (W. Ger.)

NOTES

□

In equestrian competition, Brazil's only Olympic three-day event rider, Joao Carlos Cavalcanti, had to withdraw after his horse was injured in a stall Saturday at Santa Anita.

Soberano, an 11-year-old bay gelding from Brazil, suffered a deep wound on the left side of his neck that required 60 stitches.

Competition Director Alan Balch said investigation indicated that Soberano had kicked loose a piece of metal molding and was cut on the neck by the protruding metal.

—LYNN SIMROSS

□

How moving were Saturday's Opening Ceremonies for the athletes? Apparently, quite. Coach Vonnie Gros of the U.S. women's field hockey team, said she was happy that her team, which will begin play Wednesday, didn't have to play Sunday. "With the all emotions from Saturday, I'm really glad we didn't have play," she said.

—ALAN DROOZ

□

ABC made no friends in the Malaysian community during its Opening Ceremonies telecast, which switched to a commercial and missed Malaysia's entrance. Vocal Malaysian supporters at the country's field hockey game Sunday waved flags and held up a large sign that said in part, "You didn't see them on ABC but Malaysia is here."

—ALAN DROOZ

□

No, Ozzie Smith wasn't at the men's field hockey games Sunday. That was a large Australian contingent chanting, "Aussie! Aussie! Aussie!" and holding up a sheet showing a boxing kangaroo. The Aussies had a lot to cheer about, winning, 5-0. Among those cheering, to the dismay of some in the press box, were most of the Australian reporters.

—ALAN DROOZ

□

The most-cheered team? How about Mexico's, which found surprising favor among the 7,429 who showed at Pauley Pavilion to watch men's gymnastics Sunday morning.

But then why not? The Mexico team is actually a UCLA freshman, Tony Pineda, coached by his UCLA coach, Art Shurlock.

He isn't the only "home team" to be performing here—three of the U.S. gymnasts are from UCLA—but he's the only one wearing white and green national colors. Pineda scored 57.05 in the compulsory exercises, meaning his "team" lags a bit behind China's.

—RANDY HARVEY

United Press International

Steve Lundquist rejoices after setting world record of 1:01.65 in 100-meter breaststroke Sunday.

LUNDQUIST

Continued from page 32

Moffet said he received an injection, but that his leg hurt "real bad, too bad to kick. I knew I was in trouble when I warmed up. I had no legs."

The injection Moffet received, which was not identified, immediately created a minor furor. Swimming officials said that Dr. Robert Leach, who has been designated by the International Olympic Committee to make all medical statements, would have a comment on the Moffet matter today.

Moffet reportedly was considering not swimming in the race but was talked into it by U.S. Olympic Coach Don Gambril.

"I told him he should at least make the effort," Gambril said. "Sometimes when you don't try something, you look back years later and regret it. I think he would have regretted it if he hadn't at least tried."

Moffet said he would swim the 200-meter breaststroke Thursday.

Lundquist, who had dominated the 100-meter breaststroke for the past three years until he was upset by Moffet at the trials, was effusive in praise of his rival.

"He's such a tough competitor, I'm going to miss him. I wouldn't be where I am without him."

Lundquist can also identify with an injury.

He hurt his shoulder water-skiing last October, and it kept him out of the water for several months and caused his weight to soar from 185 to 205. A diet of salad, water and iced tea got him back in shape.

"Injuries are one of those things," Lundquist said. "I had mine, but I had time to get back. But what happened to John (Moffet) was one of the worst tragedies."

THE MEDALISTS

MEN'S

Swimming

100-METER BREASTSTROKE

1. Steve Lundquist (U.S.)
2. Victor Davis (Canada)
3. Peter Evans (Australia)

JAYNE KAMIN / Los Angeles Times

Alexi Grewal's celebration goes almost to disbelief moments after he wins gold medal by split second for U.S. in road racing.

GREWAL

Continued from page 32

time ago. Now was now."

And *now* Bauer was with him with a little less than nine miles to go for an Olympic gold medal. Grewal seemed to pick up, and they took turns in the lead, neither of them trying to pull away, but neither one falling back.

"Bauer was killing me," Grewal said. "I was tired, and he kept saying, 'Let's go, let's go.' I told him I was going as fast as I could."

And the leaders seemed more preoccupied with their pursuers than they were with each other. At times, they would both be looking over their shoulders.

The Norwegians—Lauritzen and Saether—were maybe 25 seconds back, but they were working together. They took turns riding in each other's drafts to conserve energy, and thus 25 seconds can be eaten up rather quickly.

"We think we can catch them," Lauritzen said, "because they keep looking at each other. We think maybe they stop racing, but they were going very fast."

Lauritzen and Saether also had lost the pack at the Vista del Lago hill.

"We didn't attack," Lauritzen said. "We just went a little faster than they did. They must have been tired. We looked around from the top of the hill and didn't see anyone."

However, Grewal and Bauer were not aware that the Norwegians had broken so clear that they ultimately would finish 58 seconds ahead of Phinney.

Bauer was particularly sensitive to the threat of both the Norwegians and the Americans because he had the feeling he was outnumbered.

"With three Americans and two Norwegians," he said, "it was a disadvantage. It was like having five riders against me."

Thus Bauer, whose teammates had made it easy for him early, had to force the pace and work a little harder to keep the Norwegians at bay.

"I had to keep going," he said, "because I knew the chasers were coming."

Grewal and Bauer seemed almost at a standstill, however, as they came around the final turn to a 200-yard climb to the finish line.

"I was worried about the sprint all week," Bauer said, "because uphill sprints aren't my forte."

And Grewal was ready.

"Steve didn't know how fast I was," he said. "I've been working on my finishes."

That might have been optimistic for a fellow who did not even know he would be *starting* a week ago.

THE MEDALISTS

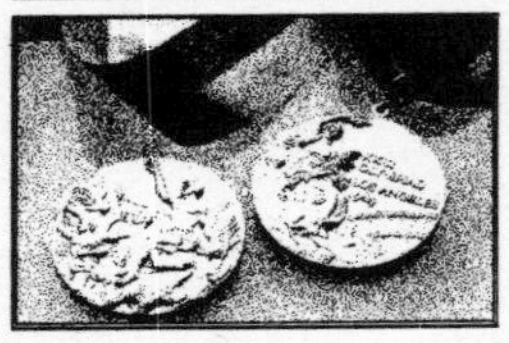

MEN'S

Cycling

ROAD RACE

1. Alexi Grewal (U.S.)
2. Steve Bauer (Canada)
3. Dag Otto (Norway)

Swimming Against Tide, Gross Comes Through

West German Beats Heath in World-Record Time and Ends America's Streak

By RANDY HARVEY, *Times Staff Writer*

Through the first three finals at USC's Olympic Swim Stadium Sunday, the United States had won four gold medals. But the tidal wave could not last forever, and it did not as West Germany's Michael Gross broke his own world record in winning the 200-meter freestyle.

The result was hardly unexpected. For Gross, the 1982 world champion in the event, the 1:47.44 he swam Sunday was his third world record in two years. His previous best was 1:47.55.

But on a day when two American women tied for a gold medal in the 100-meter freestyle, the crowd figured that anything could happen.

In this case, it would not have been out of the realm of possibility for Mike Heath, a 19-year-old Texan who holds the American record, to pull off the first major upset of the Olympic swimming competition.

In setting the American record of 1:47.92 at the U.S. trials, Heath became the only other man in the world with a time that was within one second of Gross' world record.

After the first 100 meters in the final Sunday, Heath's chances looked better than ever. Gross led from the beginning, but Heath was gaining.

During the qualifying Sunday morning, Gross appeared vulnerable in the final 50 meters. He made the turn after 150 meters almost two seconds ahead of his world-record pace but slowed considerably at the end to finish in 1:48.03.

Even though that broke the Olympic record of 1:49.81 set in 1980 by the Soviet Union's Sergei Kopliakov, Heath must have been encouraged by Gross' slow finish.

That was uncharacteristic of Gross, who normally is stronger at the end of a race than the beginning.

In the final, he reverted to form. His start was not particularly impressive as far as his time was concerned, but he obviously was saving his energy for the final half of the race.

He pulled away in the final 50 meters to win easily over Heath, who was second. Gross' West German teammate, Thomas Fahrner, who will attend USC this fall, finished third ahead of American Jeff Float.

For the first time all afternoon, as Gross stood on the top level of the victory stand, an anthem was played other than "The Star Spangled Banner."

"The first 100 meters was very easy because I realized after the heats that if I go too fast, I will be a little slow in the last 25, perhaps 40, meters," Gross said later. "Therefore, I go a little bit slower than that in the afternoon."

It might also have been wise for Gross to pace himself because of the schedule he is facing here.

Gross, 20, is 6-6, 176 pounds. His nickname is The Albatross, one German reporter explained, because of the way Gross swoops through the water in the butterfly. He swims both the 100 and the 200 butterfly and also will compete in three relays before the end of the swimming competition.

Heath, 19, is assured of swimming in four events here and could be in a fifth if his finish in the 100-meter freestyle earns him a berth on the 400 medley relay team. It would be his third appearance on a relay.

As for winning an individual gold medal, the University of Florida swimmer thought he had his best chance in the 200 freestyle. He was disappointed, not necessarily because he won the silver medal but because he did not feel he swam well.

"I felt strong in the first 100 meters," said Heath, who emerged as a world-class swimmer this year by winning the 100 and the 200 freestyles at the U.S. trials.

"I thought I was going to come close, if not breaking the world record, then touching out Michael Gross. But in the second 100, I felt like I was spinning.

"Michael Gross was in control, I could see that, and I knew my stroke wasn't right."

The spectators, many of whom were waving American flags, were more excited when Heath appeared to make his move before the final turn than he was.

"I was closing the gap a little bit," Heath said, "but he was so far ahead that there wasn't a chance of me touching him out."

Heath said he was not intimidated by Gross.

"That didn't have anything to do with the way I swam," he said. "He is a big man. I'm sure he does intimidate some people. But I'm used to swimming against big men. Both my brothers were big. I've swum against world record-holders before."

The race for third place was not decided until the final 10 meters, when Fahrner came from behind to pass Float.

"I really wanted to get a medal," Float said. "I didn't care what color it was."

MEN'S

Swimming

200-METER FREESTYLE

1. Michael Gross (W. Ger.)
2. Michael Heath (U.S.)
3. Thomas Fahrner (W. Ger.)

THE MEDALISTS

CON KEYES / Los Angeles Times

Tracy Caulkins is on her way to American record of 4:39.24 in the 400 individual medley Sunday, winning by more than nine seconds.

The Queen, at Last, Is Crowned With Gold

Tracy Caulkins Wins Her First Olympic Medal With Ease

By TRACY DODDS, *Times Staff Writer*

At last, at last, at very long last, Tracy Caulkins is wearing an Olympic gold medal around her neck.

On the first day of competition of the 1984 Olympic Games, Caulkins took her rightful place at the top of the victory stand after going through the formalities of winning the 400-meter individual medley relay for women.

Long a member of the royal family of world-class swimmers, at last she is crowned queen in one of the premier events, the decathlon of swimming.

Caulkins has no weakness among the four strokes and Sunday evening, she had no peer in the final heat.

With big, smooth, graceful stokes she pulled away on the first leg of the butterfly. At 100 meters, she had a full second lead.

She glided through the next 100 meters with a backstroke that looked so effortless, so restful and easy it was hard to believe that with each stroke she was leaving the field waves and waves behind. At the end of 200 meters, she led by almost five seconds.

And then it was time for the breaststroke, a stroke that she was having trouble with at the Olympic trials just a few weeks ago. But she swam her best breaststroke split ever to lead by almost nine seconds at the end of 300 meters.

In the final leg, a freestyle sprint, she maintained that awesome margin, leaving the others to do the only racing.

The American record-holder finished in 4 minutes 39.24 seconds, her best time ever, and she did it swimming all alone.

Caulkins said, "I am really happy with my time because it's been four years since I've done a personal best."

Suzanne Landells of Australia, the silver medalist, came in at 4:48.30. Petra Zindler, the bronze medalist from West Germany, finished in 4:48.57.

Sue Heon of the United States was fourth, missing a medal by less than a second.

Yes, Caulkins might have been even faster if she had been swimming against the world's best, but the ranking best in the 400 individual medley swims for East Germany, one of the countries boycotting these Games.

Do not doubt Caulkins when she says that having the East German women here would have been better. "It would have been a great race," she said. "We could have pushed each other. . . . It's very difficult being out in front to keep pushing yourself. . . ."

Caulkins is still about three seconds off the world record, which is held by Petra Schneider of East Germany. And in the last world rankings, she finished behind Kathleen Nord of East Germany. But that it not to say that had there been no boycott, Caulkins would not have won the gold. Not at all.

Schneider set her world record of 4:36.10 in August of 1982. She has not been nearly so fast since. Caulkins' main competition would have come from Nord.

"It would have been Nord, based on what she did in the world championships and what she did in their trials," Caulkins said.

But Caulkins would not have conceded anything in this race. Last January, at the U.S. Swimming International meet at Austin, Caulkins beat Nord in head-to-head competition in both the 400- and the 200-meter individual medleys.

It would have been better to win the gold by beating the best, but Caulkins learned long ago that a mere swimmer has no control over world politics.

She was one of the many athletes hurt by the boycott of 1980. At that time, she was on top. After that, she suffered through something of a letdown. As these Games drew near, though, she found that old motivation and brought it all together again.

"I had a lot of confidence about the race today," she said. "I expected a lot out of myself. . . . This is the best time I've ever had in the 400 IM, so that makes things look bright for my other events. This is my most demanding race. They're all demanding, but this is the hardest one. My other two events coming up are my favorites (the 200 individual medley and the 100-meter breaststroke.) I feel like I'm off to a good start.

"We've gotten the jitters out. the American team is doing well."

It was noted that she and Steve Lundquist (who won the gold medal in the men's 100-meter breaststroke) and Nancy Hogshead (who won one of the gold medals in the women's 100-meter freestyle) had all come back from the disappointment of the 1980 boycott.

"I hadn't really thought about that, but it's true," Caulkins said. "I think that's an indication of the type of people we have on our team. We have all stuck around and have had to overcome obstacles."

All worth it, obviously, for that gold medal.

Caulkins has won gold medals at world championships, at Pan-Am games, at every national meet she has ever entered. She has won more national titles (48) than any other American swimmer, ever. And yet, never that Olympic medal.

Asked about the emotion involved, the usually cool young lady of 21 answered in a quivering voice, "I start getting all teary-eyed just thinking about it. It's really something special. When I stood up there for the anthem, I saw my sister (Amy, who also is a swimmer) and my family. . . . It's just really special."

And with that, she ended the interview, tears streaming down her face.

THE MEDALISTS

WOMEN'S

Swimming

400-METER INDIVIDUAL MEDLEY

1. Tracy Caulkins (U.S.)
2. Suzanne Landells (Australia)
3. Petra Zindler (W. Germany)

American Athletes Open Games in Style—Gold Style

The United States, showing both speed and depth, won six gold medals in swimming and cycling Sunday as competition began in the 1984 Summer Olympic Games.

In swimming, Steve Lundquist set a world record in the 100-meter breaststroke, Tracy Caulkins won the gold in the 400-meter individual medley, and Carrie Steinseifer and Nancy Hogshead finished in an unprecedented tie for first in the women's 100-meter freestyle.

In cycling, Americans won the women's and men's road-racing events. American's also took the lead in men's team gymnastics, ahead of the favored Chinese. The Americans clobbered China in basketball, beat Argentina in volleyball, Costa Rica in soccer, and America's No. 1 amateur boxer came back to win after taking a fierce blow.

It was a big day for China, making its first Summer Olympics appearance since 1952. Xu Haifeng, a fertilizer salesman, became an instant hero by winning that country's first Olympic gold medal, at pistol shooting. And Chinese placed one-two in flyweight weightlifting.

With Soviet-Bloc nations boycotting the Games, the United States' performances presaged a possible large medal haul.

The leading medal winners: The United States six golds and three silvers; China two golds, a silver and a bronze; West Germany a gold and three bronzes; Canada two silvers and a bronze, and Australia a silver and a bronze.

Sunday's Roundup

Highlights:

—Swimming. Lundquist, of Jonesboro, Ga., swam a 1:01.65 and regained the record taken from him by teammate John Moffet of Costa Mesa, who had swum 1:02.13 at the trials. Moffet, who has a groin injury, finished fifth.

Caulkins, of Nashville, who has won more titles than any U.S. swimmer, finally got the big one that had eluded her when she easily won the 400 individual medley in American-record time, 4:39.24.

And for the first time in Olympic swimming history two women—Hogshead, of Jacksonville, Fla., and Steinseifer, of Saratoga, Calif.—shared a gold medal. They overcame an early lead by Holland's Annemarie Verstappen and won in 55.92 seconds.

Only West Germany's Michael Gross prevented an American sweep of the day's gold when he won the 200-freestyle in 1:47.44, 11/100ths of a second under his world-record time.

—Cycling. Alexi Grewal, only days after having a suspension lifted, and Connie Carpenter-Phinney ended a 72-year-old U.S. medal famine as both won golds.

Grewal, 23, of Aspen, Colo., won the 190-kilometer race (118 miles) in a stirring sprint to the finish line with silver-medal winner Steve Bauer of Canada.

Carpenter-Phinney, of Boulder, Colo., a four-time world champion, also sprinted the final 200 meters to edge teammate Rebecca Twigg, of Seattle, in the 79-kilometer event (49-miles) for the first women's cycling medal in Olympic history.

Grewal almost didn't make the Games. He was suspended for 30 days by the U.S. Cycling Federation after a banned substance was found in his system after a race. He appealed and was reinstated last week after it was determined that the substance had been taken for asthma.

—Basketball. The U.S. men, led by Alvin Robertson with 18 points and Michael Jordan with 14, crushed China, 97-49. Before a flag-waving Forum crowd, the Americans set out to recapture the gold they last won in 1976 in Montreal.

—Gymnastics. China started the men's compulsories by getting six of eight perfect scores of 10, with Japan getting two others. When it was the United States' turn, however, the Americans moved into first place in the team competition. UCLA's Peter Vidmar got a 10 on the pommel horse, and no lower than 9.8 in the other events, to tie Japan's Koji Gushiken in individual scoring. Bart Conner, of Morton Grove, Ill., tied for third with China's dazzling but inconsistent Li Ning, who had two 10s. Mitch Gaylord, of Van Nuys, became the first American to get a 10, on the parallel bars. Never before had Americans earned 10s in Olympic gymnastics.

—Boxing. Brooklyn's Mark Breland, a 147-pounder considered the world's finest amateur, survived a wild second-round right to the jaw that buckled his knees. After taking a standing eight-count, he went on to defeat Canada's Wayne Gordon 5-0.

THE MEDAL COUNT

THE TOP FIVE MEDAL WINNERS (THROUGH SUNDAY)

COUNTRY	GOLD	SILVER	BRONZE	TOTAL
U.S.	6	3	0	9
CHINA	2	1	1	4
W. GERMANY	1	0	3	4
CANADA	1	2	0	3
AUSTRALIA	0	1	2	3

Scott Ostler

They Came, They Saw, They Got Hard Lesson

After weeks of tuning up against people such as Magic Johnson, Larry Bird and Bill Walton, the U.S. Olympic Basketball Team hit the small time Sunday.

Don't get me wrong. China has a decent basketball team, even if it did lose to the Roundballers of the Knight Table, 97-49.

But the Chinese team spotted the Americans a few centimeters in height and about 85 years in experience. This is still America's Game.

Sure, the rest of the world is catching up, but can they do this?: Near the end of the first half, U.S. guard Leon Wood whipped a pass behind his back to Wayman Tisdale, who did a no-look slam-dunk behind his head.

This move does not translate into Chinese. Nor do a few of the other moves the Americans threw at their worthy opponents Sunday. If Leon Wood moved to China he could get his own nightly TV show, a half hour of Leon dribbling through traffic.

After one of Wood's more creative journeys through the defense, the players on the Chinese bench nodded in appreciation, and one assistant coach smiled broadly and gestured in wonderment.

Don't feel bad, guys. Our walls aren't so great. Every country has a specialty.

China isn't alone in looking up to the U.S. team. China doesn't have a Michael Jordan, but who does? Sunday Jordan, the team's glamour guy, scored only 14 points, but he set some kind of tone. At one point early in the first half Jordan was personally ahead of the Chinese team in scoring, 13 to 11.

American players and writers are still talking about a shot Jordan threw up last week against some NBA All-Stars in San Diego. It was a reverse, switch-hands, alley-ooooop layup in traffic.

□

"I've seen him do stuff I never saw anybody do," said teammate Jon Koncak after that particular shot. "All the pros were just standing there looking at him."

That's the thing about American basketball—our players even amaze each another. The Jordan layup—who can explain how such moves are accomplished? You don't diagram this kind of shot. You learn it by playing ball eight hours a day on some hot playground, year after year; by watching people named Dr. J and Elgin and Magic.

It just sort of sinks in, and comes back out at the darndest times.

The American kids came to the Forum well prepared Sunday. And, amazingly, all in one piece after a nine-game barnstorming tour against various teams of NBA (No-holds Barred Assn.) stars, whose play would have shocked hockey fans.

Professional wrestlers wouldn't use some of the holds, slaps and cheap shots the NBA guys used on the American lads over the last few weeks.

Apparently the lessons were not lost on the Americans. When the Chinese players left the floor after Saturday's game, at least three of them had fresh blood stains on their uniforms.

The U.S. players, under coach Bob Knight, learned well from the NBA thugs.

But the Americans don't play NBA ball. They play Bobbyball.

In Bobbyball, for instance, you don't necessarily start your monster big man. Pat Ewing was on the bench to open Sunday's game, and played only 13 minutes. Some say that's because Bob and Pat don't see eye-to-eye on a lot of things. Knight says it's because Ewing isn't 100%. Given Knight's rapport with the world's press, the truth may never be known.

□

In Bobbyball, in pregame warmups, you don't shoot the ball for the first two minutes. You *pass* it. For two minutes. Then, after layups, you do a defensive drill. An NBA team would no more warm up this way than it would roll out a baseball backstop and take batting practice.

In Bobbyball, you swarm on defense like hungry college kids, and swoop to the hoop on fast breaks like the big guys in the NBA.

This Olympic basketball in general is a different kind of ball than what locals are accustomed to. Even the crowd is different. The Forum fans Sunday popped a million flash bulbs at each center jump, as if this sight were as rare as a moon-missile launch. And Sunday, with the United States leading by almost 50 points in the closing minutes, most of the fans were still in their seats.

Yes, there were many unusual sights. Knight, for instance, amazed veteran observers with his bizzarre behavior. Not once did he attempt to strangle one of his own players or fly into a frothing rage at an official. Maybe he is suddenly aware that the world's hoopsters, and coaches, copy American moves, good and bad, and has decided to set a good example.

After the final horn Sunday, one member of Knight's coaching staff picked up a sack of basketballs in one hand and a portable water cooler in the other and trudged across the court toward the lockerroom.

Who was the guy? Why, it was Bob Knight himself.

There seemed to be a message here: Who says all Bobby Knight can do is coach?

Due to Knight's influence, in future years we'll see coaches on the international scene behaving like gentlemen on the sidelines and helping move team equipment.

Unfortunately for the rest of the world, such moves are easier to imitate than those of Leon Wood and Michael Jordan.

Fertilizer Salesman Wins the First Gold of '84 Games

By ELLIOTT ALMOND, *Times Staff Writer*

Olympic tradition dictates that the Games' first gold-medal winner is the men's free pistol champion. It seems the International Olympic Committee wanted to start the competition with a bang.

So, to the delight of IOC President Juan Antonio Samaranch and a crowd of 7,000 in the Chino Valley for the Games' first medal, a fertilizer salesman from China, who began shooting competitively about three years ago, won his country's first-ever gold medal.

Xu Haifeng, who used to shoot birds with a slingshot when he was a boy, scored 566 points out of a possible 600 to upset Sweden's 1972 gold medalist Ragnar Skanaker (565) and Chinese national champion Wang Yifu (564) for the gold. Skanaker won the silver after bombing in Montreal in 1976 and Moscow in 1980 whereas Wang won the bronze.

In the sports pistol—the first-ever all women's Olympic shooting event, Canadian Linda Thom defeated American Ruby Fox of Parker, Ariz., in a shootoff for the gold medal and Australia's Patricia Dench outshot China's Liu Haiving for the bronze.

The tall, slender Xu, 27, was beside himself after realizing he was the victor. From the moment he left the firing line after 2½ hours of shooting a .22 caliber pistol at a 50-meter target to the time he stood atop the winner's platform to receive his medal, he never let go of a big smile.

His victory was so surprising that he caught the Chinese press off guard. "We didn't expect this," a Peking journalist said.

Xu lives in the eastern section of China in He Xian county—"a very small village," he said. The county's population, however, is 700,000.

Whereas most of the Olympians on the range had years of experience, Xu has competed in only two international meets—the Asian Games championships and a pre-Olympic tournament at the shooting site last April. Xu finished second to Wang in China's national championships.

So what made Xu so good so soon?

Chen Jiyuan, his coach, has an explanation:

"Xu separates himself from other shooters because of his psychological control. He has great ability to withstand pressure for a long time and a tremendous sense of balance.

"He devoted himself completely to shooting."

Skanaker, who has been competing on a world-class level for 20 years, including four Olympic Games, said he felt the pressure of the throng following his every move at the rifle range.

"I've won 700 medals in my life, but I still can't get over the pressure; it's impossible to get used to."

Fox, 37, hadn't shot well in an international competition since 1979 when she won the World Air Pistol championship, so losing the gold was not a total loss. She placed second at last June's U.S. trials to barely make the team.

NOTES

From Times Staff Writers and Wire Services.

Olympic trapshooting started with a fizzle rather than a bang Sunday. A mouse had gnawed through a conduit, short-circuiting the machine that launches clay pigeons for the shotgunners.

The trouble was discovered during the morning competition at the shooting site at Prado Regional Park near Chino. Shooters call for the bird by yelling, "Pull!" into an acoustic microphone. Because of the short, the releasing device did not respond. Competition was delayed while workers put in new wires at the range—one of three—and some marksmen had to make up rounds later in the day.

Most seemed unaffected. Said Wally Zobellof the U.S. team, pointing to his head, "It's all up here. This won't change anything."

—ELLIOTT ALMOND

□

Mayor Jacques Chirac of Paris submitted a bid to the International Olympic Committee for his city to hold the Summer Games in 1992.

Seoul, South Korea, will be host for the 1988 Games.

Barcelona, Spain, and Amsterdam, The Netherlands, will submit 1992 offers later this week. Chirac invited the mayors of those cities, Parqual Maragal and Ed Van Thijn, to his presentation luncheon at a downtown hotel.

The Indian capital, New Delhi, and Brisbane, Australia, also are expected to make bids.

Paris did not create a special exhibit for IOC members and international sports officials. Amsterdam, however, built a typical Dutch tavern in the basement of the hotel where the IOC has headquarters, and free beer was served.

□

Before about 300 coaches, referees-judges and media people in the Sports Arena last Friday, Col. Don Hull, president of the International Amateur Boxing Assn., made a short speech about amateur boxing entering the wonderful age of computers.

"We're about to have the first computerized draw in the history of the Olympics," Hull said, then he turned the proceedings over to boxing's new high-tech generation.

As an afterthought, he cracked, "This will be great, if it works."

Said another amateur boxing official, "It should take only a few minutes" to do the computerized draw for the entire tournament.

Two hours later, the draw was just past the halfway point. The computers, or the computer operators—it wasn't determined which—functioned with painful slowness. The procedure took 2 hours 28 minutes.

As the process dragged into late afternoon, U.S. referee-judge Rolly Schwartz cracked:

"They should have flown in a Las Vegas keno operator with a sackful of numbered Ping-Pong balls, dumped them in a glass bubble, knocked them around with an air hose, pulled them out by somebody in a blindfold, and we'd be done by now."

—EARL GUSTKEY

□

Who ignited the Olympic flame in 1932, the last time Los Angeles had the Games? A gas company employee, Virgil Raymond, 84, of Eagle Rock, says he did.

"I was working for the Los Angeles Gas and Electric Co.," Raymond recalled. "I was instrumental in helping build the Coliseum." When it was time to light the torch, "they said the honor should be mine, " he said.

He said he lighted the flame from a metal ladder behind the giant shaft, where he could not be seen by the more than 100,000 spectators.

Bill Schroeder, director of the First Interstate Athlete Foundation, who was present that day, said no one attached much importance to the Olympic flame lighter 50 years ago.

The tradition of having some honored person light the flame began at the 1936 Berlin Olympics.

□

LARRY BESSEL / Los Angeles Times

Men's compulsory exercises, usually not popular in gymnastics, draw a crowd at Pauley Pavillion.

Rafer Johnson was vacationing in Colorado when Peter Ueberroth, president of the L.A. Olympic Organizing Committee, informed him that he would be the final torch bearer and would light the Olympic flame at the Opening Ceremonies.

"Last night (Saturday) I got a good night's sleep for the first time in 11 nights," the 1960 decathlon gold medal winner said Sunday.

"When I was competing and training regularly, everything was a set regimen. I knew what I had to do and didn't worry. But this I really worried about, especially the secrecy thing.

"And with the cramps and shin splints (recent ailments), there was some apprehension. I never thought I couldn't do it (run up the steps with the four-pound torch to light the flame), but I thought about it a lot. I was totally prepared physically for it."

Johnson, 48, said he trained hard, carrying a 15-pound weight while running, and spending a lot of time running up long, steep flights of apartment stairs.

There was a contingency plan in case he wouldn't have been able to run. Bruce Jenner, the 1976 decathlon champion, was an alternate.

Gina Hemphill, who handed the torch to Johnson after running one lap around the track, said later: "That was something that only Rafer Johnson could have done as dramatically. He looked like an ebony god up there."

—BOB CUOMO

□

How significant is it to win an Olympic gold medal in swimming?

Well, Deryk Snelling, coach of the Canadian women's team put it this way:

"With the boycott in 1980, it is like everyone in the world has been going to medical school for the last eight years and only one person is going to pass the final exam."

—SEYMOUR BEUBIS

□

Even though competition in the modern pentathlon was scheduled for early Sunday morning at Coto de Caza in south Orange County—about 50 miles from Los Angeles—the four-man U.S. team attended Saturday's Opening Ceremonies.

Mike Storm, Greg Losey, Dean Glenesk and Rob Stull got back to Coto de Caza at midnight. Because they had to report at 7 a.m. Sunday for the equestrian portion of their competition, they slept during the ride back from the Coliseum.

"We were a little tired coming back," said Losey. "But you can't miss that. You can't miss the Opening Ceremonies. The positive effect far outnumbered the effect of the sleep we lost."

Losey said he strayed from the parade of U.S. athletes into the Coliseum to say hello to his parents in the stands and to introduce himself to actresses Linda Evans and Brooke Shields.

—SAM McMANIS

□

Thomas Keller, president of the federation that governs international rowing, said Sunday that the Soviet-led boycott would dilute the competition at Lake Casitas and that he was saddened that so many participating countries refused to beef up their squads for the races here.

Keller, who heads the international rowing federation, said that the absence of the Soviet Union, East Germany, Bulgaria and other countries meant that the rowing fields had been reduced by 40% in the women's competition and by 30% on the men's side.

Of the 42 rowing medals awarded at the 1980 Games in Moscow, 33 were won by countries boycotting this year's Olympics.

—BILL CHRISTINE

□

"Official Headquarters of the Martian Olympic Team," says the sign outside A Change of Hobbitt, Santa Monica's sci-fi bookstore, and who are we to argue?

Asked what events her wards would be competing in, Linda White, Hobbitt Olympic hospitality director, said, "Well, there's the high jump, naturally, though we're not sure they'll be allowed to compete. Martians, of course, are 18 feet tall."

Of course.

"Then, there are the shooting events," King said. "Again, we may run into technical difficulties. Is there an Olympic rule against ray guns?"

We said we would check.

By far the largest Martian contingent, though, is entered in the swimming competition, at the longest possible distances.

Swimming? "Oh yes," said King. "They're quite proficient. The canals, you know."

—DICK RORABACK

DAY 4 OLYMPICS '84

Jim Murray

A General Who Rules His World

One of the most enduring—indeed, endearing—of Americans is the tough, unbending, iron-willed commander of men, the leader with the jaw of granite and the heart of gold you don't get to see till the last reel. He was the hero of a hundred John Wayne movies. He was "The Iron Major," "Old Blood And Guts," "Old Hickory" and a dozen other sobriquets of the war zone.

His job was to whip up a bunch of wimps into men, to fit them for the battlefield in the shortest possible time. March them in snow, bust them to private, throw them in the brig. "What do you mean, your wife's pregnant? This is a war, son, not a maternity ward!"

George C. Scott got the part. You all know the dialogue. "You'll hate him, son, but some day, when the going is tough and you're pinned down on that beachhead by Tojo's Imperial Marines, you'll thank your lucky stars for him!"

It was all very heady stuff and it carries over into the last vestiges of war in polite society, sports. Sports lore has its hard-bitten officer-corps heroes, too. The coaches.

□

There's Woody Hayes, bopping a guy on the helmet in the practice field so he won't flinch on Michigan game day, Rockne exhorting his troops or referring to them contemptuously as "girls." "You can tell your grandchildren you're the first Notre Dame team that ever quit!" He's Frank Leahy looking at a boy's broken wrist and snarling "Don't bother me with details! Rub a little dirt on it and get back in there!" He's Howard Jones snapping, "I don't want to see this game, I want to *hear* it!"

And he's Bobby Knight.

You can never be sure whether a great coach is a great psychologist—or needs one.

They all have one thing in common: A vast contempt for anything or anybody that has nothing to do with winning. No one knows who said it first, but it's for sure it was a coach: "Winning isn't everything, it's the only thing."

Bobby Knight is a fascinating study of the breed. Sarcastic, sentimental, implacable, impervious to criticism, impatient of mistakes, infuriated by indifference. He has that marvelous ability to convince himself that the most important things in the world are going on between the free-throw lines. If coaches have outside interests they're usually the Peloponnesian Wars or Grant's campaigns in the Wilderness, something long gone, the intellectual equivalent of playing with toy soldiers.

□

Putting a Bobby Knight in charge of the Olympic basketball movement is one of two things: It's either putting a rear admiral in charge of a rowboat, or it's assembling an aircraft carrier and crew to ply the waters between Staten Island and the Battery.

It's well known that a U. S. Olympic team could be recruited by phone or by sticking a pin in any one of a dozen major college lineups in the country. and picking one player from each.

But that'd be like asking General Patton to lead a party of college professors into the Kasserine Pass. Coaches, like generals, like to handpick their troops. And once they get them, they slap them around to make them better. It's called "building character."

Bobby Knight is incapable of just getting a basketball, a hoop and an arena and any 12 players and setting forth in quest of the Holy Grail, a gold medal. First, he gathered 72 of the quickest, fastest, meanest desperadoes on the American boards; he got four of the best coaches in the land; he ran a boot camp that made Parris Island look like a weekend on the Riviera.

All this to beat Uruguay. He cut some players who could have won the gold medal easily for any nation

Please see MURRAY, page 37

United Press International
Mary Lou Retton is up in the air during a 9.85 routine in compulsories on the balance beam.

It Takes 4 Americans to Finally Stop Gross

U.S. Edges West Germany in Record Time

By TRACY DODDS, *Times Staff Writer*

Flag-waving and patriotic emotionalism reached a new all-time high at the Olympic Swim Stadium Monday night when Bruce Hayes, from UCLA, swam the toughest, gutsiest race of his life to hold off the challenge of Michael Gross and give the United States a world record and a gold medal in the men's 800-meter freestyle relay.

Going into the morning preliminary heats, the West Germans held the world record. The Americans lowered it by almost two seconds in the morning, with Geoff Gaberino and Rich Saeger swimming along with Hayes and David Larson. For the final, the Americans' top two 200-meter freestylers, Mike Heath and Jeff Float, teamed with Hayes and Larson to—incredibly—take another three seconds off the world record.

Heath led off and gave the Americans a lead. At the end of the first 200 meters, Sweden was second and West Germany third.

Larson swam the second leg and maintained the lead for Float, who opened it up a little more for Hayes.

It was then left up to Hayes to hold off the man who had already won two gold medals and broken two world records in these Games, the man U.S. Coach Don Gambril calls, "the most talented swimmer in the world."

And he did it. But it was no small task.

Please see HAYES, page 37

Gross Beats Morales —Who Does His Best

West German Sets Another World Record

By TRACY DODDS, *Times Staff Writer*

Michael Gross, a long and gangly West German known as The Albatross, spread his wings and flew through the 100-meter butterfly to win his second Olympic gold medal with his second world-record swim in two days at the Olympic Swim Stadium Monday.

Gross, who set a world record in winning the 200-meter freestyle on the first day of competition, is fast becoming the star of these Games, threatening to do to Mark Spitz's legendary Olympic feats what Carl Lewis is threatening to do to Jesse Owens' legendary Olympic feats.

Gross set the world record in the 100-meter butterfly at 53.08 seconds, touching out young Pablo Morales of Santa Clara, who got the silver medal with a time of 53.23. Glenn Buchanan of Australia picked off the bronze in 53.85.

For Morales, 19, the silver medal was a major disappointment. He had gone into the race as the world record-holder. He lowered his time in the final heat and still came in second.

Morales, who said before the final that he would have to take it out a little faster, went out maybe a little too fast. But he was pushed from the start. Gross was right with him at the turn. Morales beat him out of the turn, but in the final sprint, Morales faded.

"I could hardly move with 10 meters to go," Morales said. "I really

Please see GROSS, page 37

This Figure Doesn't Lie: U.S. Trails Romania by a Fraction

By RICHARD HOFFER, *Times Staff Writer*

As sometimes happens in gymnastics, the twisting figures on the mats were replaced by the twisted figures on the scorecards as figures of interest, and some righteous fury over arithmetic enlivened an otherwise dull compulsory. It is always so. And so it was again Monday night during the second day of Olympic gymnastics at UCLA.

You can thank fierce national pride (theirs, ours, whomevers) for the sometimes fascinating, sometimes hilarious intrigue it occasionally endows on women's gymnastics.

At issue in the women's first round of compulsory exercises was the scoring of Romanian judge Julia Roterescu, who, in the words of American gymnasts and coaches alike, "hammered" the U.S. on balance beam. She flashed the low score for each of the U.S. women in the morning, then flashed the high ones for the Romanians later in the evening.

The blatant unfairness of it all caused Bela Karolyi, a reformed Romanian, to cheerfully promise he would "catch her neck" should he meet his old friend again, even though American judge Sharon Valley was performing a similar function on behalf of the United State at the same time.

But all this exciting talk came to naught. When the chalk dust settled, a fairly fair event emerged. Even U.S. Coach Don Peters had to admit that, while he wasn't pleased, he was relieved. Karolyi, an adjunct to the coaching staff who trains U.S. stars Mary Lou Retton and Julianne McNamara, was not available. He may have been still trying to catch Roterescu's neck.

When it was all over, the much-favored Romanians had a lead of just .45 of a point over the United States going into the optional exercises Wednesday night. That is not a big lead in gymnastics. As Peters points out, the first Romanian to fall from the beam gives the United States a .05 lead. In any event, the United States seems certain to nail its first team medal since 1948.

Peters had been afraid that the scoring would loosen up quite a bit more in the evening session, a documented fact in gymnastics as judges tend to reserve room for excellence later on. If the judges loosened up too much, the United States might have found itself off the board with its team score of 195.70. "But the scores didn't inflate as badly as I thought," he said. "It went better than expected."

So going into the optionals,

Please see GYMNASTICS, Page 37

A Little Man Pumps Some Heavy Iron

Albert Hood, the United States' best bantamweight weightlifter, was no match for the rest of the world Monday night, finishing eighth in his division (123¼ pounds), but he set two American records—248 pounds in the two-hand snatch and 534.5 pounds for total (snatch plus clean and jerk). China's Wu Shude won the gold medal with 589.5 pounds, far below the world record of 661.25 pounds held by the baby Bulgar, 16-year-old Naim Suleimanov. The Soviet boycott probably cost Suleimanov the first of many gold medals.

Photo: THOMAS KELSEY
Los Angeles Times

U.S. Stays in the Swim; Women Gymnasts in Close Battle

American swimmer Bruce Hayes edged West Germany's Michael Gross on the anchor leg Monday in the most thrilling race of the two-day-old Olympics—the 800-meter relay—in a busy day that had these highlights:

Gross became the Games' first double gold medal winner, the United States won two golds in swimming and one in shooting, the U.S. women won big in basketball, U.S. women gymnasts started strong, three U.S. boxers won easily, a U.S. cyclist set a record that was disallowed, and Canada won two swimming golds. A look at the action:

—Swimming. Gross got his second gold by nipping favored Pablo Morales of Santa Clara, Calif., in the 100-meter butterfly in a world-record 53.08 seconds. He was denied a third when Hayes, of Dallas, somehow overtook him and won by a fingertip in the relay. "Unbelievable," said Gross. The time: a world-record 7:15.69.

Mary Wayte of Mercer Island, Wash., and Cynthia Woodhead of Mission Viejo were one-two in the 200-meter freestyle. And Canada got its first swimming gold in 72 years when Alex Baumann won the 400 individual medley in a world-record 4:17.41 and Anne Ottenbrite won the 200 breaststroke.

—Cycling. Steve Hegg of Dana Point rode an innovative cycle to a world outdoor record of 4:35.57 in a 4,000-meter pursuit qualifying race, but officials disallowed it as he broke a rule by passing a competitor, hence no pursuit. West German Freddy Schmidtke won the gold in the 1-kilometer time-trial event with a 1:06.4. Canadian Curtis Harnett was second, France's Frabrice Colas third.

Monday's Roundup

—Gymnastics. Led by spectacular Mary Lou Retton of Fairmont, W. Va., the U.S. women started impressively in the team compulsories. Retton got a 9.90 in the vault and was individual high scorer in the opening session. The U.S. coach blasted a Romanian judge for "prejudiced" scoring. In the evening session, the Romanians came on strong and had a lead of .45 going into Wednesday's optionals.

—Basketball. USC's Cheryl Miller scored 23 points as the favored U.S. women's team began a quest for its first-ever Olympic gold medal with an 83-55 victory over Yugoslavia. The 6-3 college Player of the Year led her team's fast breaks, igniting several with her steals. China beat Australia, 67-64, and Korea downed Canada, 67-62. In men's basketball it was Italy over West Germany, 80-72, Brazil over Egypt, 91-82, and Yugoslavia over Australia, 94-64.

—Boxing. Paul Gonzales, fighting before a frenzied hometown crowd, eliminated his stiffest competition for a gold medal with an easy 5-0 win over Korea's Kwang Sun Kim in the 106-pound class, flooring him three times. In the 165-pound class, Virgil Hill of Williston, N.D., scored against Edward Neblett of Barbados with left hooks and staggered him with a right in the second round, and the referee stopped the bout. At 178 pounds, Evander Holyfield of Atlanta advanced, stopping Taju Akay of Ghana in the third.

—Shooting. Ed Etzel of Morgantown, W.Va., won the men's English match small-bore rifle competition. Michel Bury of France was second, Michael Sullivan of Britain third.

—Volleyball. The U.S. women defeated West Germany, 17-15, 15-8, 15-10, but didn't look as strong as some had expected off their rave reviews. The first set went 14-14 and 15-15 before substitute setter Carolyn Becker of Laguna Hills pulled it out with a pair of blocks. Earlier, China downed Brazil, 15-13, 15-10, 15-11; Japan beat Korea, 8-15, 15-11, 15-2, 15-7, and Peru took Canada 15-9, 15-10, 15-4.

—Weightlifting. China finished one-two for the second day when Shade Wu won in the 123-pound class and Runming Lai finished second. Japan's Masahiro Kotaka was third. America's best medal hope, Albert Hood of Los Angeles, finished eighth.

In field hockey, New Zealand achieved a 3-3 tie with Pakistan, the World Cup champion. The Netherlands beat Canada, 4-1, and Great Britain took Kenya 2-1.

In equestrian competition, the United States held a strong early lead over Sweden, France and Britain after dressage riding in the three-day event.

In soccer, Canada and Iraq tied at 1-1, Yugoslavia beat Cameroon, 2-1, Brazil defeated Saudi Arabia, 3-1, and West Germany topped Morocco, 2-0.

In rowing, Romanians won all four of their women's elimination heats, and the United States and Britain each had two wins.

In modern pentathlon, Italy led after Monday's fencing competition and the United States stayed in second place after upsetting France, considered the event's strongest fencing team. In Greco-Roman wrestling, Steve Fraser of Ann Arbor, Mich., became a wild-card favorite in the 198-pound division when Finland's Toni Hannula was disqualified for tearing Fraser's uniform.

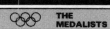

THE MEDAL COUNT

TOP FIVE MEDAL WINNERS (THROUGH SUNDAY)

COUNTRY	GOLD	SILVER	BRONZE	TOTAL
U.S.	9	6	0	15
W. GERMANY	3	1	3	7
CANADA	3	3	0	6
CHINA	3	2	1	6
AUSTRALIA	0	1	4	5

GROSS

Continued from page 36

pushed myself to the limit. That's a credit to Michael. He swam a great race. His experience showed in that one."

The times the two swam, both in the morning and in the evening, were a credit to both. But after all, these are the Olympic Games.

In preliminary heats in the morning, Gross had broken the oldest Olympic record on the books when he swam a 54.02 to break the record set by Mark Spitz in 1972 at Munich. In the next heat, Morales beat the record set by Gross when he swam a 53.78.

After winning the gold medal, Gross galloped along the side of the pool in jubilation. Later, he said, "This is absolutely unbelievable. I cannot believe it. It is amazing. Can it be? I thought that perhaps I could swim a 53.5, but 53.0? That is amazing. . . .

"I concentrated on the last 10 meters of the race, since I thought that Morales would die at that point, which he did. So I really concentrated on making a good touch.

"But what a time. I am almost speechless."

And what could Morales say? Morales, who grew up swimming in the same hometown that Spitz grew up swimming in, had his own designs on the Spitz events and records. Now he's up against a man who is inspiring awe in everyone around him.

Morales claims that he was not in the least intimidated by the 6-7 superstar. "When you see a human unique in any regard or size, there's an aura about them," Morales said. "But I was the world record-holder. I had my own confidence to drain off of. There is no way you can be intimidated if you know what you can do."

Morales said that he was not surprised that Gross came through to win the event. "I was surprised at the time," Morales said. "That was a real drop for Michael. You can't expect not to be challenged by someone that talented."

THE MEDALISTS

MEN'S

Swimming

100-METER BUTTERFLY

1. Michael Gross (West Germany)
2. Pablo Morales (U.S.)
3. Glenn Buchanan (Australia)

Morales was a little upset with himself for going out so fast. He said, "I took it out a little bit harder than I should have. I was a little excited. . . .

"This is the first time I've been that close to him, much less swum against him."

In his immediate disappointment, Morales was having some trouble putting his silver medal into perspective. It was his all-time best. The time has to give him confidence for his final two individual events.

As the top American finisher in this 100-meter event, he'll also be on the 400-meter medley relay team.

Matt Gribble, the other American in this event, had trouble, again, with his back and did not even make the final. Gribble had been the world record-holder in the 100-meter butterfly until the Olympic trials last month when Morales beat him and took the world record.

"I'll have to take some time to gather my thoughts," Morales said. "This is all going by so quickly. I do have two more events to swim. No way can I let this get me down. . . .

"Oh, sure, there is definitely a positive side to this. It was a lifetime best. I think one race like this gives you a lot of experience."

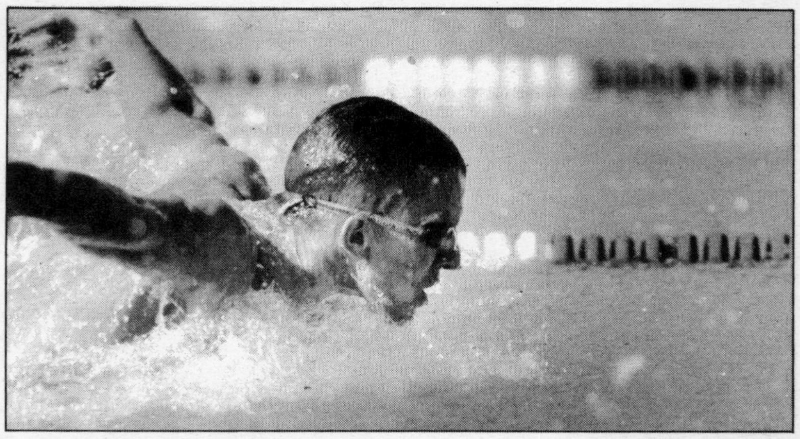

DAVE GATLEY / Los Angeles Times

Michael Gross of West Germany swims to victory in heat of 100-meter butterfly Monday. In the final, he set a world record of 53.08 as he won his second gold medal of the Games.

HAYES

Continued from page 36

Halfway through his come-from-behind challenge, Gross had caught up with Hayes. He even took a slight lead off the wall on the third 50.

But Hayes kept churning away, inching up on Gross, whose unusually long arms allow him to take fewer, longer strokes. On and on, Hayes charged until, at the touch, he sent the crowd into a frenzy.

Gross, who had set a world record and won a gold medal in the 100-meter butterfly earlier in the evening, said that he did tire at the end. Gross said, "I simply didn't have any more to give. I just ran out of gas. My time was 1:46.9. How much faster do I have to swim? That was really a hot race."

THE MEDALISTS

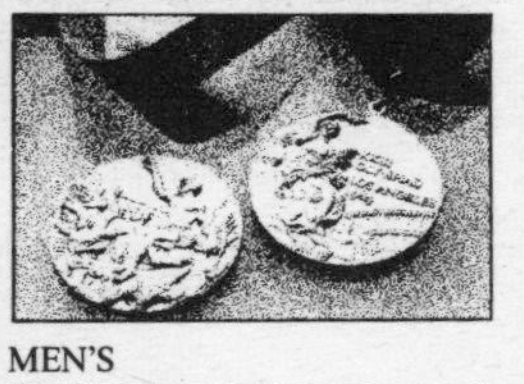

MEN'S

Swimming

800-METER FREESTYLE RELAY

1. United States
2. West Germany
3. Great Britain

Indeed, Gross' split was the fastest relay split ever for the 200.

But it wasn't enough.

Float, who seemed about to burst with joy, climbed up onto the starting block, spread his arms to the heavens and basked in the roar of the crowd, his home crowd, on the campus of his alma mater, USC.

Later, on the victory stand, with the gold medal around his neck, Float tried to cry, smile and sing the Star Spangled Banner, all at the same time. He succeeded only in bringing tears to a lot of other admiring eyes.

"There are not too many words that can express the emotionalism of the moment," said Float, who speaks remarkably well considering his serious hearing impairment. "I have never been so happy. This is one of the greatest moments ever. After all these years, and the boycott and everything, this was the way I had hoped it would be. I'll be retiring after this, and this is a great last swim."

Float finished fourth in the 200-meter freestyle event on the first night of competition when Gross won the gold medal and Heath took the silver.

The expected order of the relay would put Gross and Heath on the anchor leg for that final sprint. Instead, Gambril led off with Heath.

Gambril explained, "Gross paid too much (in effort) to catch Bruce early in the race. That's exactly what we wanted him to do. . . . Bruce swam a cool race. He did what he had to do to get us the win. He has anchored enough relays in the NCAA meet to know how to handle this kind of pressure. We told him exactly what was going to happen and he was ready for it.

"I didn't expect Gross to catch him that quickly."

Larson, who, like Float, was a member of the 1980 Olympic team that did not get to compete, said that this was worth sticking around for four more years. He said he would have been happy for the four years even if he had not won the gold medal because, he said, "I would have known that I gave it my all."

He added, "I have been on a lot of U.S. relay teams, but the main difference in this one was that we were at home with the people who love us and who were behind us. I think we had a lot of confidence based on the fact that we broke the world record in the morning with what our coaches affectionately call our 'B' team. A lot of countries would drool over that team."

MURRAY

Continued from page 36

on earth. He packed off guys who could go in the pivot for the Pistons tomorrow.

He got 12 players who could go out and beat the NBA. And did. He had a battleship to fight Chinese junks, a railroad gun to hunt rabbits.

But, what a lot of people were afraid of was that this stormy Knight might embarrass not only every other basketball team in the world but the home front as well.

An Olympics is supposed to be a polite, gentlemanly, sporting type of proposition, conducted in icy formality with protocol, bows, declarations of good sportsmanship rather like high tea at a cricket match. Bobby is not your hand-kissing, heel-clicking type. Bobby is not your basic genial host, your gracious guest. Bobby punches cops in host countries.

His press conferences are models of sarcasm as wit. When some unsuspecting foreign reporter blundered into asking him how he thought the back injury to a foreign player would affect the play, Bobby retorted sharply, "I have not recently examined his back."

When one reporter (KABC's Ted Dawson) kept asking repeated questions, Knight asked testily "Has this guy got his own microphone?" When asked how a given game might go, Knight snapped, "It would take a trained observer to see and I don't see many of those in this hall." When someone asked about the Russian absence, Bobby bristled. "Who cares whether the Soviets are here? They didn't win the gold medal at Moscow and they wouldn't have here."

At a multilingual press conference, Knight got impatient with the American moderator. "I could do your job better than you could. The only one I couldn't handle is hers," he said, pointing to the girl translating his remarks into French. Knight is prone to lapse into scatology when the questions are going too slow to suit him.

In the game against China which Bobby's battleship sank without a trace, his team was winning the match 97-45, an outcome which appeared to bore his team at one point. But not Bobby. He jerked the entire lineup out of the contest and, loud enough for spectators to hear, told them if their lackadaisical attitude persisted he would not only do that in a 97-45 game but would not hesitate to do it in a close game in the final minute.

A reporter approached one of his players, the deft Leon Wood. "Are the players afraid he (Knight) will cause an international incident?" he asked. Wood laughed. "Not unless the world provokes him," he said.

Of course, if the world really provokes Bobby Knight, he'll march it into a swamp.

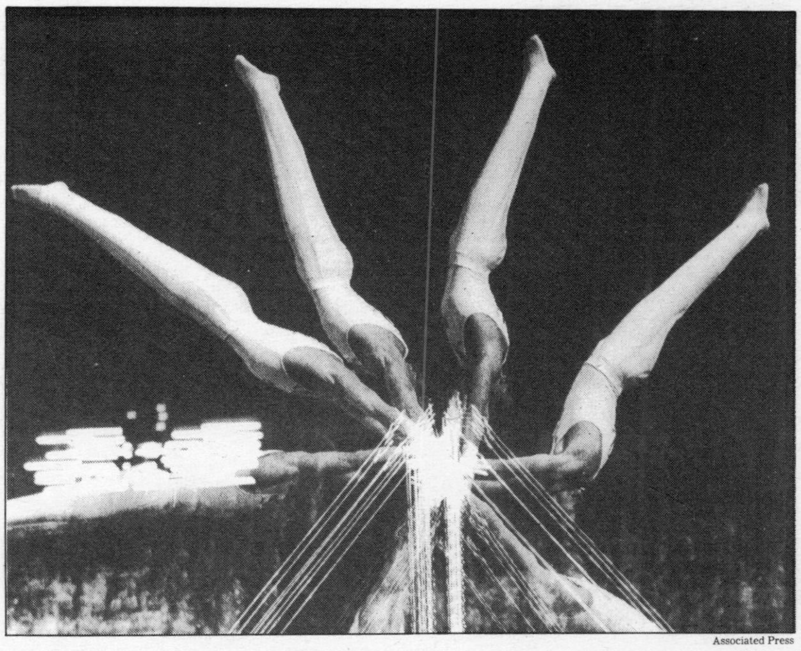

Associated Press

A multiple exposure shows Mitch Gaylord of the U.S. performing his routine on the high bar.

GYMNASTICS

Continued from page 36

which will be combined with the compulsory scores to decide the team competition, the United States is very much in the hunt. China, which had finished ahead of the United States in the 1983 World Championships, finds itself behind, in third, with 194.15. China's chances of catching Romania, which scored 196.15 Monday, are remote, at best.

"I was afraid we'd be behind more than a point," Peters said. "Then it would have been no contest."

It's still a contest, in more ways than one. Not only is the team event up for grabs but so is the individual all-around title. The two Romanian stars, Lavinia Agache and Ecaterina Szabo, are tied for first with 39.55. The U.S. sensation, Mary Lou Retton, is in second with 39.50, followed by teammates Julianne McNamara at 39.45 and Kathy Johnson at 39.10. There looks to be an individual medal for a U.S. gymnast as well. That will be the first since in this sport since the game's creation.

Some complaints remained, however. Neither Peters nor Karolyi could imagine how Retton's vault could be scored anything but perfect, although judges thought 9.90. Retton, whose stock in trade is tne power she derives from her stocky legs, usually amazes judges with the sheer distance of flight. As Karolyi explains, distance is the one factor that can make up the point-grabbing element of risk. "It is the only way you can show risk in compulsories," he said. "You can not, after all, break your neck in compulsories." That opportunity is reserved for the hair-raising optionals.

On the other hand, both Agache and Szabo scored 9.90s with vaults that included distinct little hops on dismounts.

Szabo, however, scored the evening's only 10, getting the perfect score in floor exercises. The entire day of scoring stood out in contrast to the men's compulsories the day before when 10 perfect scores were awarded. Women's judges are harder to impress. "It's just a trend," Peters explained. "The women went through this in 1976 when 10s were being thrown like crazy. They've since tightened up. The men are just now going through that."

So the judges' math didn't have as much to do with it all as first supposed. So it will come down to the twisting figures of Szabo, Retton *et al.* "We've got a chance," Peters said. "But don't expect the Romanians to fold. They didn't have a major break the whole night. They have very strong optionals, too."

Watching them once more from the stands Wednesday night, you can be assured, will be Nadia Comaneci, the Romanian who first made the notion of perfection seem possible. Her silent and mysterious benediction, which flows from her legacy to powerful Romanian gymnastics, may do more for the Romanians than Julia Roterescu could ever do.

Olympian Appetites Go for Culinary Gold

From Associated Press

Tons of charbroiled steak, hundreds of thousands of apples and nearly 2 million cups of ice cream are being devoured by Olympic athletes with appetites rivaling a Pac-Man army.

It's a food fiend's paradise, according to Ed Krein, food production manager for ARA Services Inc., the official cooks for the Los Angeles Games.

"While we can't compete with mom's cooking, you won't find this kind of quality anywhere," said Krein.

By the time the Summer Games end in two weeks, Krein's 3,000-member staff expects to have served 1.2 million meals, including 20,000 box lunches per day and 15 tons of T-bone steak. Each day, 10 trucks arrive at the main villages with the makings for 60,000 meals.

"We're not talking pounds, we're talking tonnage," Krein said.

Incorporating staples from all five continents, Krein has made up one of the most extensive menus in Olympic history. With fare that runs from A to Z—chilled avocado soup to zucchini Parmesan—the list of provisions is almost endless.

"This is paradise for all of 'em. Even Americans are complimenting us for the freshness of the product," said Krein, 41, also head chef of the USC Olympic Village kitchens. Krein expected to serve between 6,000 and 7,000 12-ounce steaks a day at USC, but he got a surprise.

"We anticipated fish to equal the demand of steaks, but it's been half of what we expected, and steak has doubled," he said.

He attributes a heavy run on milk and other beverages to a heat wave that sent temperatures here into the 90s during much of July.

Athletes are finding something for everyone.

If tastes run toward French cooking, there are three types of pate—liver, shrimp and artichoke-plus goat cheeses and vichyssoise.

There are pasta, pepperoni and canneloni for Italian-food lovers; couscous, lamb curry and countless rice dishes for those with a bent for African cuisine.

Kosher foods are available on request, and the cooks, operating 24 hours a day, are lending a hand to cater every need.

The most unusual request, Krein said, has come from the Japanese, who arrived with 1,000 pounds of fresh eel, a delicacy in Japan. "We help them cook it," said Krein.

From the Koreans came a request for large supplies of kimchi, a fiery pickled vegetable. "They are eating it seven days a week, three times a day," Krein said.

Under Olympic bylaws, all food is to be shared, a tradition that keeps the Italian chefs especially busy.

"In Sarajevo, after one week, they had the longest lines, and they are getting longer here," Krein said.

Traditionally, fresh fruit is the favorite snack of Olympians, and it has been by far the most popular item in Los Angeles. Krein expects 250 tons will be eaten by the time the Games end Aug. 12, possibly surpassing the average of 16 pieces of fruit consumed each day by each athlete at the Montreal Games in 1976.

The supply of ice cream, 1.7 million five-ounce cups, is melting away fast.

"They eat ice cream like it's the end of the world," said Faye Clarke, vice president and general manager of ARA.

In Moscow four years ago, native specialities included chicken Kiev, shish kebab and sturgeon.

In America, "it wouldn't be the Olympics without hot dogs, hamburgers and popcorn. And we've got 'em," Krein said.

Swimming

Women's 200 Freestyle

Woodhead Gets a Second—and She Relishes It

By MIKE PENNER, *Times Staff Writer*

So this, finally, was Sippy Woodhead's Olympic moment—second to finish, overshadowed by American teammate Mary Wayte, left to clutch a single silver medal.

Once, the scenario appeared so different, so promising. Four years ago, she was primed for a gold rush in Moscow. Her challenge was the possibility of winning six gold medals; her story seemed destined to become the female version of the Mark Spitz saga.

But then came the 1980 boycott. And, then, the injuries and the substandard performances, followed by the self-doubts and the despondence.

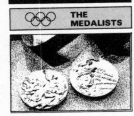

THE MEDALISTS

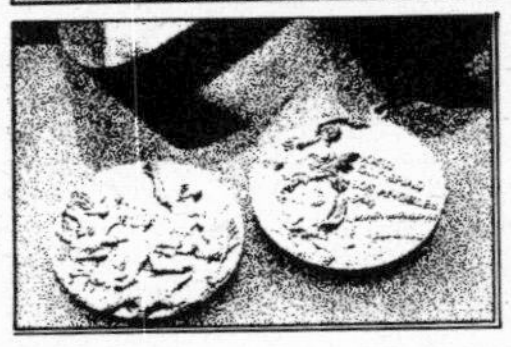

WOMEN'S

Swimming

200-METER FREESTYLE

1. Mary Wayte (U.S.)
2. Cynthia Woodhead (U.S.)
3. Annemarie Verstappen (Netherlands)

Woodhead's runner-up finish to Wayte Monday in the women's 200-meter freestyle competition, the only race in which she will swim during these Olympics, might have the initial look of disappointment. This wasn't the way it was supposed to turn out.

But during the medal presentation and throughout all post-race interviews, Woodhead couldn't stop smiling. Letdown? If so, Woodhead wasn't letting on.

"If you were with me when the times were bad," Woodhead said, "you'd realize how much this means to me. . . . I'm really happy I stuck through all this. Sometimes, it was as if I didn't want to see the world.

"But when I touched the wall at the end of the race, I was as happy as if I had won the gold."

In what will probably go down as her only Olympic appearance, Woodhead of Mission Viejo swam a time of 1:59.50. It was her best mark in nearly five years, when she then held the 200-meter world record, but it was a quarter-second slower than her longtime rival, Wayte of Mercer Island, Wash.

Coming on strongly in the last 50 meters, Wayte overtook Woodhead and beat her to the wall in 1:59.23. Wayte had never before broken two minutes but she produced her best when she needed it the most.

The two had met many times before, usually with Woodhead getting the better of things. In the U.S. trials, Woodhead edged Wayte for first by four-hundredths of a second.

And there they were again at the USC Olympic Swim Stadium, side by side, driving for the finish stroke-for-stroke. This time, it was Wayte who out-touched Woodhead for the win, also outdistancing the Netherlands' Annemarie Verstappen (1:59.69), who took her second bronze medal in as many days.

And thus it was Wayte, not Woodhead, who took the top step on the victory stand.

"I'm just glad it's over," Wayte said. "At the trials, I remember being so close to her (Woodhead). Randy (Reese, Wayte's coach) told me, 'It's OK to finish second in the trials, as long as you win the Olympics.'

"Today, he said, 'You've done everything I've told you to do—now do it.' This is something I've been waiting my whole life for."

So had Woodhead. A holder of 12 national titles, Woodhead saw her moment of triumph snuffed out by politics in 1980 and then had to overcome mononucleosis in 1981, bronchitis and a broken leg in 1982, along with periodic bouts of depression just to get this far.

One event, one brief race would be all for Woodhead. It resulted in silver, not the legend that might have been.

Might have been. Woodhead has considered those words before—and hates them now.

"We can all think like that," she said. "But that's no way to live life. The boycott in '80 took away the whole incentive for a lot of us. It was damaging to our sport."

All Woodhead could do was make the best of her chance, however limited it might be.

And she believed she did.

"I'm really happy with my time and what I accomplished," Woodhead said. "I went out to swim my race and I did it. I'm comfortable with it."

And Wayte was ecstatic. Her time was about 1½ seconds off the world record (1:57.75), but in this field, it was plenty fast.

Wayte was smiling from start to finish, grinning broadly and waving to relatives in the stands before the race—and carrying on even more afterward.

"In the trials, I swam well because I was very relaxed," Wayte said. "So I just decided to keep smiling and get through this."

Sippy Woodhead also got through it. And, at last look, she was smiling, too.

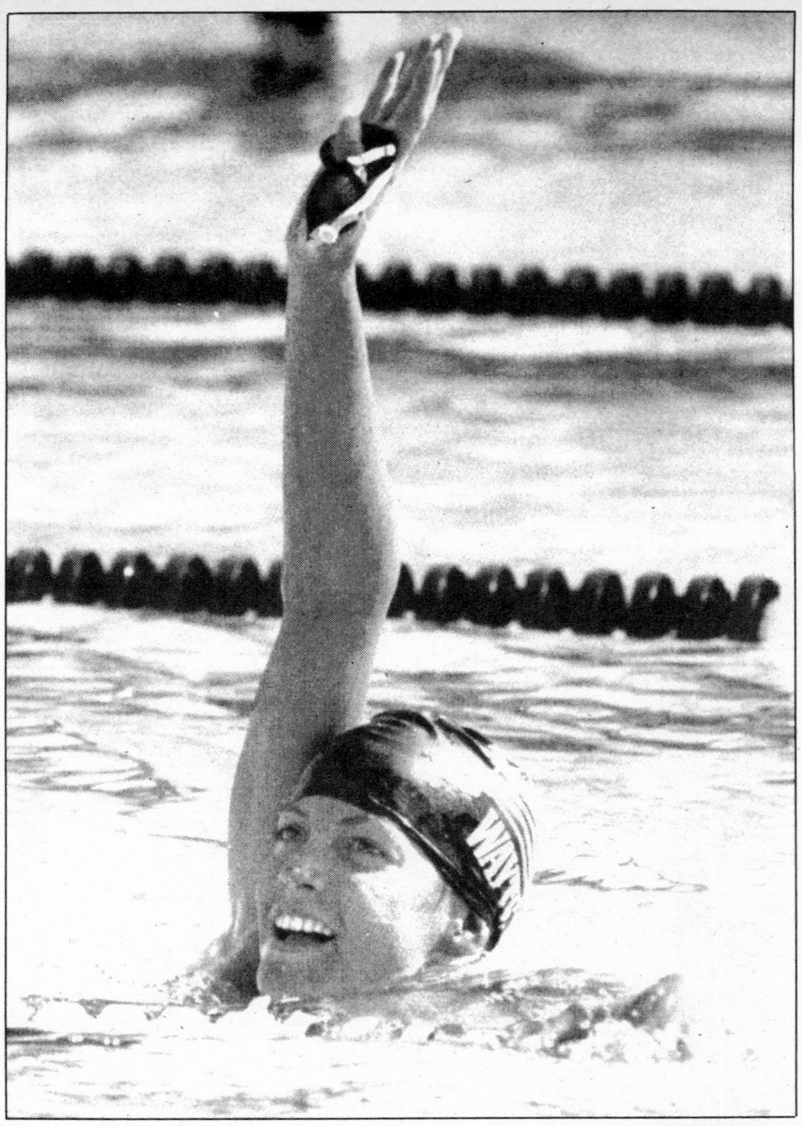

United Press International

Mary Wayte of the University of Florida celebrates victory in the women's 200-meter freestyle after edging U.S. teammate Cynthia Woodhead. Wayte's time was 1:59.23.

Canada's Baumann Makes Up for Lost Time

By SEYMOUR BEUBIS, *Times Staff Writer*

Until Monday, Canada hadn't won an Olympic swimming gold medal in 72 years.

But then Canada never had anyone like Alex Baumann before. In fact, the entire swimming world has never seen an individual medley swimmer as good as Alexander the Great.

Baumann, 20, of Sudbury, Ontario, shaved time off his own world record in the 400-meter individual medley and finished in 4:17.41 to beat a rugged challenger, Ricardo Prado, 19, of Brazil, the former world record-holder, by slightly more than a second.

Robert Woodhouse, 18, of Australia took six seconds off his best time to capture the bronze.

The two U.S. swimmers in the race, Jesse Vassallo, 22, of Mission Viejo and the University of Miami, a one-time world record-holder in the event, and Jeff Kostoff, 18, of Upland and Stanford University, finished fourth and sixth.

Prado, who moved to Mission Viejo to train under Mark Schubert when he was 15, started out as if he was trying to recapture the world record from Baumann.

He led by more than a second over Baumann after the 100-meters of butterfly, and extended it to just under two seconds after the backstroke leg.

But Baumann, a fantastic breaststroker, took the lead on that leg by just over a second and maintained it through the 100 meters of freestyle.

Baumann bettered his old world record of 4:17.53 set last June. Prado had his best time ever, a 4:18.45, and Woodhouse finished with a 4:20.50.

Regarded as the most versatile swimmer in the world (he has no weak stroke), Baumann, who has a maple leaf tattoo on his chest, said after his winning race that he is "very proud to be a Canadian."

"It's been a long grind for me the last 10 years. It's been a long grind for Canadian swimming over the last 72 years. I'm glad we finally hit gold again."

Prado said he gave it his best shot. He said he knew that he had to have a big lead over Baumann going into the breaststroke.

"I had to swim my own race," Prado said. "I knew that he (Baumann) would be coming strong at the end.

"That's life, what can I say. You always want to win, but sometimes it does not work out. He (Baumann) was better today. He swam faster, and he won."

Baumann's victory apparently spurred on the Canadian team. Immediately after he won the individual medley, Anne Ottenbrite, 18, captured the Olympic gold medal in the women's 200-meter breaststroke.

Watching Baumann win the Olympic gold medal was his mother, Vera, a world-ranked breaststroker in her native Czechoslovakia in the 1940s.

Baumann was born in Prague. His family moved to New Zealand in 1967 and then to Canada two years later.

He began swimming at the age of nine and was an immediate success, establishing nine national records in the 10-and-under division.

Until his win at the Olympic Games Monday, Baumann's greatest victory was in the 1982 Commonwealth Games when he set a world record in the 200-meter individual medley with a clocking of 2:02.25—a mark which still stands.

Baumann will be out to better it when he swims the 200 individual medley Saturday.

In the preliminaries Monday morning, Baumann swam a controlled race to edge Kostoff. He finished in a 4:22.46 to Kostoff's 4:22.55.

But Baumann's coach, Dr. Jeno Tihanyi, predicted that his swimmer would go a lot faster in the afternoon session, and he was right on the mark.

The fourth-place finish was a crushing blow to Vassallo, who came close to an Olympic medal. He finished less than a second behind Woodhouse.

He made the Olympic team after overcoming a serious knee injury that required surgery and kept him out of action for nearly a year and a half. He set a world record in 1978 and was one of the best swimmers in the world in 1980 when the United States decided to boycott the Olympics.

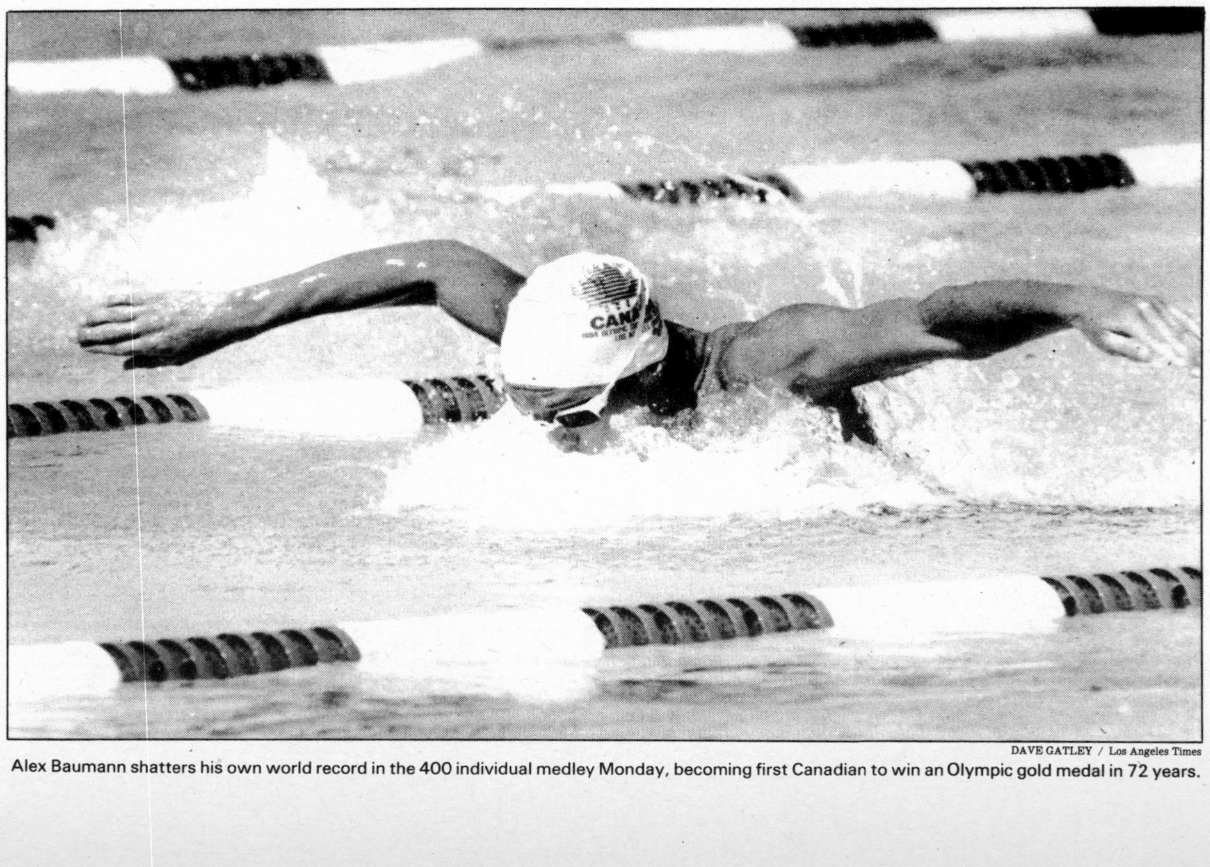

DAVE GATLEY / Los Angeles Times

Alex Baumann shatters his own world record in the 400 individual medley Monday, becoming first Canadian to win an Olympic gold medal in 72 years.

An Old Rivalry to Resume at Lake Casitas
Pertti Karppinen and Michael Kolbe Will Meet Again This Week in Single Sculls

By BILL CHRISTINE, *Times Staff Writer*

Michael Kolbe

OJAI—The only thing Pertti Karppinen and Michael Kolbe have in common is that they are tall, handsome and world-class scullers. Otherwise, they are as different as a Finn (Karppinen) and a German (Kolbe).

Karppinen, a 6-7, 31-year-old blond, must rank as one of the world's tallest fire chiefs. He probably doesn't even have to slide down the pole. He's definitely the world's best sculler, having won the Olympic singles at Montreal in 1976—Finland's first rowing gold medal—and at Moscow in 1980.

The 6-4 Kolbe, who will be 31 Wednesday, is a dark-haired, ball-bearings salesman who, with an asterisk, was the world's best sculler in 1981 and 1983. Those were years when Karppinen skipped the singles to row with his brother, Reina, in the pairs.

So Pertti, who has beaten Kolbe in two of three races in Europe this year, is still favored to win a third straight gold medal in the Olympic Games this week on Lake Casitas.

Kolbe had Karppinen's number a couple of times in the 1970s—he was first and Karppinen was fourth in 1975 and the West German won again in 1978 while Karppinnen struggled to get sixth—but enough with history. More about the contrasts.

On the water, their styles are as different as Rembrandt and Andy Warhol. Kolbe is a paragon of technique, a stylist who does everything by the book. Karppinen wouldn't win any points for smoothness—"He's not pretty," says U.S. men's sculling Coach Harry Parker—but he's strong and an extremely consistent stroker, from starting point to the finish line, 2,000 meters later. Kolbe's way with an oar is more modeled after a piranha. "He's an exceptional sprinter," Parker says. "He kills off most of the opposition in the first 1,000 meters."

Off the water, there's no mistaking Kolbe for Karppinen, either. Karppinen is all business, a reluctant interview whose predominant look is a flinty glare. Watch out for potential sparks if you get close to him. He wants to win that third gold badly, which would match the three in a row by the Soviet Union's Vyacheslav Ivanov in 1956, 1960 and 1964, because Kolbe is retiring after these Games.

Kolbe is an easy interview, an oarsman who doesn't putter around with his boat. His eyes dance when the questions come partially loaded. The other day he appeared unannounced in the press tent at Lake Casitas, not for any formal interviews, but to chat with some German journalists, make a couple of phone calls, have a soft drink and see how a prosaic aspect of the Games works.

Seppo Nuuttila, Finland's rowing coach, feels that Karppinen would be 3 for 3 over Kolbe this year but for some unfavorable conditions in a race at Mannheim, Germany. "Kolbe had a better lane," Nuuttila said. "His lane was protected from the wind by a mountain."

Asked about this, Kolbe rolled his eyes and smiled. "I think that's the way it was," he said in perfect English. "I don't know for sure. But at least the conditions for the Olympics will be equal for everybody. All of the lanes are a long distance from the shore."

After their last meeting in Lucerne, Switzerland in June, there were published reports that Kolbe gave up after losing to Karppinen and skipped a rematch the next day.

Kolbe shook his head. "I don't like to row twice on a weekend," he said. "I had already made up my mind, before the first race, that I was only going to row one day."

Karppinen and Kolbe are not friends, although they've been kicking around international waters since 1974. "It would be hard (to be friends)," Kolbe said. "The language is a problem. He speaks Finnish (and no English), and I speak German."

The rivalry will end here, at least as far as Karppinen is concerned. "I was married a year and a half ago," he said through Nuuttila, acting as an interpreter, "and I have a son eight months old. I have been rowing for 12 years, taking off four months each year, and this would be a good way to end my career, with a third gold that would give me a high place in the history of the sport."

Kolbe's future is less certain. "When the Olympics end," he said, "I will go on holiday with my family (he is married to a Norwegian and they have a 3-year-old son), and then we will decide. I have lived in Norway the last two years, and I do not know what I will do."

Karppinen and Kolbe were expected to meet in the six-man final Sunday morning, but they unexpectedly drew into the same preliminary heat, scheduled for 8 a.m. today. The race that also includes John Biglow, who finished third in the world championships in both 1981 and 1982.

It's just a heat, but it promises to be the most rousing race during the opening days of the seven-day competition that started Monday. Because of rowing's repechage (second-chance) system, Karppinen, Kolbe and Biglow could still wind up in the final no matter what happens in today's heat.

Biglow is a realist. "Overall, I wasn't pleased with the way I rowed during our European tour," the Yale University graduate from Bellevue, Wash., said. "I think I have a chance here because I expect to row faster, but right now I'd rank myself as fifth best in the world. But you have to take each race individually. In 1981, for example, I wasn't the third best sculler in the world, but I finished third in the world."

Biglow has come into the Olympics using a relatively new boat, having switched from a German-made Empacher model to an American-made Van Dusen while the Americans were halfway through their European swing.

Rowing shells are like baseball gloves, there's something for everybody. The Van Dusen has a different hull than the Empacher and is an especially light boat. Some of the Van Dusens are so light, in fact, that scullers have to add lead to the boats to make the minimum weight of about 32 pounds.

An advertisement for a Van Dusen in Rowing USA magazine reads: "The fastest way down a racing course."

Jos Compaan of the Netherlands agonizes over her loss in trial heat of women's 1,000-meter single sculls to Charlotte Geer of the United States.

Far left: Italy's Giovanni Suarez, far left, raises his arm in jubilation as his four-oar with coxswain crew wins 2,000-meter preliminary. Left: Americans Joan Lind and Virginia Gilder, with finger raised, after their victory in the trial heat of the 1,000-meter quadruple sculls with coxswain. Lind was a women's single sculls silver medalist in the 1976 Montreal Olympics.

Photos by Steve Fontanini

DAY 5 OLYMPICS '84

U.S. Pulls Off Miracle of L.A.

Peter Vidmar (right) and Bart Conner rejoice after Vidmar's 9.95 routine on the high bar finished off world champion China's chances and gave the United States its first-ever team gold medal in Olympic gymnastics Tuesday night.

Associated Press

American Gymnasts Upset China

By RICHARD HOFFER,
Times Staff Writer

They stood wreathed in ribbons, the weight of their new gold all that was holding them to this earth. They had flown, flared and floated all Tuesday night, soaring above the mats in a rarified atmosphere. Would they ever come down? Only to alight briefly on the podium, to be acknowleged as champions of the world, the true winners of the space race.

Olympic champions at last, for the first time ever, medalists for the first time in 52 years, the United States men's gymnastics team seemed at turns delirious and hysterical as the golden weight of achievement settled against their chests.

Otherwise, without that winking weight, they surely would have floated once again into space, adrift in a sparkly ether of accomplishment.

Yes, the United States had won a gold medal in the team event, beating world champion China. Would they have beaten the Soviet Union? East Germany? Any East European power, traditional forces in this competition? Hadn't China? Yes.

Complaints of the Soviet-led boycott must remain mere anecdotage. Do not imagine that Peter Vidmar, the tears rolling down his cheeks, his stoic chin fractured by massive trembling, doubted what

Please see GYMNASTICS, page 41

TONY BERNARD / Los Angeles Times
Tim Daggett virtually clinches gold medal for U.S. with a perfect routine on the high bar.

Carey Wins the Gold; You'd Never Know It

By JOHN WEYLER, *Times Staff Writer*

It had to be an Olympic first.

There were no raised fists, no jubilant shouts or tears of joy. Not even a polite wave of acknowledgment to the crowd.

Rick Carey just held onto the gutter of the Olympic pool, stared down into the water and slowly shook his head from side to side in obvious dejection.

It's not the kind of behavior we've come to expect from athletes who have just won gold medals. But make no mistake, Rick Carey is not your average athlete.

This man, who has completely dominated the backstroke events for the past three years, had just won his first-ever Olympic race, the 200-meter backstroke. But his winning time, 2:00.23, was more

than a second and a half off his world record, and he was, well, disgusted.

"I've swum faster in workouts," he said. "I don't know what happened . . . I just don't know. I just know I don't find it the least bit satisfying. It just hurts."

He didn't get over the disappointment in a hurry, either. He hung his head on the victory stand while silver-medalist Frederic Delcourt of France and bronze-medalist Cameron Henning of Canada beamed with wide grins. Carey didn't even wave to the crowd as the medalists paraded along the pool after the awards ceremony.

He did stop long enough to hand

Please see CAREY, page 41

He's More Than Poetry in Motion

Jim Murray

The first look you get at Sebastian Coe, you figure this is what Lord Byron must have looked like. This is not a major British athlete, this is a minor British poet.

You see him on the track and you're tempted to ask: "Shouldn't you be composing odes to a waterfowl or sonnets to the Portuguese or reading verse beneath a balcony in Venice?" Or: "How is Keats these days?" You politely ask him if his first names aren't Percy Bysshe.

He looks—well, "effete" isn't the word, but it's close. Put it this way: You wouldn't be too surprised if he had posed once for Gainsborough's Blue Boy.

First of all, there's the dark curly hair, the aquiline nose, pale forehead. The faintly haunted look. This is either David Copperfield or a character out of "The Barretts of Wimpole Street," not a locker room. He should be sniffing a rose, harking a lark, eulogizing an urn, not running around in his underwear. He should be a sad, melancholy young troubadour brooding on the fate of a buttercup, not

running down the flower of the world's racers. There's the look of the perennial English schoolboy about him. A "Chariots Of Fire" scene come to life.

Even the name is evocative of the England of *belles lettres* and Romantic poets. Sebastian Coe. It's not a runner's name, it's a writer's. Runners are named Chuck or Steve or Emil or Ivan. Sebastian Coe suggests somebody who writes with a feather and calls his mother Mater, lives in the family castle at Brideshead.

Mile runners, to be sure, are not NFL linebackers as a class. There's a neurasthenic quality to the best of them. But Coe adds another dimension to it. The bard's "wan and palely loitering" look.

It's nature's joke. This pale and skinny little Brit is one of history's

toughest competitors. You watch him and you'll understand where they got that empire.

The camouflage exists right into the race. If Seb Coe were an animal, he'd probably be a spotted deer, a modern Bambi. He runs with the loping grace of a startled fawn. He does not appear so much to be running a race as chasing a butterfly. You wonder what he did with his net.

When he first came to Moscow four years ago, a lot of people there thought Britain had made a mistake and sent its poet laureate. The other British runner looked more the part. There's nothing poetic about Steve Ovett, but the hard-bitten press corps wondered about this other youngster who looked like an angel in a school play.

The Soviets called him "the young English lord" or "young Master Coe," and when he lost the 800 meters after getting pushed around to the outside of the track, they thought he was just another

Please see MURRAY, page 41

Sebastian Coe

Italy Beats U.S., 1-0

63,624 Fans at Rose Bowl —but Is It a Soccer Boom?

By RANDY HARVEY, *Times Staff Writer*

In Dallas millionaire Lamar Hunt's dream, there were 100,000 fans at the Rose Bowl to see the United States play Italy in football.

Not the kind of football played by his Kansas City Chiefs of the National Football League, but the kind of football played by his Dallas Tornado of the North American Soccer League.

The dream did not materialize Tuesday night, but the time that it will come true may be drawing closer. On the third night of Olympic football (soccer) competition, a crowd of 63,624 watched Italy beat the United States, 1-0.

The truly amazing thing was not that there were 63,624 fans in the Rose Bowl, although that was certainly remarkable.

The truly amazing thing was that tournament officials were disappointed because there were not more fans there. That is akin to gymnast Mary Lou Retton being

disappointed Monday because she scored a 9.95 in the floor exercises instead of a 10.0. Some people are never satisfied.

While no one realistically expected to fill the Rose Bowl, which seats about 98,000 for the Olympics, original estimates were that the crowd would exceed 80,000.

That would have broken the U.S. attendance record for the sport of 78,265 set Sunday night in Palo Alto, where the United States beat Costa Rica, 3-0, in the opening round of Olympic competition. The record probably will fall at least twice more before the end of this tournament. Sellouts are anticipated for both the semifinals and the final at the Rose Bowl.

Many fans were walking around before the contest Tuesday night with signs expressing their desire for tickets for the Aug. 11 final. Not all of the signs were in English.

Please see CROWD, page 41

CAREY

Continued from page 40

his flowers up to his mother, but that was it. Asked the significance of the gesture, Carey replied: "She gave birth to me."

It was a classic example of the sort of behavior that has earned Carey a reputation as a pouting prima donna, an absolute perfectionist who cannot handle defeat or even a poor performance. It's also an example of the intensity that has driven him until he is the best there is.

Ironically, Carey started swimming when he was 10 years old because his parents forced him to. They were tired of his tendency to start a fight every time he lost in gym class at elementary school and wanted him to learn how to lose gracefully.

But the young man who would one day own two world backstroke records learned only how to win. And, obviously, he can't do that very gracefully, either.

"I expect a little more out of myself," Carey said. "The Olympic Games are supposed to be special, supposed to be exciting. I guess I caught Olympic fever and I don't swim well with a fever. It was a little overwhelming out there."

To his credit, Carey would not blame a stiff head wind or even the setting sun, although he did say it got in his eyes a little when he made a poor turn after 150 meters.

Carey, who established an Olympic record of 1:58.99 in the preliminaries Tuesday morning, predictably predicted he would break his world record (1:58.86) in the final. But it certainly wasn't the first time he's put that kind of pressure on himself.

"I always saw this moment as finishing with a world record," Carey said. "I really wanted to do it for my parents and for the crowd. I felt the disappointment in the crowd when I touched. I know a lot of them came here wanting to see a world record."

There were about 14,000 people in the Olympic swim facility (the official attendance was 11,047) Tuesday and not one could have been as disappointed as Rick Carey. But more than a few saw fit to eventually boo him when he refused to so much as raise his hand in appreciation for their standing ovation.

The slow win may have put Carey in a dark mood, but it certainly didn't put a damper on his arrogance.

Asked if the absence of some of the Soviet Bloc backstrokers may have led to the slow times, Carey said, "I would have won no matter what. No one can beat me, no matter how bad I feel. I had control of the race all the way and I would have won no matter who was here. And that's not cockiness, either."

Some might argue that point.

In any case, the other two swimmers in the press tent after the race were a sharp contrast to the downcast Carey.

Delcourt: "I'm very, very happy."

Henning: "I'm ecstatic."

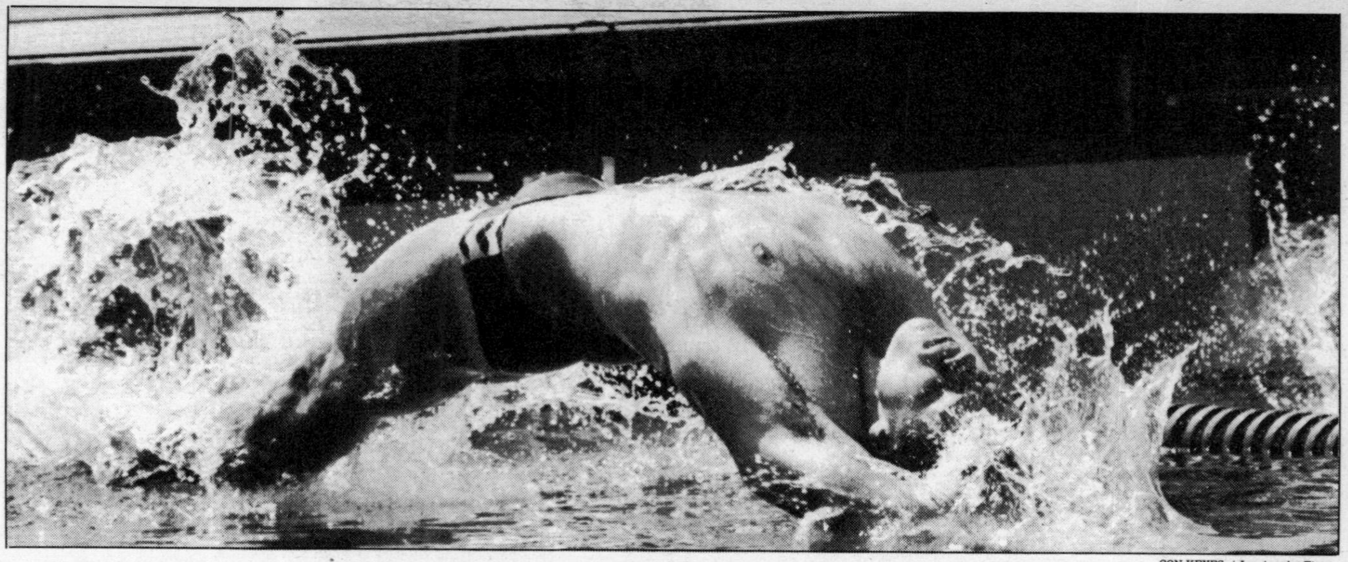

CON KEYES / Los Angeles Times

Rick Carey arches his back at the start of the 200 backstroke. Although he won gold medal with a time of 2:00.23, he was disappointed at not breaking the world record.

GYMNASTICS

Continued from page 40

the United States had attained Tuesday night.

This has been a long time coming. Ever since gymnasts have hauled in the rope and put away the Indian clubs, the United States has been as chained by gravity as statuary. The Soviet Union soared beyond all others in terms of accomplishment, dominating this sport, except for a brief reign by the Japanese. Then came China, led by the wonderful Li Ning, which surpassed the Soviet Union last year, winning the World Championships.

The United States, anybody could plainly see, was catching up. Also, as anybody could plainly see, they were still way behind. They won an individual medal in the 1976 Olympics, some medals in the 1979 World Championships. They were in the ball park, but nowhere near home plate. While China was unsettling the Soviet Union last year, the United States was fighting for its life just to get fourth, behind Japan.

But, hey, look them over. With a 1.05 lead over China from Sunday's compulsories, the United States could afford a little slippage at UCLA's Pauley Pavilion in the optional exercises, hanging in to beat second-place China, 591.40 to 590.80. Japan was well back in third place with 586.70.

It was an emotional scene for the athletes, for the 9,356 in attendance and probably for a nationwide TV audience, as well. Settled under the "festive federal" banners that hung from the roof, the U.S. gymnasts turned and waved to a flag-waving crowd. Three-time Olympic team member Bart Conner, who missed the 1980 Games because of the U.S. boycott, faced the people, tears coursing down his face. Vidmar wept openly.

Their score was an Olympic record, topping the Soviet Union's score in 1980 by nearly two points. But what you will remember is Mitch Gaylord shooting the works on his patented and risky Gaylord II on the horizontal bar, poised to either catch the bar after a one-and-a-half twisting somersault or fall to the floor and jeopardize the U.S. lead.

Yes, they went for the gold, did not settle for it. U.S. Coach Abie Grossfeld knew well what was at stake, but what the hell? "I knew how bad he wanted it," he said and shrugged. "He could have had an automatic 9.8 (with a more conservative routine), but it meant so much to him." He got a 9.95. It was that kind of gold medal.

You will remember Gaylord's UCLA teammate Tim Daggett getting one of the night's seven perfect scores, dismounting from the horizontal bar with a full twisting double flyaway somersault and raising his fist to the crowd before the judges knew what happened, almost before his form reappeared from a cloud of chalk.

You will remember other 10s, besides: Gaylord on rings, after a twisting double-back dismount; Conner on parallel bars. They matched the great Chinese gymnasts, Li Yuejiu, Tong Fei and Li Ning 10 for 10.

You will remember shootouts during several of the rotations. The Chinese had knocked a full 6/10ths of a point off the U.S. lead after the second rotation when Tong Fei and Li Ning were scoring 10s on rings and the United States was scoring in a low range on pommel horse. The arena seemed to echo with cheers after that. The United States took rings and drew gasps there as the Chinese were nailing routines on vault. On horizontal bar, no Chinese gymnast scored lowered than 9.9. Working on parallel bars at the same time, the U.S. gymnasts had a throwaway 9.8, four 9.9s and a 10.

MEN'S

THE MEDALISTS

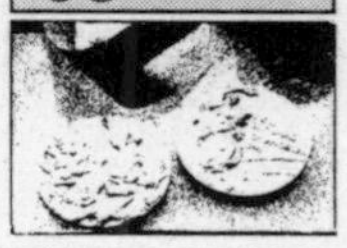

Gymnastics

■ TEAM COMPETITION

1. United States
2. China
3. Japan

Oh, it was exciting all right. Flushed with success—he is the leader in the all-around, qualifying into Thursday's all-around finals along with Conner and Gaylord—Vidmar annointed his team "a new world power, for years to come. We made history for the U.S. today."

Conner, who is fourth after half of the all-around scoring, behind Li and Tong, was more modest about the impact, although he did admit, "It has to be the biggest moment for all of us. . . . Now, we've proved we're at the level of China and Russia," he said. "Nobody's going to blow us away."

Even the laconic Grossfeld, a realist above all else, seemed surprised at the victory. He announced it was at least on a par with the U.S. hockey team appearing from nowhere to beat the Soviet Union in the 1980 Winter Olympics. "It's certainly equal to that in every way," he said. "In the gymnastics world, no one who knows gymnastics ever thought we would beat the Chinese (pause) except our own people."

So how could this happen? Well, the U.S. gymnasts are very good and they certainly improved after the World Championships when they yielded points on simple things, like dismounts. No doubt the home-field advantage helped, too. China Coach Zhang Jian said as much of the crowd enthusiasm. "Our performance was impaired," he allowed. Also, the U.S. lead from the compulsories of 1.05 helped. It was a relatively poor performance for the Chinese, who when gunning for the top-dog Soviet Union, scored a compulsory exercise of one point more than they did here.

The United States gymnasts have been preparing in a kind of shadow, dim figures due to their non-appearance in the 1980 Games. They were working at it all along. Vidmar, much later Tuesday night, recalled how he and Daggett, his best friend, used to practice on the horizontal bar, the apparatus they used to put the world at bay. They would turn off the radio, tell each other to get serious, do their best possible trick. This was for the gold, they would tell each other. And they would laugh.

□

After winning its first team gymnastics gold medal ever, the United States goes for still more. The United States has qualified the allowable three gymnasts into the 36-man all-around field, which will be contested Thursday. With their scores from the compulsory and optional exercises combined to provide 50% of the all-around score, these gymnasts go for the remaining 50% in optionals Thursday. They are Peter Vidmar, in first place with 59.275 points; Bart Conner, fourth with 59.150, and Mitch Gaylord, tied for sixth with 59.075. China's Li Ning and Tong Fei are Nos. 2 and 3; Japan's Koji Gushiken is fifth.

CROWD

Continued from page 40

Most of the Olympic venues have at least a hint of international flavor, but this one is truly worldly. Concession stands sell souvlaki, gyros, fish and chips, tacos, burritos, churros and, naturally, hot dogs.

Vendors outside the stadium Tuesday night were selling Italian-language newspapers from Rome, Milan, Turin and New York. They were doing a brisk business.

Il Progresso headlined *"La battaglia di Pasadena."* The battle of Pasadena.

The article told of Italy's 1-0 victory Sunday night over Egypt, which resembled a back-alley rumble. Or an ice hockey game.

The match between Italy and the United States was played on friendlier terms but had its tense moments.

This was not the night of shooting stars for the United States, but it did mount enough charges in the second half to keep the hundreds of American flags in the stands waving until the very end.

Perhaps someday, if the sport ever finds its way into the nation's heartland, this will be remembered as the tournament that started it all.

It is too late for Lamar Hunt. Rising costs and decreasing fan interest drove him and the Tornado out of the sport in 1981. The only thing the millions he invested in the sport bought him was a kick in the grass.

Even though it is unquestionably the world's most popular sport, Americans have had difficulty relating to it.

When he came to the United States as the national coach in 1975, West German Dettmar Cramer complained that Americans would never pick up the sport as long as they continued to pick up the ball with their hands.

Throw a ball to a South American or European child, he kicks it. Throw a ball to an American child, he catches it.

Cramer threw up his hands and returned to Munich less than a year after he arrived.

But not only do Americans not have an instinct for the sport, they do not speak the language. They call a match a game and the pitch a field. They do not even call it by its proper name, saying soccer instead of football.

That was all supposed to change when professional soccer came to this country in 1967.

Ever since then, soccer enthusiasts in this country have been a little like the religious fanatics who parade around on street corners with signs forecasting the end of the world.

Whether they were promoting the National Professional Soccer League, the United Soccer Assn., the North American Soccer League, the American Soccer League, the Major Indoor Soccer League or the United States Soccer Federation, they all preached about the forthcoming soccer boom in the United States.

Why not? The sport has more action, less injuries and fewer costs than American football. And everybody on the field gets to play with the ball.

The complaint heard most often from American sports fans is that there is not enough scoring in soccer. But unless it is the Raiders against the Redskins, or the Chargers against anybody, there are probably fewer scoring opportunities in American football than in soccer. It is scoring opportunities that provide the excitement, no matter what the sport.

Besides, nobody complains when the Dodgers win a game, 1-0.

About the only thing soccer did not have when it arrived in the United States was an established star. That was solved when the sport's greatest player, Brazil's Pele, signed to play for the NASL's New York Cosmos in 1975.

Two years later, in Pele's final NASL season, the Cosmos drew 77,691 fans for a playoff game, a U.S. soccer attendance record that stood until Sunday night.

The Cosmos did not have Pele in 1979, but they did have West Germany's Franz Beckenbauer, Italy's Giorgio Chinaglia and a supporting cast of several other international stars. Their average attendance was 47,000.

But, with apologies to Frank Sinatra's "New York, New York," if you can make it there, it does not necessarily mean you can make it anywhere. Guys with accents who wear short pants and run around "keeking touchdowns" do not play in Peoria. Sorry about the stereotype, but that is the way the sport is seen in Middle America.

St. Louis probably has more youth league soccer players than any other city in the country but would not support the NASL's Stars. Not even Hunt's millions could save the NASL's Tornado in Dallas.

Hunt argued that the United States needed an international presence in the sport before it would be accepted here.

To prepare a representative World Cup team, Team America was formed last year. It was supposed to bring together the best young Americans, provide them with quality competition and mold them into a unit capable of at least staying on the same field with the Europeans and South Americans.

If that field happened to be in the United States, in front of a national television audience, the result, the promoters said, would be—you guessed it—the soccer boom. Thus an effort was made to bring the 1986 World Cup to the United States. Presenting this country's case was none other than Dr. Henry Kissinger.

Team America drew 50,000 for one match in its home of Washington, D.C., but in retrospect, the attendance probably had to do more with a concert given afterward by the Beach Boys.

Team America's average attendance was less than 5,000. It finished the season with a 10-20 record against NASL competition, losing 13 of its last 17 games, and was mercifully put out of its misery.

The effort to bring the World Cup to the United States was no more successful. It was awarded to Mexico. "The U.S. was not prepared yet," an International Federation of Football (FIFA) spokesman said Tuesday.

There obviously is still some interest in soccer in the United States. In three matches against international teams this year, the Cosmos averaged 36,368 fans. But in matches against other NASL teams, the Cosmos are down to 14,407.

"That is very sad," Dick Berg said before the match at the Rose Bowl Tuesday.

Berg is a Los Angeles Olympic Organizing Committee vice president. As general manager of the Dallas Tornado in the mid-70s, the former Stanford quarterback was one of those promoters who believed the soccer boom was around the next corner. He felt it so strongly he could make even Cowboy fans believe it, which is why soccer flourished in Dallas for a couple of years.

But he has been disappointed so many times that he has not allowed himself to become too excited about the Olympic soccer attendance.

It might be another apparition.

"If the crowds are as pro-American as they have been so far, and if we win, we'll at least be back in the same spot where we were in 1977, which I consider the high-water mark," Berg said. "We'll have our foot in the door.

"But the U.S. has to win. I really believe that a good showing is not good enough. It would be a remarkable accomplishment if this team reaches the quarterfinals, but it has to be in the final to make an impression.

"The response from Americans for the ice hockey team in 1980 was unbelievable, but I don't think it would have been there if we had not won the gold medal.

"I'm forever hopeful, but I wish I could be more optimistic."

Who knows? The 1980 U.S. hockey team had its "Miracle on Ice." The 1984 U.S. soccer team may have its "Splendor in the Grass."

Just in case, representatives from the Los Angeles Lazers were outside the Rose Bowl Tuesday night to sell tickets to the team's indoor soccer games—uh, matches—next season at the Forum.

They had trouble selling tickets to games last season even when they were giving away free trips to Hawaii. But the team's assistant to the president, Jodi Graffio, said Tuesday that if soccer catches on at the Olympics, maybe it will catch on at the Forum.

Now, that would be a miracle.

MURRAY

Continued from page 40

picture runner, pretty to look at and dangerous to a clock but no threat at all when it came to the rough-and-tumble of the Olympic Games.

Steve Ovett, the eventual winner in the 800 at Moscow, thrashed his way through tightly bunched packs of competitors like a peer of the realm caning his coachmen. Coe ran his usual esthetic race parked outside two or three runners the whole way. "Seb must think it's a bloody ballet!" growled one of the British newsmen watching. At Moscow, winner Ovett was not the most popular athlete over the gin-ands of Fleet Street.

Coe himself recalled the race over lunch at the UCLA Olympic Village the other day. "I made the cardinal mistake of losing contact with the true competition," he said. "When the opportunity came, I didn't respond quickly enough." He spent the whole race in Lane 2, which meant ultimately that, in 800 meters, he ended up running 10 to 11 meters more than any other leader in the race.

When the metric mile came along, even Track & Field News was ready to give up on the great Brit who had set four world records. It was sadly concluded that he belonged on the roll of British runners who ran best over foggy moors, like Roger Bannister, breaking four-minute barriers but not Olympic tapes.

Coe himself was made of sterner stuff. A reporter ran into him in a top-floor corridor of the Hotel Rossia near Red Square on the eve of the 1,500-meter final. "A lot of people are hoping you can bring it off," he said. "Oh," said Coe. "I'm sure I can."

In the ensuing race, the crowd fancied Ovett, who had won 41 straight races at that distance, or the East German, Jurgen Straub, another noted infighter.

But Keats and Shelley or Lord Byron would have loved Sebastian Coe's race. Because of the conditions of the race—Straub and Ovett bristling away—Coe was able to run freely. "It's what I do best." He struck his beautiful form like a hunter going over hedges. He swept past the German on the turn, blazed the final hundred in 12 flat and flashed across the finish line. He had finally run a race that rhymed.

Seb Coe is back at the Olympic Games this year, as usual discounted as a semi-literary figure. As at Moscow, he is deemed not at top form, a debilitating glandular disorder akin to the dormitory disease, mononucleosis, having drained some of his energy for training. (You would imagine Lord Byron would have glandular disorders, too. It fits the image.)

But Steve Ovett, Steve Cram, Steve Scott, Sydney Maree and Jim Spivey would do well to check that fragile little Englishman at their shoulder. He's not as ethereal as he might look. This is one of the great athletes in the world, never mind if he looks like Childe Harold in cleats.

Gaines Finally Gets on a Roll, and There Is No Stopping Him

By TRACY DODDS,
Times Staff Writer

Rowdy Gaines got off to a fast start—a fast, rolling start—and bolted into a lead that he held for the entire sprint to win the gold medal in the men's 100-meter freestyle Tuesday night at the Olympic Swim Stadium.

Gaines, who holds the world record with a time of 49.36 seconds, won his first Olympic gold medal with a time of 49.80, beating the Olympic record of 49.99 set by Jim Montgomery in Montreal in 1976.

It was truly a golden moment for Gaines, who came back at the age of 25 to try for the glory that was denied him by the 1980 boycott.

"I'd swim another eight years and go through another boycott for this feeling right now," Gaines said. "I know you've heard it before from people like Lunk (Steve Lundquist) and Tracy (Caulkins) and Sippy (Woodhead) and Jill (Sterkel) but for us, it's true. We all went through hell in '80, but this makes it all worth it."

No one was begrudging Gaines his gold medal. Indeed, he deserved it and, indeed, he might well have won it anyway, but there were tempers flaring about the quick gun on the start.

Several coaches expressed their displeasure with the start, including U.S. Coach Don Gambril. The Australians issued the only official protest, which was disallowed by a FINA jury. Gambril recommended that the starter, Frank Silvestri of Panama, be replaced. But as the coach of the winner, he would hardly protest the race.

The swimmers had stepped onto their starting blocks and were just leaning over to take their positions when the gun sounded. Gaines was closer to his position than the others. He uses a track start, with one foot back to push off, and he was in a forward motion when the gun went off.

Mark Stockwell of Australia, who was the top qualifier in the morning heats and who finished second in 50.24, was caught unaware.

Immediately after the race, Stockwell fired off this response: "That was not a fair start. I didn't know what to expect. I thought that the starter would call everyone back. I didn't know what was going to happen. Do they think that they can change the rules here in America in order to win or what? I'm trying to be a good sport about this, but I really am disgusted. I expect things to be fair and the same for everyone. Heath was really left standing on the block."

Mike Heath, who beat Gaines at the U.S. Olympic trials to qualify for this event, finished fourth Tuesday night, behind bronze-medalist Per Johansson of Sweden.

Heath said, "Several of us got robbed on the start. I was just coming down to grab the block when he shot the gun off. I have a pretty slow start, anyway, and that sure didn't help me."

Gaines was not denying that it was a quick start. He said, "I have no control over who starts the race. All I can do is swim it. . . . I did get down quick. My coach, Richard Quick, talked to me during the day and told me to be ready. I've been taught to get down quick because I've been left on the blocks before, myself."

There has been comment for several days on how quick the starts have been. So maybe it wasn't all luck that Gaines was the only one not complaining. Maybe it was experience, too.

Later, being interviewed alongside Gaines, Stockwell toned down his reaction to the start. He said, "I don't want to take anything away from Rowdy. He's having a good time. So am I. He's a good guy, actually.

"He's been around for a long time. He knows what to look out for."

As the top American finisher in the 100-meter freestyle, Gaines earned a spot on the 400-meter medley relay. He was already on the 400-meter freestyle relay because he finished among the top four in the 100 at the trials.

So this could well be the first of three gold medals for Ambrose Gaines IV.

Gaines said a year ago, when he made the decision to come back, that he was going for the gold. He said, at that time, that he did not intend to go through a year of hell for a silver medal. He backed off that a little bit after winning the gold. He said, "This afternoon, I prepared my loser's speech. I was going to say that I felt honored and proud to swim against the guy who won—I do feel honored and proud to swim against these guys—and I was going to say that it's been worth it to have the career that I've had.

"I've set three world records in individual events and half a dozen on relays. That's nothing to be ashamed of."

But it's also nothing compared to a gold medal.

His elation showed at the finish, when he shot his fist into the air.

Asked to comment on that show of emotion, he gave a typically Rowdy answer, saying, "I was going for that Sure underarm commercial, I guess."

DAVE GATLEY / Los Angeles Times
A jubilant Rowdy Gaines raises his fist after breaking an Olympic record in the 100 freestyle.

CON KEYES / Los Angeles Times
Rowdy Gaines places hand on his heart during national anthem.

With the Stars and Stripes as a backdrop, a victorious Rowdy Gaines reaches out to his friends.
United Press International

Bertrand and Three Other American Sailors Win on First Day of Races

By RICH ROBERTS,
Times Staff Writer

Yachting

It had been one protest, a redress, some review board and executive committee hearings and several arbitrations since John Bertrand was in a sailboat race, so anything short of falling out of the boat Tuesday would have been considered a success.

But the first Finn class race of the Olympic yachting competition at Long Beach went better than that. Bertrand not only won it but made it look so easy that he appeared to be sailing in his own fair wind.

Three other American sailors also won: Bill Buchan in Star, Randy Smyth in Tornado and favorite Robbie Haines in Soling. Smyth's arch-rival, Chris Cairns of Australia, with his hair dyed green and gold, finished fourth. Tuesday's races were the first of a series of seven (with one throwout) in seven classes to determine the gold-medal winners.

Jonathan McKee, with Buchan's son Carl as crew, tried to make it five wins for the United States, chasing the Moeller brothers, Jorgen and Jacob, of Naerum, Denmark, to a close second around the Flying Dutchman course.

Then the Moellers had to survive another close call when officials weighed their clothing, which barely made the 20-kilo (44-pound), soaking-wet maximum on the third try.

America's Steve Benjamin brushed the port end starting buoy with his 470 dinghy, had to reround and finished a disappointing 10th as the Hunger brothers, Wolfgang and Joachim, of Berlin sailed to a 35-second win over France's Thierry Peponnet.

France's Gildas Guillerot finished first in the sailboards, but the jury disqualified him for violating Rule 60.2 (b): using illegal body kinetics to enhance speed. Yacht rules forbid the rocking of the boat or board, or the deliberate shifting of body weight, for the purpose of gaining speed.

Germany's Dirk Meyer inherited the win, but it was America's day.

"Oh, boy," Smyth said, "the U.S. had a fabulous day. It looks like a good year."

Buchan, at 49 the oldest American sailor, said, "I'm impressed that John Bertrand won. That says a lot for his skills."

Bertrand, 28, of Anaheim Hills only last Thursday won a 2½-month-long dispute involving Russ Silvestri to determine the U.S. Finn representative. He tried not to take it too seriously when he sailed with the leaders in Monday's practice race—his first competition since the disputed final race of the trials May 11.

"They're holding back, letting us old guys look good," he said of his rivals. "Lasse (Hjortnaes of Denmark, the world champion) gave up and just sat there. The Swede (Ingvar Bengtsson) was going fast, and he wasn't even hiking out (leaning out over the water to balance the boat) . . . just sitting there laughing at everybody."

But it was deadly serious Tuesday, especially for Bertrand, who entered the Olympics carrying the extra burden of proving he belongs.

His fiancee, Andrea Adame of San Francisco, said: "I don't know what's going to happen in the rest of the series, but I think his victory has already been won."

Bertrand led at every mark by as much as 1 minute 8 seconds and beat runnerup Russell Coutts of New Zealand by 30 seconds.

But wouldn't you know, he wound up in the jury room late Tuesday night on a port-starboard protest by Coutts. The jury's decision is to be announced this morning.

That problem aside, Bertrand said, "Getting around that first mark first was a boost. I was a little surprised, I guess."

He had said he was "out of shape" from too much litigation and not enough sailing and was "pretty tired" afterward, with "a lot of those big, strong boys coming on at the end. But what happened to Lasse?"

What happened to Lasse, who finished 21st, was a broken outhaul, the line that controls sail tension along the boom. The Dane suspected sabotage.

"Probably," he said. "It shouldn't break because it's only a week old."

Tuesday's winds were moderate 8-to-10 knots at the 1:30 start, building to nearly 20 at the finishes some two hours later.

KEN HIVELY / Los Angeles Times
Wolfgang Hunger (left) and his brother, Joachim, hiking out on their way to victory in the first Olympic 470 yacht race Tuesday.

OLYMPICS '84/NOTES

Compiled By JERRY GILLAM

Will the Signals Be 'One If by Land, Two If by Sea'?

From Times Staff Writers and Wire Services

The next few days will not be a good time to smuggle anything into Los Angeles by boat—unless you own a submarine.

The Coast Guard is patrolling the Olympic yachting courses off Long Beach with three helicopters and vessels ranging from the 400-foot icebreaker Polar Star to 45 high-speed inflatable dinghies with twin 70-horsepower outboards.

During a recent practice race, the Polar Star noticed an unmarked boat entering one of the courses and ordered it intercepted and boarded. On board were Pelle Pettersson and three other members of the Swedish support team, who were escorted back to the Olympic harbor.

Pettersson is Sweden's most distinguished sailor—a former America's Cup campaigner and winner of Olympic bronze and silver medals in the Star class.

If you aren't flying the right flag, however, it doesn't matter who you are.

—RICH ROBERTS

□

Muhammad Ali, former heavyweight boxing champion making his first appearance at the Sports Arena, sat in the partitioned VIP ringside area, guarded by two uniformed police officers.

Asked if he had any regrets about throwing his Olympic gold medal into the Ohio River in Louisville—a story documented in his book and on film—he nodded slowly but said nothing.

Pressed for a reply, he commented, almost inaudibly: "I do now. I wish I'd kept it."

Ali, who won a gold medal as a light-heavyweight in the 1960 Rome Games when he was known as Cassius Clay, later threw the medal into the river after he had been refused service in a restaurant because he was black.

Officials, upset about a reporter nudging between the two officers to speak to Ali, finally ushered the reporter away.

—JACK HAWN

□

When the Olympics are over and Rob Stull returns home to San Antonio, Tex., the first thing he is going to do is find a job. Any job.

"I've got to earn some money to pay all my legal fees," Stull said.

Stull, the alternate on the U.S. Olympic modern pentathlon team, wasn't kidding. It took him two months of legal maneuverings and a 12-hour hearing to confirm his spot on the four-man Olympic team.

After the May trials, in which Stull finished third, seven athletes accused him of soliciting friends to throw fencing matches to him. Officials of the U.S. Modern Pentathlon Assn. eventually called a hearing, at which time Stull was finally cleared.

Three days before the start of the competition, however, the coaches designated Stull as the alternate. So Monday, he looked out at the fencing strip at Coto de Caza in south Orange County and said: "This is the day I've trained the last four years for . . . and I'm standing here talking to you.

"It's been a long road for me. I go through all that to make the team, and then I'm hit with being the alternate, and I thought I was being robbed again. But now, I'm trying to be the best alternate I can."

The same day the coaches made Stull the alternate, his teammates elected him captain.

Stull, 24, said he would stay in the sport and try to qualify for the 1988 Olympics.

—SAM McMANIS

□

It's easy to get caught up in the pomp and pageantry of the Olympics. The nearly continuous coverage on television and the volume of stories in newspapers can't help but get many people excited—but not Times staff writer Dan York, who had this negative reaction: "The bad thing about the Olympics is that it legitimizes trash sports every four years."

□

Weightlifting events aren't usually fraught with hazards to referees or spectators, unless a fully loaded iron bar bounces off the performing platform.

That's what happened in Monday afternoon's session. Tunisia's Taoufik Maaouia lost control of the bar while trying to snatch 209.25 pounds, lurching forward and dropping the barbell.

It bounced over a barricade toward an official sitting in front of the platform, coming to rest within inches of his lap.

□

The announced crowds at the sold-out Olympic volleyball competition at the Long Beach Arena are not quite what they seem to be.

The Los Angeles Olympic Organizing Committee has listed the official crowd at each of the volleyball sessions as 12,033. Actually, the paid attendance for each session has been closer to 9,000.

The LAOOC's figures include players, coaches, officials and statisticians, plus 700 seats for non-competing athletes, another 700 for the LAOOC, 300 for the Olympic family (VIPs), 100 for the volleyball commissioner and the 350 seats that have been replaced by the press area.

—JERRY CROWE

□

USC's Cheryl Miller had a fainting spell last season that was remedied in part by better nutrition.

Still, she hasn't quite eliminated a sweet tooth, particularly for chocolate.

While talking with reporters after Tuesday's victory over Australia, Miller couldn't keep her hands away from a plate of chocolate cookies and a bag of M&Ms.

She was so intent on eating that she couldn't be quite as informative as usual.

Asked for the umpteenth time if she is too flamboyant, Miller paused dramatically, rolled her eyes upward and said, "No."

She's an entertainer, and a diplomat, too.

"I have a lot to learn," she said. "The reason it looks so easy for me is, my teammates complement me so well."

—CHRIS COBBS

□

Flo Hyman of the U.S. women's volleyball team lashed out at the media Monday night for what she said were unwarranted attacks against Coach Arie Selinger.

"It doesn't matter what you all think," she said. "It's what the players think. We're the ones who have to train and we're the ones who have to do the work. You guys don't have to do nothing. And as long as we're happy, just leave us alone and let us do our job."

—JERRY CROWE

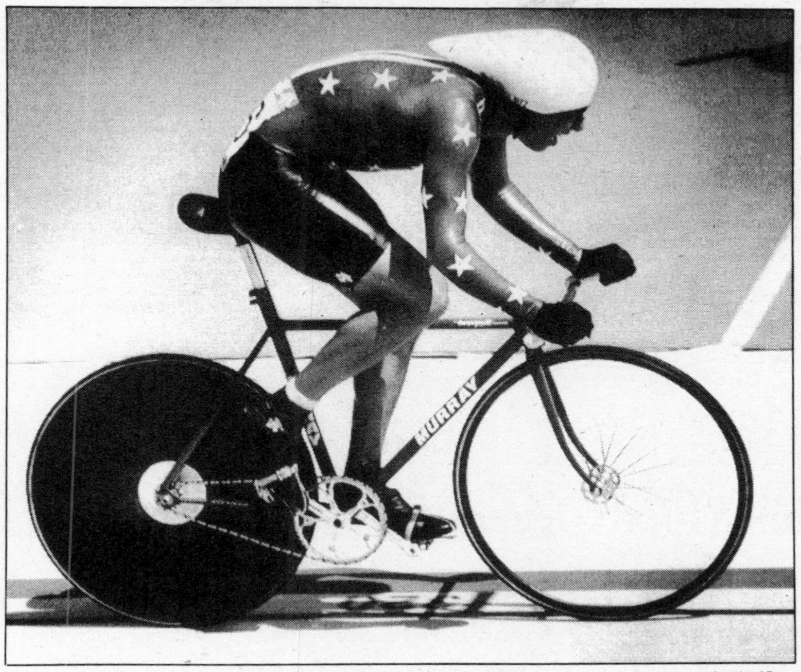

Associated Press

Cutting a startling figure in his streamlined racing helmet, American cyclist Steve Hegg tops qualifying Monday in the 4,000-meter pursuit race on a bike with a solid rear wheel.

Instead of each country having its own cycling repair and maintenance shop at Cal State Dominguez Hills, Campagnolo U.S.A. is serving every cyclist and team riding at the Olympic Velodrome.

A dozen mechanics, gathered fRom all over the country, are equipped with 30 spare bikes, 80 wheels, $75,000 in spare parts and $2,000 in tool kits. They can change a rear wheel, racing sprocket and all, in eight seconds.

"We're totally neutral," said R. Brook Watts of Houston, the crew chief. "We'll rebuild a bike completely, like we did for a rider from Antigua, to try and put him on an even keel with the rich teams—at least as far as his equipment is concerned.

"Or we'll replace any part any rider on any team might want replaced. Everything is free. We just trade new parts for dead parts, and when the Games are over, all the dead parts become property of the LAOOC."

—SHAV GLICK

□

Julie Vollertsen of the U.S. women's volleyball team attributed the Americans' subpar performance in their victory over West Germany Monday night to nervousness.

"This is like graduation day and you're always worried that you're going to trip on the steps going up to get your diploma," she said.

—JERRY CROWE

□

Dutch field hockey Coach Wilhemus van Heumen fears the heat at East Los Angeles College will take more of a toll on European teams than others by the end of the tournament, but not even all his players agree.

Dutch star Ties Kruize said, "I like it. It's not so wet (humid)."

West German Coach Klaus Klieter said the weather was "nice . . . for swimming." He added, "Actually it was worse at tournaments in Kuala Lumpur and Bombay."

Asked the temperature on the artificial turf, German player Michael Peter said, "We came to play hockey, not measure the temperature."

—ALAN DROOZ

□

Indian field hockey officials filed a protest with stadium officials after one spectator tore up another spectator's Indian flag during a game between India and the United States, India's team manager said Tuesday.

The manager, Nandy Singh, called it a minor incident and said he was waiting to see what action was taken to prevent it from being repeated. He said there was no talk of the Indian field hockey team withdrawing.

"Someone grabbed a flag on the first day and tramped on it and we are quite upset," he said.

□

While Britain's Princess Anne goes about her duties as president of the British Olympic Association, her husband pulls shifts as just another working bloke at the Los Angeles Games.

Well, almost.

Capt. Mark Phillips is working the games as a television commentator covering equestrian events for Australia's Network 10.

While Phillips lodges with his colleagues at the Hollywood Holiday Inn, his wife is staying 18 miles away in Pasadena at the plush Sheraton hotel.

They see each other when they can.

"I don't want to be asked stupid questions about my wife," Phillips, an accomplished horseman, snapped to a fellow journalist at the Santa Anita race track, where the Olympic equestrian events are being held.

"We see each other whenever our two programs allow."

□

Much has been said and written about the Olympic villages at USC and UCLA, but wrestlers have a mini-village in Anaheim only a few steps from the Convention Center arena.

Because the afternoon session ends at 3 p.m. and the evening session begins at 6 p.m., there obviously is not enough time for athletes to return to their villages and get back. They would be on the road for all three hours.

Thus, an exhibition hall behind the arena serves as a home away from the home away from home for wrestlers.

Each country entered has its own area, complete with beds, tables and chairs. Athletes can sleep, play cards, read, whatever. Only draperies separate them, so national secrets are kept to whispers.

There also is a lounge area with television sets, six warmup mats, saunas for those who have to shed ounces (or pounds), and scales.

Of course, the losers widen their options. And Disneyland is right across the street.

—DAVE DISTEL

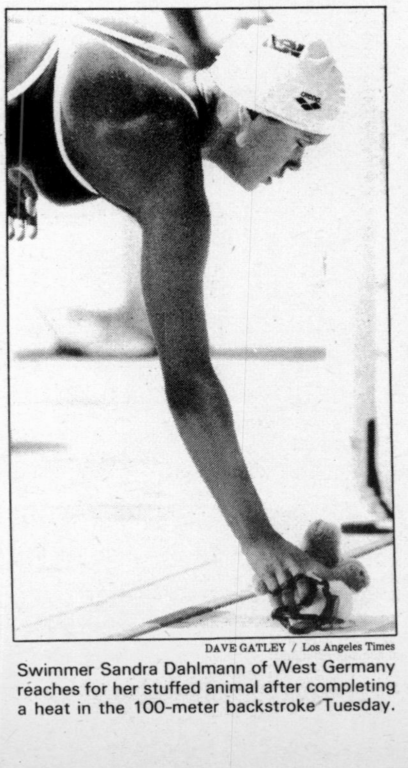

DAVE GATLEY / Los Angeles Times

Swimmer Sandra Dahlmann of West Germany reaches for her stuffed animal after completing a heat in the 100-meter backstroke Tuesday.

□

With the bodies as ready as they'll ever be and degrees of skill virtually identical at the top, the Olympic judo teams have settled down to a little quiet psychological warfare. "It's all mental now," said American Bobby Berland. "Mental and emotional."

Britain's Neil Adams agreed. The consensus favorite at 172 pounds after finishing second in the world championships in 1983, and second in the '80 Olympics at 156, Adams said, "It's now a matter of motivation—and the British team has it in abundance."

Questioned on his own strengths, Adams, an exuberant 26-year-old from Coventry who is a prominent model and a national hero back home, conceded, "I'm a pretty good all-around fighter. I can play the technical game, but I can use the muscle if I have to."

His weaknesses? "Do you suppose Brett Barron will be reading this?" asked Adams. Barron is the U.S. 172-pounder who poses one of Adams' stiffest challenges. "Yes? Well, then I can say in all honesty that I haven't a single weak point."

—DICK RORABACK

□

The 3-0 victory over Costa Rica by the United States in its opening soccer game last Sunday was not only the first American Olympic victory in 60 years, it was a reversal of a very definite trend.

In its first Olympic soccer game, in 1924, the United States beat Estonia, 1-0. It has been all downhill since then.

The composite U.S. result before Sunday was one victory, eight defeats, one tie, four goals scored and 51 goals given up.

—TERRY SHEPARD

□

American Ed Etzel, winner of Monday's English match competition at the Prado Regional shooting range in the Chino Valley, says there is a stigma attached to the prone small-bore riflemen.

"Prone shooters are known as an overweight bunch," Etzel, a slender, dark-haired marksman, said. "They're called belly shooters. I hope I can do well in the three-position on Wednesday so I won't be known as only a prone shooter."

—ELLIOTT ALMOND

□

H.D. Thoreau, the co-commissioner of track and field for the Games, has wanted to see Pickfair, the storied home of Douglas Fairbanks and Mary Pickford, since he was a boy growing up here in the 30s.

Thoreau got his chance one night last week when Jerry Buss, the new owner of Pickfair, held a garden party for International Amateur Athletic Federation and other officials.

Fairbanks and Pickford held the same type of party for Olympic officials here for the 1932 Games. Thoreau suggested it would be appropriate to continue the theme. Buss agreed. Thoreau got his invitation.

—MAL FLORENCE

□

Vonnie Gros, coach of the U.S. women's field hockey team, says Los Angeles' smog has been greatly overhyped.

"In my mind, I had built the problem to be much greater," she said.

She joked that when the team trained at Ursinus College in Pennsylvania, "I had scheduled four cars to back up to our practice gym. But Ursinus wouldn't let us do it."

—ALAN DROOZ

□

Geoff Gaberino, the leadoff swimmer for the men's 800-meter freestyle relay that set a world record in the preliminary heat Monday morning, did not swim in the final Monday night. He was one of the two alternates scheduled to swim just the preliminaries.

He said, "It's hard to just jump up in the morning and swim, knowing you're not going to swim at night. But the world record was a nice little bonus. We wanted to shake the Germans up a little and set a world record with—quote, not the best, unquote—team we had."

—TRACY DODDS

□

Young-Sin Kim and Soon-Chul Lee, two members of South Korea's baseball team here to participate in the demonstration tournament, apparently would prefer to play in cooler weather.

During a practice session at Dodger Stadium Monday, they practically staggered into the dugout, gasping for air. After quenching their thirst, they were asked how they liked the Southern California weather. They shook their heads and said, in effect, that it was much too hot to play baseball in Los Angeles.

That happened at 12:10 p.m., when the temperature was only about 84 degrees.

—BOB CUOMO

□

Mike Tyson, the hard-punching New Yorker who was eliminated by Los Angeles heavyweight Henry Tillman in the Olympic trials boxoff in Las Vegas, was asked for his autograph by a young fan with an American flag sticker pasted on his forehead.

"Do you know who he is?" the fan was asked.

"No," he replied.

The boxer stopped writing.

"Then why do you want my autograph?" he asked.

Slightly embarrassed, the fan shrugged . . . and Tyson resumed writing.

—JACK HAWN

□

Bela Karolyi's impromptu press conference may have been the highlight of Monday's gymnastics action. The former Romanian coach, who is now coaching U.S. Olympians Mary Lou Retton and Julianne McNamara, dumped on Romanian judge Julia Roterescu with a comic fury.

Asked if he understood why she was so blatantly underscoring the Americans, he said, "She is judging just as she does in Europe. But I think this time she has lost her mind and forgotten she is here alone."

And so on. After 10 or more minutes of such cheerful denigration—"I tell you, she is not a smart one!"—several of the journalists listening held up sheets of paper, giving him a 10, traditionally a perfect score in press conference competition.

—RICHARD HOFFER

□

Art ("Say something nice") Aragon, California's Golden Boy of professional boxing 25 years ago, showed up at the Sports Arena with his sense of humor on the front burner, as usual.

"How many amateur fights did you have, Art?" he was asked.

"Thirteen," he replied. "I won all but 12."

Actually, he was unbeaten and said he would have remained an amateur during and after World War II years until 1948, "if I'd known about the Olympics."

He turned pro in 1943 and retired in 1960. Although never a world title contender, his fights were never dull and filled the Hollywood Legion Stadium, Olympic Auditorium and other Southland arenas for years.

Now a bail bondsman, his cards promise "I'll get you out if it takes 10 years."

—JACK HAWN

□

Soviet reports from Tass critical of the Olympics apparently weren't relayed to Soviet officials on hand for the cycling competition.

Miron Baramia of the USSR was chief commisairre for the women's road race Sunday, and Valeri Syssoev, president of the Interntional Cycling Federation, presented the medals to Connie Carpenter-Phinney, Rebecca Twigg and Sandra Schumacher.

"Both of the Soviet officials praised the course and conduct of the crowd and the competitors," said Peter Siracusa, LAOOC commissioner of cycling.

—SHAV GLICK

□

Los Angeles Olympic Organizing Committee members probably made a mistake when they scaled the house at Cal State Fullerton's gymnasium (capacity: 3,300) for team handball. Tickets were priced at $10, $6 and $3 for the preliminaries.

The $10 seats are located on the gymnasium floor, with a clear, unobstructed view of play. The $6 seats are behind the goals, where spectators will be viewing play through a four-inch mesh net that will protect them from errant shots that travel up to 80 mph.

The $3 seats are located on the second level of the gym. They really offer fans the best view of the action, especially from the fourth row up where a railing doesn't inhibit viewing.

—TOM HAMILTON

Italy Gets Win Over U.S. Team

By GRAHAME L. JONES, *Times Staff Writer*

Three months ago, shortly after taking over as coach of the U.S. Olympic soccer team, Alkis Panagoulias issued a blunt warning.

"The Europeans are coming to slaughter us, not just to beat us," he said. "There is no mercy in international soccer. We are in very deep water, surrounded by sharks."

On Tuesday night, before a crowd of 63,624 at the Rose Bowl, the United States found itself confronted by one of the most dangerous sharks of all—the Mediterranean Blue.

Italy's *Forza Azzurri* came into the game determined to swallow the Americans whole. The Italian team had been ridiculed by the press in Rome after its 0-0 tie with the United States at Giants Stadium in May. This time, it wanted a convincing victory.

But the United States, fresh off a 3-0 win over Costa Rica on Sunday, proved itself no pushover. Italy won, thanks only to a 54th-minute goal by Pietro Fanna, but it was hardly convincing.

The game's lone goal was well taken, however. Riccardo Ferri floated a cross into the left side of the goal area, where Aldo Serena leaped above the American defenders and headed the ball down across the goalmouth to the onrushing Fanna. Spotting an opening, Fanna caught the ball on the half-volley, and his right-footed shot was spinning in the back of the net before U.S. goalkeeper David Brcic had a chance to react.

"The player who scored the Italian goal actually mis-kicked," Panagoulias claimed afterward.

"I would like to mis-kick shots like this all the time if this is the result," Fanna replied when told of the U.S. coach's remark.

Far from being discouraged by the setback, the Americans began mounting offensive forays of their own. They found their way blocked by a strong Italian defense, however, and never seriously troubled Italian goalkeeper Franco Tancredi.

In fact, Tancredi's most nerve-racking moment came as the result of a miscue by one of his own defenders that almost resulted in the United States taking an early lead.

Fifteen minutes into the game, Pietro Vierchowod rose to head away a U.S. corner kick, only to see the ball fly toward his own net. Tancredi had to fling himself to his left to bat the ball away.

That was as close as the United States came to scoring.

This was the fourth meeting between the teams in Olympic competition and the Americans are still seeking their first win and their first goal. They have been outscored, 19-0, in four losses.

Tuesday's victory virtually assures the Italians of a spot in the quarterfinals, while the United States will have to beat Egypt at Stanford Stadium on Thursday night in order to advance.

Midfielder Ricky Davis, captain of the American team, said the Italian defense proved too much for the United States.

"The Italians are very tough," he said. "It seems like you're playing against 35 of them when you try to attack."

After Italy had taken the lead, Panagoulias sent Californians Jeff Hooker and Michael Fox in place of Chico Borja and Jean Willrich, but it was not enough. Whenever the United States threatened, Italy dropped as many as nine players back on defense, effectively thwarting the U.S. attack.

With the crowd chanting the now popular "USA . . . USA . . . USA" and rising to its feet every time the Americans moved forward on offense, the United States seemed to have a chance.

But a shot by Hooker flew wide to the right in the 80th minute and, when Hugo Perez skied a free kick over the goal in the dying seconds, the last chance had gone.

Now, it all comes down to Thursday night's game. Because of Egypt's 4-1 win over Costa Rica Tuesday night, a tie will do the United States no good. To reach the quarterfinals, it will have to win.

Soccer Notes

During halftime of Tuesday's game, a fan carrying an American flag ran across the Rose Bowl field, eluding security personnel before finally being collared and escorted out of the stadium. Four other fans tried the same thing and also were wrestled to the ground and led out. . . . Stars and Stripes were everywhere in evidence, but one fan who tried to buy an Italian flag was told, "Go to Rome." . . . If anyone knows the correct score of the United States' win over Estonia in the Paris Olympics of 1924, please tell the United States Olympic Committee. On Tuesday, there was a minor squabble over whether it was 1-0, as the United States Soccer Federation claims, or 11-2, as USOC first said, or 2-1, which is what USOC now says was the score. . . . Total attendance halfway through the first round of the 32-match tournament now totals 391,947, or an average of 32,662 per game.

U.S. Piles Up Gold Medals in Swimming, Gymnastics

U.S. Olympians swept Tuesday's five swimming events and then stunned world-champion China by winning the men's team gymnastic title—the men's first gold medal in that sport in 80 years. A woman shooter also won a gold.

The seven golds gave the Americans 16 for the Games' first three days, four more than all other countries combined. The U.S. total is 24. China is second with 11.

The men's and women's basketball teams and the men's volleyball teams all had easy wins, but the U.S. soccer team lost. Two American boxers won their bouts, U.S. yachtsmen won in four of the seven races, and China won its third straight gold medal in weightlifting.

The day's highlights:

—Gymnastics. Mitch Gaylord of Van Nuys, Bart Conner of Morton Grove, Ill., and Tim Daggett of West Springfield, Mass., got perfect 10s (among seven awarded) in, respectively, the rings, parallel bars and high bar. UCLA's Peter Vidmar was the high scorer. The American win (with 591.40 points to 590.80 for China and 586.70 for Japan), touched off a wildly emotional celebration at Pauley Pavilion. Although China was strongly favored, the U.S. team in the six-discipline sport built confidence in the compulsory exercises Sunday and could not be denied in the optionals Tuesday night.

—Swimming. Tiffany Cohen of Mission Viejo started the medal parade by winning the women's 400-meter freestyle in American-record time, 4:07.10. Rowdy Gaines of Winter Haven, Fla., took the men's 100-meter freestyle in Olympic-record time of 49.80.

Tuesday's Roundup

Theresa Andrews of Annapolis, Md., won the women's 100 backstroke in 1:02.55. Rick Carey of Mount Kisco, N.Y., won the men's 200 backstroke in 2:00.23. And the team of Jenna Johnson of La Habra, Carrie Steinseifer of Saratoga, Calif., Dara Torres of Beverly Hills and Nancy Hogshead of Jacksonville, Fla., took the women's 400 freestyle relay in 3:43.43. The performance brought the three-day total of U.S. swimming medals to 10 golds and five silvers.

—Basketball. The favored U.S. women soundly defeated Australia, 81-47, with their stars on the bench much of the time. Aussie Coach Brendan Flynn called them the best of all time. Unbeaten South Korea defeated Yugoslavia's women, 55-52. The favored U.S. men, with North Carolina's Michael Jordan scoring 20 points, easily subdued Canada, 89-68. In other men's action, China beat France, 85-83.

—Boxing. Two fighters from Detroit's Kronk Gym won bouts. Frank Tate, world champion at 156 pounds, beat Sweden's Lofti Ayed 5-0, but got booed as Ayed was more aggressive. Steve McCrory won without fighting when Tad Joseph of Grenada couldn't make the 112-pound limit.

—Rowing. The United States and New Zealand won their elimination heats in the men's eights, making them the favorites in Sunday's finals. The two countries also placed first in their four without coxswain heats.

—Shooting. Pat Spurgin of Billings, Mont., won the women's air-rifle, with Italy's Edith Gufler second and China's Wu Xiaoxuan third. In a three-way shootout, Luciano Giovannetti of Italy won the trapshooting, with Peru's Francisco Boza second and Dan Carlisle of Fort Benning, Ga., third. Li Yuwei got China's second shooting gold, winning the running-game target event, with Colombia's Helmut Bellingrodt second and China's Huyang Shiping third.

—Weightlifting. Chen Weigiang won in the 132-pound class, giving China its third straight medal. Gelub Radu of Romania was second, Tsai Wen-yee of Taiwan third.

—Cycling. Steve Hegg of Seal Beach and Leonard Nitz of Sacramento advanced to the semifinals in the 4,000-meter pursuit event, giving the U.S. a good chance at a third cycling gold medal.

In yachting, U.S. sailors won first-day races in four of the seven classes—Finn, Star, Soling and Tornado.

In the Games' first exhibition baseball game, at Dodger Stadium, Italy defeated the Dominican Republic, 10-7, on Roberto Bianchi's two-run single that highlighted a five-run ninth inning.

In wrestling, Steven Fraser of Ann Arbor, Mich., positioned himself for a medal in the 199-pound Greco-Roman division by upsetting Sweden's three-time world champion at 199 pounds, Frank Andersson. Jeffrey Blatnick of Niskayuna, N.Y., defeated Refik Memisevic of Yugoslavia on a disqualification at 221 pounds.

In volleyball, the U.S. men stayed unbeaten by downing Tunisia, 15-3, 15-2, 15-3. Italy beat China 15-5, 16-14, 15-13. Canada downed Egypt 15-10, 15-9, 15-3.

THE MEDAL COUNT

THE TOP FIVE MEDAL WINNERS

COUNTRY	GOLD	SILVER	BRONZE	TOTAL
U.S.	16	7	1	24
CHINA	5	3	3	11
W. GERMANY	3	1	4	8
CANADA	3	3	1	7
AUSTRALIA	0	2	4	6

Weightlifting

China Wins More Gold as Strategic Ploy Works

By CHRIS BAKER, *Times Staff Writer*

The Soviet Union and Bulgaria are the real big red machines in the world of weightlifting, but maybe they had better make room for China, apparently an emerging power in the sport.

Featherweight Chen Weiqiang, a 26-year-old graduate student in physical education from Guandung province, gave China its third straight gold medal in the first three days of Olympic weightlifting competition when he upset Gelu Radu of Romania by just 5.5 pounds Tuesday night before a paid crowd of 1,347 at Loyola-Marymount University.

China has won five medals, three gold and two silver, and could win another medal tonight in the lightweight class.

"I'm very excited and happy that the Chinese have gotten three gold medals," Chen said. "It's a great pleasure."

Chen lifted a total of 622.5 pounds to Radu's 617. Chen's performance, however, was far off the world-record total of 694.25 pounds set by Stefan Topurov of Bulgaria last April.

Lending a political twist to the evening's activities, Tsai Wen-Yee of Taiwan won the bronze medal with a total of 600.5 pounds.

The lifters, however, downplayed the politics, shaking hands on the victory stand and congratulating one another.

Said Chen, "First of all, I have congratulations to a brother (Tsai). Secondly, it's a glory to the People's Republic of China."

Said Tsai, "I'd like to return congratulations to Mr. Chen . . . I hope that the sport will remain in a sport spirit and not get into the political realm. This is very important to me."

Radu, who finished third in the 132-pound division at the 1983 world championships in Moscow behind Yurik Sarkisian of the Soviet Union and Topurov, was a heavy favorite here. Chen was sixth at the world championships.

A strategic ploy in the clean and jerk backfired on Radu, however, costing him the gold medal.

Radu and Chen had each called for an opening weight of 352.5 pounds, but started playing games and changing their weights.

Radu reduced his weight to 341.5 pounds and handled it easily on his first try. Chen reduced his opening weight to 347 pounds, and made it just as easily.

Radu was set to lift 358 on his second attempt, which would have tied his personal best and bettered the Olympic record of 352.5 pounds set by Nikolai Kolesnikov of the Soviet Union in 1976.

Instead, he decided to go up to 363.75 pounds in an attempt to put pressure on Chen, who had also called for a second weight of 358 pounds. Chen's personal best was 352.5.

Then Chen announced that he was also moving up to 363.75. If Chen had not increased to 363.75 he would have had to lift before Radu.

With Chen also going higher, Radu was called to the platform to lift immediately. He cleaned the bar to his shouders but he couldn't jerk it. Chen also got the bar up to his shouders but then dropped it.

On his third attempt, Radu barely got the bar above his knees before the two-minute bell rang, giving the medal to Chen. With the gold medal already in the bank, Chen made a half-hearted attempt to lift the weight.

Said Chinese weightlifting Coach Huang Quianghui: "First of all the Romanian (Radu) and Chinese (Chen) athletes put up 160 kilos (352.5 pounds) as their first attempt. Later, when the Romanian reduced his attempt to 155 kilos (341.5 pounds) we decided to reduce to 157.5 kilos (347 pounds) so that we would still be ahead by 2.5 kilos (5.5 pounds), assuming that we both had successful lifts.

"With this strategy, in the end, we would come out with the total result being the same at 162.5 kilos (358 pounds) in the jerk. Since Chen's bodyweight is less he would have won."

Said Radu: 'It was a technical move. I should have pulled the 165 kilos (363.75 pounds) up to 170 kilos (374.75 pounds). If I had been more careful I could have won the gold medal."

Tsai was in first place after the snatch on the basis of bodyweight. He lifted 275.5 pounds on his third attempt. He let out a loud yell before approaching the bar, then waved to the crowd after successfully completing the lift.

Tsai weighed 130.51 pounds, Chen 130.95 and Radu 131.94. Chen also snatched 275.5 pounds on his second try, but he missed at 281 on his third try and had to settle for second place because he was heavier than Tsai.

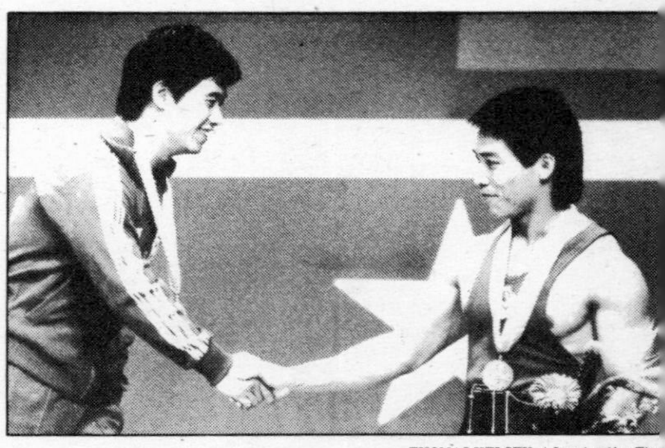

THOMAS KELSEY / Los Angeles Tim

Gold-medal winner Chen Weiqiang of China (left) shakes hand with bronze medalist Tsai Wen-Yee of Taiwan after feathe weight-class weightlifting competition Tuesday nigh

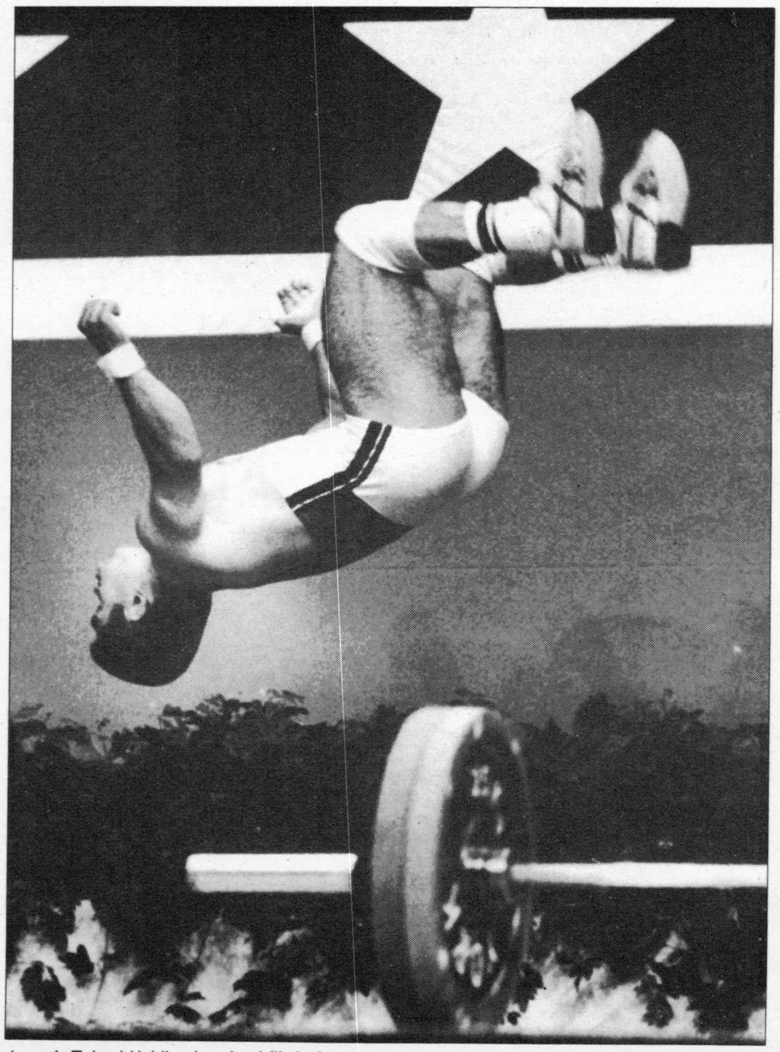

Japan's Takashi Ichiba does backflip before attempting a clean and jerk in the 123-pound division.

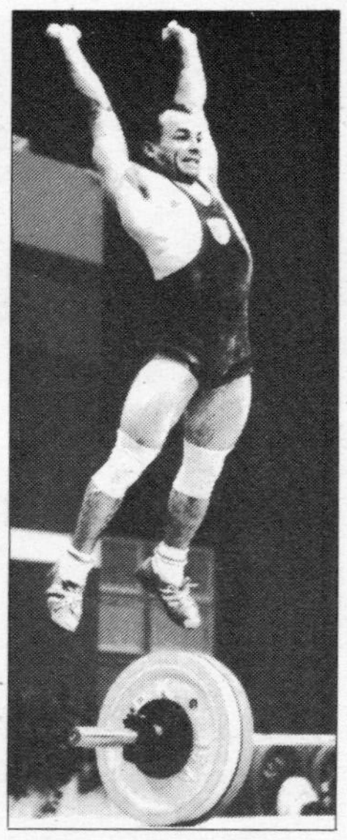

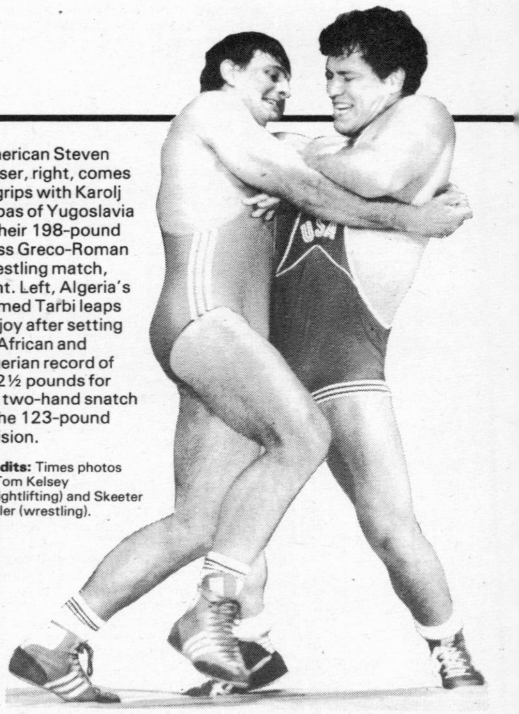

American Steven Fraser, right, comes to grips with Karolj Kopas of Yugoslavia in their 198-pound class Greco-Roman wrestling match, right. Left, Algeria's Ahmed Tarbi leaps for joy after setting an African and Algerian record of 242½ pounds for the two-hand snatch in the 123-pound division.

Credits: Times photos by Tom Kelsey (weightlifting) and Skeeter Hagler (wrestling).

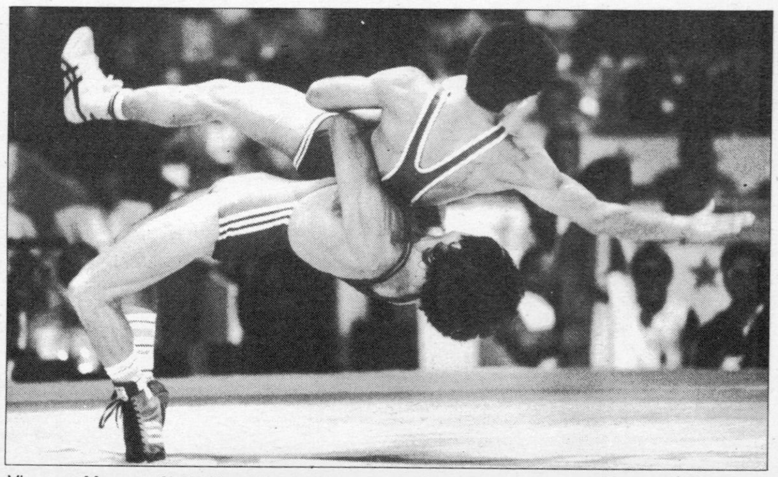

Vincenzo Maenza of Italy flips China's Haisheng Li on the way to winning his 106-pound class preliminary Greco-Roman wrestling bout.

Designed By TOM TRAPNELL

DAY 6 OLYMPICS '84

Jim Murray

Mermaid Who Started a New Olympic Sport

No one knows exactly the derivation of about half the sports in an Olympics. The javelin is pretty easy to figure out. How else could you kill a dinosaur in 1 million BC? The discus is a little harder to figure. So is the hammer throw. Come to think of it, the backstroke seems a pretty inefficient way to get away from crocodiles.

The inventors of a lot of the ball sport events are no longer with us. Dr. James Naismith of basketball fame, for example, has gone to a higher tournament. Whoever invented kayak pairs; small-bore rifle, prone; the coxless fours, or the clean-and-jerk weightlift and the uneven bars has gone to his reward. Presumably, they were all dour, pipe-smoking, gym-teacher types with handlebar mustaches, festooned with stopwatches and charts.

But the inventor, or at least, the popularizer, of one Olympic sport is none of the above. She is, in fact, an American Aphrodite, an orchidaceous goddess of the sea who put a whole generation of her contemporaries in back-yard swimming pools and was the mermaid of a thousand schoolboy dreams.

Esther Williams did more for a bathing suit than John Wayne ever did for a cowboy hat, Tom Mix for a horse, Errol Flynn for a sword, Ronald Colman for a pith helmet or Cary Grant for a tuxedo.

She put a generation of shopgirls not only in handkerchief bathing suits but in upswept hairdos. She practically made the suntan-oil industry and wrecked the parasol business by herself.

□

Esther was a dirt-poor Los Angeles schoolgirl who became the best swimmer in the world in the hectic prewar year of 1940, when she won gold medals in 100-meter freestyle, butterfly and medley swimming at the national championships in Des Moines that year. Esther was 17.

When you shed a tear for the poor boycotting athletes of 1980 and '84, consider that Esther's generation was one of the first to be deprived of its gold-medal shot. The Helsinki Olympics of 1940 were canceled. The Red Army was at the gates of Finland, and Hitler was rolling through France. Esther, instead of winning a gold medal in Helsinki, was working in the windows of I. Magnin's Wilshire Boulevard store pinning scarves on mannequins for $78 a month.

It was a time when Billy Rose was married to Eleanor Holm, the unfrocked swim star of the '36 Olympics, and was staging an "Aquacade," i.e., a Ziegfeld Follies in a tank at the San Francisco World's Fair. Rose figured it was a swell way to undress some of the most gorgeous chorus-girl shafts in the country.

Esther Williams was tall, green-eyed and voluptuous. She really didn't have to swim, but she did. Johnny Hyde, Sam Katz, L.B. Mayer himself came waving blank contracts. Esther, a practical sort, balked. She already had a career—after all, they promised to make her assistant buyer with a raise to $200 a month at Magnin's.

She made a screen test with Clark Gable, no less. The studio figured once Gable kissed her, a movie career would look infinitely better. They were right. "I melted," admits Esther, who always had a lusty interest in the other sex and romance. "You're tall," Louis B. Mayer told her accusingly. "You're short,"

Please see MURRAY, page 46

ANACLETO RAPPING / Los Angeles Times

Baptism—Ireland's Fiona Wentges, aboard Ballylusky, clears a water jump during the equestrian competition at Fairbanks Ranch.

GARY FRIEDMAN / Los Angeles Times

Wednesday night was a nail-biter for gymnast Mary Lou Retton and Coach Bela Karolyi.

American Women Just Miss L.A. Miracle II; Romania Wins

By RICHARD HOFFER, *Times Staff Writer*

If there was magic in the air, it was leftover, gone stale, polluted by defeat. The U.S. women's gymnastics team would not draw the same purity of breath the U.S. men did the night before, when the men won this country's first Olympic gold medal.

The U.S. women, although they flew high, did not fly quite high enough to escape the ozone layer of disappointment. They did not, as dreamed, win a gold medal.

They did win a silver, though, coming in second, one point behind the Romanians, new Olympic champions. For the United States, this is only a disappointment in light of their own great hopes and in comparison with the men's miracle finish over the Chinese in their team competition Tuesday.

As the U.S. women have long been regarded as the most earth-bound of athletes in world gymnastics (they have not won a team medal since 1948), their medal finish is remarkable in its own right.

It is true that it was accomplished in the absence of the Soviet Union, a gymnastics program that has dominated this sport, winning every Olympic team competition since it was embraced by the Olympic family in 1952. The Soviet team, the defending world champion, just might have nudged their longtime rival Romanians from the top step of the podium had they been here. But then, they were invited weren't they?

If it is impossible to say whether Romania is truly the best in the world, it is at least possible to say that the United States is getting better, a lot closer to the best. The U.S. team finished seventh in those championships last year, and although four of the top six teams

Please see ROMANIA, page 46

Breland Easily Stops Foe in Third Round

By EARL GUSTKEY, *Times Staff Writer*

Two down, three to go for gold. That's where Mark Breland stands in the Olympic boxing tournament's welterweight bracket. He doesn't have the gold medal yet, but against a hopelessly outclassed Puerto Rican Wednesday night at the Sports Arena, it seemed as if there must surely be one in the LAOOC's vault with his name on it.

From the start, it was only a matter of time. Carlos Reyes is short and slow, Breland 6-3 and quick. The mismatch made it seem the punches were pounding down upon Reyes from a man 7-3.

Breland began conservatively, cautiously. In deliberate fashion, he went on the hunt slowly against an opponent he wasn't even supposed to box. Reyes was hauled down from the top of the welterweight bracket, kicking and screaming, to box Breland following a mid-day readjustment of the welterweight bracket.

With 2:05 left in the first round, Breland landed a short left hook that didn't appear to hurt Reyes, but referee Noureddine Addala of Tunisia counted off a standing-8. Three 8s in one round or four in one bout stops an amateur bout.

With a minute left in the first,

Breland backed up the Puerto Rican with a four-punch flurry that wobbled Reyes' knees, precipitating another standing-8. In the last 45 seconds of the first round, Breland battered Reyes with several long lefts and rights.

Five seconds into the third, Breland hit Reyes with a short left, and Reyes dropped briefly to one knee. Seconds later, in center-ring, Breland unleashed a storm of punches, and the referee waved him off.

Breland, now 106-1, was almost flawless defensively Wednesday, slipping punches almost effortlessly. Even former light-heavyweight pro champion Jose Torres couldn't land a glove on Breland. He tried to pull Breland's name out of an M&Ms candy box with a straight right into, but Breland slipped that one, too.

Reyes, because he'd drawn a prelims bye and because his second opponent failed to make the weight Wednesday morning, had to be put in the lower bracket. International rules prohibit a boxer from beginning a tournament with, in effect, two consecutive byes.

Please see BRELAND, page 46

KEN HIVELY / Los Angeles Times

Splash—David Sweeney is at helm and Brian Sweeney hikes out as Canadian yacht competes in Tornado class.

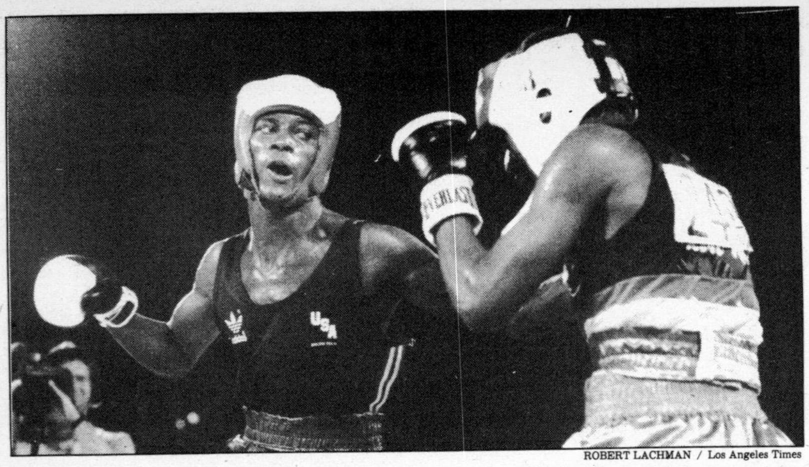

ROBERT LACHMAN / Los Angeles Times

Mark Breland (left) lands a left hand en route to his win over Carlos Reyes Wednesday night.

BRELAND

Continued from page 45

The Puerto Ricans protested when Reyes was sent up against Breland, but to no avail. Breland was paired to box South Korean An Young Su, but he was moved upstairs, to Reyes' slot.

Breland next boxes Romanian Rudel Obreja in the quarterfinals Monday morning.

Afterward, someone wanted to know why Breland hadn't knocked out Reyes.

"A lot of people know me for quick knockouts," he said, "but I didn't want to go out and do a lot of banging so early in the tournament. Maybe I will in the final. I knew after the first round that sooner or later, he'd go."

□

Salulolo Aumua, the Western Samoan boxer hospitalized Tuesday after suffering a neck injury, was released from Orthopedic Hospital Wednesday.

David Zeitman, chief medical officer of the Los Angeles Olympic Organizing Committee, said Aumua was released wearing a cervical collar. He was declared "neurologically clear" after tests, Zeitman said.

Aumua, a light-middleweight, was hospitalized and placed in traction as a precaution after he injured his neck in his bout with Gnohere Sery of the Ivory Coast. The bout was stopped by the referee when Aumua indicated he was hurt.

MURRAY

Continued from page 45

Esther told him, accurately enough. From then on, she was studio pet.

Hollywood had a canny history of turning Olympic sport into beauty pageant and a welcome break in the programs of gangster movies, war dramas and horse operas. In the silent era, they had signed up Annette Kellerman, the bathing beauty who had popularized the one-piece bathing suit and took ankles out of the closet, and made a fortune with her. They found Sonja Henie, a Dresden doll in skating costume at Hitler's Olympics and not only made "Sun Valley Serenade" but launched a dozen Ice Follies-type touring shows.

Esther Williams and Busby Berkeley turned a swimming pool into a seraglio, a sultan's dream with breathtaking production numbers of gorgeous girls swimming in geometric shapes around blue water while Esther, with orchids and exotic plants wound round her hair framing that beauteous face, was the centerpiece.

The plots weren't much. The titles should tell you. "Neptune's Daughter," "Jupiter's Darling," "Million Dollar Mermaid," "Bathing Beauty," "Pagan Love Song," "Easy To Love," "Andy Hardy's Double Life." Esther got to kiss her leading men, including Mickey Rooney, under water. The critics were beside themselves with gnashing teeth, of course. The critics always want Hollywood to make Ibsen and Grapes Of Wrath in that order. "Wet, she's a star. Dry, she ain't," they jeered.

"I never had a picture that was praised by Time, Bosley Crowther or The New Yorker," Esther lamented. But she never had a picture that lost money. "Million Dollar Mermaid" was the second-biggest grosser (to "Gone With the Wind") in Metro history at the time.

The songs were toe-tapping. "Magic Is the Moonlight," "Baby, It's Cold Outside." Recalls Esther: "More girls between the ages of 12 and 18 went to my movies than any others on the lot or in the town." She was the hottest single property the town had since Shirley Temple.

But what was more important, her films introduced the world to the beauty of choreographed swimming. "We called it 'Water Ballet,' " she said.

Stage 30 at MGM became the most important swimming hole in history. When Esther first showed up on camera, she splashed down the pool in near-world record time. Mayer was disgusted. "I don't want fast, I want pretty!" he shouted.

They've been getting it pretty ever since. A new sport was spawned. It was called "synchronized swimmming." Women who had been trying to get it certificated for years saw its acceptance grow by quantum leaps every time Esther surfaced through leis of plumeria and birds of paradise to fall into the arms of Fernando Lamas.

Esther got rich huckstering swimming pools (Hollywood didn't give residuals in those days), but synchronized swimming became an Olympic event and gave a new meaning to the term "breaststroke" at least for the men in the audience who had popped for $200 a seat to watch medleys.

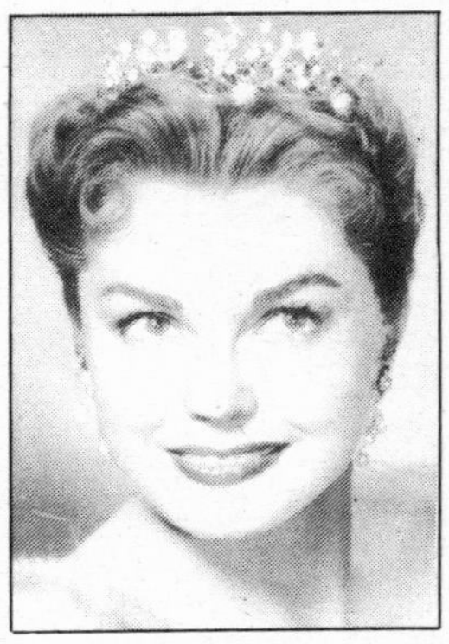

Esther Williams

Avery Brundage, the crusty old czar of the Games, had resisted the event for years. "It's not sport, it's show biz," he growled.

Esther, still the unlined beauty who used to rise out of a sea of chorines and corsages, is finally getting her Olympics. She will be an ABC-TV commentator for the swimming, diving, and of course, synchronized swimming events in the Olympics.

She sternly defends its inclusion in the Games. "It's a grueling sport. You have to do acrobatic lifts, you can't touch bottom, you have to train for years, you have to be precise, skilled and athletic."

And of course, in the old days, you got kissed by Clark Gable.

ROMANIA

Continued from page 45

refused to come to the Olympics, the United States still managed to improve its position in world rankings by overcoming the Chinese, the other high-ranking team to come. The United States' score of 391.20 was a full point behind Romania's but a big 4.60 ahead of the Chinese.

The United States came into Wednesday's optional exercises in UCLA's Pauley Pavilion trailing the favored Romanians by just .45 of a point after compulsories. In women's gymnastics that is a good lead but not an insurmountable one. However, the Romanians, from the first apparatus on, enlarged that margin. They did not yield so much as a tenth of a point until the final apparatus when the United States, led by Julianne McNamara's second perfect score of the evening, outscored them.

The Romanians actually clinched the victory by outscoring the United States on the balance beam by 1.60 points. Had Tracee Talavera not dismounted to her knees, had not the usually steady McNamara toppled right off, like a logger going into the drink, the United States might have accomplished a miracle for the second night in a row. But they did, they did. The Romanians did not.

Although the U.S. women performed spectacularly, with McNamara getting 10s on uneven bars and floor and Mary Lou Retton scoring one on vault, their second place score resonates with the particular failure of the balance beam. Talavera's 9.15, as the low score, did not count; it was a throwaway. But then came McNamara's 9.20. Had to count.

Bela Karoyli, the former Romanian national coach who has found himself on the other side of the fence as McNamara's and Retton's personal coach (and unofficial assistant coach of the U.S. team), explained McNamara's sudden lack of balance as a lack of concentration. But that can be understood; she had to wait several minutes on the podium before performing while the judges conferred over Kathy Johnson's score.

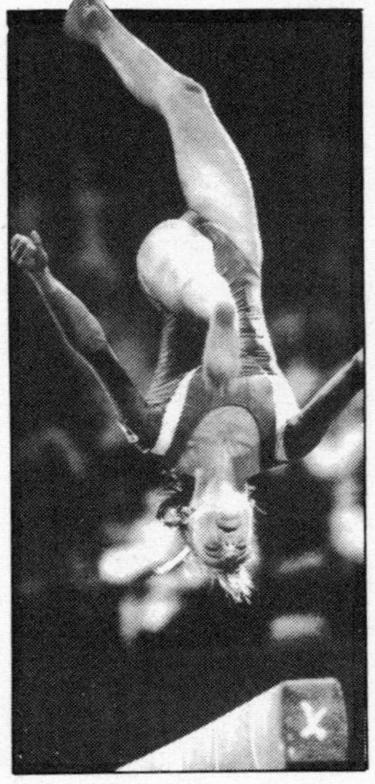

Associated Press

Bettina Ernst of Switzerland is head-over-heels during her routine on the balance beam in the gymnastics optionals.

That consultation even included a short-distance phone call from superior judge Jakie Fie to Yuri Titov, president of the Federation of International gymnastics, who was sitting 30 yards away. Whatever it was about, it was about a 9.60.

If Johnson wasn't upset, Karoyi was. While the judges talked it out and while McNamara stood looking at that awful, four-inch wide slab, Karolyi fumed. "No woman in the world can keep her concentration for that length of time . . . Her mental concentration disappeared."

Said McNamara of her fall, more or less agreeing with her coach: "That was really a freak thing. I've never, ever done that before . . . I had to wait up there a long time . . . I was up there thinking, but that's the way it goes." Even had McNamara stayed upright, however, the U.S. would not necessarily have won. The Romanians, who had suffered greatly on that apparatus in the World Championships (both stars Lavinia Agache and Ecaterina Szabo had fallen), performed wonderfully. Simona Pauca scored a 10, Szabo a 9.95.

The beam hurt McNamara individually, though, dropping her to a tie for third place in the all-around competition, which is decided Friday with another round of optionals. On the other hand, her 10 on uneven bars, which qualifies her into that apparatus final on Sunday, will be remembered as well as the first perfect score by a U.S. gymnast in the Olympics.

The United States remains in contention for gold—no U.S. women gymnast has ever won a medal of any alloy in Olympic competition—in several individual categories. Retton, who scored 9.90 or above (including a 10 on vault) in all but beam, leads the all-around with a score of 39.325 (an average of compulsories and optionals). Szabo, who scored the first 10 of the night on vault, is second with 39.375. Teammate Laura Cutina is third with 39.200.

The other U.S. gymnast to qualify into the all-around are Kathy Johnson, who was in sixth place 39.050.

The U.S. gymnasts did not view their second-place finish as failure. Silver shines brightly, too, especially, if it's the only jewelry you have. Kathy Johnson, a two-time Olympian and at 25 the elder stateswomen, said: "This is the fulfillment of a dream. I've wanted an Olympic medal almost even before I got into the sport. Sitting outside (the press room), I almost put myself back when I was 12 years old. I used to wonder how it would feel to win a medal, and it feels exactly like I thought it would. I was looking down at it, and I thought I was looking at a lollipop."

Retton, at 15 no stateswoman at all, thought she discerned a difference. As they were leaving the podium after the medals ceremony, she turned to U.S. Coach Don Peters and said: "Hey, theirs are shinier than ours," of the Romanian medals. He said: "Yes, gold is a little bit shinier than silver, but we're still proud."

Weightlifting

Surprising China Wins Fourth

By CHRIS BAKER,
Times Staff Writer

China, the big surprise in Olympic weightlifting competition, kept its startling streak alive Wednesday night.

China earned its fourth consecutive gold medal as Yao Jingyuan, 26, a physical-education teacher, won in the lightweight class, 148.75 pounds, Wednesday night at Loyola-Marymount University.

Yao, who finished fifth in the 1983 world championships, lifted a total of 705.25 pounds—314 in the snatch and 391.25 in the clean and jerk.

China has now won six medals in the four lighter classes, four gold and two silver.

"We didn't expect so many gold medals," Yao said. "We expected one of the first three places in these four categories."

The good fortune the Chinese have enjoyed so far, however, is about to end, according to their coach, Huang Qianghui, who said he was not looking for any more medals in the remaining six classes.

"We have to stop today," he said. "Tomorrow we have no promising lifters."

Yao's winning total was well under the world-record total of 760.5 pounds set by Joachim Kunz of East Germany in 1981.

Asked if he thought that his gold medal had been cheapened because of the Soviet-led boycott, Yao said, "It's a great pity that the Bulgarians and the East Germans didn't participate in the Olympic Games. They are the high-standard weightlifters. And this time I won a gold medal. I think it is through my great efforts."

Andrei Socaci of Romania and Jouni Gronman of Finland tied for second with 688.75 pounds but Socaci took the silver medal because he weighed less than Gronman, who got the bronze. Socaci weighed 147.92 pounds, Gronman 148.14 pounds.

Socaci, 18, a schoolboy who said he has been lifting since he was six, lifted 314 pounds in the snatch and 374.75 in the clean and jerk.

"This was my first international competition," he said. "I have not participated in any competition where there is so much attention. I trained at home for this meet and did a great deal of preparation, studying my competition.

"I did come here with expectations for a medal, but certainly not a silver or gold."

Gronman, who said a silent prayer on the platform before each lift, clasping his hands and raising his head, snatched 308.5 pounds, then hoisted 380.25 in the clean and jerk.

Asked about the bodyweight factor, Socaci said, "It added to the suspense of the competition and was nerve wracking to the competitors. It was definitely a factor."

Gronman had a chance to move from third to first on his last clean and jerk attempt of 396.75 pounds. He managed to clean the bar to his shoulders but he couldn't jerk it above his head.

"I had enough self-confidence but I didn't have the strength," Gronman said.

The competition was particularly keen in the snatch as the top six lifters were separated by just 11.02 pounds.

Socaci beat Yao in the snatch on the basis of bodyweight. Both men lifted 314 pounds on their last attempts, but Socaci weighed 147.92 pounds, Yao 148.14 pounds.

Gronman, who opened with a successful lift of 308.5 pounds, had a chance to pass Socaci. Gronman had the weight increased to 319.5 pounds, then missed twice and had to settle for fifth place behind Dean Wiley of England and Yasushige Sasaki of Japan.

Wiley and Sasaki both lifted 308.5 pounds and both weighed 148.03 pounds. Wiley, however, took third place in the snatch because he was lighter than Sasaki when the lifters were weighed again between the snatch and clean and jerk.

Yao opened the clean and jerk with a lift of 380.25, then went up to 391.25, which he handled easily. Gronman couldn't lift the same weight, however, and was supposed to follow himself. Gronman's coaches, however, had the weight raised to 396.75, forcing Yao to go ahead of him.

That gamble paid off because Yao couldn't handle the weight, leaving Gronman, who had the last lift of the competition, going for first place, at best, or third, at worst, when he lifted.

He bounded up the stairs to the platform and paced the stage behind the bar, then began to pray. Finally lifting, he got the bar to his shoulders and the crowd began to go wild. His coach waved his hands to quiet the crowd, but Gronman couldn't get the bar over his head.

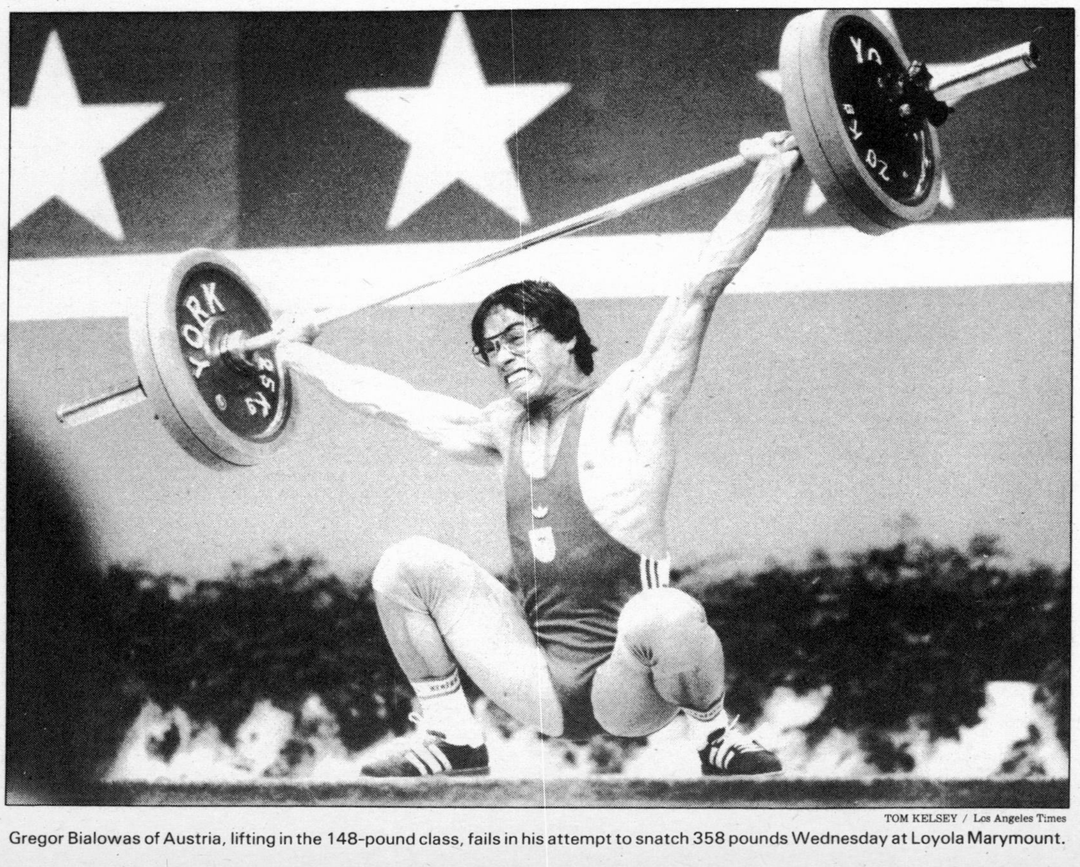

TOM KELSEY / Los Angeles Times

Gregor Bialowas of Austria, lifting in the 148-pound class, fails in his attempt to snatch 358 pounds Wednesday at Loyola Marymount.

U.S. Rallies From 2 Games Down to Beat Brazil

By JERRY CROWE,
Times Staff Writer

In the face of a raucous, flag-waving American crowd, Brazil nearly shattered the dreams of the U.S. women's volleyball team Wednesday night.

But the Americans, staging an improbable comeback that sent the capacity audience of 12,033 out of the Long Beach Arena buzzing, rallied to beat the upset-minded Brazilians, 12-15, 10-15, 15-5, 15-5, 15-12, in a grueling 2-hour, 20-minute match.

The United States, expected to challenge Japan and China for the gold medal, would have dug a big hole for itself if it hadn't scored the final six points of the match to cap the comeback.

They would have had to beat the world champion Chinese Friday night just to reach the semifinals.

With the victory, the United States assured itself a berth in the medal round, which begins Sunday.

"They needed confidence under pressure," U.S. Coach Arie Selinger said. "They demonstrated they could do it. This should make them believe."

Selinger said he expected the Brazil match to be tough "because it was critical as to who would go to the medal round. Its a positive experience for our players."

The Americans went to 10-year veteran Flo Hyman in the late stages of the fifth game. A pair of crushing spikes by the 30-year-old Hyman tied the score at 12, and an off-speed spike by Hyman put the Americans ahead, 13-12.

Rose Magers' block and a spike by Paula Weishoff gave the United States its final two points.

And the Americans, who struggled to beat lightly regarded West Germany in their opener Monday night, somehow had survived against another lightly-regarded opponent. Brazil, runner-up to Peru in South American zone, was beaten in straight games Monday by China.

West Germany's Terry Place-Brandel, who played for the U.S. team from 1978-80, may have seen the Americans' struggles coming the other night when she said of her former teammates, "They're afraid to lose, and that's scary."

In other words, the Americans are feeling so much pressure to win at home that they haven't been able to relax and play their best.

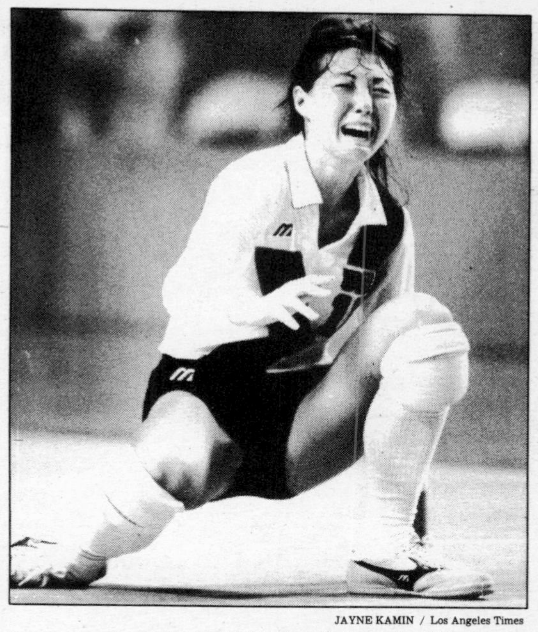

JAYNE KAMIN / Los Angeles Times

Tears of joy stream down Debbie Green's face after U.S. victory.

After Monday's win over West Germany, Julie Vollertsen—one of the Americans' seven veterans of the 1980 boycott—said: "This is like graduation day and you're always worried that you're going to trip on the steps going up to get your diploma."

The Brazilians, led by Vera Helena Bonetti Leme and Maria Isabel Barroso Salgado, stuck their foot out Tuesday night.

Almost every hit the Americans tried to put down in the first two games, the Brazilians put right back up. The Americans connected on only 29% of their kill attempts as the Brazilians stunned the Americans.

Selinger made wholesale changes in his lineup, trying to find the right combination.

By the start of the fifth game, he had gone back to his starters—Hyman, Weishoff, Magers, Debbie Green, Rita Crockett and Sue Woodstra.

Weishoff sparked the comeback with her all-around play—digging, hitting, blocking and passing. And Green's setting improved as the match wore on.

Weishoff was the Americans' leading hitter (18 of 42 for 43% kills), and also had 11 blocks, which tied her for a match high with Magers.

In the fifth game, it was the Brazilians who seemed to be feeling the pressure. In that game alone, they had eight service errors.

And now comes the hard part.

Next up for the Americans (Friday night at 8:30) are the Chinese, who beat them seven times in eight meetings last spring.

If Selinger's team was nervous Monday night against an unheralded West German team that it had handled easily in several exhibitions last month, it may be even tighter emotionally against a Chinese team that won the World Cup in 1981 and the world championship in 1982.

A lot is at stake. The loser gets a semifinal date with Japan, the team Selinger regards as the favorite.

The winner gets Peru or South Korea.

Selinger has put his players on the spot, calling Friday's match the key to the tournament.

"They're under a lot of pressure to win," West Germany's Place-Brandel said. "They've been working toward a goal for more than 10 years and when it comes down to one day, that's a hard thing to handle."

Japan vs. Peru. What was expected to be a fairly competitive match turned out to be a rout for the Japanese, 15-8, 15-7, 15-5.

"We fought very strongly," said Yumi Egami, who hit on 15 of 26 kill attempts to lead the Japanese. "Peru being very strong, we thought we had to fight with all our power."

Peru must beat South Korea on Friday to advance to the semifinals.

China vs. West Germany. The United States may have struggled against the West Germans, but the world champion Chinese certainly didn't. They romped, 15-5, 15-6, 15-3, in 55 minutes.

The West Germans' hitting (25 of 102 in kill attempts for 25%) reflected China's superiority. China hit 47% of its kill attempts.

South Korea vs. Canada. The South Koreans were dominant, crushing the lightly regarded Canadians in 46 minutes, 15-10, 15-1, 15-3.

"They live in the gym and it shows," said Canadian assistant coach Mike Burchuk, adding that the South Koreans had played an "average" match.

Unfortunately, the Canadians are below average. They hit on just 22% of their kill attempts, while South Korea was connecting on 40%.

Volleyball Notes

Setter **Dusty Dvorak** of the U.S. men's team was elbowed by teammate **Steve Salmons** in Sunday's match against Argentina and has been complaining of stiffness in his neck, but he didn't seem to be bothered by the injury Tuesday night against Tunisia. . . . The unbeaten Americans will meet South Korea (1-0) in their third Pool A match tonight at 8:30. Other matches today as the men's preliminaries continue: Brazil (1-0) vs. Tunisia (0-2) in Pool A; China (0-2) vs. Egypt (0-1) and Japan (1-0) vs. Italy (2-0) in Pool B.

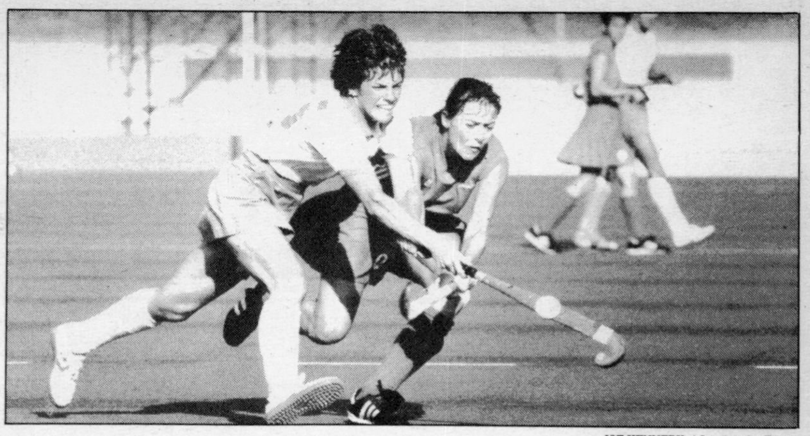

JOE KENNEDY / Los Angeles Times

Leslie Milne (left) of the United States is on the stick, keeping the ball away from Diane Virjee of Canada in a 4-1 victory, the first-ever field-hockey win for Americans in Olympics.

Women's Field Hockey

U.S. Wins, and Makes History, 4-1

By ALAN DROOZ,
Times Staff Writer

When it was over, the U.S. team took a victory lap. And why not?

It's not every day an American team wins a field hockey game, let alone an Olympic opener. The 4-1 victory over the Canadian women was not only overpowering, it was the first Olympic field hockey victory for any American team. Ever.

A crowd of 4,100 at East Los Angeles College had a lot to cheer about as the American women provided the most entertaining game of the tournament and dominated from the start.

Beth Anders powered three penalty corner shots into the net. Anders, known for her prowess as a penalty corner hitter, missed on her first two chances but hit her third seven minutes into the game. About 10 minutes later she was 2 for 4 and the American women had a 2-0 halftime lead.

The powerful, 5-11 Anders downplays her standing as a hitter—"I've never even thought about where I rank"—but her hitting was the topic on the minds of the Canadian players, who missed nine of their own penalty corners.

Anders said she was even worried after her second hit was stopped. "I thought at that point we were in trouble because I'm not gonna hit a ball better," she said. But her next two shots went in and her last shot with 6:40 left was so hard it hit a defender in the thigh and knocked her back into the net.

"They've always had a lethal penalty corner," Canadian captain Shelly Andrews said. "The thing is to stop them outside the circle."

Laurie Lambert added, "Yeah, we don't have anybody 6-2 with a 25-ounce (very heavy) stick."

The U.S. took a 3-1 lead on Beth Beglin's rebound shot before Canada's top scorer, Darlene Stoyka, scooped in a shot. Stoyka was generally smothered—mugged might even be apt—by U.S. defender Anita Miller.

Stoyka said, "Anita's probably one of the best in the world. The other countries probably won't be that tight." Andrews said, "They crowd. And everybody gets back."

Anders said the team "definitely did an excellent job of marking. We didn't let them get going. Because when they do get going they're trouble."

Canada was little trouble Wednesday, which pleased U.S. Coach Vonnie Gros, who was worried what a four-day wait might do. "Sometimes you waste too much energy in mental preparation," she said. "It was a very difficult wait. Some men's teams already had two games under their belt. But after the second goal I thought we had it under control."

The U.S. next plays top-seeded Holland on Friday morning. Goalie Gwen Cheeseman, who said she felt so good, "You almost know where the next ball is gonna go," suggested the team won't relax.

Australia 2, West Germany 2— Australia erased a 2-0 halftime deficit and produced a draw when Sandra Pisani scored her first goal ever in international competition with 35 seconds left. It was the opener for both teams.

Germany completely dominated the first half, applying constant pressure that produced 10 penalty corners and 10 shots on goal to one each for Australia. Martina Koch and Corinna Lingnau scored the goals.

But Australia was in charge most of the second half, with Sharon Buchanon getting on the board eight minutes into the period. With time running out, Buchanon charged the German goalie and got off a shot but was rejected. However, Pisani slashed the rebound into the bottom left corner of the net for the tie.

U.S. Medal Count Reaches 29; China Next With 13

Romania ruined the American women's dreams of an Olympic gold medal in team gymnastics Wednesday night, winning the two-day competition by a single point.

The Americans had hoped to match the U.S. men gymnasts' stunning gold-medal upset of powerful China Tuesday night. But the women had to settle for the silver. China got the bronze.

In other Wednesday action, a U.S. yachtsman was disqualified, a U.S. cyclist and a U.S. wrestler got gold medals, and American men won in boxing, basketball and water polo. China won a fourth straight gold in shooting.

The United States upped its gold-medal count to 18 for the first four days. Its total is 29. China is second with 13 medals, six of them golds.

The day's highlights:

—Gymnastics. Romania scored two perfect 10s in the optional exercises and went on to win. The Americans had three 10s but made some costly mistakes. The Romanians got 392.20 points over the two days, the United States 391.20.

—Yachting. John Bertrand of Anaheim Hills, who finished first in the Finn class Tuesday, was disqualified when a New Zealand protest was upheld. The accusation: Bertrand tacked in front of the other boat, causing a collision. In second-day races, Scott Steele of Annapolis, Md., won the sailboard and Jonathan McKee (Seattle) and Carl Buchan (Kirkland, Wash.) won the Flying Dutchman.

—Cycling. The United States got its fifth cycling medal as Steve Hegg of Dana Point won the 4,000-meter pursuit event from West Germany's Rolf Golz. Harvey Nitz of Sacramento earlier won the bronze medal, defeating Australia's Dean Wood.

Wednesday's Roundup

—Greco-Roman wrestling. Steven Fraser of Ann Arbor, Mich., won the 198-pound title—America's first-ever in Greco-Roman— defeating Romania's Ilie Matei. Frank Andersson of Sweden was third. Other medal winners: 106 pounds—Italy's Vincenzo Maenza, West Germany's Markus Scherer, Japan's Ikukzo Saito. 136 pounds—Korea's Kim Weon Kee, Sweden's Kentolle Johansson, Switzerland's Hugo Dietsche.

—Basketball. The American men stayed unbeaten with another runaway win, 104-63, over Uruguay. Patrick Ewing, the seven-foot center from Georgetown, led U.S. scorers with 17 points in his 18 minutes of play and had nine rebounds. North Carolina's Michael Jordon had 16 points. Also: Australia 67, West Germany 66; Yugoslavia 100, Egypt 69; Canada 121, China 80.

—Boxing. Mark Breland, amateur boxing's best, stopped Carlos Reyes of Puerto Rico in the third round of their 147-pound bout after two knockdowns.

—Weightlifting. Yao Jingyuan gave China it's fourth straight gold medal by winning the 148-pound class. Romania's Andre Cocaci was second, Finland's Jouni Gronman third.

—Water polo. The favored United States, in its first Olympic game since 1972, downed Greece, 12-5. Joe Vargas of Hacienda Heights, Calif., scored three goals. Also: Yugoslavia 13, Canada 4. The Netherlands 10, China 8. Spain 19, Brazil 12. Italy 15, Japan 5. Morocco 1, Saudi Arabia 0.

—Shooting. Malcom Cooper won Great Britain's first rifle gold medal in 72 years in the three-position small-bore event. Daniel Nipkow of Switzerland was second, Britain's Alistair Allan third.

— Modern pentathlon. Favored Italy won the team gold medal and the United States took the silver, its first team medal ever. France got the bronze. The individual winner was Daniele Masala of Italy. Svante Rasmuson of Sweden was second, Carlo Massullo of Italy third.

—Team handball. West Germany 12, Yugoslavia 11.

—Field hockey. Women: Australia and West Germany tied, 2-2. Men's scores: Great Britain 3, Canada 1. Pakistan 3, Kenya 0. The Netherlands 3, New Zealand 1.

—Fencing. Peter Lewison of Brooklyn surprised observers with upsets in several bouts to advance in men's foil.

—Rowing. The U.S. women's four oars with coxswain made the finals and single-sculler John Biglow made the semifinals in their events.

—Equestrian. The United States led in team scoring and Karen Stives of Dover, Mass., led individually after the endurance phase of the three-day event.

—Volleyball. Men: South Korea over Canada, 15-10, 15-1, 15-3. China over West Germany, 15-5, 15-6, 15-3. Japan over Peru, 15-8, 15-7, 15-5. Women: The United States defeated Brazil in a thrilling five games, 12-15, 10-15, 15-5, 15-5, 15-12.

—Soccer. Yugoslavia 1, Canada 0. Cameroon 1, Iraq 0. Brazil 1, West Germany 0.

THE MEDAL COUNT

THE TOP FIVE MEDAL WINNERS

COUNTRY	GOLD	SILVER	BRONZE	TOTAL
U.S.	18	9	2	29
CHINA	6	3	4	13
W. GERMANY	3	3	4	10
CANADA	3	3	1	7
ITALY	4	1	1	6

■ **Note:** Italy is tied for fifth in overall medals with Britain and Australia but has more gold medals.

Europeans Advance; So Does Lewison

By JOHN DART, *Times Staff Writer*

European favorites advanced as expected on the first day of fencing Wednesday, yet joining the top 16 in men's foil was an American with little international experience but a vocal following.

Andrea Borella of Italy, this year's top foilist on the World Cup circuit, went undefeated in 13 bouts through three preliminary rounds fought before 1,578 persons at the Long Beach Exhibition Hall.

However, most of the audience, which was divided into two distant grandstands, tended to cluster near the fencing strip where New Yorker Peter Lewison, 22, survived the second round with comebacks from 4-0 and 4-2 deficits in the five-touch preliminary bouts.

Chants of "Peter, Peter" and a long banner reading "Go Lewison" accompanied Lewison through a 5-3 win over Stephan Joos of Belgium and a 5-4 overtime victory against Gregory Benko of Austria.

After his last third-round bout, a 5-2 loss to leading contender Mathias Gey of West Germany, Lewison gave his following of about 800 the traditional salute with his blade and added a kiss as well.

"This is fantastic. The crowd made the difference," Lewison said, as he signed autographs. And Lewison signed lengthy autographs, after asking the person's name each time. American fencers aren't used to this kind of attention, or even success.

Lewison said he has only competed in three previous international tournaments and this was the best he has ever done. On his comebacks in the second round, he said, "I feel I'm strongest when I'm down."

Lewison, who placed third in the U.S. championships this year, still has great potential, says his coach, Semyon Pinkhasov. "And he was patient in his bout with Benko; that was the difference in that bout," Pinkhasov said.

Two other Americans, 1984 U.S. champion Michael McCahey and veteran Gregory Massialas of San Jose, did not survive the second round. American fencers have not won an Olympic medal since 1960. They came into the 1984 Games with their best chance in the team saber event. Nevertheless, Lewison was the first U.S. foilist to reach the top 16 since the present tournament procedure was set in 1968.

Borella, who appeared to some to be fencing just well enough to win despite his unblemished string, said he felt strong psychologically. He said through an interpreter that he hoped to maintain that same mental state today in the direct elimination stage.

He said he expected to see his toughest fights from France's Phillippe Omnes and teammates Stefano Cerioni and Mauro Numa.

Gey and German teammate Matthias Behr are also top prospects to make the final eight tonight, but Borella said he did not see them fence Wednesday.

Fencing Notes

Gregory Massialas would have advanced to the third round if Romanian **Adalbert Kuki**, who had clinched his step to the next round, had defeated an underdog Egyptian opponent, **Abdelmonem Elhousseiny.** Massialas, in fact, urged the Romanian to fight tough before Kuki's bout began. But Kuki lost, 5-1, prompting some U.S. officials, including team captain Jack Keane, to say the Romanian's loss was unusual . . . Among those eliminated Wednesday were **Pascal Jolyot** of France, who was recovering from a January knee operation, and veteran **Harald Hein** of West Germany . . . The official count has 466 fencers here representing 41 countries. Four individual and four team gold medals are at stake.

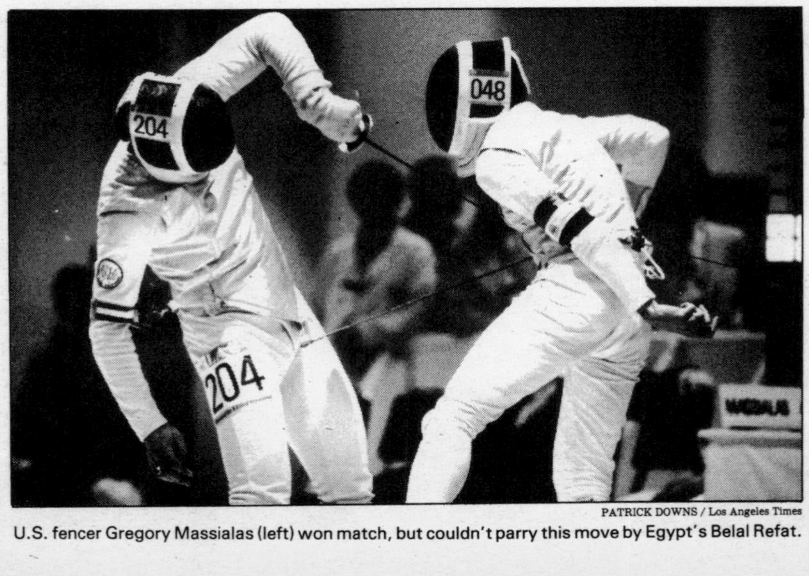

PATRICK DOWNS / Los Angeles Times

U.S. fencer Gregory Massialas (left) won match, but couldn't parry this move by Egypt's Belal Refat.

OLYMPICS '84/NOTES

Compiled By JERRY GILLAM

Dispute Brings Discord to the Jamaican Track Team

Five-time Olympian Don Quarrie of Jamaica, the 200-meter gold medalist in 1976, says a dispute involving sprinter Colin Bradford threatens to "destroy our team."

Bradford, a member of Jamaica's 1976 and 1980 Olympic team, was dismissed from the squad in mid-July after a dispute with Coach Herb McKenley after qualifying in the 200 meters.

Quarrie, a three-time medalist, said he has been leading the fight for Bradford and is now under fire from the coaching staff himself.

"They're trying to get rid of me," said Quarrie, 33. "They've destroyed Bradford and they're trying to destroy me."

L.A. attorney Howard Silber, hired to present Bradford's case, said he was informed Wednesday by Mike Fennel, president of the Jamaican Olympic Committee, that Bradford's case had been reviewed and "the decision is final."

Silber said attempts to resolve the dispute by meeting with McKenley and Ed Bartlett, Jamaica's minister of youth and sports, had fallen through when no meeting could be arranged.

Bradford, 29, was dismissed from the team in mid-July after an argument with McKenley. According to Bradford, the heated exchange came after McKenley refused to explain why no information about the team's Olympics plans had been passed along to Bradford, who had qualified by finishing third in the 200 meters.

Attempts to reach McKenley and other Jamaican officials were unsuccessful.

□

Zola Budd, the expatriate South African who won a long battle to compete in the Olympics for her new homeland Britain, won't win a gold medal, and she will be lucky to win any medal, her coach says.

The 18-year-old Budd, who ran the world's fastest time in the 5,000 meters earlier this year, will try to finish in the top five, according to her South African coach, Peter Labuschagne, the London Daily Mirror reported.

Budd's 5,000-meter time was 6.43 seconds under the world record time of American Mary Decker, but that distance is not run at the Olympics. Budd will compete in the 3,000 with Decker, who will win the event, Labuschagne says.

"The people surrounding her—the only people she can trust, such as me and her family—will be very happy if she is running under the first five in the Olympics. That's what we are aiming for," the coach said.

The Daily Mirror said the coach's comments, made in Los Angeles, were in "an exclusive tape-recorded interview with American writer Patricia Franklin, due to be published in the States later this week."

□

Jack Donohue, the Canadian men's basketball coach, tells a story about riding in a car with his friend, Bob Knight, the U.S. men's coach.

Donohue notices they're getting low on gas, and then watches Knight pass up a gas station. Donohue asks why.

"I don't like that kind of gas," Knight says.

"You look like a man who's never run out of gas," Donohue tells him.

"Thirty-eight times in the last year-and-a-half," says Knight.

—MARK HEISLER

□

If they awarded gold medals for flag-waving, Colombia surely would hold a commanding lead in boxing.

After almost three days of so-so flag-waving competition at the Sports Arena (Great Britain, Japan, South Korea and even North Dakota), Colombian Marco Lopez unfurled his country's colors and ran around the arena to the delight of the roaring crowd.

As Colombian boxer Alvaro Mercado battled a Spaniard in the ring, Lopez hassled with officials, who politely attempted to escort him from the floor, and eventually did.

But Lopez, a 29-year-old bachelor from Medellin, Colombia, couldn't be happier about his first trip to Los Angeles.

Moments later, an unidentified American, waving Old Glory, made a brief appearance on the arena floor, and later two more Yanks holding an even larger U.S. flag trotted around a bit, but all came up far short of Lopez's flamboyant demonstration.

And, when the boxing decision was announced, Lopez gave the Colombian colors a final, triumphant flourish.

His countryman had won.

—JACK HAWN

□

Jeff Float, a member of the world record-setting American 800-meter freestyle swimming relay team, is 80% deaf in one ear and 60% in the other. His sense of humor, however, is intact.

Float, the leadoff leg, told a news conference he had noticed crowd noise for the first time after his first 100 meters.

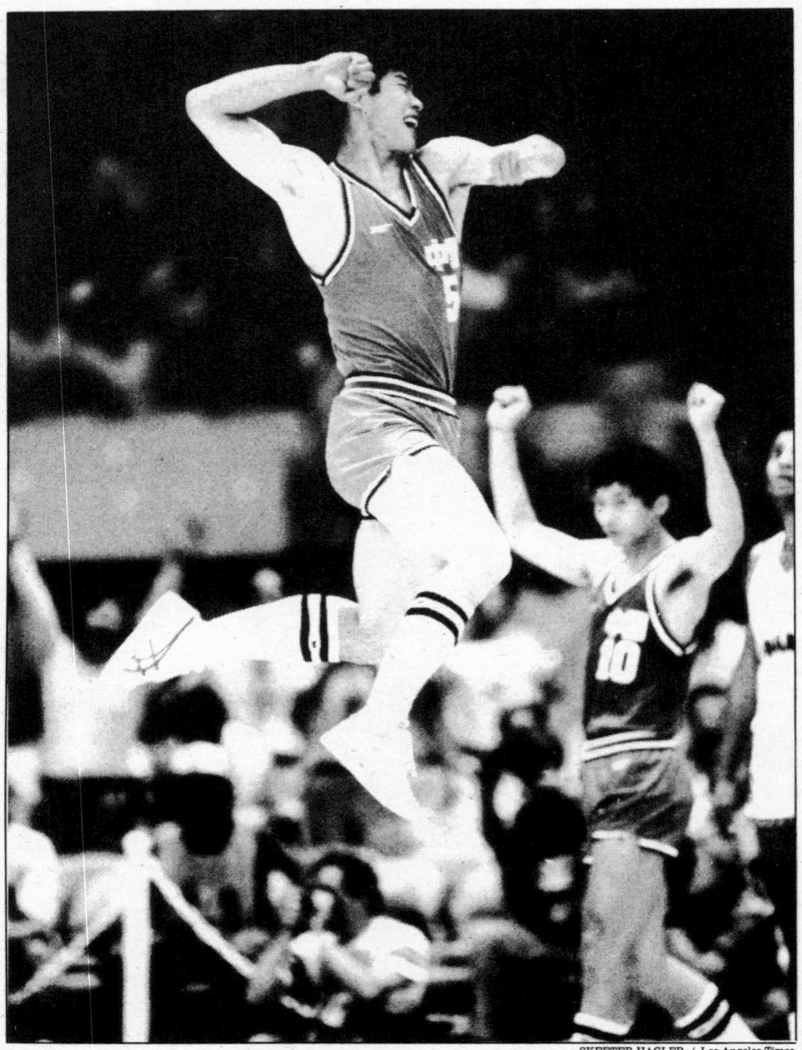

SKEETER HAGLER / Los Angeles Times

Lu Jinqing of China leaps to celebrate his team's 85-83 basketball victory over France.

"When I hit the wall, it was unbelievable. The noise was just . . . deafening," he added, without at first realizing the pun until his teammates broke up laughing.

□

Tunisia has been the brunt of a lot of jokes at the Olympic men's volleyball competition.

After the United States had crushed the Tunisians, 15-3, 15-2, 15-3, Tuesday night, several LAOOC press aides were trying to fly paper airplanes from the press area to the court, about 30 feet away.

One of the competitors' planes took a nosedive and landed on the step in front of him.

"Tunisian Air Lines?" asked a passer-by.

—JERRY CROWE

□

Trying to get the score of the U.S.-Italy soccer game from passing motorists in Pasadena proved to be a problem Tuesday night.

Stopped in post-Rose Bowl traffic on Arroyo Parkway, two locals decided to find out the score from the driver in the next lane.

The problem was that driver and his passengers frantically pushed every button on their rent-a-car—but couldn't get any window down before the light changed.

An attempt at the next light netted results as the second driver was able to find the window button just as the light changed. "Etaaaaly 1-0," he shouted as he flashed a thumbs up sign and drove off.

—VIC JOHNSON

□

Add this from Jack Donohue, Canadian men's basketball coach, on Olympic villages and security:

"I love the village here. To understand about security, you have to leave North America. Here they have security people on the buses, you see them, but they don't have weapons. They don't jam it up your nose.

"In South America, you've got 12-year-olds with machine guns. They all have acne. And they all look like they want to use them."

—MARK HEISLER

□

International Amateur Boxing Assn. (AIBA) rules have always stressed safety, but this Olympic tournament has four new ones:

—The two-inch-thick Ensolite padded mat the boxers compete on is now mandatory for major AIBA events, to prevent head injuries. One official said an egg dropped on the mat from eye level won't break.

—The use of four ring ropes, tied together twice on each side, to prevent boxers from being knocked out of the ring.

—Headgear, to prevent eye cuts and, possibly, head injuries, is mandatory and being used for the first time in the Olympics.

—Referees, on knockdowns, are under orders to not complete a count if, in their opinion, a boxer won't beat the count. They're to stop counting, declare the bout over, remove the fallen boxer's mouthpiece, and summon the ringside doctor.

A fifth rule, mandatory fitted mouthpieces, was to have been employed, but was dropped before the first session. Reason: Most of the African nations simply didn't have them. They had only the rubber, one-size-fits-all type.

—EARL GUSTKEY

□

Drazen Petrovic, the 19-year-old guard who's leading the Yugoslavian men's basketball team in scoring, was supposed to be headed for Notre Dame this fall. But now he says he'll stay home, that he'd be "homesick" outside Yugoslavia.

Irish Coach Digger Phelps, here doing color commentary for ABC, says Petrovic "signed with us," but won't say anything else about it "until the Olympics are over."

Petrovic says he does speak enough English to attend school in the United States. Of course, he said it through an interpreter.

—MARK HEISLER

□

West Germany's women led Australia 2-0 halfway through their field hockey game Wednesday but ended up with a 2-2 tie. German Coach Wolfgang Strodter said he was pleased with a draw but when a reporter asked how he would deal with the disappointment, he smiled and replied: "Whisky and Coke."

—ALAN DROOZ

□

Marvin Earley was selling the "Official Olympic Watchdog," in front of the Olympic Swim Stadium Tuesday.

Although the dog appeared to have as many origins as there are countries in the Olympics, Earley insisted the animal was "100% pit bull."

Above the snoozing dog, Earley tacked a homemade sign to a tree proclaiming that his pet was indeed the official watchdog of this Olympiad. Oh yes, he was asking $50.

—MILES CORWIN

□

An Olympic swim final is usually serious business. There's work to be done and most of the competitors approach it precisely that way.

But before plunging into the pool for her 200-meter freestyle race Monday, the United States' Mary Wayte was all smiles and beaming eyes. Why?

Part of the reason was an inside joke between Wayte and her 17-year old brother, Mike. "We have this little thing where we call each other 'Grandma,' " Wayte said. "I don't know how it started, but we've always done it. He yelled it out right before the race. I looked over at him in the stands and just started laughing."

"Grandma" Wayte then went out and won a gold medal.

—MIKE PENNER

□

You never know where you'll find a benefactor. Take the distance runners on the U.S. Olympic team, for example.

Bill Dellinger, the distance running coach, said he and the athletes came across what seemed like almost an abandoned ranch in the Lake Cachuma area near Santa Barbara recently.

It seemed like an excellent place to run because the temperature—90 degrees-and humidity—50 to 65%—simulated conditions in Los Angeles.

Permission to run on the 40,000-acre cattle ranch was obtained from the absentee owner, Sir John Galvin. Now the runners have the run of the ranch. There's also a swimming pool on the premises where they can cool off afterwards.

Galvin was more than happy to accommodate the athletes. His daughter, Patricia Galvin, represented the U.S. Olympic equestrian team in the 1960 and 1964 Olympics. She finished sixth in individual dressage in the 1960 Games.

—MAL FLORENCE

□

A skimpily-clad young woman approached Sebastian Coe, the British middle-distance star, the other day at a West Los Angeles book store where he was autographing his fitness book. "May I have your autograph?" she asked.

Coe signed a scrap of paper. The woman looked at it and asked, "Are you running in the Olympics?" Coe replied he was. "What races?," the woman asked. She didn't buy a book.

A man stopped, looked at the book, put it down and stayed to chat for five minutes. As he left, he asked Coe, "What is your name please?" He didn't buy a book either.

—BILL SHIRLEY

□

When U.S. super-heavyweight Jeff Blatnick scored an upset of super-heavyweight proportion in Tuesday's Greco-Roman wrestling in Anaheim, he arrived in the media zone to find that the media had abandoned him.

The writers had all scrambled back to the arena to watch Blatnick's teammate, Steve Fraser, meet—and ultimately defeat—1982 world champion Frank Andersson of Sweden.

When the writers returned to the media zone, Blatnick kept them waiting because he was watching Fraser and Andersson on television.

"We don't get much TV time," Blatnick said. "It isn't often that Greco-Roman gets out of the closet."

—DAVE DISTEL

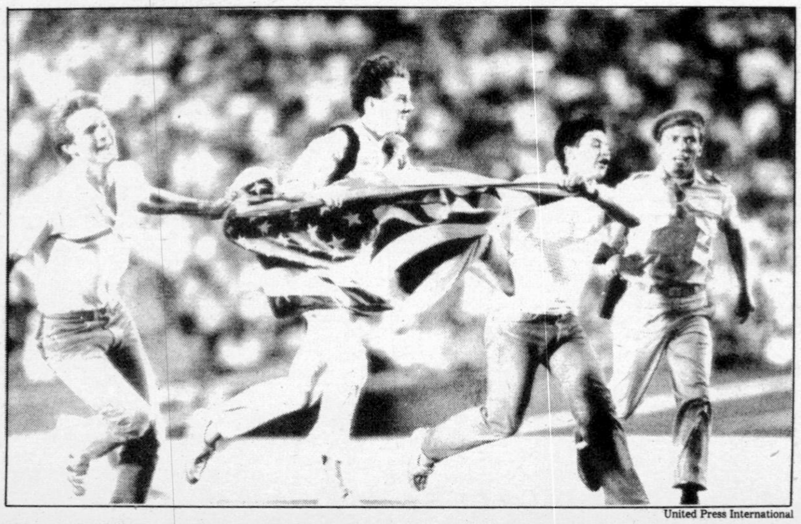

United Press International

With a security man in hot pursuit, three jubilant American fans run across field at Rose Bowl during Tuesday's soccer game between United States and Italy. The Italians won, 1-0.

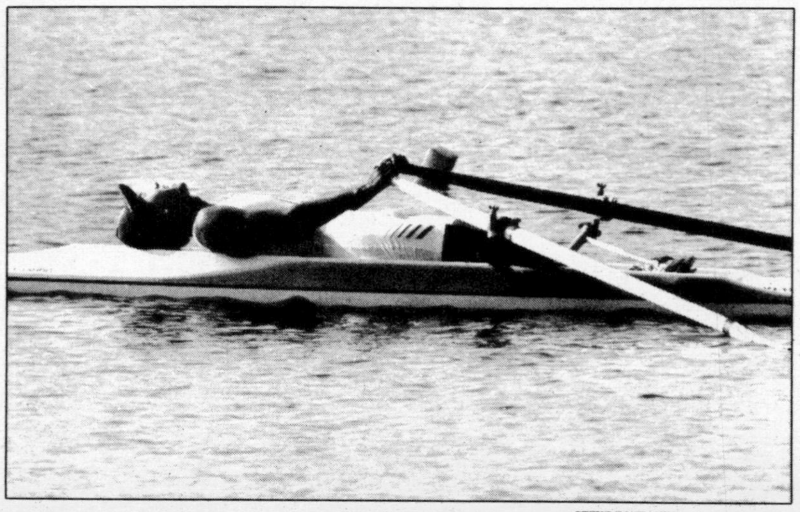

STEVE FONTANINI / Los Angeles Times

Home is the sailor, home from the race, bone-weary and in last place. Shunsuke Horiuchi of Japan glides across finish line in men's single sculls competition at Lake Casitas.

OLYMPICS '84/STOP ACTION

Mitch Gaylord of the American gymnastics team finishes a gold-medal routine.

America's Steve Hegg, above, celebrates victory in 4,000-meter individual pursuit cycling. He won gold Wednesday. Edward Neblett of Barbados, left, on the canvas after a TKO loss in 165-pound division to Virgil Hill of the United States.

Winners and Losers

Boxer Sanpol Sang-Ano of Thailand lowers his head and cries after being stopped by Daniel Mwanci of Kenya.

Cheryl Miller of the U.S. women's basketball team high-fives a teammate during 83-55 victory over Yugoslavia. Americans are favored.

Canadian Alex Baumann lets out a yell after swimming the men's 400-meter individual medley final in 4:17.41 to set a world record.

Michelle Duserre of Huntington Beach is congratulated by teammates after her performance on the uneven bars.

Morocco's Abdelmalek Elaouad is helped off the mat after dislocating an arm during first-round loss in 106-pound division of Greco-Roman wrestling.

Designed By TOM TRAPNELL

Meir Daloya of Israel lifts himself up after dropping the weights during the 114½-pound division competition.

Credits: Except where noted, photos for this page were taken for The Times by Rick Corrales, Gary Friedman, Skeeter Hagler, Tom Kelsey and Rosemary Kaul.

OLYMPICS '84

DAY 7

Jim Murray

Now We Have Charlie Hustle in a Leotard

She's 4 feet 9 inches tall and about 3 feet 7 of it is eyes. They're big and dark and have these incredibly long lashes. When she has them wide open, you can't see the rest of her. Russians write songs about eyes like that.

She's 94 pounds. Her heart weighs about 65 of them. She's America's tomboy, everybody's kid sister. She has this kind of husky contralto type of voice, Doris Day crossed with Jennifer Beals, and she never sits still. She wears her hair in what used to be called a boyish bob and it constantly seems to be flying. This is what J.M. Barrie had in mind when he wrote Peter Pan. Disney would love her.

If you could compare her to any other athlete, it would be Pete Rose. She manages to convey the wide-eyed joy in her competition of the little girl who has just come downstairs on Christmas morning and found a pony.

Olympic Games, which are supposed to be playgrounds for brutish muscular runners, oarsmen, cyclists, pugilists and guys who can lift freight trains have been given over lately to the toy people department. Babes in Toyland. Athletes in teeth braces. Gold medalists in ponytails. Kiddies who bring teddy bears to press conferences.

□

Mary Lou Retton is the latest in a lengthening line of windup dolls who have made the glamour event of an Olympics not a (ugh!) common foot race or lunge with a round plate but a child on a high bar. Not since Shirley Temple danced down stairs with Bojangles has any moppet so captured the heart of the world. The competitors look like the crew of the Good Ship Lollipop.

It all began in Munich with this little pigtailed pixie with the soulful eyes and rouged cheeks of a Raggedy Ann doll. Olga Korbut was not the best gymnast at the '72 Olympics, but she was the most lovable. She won the hearts of the world one night when she missed a backward somersault on the balance beam and cried.

No one knew gymnasts had feelings before. They marched in like the Parade of the Wooden Soldiers, performed their routines stolidly and uninspiredly, and no one knew whether they even bled or cried or had feelings or whether they were whittled in a laboratory some place or even made out of gingerbread in a treehouse in the Black Forest.

Olga changed all that forever. She also forced them to put padding in the balance beam since no one had ever done a backward somer-
Please see MURRAY, page 51

Things got turned upside down Thursday night for China's Li Ning, favored to win the men's gymnastics all-around. He had spectacular

JAY DICKMAN / Los Angeles Times

moments, including this 9.9 on the rings, but in the end, Li finished third, behind Koji Gushiken of Japan and Peter Vidmar of the U.S.

Gushiken Returns Rising Sun to Its Place in Rafters

By RICHARD HOFFER,
Times Staff Writer

At 27, Koji Gushiken is something of a relic. In the severe discipline of gymnastics, few men persevere beyond their teens, never very far into their 20s. It's a hard sport. And when the athlete fails to find any reward for his persistence—when he misses Olympics after Olympics because of injury or because of politics—the sport becomes harder than hard. It becomes impossible.

But there was Gushiken, whose glory came to him late but deservedly, standing on the podium, blinking back the tears after he had won the men's all-around competition Thursday night. Finally composed, he took up the last words of Japan's anthem, his flag rising to the rafters. "To be part of a rock," he managed to sing, articulating his country's determination to survive, to be there when the force of age, politics, whatever, would seem to dictate otherwise.

He had come from almost nowhere to edge the United States' Peter Vidmar—this country's first medalist ever in the all-around. The Japanese gymnast was in fifth place after the first half of this competition, with such formidable athletes as China's Li Ning and Tong Fei ahead of him. But he stormed through the apparatus—scoring a 10 on vault, 9.95s on rings and horizontal bar, 9.9s on the rest to finish with 118.700, just 25/1000ths of a point in front.

Was Li Ning, the irrepressible youth whose crowd-pleasing flair may as well cause him to be renamed the Li Ning Tower of Pizazz, surprised? "Yes, I was sur-

Koji Gushiken of Japan, gold medalist in the men's all-around gymnastics event.

prised," he admitted, sheepish for once. He played it conservatively and, although he hit 9.95 on pommel horse, was scored accordingly, settling into third with 118.575.

And what about Vidmar, the former Bruin who performed on this same Pauley Pavilion floor in anonymity before becoming a name while leading the United States to the team championship Tuesday? Was he surprised?

Not hardly. He was served notice earlier in the day when he went to
Please see GYMNASTICS, page 51

IOC President Protests Focus of ABC's Coverage

By PATT MORRISON and KENNETH REICH, *Times Staff Writers*

Amid complaints from foreign Olympic athletes and coaches that their high-caliber performances are being slighted by ABC-TV's euphoric focus on Americans, the president of the International Olympic Committee has written a "stern" letter registering a "formal complaint" against the network's coverage.

That was how Peter Ueberroth, president of the Los Angeles Olympic Organizing Committee, described a letter that he received Thursday from IOC President Juan Antonio Samaranch. The letter, Ueberroth said, represents "quite a consensus" of the nine-member

executive board, which governs the IOC.

"They wished me to talk to ABC to be sure they'd give equal coverage," Ueberroth said at a press conference Thursday night. "They mentioned that some medals won by other countries are not being announced in the entire daily show."

The coverage, board members indicated, threatens to diminish the "international flavor" of the Games in the eyes of the American public, Ueberroth said. He did not attend the IOC meeting earlier in the day when the subject was discussed.
Please see MEDIA, page 51

Nobody Even Comes Close to Davis as He Shatters Own World Record

By SEYMOUR BEUBIS, *Times Staff Writer*

Despite swimming the second fastest time ever, a 1:01.99 in the 100-meter breaststroke, Victor Davis of Canada wasn't pleased with his second-place finish last Sunday behind Steve Lundquist of the United States.

In fact, he was downright annoyed.

"I came here to win two gold medals," Davis said after the race.

Lundquist, with his explosive starting power, may have stopped Davis from winning Olympic gold in the 100, but no one was going to deny him in his specialty, the 200-meter breaststroke.

The world record-holder at that distance (2:14.58) entering the Olympic Games, Davis, 20, lowered his mark to 2:13.34 Thursday as he coasted to the most-lopsided victory thus far in the men's competi-

tion, winning by almost 2½ seconds before another capacity crowd at the Olympic Swim Stadium.

His time also broke one of the longest-standing Olympic records of them all, a 2:15.11 set by David Wilkie of Great Britain at Montreal in 1976.

Taking second place was Glenn Beringen of Australia, with a time of 2:15.79. He was followed by Etienne Dagon, whose 2:17.4 was fast enough to give Switzerland its first-ever Olympic medal in swimming.

Richard Schroeder, 22, of the United States was fourth in 2:18.03. American John Moffet was scratched from the race after suffering a leg injury while swimming in a preliminary heat of the 100-meter breaststroke Sunday.

Davis, spurred by a large Canadian following that began shouting, "Here we go, Victor," as he approached the starting blocks, gave his fans what they wanted: He went.

Davis jumped into the lead in the first 50 meters and was on a record pace at each split thereafter.

"I wanted to set a record that would be unreachable for several years," Davis said.

Asked if he was satisfied with his performance, Davis said: "I'm totally satisfied for now, but give me a couple of months."

It is well known that Davis also wants the 100-meter breaststroke record owned by Lundquist.

Calling the win, "the most satisfying of my life," Davis said the gold medal means "everything to
Please see DAVIS, page 51

CON KEYES / Los Angeles Times

Victor Davis of Canada breaks his own world record in winning the 200-meter breaststroke.

Japan Breaks Through, Slows U.S. Gold Rush

Compiled From Times Wires Services

U.S. swimmers won three more gold medals Thursday but Japan thwarted the hopes of the American men for a second gold in gynastics when Koji Gushiken won the all-around event. UCLA's Peter Vidmar was second, China's Li Ning third.

Also in Day 5: An American who had battled Hodgkin's disease won the super-heavyweight gold medal in wrestling. Canadian and Dutch swimmers each won golds. Japan got three golds for the day. The United States clinched a gold in cycling, remained undefeated in women's basketball, men's volleyball, boxing and water polo, but got a tie in soccer and lost in men's team handball and men's field hockey.

The U.S. medal total is 37, with 22 golds. China is second at 15, with 7 golds.

Thursday's highlights:

—Swimming. George DiCarlo of Denver won the men's 400-meter freestyle, with John Mykkanen of Placentia second, Justin Lemberg of Australia third. Mary T. Meagher of Louisville won the women's 100-meter butterfly, with Jenna Johnson of Santa Rosa second, Karin Seick of West Germany third. Victor Davis of Canada stopped the U.S. gold-winning streak at eight by winning the men's 200-meter breaststroke in a world-record 2:13.34, with Glenn Beringen of Australia second, Etienne Dagon of Switzerland third. Petra van Staveren of Holland won the women's 100-meter breaststroke, with Anne

Thursday's Roundup

Ottenbrite of Canada second, Catherine Poirot of France third. The U.S. men won the 400-meter medley relay in a world-record 3:19.03.

—Gymnastics. Japan's Gushiken got a 10 in vaulting and had no less than 9.9 in the five other all-around events, scoring 118.700. Vidmar had 118.675, Ning 118.575.

—Greco-Roman wrestling. Jeffrey Blatnick of Schnectedy, N.Y., beat Thomas Johansson of Sweden. Blatnick, who had his spleen removed two years ago, said tearfully as the crowd cheered: "I'm a happy dude." Other gold medalists: 163 pounds, Joukon Salomaki, Finland; 114 pounds, Atsuji Miyahara, Japan.

—Basketball. The American women routed South Korea, 84-47, USC's Cheryl Miller scoring 16 points.

—Boxing. Meldrick Taylor, 17, of Philadelphia, the youngest U.S. boxer, beat Romania's Nicolae Talpos, 5-0, in the 125-pound class. Robert Shannon, Edmonds, Wash., topped Sami Mwangi of Kenya and won, 5-0, in the 119-pound class, making the team 10-0.

—Volleyball. The American men rolled over unbeaten Korea, 15-13, 15-9, 15-6.

—Water polo. With Kevin Robertson of Concord, Calif., and Gary Figueroa of Salinas getting three goals each, the United States defeated Brazil, 10-4.

—Shooting. China's Wu Xiaoxuan became her country's first-ever double-medal winner by taking the women's three-position rifle. Tuesday, she won the air-rifle bronze. West Germany's Ulrike Homer was second, Wanda Jewell of Wahiawa, Hawaii, third. Japan's Takeo Kamachi got his country's first gold medal in the men's rapid-fire pistol.

—Cycling. Mark Gorski of Costa Mesa and Nelson Vails of New York ensured a fourth U.S. gold medal in cycling by qualifying for the final in the 1,000-meter pursuit.

Also: In fencing, Italy's Mauro Numa the gold in individual men's foil. In weightlifting, Karl-Heinz Radschinsky of West Germany won the gold at 165-pounds. In soccer, the U.S. and Egypt tied, 1-1. In team handball, Sweden defeated the U.S. men, 21-18. In field hockey, the Americans lost their third straight game, to Malaysia, 4-1. In rowing, the International Olympic Committee ordered the names of commercial sponsors removed from boats. In yachting, the U.S. leads in only one of seven classes, the Flying Dutchman. In exhibition baseball, it was the U.S. (with four homers) 16, Italy 1, and Taiwan 13, the Dominican Republic 1.

THE MEDAL COUNT

THE TOP FIVE MEDAL WINNERS

COUNTRY	GOLD	SILVER	BRONZE	TOTAL
U.S.	22	12	3	37
CHINA	7	3	5	15
W. GERMANY	4	4	5	13
CANADA	4	5	1	10
AUSTRALIA	0	4	5	9

GYMNASTICS

Continued from page 50

the gym to work out and couldn't get the doors open. Inside was Gushiken, all alone. Vidmar told his U.S. coach, Makoto Sakamoto, that Gushiken was reciting some kind of Japanese mantra, some kind of Samurai ritual. Gushiken looked up and was shocked to see Vidmar. Which was fair. Vidmar had been plenty shocked to see Gushiken applying a metaphysical conviction to his sport.

"Peter is very religious, too," Sakamoto says. "To see that kind of religious concentration, well, he knew it would be a tense night."

Tense underplays the drama. Vidmar's lead of five-hundredths after the averaged compulsories and optionals was destroyed after just three rotations. Li Ning, whose team had already suffered embarrassment by losing to the United States in the team competition, made up the difference on floor and pommel horse, even though Vidmar started the evening by scoring a 10 in his first event, the horizontal bar, to the delight of a flag-waving crowd of 8,834.

THE MEDALISTS

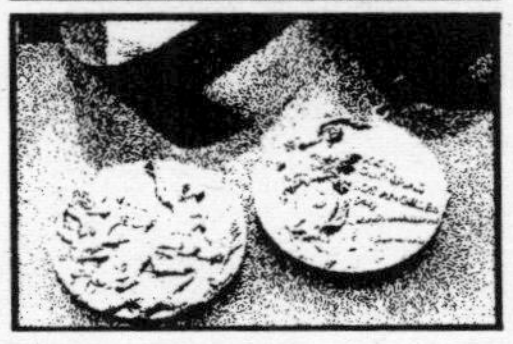

MEN'S

Gymnastics

■ ALL-AROUND

1. Koji Gushiken (Japan)
2. Peter Vidmar (U.S.)
3. Li Ning (China)

It appeared to be a two-man race at that point. Maybe Tong Fei, who also scored a 10 on horizontal bar could sneak in there and turn it into a Tong Show. Except he broke slightly on parallel bars and was scored 9.75, a kind of shutout at this level of competition.

But then came Gushiken, a lecturer at the Nippon College of Health and Physical Education in Tokyo half-days, gymnast the other half. Vidmar, who may have been prepared for Gushiken's bushido bravado, nevertheless did not know where Gushiken was in the standings. Nor where he was.

Even in the last dramatic rotation, when Vidmar was leading off on parallel bars the same time Gushiken was leading off on floor? "I had no idea where I stood in the competition," Vidmar said, although he did notice on the leader board that after five rotations he was 25/1000ths behind Gushiken. Gushiken was first, scoring a 9.9. Did he watch Vidmar then? "I didn't watch him play," he said. "A tear was running down my eye and I couldn't tell."

It was a 9.9 routine for Vidmar. Vidmar dismounted, walked over to Gushiken, who was taking some tape off his legs. "I asked him if he was done; he said yes, finished. Then I found out he did a 9.9"

That was that. Vidmar's 9.9 on parallel bars was not enough. Gushiken's 9.9 was too much.

Vidmar was not terribly disappointed. He said later that the team gold medal meant more to him than any individual achievement. Anyway, how could anybody begrudge Gushiken, a warrior who has fought time among other things?

Gushiken, who bows and smiles at almost any opportunity, has not been on what you'd call the Orient Express when it comes to gymnastics development. A first-time Olympian at 27? It doesn't happen in this game. At that age, a gymnast requires orthopedic help to get through routines. What is apparatus to such a gymnast? A cane?

But it is a fact that Japanese gymnasts mature later in life. That is their system. The best gymnasts usually train after college, when they are able to acquire some kind of company sponsorship.

Even so, Gushiken is old by any standards. But "two great accidents," a broken ankle that threatened his career nine years ago and a ruptured Achilles tendon eight years ago, kept pushing his future back. He says he wasn't good enough for the Montreal Olympics, that he was the 13th best gymnast in Japan. By 1980, he was good enough. But then he was stymied by the same boycott that kept Vidmar home from Moscow.

"That is why I trained so hard for this," he said, "to win double gold."

Others besides Vidmar should have seen him coming. No Olympic medals, true. But his world rankings have been consistently improving. He was third in the all-around at the 1979 World Championships, second in the all-around to the Soviet Union's 17-year-old Dmitri Bilozerchev last year, another year in which youth was served.

But not this time. Patience was rewarded. "I have been doing gymnastics for 16 years," he said. "At my pace, I knew eventually a medal would come."

This will be a mighty consolation for Japan, a faded power in gymnastics. Once the dominant force, before the Soviet Union regained control, Japan has now slipped badly. They weren't even in the running for the silver team medal Tuesday. But as Sakamoto said, "If all their gymnasts had his fighting spirit, it would be otherwise."

The U.S. consolation prize, meanwhile, is not regarded lightly. The only medal the United States has won at all since 1932 was a bronze medal on the apparatus in 1976. And that was regarded as a fluke by many. Vidmar's second place can hardly be considered that. And you can reconsider the United States' place in this sport when you know that U.S. gymnasts Mitch Gaylord and Bart Conner finished fifth and sixth in the all-around.

The United States will probably carry this legacy of excellence into another Olympics. For that matter, so, probably, will Gushiken.

DAVIS

Continued from page 50

me . . . now I can sleep."

Davis, who plans to swim for two more years, was one of the most animated of all the Olympic champions.

As he was ushered to the victory stand to receive his gold medal, the jubilant winner tossed Frisbees into the stands. "They have the Canadian emblem on them. I wanted to show my appreciation to the people."

After he received his medal, he threw his arms into the air. As he left the swim stadium, he bestowed a kiss on a woman in the stands, continued to toss Frisbees, slapped hands with people in the stands and posed for pictures.

Davis said the woman he gave flowers and kissed was his mother. "Who did you think it was? I don't kiss strange ladies." Davis said.

Then revealing his sense of humor, he added: "I hear there are a lot of strange ladies in Los Angeles."

Davis admitted that for the first time in his life, he felt pressure.

Everyone expected Davis to win the race—swimmers, coaches and the press. The only question was what the margin would be and by how much he would break his world record.

There was some talk before the race that Davis was boldly predicting victory, but he denied it. "I don't know where you heard that. It isn't true."

Davis said that he expects his chief competition in the next few years in the 200-meter breaststroke to come from Europeans or Australians.

"The U.S. swimmers are more sprint-oriented," Davis said.

The road to the Olympic Games has been a rocky one for Davis, at least from a physical standpoint.

He had mononucleosis in June 1983, and his weight dropped from 185 to 170. Then he suffered from a swollen spleen that kept him out of the water for several months. Last spring, he was bothered by a sciatic nerve condition.

But Davis recovered and, in June at the Canadian Olympic trials, lowered his world record from 2:14.77 to 2:14.58.

The 6-2, 185-pound Davis began swimming in lakes as a youngster, but his competitive career didn't begin until he was 12.

Davis first began to make waves in the swimming world in January 1981, when he recorded breaststroke victories at meets in New Zealand and Australia.

Since then, his reputation has grown and grown, culminating with the Olympic gold medal.

The victory Thursday by Davis provided Canada with its third swimming gold of the Olympics, not bad for a nation that had not won a swimming gold medal in 72 years until Alex Baumann ended the drought last Monday, taking the 400-meter individual medley. The other Canadian gold medal winner was Anne Ottenbrite in the women's 200-meter breaststroke.

MEDIA

Continued from page 50

Acting on behalf of the IOC, Ueberroth indicated he had asked ABC "to consider trying to give a good focus (to its coverage)," and added that "ABC is being sensitive on the subject . . . and I think you will see their focus change."

But Ueberroth, in distancing himself from the IOC's disagreements with ABC's coverage, said that although he had not "seen very much (TV) to judge," he had "no personal complaint" with what he had seen, which he said "seems to be quite good and quite across the board."

Still, he conceded, he has received "several" letters from the public complaining that ABC's coverage—and that of a few radio stations—is too chauvinistic. But Ueberroth added that he thinks "the mass media (are) doing a good job covering the Games and basically are giving the American public what it wants."

Tom Mackin, ABC's director of program information, said late Thursday that he knows of no letter of protest. "I know of no formal protest that has come from Juan Samaranch to ABC . . . I don't know. I can't ask the question (of Roone Arledge, president of ABC sports) while we are on the air."

Mackin told The Times earlier Thursday that while "we obviously are emphasizing the Americans," the network, which has exclusive rights to the Olympic broadcasts, is "trying to be as balanced as we possibly can."

Foreign broadcasters, who provide their own comments to the ABC footage, "probably are emphasizing their athletes in the coverage that is going back to their countries," Mackin said. "I don't know that, but it seems reasonable."

Here, he said: "I think an American audience wants to see Americans. They want the other athletes, too, of course, and I think they're seeing them."

Even as the IOC drafted its complaint, foreign athletes were airing their own.

The athletes and coaches say they know a good performance when they see one and that the United States' near-monopoly of gold medals is laudable. But they say they have seen other good performances too, from other nations—they just haven't always seen them on television.

When Canadian Olympic basketball forward Sylvia Sweeney switches on the television set to watch the Games, she said Thursday, "It's like this is the U.S. Open, not the Olympics."

Yugoslavian shooter Raymond Debevec, said: "It looks like it did in Moscow, except now we're in America."

To Australian race walker David Smith, "It looks like America versus the rest of the world. There's an overemphasis that it's America's Games, and the rest of the world is invited . . . All they (ABC) are worried about is the medal count, and to me that's the worst thing about the Olympics."

John McGouran, press officer for the Irish Olympic team, said: "On the news last night, the ABC news, they said that the Americans in the ladies' gymnastics didn't win the gold—but they didn't say who did. We thought that sort of coverage was bad in Moscow, but the Americans have outstripped them by far—very chauvinistic. I just can't tell you enough about what the people in the camp (Olympic Village) say about the coverage."

A Chinese consular official, who asked not to be named, said: "We have all complained. No other teams are shown but the Americans."

At the villages on Thursday, some of the athletes had a few words of their own.

Canadian gymnast Kelly Brown said she felt sorry for the short shrift she felt Rumanian and Chinese women gymnasts got.

"(Yanhong) Ma scored a perfect 10, but (television) was looking at (American Mary Lou) Retton and didn't even see the Chinese team," Brown said. "They could've shown her routine. It is the host country, but they're overdoing it."

A New Zealand team member who did not give his name—and who said U.S. fans made him afraid to cheer for Chinese gymnasts lest he "get shot or end up with a beer in my back"—said the coverage is "virtually a joke—all we're doing is watching America. The whole (UCLA) village is talking about it. . . . You wouldn't know there was anybody else in the Olympics."

For Puerto Rican swimmer Miguel Figueroa, what hurts is American TV dominance rather than American medal dominance.

"You get frustrated. You feel like the underclass," he said. "If you're here, it's because you're the best in your country, and they (TV) should respect that."

Other athletes complained that in a multiracial city like Los Angeles—whose ethnic populations from Latin America, Asia, and the Mideast rival in size many of the major cities abroad—many people have two teams to cheer for, but sometimes only one team to watch.

"That's the big problem," said Lebanese swimmer Percy Sayegh. "It really does hurt . . . all the interviews, everything's American. The Lebanese people here, they say, 'Why don't we see you on TV?' When everybody comes here, he shows his best, but his best is not on TV . . . Just let it be fair."

French track and field team member Liliane Gaschet, a 100- and 200-meter women's competitor, believes "it's too much. They don't show anything but Americans. And after seeing the Americans, they change (cameras) to another sport. One wants to see how the others do—and we can't do it. The camera is always fixed on the Americans. The sites are full of Americans, cheering their team. They don't need all the television, as well."

But a teammate, Didier Dubois, tended to dismiss the focus on American achievements. "It's natural—it would be the same in France, in Moscow," he said. "And after all, they are winning a lot, aren't they?"

One American women's handball team player's response to criticism of TV coverage was blunt: "Tough . . . We're winning medals—we're winning gold medals."

Don McRae, Canadian women's basketball coach, criticized both ABC and The Los Angeles Times' coverage as "skewed . . . you're looking at 75-80% American athletes . . . It's unforgivable and irresponsible. Even the Soviets would not be so biased."

What about an athlete "who puts together his best-ever performance and is just as proud as if he won a medal—why not write about that, or about the disappointment an athlete feels when he doesn't live up to his expectations?" suggested McRae.

Everyone is "aware of how proud Americans are. God knows there has been a celebration every hour at these Games. But just to focus on American successes is irresponsible."

He was so upset by media hype of the U.S. women's volleyball team, he said, that he found himself cheering against them. "I've had it up to here," he said, pointing to his neck. "I know the American volleyball team went through a lot to get here, and I was disappointed in my reaction (rooting against the U.S.)."

George Cotliar, managing editor of The Times, defended the paper's coverage, saying that "over the last 13 days, since before the opening of the Olympics, I believe we've done a more than adequate job of covering foreign athletes."

Cotliar added: "There's no Nadia Comaneci in these Olympics, yet; and no Olga Korbut, yet. When the time comes, we'll address that situation, whether it be a Canadian woman, a Canadian man or whoever. Until then, we'll write about what's happening, and that is, the Americans are winning the majority of the medals."

Times staff writers Sandy Banks, Chris Cobbs, Maura Dolan and Joel Sappell contributed to this story.

MURRAY

Continued from page 50

sault before. If she was not the best, she was the most innovative.

In '76, a wispy, boyish 14-year-old with the haunted eyes of a gypsy violinist not only stole hearts, she stole gold medals. Nadia Comaneci flew through the air of Montreal's Forum like a flight of doves off a backwoods lake when the sun hit it. Stunned judges awarded her the first 10 ever seen in gymnastics competition, and it seemed hardly enough.

Americans looked on in envy and ached to get into this fairy-tale world. At international events, including the Olympics, the American team always came out with the second string of competitors—the English, Philippines or some lesser group. The country was not scoured for athletes a la Iron Curtain countries, but the sport, so to speak, came to the athletes. Young girls who could run fast, jump high, take chances and have natural rhythm were attracted to a sport that made you an international celebrity.

Mary Lou Retton was one of these super athletes. Buried in West Virginia, where Dad had been a teammate of Jerry West's, no less, in basketball, Mary Lou could outrun any boy in the neighborhood. She had the strength and speed of a tough little flyweight boxer and she was fearless.

And she loved the limelight. Whirling like a pinwheel around two uneven parallel bars in front of 20,000 flag-waving spectators is no place for Louisa May Alcott or the Bronte sisters. You need the mental toughness of a spitball pitcher, a Burleigh Grimes.

The longtime coach of Nadia Comaneci, the volatile Bela Karolyi, defected from Bucharest to America—and was glad he did when he got a look at Mary Lou Retton. This was the sight to gladden the heart of anybody who wanted to break the Soviet stranglehold on the sport of women's gymnastics once and for all.

Mary Lou combines grace and agility with raw power. And she loves what she's doing. Whether it's TV interviews, press conferences or a simple vault over a side horse, Mary Lou does it with the zest and love of Pete Rose sliding into second. Her eyes sparkle, her cheeks glow, she does everything on the dead run and smiles a lot.

"I'm hyper," she admitted the other night after a full flawless night on the floor. "That's why I love optionals (events that allow the free flow of exercises not bound by mandatory figures). I can let myself go."

The balance beam is the torture rack of gymnastics competition. Barely 3½ inches wide, it is a piece of lumber 16 feet long and 4 feet above the floor. It is very easy to fall off. It's doubtful if the average citizen could walk across it without slipping.

Girl gymnasts do back and forward somersaults on it. If they fall, they get deducted half a point. To get an idea of the degree of difficulty, try to imagine a guy crawling along a hotel ledge high in the air and doing periodic flips.

The balance beam proved the downfall of the American four in the team competition at Pauley Pavilion the other night. It usually does. It is the gymnasts' wall of pain, their version of the road hole in a British Open or trying to score from the Raiders' three-yard line.

Gymnastics are the Balkans of Olympic sports. Wars break out all the time over scoring. A fall is easy to score, but the rest is highly subjective, and the notion of fair play never seems to have made much headway east of Eton and Harrow.

While the judges were in a scream-into-the-telephone snit over a score for American Kathy Johnson in the balance beam competition the other night, one of our best artists, Julianne McNamara, was forced into an eight-minute delay. She lost her concentration, fell off the bar once and settled for a 9.2 score. That's a strikeout in this sport, or at least, a popup with the bases loaded.

The American girls finished second. But that's higher than they ever did before. In fact, that's the first medal they've ever won.

And the scoring counts toward the all-around gold medal, meaning that Mary Lou Retton, who found herself with one 10 and a whole bunch of 9.9s, is leading the world at the moment in that gold medal chase.

If she wins it, and breaks Nadia's record, she's going to replace the Cabbage Patch Doll as next Christmas' prize gift to the country. And why wouldn't she win it? The other Mary Lou Retton, Pete Rose, is going to break Ty Cobb's record, too, isn't he?

Scott Ostler

Taiwan Kids Are Older, but They Play Same Game

You've heard of books banned in Boston.

How about a baseball team banned in Williamsport, Pa.?

A team of pre-teen-agers, yet, kids who were polite, respectful and conscientious, and whose main passion in life was baseball.

The kids were from Taiwan, and they were so fantastic, year after year, that the country was finally banned from the Little League World Series in Williamsport.

What becomes of kids such as these? They go on to the Olympic Games, of course. Half the starters for the Taiwan team in this Olympic Games once played on a Little League World Series championship team.

The Taiwan team found the competition a little stiffer here at the Olympics than it was in Williamsport. They lost to the United States, 2-1 Tuesday. But they came back Thursday to beat the Dominican Republic, 13-1.

Now that's more like the Taiwan players we grew to know and love—and some grew to hate—in Little League.

Brief history: Little League baseball was introduced to Taiwan in 1969. That season a regional all-star team from that country won the Little League World Series.

The country went wild. Not since C.K. Yang challenged Rafer Johnson for the decathlon title in the 1960 Olympics had Taiwan had a national sports hero. Now they had a whole team of 'em.

Taiwan teams won the Little League World Series in 1971, 1972, 1973 and 1974. In the 1973 Series they outscored their three opponents 57-0 and outhit them 43-0.

The Taiwan kids were no longer the cute little underdogs. They had become monsters, accused of cheating, booed by the American crowds. None of the charges were ever substantiated, but in 1975 Little League officials excluded foreign teams from the "World" Series.

If you can't beat 'em, ban 'em.

The ban was lifted after one season. Japan won in 1976, then Taiwan teams won the Series five straight years, 1977 through 1981.

This country, you get the feeling, knows something about baseball.

For starters, it knows how to work.

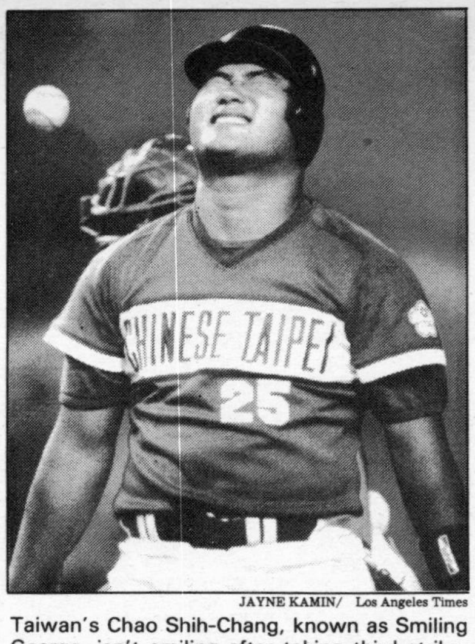

JAYNE KAMIN / Los Angeles Times

Taiwan's Chao Shih-Chang, known as Smiling George, isn't smiling after taking third strike.

"They drill with intensity," says Rod Dedeaux, coach of the U.S. team, who has seen the Taiwan Olympic team play many times. "It's not unusual for them to work 10, 12 hours a day in practice.

"They played us (USC) at our park, a night game, and we won. After the game they asked if they could use the field to practice. They practiced two hours, after a night game, and the first hour they worked without a ball or bat, doing agility drills."

This is the kind of attitude that made the Taiwan Little League teams the scourge of the world.

"The way we train is difficult," said Lo Liang-Han, secretary of the country's Olympic team. "Our boy, I think, is much more disciplined. He does what the coach say."

Mike McGrath, an American who attended high school in Taiwan and later earned a doctorate in Chinese studies at Princeton, once told Sports Illustrated, "It wasn't the longer practices alone that did it. They also applied themselves better (than American kids in Taiwan) in training. It is simply that their lives are more regimented and diligence is probably more highly prized."

Now the Little Leaguers have grown up. They don't steamroll a world tournament as they did as kids, but their Olympic team is rated second best to the United States in this eight-team demonstration tournament.

The Taiwan team doesn't beat you with muscle. In batting practice before Thursday's game, only one hitter knocked a ball over the Dodger Stadium fence. This is a team of 20 Rod Carews, slapping, slashing and spraying the baseball.

Size dictates style; only one player on the roster (a pitcher) is six-feet tall.

The lone power hitter is rotund first baseman Chao Shih-Chiang (Smiling George), who is also the team's designated character.

"I like American food," George says. "I like the hamburger. I like the taco, which is Mexican."

During Taiwan batting practice, silence reigns except when George steps to the plate and provides a running commentary of his own hits.

"Sank you," George says, bowing to the batting practice pitcher as he steps out of he cage.

George—he got his American nickname from Dedeaux, and has kept it—is an assistant professor of Physical Education at Chinese Culture University and hopes to play baseball in the American major leagues. He says the Yankees have shown interest.

Would he like to play for the Dodgers? They're always looking for a first baseman with power.

"This field is too big for me," George says with a laugh.

I don't have the heart to tell George about the size of Yankee Stadium's left field. Or about George Steinbrenner.

Dedeaux says George has major-league power, but the real big-league prospects are the pitchers, especially Kuo Tai-Yuan, who showed a 95-m.p.h. fastball to the U.S. hitters Tuesday.

"And I'll tell you about their pitchers," Dedeaux said. "They can pitch every other day, or every day if they have to. Their guy (Kuo), I have no doubt, could have pitched the next day if he had to."

American big leaguers should be thankful only one Taiwanese player ever made it to the majors here. Pitching every day? Working out 10 hours? These guys could spread dangerous ideas.

How dangerous? Just ask the Little League bigshots in Williamsport.

French Boat Is Hit by Saboteur

By BILL CHRISTINE, *Times Staff Writer*

OJAI—Is there a saboteur on the loose in international rowing circles?

For the second time in two weeks, a boat has apparently been tampered with. The latest incident came Thursday in the men's eight-oar repechage heat at Lake Casitas, where the French boat lost all chance at 700 meters into the 2,000-meter race.

Jean Jacques Martigne, France's six oar, was knocked out of the race because of an oarlock gate that was sheared and came loose. The gate is a small metal rod that serves as a cover for the oarlock, keeping the oar in place. When Martigne's gate snapped open, he lost his oar.

An identical incident happened to the U.S. four-with-coxswain crew two weeks ago in the International Junior Championships in Sweden. Because of the first incident, Olympic officials checked the French oarlock after Thursday's race and found evidence of foul play.

Later, Thomas Keller, president of the International Rowing Federation which governs the sport, ruled that the French eight crew deserved another chance. So, despite finishing last in Thursday's five-boat loser's heat, France will be added to the Sunday's final, making it a seven-boat race.

"The other countries agreed with my decision," Keller said. "There was applause when they heard it."

Keller labeled the damage to the oarlock as "willful."

"It was very cleverly done," he said. "I would say that a file was used to do the job."

Keller, who has a background as a chemical engineer, said the evidence indicated that the damage was probably done before France rowed in its first Olympic race on Tuesday, and probably occurred before the shell arrived at Lake Casitas.

"We have no idea who would have enough of an interest to do something like this," Keller said. "It's very sad that things like this do happen."

Keller's decision allows France to advance to the finals even though it has finished last in both of its preliminary races. On Thursday, France finished behind Australia, Canada, Great Britain and Chile. Four of the five boats were supposed to make the finals, joining the United States and favored New Zealand, which both won opening heats Tuesday.

"I was left no choice but to keep the French in," Keller said. "They were left in a position of trying to beat out Chile (which finished fourth) with only seven people."

According to Keller, there will be no investigation into the oarlock incident. "Since we are convinced that it happened before the boat got here, nothing could be accomplished," he said. "And besides, we are not investigators. Crews are responsible for their own equipment, and they must check their boats carefully in view of all this."

Meanwhile, in the single sculls semifinals Thursday, there were no surprises in either the men's or women's races.

Valeria Racila, the tall, tanned Romanian who's heavily favored to win the gold medal Saturday, won her heat by more than three seconds, finishing ahead of Carlie Geer of the United States and Andrea Schreiner of Canada. Lisa Marian Justesen of Denmark, Ann Haesebrouck of Belgium and Beryl Mitchell of Great Britain finished 1-2-3 in the other semifinal race to advance to the finals.

In the men's division, favored Pertti Karppinen of Finland, while rowing at a reduced pace of less than 30 strokes per minute, still won his semifinal heat, with Robert Mills of Canada and Kostantinos Kontomanolis of Greece finishing immediately behind him and qualifying for Sunday's final. The other finalists are Michael Kolbe of West Germany, Ricardo Ibarra of Argentina and John Biglow of the United States, finishing in that order in their semifinal heat.

The Americans have more finalists than any other country—13 out of a possible 14 events. Today's action will settle places seven through 12. The women's finals are Saturday, with the men taking over Sunday. Both sessions start at 8 a.m.

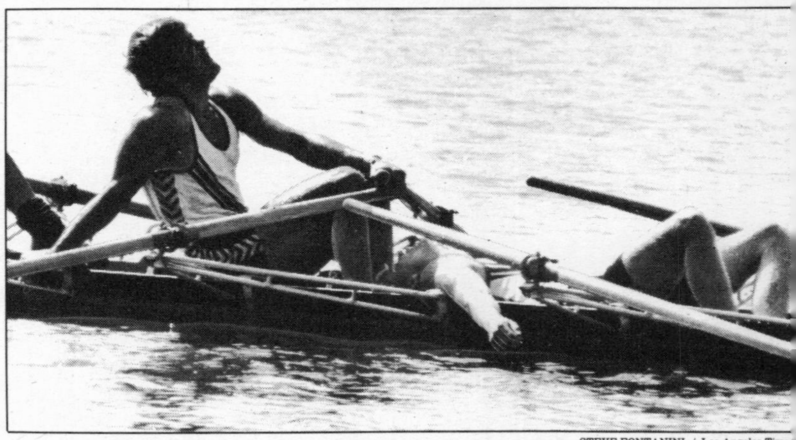

STEVE FONTANINI / Los Angeles Times

Velte Vinje (left) and stroke Ivan Enstad of the Norwegian quadruple sculls without coxswain, have nothing left to give after failing to qualify for semifinals Thursday at Lake Casitas.

Men's Team Handball

Sweden Ends U.S. Hope for Medal

By TOM HAMILTON, *Times Staff Writer*

The patriotic cries and American flag-waving were not enough to keep the underdog United States men's team handball players in the running for a medal of any kind in the 1984 Olympic Games.

That reality materialized Thursday as the United States lost to Sweden, 21-18, before 3,300 fans at Cal State Fullerton. It was the second consecutive defeat for the men's team in Group B, where Sweden, Denmark and West Germany have 2-0 records among the six teams.

The two teams with the best records in the group will advance to the medal round Aug. 11 at the Forum in Inglewood. The American team has three games remaining in pool play, and it's becoming more apparent that their last-place ranking in the tournament was justified.

"Realistically, our dream of a medal is over," winger Joe Story said. "Now, we can only look forward to playing our best and hope to come away feeling we've done our best."

Center back Bob Djokovich put things into perspective when he said: "We knew from the outset that this was going to be a longshot. Most of the guys on our team have only been playing the game for two or three years, and we're playing the best teams in the world."

Oh, there were some moments for the U.S. team Thursday afternoon. They opened a 2-0 lead on goals by Peter Lash and Steve Goss, and goalie Billy Kessler provided the capacity crowd with a few spectacular saves.

But Sweden took a 5-4 lead on a penalty shot by Bjorn Jilsen with 13:18 left in the first half and never trailed thereafter. Sweden led by seven goals in the second half and only reinforced what its coach, Roger Carlsson, said two days ago.

Carlsson boldly told the press: "I expect to win" the game against the United States. And why not? Carlsson has two professionals on his team.

Goalie Claes Hellgren and Jilsen both play for the Tres de Mayo club out of the Canary Islands in a Spanish league. They reportedly earn $50,000 a year and looked like a million dollars against the United States.

Jilsen scored eight goals, and Hellgren protected his 10-meter goal as efficiently as the Olympic security force is guarding the athletes.

Lash was the only American who could overcome Jilsen's mastery. He scored nine goals, and later, Hellgren said he could play for any team in Spain. But teammate Jim Buehning was shut out, and no other U.S. player scored more than two goals.

"We had a lot of opportunities to score in the first half and didn't," U.S. Coach Javier Garcia Cuesta said. "Our offense needs a little more mobility if we hope to play with the best teams in the world.

"We have a long way to go, but I am amazed how far we've progressed in three years. At first, we were hoping just to be competitive. Now, we're losing by just three goals, and it's very frustrating to be so close."

Romania 26, Iceland 17—Although Iceland had stunned gold medal co-favorite Yugoslavia with a 22-22 tie in the first round of Group A play Tuesday, the other favorite, Romania, never trailed in Thursday's one-sided game.

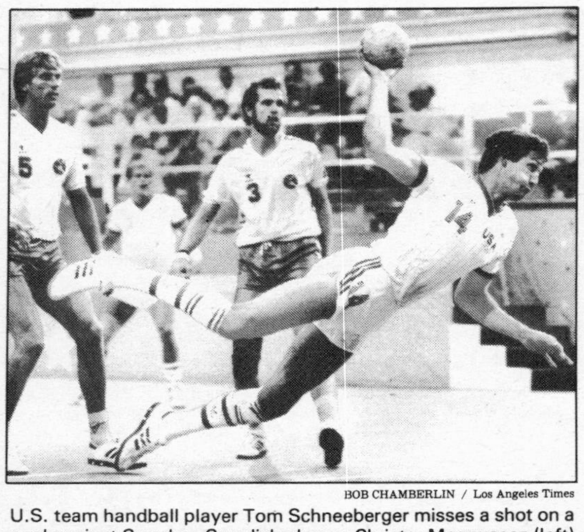

BOB CHAMBERLIN / Los Angeles Times

U.S. team handball player Tom Schneeberger misses a shot on a goal against Sweden. Swedish players Christer Magnusson (left) and Danny Augustsson (right) watch their opponent fall.

NOTES

A Swedish wrestler, Frank Andersson, is currently contemplating a post-Olympic job as the national coach of Kuwait. It may not sound very exciting, but Kuwait—an oil-rich country—is reportedly willing to part with "millions of dollars," according to a Swedish journalist.

"I haven't decided yet," Andersson said. "I really want to try professional wrestling in this country, but I don't know what it is."

Advised that professional wrestling in the United States is a cross between a circus and The Three Stooges, Andersson shook his head.

"Serious wrestling," he said. "Maybe freestyle. It would be nice to have serious wrestling and get paid for it."

Bottom line: Andersson has been criticized in his homeland, at times, for being more serious about night life than wrestling.

—DAVE DISTEL

□

Police officer Alan Sherwood scored something of a goal Monday night while patrolling the crowd of 40,800 at an Olympic soccer match at the Rose Bowl.

Amid the sea of spectators, Sherwood thought he recognized a man he had investigated in the past. The man was wanted on a $5,000 narcotics arrest warrant.

After a quick radio check confirmed his suspicions, Sherwood arrested Howard Wayne Woodson, 21, who was booked for investigation of possessing marijuana for sale.

"That was pretty good police work," a police spokesman said. "Of course, for that one there's probably 200 we missed."

□

So, you think target shooting isn't physically demanding? American Mary Schweitzer, who competed in Tuesday's air rifle competition might disagree.

"Wearing a T-shirt, under a sweatshirt, under a leather shooting jacket, she lost five pounds during the heat of competition—a 40-shot, 1½-hour event.

"There was sweat pouring off my head onto my face," she said. "On the line the temperature seemed to rise because of all the people behind us."

About 500 jammed the cramped indoor air gun range at the Olympic shooting site in the Chino Valley to watch American Patty Spurgin win a gold medal.

—ELLIOTT ALMOND

Carl Lewis, please note: The lineup of the planets bodes ill for the man who is trying to become the brightest star in the Olympic heavens.

This cosmic memo is from Future Forecasts, a Westwood instant horoscope shop, where you can plunk down your $9.95 for the Olympic Special, and in five minutes, presto! Planetary print-out prognostications.

For Lewis, who will try to win four track gold medals within the next two weeks, the stars are dim. In a 15-page projection, the computer warned: "Projects or plans that began up to six years ago may come to fruition now, but only if you have been careful about details . . . as long as you avoid certain pitfalls.

". . . The primary problem is to avoid thinking too big or attempting something that is totally grandiose and impractical.

"The pace of events may become rather fast-moving for you at this time. . . . The scale of events may be too large for you to grasp."

Then again, it was a computer that picked the Chicago Cubs to finish last.

—JULIE CART and RICK REILLY

48,491 See United States Turn on Power in 16-1 Rout

By BOB CUOMO, *Times Staff Writer*

Baseball

Before the Olympic baseball demonstration tournament began, U.S. Coach Rod Dedeaux said that one of his team's strengths was power, although he said he doubted whether it would be a factor against the mature and experienced pitchers the Americans were scheduled to face.

Thursday night, for one of the few times in his career, Dedeaux was wrong. The United States flexed its muscles, hitting four long home runs en route to a 16-1 rout of Italy before a crowd of 48,491 at Dodger Stadium.

The United States, which beat Taiwan, 2-1, in its opening-game Tuesday night, is 2-0 and leads the White Division. Italy and Taiwan, a 13-1 winner over the Dominican Republic in Thursday's first game, are both 1-1. The Dominican Republic is 0-2.

Another large crowd saw the United States do the majority of its scoring in the first inning when 13 men went to bat. Seven hit safely, two walked and one was hit by a pitch. Nine scored during the 23-minute inning.

The big hits were home runs by Shane Mack, Will Clark and Oddibe McDowell. Mack followed a leadoff walk to McDowell with a high drive over the 385-foot mark in right-center field. Clark, the next batter, drove the next pitch halfway up the right-field pavilion. McDowell capped the scoring with a three-run homer into the right-field seats.

The victim of the U.S.'s power output was Luigi Colabello, a 34-year-old left-hander who was born in Milford, Conn., and attended the University of Massachusetts. Colabello, one of 10 American-born players on the Italian team, lasted just a third of an inning and gave up all nine runs.

Italy, meanwhile, had little success against U.S. starter Scott Bankhead. The All-American from the University of North Carolina pitched the first five innings and allowed only three hits, one walk and one unearned run while striking out four.

McDowell, the All-American center fielder from Arizona State, had three of the 18 hits the United States totaled off three Italian pitchers. He also drove in five runs, the last when he lined his second home run of the game over the 370-foot sign in left-center.

Taiwan 13, Dominican Republic 1—Taiwan bounced back from its 2-1 loss to the United States Tuesday night, scoring five runs in the second inning and seven in the third to even its White Division record at 1-1. The victory also kept alive Taiwan's chances of advancing to the semifinals.

Limited to four hits by the U.S.'s John Hoover, Taiwan collected 16 hits off three Dominican pitchers, including six in the second inning and five in the third. Taiwan also benefited from poor defensive play by the Dominican Republic. Three errors, including two by shortstop Ivan Crispin, were committed in the third inning.

Shortstop Wu Fu-Lien, who made several fine plays, had three hits and drove in two runs. Center fielder Lee Chu-Ming and catcher Twu Jong-Nan each had two RBIs.

The Dominican Republic, limited to just four hits through eight innings, averted a shutout when Pedro Gomez scored on a two-out ninth-inning double by third baseman Aristedes Taveras.

Compiled By JERRY GILLAM

Legendary Yamashita May Be the Ultimate Weapon

From Times Staff Writers and Wire Services

More certain than a Carl Lewis parlay or an Edwin Moses romp is the prospect of a gold medal for Yasuhiro Yamashita.

If ever there was a mortal lock in Olympic judo, it is Yamashita, a 5-11, 280-pound Japanese legend whose winning streak eclipses even Moses' 89 straight victories in the intermediate hurdles.

Yamashita has not come close to losing a bout since 1977, a string encompassing 194 fights—189 of them won by *ippon*, the judo equivalent of a knockout.

Not counting his opponents in the open division, Yamashita is a unanimous choice among the world's judoists.

Polled informally on their gold-medal predictions, judokas from China to Canada invariably begin: "Well, there's Yamashita, of course, and . . ."

Naturally enough, Yamashita's open-class rivals—including America's Dewey Mitchell, fit, feisty and 40 pounds lighter—concede the gold to nobody this side of Ft. Knox.

Still, when asked by Sports Illustrated what could stop Yamashita, Noboyuki Sato, his *sensei* (coach/master), replied: "A nuclear war."

—DICK RORABACK

□

Liselott Diem, widow of Carl Diem, the chief organizer of the 1936 Berlin Olympics, is in Los Angeles this week, attending yet another Olympic Games in a press capacity. Diem also attended the 1980 Moscow Olympics.

She says she thinks the L.A. opening was even better than Moscow's, although, as Olympic openings go, she regarded Moscow's as "first-rate."

Diem gives high marks to the LAOOC in all particulars except for the spread-out character of the Games. Now well past 70, she says it is a hassle to get around L.A. Accordingly, she plans to return home Saturday, only a week into the Games.

—KENNETH REICH

□

Flo Hyman of the U.S. women's volleyball team lived up to her nickname Wednesday night in her team's come-from-behind victory over Brazil.

"My nickname is Clutchman," Hyman said. "And my captain was saying, 'OK, Clutchman, whatcha gonna do?' So I said, 'OK, turn it on.' "

Then Clutchman not only turned it on, she turned the last game inside out.

Hyman slammed a half-dozen winning crucial spikes in the final minutes of the fifth game, including the match-winner.

□

Charles Shields says he was so overcome with emotion when he saw his grandson, Tim Daggett, score a perfect 10 at the Olympics that he started crying and ran outside in the middle of the night to turn on the lights and raise an American flag.

"I was so thrilled that I had to tell everyone who went by that something had happened," Shields, 84, said.

The 22-year-old UCLA psychology major's performance on the horizontal bars was the third perfect American routine and enabled the U.S. to earn its first gold medal ever in Olympic gymnastics.

Shields said he left the flag flying from a five-foot pole on the side of his house all night and kept it there Wednesday as family, friends and neighbors came by to congratulate him.

□

When U.S. gymnast Bart Conner underwent arm surgery last December to repair a torn biceps muscle, he came away from the operation with several souvenirs—about 40 bone chips.

One was as big as Conner's thumb. His mother kept it, and now that her son is a (team) gold medalist, she has definite plans for it.

"She wants to have the bone chip plated in gold and make a necklace out of it," Conner said. "Pretty tacky, huh?"

—MIKE PENNER

□

The Dodgers are playing on the road while the Olympic baseball demonstration tournament is being held at Dodger Stadium, but there are some reminders of the team that normally occupies the third base dugout.

Italy's uniforms are an exact replica of those worn by the Dodgers when playing on the road. They're gray with blue and white trim, and the number on the front of the jersey is red. The only difference is that instead of Dodgers on the front, it says Italia. Maybe Tom Lasorda helped design them.

The Dominican Republic has a player named Mota. He's a 17-year-old outfielder, whose first name is Miguel. He's not related to Manny Mota, but he received loud cheers during the player introductions.

—BOB CUOMO

□

The Olympic pool is being kept clean with injections of ozone gas instead of the usual chlorine. The method has been tested for the past four months at the Mission Viejo Swim Complex and seems to help reduce eye irritation.

Many swimmers still wear goggles, however, because they improve visibility.

"It works great," said Mark Schubert, the Mission Viejo coach and an Olympic assistant. "They inject it (ozone) once in the morning and it works all day. It's like 50 or 100 times more powerful at killing bacteria than chlorine, and there's no residual like with chlorine. Your eyes never hurt after a workout."

—JOHN WEYLER

□

The executive board of the International Olympic Committee banned a masseur for the Japanese team from the Games and delivered a "severe warning" to that country's delegation for allowing him to give an herbal product to one of its volleyball players as a cold treatment.

The IOC did not ban the athlete, Mikiyasy Tanaka, from the Olympics, according to a statement released by the IOC Thursday. But the masseur, Yoshi Yahagi, will no longer be allowed to participate in the Los Angeles Games or the in next two Olympics.

A test of Tanaka's urine revealed that he had taken a Japanese product containing the herb ephedra.

The IOC found that Yahagi gave Tanaka the herb for a cold and told the athlete that the product was not a drug but a "simple herbal remedy" which would not lead to a problem in a dope-control test.

Following the recommendation of the IOC Medical Commission, the executive board decided that the Japanese delegation should "receive a severe warning of the potential danger in taking or administering herbal preparations or allowing their athletes to take any products for medical application other than those recommended by a team doctor."

MAKING A SPLASH

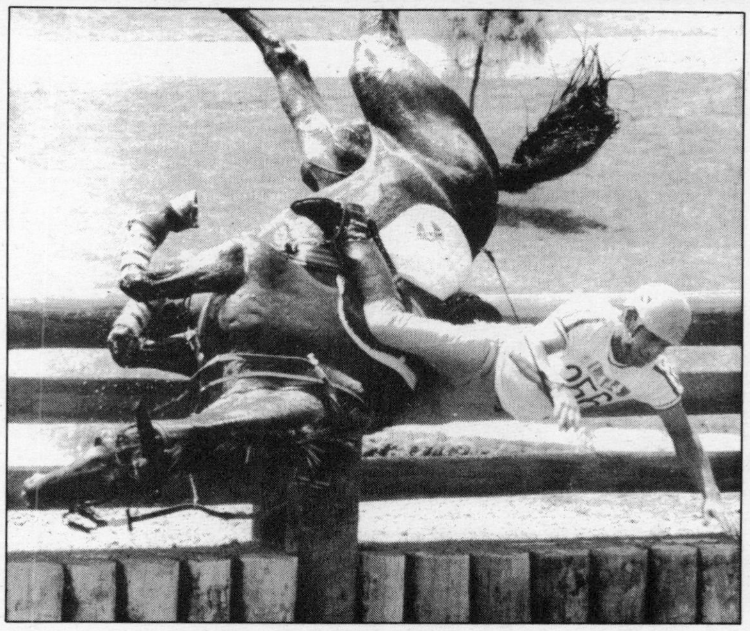

United Press International

Armando Romero of Mexico takes a dive (top) in the three-day endurance equestrian competition at Fairbanks Ranch in Rancho Santa Fe when his horse, Homenaje, tumbles on a water jump. Romero goes under (bottom), but neither the rider nor the horse was injured.

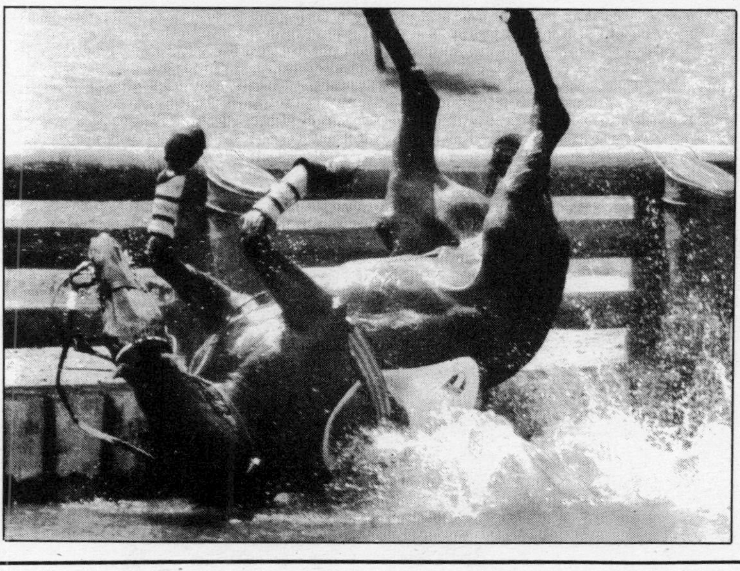

□

One of the best things about the upset victory in men's gymnastics, according to U.S. team member Bart Conner, is the effect it has had on the mood at the Olympic Village.

"So many people came to the Village worrying about what was going to happen during the Olympics," Conner said. "Forty people get run down by a car in Westwood. People wondered if there were going to be bombings at the Coliseum.

"Then this happens early in the Games, and people are walking around smiling. They're saying, 'Hey, this is going to be a good Olympics after all.' "

—MIKE PENNER

□

Team handball is a family affair for the Buehnings of Short Hills, N.J. Peter Buehning Sr. was a founder of the U.S. Team Handball Federation in 1959 and has served as the organization's president since 1961.

His wife, Renate, is a vice-president of the federation and served on the organizing committee for the International Handball Federation Congress held in San Diego before the Olympics.

Their oldest son, Peter Jr., is one of two accredited American referees officiating the Games. Finally, Jim Buehning is a starter for the U.S. men's team and has been a member of the national team since 1977.

—TOM HAMILTON

Las Vegas Bookmaker Posts Odds on Games

LAS VEGAS (UPI)—Great Britain's Daley Thompson has been installed as a 2-1 favorite to defeat West Germany's Jurgen Hingsen for the decathlon title next week in the Olympic Games at Los Angeles, a Las Vegas bookmaker said Thursday.

Vic Salerno of Leroy's Horse & Sports Place also posted proposition odds for four track and field events, offering 6-5 odds on whether the pole vault will be won at 19 feet 3¼ inches, the high jump at 7-10, long jump at 28-1 and the shotput at 71-10.

Salerno said the volume of sports betting in Las Vegas is down due to the Olympics being shown on television.

"That's why we decided to put some numbers on the Games up on the board, just to draw some attention," he said. "We're getting some action, but nothing like we get during football season."

□

A mistake by a Los Angeles Olympic Organizing Committee press aide temporarily threw the International Volleyball Federation into a panic late Wednesday night, triggering an emergency meeting of the sport's governing body to determine the fate of the Italian Olympic men's team.

A fact sheet distributed by the LAOOC following Italy's victory over China Tuesday included this quote from Italian Coach Silvando Prandi: "Six of our players are from the Italian pro league."

The only problem was, Prandi never said that—at least in a formal interview. And there are no professional volleyball leagues in the world.

The Italian club leagues, which attract many foreign players by paying them up to $50,000 a year in "expenses," are considered amateur competition by the IVBF.

An LAOOC press aide made them "pro leagues" in paraphrasing a Prandi answer to a reporter's question.

In the end, the fact sheet was revised, and everybody went home—but later than they had expected.

—JERRY CROWE

□

Paul B. Zimmerman, retired sports editor of The Times, covered the 1932 Games in Los Angeles and is now an accredited journalist at the 1984 Olympics. In all, Zimmerman has covered eight previous Olympics. He presently is filing special features to the Sankei Sports Shimbun, the largest sports daily in Japan.

□

Canadian women's field hockey Coach Marina van der Merwe, a tough taskmaster tabbed "Vince Lombardi in lipstick" by some of the press, was surprised to find a roomful of reporters waiting for her after Canada's 4-1 loss to the United States Wednesday. "Sorry I'm late," she said. "I didn't realize losers were in demand."

Asked if the Lombardi comparison fit, Canadian captain Shelley Andrews replied: "I don't know. I've never met Lombardi."

—ALAN DROOZ

□

The coach of the Greek water polo team, Gose Brasco Cata, was asked at a press conference if Greece had ever beaten Spain.

Cata laughed and said he remembered the one victory well. He was the coach of the Spanish team at the time.

"I cannot forget it," said Cata, who is Spanish and has been coaching the Greek team for only a few months. The score was 6-5, the year was 1978, it was a night game, it was raining . . ."

—MILES CORWIN

□

There was an added touch to "Star Wars Marathon" at the USC Olympic Village Tuesday night—a special guest appearance by Darth Vader.

Vincent Sarnelli of France strolled up to the black-caped villain and showed him the boxing gloves imprinted on his Olympic identification tag.

"I'm not afraid of you, I'm a boxer," Sarnelli said as he pretended to box with Vader.

The USC Village cinema showed all three of the film hits produced and directed by George Lucas—"Star Wars," "The Empire Strikes Back" and "Return of the Jedi." Lucas is a USC graduate.

Between movies, Vader strolled through the village greeting athletes along the way.

He often stopped to have his picture taken with athletes, teasingly placing his hands around the necks of male athletes and drawing female athletes under his black cape.

The only problem Vader faced in the village came from security guards who repeatedly stopped him, asking for his identification since he wasn't wearing an accreditation badge.

□

George Haines is the dean of the U.S. Olympic swimming team's coaching staff.

Haines, 58, head women's coach at Stanford, is an Olympic coach for the seventh consecutive time.

His first Olympic coaching assignment was in 1960 at Rome. He was the head coach in 1980, but the United States boycotted the Games at Moscow.

Some of his former pupils are among the legends in the sport, including Mark Spitz and Don Schollander.

This time, Haines is serving as an assistant under Coach Don Gambril, who is on the Olympic coaching staff for the fifth time.

—SEYMOUR BEUBIS

□

What's the use of winning a gold medal if you can't call anybody and tell 'em?

American gymnasts Tim Daggett and Bart Conner were tooling around in a luxurious white ABC-TV limousine—complete with phone—after a late-night interview Tuesday and found themselves in that circumstance.

Here they were, just a few hours after winning the team gold medal—riding high and in style—and nobody home to answer the phone.

"Boy, was that frustrating," Daggett said.

The new heroes, thus exasperated, told the chauffeur (not named James) to take them back to the USC Olympic Village, where they were greeted with a worthy welcome and stayed up till . . .?

"I better not say," Daggett said, checking for Coach Abie Grossfeld.

Of course, Grossfeld wasn't one to talk. "I got to bed at 4:30 (a.m.)," he said.

Mitch Gaylord, Daggett's fellow gold medalist, one-upped him.

"I never did get to sleep," he said.

—RICK REILLY

□

Canadian field hockey player Laurie Lambert casts one vote for tranquility at East Los Angeles College, where a new sound system plays popular music between games and a high school band sometimes entertains.

"I don't like all the music. I'd rather have peace and quiet and two people in the stands like usual," she said as teammates winced.

—ALAN DROOZ

□

Among the hundreds of telegrams and messages the American gymnasts received Wednesday morning was this one from Diana Ross to Bart Conner:

"My daughter and I watched you on TV last night. We just wanted to say we love you."

Noticeably absent from the salutations, though, was one from President Reagan. "Hey, that's right," said Tim Daggett, Conner's teammate. "We haven't heard from Ron yet."

—MIKE PENNER

□

Ryan O'Neal and his companion, Farrah Fawcett, were among the boxing fans at the Sports Arena Wednesday night, and both the actor and actress insisted that they are, indeed, fight fans.

O'Neal has managed professional boxers in the past and said he hopes to sign Canadian heavyweight Willie deWit to a pro contract after the Olympics. His partner, he said, would be rock music promoter Shelly Finkel of New York.

Asked if he had ever boxed as an amateur, O'Neal replied: "I had 12 fights."

However, the exact number of victories was hazy.

"I won the majority of them," he said.

Majority?

"That's right . . . more than half."

Other ringsiders included singer Andy Williams and former champions Carlos Palomino and Sugar Ray Robinson, whose ring career—including more than 200 amateur bouts—was legendary.

—JACK HAWN

□

Athletes in every Games, although fiercely competitive, are still charitable to their foes.

In the 148-pound (67.5-kilogram) weightlifting session Wednesday, Hatem Bouabid of Tunisia and Surendra Hamal of Nepal shared a lifting belt because Bouabid inadvertently forgot his belt at the Olympic Village.

Bouabid, however, failed to complete a snatch lift and wound up scoreless.

□

Team handball might be the only Olympic sport that requires an explanation before play begins.

Public address announcer Steve Jacobson begins each session at Cal State Fullerton by explaining the techniques and rules of the game to the fans, most of whom are watching the sport for the first time.

But the estimated 150 Danish fans who attended the opening session Tuesday obviously didn't need any explanation. Team handball is rapidly gaining on soccer as the country's No. 1 sport, and many of the fans at Fullerton were dressed in the country's colors of red and white and waving Danish flags.

"We thought the sport would delight American fans because it's a speedy game with high scores and acrobatic goalkeeping," Danish Coach Leif Mikkelsen said. "It is very popular in Denmark and the sport has everything Americans seem to enjoy in basketball or football."

—TOM HAMILTON

Pat Head Summitt, U.S. women's basketball coach, shouts to her players during their victory over Yugoslavia.

U.S. fencer Gregory Massialis, left, tries to block an attack by Belal Refat of Egypt. Massialis won the match.

U.S. pursuit cyclist Brent Emery on his way down during qualification race.

R. Patrick McDonough leads U.S. cycling team onto track, prior to start of 4,000-meter team pursuit competition.

Associated Press

Associated Press

Star class boats head to the weather mark during the third race.

America's Nelson Vails, left, blows a kiss, then celebrates with the crowd, below left, after winning a sprint cycling semifinal.

Credits: Except where noted, photos for this page were taken for The Times by Rick Corrales, Patrick Downs, Ken Hively, Rosemary Kaul and Craig Wright.

Designed by Tom Trapnell

Los Angeles Times

Saturday, August 4, 1984

DAY 8 OLYMPICS '84

Retton Vaults Past Szabo to Win Gold Medal

SKEETER HAGLER / Los Angeles Times

Mary Lou Retton stretches out on the balance beam, where she scored a 9.8 en route to the gold medal in the all-around competition.

She Throws a Pair of 10s at End, Takes All-Around

By RICHARD HOFFER, *Times Staff Writer*

She's a calculating coquette. You give her a chance, she'll take your heart. She's a shrewd, brown-eyed gold digger. Yeah, you give her a chance, she'll take your gold, too.

Mary Lou Retton, who has restored pixie to our vocabulary, stole both Friday night, winning, in order, U.S. hearts and Romanian gold. The little sneak. Who saw her coming, padding down the runway in those size-3 feet?

Ordinarily you'd want to hang her from your rear-view mirror. But Friday night, much of America, certainly most of the 9,023 in Pauley Pavilion, wanted to suspend this 4-foot-9 doll in the stratosphere of Olympic tradition, where the heroes belong.

This is what she did, relying on all the nerve and cunning normally available to 16-year-old girls with crushes on Matt Dillon. Battling back in her final two events, needing perfect scores and no less, she beat Romania's Ecaterina Szabo by 5/100ths of a point and Romania's Pauca Simona by 5-10ths to win the women's all-around title, literally vaulting into history.

Some quick perspective: This is only the first individual Olympic medal ever won by a U.S. women's gymnast. Ever.

In the days and months and years that follow, this victory will no doubt be translated into a renewed boom in women's gymnastics, with new clubs opening and every pre-teen worth her pigtail paying money to learn how to somersault. Funny that the last big boom was in 1976, when another little pixie, Nadia Comaneci, transformed her sport. Try to picture seven-year-old Mary Lou,

lying in her living room back in Fairmount, W. Va., watching Nadia, suddenly inspired. "I thought, 'Oh, my gosh, she's so wonderful,'" she said. "Who would have thought?"

Yeah, who would have thought? Nadia, a guest of honor at Pauley Pavilion for these Olympics, offering her silent benediction to the Romania girls? Romania's star gymnast, Ecaterina Szabo, who began the night with a 10 and a 9.95 to take a quick .15 lead?

Only Retton, as nerveless as plant life, could have thought it. And did. She knew that the order of events indicated Szabo taking the early lead. What's to worry. While Szabo was performing in her strongest events, Retton was performing in her weakest. Wait for the finish to announce this winner. "It was the luck of the draw," she admitted.

Szabo, a gymnast who is much like Retton in form and style, began the evening with a 10 on beam. Retton was struggling through an uneven bars set with a 9.85. Suddenly Retton's preliminary lead (from the team event) of .15 was gone, wiped out. Then while Szabo was scoring 9.95 on her floor exercises, dancing to a whacky medley that alternated "Rhapsody in Blue" with "Camptown Races," Retton was getting a 9.8 on her least favorite apparatus, the beam. Szabo, the 17-year-old heir to Nadia, a veteran international competitor who placed third in the most recent World Championships, was leading America's in-

Please see RETTON, page 56

IOC, ABC Discuss Coverage

By KENNETH REICH and JAY SHARBUTT, *Times Staff Writers*

International Olympic Committee leaders who had complained about ABC-TV's alleged over-concentration on Americans in its coverage of the Olympic Games, met with network executives Friday and later expressed satisfaction with certain phases of the coverage.

But the statement by IOC President Juan Antonino Samaranch of Spain and IOC Executive Director Monique Berlioux of France did not address directly the question of the American focus that was raised Thursday.

After Samaranch and Berlioux had met with Roone Arledge, president of ABC news and sports, an ABC spokesman indicated the network will continue its emphasis on the accomplishments of American athletes.

Tom Mackin, the network's director of program information, said there had been no directive from Arledge or any other ABC official to change the American broadcasts.

Samaranch and Berlioux, in their statement, said they had accepted ABC's assurances that it was providing more "neutral coverage of the competitions" to foreign broadcasters.

Meanwhile, another network spokesman, Tom Osenton, declared:

"Our responsibility is to put on a show for the American audience . . . That's ABC's prerogative, to shape a show." He said the prime story of the Olympics thus far had been "the success of the American team."

Even as Samaranch and Berlioux went to the ABC broadcast center to confere with Arledge, the IOC released the text of Samaranch's Thursday letter to Peter V. Ueber-

Please see ABC, page 56

DAVE GATLEY / Los Angeles Times

Sieben Flies Past Gross

Australian Breaks World Record in Upset Win

By TRACY DODDS, *Times Staff Writer*

While the world record-holder, Michael Gross of West Germany, was racing in Lane 4, concentrating on his battle with Rafael Vidal of Venezuela in Lane 5 and Pablo Morales of the United States in Lane 3, a funny thing was happening over in Lane 6. Jon Sieben of Australia was pulling off an upset.

Sieben, 17, came charging from behind on the last leg of the 200-meter butterfly at the Olympic Swim Stadium Friday to pass Morales, Vidal *and* Gross and win the gold medal in the world record time of 1 minute 57.04 seconds.

Americans, meanwhile, had another big day in swimming before a crowd of 11,764,

earning gold medals in the other four events, plus three silvers. The winners: Tracy Caulkins, 200-meter individual medley; Tiffany Cohen, 800 freestyle; Rick Carey, 100 backstroke, and Theresa Andrews-Caulkins-Nancy Hogshead-Mary T. Meagher, 400 medley relay.

But it was Sieben who stole the evening. As of Friday morning, Sieben's fastest time ever was a 2:01.17.

Nobody takes four seconds off his time in one day. It just doesn't happen.

The swimmer from Brisbane turned in a 1:59.63 for his best time ever in the morning preliminary heats to qualify fifth

Please see SIEBEN, page 56

CON KEYES / Los Angeles Times

Australian Jon Sieben yells after upsetting Michael Gross (top, right) in the 200 butterfly.

Chinese Fall to U.S. Women

By JERRY CROWE, *Times Staff Writer*

Into the madhouse stepped the world champion Chinese, who met the same fate as two previous victims of the U.S. women's volleyball team.

This one was more impressive for the Americans, who remained unbeaten in the Olympic tournament with an emotional 15-13, 7-15, 16-14, 15-12 victory Friday night over the Chinese before another screaming, flag-waving crowd of 12,033 at the Long Beach Arena.

The fans erupted when China's Lang Ping spiked a ball long to end the match, enabling the Americans to avoid meeting Japan in Sunday night's semifinals.

Instead, they'll meet Peru, which beat them in a controversial semifinal match two years ago in the world championships at Lima, Peru.

China must play Japan, which beat the Chinese last November to win the Asian championship and is regarded by U.S. Coach Arie Selinger as the favorite for the gold medal.

China had beaten the Americans seven times in eight meetings last spring, but most of those matches were exhibitions.

Friday night's match, of course, was much more than an exhibition.

The psychological warfare between the teams started long before the opening serve.

In a meeting last week, representatives of both teams insisted on wearing blue uniforms in the match. Selinger told a Los Angeles Olympic Organizing Committee official that his team had never lost to the Chinese when it was wearing blue.

After about 30 minutes, the Chinese relented and agreed that they would wear red.

The Americans were *seeing* red

Please see VOLLEYBALL, page 56

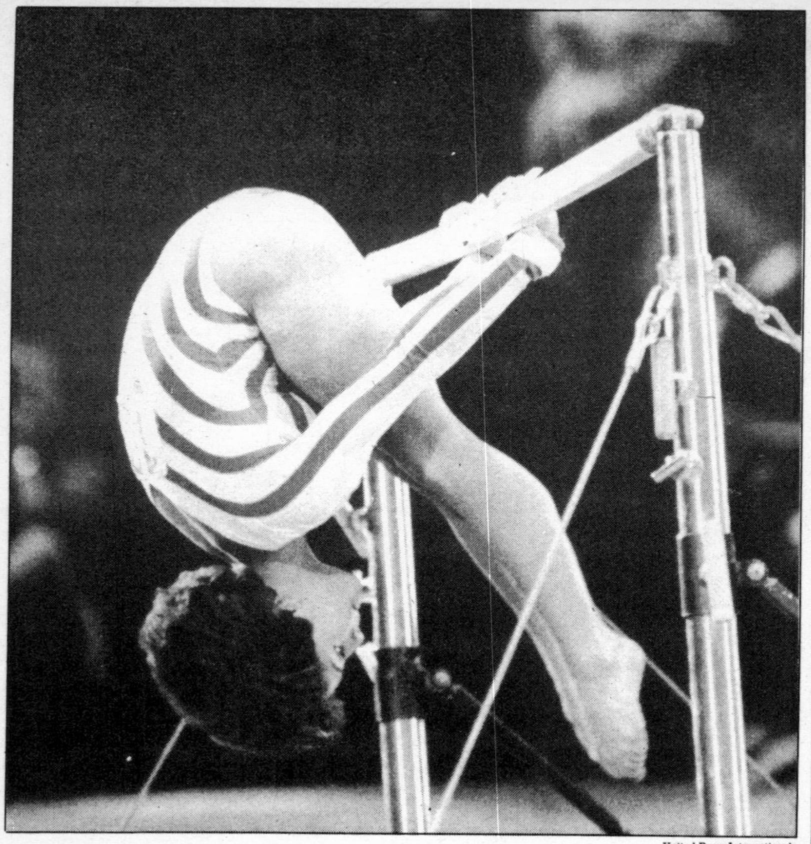

United Press International

Mary Lou Retton's picture-perfect move on uneven bars helped her to women's overall gold medal.

RETTON

Continued from page 55

genue by 15/100ths.

U.S. Coach Don Peters was unmoved by this apparent momentum. "I knew that after the first two events, Mary Lou might be behind, just because they were Szabo's strongest and Mary Lou's weakest. It was just a matter of order."

Then Szabo got a surprising 9.9 on vault, her legs slightly splayed as she dismounted. Retton took the floor, where her tumbling power is most evident and best rewarded. She vamped through the old song "Johnny, My Friend," playing the crowd shamelessly, grinning out of each somersault. A double layout somersault on her first pass. Grin. A double tuck. Grin. Another. Then a smile that revealed what must have been hundreds of the whitest teeth you ever saw. On the side, Peters held up all the fingers he had. The judges didn't have it in them to argue. A 10. Szabo's lead was cut to 5/100ths.

On the last rotation, Szabo was up on uneven bars first, while Retton cooled her heels waiting to vault. "I watched her on bars," Retton admitted. "It was a nice set, a clean set, but she took a step on her dismount, and I knew it was a 9.9. I knew I had it."

Oh, and who does your arithmetic, Mary Lou? She only had it if she scored a 10, as in perfect. A 9.95 tied her for the gold. Anything less and she was trying to beat Simona going for silver.

"I knew the takeoff was good," she said, recreating her event, "and I knew the vault was good. And I knew I'd stick it." The way people talked afterward, everybody seemed to know as much.

"It was the biggest vault ever," proclaimed her private coach in Houston, former Romanian national coach Bela Karolyi, the Texan with the Transylvanian drawl. "When she hit the floor, there was no question."

Said Peters: "You have to give it a 10. It's the best vault I've ever seen."

Mary Lou didn't doubt as much. She pogoed halfway back to the runway for her second vault, arms in the air, arrested only by Karolyi himself who had vaulted the railing. As far as Peters was concerned, that was the only moment of suspense. "I thought we'd get slapped with a deduction," he said, noting that Karolyi, not officially on the U.S. staff, was performing what might look like a terrorist act to the judges. "But I guess that only happens in movies."

It was a 10, all right. Her second, meaningless one, was a 10 as well. Mary Lou, her eyelashes reaching into the first row, saluted the crowd, and a lot of people, as Peters always notes, "wanted to reach out and hug her."

Szabo stood quietly behind the horizontal bar, staring. Wistfully? Sadly? Who could know what those silver-dusted eyes were seeing.

Later Retton rolled the gold medal between her fingers, looking up into the stands, spotting parents, friends and fans. And her coaches talked about this prodigy, the new wave in gymnastics, "this chunky leetle thing," as Karolyi describes, "not quite a butterfly."

What they talked about, even more than her effervescence, was her nerve. Karolyi, the man who developed Nadia and who started, for that matter, Szabo before defecting to this country, talked in his usual hyperventilating chatter.

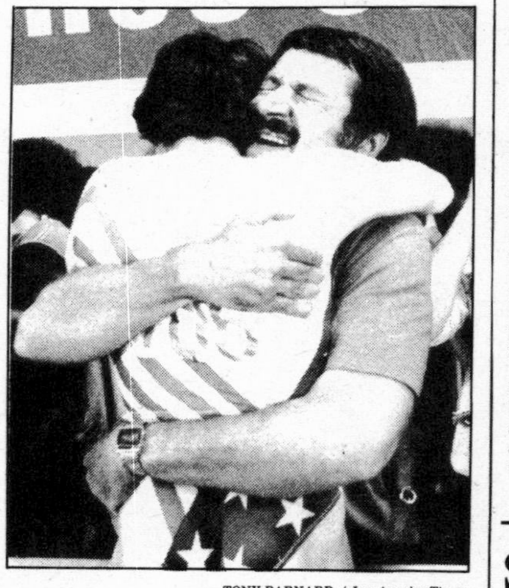

TONY BARNARD / Los Angeles Times

When it's over, Retton gets a gold-medal hug for her efforts from her coach, Bela Karolyi.

"She shows this fantastic ability, an aggressiveness," he said. "Who could do it? Who could come back and do it? Nadia was a great champion, but I am telling you Mary Lou is bigger. I guarantee no gymnast in the world could have done what Mary Lou has. To have that strong a personality is fantastic, unbelievable."

Peters, somewhat more subdued, agreed that there are few athletes as mentally strong as Mary Lou. "She thrives on pressure. She never gets tight," he said. The pressure is what did it, when she needed those 10s. That kid thrives on it. A great champion."

Retton, finally put atop a chair so she could stand eye-to-eye with reporters, shrugged. "Yeah, I work best under pressure." What more was there to say? One thing that is unavailable to this 16-year-old is perspective. When you're that small, it can be hard to understand how you suddenly get so big.

□

West German gymnast Elke Heine fell from the balance beam during warmups prior to the women's all-around competition and reportedly suffered a hyperextended back. She was examined at the UCLA Medical Center, but the extent of her injury was not immediately known.

Heine was carried from Pauley Pavilion, the site of the gymnastics competition on the UCLA campus, by UCLA medical personnel.

China's Wu Jiani withdrew from the all-around finals after hyperextending her elbow during an afternoon workout at the Wooden Center, also at UCLA. Wu would have entered the finals in eighth place.

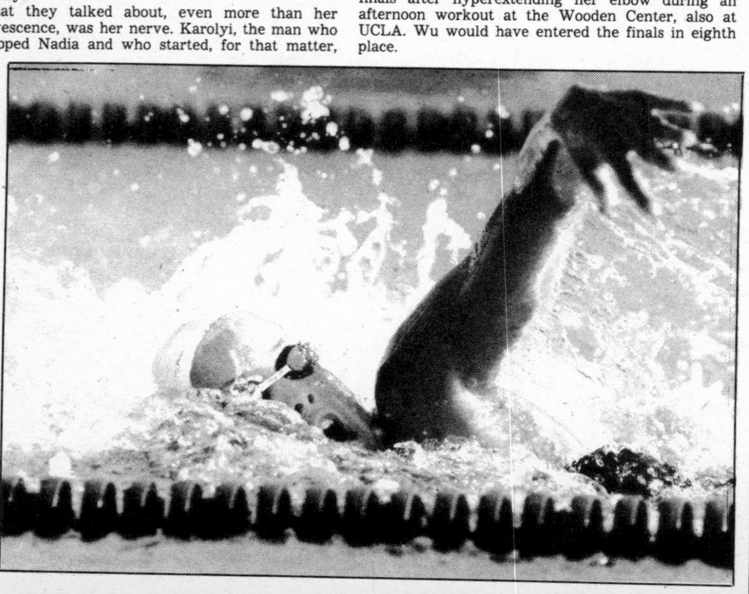

DAVE GATLEY / Los Angeles Times

Tiffany Cohen of the United States is on her way to an Olympic record in the 800 freestyle.

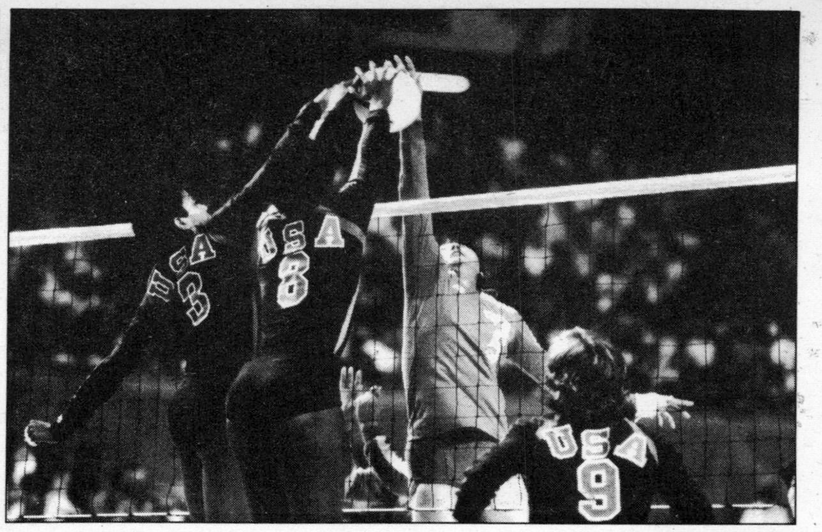

RICK MEYER / Los Angeles Times

Rita Crockett (3) and Rose Magers (8) of the United States block shot by China's Xilan Yang Friday night in women's volleyball match at Long Beach Arena. U.S. won in four games.

VOLLEYBALL

Continued from page 55

after China opened a 13-9 lead in the first game.

They stormed back at that point, Flo Hyman and Paula Weishoff combining on a block to make it 13-10 and an ace serve by Rita Crockett making it 13-11.

Julie Vollertsen, inserted into the U.S. lineup for Sue Woodstra in the first game for the third straight match, followed with two kills off the Chinese block, the second made possible by Crockett, who dug a wicked hit by Ping.

Rose Magers then blocked Ping for another point, and Hyman ended the comeback with an ace, the fifth of the game for the Americans.

In the opening game, Ping, considered by many to be the world's best hitter, was 0 for 11 in kill attempts as the Americans played much more aggressively than they had in uninspired performances against West Germany and Brazil.

Ping came back strong in the second game, putting down 7 of 9 kill attempts as the Chinese improved their hitting percentage from 39% to 59%.

The third game went to 14-14 before Weishoff and Hyman combined on a block for the 15th point and Crockett ended it with another ace, this one more controversial than the others.

Liang Yan dove for it and sent it back to the Americans' side, but the referees ruled that it had hit the floor before it hit her hands.

Ping was 5 of 16 in the third game, limited by an effective defense by the Americans.

Earlier Friday, Selinger called the China match the key to the whole tournament for the Americans because of its bearing on the semifinal matchups.

After the tough victory late Friday, Hyman seemed to agree, saying that she was "happy because we accomplished one of our goals, which was to get an easier draw in the medal round and let the Oriental teams fight it out (in the other semifinal)."

For the past year, Selinger has said that Japan—which has never won less than a silver medal at the Olympics—is stronger than China, and most of the coaches here seem to agree with him.

The crowd was again a factor Friday, roaring its approval as the Americans, serving tough to make it difficult for the Chinese to get into their offense, came from behind to win the first, third and fourth games.

Peru vs. South Korea. The Peruvians, after squandering a two-game lead, staged their own comeback to win, 15-8, 15-6, 7-15, 6-15, 15-13, and join the big three of China, Japan and the United States in the semifinals.

In the fifth game Peru rallied from an 11-8 defecit to score six straight points. Then, after South Korea closed to 14-13, all-world hitter Cecilia Tait crushed a spike through the block for the match-winner.

Peruvian Coach Park Man Bok, a former coach of the South Koreans, said he had mixed emotions about the win, but assured the South Korean media that "my blood is Korean and my heart always belongs to Korea."

Japan vs. Canada. The Japanese rolled into the semifinals against the winless Canadians, 15-6, 15-6, 15-6. Japan has won 23 of 25 matches in Olympic competition, and has won 21 of those matches in straight games.

Brazil vs. West Germany. The West Germans, who had geared their training toward this match, surprised the Brazilians, 15-9, 16-14, 15-11.

Brazil, which took the United States to five games before losing, wound up winless in Pool A.

Volleyball Notes

Italian men's **Coach Silvando Prandi,** misquoted by the LAOOC after Tuesday's match, refused to meet with the press following the Italy's loss to Japan on Thursday night . . . Men's preliminaries continue today: Argentina (0-2) vs. Tunisia (0-3) and Brazil (2-0) vs. South Korea (1-1) in Pool A; Japan (2-0) vs. Egypt (0-2) and Canada (1-1) vs. China (1-2) in Pool B. The United States (3-0) has a bye today and will meet Brazil Monday night at 8:30.

SIEBEN

Continued from page 55

for the final. That was incredible enough. But to upset Michael Gross with a world-record time a few hours later?

"It's a miracle," U.S. Coach Don Gambril said. "It really is phenomenal. A personal improvement like that—I don't know how to even compare that to something else to show how impossible it is."

Gross, whose world-record time had been 1:57.05, took the silver medal in 1:57.40. Vidal got the bronze in 1:57.51 to give Venezuela its first swimming medal ever. And Morales, the world record-holder in the 100-meter butterfly until finishing second to Gross Monday night, had his best time ever, a 1:57.75 that left him fourth.

It was the fastest 200-meter butterfly field ever.

"I can't think of anything I've ever seen that would even be close to a race like that and an upset like that," Gambril said.

Gambril was smiling. As a swimming *aficionado*, he had to appreciate the race itself. As the U.S. coach, he had to be pleased with Morales. Gambril said: "It was the best swim of his life. He's young (19). You haven't seen the last of Pablo Morales." And as the coach of the University of Alabama, he had to be drooling.

Sieben will be a freshman at Alabama this fall.

Did Gambril have some way of knowing that Sieben had this kind of latent talent?

"I was going on the word of Laurie Lawrence," Gambril said. "He and I are good friends. We've coached together before. He recommended both Sieben and (Australian) Justin Lemberg, who won the bronze medal in the 400 free. They'll both be at Alabama." There was no need to ask which of the coaches was Sieben's. For starters, Laurie Lawrence was wearing a sailing shirt that said, "It's What's Down Under That Counts." If that wasn't enough of a clue, he was the one who wasn't walking, he was skipping and jumping for joy. He wasn't smiling, he was glowing. He wasn't discussing the upset, he was bubbling over.

"He really came on like gangbusters, didn't he?" Lawrence said. "He's a scrambler. He just really used his legs coming home. I told him before the race, 'You're the best flier in the field, now go out and show it.' He told me not to worry. He said, 'I still have a bit up me sleeve.' He said, 'You don't show all your cards in the heats.'

"I knew he was one of the toughest, mentally. I knew he could do it. He was frightened of no one here. . . . There are only 15 million of us in Australia, but that means there are 15 million big hearts."

With that, he bounded away. The awards ceremony was about to begin. Lawrence shouted over his shoulder, "I have to 'ear the song."

No one, not even Sieben, really expected to hear the Australian national anthem after the 200-meter butterfly.

"I had no idea what was going to happen tonight," Sieben said. "It just went through my mind that I was feeling good. . . . I could see Rafael beside me in Lane 5 and coming home, that last 50, I knew I was a definite medal chance. Once I got in front of him, I wasn't going to look again. I was just going for the wall."

Gross, the overwhelming favorite, said nothing actually went wrong with his race. He said, "In the morning, I realized that I was not in so good shape as Monday and Tuesday when I won the 200 free and 100 butterfly. I hoped that it would be enough to swim around my world record to win. I didn't expect Jon to go so fast. I was concentrating on Rafael and Pablo, of course. And of course, I cannot see him in Lane 6 or 7."

Morales, who, of course, was not brought to the interview with the medalists, stopped briefly to talk with reporters over a fence. He was more soft-spoken than usual but seemed to be dealing pretty philosophically with the fact that, for the second time, he had turned in his lifetime best time only to come up short. And he added, "When a person takes four seconds off his time to set a world record and win the Olympics, it's a beautiful thing.

"That's what the Olympics are all about."

ABC

Continued from page 55

roth, Los Angeles Olympic Organizing Committee president, complaining of ABC's coverage.

The complete text of the Samaranch letter was this:

"Many complaints have been transmitted to me regarding coverage by ABC of Olympic events. The coverage should be of an international nature, particularly for the victory ceremonies.

"I therefore insist that you take the necessary action to have this situation rectified, as the Games belong to the whole world."

Ueberroth subsequently relayed the complaint directly to Arledge, although the LAOOC president told reporters Thursday night that he personally did not share it.

The complaints by Samaranch and a number of foreign athletes and coaches had to do mainly with ABC's domestic show within the United States, which all have been watching, and not its separate world feeds to foreign broadcasters at the International Broadcast Center in Hollywood.

The center was built and serviced by ABC in its role as "host broadcaster" for foreign radio and television organizations that have signed with the LAOOC to broadcast their own coverage of the Games back to their respective countries.

A check Friday of some of the foreign broadcasters showed a mixed reaction to the feeds ABC has been giving them. Most of those interviewed said the feeds are fairly international in content, but some complained that they were too over-Americanized.

Jarle Hoeysaeter, a Norwegian who heads the 39-nation European Broadcasting Union, expressed satisfaction, saying it is important to realize that what is seen in foreign countries is not for the most part what the American audience is seeing. He noted that the foreign broadcasters can pick what they want out of what ABC describes as an "unbiased neutral" feed and weave it into their own productions.

Hoeysaeter said he thinks some of the athletes' complaints may be based on a "misunderstanding" that what they are seeing in America on ABC is precisely what is being relayed back to their own countries.

Alec Weeks, leader of the British Broadcasting Corporation's 125-member radio-television team, said he thinks ABC has been balanced and fair, and that even the criticism of ABC's domestic coverage "is making a mountain out of a bloody molehill."

But Hisanori Isomura, head of the Japanese television pool covering the Games, said he believes the ABC coverage even in the international feed is biased toward winners, many of whom have been Americans, and isn't putting enough emphasis on the other participating athletes.

"In Japan, we tend to do stories on those who lost, to ask them why they lost and what it means to them," he said. "We have rather an underdog mentality, you might say."

U.S. Team Wins Gold in Three-Day Event

Stives and Ben Arthur Lead Way; New Zealander Wins Individual Title

By LYNN SIMROSS, *Times Staff Writer*

The Olympic three-day event team gold medal came down to the last strides of Karen Stives and her mount, Ben Arthur, Friday, and they hung on to win it for the United States by a scant 3.20 points.

Stives and her 11-year-old gray gelding, "Benny", surrendered the individual gold medal, however, by knocking down a rail at 11 B, the third to the last fence in the show-jumping competition, the final phase of the three-day event.

New Zealand's Mark Todd, who completed a perfect ride just minutes before Stives began the course, won the gold, his country's first equestrian medal. Stives took home the silver and Virginia Holgate of Britain, who also rode a clean round, won the bronze.

Demonstrating their resilience, Stives and Ben Arthur negotiated the final jumps without incident. Had the pair caught another rail at obstacle 12—each rail down is a five-point penalty—the United States would have lost the team gold, too.

But on this day, it was to be the members of the U.S. team standing on the winner's platform as they played the national anthem before the huge, cheering crowd of 27,502 at Santa Anita.

Led by Stives, the United States totaled 186 points overall to 189.20 for Britain. The West German team took the bronze with 234; France was fourth with 236.

"My first thought (at the last fence) was not to have that down, too," said Stives, 33, of Dover, Mass. "I knew I had to be very careful. Mike (team captain Plumb) had had it down."

Plumb, the first of the American riders to jump, knocked down the rail at the last obstacle.

He said later that he thought his horse Blue Stone had reacted badly coming into the last jump because he saw the judge raise his orange flag.

"I had the feeling he thought after the triple (obstacle 11, with three fences) that we might be done," Plumb said. "When we got to 12, I felt him look and suck back and he did get a jump behind. He saw the flag."

After Plumb got his five-point penalty, Britain's Ian Stark got one, too, hitting the rail at 11 C.

From then on, it was up to the women riders. Torrance Watkins Fleischman and Stives for the United States; Holgate for Britain. World champion Lucinda Green from Britain already had finished the course without faults.

"It was real pressure for the team medal," Stives said. "I knew we had one rail (to spare) and once over 12, I knew we had the team gold."

Coming into the show-jumping phase, Stives and Fleischmann both had scored clean rounds in the Wednesday cross-country phase at Fairbanks Ranch to give the United States a cushion of 8.2 points.

Todd seemed overwhelmed by his feat. After the medal ceremony, he was ecstatic and had a hard time expressing his feelings. He kept repeating, "I feel fantastic, just fantastic."

Of Charisma, his 11-year-old New Zealand-bred brown gelding, he said: "He's just one hell of a horse. He's good at dressage, a machine across the cross-country and a good show jumper."

Friday, Charisma was more than just a good show jumper, he rose to the occasion, delivering a perfect ride.

"Show jumping," Todd said, "is Charisma's weakest phase. But it wasn't today."

Asked if he watched Stives' ride, Todd smiled and said: "I watched bits of Stives' round. I must admit I saw the rail go down. I said to myself, 'It's finally happened.'

"I felt very sorry for Karen," he said. "I know how she must have felt."

Todd, 28, is a dairy farmer who rode show jumpers before going into three-day event competition.

A rider since he was 8, Todd began to compete internationally in the three-day in 1978 when he came to the world championships in Lexington, Ky.

He has been competing in the United States and in Europe ever since, but his future is uncertain, he explained, because he has to find out what Mrs. Fran Clark, owner of Charisma, wants him to do. He would like to go on to England and compete at the three-day championships at Badminton this fall.

"I was a farmer before I left in March this year to compete," said Todd. "But the future is uncertain until I talk with Mrs. Clark."

Todd said he was unable to estimate how much money he has spent competing in international competition.

Until recently, he had to pay for everything himself. But in the 18 months he has been riding Charisma he has acquired a sponsor, a ranching and livestock firm in New Zealand.

"I wouldn't have any idea what I have spent," Todd said. "I had to sell several good horses to keep me going. We are basically amateurs in this sport.

"But everybody has been great, here, and in New Zealand. I've gotten a lot of support telegrams."

Everyone in Todd's hometown of Cambridge, about 80 miles from Auckland, was able to watch him compete in the three-day on New Zealand television.

During the medal ceremony, Todd was nearly overcome with emotion, as were most of the winning team members.

"I don't like to cry," said Plumb, the gold medal hanging around his neck. "But it entered my mind."

With his medal Friday, Plumb, 44, upped his Olympic medal total to six, an American record.

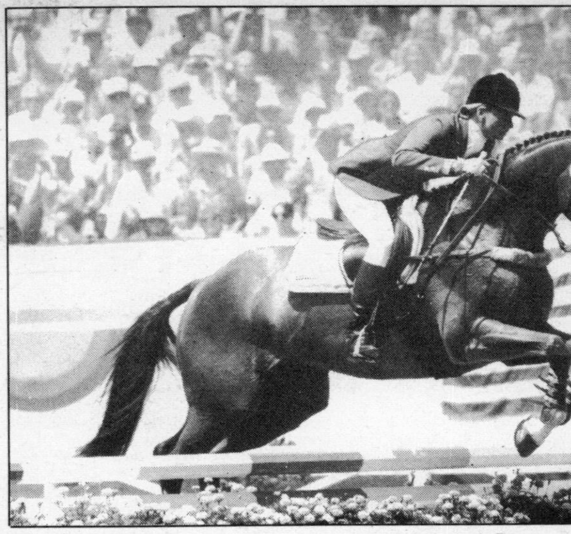

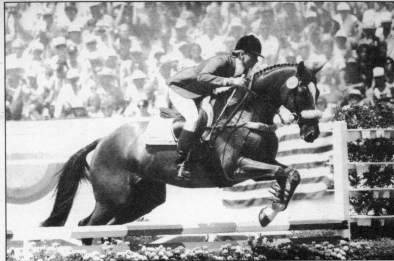

KEN LUBAS / Los Angeles Times

Torrance Watkins Fleischmann of The Plains, Va., clears fence during clean ride in show jumping phase at Santa Anita Friday.

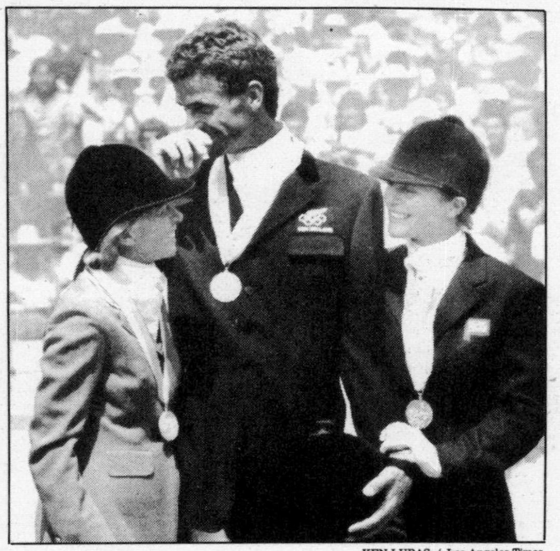

KEN LUBAS / Los Angeles Times

Karen Stives (left), Mark Todd and Virginia Holgate share words of congratulations on the victory stand after three-day event.

Wrestling / Greco-Roman

Romania Wins Two Gold Medals

By DAVE DISTEL, *Times Staff Writer*

Romania awakened this morning to the news it had been anticipating all week.

It won two gold medals Friday night and added the Romanian national anthem to the hit parade on the victory stand for Greco-Roman wrestling at the Anaheim Convention Center.

But it had to wait until the last night before Ion Draica won at 180.5 pounds and Vasile Andrei beat America's Greg Gibson at 220 pounds.

"We were expecting more," said Andrei, "but we are happy with what we have."

Andrei's young daughters, his pride and joy, will hear the news on the radio this morning. And so will Draica's ill father, who told his son the only medicine he should bring home was a medal.

"He told me if I take a medal he will feel good," Draica said, "and I bring him a gold one."

West Germany's Pasquale Passarelli, an Italian-born 125.5 pounder, and Yugoslavia's Vlado Lisjak, given new life at 149.5 pounds by an upheld protest, were the other gold-medal winners.

The United States added to its medal collection with the silver won by Gibson and a bronze by James Martinez at 149.5. Martinez won with a pin of Romania's Stefan Negrisan 25 seconds into the match, the second-fastest pin of the week. Afterward, Martinez said, "I can't even describe how good I feel."

Passarelli's win was easily the most dramatic of the night. He beat Japanese world champion Masaki Eto, 8-5, even though he spent the last 1:36 on his back with his body arched upward to avoid a pin.

"This is not swimming or chess," said the 27-year-old insurance agent. "Wrestling is a fighting sport and we have to hold on, even if 1 minute and 30 seconds is a very, very long time."

Passarelli's back was arched so that he could watch the clock, and it certainly did not make it go any faster.

"All kinds of things were going through my head," Passarelli said, "but I just couldn't let myself lay down."

Eto, for his part, thought he had achieved a pin. And he did not think Passarelli should have been allowed to use his arm to brace his body upward.

"I thought I pinned him within five to 10 seconds," he said. "And I appealed three times to the referee to remove his arm and the referee refused three times."

The Japanese also appealed to the International Wrestling Federation protest committee, but the protest was rejected.

Another protest led to Lisjak's gold medal—and the ultimate dethroning of another world champion. Lisjak, whose Thursday night loss to Negrisan was reversed, pinned Finland's Tapio Sapila in 57 seconds.

It was a major upset, because Lisjak is a 22-year-old truck driver virtually unknown in Yugoslavia outside the village of Petrinca.

"I felt I had nothing to lose," Lisjak said. "He was the world champion and the absolute favorite."

The Romanians, after their long wait, were the last two Greco-Roman medal winners.

Draica broke the Romanian drought when he beat Greece's Dimitrios Thanapoulos, 4-3. And it was also a long drought for Draica, who said he was retiring at 26.

"I have a world championship," he said, "and many times European championships, but I never had the medal in the Olympics."

Andrei beat Gibson, 12-0, in 4:16 after Gibson hurt one of his gimpy knees in the opening seconds of the match and never got untracked. He had been postponing surgery because he did not want to miss the Olympics.

"I thought if I got on top of him I'd have a chance to turn him," Gibson said, "but I never had a chance. He was doubled over to protect himself in a football stance, and I couldn't believe he was never cautioned."

Andrei turned 29 on the day of the opening ceremonies, and he laughed at the suggestion that the Los Angeles Olympic Organizing Committee had thrown quite a birthday party for him in the Los Angeles Memorial Coliseum.

"Now," he said, "I have more to celebrate."

Winning bronze medals were Greece's Haralambos Hilidis at 125.5 pounds, Soren Claeson of Sweden at 180.5 pounds and Josef Tertalje of Yugoslavia at 220 pounds.

Wrestling Notes

It was announced during the afternoon session that it was a sellout, but the crowd was only 4,130. The announcement meant that on-site tickets were sold but tickets were undoubtedly available at Hollywood Park. The evening session drew 5,688 . . . If Greco competition was scored like a world championship, Romania would have won with 30 points. The United States and Sweden would have had 26 . . . **Steve Fraser** is 26 years old, not 31 as previously reported. The U.S. Olympic media book lists 1953 as his year of birth.

Track and Field / 20-Kilometer Walk

Mexico 1-2 as 'Home' Fans Cheer

By MARLENE CIMONS, *Times Staff Writer*

Jimmy Lopez of Lynwood probably spoke for the 1½ million Mexican-Americans who live in the Los Angeles area Friday night when he leaped from his seat, jumped onto the track and lifted Mexico's Ernesto Canto off his feet in a giant hug.

Canto had just won the gold medal in the 20-kilometer (12.4-mile) racewalk with a new Olympic record of 1 hour 23 minutes 13 seconds, and Lopez and his friends could not contain their emotion.

And the joyful outpouring became even more overwhelming when, seven seconds later, Raul Gonzalez, also of Mexico, crossed the finish line to take the silver in 1:23:20.

"I am American, but I am Mexican," Lopez said, nearly in tears. "I feel great. This is the greatest moment in my life."

Canto, world champion and world record-holder in 1:18:40, joined his countryman for a brief celebration. They showed off the silver-and-black sombreros someone had put on their heads and took a victory lap around the Coliseum, holding a hand-painted sheet that said, "Viva Mexico" in red.

Almost lost amid this display of national pride was bronze medalist Maurizio Damilano of Italy, the 1980 Olympic champion who finished third in 1:23:26.

Canto said he was deeply affected by the sentiment shown by the Mexican-American community both inside the Coliseum at the finish and on the course outside the stadium.

"We did receive very strong support," he said. "Los Angeles has a large Mexican community, second only to Mexico. I felt tremendous emotion, especially when I came into the Coliseum."

He added: "It was a great experience, but I didn't realize I was going to be a winner—Raul Gonzalez was right behind me. But it was an opportunity I could not let pass. It was now or never."

Canto was in front almost immediately during the first of five laps inside the stadium, although he lost the lead to Canada's Guillaume Leblanc after they began their six laps outside, around Exposition Blvd. Canto got the lead back after 10 kilometers but it was never a commanding one.

"It was very strong competition," Canto said. "We were not sure what was going to happen. It was hot, and there was a lot of humidity. Raul came very close to me. It was a very difficult race."

American Marco Evoniuk, of Longmont, Colo., placed seventh in 1:25:42. His teammates, Jim Heiring, of Kenosha, Wis., and Dan O'Connor, of Westminster, Calif., placed 23rd and 33rd respectively, in 1:30:20 and 1:35:12.

Evoniuk, who will also racewalk the 50-kilometer (about 31-mile) event next weekend, said he was not unhappy with his performance. He considers the longer distance his better event.

He said he was impressed with Mexico's domination of the sport. "They train full-time at altitude," he said.

Then, of the Mexican-American support along the course, he added, a bit ruefully: "It helped them—and not us."

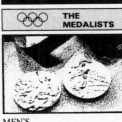

THE MEDALISTS

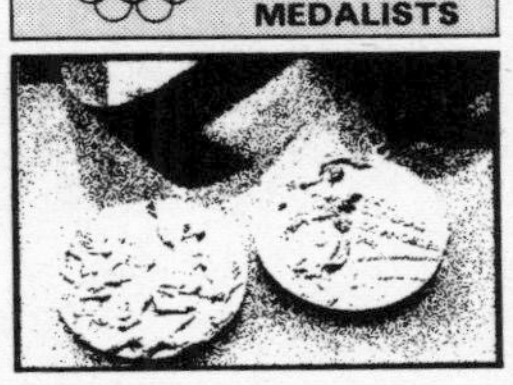

MEN'S

Track

20-KILOMETER WALK

1. Ernesto Canto (Mexico)
2. Raul Gonzalez (Mexico)
3. Maurizio Damilano (Italy)

Yachting

U.S. Skippers Sail Into Contention

By RICH ROBERTS, *Times Staff Writer*

Scott Steele is 26 but looks about 18, which makes it better when he lists his occupation as "U.S. boardsailing team member."

It isn't quite like being unemployed, but he can upgrade it now. Make it: U.S. Olympic yachting team member.

Steele has been formally accepted into the most successful sailing aggregation in the current Olympics. After the first four of seven races and using the one alloted "throwout" to discount the worst race, Americans lead two classes and are second in the other five, with the unheralded young man from Annapolis, Md., coming from out of nowhere to lead the way.

Steele, John Bertrand in Finn and Randy Smyth in Tornado all won their second races Friday to lead a United States surge.

Bill Buchan placed second to rebound in Star, while Robbie Haines placed fifth but held his lead in Soling. Jonathan McKee was third in Flying Dutchman as Canada's Terry McLaughlin won for the second day in a row, while Steve Benjamin was fourth in 470 after a bad start.

Smyth said, "We knew we had a real strong team coming into this. The big surprise has been Scott—the one guy nobody thought had a chance for a medal—and there he is winning races."

It wasn't only that Steele had had little success against the Europeans. His event was new to the Olympics and—well, is boardsailing really *yacht* racing?

Steele won the last round of U.S. yacht trials in June, almost as an afterthought, it seemed, when his Olympic chances were compared to those of Smyth and the others.

"I felt like I wasn't getting the respect I should have from the others," Steele said. "I came into this being the underdog. But I'll tell you one thing, it made the whole situation pressure-less. Nobody expected me to do well. I was a lot more nervous at the trials."

Steele won Friday by 1 minute, 17 seconds—about a city block in sailboat racing. Equally amazing was the position of Stephan Van den Berg, the five-time world champion from Holland who finished 11th.

Anyone up on his or her boardsailing would check those results and immediately guess that the winds continued to be unusually light, and they'd be right. It blew from 7 to maybe 12 knots on the boardsailing course inside the Long Beach breakwater Friday.

Steele weighs only 129 pounds—"I might get to 130 if I eat a big meal," he said—so he has an edge over his larger rivals in light air.

But Major Hall, the U.S. boardsailing coach, said if Steele goes on to win the gold medal, it won't be a fluke.

"Everybody says Scott is getting his conditions, which is fine," Hall said. "But when the wind comes up he won't get blown away. He may not dominate, but he'll hang in there."

Benjamin said, "Scott is an excellent sailor, not only on a board."

A ripple of controversy rolled through the boardsailing fleet Friday when it was learned several sailors had applied duct tape to their daggerboards Thursday to reduce the play in the slot, while others complained that the rules forbid any changes.

The jury responded by granting redress to eight boards. Instead of Thursday's score, they'll receive points for the third race equal to the average of their five other best races of the series.

Steele didn't use tape but didn't ask for redress because he placed second Thursday to Van den Berg—and, besides, he disagreed with the jury's action.

"I thought it wasn't a good thing they did at all," he said. "I don't think it (the tape) makes any difference in the speed. It's not that critical a thing to give people redress on it."

Steele has finishes of 7-1-2-1.

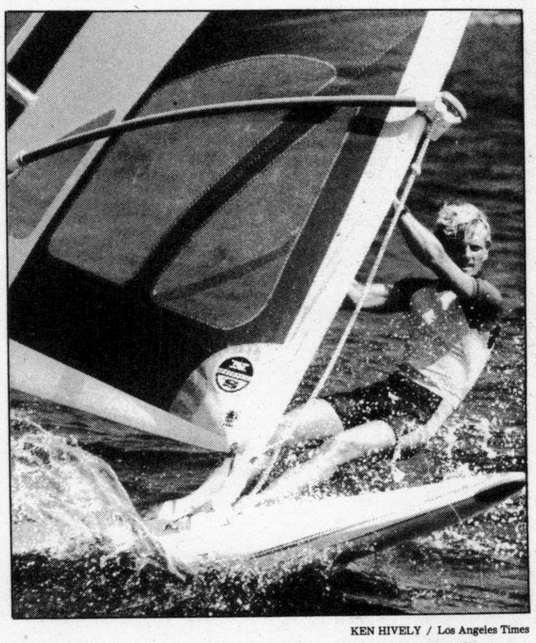

KEN HIVELY / Los Angeles Times

Scott Steele of Annapolis, Md., won the fourth boardsailing race of the series Friday to take the lead for the gold medal.

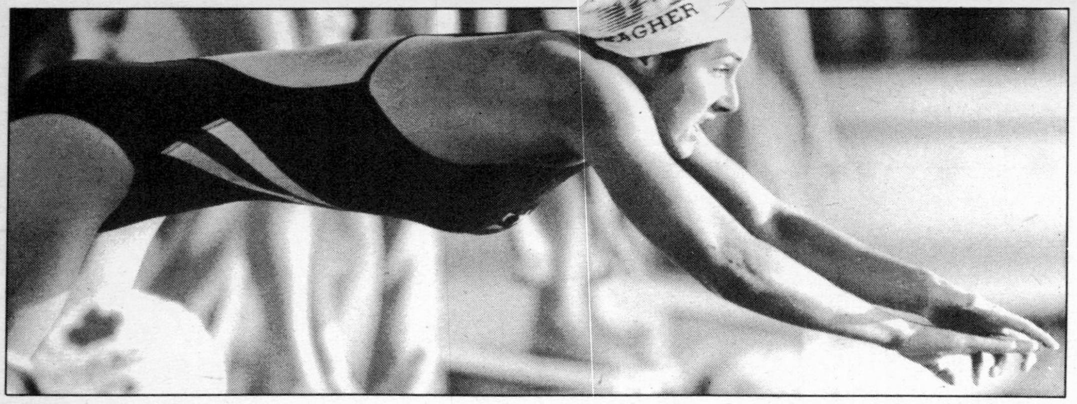

DAVE GATLEY / Los Angeles Times

Mary T. Meagher takes the plunge into her butterfly leg as she leads the United States to a gold medal in the 400-meter medley relay.

Retton, Karolyi Apply the Crusher

Teacher Almost as High as the Student on Golden Leap

By RICK REILLY, *Times Staff Writer*

Sometimes in journalism, you have to get your spleen crushed.

Then again, that's what I get for standing along the railing at Pauley Pavilion next to Bela Karolyi just as his prize pupil, Mary Lou Retton, was set to make the vault of her life.

And when Retton hit the perfect vault, a 10 if it was a 1, Karolyi knew it meant the Olympic gold medal. First he scissor-hopped the barrier, whooping as he went—a 9.9 jump and a 10 whoop. American Olympic Coach Don Peters, terror on his face, chased him back over. ("I thought we might get a penalty deduction," Peters said later. "But I guess that happens in the movies.")

So Karolyi jumped back over the barrier. He was wild-eyed and in desperate need of somebody to hug.

He looked at me.

I took a step back. I offered my hand in hopes that would be enough. That, I could tell, would not be.

"Yawooooo!" he bellowed as he put me in a half-nelson.

"Gmmphmph!," I said, "gmmphmph" being the only literate thing I tend to manage when my lungs have been collapsed.

The next huggable thing Karolyi found was Retton, considerably more deserving and tenfold more huggable.

For two years they worked together for this moment and it was theirs now. She bounded over to him and he swallowed her up in his arms and lifted her over his head. She shrieked and closed her eyes, let her head drop back so that she was suspended there, her legs against the banner, her arms around Karolyi's neck. She stared at the banners hanging from the ceiling, awash in the sweetest moment of her 16 years.

And there was no sign of the clutch ever breaking up. Mary Lou Retton and Bela Karolyi had invented the Endless Hug. (And why not, seeing as how much the warm-up hug lacked.)

"We did it, Little Body!" Karolyi screamed. "We did it! Unbelievable!"

Retton just smiled a smile that took up most of her face. She could not answer. She did not have to.

Sweeter still is how Little Body and the Mad Romanian did it.

Moment-by-moment, here is one of the darndest gold medals in Olympic history:

Rotation 1, The Uneven Bars— Retton's lead over Romania's Ecaterina Szabo is a 15th of a point, a comfortable lead in world-class gymnastics. Still, Karolyi is already nervous. He must split his time between Retton and American Julianne McNamara, who is in fourth place and beginning on the balance beam.

But McNamara's night ends immediately. Her 9.55 on the beam virtually eliminates her from a shot at a medal. Karolyi runs down to the other end of the gym to holler instructions at Retton. With Szabo already scoring a 10 on the balance beam, the heat is on.

"Arms . . . arms . . . long . . . good . . . powerful," he yells as she performs, and then, on the dismount, "Action!" But Retton falters, taking a step.

Karolyi's face is a wince, but as Retton hurries over, he snaps on a new one.

"Pretty good," he says, but they both know it is not pretty good. It is a 9.85. Szabo has reeled in Retton in one turn. They are tied.

Rotation Two, The Balance Beam— Retton is nervous during the warmup. She runs through her routine on the carpet eight or nine times before Karolyi calls her over. "Stop now. You rest."

All around them, gymnasts are falling off the deadly beam. American Kathy Johnson is one. Johnson folds into her coach's arms and cries. Retton tries not to look.

Again, the routine is good, but not great. Retton is off-balance twice. The scoreboards flash a lowly 9.8. "Ahhh," Karolyi says. "The Italian judge has got a deal with the Romanians."

Worse news: Szabo has gone 9.95 on the floor exercise. Retton now trails by .15. Karolyi looks down.

"It is killed," he says. "It is over."

But here comes Retton again, looking like she'd just been told she will have to wear braces.

"It is all right," he says. "You have to work now like you have never worked in your life! OK? Never!"

Retton just bites a quivering lip and tries to nod with optimism.

"Hey, it's going to be all right I tell you!" Karolyi says.

Neither one look like they believe it.

Rotation 3, The Floor— Karolyi sends Retton off with, "Be a lady now," but again it seems hopeless. Szabo has gone 9.9 on the vault.

The music begins and Karolyi leads the clapping to the beat. Pauley tries to help, but it a complicated clap and this isn't the UCLA student body. It fizzles.

Retton, however, doesn't. Her three flips are executed perfectly and on the final one, Karolyi is four feet off the ground with her.

It is a 10.

"Go back!" he screams, waving ather to go back onto the stage to play the crowd. "GO *back!!*" Retton doesn't hear.

Szabo's lead, incredibly, has been cut to .05 and the Romanian hasn't had a routine under 9.9 all evening. Better yet, Retton's best event remains and everybody inside the railing knows it—the vault.

Rotation 4, The Vault— He is a walking collection of frayed synapses now, Karolyi is, and he moves to a different spot along the railing every 15 seconds. At every other spot, he calls Retton over to drill into her the same lesson he has been drilling into her for two years.

"Run strong! Then, bang! Hit it! Then, high! OK? Strong! Bang! High! OK?"

"OK."

"Bang! OK?"

"OK."

"Relax. The biggest vault in the world. And stick it! OK, Little Body?"

Little Body promises she will.

Across the way, Szabo's dismount from the uneven bars includes a hop—9.9.

Retton needs a 9.95 to tie for the gold medal. A 10, and it is hers and hers alone.

She is next. Once more, Karolyi calls her over.

"Now or never, OK?"

"OK."

The green light on the scoreboard signals that Retton's time has come . . .

Strong! Retton pounds down the runway.

Bang! She hits it.

High! She is very high.

"*Yes!!!*" Karolyi screams.

She sticks it.

Over the wall he goes, only to be chased back.

There is that look in his eye.

Gmmphmph.

They never mentioned this in the job description.

Swimming / Women's 400 Relay

U.S. Team Almost Takes It Too Easy This Time

By JOHN WEYLER,
Times Staff Writer

With their best competition disqualified in the preliminaries, the U.S. women's 400-meter relay team went into Friday night's final with a relaxed sense of confidence.

Backstroker Theresa Andrews, breaststroker Tracy Caulkins, butterflier Mary T. Meagher and freestyler Nancy Hogshead came up to the blocks feeling pretty sure of themselves. After all, the Dutch and Australian teams that were expected to give the U.S. contingent their biggest challenge had been disqualified when swimmers left the blocks too early in the the morning's heats.

But until Meagher got in the water and turned in the fastest 100-meter butterfly leg in women's relay history (58.04), it looked like the queens of American swimming were in the counting house counting the gold a little too early.

Britain got out to an early lead before the West German team grabbed the advantage after the first 100 meters (the backstroke leg). Caulkins had a good first 50, but she faded coming into the wall, and the West Germans had almost a half-second margin after the breaststroke.

But Meagher, who owns both butterfly world records, is without peer when she's swimming well, and she was churning up huge chunks of water in long, easy strokes at this point. She turned the deficit into a two-body-length lead 100 meters later, and Hogshead outsprinted West Germany's Karin Seick to win going away.

The U.S. won the gold in 4:08.34, almost two seconds off the Olympic record and nearly three behind the world record (4:05.79 set by the East Germans in the 1983 European Championships). West Germany won the silver in 4:11.97 and Canada took the bronze in 4:12.98.

"I was feeling really good in warmups and I felt like I had a good race in me," Meagher said. "Having the one gold medal under my belt (she won the 100 butterfly Thursday) must have helped because I really wasn't nervous at all.

"I have a lot of confidence in these girls and I know they feel the same way about me. I was really happy when I found out what my split was. It makes me feel good going into tomorrow's 200."

Hogshead admitted that this team—which together represents more than a quarter of a century of swimming experience—was relaxed, but she also insisted that they "knew they had a job to do."

Hogshead: "I don't know about Tracy, but I was feeling a little down because we had been up so high after the 200 IM (Caulkins won and Hogshead took the silver) and then there was a sort of letdown. That, combined with the fact our main competition was disqualified had us all feeling a little blah-de-blah-de-blah.

"After the breaststroke it was really close. I'm just glad I didn't have to pull it through . . . I'm glad T. had such a great split because it put me in a good position. I have to admit I was a bit tired coming out of the IM."

Caulkins: "When we found out Holland was out of it, it was pretty hard to get back up. We'd been talking about beating them all week. After that, we just all talked about getting safe starts."

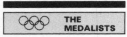

THE MEDALISTS

WOMEN'S

Swimming

■ 400-METER RELAY

1. United States
2. West Germany
3. Canada

Chinese Get Their First Fencing Gold

By JOHN DART, *Times Staff Writer*

China's Luan Jujie, a tomboy who sometimes got into fights with neighborhood boys in Nanking, dueled Europe's best Friday night and won the women's foil gold medal.

Luan was the first Asian ever to win a fencing gold medal and the first Chinese ever to capture any Olympic fencing medal.

The 26-year-old lefthander handily beat Cornelia Hanisch of West Germany, 8-3, in the final bout at the Terrace Theater in Long Beach. She earlier trounced Elisabeta Guzganu of Romania, 8-0, and Sabine Bischoff of West Germany, 8-5.

Earlier Friday, two American men advanced to today's direct elimination in individual saber competition—eight-time U.S. champion Peter Westbrook and Steve Mormando.

In women's fencing, Luan had already served notice to women foilists by taking second place and third place in the 1981 and 1983 world championships respectively.

For Hanisch, 32, it might have been the chance to win the gold she missed when West Germany joined the U.S.-led Olympic boycott in 1980. She was at the height of her game then, winning the world title in 1979 and 1981.

Hanisch had defeated pre-tournament favorite Dorina Vaccaroni in the semifinals, 8-6. But Vaccaroni's steady progression from third, to second, to first in the world championships in previous years was not to culminate in the Olympic title this time. Vaccaroni had to settle for the bronze medal, beating Guzganu 8-5.

In Vaccaroni's first finals bout she benefited from the calls of an American judge, Marius Valsamis. He warned Vaccaroni and her opponent Veronique Brouquier of France for covering their torsos—the target—with their free arm. Valsamis called Brouquier a second time with Vaccaroni ahead 9-8.

Eight points is the goal in the women's finals, but one has to win by two points in regulation time. The second call against the Frenchwoman cost her a point, giving Vaccaroni the win.

Two strong foilists, Carola Cicconetti and Margherita Zalaffi, both went quickly in Friday afternoon double elimination bouts, leaving Vaccaroni alone to hoist Italy's colors in the finals. Cicconetti, runner-up in the 1983 world championships, was eliminated by Luan, 8-5.

Luan herself was thrown into the losers' bracket in an upset by the "grandmother" of women's fencing—Sweden's Kerstin Palm, age 36—but made the final eight by downing Aurora Dan of Romania, 8-7.

After the opening three rounds of saber competition Friday, Gianfranco Dalla Barba of Italy and Jean Francois Lamour of France were both undefeated and seeded 1-2, respectively. Favorites for medals, they would have been contenders even if the dominant saber-rattlers from the Soviet bloc had come to Los Angeles.

New Yorker Westbrook, 32, and New Jersey's Mormando, 28, were seeded sixth and ninth among the field of 16 saber fencers—despite the fact both said they were not fencing too well in early bouts.

Mormando said Friday's competition was the "worst fencing I have ever had in one day. I more or less used experience and muscle to get through."

Westbrook started slowly, but finished the third round with a 3-2 record. He said it should have been 4-1 except for a bad call.

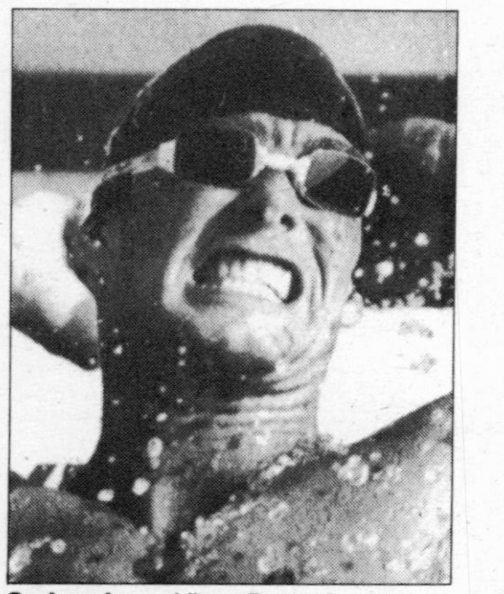

Swimming—Victor Davis, Canada.

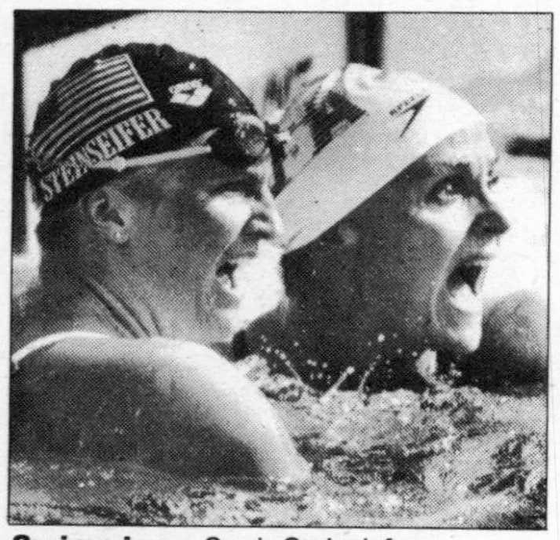

Swimming—Carrie Steinseifer, Nancy Hogshead, U.S.

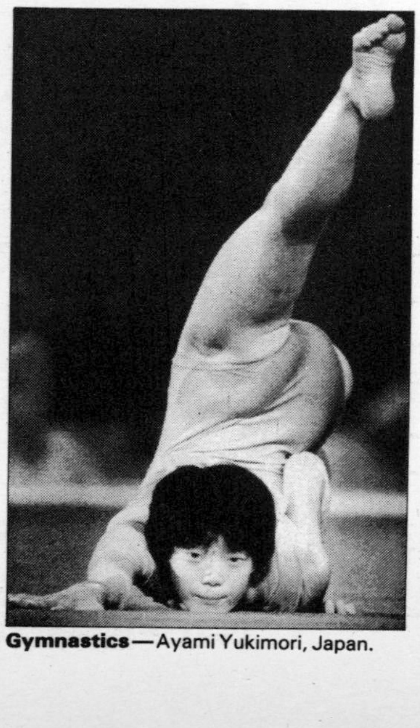

Gymnastics—Ayami Yukimori, Japan.

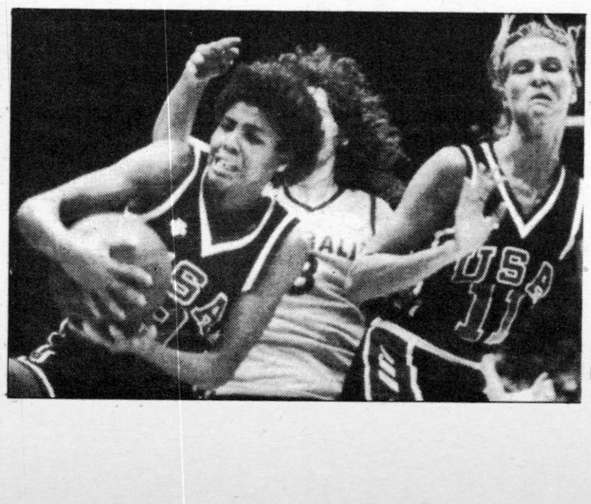

Basketball—Cathy Boswell, left, and Cindy Noble, U.S.

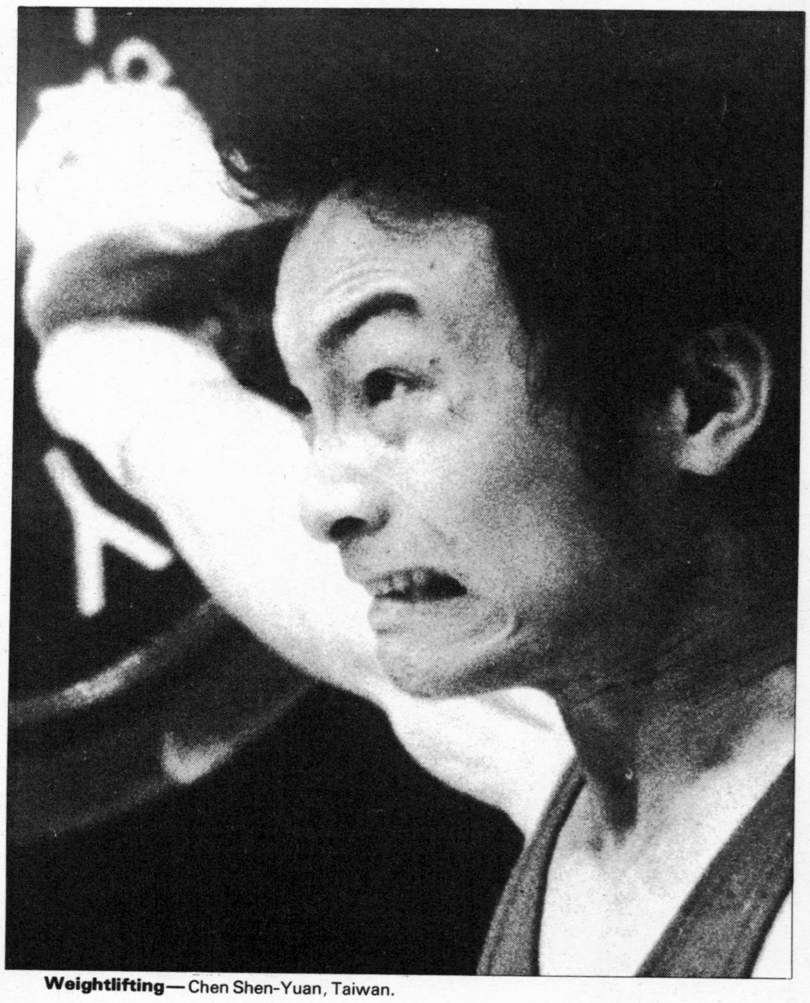

Weightlifting—Chen Shen-Yuan, Taiwan.

OLYMPICS '84/NOTES

Compiled By JERRY GILLAM

Nude Swimmers Make Waves at Cal State Fullerton

From Times Staff Writers and Wire Services

The original idea of opening Cal State Fullerton's 25-meter pool to the team handball athletes was to offer some recreational swimming and a lounge area for the players between playing sessions. But the campus pool has presented some problems.

Last week, Swiss athletes alarmed the SWAT team that patrols high above the venue on the library roof when they went skinny-dipping.

Someone forgot to tell them it's fashionable to wear a bathing suit in Southern California.

This week, Yugoslavian Coach Branislav Pokrajac lost one of his top players, Milan Kalina, for the team's first game when Kalina suffered a neck injury attempting to do a back flip off the pool's high dive. With Kalina out of the lineup, Iceland tied the gold medal co-favorites, 22-22.

Consequently, the high dive has been ruled off-limits for all players. The pool is still open, however. Providing one wears a swimsuit.

—TOM HAMILTON

□

Jesse Robinson, a steward in the press area of the boxing tournament at the Sports Arena, wants to make sure the world's sports reporters go home knowing where the "Cradle of Olympians" is.

It's Compton, if you didn't know.

Robinson, 72, is passing out a 22-page brochure about Compton's Olympians, which he sent to many of the 8,200 journalists here.

He'll be hauling his satchel full of booklets to the Coliseum, too, since he's also a shotput judge in the track and field competition.

Robinson's booklet chronicles the Olympic achievements of 10 past Compton athletes who competed in the Olympics: Ken Carpenter and Cornelius Johnson, 1932-1936; Ed Sanders and George Brown, 1952; Earlene Brown, 1956-1960-1964; Charles Dumas, 1956; Herman Stokes, 1960; Ulis Williams, 1964; Reynaldo Brown, 1968, and Hugo Salcedo, 1972.

And this year, Compton has an 11th—sprinter Jeanette Bolden.

—EARL GUSTKEY

□

The sport of kings is not necessarily horse racing. The exiled King Constanin of Greece has been watching the Olympic yacht racing at Long Beach from a spectator boat, along with Prince Albert of Monaco.

Constantin, then 20, skippered a Dragon-class boat to a gold medal at Naples in 1960. His mother, Queen Frederika, celebrated by shoving the crown prince into the water.

—RICH ROBERTS

□

Friday, the Taiwanese government-owned Chinese Television Service showed, for the first time, a mainland Chinese athlete competing in the Olympics after a five-day blackout of Chinese competitors.

The station focused on weightlifter Yao Jingyuan, who won a gold medal in the 149-pound (67.5-kilogram) class.

All three Taiwan stations previously had cut film footage of mainland Chinese Olympic athletes competing in the Games due to government censorship. Newspapers have been allowed to carry stories and photos of Chinese competitors.

Chu Tsong-ke, the Director of Government Information Office's domestic affairs, said since local newspapers were carrying reports of the records of mainland Chinese athletes at the Games, it seemed "improper" to have a total ban on television of the Chinese team.

In a telephone interview, Chu said that sports should not be mixed with politics.

"We consider victories of the mainland Chinese team as victories of our Chinese compatriots," he added.

The Los Angeles Olympics mark the first time that both teams are competing together in the Games although as separate entities.

Taiwan, which was barred from the last two Olympics, was readmitted to the Games after it agreed to compete as the "Chinese Taipei Olympic Team."

□

There have to be less dangerous ways to have fun than the sport of field hockey. In the first six days of competition at East Los Angeles College, several players have taken direct hits from batted balls, which are harder than baseballs, to unprotected parts of the body.

Since players who are removed may not return, most try to shake off injuries and continue. The most amazing competitor may have been Holland's Irene Hendriks, who was hit in the head from about six feet, appeared to be out cold for several moments but went on to finish the game.

One male player was hit in the crook of the neck from about 60 feet and came out of the game. But Norman Hughes of Great Britain took a blast in the same general area from about 30 feet and stayed in.

Except for the goalie, the players wear no padding other than shinguards.

—ALAN DROOZ

□

Olympic horses are up for sale at the Los Angeles Games.

In the privacy of the competitors' village and the seclusion of the stables, a discreet but potentially lucrative market exists for horse-trading.

The unusual situation has come about because the poorly financed teams from Australia and New Zealand are obliged to sell most of their horses after the Games since the cost of shipping them home is too great.

The likely buyers are a small number of wealthy riders who are always looking to snap up a potential champion.

In 1980, Britain's Lucinda Green bought Regal Realm from Australia's Merv Bennett after the Alternative Olympics, a three-day event in Fontainebleau, France.

Two years later, the combination won the world championship.

Prices of horses are rarely disclosed by those involved in the deals. But equestrian experts believe a potential champion could fetch more than $100,000.

□

Volleyball must be starting to arrive—the coach is complaining about the media.

"I don't have time to educate reporters during the Olympics," said U.S. men's volleyball Coach Doug Beal.

Just one victory away from a possible medal, Beal also is irked by the buildup the press is giving his team.

"I don't want the burden of popularizing volleyball as a sport in the United States," Beal said. "My shoulders aren't that big. Just the burden of coaching this team is big enough for me.

"Unfortunately, ever since the U.S. hockey team won the gold medal in 1980 and got all that publicity, you guys have been looking around for a replacement. You've been waiting to grab anything that comes around the corner."

OVER WEIGHT

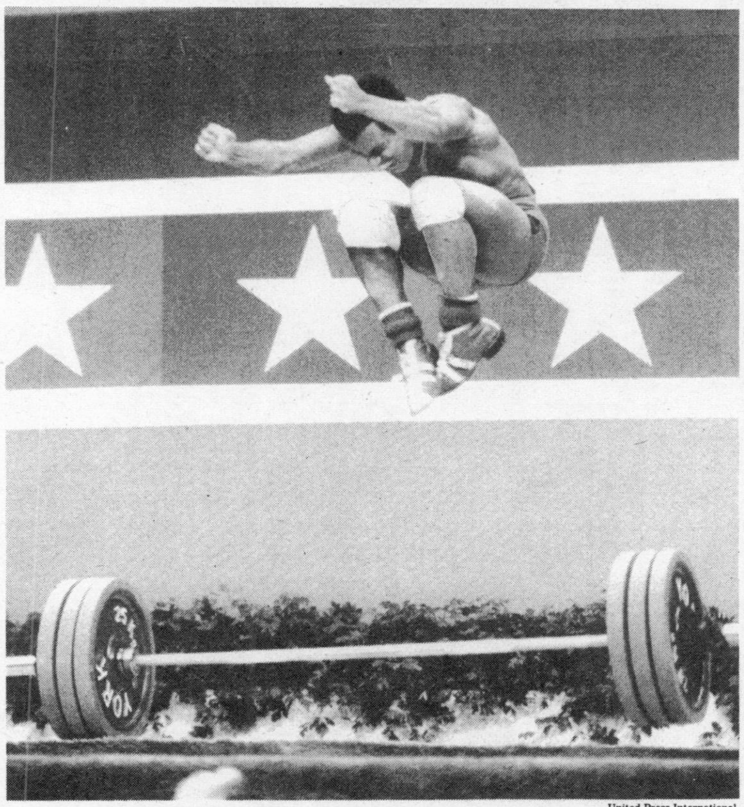

United Press International

Mercado Gilberto of Colombia leaps high in the air after completing a successful lift in the 165-pound classs during the weightlifting competition at Loyola Marymount Thursday.

The British are coming: Britain's field hockey team, which only got into the men's pool as a last-minute replacement for the Soviet Union, has been one of the surprises of the Olympics, running its record to 3-0 Friday.

It's an astounding accomplishment considering that the team was only thrown together earlier this year and has little international competition as a unit. The players usually play for the separate teams of England, Scotland and Wales.

IT seems that the British, who spread the game around the world but were eclipsed by their colonies, can still teach a few lessons of their own.

—ALAN DROOZ

□

Paid attendance for all events during the first five days of the Olympic Games, including the opening ceremonies, was 1,580,928.

Soccer was by far the most popular event with total crowds of 149,617 for the matches at Annapolis, Md.; Cambridge, Mass., Palo Alto and Pasadena.

There were more than 200,000 specators at the cycling road races Sunday in Mission Viejo, but that was a free event.

Basketball drew 32,899 for its first three sessions. Volleyball drew 24,066 for its first two sessions.

□

President Reagan has autographed baseballs that will be presented to U.S. team members after their baseball game with the Dominican Republic today.

Ron Lane, commissioner of Olympic baseball, will make the presentations, and Baseball Commissioner Bowie Kuhn is scheduled to participate.

"We wanted to provide this great USA team with the recognition it deserves, win or lose. The White House concurred," said Ted Sizemore, a former major league player and representative of the Rawlings Sporting Goods Co., provider of baseballs for the Games.

□

The West Germans seem to have found something of a secret weapon in a compound called Revital Energen, a unique combination of bee pollen, cereal germ, hawthorn and ginseng that also supplies a balance of amino acids, enzymes and vitamins.

It was originally manufactured as a health product for the general public and has received wide acclaim in West Germany by executives for its use in helping to focus concentration and control stress.

Most of the athletes on the West German team use Revital Energen, including gold-medal-winning cyclist Fredy Schmidtke and track stars Juergen Hingsen, Ulrike Meyfarth and Dietmar Moegenburg.

Swimmers Michael Gross and Thomas Fahrner recently took part in one of the research projects with the compound, which is designed to be taken in 40-day stretches once or twice a year.

Research results reportedly have been very positive. They has shown positive immunization effects, too. Meyfarth, who had been susceptible to flu in the winter and in the spring, found that the compound produced a marked increase in her resistance while she continued with regular training.

—TRACY DODDS

□

Neil Ayer, course designer for the Olympic three-day equestrian endurance phase, constructed a tough course for the cross-country riders at Fairbanks Ranch, but not without some wry humor.

Although the 44 riders were too busy concentrating on getting around the course to notice, the 14th obstacle, a Western town, not only had store fronts, a saloon, hotel, sheriff's office and livery stable, it was complete with a Boot Hill.

One tombstone read:

1892
Neil Ayer
A Man of Olympic Stature

Considering that only four riders finished the course without penalty, surely they would agree.

—LYNN SIMROSS

□

Several water polo players met with a Broadway department store executive in January. They were hoping to land modeling jobs.

The executive was enthusiastic, and she suggested that the players model Ralph Lauren Polo shirts.

"The woman told the players that she wanted pictures of them on their horses, holding mallets," recalled Noel Gould, the attorney for the water polo team, who was representing the players. "When we told the woman that they were *water* polo players, she lost interest.

"We never heard from her again."

—MILES CORWIN

□

Terry McLaughlin, Canada's Flying Dutchman sailor, has a sense of the dramatic. Or at least, he's looking forward to a sure thing.

His Olympic effort is developing into a two-boat battle with Jonathan McKee and crew Carl Buchan of the United States, and McLaughlin is looking forward to a showdown on the final day.

"My dream in the Olympics is to come down to the last race in a match-race situation where you can win the gold medal but can't lose the silver," he said.

—RICH ROBERTS

□

Relying on what it said was evidence from "underground Soviet sources," a Ukrainian human rights organization Thursday charged that an abnormally high number of former Olympic athletes from the Soviet Union have died, victims of that country's "widespread drug use and physiological experimentation" to bolster its athletic achievements.

"The Soviet Union is literally sacrificing its Olympic athletes for the sake of its own glory and international prestige," said Mona Snylyk, spokesman for Smoloskyp, which claims 3,000 Ukrainian supporters living in the United States and Canada.

At a news conference, the group contended that at least 59 athletes who competed for the Soviet Union in the Olympic Games since 1952 have died, "most of them as a result of being forced to use drugs and submit to other exploitative training methods and experimentation." The average age of the athletes who died was 41.45.

Smoloskyp released the names of the 59 athletes said to be dead, saying their fate was learned by athletes still in the Soviet Union who wanted to get the word out.

A PAIR OF CUTUPS

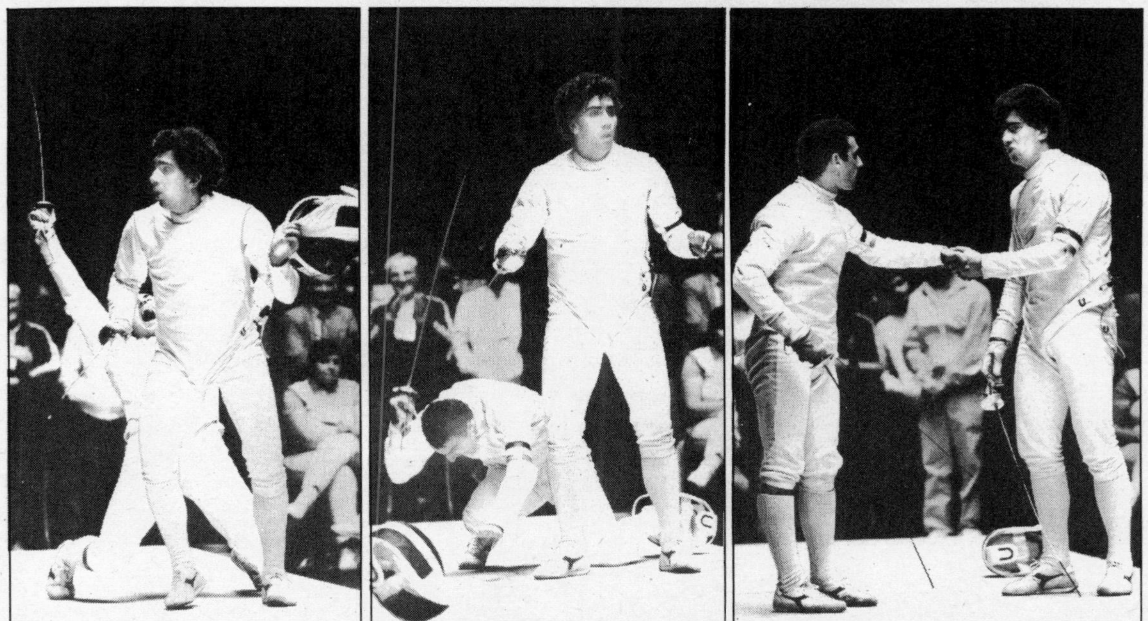

KEN HIVELY / Los Angeles Times

Mauro Numa of Italy (left) exults after scoring a touch against his fellow countryman Stefano Cerioni in fencing competition at Long Beach's Terrace Theater. While Numa continues to rejoice, Cerioni argues with the director and hurls his mask to the mat. Later, however, he congratulates Numa, who went on to win the gold medal in the foil. Cerioni collected the bronze.

Jim Murray

The Packaging of King Carl Can Now Commence

OK, Madison Avenue, everybody out of the pool! Cancel all three-martini lunches, forget the cocktail party at the yacht club, put away the Madras jacket, get out your best three-piece pinstripes and grab the 8:04 for Grand Central. Eat at your desk, hold all calls, get on a conference hookup with all the account execs. This is top priority.

Bring in all the Carl Lewis workups. See if Detroit is interested. Or do we sell Toyotas with him? The ball is in their basket. Get the cornflakes people on the phone and tell them to make an offer by midnight or we throw it open for bidding.

They have run the Carl Lewis flag up the pole, and everybody stands at attention and salutes. It flies. They have put the Carl Lewis account on the New York, New Haven and Hartford commuter, and it got off at Greenwich. They have put it on an elevator, and it got off at the executive suite. The dog will eat it. The chef will cook it. The shopgirls will buy it. It'll play in Peoria, sell tickets in Podunk. You can now borrow money on it, sell property with it, move goods or stop traffic. As they say in Hollywood, this is Picture, baby.

See if the White House wants in. Check the Vatican. See if anybody wants an audience with Carl (Himself) Lewis in person. Let's face it—this is Big! This is Michael Jackson *cum* the New York Philharmonic. John Wayne taking the fort. Bette Davis having a breakdown.

□

Carl Lewis is now a commodity. Wrap him in the flag, open the sealed bids, take an ad in The Wall Street Journal and get the money up front. Spell out the ingredients on the package, take out a series of two-minute spots, see if he'll do bar mitzvahs, weddings, ribbon-cuttings, beauty contests or celebrity roasts. See if there are any diseases left for him to chair. How about the gout? Could he stamp that out? Could Bette Davis smoke?

He's now the official legend of the 1984 Olympic Games—or about to be. Anybody who can't sell this account turns in his key to the executive washroom. Anybody who doesn't think Carl Lewis can sell cat food, razor blades, Bibles, light beer, cars, washday miracles or gym shoes turns in his ulcer.

We take you now to the main Manhattan offices of the powerful agency of Batman, Buncombe, Dreck & Dross, whose proud boast is they could sell cigarettes to the surgeon-general. As we look in, the good news is

Please see MURRAY, page 61

SKEETER HAGLER / Los Angeles Times
Carl Lewis does a victory leap after winning the Olympic 100 meters Saturday.

Lewis Dashes Away With Gold and Then Old Glory in the 100

'One Down and Three to Go,' He Says After 9.99 Victory at the Coliseum

By MIKE LITTWIN, *Times Staff Writer*

Little-girl gymnasts have stolen our hearts. Swimmers have splashed waves all over our television screens. America has been awash with patriotic fervor.

All in all, not a bad warmup. But on Saturday night at the Coliseum, these Games rolled out their main event. Welcome to the Carl Lewis Olympics.

Running a near-perfect 9.99 seconds in the 100-meter final, Lewis convincingly established himself as the World's Fastest Human. But what is that to a young man who lusts after immortality?

He is a man who after his winning race grabs an American flag from a fan in the Coliseum stands and waves it before a frenzied crowd. He is a man out to grab all there is.

And so Lewis, who collects fine crystal and silver, finally began accumulating Olympic gold—a collection that very well could run to four medals by week's end as yet another California gold rush begins.

Jesse Owens, corporate America and legend-makers await.

In the other two track and field finals, Al Joyner of East St. Louis, Ill., won the triple jump over Mike Conley of Chicago and Keith Connor of Britain, and Joyner's sister, Jackie, narrowly finished second only in the heptathlon to Glynis Nunn of Australia.

America's Sam Graddy, who matches Lewis in brashness only, finished second in the 100 meters in 10.19, two-tenths of a second behind Lewis. Canada's Ben Johnson was a surprising third in 10.22, while America's Ron Brown, nursing a sore leg, was fourth.

It was all so easy. Lewis peeled off his purple-and-black tights, waited through a false start by Johnson and then ran to daylight.

Graddy broke out quickly, but Lewis, running smoothly, began his move from the middle of the pack at about the 50-meter mark. By 80 meters, he had broken into the lead and then won going away—by perhaps eight feet. The margin of victory was an Olympic record, pushing Bob Hayes' 1964 Olympic win by .19 of a second aside. Oh, the legend-makers are going to be busy.

The funny thing is, this was the one event Lewis was worried about.

"As far as I am concerned, 60% of it is over," Lewis said in a written statement passed out to the media. "This is by far the toughest event for me because so much can happen.

"When you compete in four events such as in the Olympics, it is like going up a hill. Once I had won the 100, I felt like I'm going down."

What hope now for the rest of the world? Lewis competes in the long jump next, an event he hasn't lost in years. Then there is the 200 meters, another event he dominates. And finally, the 400-meter relay, which he will anchor for an American team that could lose only if someone drops the baton.

Those are the same four golds Jesse Owens collected 48 years ago. And it may be another 48 years before someone else comes along in that mold.

There's little enough hope when Sam Graddy, the rising junior from Tennessee, finally concedes defeat.

Please see LEWIS, page 61

U.S. Boxers Continue Triumphant March

DAVE GATLEY / Los Angeles Times
Alex Baumann of Canada is overwhelmed with joy Saturday after breaking his second world record.

Baumann Breaks Another Record

By TRACY DODDS, *Times Staff Writer*

Alex Baumann has not been back to his homeland since the Soviet Union invaded in 1968. But he was not much interested in discussing the Soviet boycott from a Czechoslovakian viewpoint.

He now has a Maple Leaf tattoo over his heart.

Baumann won his second gold medal for Canada Saturday night, lowering his own world record in the 200-meter individual medley.

He became the first Canadian to win a gold medal in swimming in 72 years when he won the 400-meter individual medley in world-record time Monday. With his second gold he matched what George Hodgson did for Canada in 1912.

He was quite proud of that. Asked if he thought the world records in both individual medleys, considered the decathlons of the swimming world, should rank him

as the best swimmer in the world or whether he thought that title should belong to Vladimir Salnikov of the Soviet Union or Michael Gross of West Germany, Baumann said: "It's hard to tell who's the best swimmer in the world. I set personal goals and let others decide if I'm the best."

Others have decided that he's certainly one of the best.

Please see BAUMANN, page 61

Holyfield and Gonzales in Quarterfinals

By EARL GUSTKEY, *Times Staff Writer*

Paul Gonzales and Evander Holyfield accounted for the United States' 15th and 16th consecutive victories in the Olympic boxing tournament at the Sports Arena Saturday night.

Today, the Americans go for 20 when bantamweight Robert Shannon and light-welterweight Jerry Page box in the day session and featherweight Meldrick Taylor and lightweight Pernell Whitaker fight on the night card.

Gonzales survived a short, thumping left hook that almost floored him in the second round to score a 5-0 decision over Ugandan William Bagonza Saturday night.

While Gonzales was contending with the dangerous Ugandan's punches, his excitable police officer-coach from the LAPD's Hollenbeck Division, Al Stankie, was having trouble with his fellow cops at ringside.

Stankie couldn't work in Gonzales' corner, so he volunteered to work in the LAOOC's boxer preparation room, wrapping hands of boxers prior to bouts. He accompanied his East Los Angeles light-flyweight to the ring and attempted to plant himself in a ringside VIP seat . . . until two policemen rousted him out of the area and into a spectator seat.

Quipped Gonzales afterward: "It's just as well—he gets too excited in the corner anyway."

Gonzales, who appears on a collision course with nemesis Rafael Ramos of Puerto Rico in next Saturday's finals, won handily on all five judges' cards: 60-55, 60-56, 60-54, 60-55, 60-56.

For a split second in the second round, however, Gonzales' dreams

Please see BOXING, page 61

Both Tineke Hidding of Holland and her ponytail fly through the air in the long jump of Saturday's Olympic heptathlon at the Coliseum. Hidding went 20 feet 10 inches for 982 points but did not get a medal in the seven-event, two-day event that was won by Glynis Nunn of Australia. Jackie Joyner of the United States was second.

PATRICK DOWNS / Los Angeles Times

BAUMANN

Continued from page 60

It was his own world record that Baumann lowered in the 200 with a time of 2:01.42. Pablo Morales of the United States took the silver in 2:03.05, and Neil Cochran of Great Britain took the bronze in 2:04.38.

For Morales, it was the third straight individual event in which he turned in his career-best time while the gold medalist lowered the world record. Morales was second to Michael Gross in the 100-meter butterfly when Morales swam lower than his own world record, and Gross lowered the record even more to win the gold. In the 200-meter butterfly, Morales had his career best and finished fourth in a race that produced the top four times ever.

Morales took the early lead, which was to be expected. The butterfly is his specialty. He maintained the lead through the backstroke, with Baumann taking over second place from American Steve Lundquist, who finished fifth.

But Baumann took over a slim lead on the breaststroke leg and stretched that lead on the freestyle finish.

Baumann said that was the way he had it figured from the start. "I knew that Pablo would go out, so my plan was to give him about 1½ body-lengths on the butterfly and to be no farther back than one second at the 100. My backstroke split was a little off, but otherwise it was a good swim for me. After the breaststroke leg, I knew that I had the race won.

"Actually, I thought that Lundquist would be my main competition. . . . I was watching him more the first half than I was Pablo. Medals are more important than records at this meet.

"But with the Soviet Bloc not here, it was important to set some world records, too, in order to prove the importance of this meet."

He does have reason to be more aware of the Soviet boycott than most of the swimmers here.

Baumann's family is originally from Czechoslovakia. His mother, Vera, was a nationally ranked breaststroker in Czechoslovakia. His father, Bedrich, a professor of sociology, took the family to New Zealand with him on a two-year pass to teach there in 1967. When the Soviet Union invaded Czechoslovakia in 1969, they decided never to return and moved to Sudbury in Ontario.

His loyalty to Canada is quite strong. Asked if he would consider coming to the United States to finish his collegiate career, he said that there was some talk of that, but he did not think so. He said: "If I did that, I'd lose a lot of the support I'm getting in Canada now. I don't think I want to do that."

Right now, Canada is as excited about Baumann as Baumann is about his two gold medals and two world records.

"It's like a dream come true for me," he said. "I think I'm still flying in the clouds. . . . It's the first time I've broken two world records in one meet. Words can't even explain how I feel right now."

MEN'S

Swimming

■ **200-METER INDIVIDUAL MEDLEY**

1. Alex Baumann (Canada)
2. Pablo Morales (U.S.)
3. Neil Cochran (Britain)

LEWIS

Continued from page 60

"Maybe Carl couldn't be beaten today," said Graddy, who had been predicting all along he would be able to beat Lewis when the time came. "I thought that if anyone could beat Carl it was me.

"At this point, since I couldn't get him, I don't see anything stopping him."

Lewis slowed down only long enough to enjoy the moment. He jumped into the air, though a little short of his usual long jump form. He waved to the crowd, shook hands with Graddy and then sighted an oversized American flag, which he grabbed from an unsuspecting fan.

He carried the flag like a true patriot while flashing a smile as wide as the 50 states. After giving back the flag, he ran along the rail to hug John Carlos, the 200-meter bronze medalist in 1968 who is remembered for his Black Power salute. Lewis remembers him as a baby-sitter back in his home town of Willingboro, N.J.

On the victory stand, Lewis waved to the crowd and blew kisses. If the win was easy for Lewis, it was not taken lightly.

"One down," he said, "and three to go."

Once again, Lewis chose not to talk to the assembled world media. He has said he won't be interviewed until after Saturday's relay—unless he breaks a world record in between. Don't bet against him.

His 9.99 was the seventh fastest time ever and just behind his best of 9.97. The world record is 9.93 by Calvin Smith, and the Olympic record is 9.95 by Jim Hines. Both were set at altitude. Lewis' 9.97 is an Olympic sea-level record, adding to all the other records Lewis holds for sea-level.

In the afternoon, Lewis easily won his semifinal heat in a fast 10.14, the second best time of the day. He was running fast then but saved faster for later.

Ron Brown was limping in the afternoon, and only a lean at the tape put him in fourth place and into the final. If he had been fit, America might have had its first sweep of the 100 since 1912. As it was, Lewis' gold was the first by an American in the 100 since 1968.

For much of the race, though, Graddy thought the gold might be his.

"I felt myself out ahead from the start," Graddy said. "At 80 to 85 meters, I was still ahead. I thought, 'Hey, I'm going to win a gold medal.'

"First I heard some steps. Then out of the corner of my eye, I could see Carl coming. I drove as hard as I could, but it wasn't enough."

Lewis said he was never concerned.

"If I am behind in the 100," he said, "I don't get worried until the 80-meter mark. I got a good start tonight, but some of the others got out faster. Once I started to come on at about 50 meters, I relaxed and felt very confident. I have the reputation of being a very strong finisher, and I established that I could take over this race about halfway through."

In other words, Graddy, who though 20 does not expect to stick around for the '88 Games, was living on false hope. Against Lewis, that's the only kind of hope there is.

Ben Johnson, a Canadian who is not even considered the best sprinter in his country, was surprised to win a medal. He was sixth in the Pan American Games, a semifinalist in the world championships and, suddenly, a bronze medal winner.

Against all evidence, Johnson wouldn't say he was awed by Lewis.

"He's not God," Johnson said. "He can be beaten."

Perhaps he can be beaten—by a fast horse. But Carl Lewis has no plans ever to run against horses. He has plans to win four gold medals and turn that gold into the real kind, the kind that awaits American heroes.

Look out, because here one comes.

Scott Ostler

Thanks to the Boycott, the Thrill Is Gone

Having a good time watching the Olympics?

Happy to see the Americans cleaning up on gold medals? Getting a charge out of the whole spectacle? Letting your spirits soar with the mood of the athletes and the city?

If so, please don't read the rest of this column. Wave your flag, hoist your beer, yell yourself hoarse. Watch the colorful TV coverage and read the happy stories. Skip this one. I don't want to go down as the Official Mood Spoiler of the 1984 Olympics.

Now. What is my grim message for the day? Just this:

I miss the Soviets. And the East Germans and Poles and Czechs and Cubans.

□

The weather is great; wish you were here.

When those crazy Commies announced that their athletes already had plans for these two weeks and wouldn't be coming to Los Angeles, the unofficial motto of the Olympics became: "Bleep 'em."

As in: "We'll have just as much fun without 'em," and "Who needs 'em?"

What else could we say? We certainly didn't want to give the Soviets any satisfaction by sulking.

So we put on our party hats, grabbed our flags and started counting American gold medals.

For the most part we've avoided mentioning the boycott bloc. Why dwell on the negative? You can't start every story with, "Thanks to the absence of the Soviets, the Americans won another gold medal today. . . ."

So we're all trying to ignore the people who aren't here. I know I tried.

But aside from the four events of the Carl Lewis Quadathlon, the shadow of the boycotters falls on every competition. The thrill is gone from basketball, gymnastics, boxing, track and field and baseball.

It's like going to a party and your date doesn't show up. You try not to notice. You laugh a lot and maybe put a lamp shade on your head. Hey, who needs her?

Bob Knight, coach of the U.S. men's basketball team, likened the Olympics to the NCAA basketball tournament. By the time the Final Four rolls around, Knight pointed out, nobody cares about the great teams that didn't make it. All that matters is what teams are there.

True, Bob, except that in the NCAA tournament, teams are eliminated on the floor. UCLA or Indiana never stayed home from the Final Four because the school president thought the hotel rooms in the host city were too small.

This whole boycott business could have been avoided if the Soviets had thought to hire an American public relations firm a year ago.

"How can we hurt the Americans without hurting ourselves?" the Russians would have asked.

"Simple, just show up," the PR people would have told the Soviets. "This will show the world your country is above such petty maneuvers as boycotting. Even if you practically invented the word."

"But how can we get even with America for boycotting our Games in '80?"

"Why bother? But if you must get your revenge, simply win a lot of medals. Also, complain to your people back home about the rooms and the traffic and the smog in L.A. You guys are great at that. If there's no smog and traffic, say there is. Who will know? Your people don't read the Los Angeles Times, do they?"

"What if some of our athletes defect?"

"Tell the folks back home they were kidnaped. Or became delirious from eating American junk food. You can turn any situation to your advantage, comrades. Staying home will accomplish nothing. Go to L.A. and you are world heroes. Even the Americans will salute you."

Lacking such sound advice, the Soviets elected to elevate the art of party pooping to new heights.

Who needs 'em? We do. The World Games last summer in Helsinki were wonderful. Until you see it in person, you can't fully appreciate the impact of watching the best athletes in the entire world competing in one meet.

Who can forget Mary Decker hitting the tape ahead of the lunging Soviet runner? Or of Jarmila Kratochvilova teaching the world a lesson in female athletic potential?

We've got the Super Bowl and the World Series, but the real World Series is the Olympics. No other event can match the festival feeling and adrenaline rush in spectators and competitors.

Will we ever see a true world competition again? Probably not in '88, because somebody—the Soviet Union, perhaps?—will be mad at the South Koreans. Sometime before the next century, maybe. . .

□

It will be sad if the Olympic Games are forced to politically neutral sites, but that would be preferable to what we've got now, these semi-world games.

There would have been no U.S. boycott in 1980 if the Games had been held in a neutral country, and no Soviet boycott in '84. It would be better to hold the Olympics at the North Pole.

It's time to find a way to get everyone to come to the party. Now that we have traded insults with the Soviet Union, it's time to bring back the Olympics.

This said, I promise to enjoy the rest of the Los Angeles Games, and not mention the chumps who didn't come.

The Soviets? Bleep 'em. Pass the lampshade.

BOXING

Continued from page 60

of Olympic gold nearly went crashing onto the powder-blue ring floor. When the Ugandan's left hook crashed onto the side of Gonzales' jaw, he had instant Jell-O knees but quickly recovered.

"Yeah, he hurt me," he said. "He stepped on my foot and I dropped my right hand when I backed up and that's when he got me."

Gonzales indicated the recent turmoil among team members over the training policy of Coach Pat Nappi hasn't fazed him. He referred to Mark Breland, Frank Tate and Steve McCrory working with their own coach, Emanuel Steward, in Santa Monica in recent days.

"If those guys feel they need to train someplace else to get ready, that's their business," he said. "I'm going to keep doing what I've been doing."

Gonzales, to use his own favorite phrase, gave the Ugandan a boxing lesson. His jab was textbook-perfect, and so was his ring movement. Responding to "Let's Go Paul!" chants in the second round, Gonzales caught Bagonza on the ropes with 25 seconds left and cut loose with four unanswered shots to the head.

The tiring Bagonza kept slugging away in the final round but was missing badly for most of the last round.

Gonzales next boxes England's John Lyon in the quarterfinals Tuesday night. He shares the card again with Holyfield, who meets Sylvaus Okello of Kenya.

Holyfield's opponent, Iraq's Ismail Salman, was unhappy that Australian referee John Davies stopped his bout in the second round. Salman had taken a fearsome assortment of body and head shots for two rounds, taken two standing eight counts, when Davies gave an "enough is enough" gesture, and waved Holyfield off.

Salman never really had a chance. He caught Holyfield with a thumping right on the jaw in the first minute of the bout, and the Atlanta light-heavyweight never blinked.

In fact, seconds later, Holyfield buried a huge right hand into Salman's midsection that nearly lifted him off his feet. You could have produced a "How to Successfully Employ Body Punching in Amateur Boxing" instructional film off this bout.

Afterward, Holyfield conceded that the bout may have been stopped prematurely.

"He (the referee) might have stopped it a little too fast," he said. "But I was hurting him with body shots. I knew if he didn't stop it, I would have knocked him out completely."

And the pressure of keeping the American winning streak going?

"We're under more pressure (than the other countries), but it makes us work harder. It's been easier than I expected. I'm hyped up, really pumped up."

□

Pressure? How about the pressure on Swedish light-heavyweight Christer Corpi? In the bout after Holyfield's, he lost a 4-1 decision to Jean Paul Nanga of Cameroon. Making the loss even more painful was the fact his king and queen, Carl Gustaf XVI and Silvia, were in the second row.

MURRAY

Continued from page 60

being relayed by the first vice president to the head man himself.

"Boss, have I got good news for you, the best news since that campaign where we sold all those ugly dolls to the public last Christmas at panic prices. Boss, our biggest promotion is off and running! I'm talking Carl Lewis is what I'm talking. He has won the 100 meters. His biggest stumbling block to the greatest athletic feat since Jesse Owens won four gold medals from Hitler in 1936.

"This is the greatest Lewis since John L. No, boss, this is not an Olympic runner, this is now *the* Olympic runner. Yeah! You got it! Like Bruce Jenner! What? Does he have as much hair as Bruce Jenner? Well, no, but he's tall and good-looking. Sure, he'll look good in a tux. No, I don't think he'll want to wear one white glove. Boss, of course, he talks nice. I mean, he's no Ronald Colman, but is Howard Cosell?

"Can he sing and dance? Play the ukulele? Boss, could Babe Ruth? I mean, we're talking legend here. What? For this kind of money you could have Ben Vereen? Boss, ask yourself: Could Ben Vereen come out to your house for the weekend and jump 28 feet for the affiliates? Could he run the hundred in 9.9? In the wind? We're talking talent here.

"What? You want to know if he can do impressions? Cagney going to the chair? Jimmy Stewart saving the homesteaders? Boss, be serious! This is the world's greatest athlete we're talking about here, not Rich Little. You want an impressionist, try Major Bowes. We're talking a hot property.

"How's this for chutzpah? Most guys try for one gold medal. This guy tries for four. And he laughs at everybody that takes him on. Laughs! I mean, this guy's John Wayne hitting the beach and slugging it out with the whole Japanese army. Is this box office? Nobody since Owens could do this.

"What? No, Jesse never made a buck. They put him to racing horses and jumping circus tents. Then they gave him a broom. But good old BBD&D wasn't around then. There was nobody to merchandise him. We're going to merchandise this guy like waterfront property in Florida or condos in Palm Springs. We might make him President, get him listed on the Big Board.

"What do you mean, in your day guys just ran for the thrill of it? What are ya, some kind of a Bolshevik? It's all set up today like Standard Oil. Whadaya think this is, a print of "Chariots of Fire?" It's all orchestrated, computed today.

"What do you mean he makes it look too easy? Oh, you say, the juggler should always drop a few plates early in the act, the aerialist should slip? Well, let me tell you, boss, this guy spots the field a five-yard head start. He doesn't even get interested in the race till it's half over. He gets out of the blocks like he was crawling out of a sewer and his coat caught. Then, just as you think he's had it, he puts it in gear and passes those guys like a train passing telephone poles. It's classic cliffhanger stuff. Perils of Pauline. The only things that can run as fast as this guy got spots.

"But I'm saving the best till last. After he wins these races, he goes into seclusion. He stiffs the media. Is that wild? Boffo stuff! Garbo, yet! Did it hurt Garbo? Howard Hughes? Boss, this kid can do it all! A natural for showbiz! I tell you we'll make more money with this guy than they did with Rin Tin Tin, hula hoops, Cabbage Patch Dolls, Bruce Jenner, Gone With The Wind and E.T. But shucks, boss, what are Olympics for anyway, eh?

U.S. Swimmers, Romanian Rowers Make Gold Rush

Carl Lewis, launching a quest for four Olympic gold medals, easily won the men's 100-meter dash Saturday at the packed Coliseum. The U.S. track and field team got a second gold when Al Joyner won the triple jump.

Americans won three golds in swimming for a total of 21, matching their best haul ever, at the 1968 Games. Holland and Canada got one swimming gold each. Romania won five women's rowing medals, the United States one.

In men's individual gymnastics, China's Li Ning won three golds, a teammate got another and the United States and Japan got two each.

Also in Day 7 of competition, the United States got a gold in skeet; three boxers, including Paul Gonzales of Los Angeles, won bouts; men's teams won in basketball and baseball but lost in field hockey and team handball, and women won in field hockey.

The United States won nine golds for a total of 38.

The highlights:

—Track and Field. Lewis accelerated with 40 yards to go and won in 9.99 seconds. Sam Graddy of Atlanta was second, Ben Johnson of Canada third. Joyner, of East St. Louis, Ill., won the triple jump over Mike Conley, Chicago, and Keith Connor, Great Britain. Glynis Nunn, Australia, won the heptathlon over Jackie Joyner (Al's sister) and Sabine Everts of West Germany.

—Gymnastics. Floor exercise—Li Ning, China, first; Lou Yun, China, second, and a tie for third between

Saturday's Roundup

Phillipe Vatuone, France, and Koji Sotomura, Japan. Pommel horse—L.A.'s Peter Vidmar and Li, tie for first, Tim Daggett, West Springfield, Mass., third. Rings—Li and Japan's Koji Gushiken tie for first, Mitch Gaylord, Van Nuys, third. Vault—Lou, first, and four-way tie for second, Gaylord, Li, Gushiken and Japan's Shinji Morisue. Parallel bars—Bart Conner, Morton Grove, Ill. first; Nobuyuki Kajitani, Japan, second, and Gaylord, third. Horizontal bar—Morisue, first; Ton Fei, China, second, and Gushiken, third.

—Swimming. Canada's Alex Bauman got his second gold and second world record (2:1.42) in the 200-meter individual medley. Pablo Morales, Santa Clara, was second and Neil Cochran, Great Britain, third. Mary T. Meagher of Louisville got her third gold in the women's 200 butterfly, with Karen Phillips, Australia second and Ina Beyermann, West Germany, third. Mike O'Brien of Mission Viejo won the men's 1,500 freestyle, with George DiCarlo of Denver second and Stefan Pfeiffer of West Germany third. Jolanda de Rover of the Netherlands won the women's 200 backstroke, with Amy White of Mission Viejo second and Aneta Patrascoiu of Romania third. The United States won the men's 400-medley relay in a world record 3:39.30, with Canada second and Australia third.

—Basketball. Michael Jordan of North Carolina led the unbeaten Americans to a 46-41 halftime lead, and when he went out with a twisted ankle they responded by defeating Spain, 101-68, for their fifth win. Chris Mullin of St. John's got 16 points.

—Rowing. Romania won five straight women's events, then the Americans edged them by a third of a length in the eight oars with coxswain to take their first gold ever in the sport. Romania's golds were in the single sculls (Valeria Racila, with Charlotte Geer of West Fairlee, Vt., second), double sculls without coxswain, pair oars without coxswain, quadruple sculls with coxswain (the United States was second) and four oars with coxswain.

—Boxing. East L.A.'s Paul Gonzales, 106 pounds, won a 5-0 decision over William Bagonza of Uganda. Steve McCrory of Detroit, 112 pounds, stopped Fausto Garcia of Mexico in the first round. Evander Holyfield of Atlanta, 178, stopped Ismail Salman of Iraq in the second round. The U.S. record: 16-0.

—Team sports. The U.S. beat the Dominican Republic, 12-0, in exhibition baseball. The U.S. women beat New Zealand, 2-0, in field hockey, but Spain beat the U.S. men, 3-1. Denmark beat the U.S. men, 19-6, in team handball.

—Other golds: Men's skeet, world-champion Matthew Dryke, Columbus, Ga. Fencing, individual saber—Jean F. Lamour, France (Peter Westbrook, New York, third). Weightlifting—181 pounds, Petre Becheru, Romania. Judo—132 pounds, Shinji Hosokawa, Japan (Edward Liddie, Colorado Springs, tied for third).

THE MEDAL COUNT

THE TOP FIVE MEDAL WINNERS

COUNTRY	GOLD	SILVER	BRONZE	TOTAL
U.S.	38	28	9	75
W. GERMANY	6	9	11	26
CHINA	12	6	5	23
ROMANIA	9	7	4	20
AUSTRALIA	6	4	8	18

STEVE FONTANINI / Los Angeles Times

The celebration begins as members of victorious U.S. women's crew toss coxswain Betsy Beard into water after winning gold medal.

Rowing

Romania Shows True Color—Gold

By BILL CHRISTINE,
Times Staff Writer

OJAI—Romania's national anthem is called "The Three Colors." It begins, "I know in this world . . ." and then proceeds to celebrate the country's colors of blue, red and yellow.

Most of the 10,000 fans at Lake Casitas Saturday didn't know the words, but they were bound to be familiar with the melody after the Romanian women's rowing team, as advertised, won five of the six gold medals in the Olympic Games.

The golds came in the first five events, which were run in less than 90 minutes, and after the procession of Romanian women to the winners' stand, the Santa Barbara City College band was sent home with the capability of playing "The Three Colors" backwards.

Other than the blue, red and yellow of Romania, the only other colors linked with Olympic gold Saturday were the red, white and blue of the United States, whose eight-oared crew prevented a sweep by holding off the Romanians by a ¼-length in the last race.

It was the first gold medal ever won by the U.S. women since

STEVE FONTANINI / Los Angeles Times

It's hugs all around for U.S. fours after taking silver medal.

female Olympic rowing began in 1976 and it was first rowing gold for any American since 1964 in Tokyo, where the men won two.

The Romanian women, who come in all shapes and sizes, have one common characteristic—speed. Led by dauntless Valeria Racila,

who defeated American Carlie Geer by more than three seconds in the single sculls, the Romanians didn't stray from the script as they reeled off these victories:

—In the fours with coxswain, with Canada about two seconds back and the U.S. boat finishing fourth.

—In the double sculls, with Holland's Hellemans sisters, Greet and Nicolette finishing second, almost three seconds behind and the United States coming in last among the six finalists.

—In the pairs without coxswain, 3½ seconds in front of Canada.

—And in the quadruple sculls, which was Romania's closest race of the day as the Americans, after a false start, finished second, crossing the line about 1½ seconds after the winners.

With eight men's finals scheduled for this morning, the Olympic rowing medal count stands at six for the Romanians, three each for the United States and Canada, two for Holland and one apiece for Australia, West Germany, Belgium and Denmark.

The question kept coming up after Romania's tour de force: What makes them row so expertly?

"Tell me why Carl Lewis is better than anybody else," said Rudy Wieler, a Canadian coach. "I don't know—all I know is that we're pleased with the way we did today and we'll just have to try to get better the next four years."

The Romanian blitz needs perspective, since the East German women, who won four out of six golds at last year's world championships, are part of the Soviet-led boycott. Racila, 27, wasn't interested in theorizing. She struck a buoy and capsized in the first 200 meters of the world championships, but Saturday there were no flaws. Racila was timed in 3:40.68, Geer in 3:43.89.

"I would have won last year but for that stupid accident," Racila said. "Since then, I have worked on my technique and changed boats. Before today's race, I had a strange feeling that I would win, because of my hard work and the four years of preparation I had done for this. I think I could have won by the same advantage even if the other teams (most importantly, the East Germans and the Soviet Union) had been here."

About 300 meters from the finish of the 1,000-meter race, Geer, a 31-year-old Dartmouth graduate from Morrisville, Vt., knew the race for the gold was over. Racila was a boat length ahead and saving

the silver became the priority.

"I thought I rowed a smart race," Geer said. "I had a little left at the end, but didn't want to blow a stroke, because you do that and you take the chance of going from second to sixth. I hit my peak this week. I rowed the three best races of my life."

Belgium's Ann Haesebrouck won the silver, with Canada's Andrea Schreiner, Denmark's Lise Marianne Justesen and Great Britain's Beryl Mitchell completing the field.

Victor Mociani, the physical-education teacher who coaches the Romanian team, said the turning point in the women's program came in 1974.

The Romanian women will remain in California for a week, Racila saying she was looking forward to seeing Disneyland, Universal Studios and the Santa Barbara Museum of Natural History. After that, they head home for their national championships.

"Those will be very, very hard," Racila said, sounding almost as though the Olympics are only a prep for the nationals.

Maybe they are. Referring to the Romanians, U.S. assistant coach Tom McKibbon said: "The East Germans and the Russians aren't here, but they sent a darn good junior varsity."

Fencing

Lamour Gets Gold; Bronze to Westbrook

By JOHN DART, *Times Staff Writer*

Saber fencer Peter Westbrook slashed his way to America's first Olympic fencing medal in 24 years—a bronze—while France's Jean Francois Lamour took the gold Saturday night in Long Beach.

The bout for the gold was between Lamour, 28, who was 14th in this year's World Cup circuit, and world junior champion Marco Marin of Italy, who turned 21 last month. It went down to the last possible moment with Lamour barely edging Marin, 12-11.

Marin had upset teammate Giovanni Scalzo in the semifinal, 10-4, while Lamour easily defeated Westbrook by the same score. In the third-place battle, Westbrook decisively beat Herve Granger-Veyron, 26, of France, 10-5.

At the final touch by Westbrook, his teammates and coaches rushed to embrace him on the stage of the Terrace Theater. The nearly full 3,000-seat arena gave the New Yorker a standing ovation and began a chant of "USA! USA!"

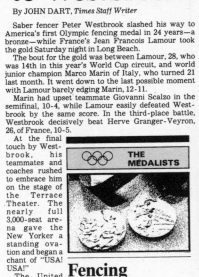

⬥ THE MEDALISTS

The United States had not won a fencing medal since 1960, when Albert Axelrod took third in men's foil. The only other saber medal for America was a silver by William Grebe in the lightly attended 1904 Games at St. Louis.

Westbrook, 32, advanced to the semifinals with a 10-8 win over Pierre Guichot, one of three Frenchmen in the finals of eight. Westbrook led all the way, but he turned his left ankle as Guichot scored to make it 9-8. He took a minute to test the ankle before resuming and scoring on the attack.

Westbrook made the finals by upsetting top-seeded Gianfranco Dalla Barba by one point, despite a disastrous start. The Italian led by 6-1 and 7-3. "I got three bad calls early in the bout," Westbrook said.

With the score 7-4, Westbrook was upset with another judging call. He dropped his mask and saber on the strip, took off his glove and started to unbutton his jacket as U.S. coaches on the sideline urged him not to quit.

While fencers are often genuinely angry, such theatrics are characteristic of saber fencing. But bout directors don't let it go too far. "I gave him a warning; we can't let fencers exaggerate too much," said Luiz Schirrhacher of West Germany, the bout director.

Westbrook tied the score at 8-8 and edged Dalla Barba at the end. "I think Dalla Barba was too sure of himself at first, then got nervous when Westbrook came back," Schirrhacher said. "I think Westbrook was helped a lot by the support of the crowd," he added, referring to the maximum of about 800 persons able to watch one bout in Exhibition Hall's divided grandstands.

Steve Mormando of the United States, who finished 12th overall, came within a hair of making the finals—but lost to Granger-Veyron, 10-9.

Fan Explains

The Flag Run Wasn't Staged

By SAM McMANIS, *Times Staff Writer*

When Carl Lewis began his victory lap Saturday night after winning the 100 meters, spectator Paul Tucker in Section 27 Row 2 of the Coliseum decided it was time to begin his own celebration.

Tucker, 50, of New Orleans, unfurled the giant American flag that he smuggled into the Coliseum in a bag and waved it at Lewis, hoping to slow down the World's Fastest Human.

Little did Tucker know that the flag would become part of Lewis' patriotic prance around the Coliseum track. When Lewis was a third of the way around the track, he made a detour and headed straight for Tucker and his flag.

Lewis didn't ask for the flag, according to Tucker, he just took it.

"As he was coming up at us, I thought he was just going to shake somebody's hand," said Tucker, who brought his two teen-age boys to the Games. "He reached out, and I swear I can't remember the moment he took it."

Tucker said he wasn't a "plant," that this wasn't a prearranged act by Lewis. But Tucker did say he saw Lewis perusing the crowd, apparently looking for a flag to wave.

"No," Tucker said. "It was improvised. But tell Carl I'll be available for the 200 meters. And (Edwin) Moses could use the flag, too, if he wants."

Tucker's biggest worry after Lewis took his flag was whether he would get it back. But after a few minutes, Lewis trotted back and returned the flag. Tucker: "Carl said, 'Thanks.' "

JOE KENNEDY / Los Angeles Times

Carl Lewis carries the flag on the track after winning the 100 meters in 9.99 seconds at the Coliseum. A fan said Lewis just came up and grabbed the flag from him, unrehearsed.

United Press International

Weightlifter Mahmoud Tarha of Lebanon, who had placed fourth in the flyweight competition, was disqualified Saturday for having taken Nandrolene, an anabolic steroid.

Pair of Lifters Barred for Life

Two weightlifters caught using steroids at the Olympics have been banned for life by the International Weightlifting Federation and disqualified from the Games by the International Olympic Committee's Executive Board, the federation announced Saturday night.

Mahmoud Tarha of Lebanon, who finished fourth in the flyweight class (114 pounds) last Sunday, and Ahmed Tarbi of Algeria, who finished ninth in the bantamweight division (123 pounds) Monday, tested positive for anabolic steroids.

Gottfried Schodl, IWF president, and Tamas Ajan, general secretary, issued a prepared statement saying, in part, that the IWF had decided in January that lifters showing positive doping results here would be banned for life .

The statement said: "We are now sorry to state that in spite of our efforts and repeated calls, Mahmoud Tarha . . . and Ahmed Tarbi . . . had a positive result at the doping controls effected here in Los Angeles . . .

"The IWF herewith confirms the disqualification of these two athletes by the IOC Executive Board from the Games and at the same time suspends them from international weightlifting for life."

ABC Isn't the Only Television Network on the Coals

From Times Staff Writers and Wire Services

ABC isn't the only network being criticized for homerism in Olympic coverage.

Viewers in Australia complained that coverage beamed there is dwelling too much on Aussie performers, and columnists in Italy ripped that country's commentators for a nationalistic stance, especially one broadcaster's pat on the back for an Italian athlete accused of cheating.

Many countries are carrying pictures supplied by ABC, but the British Broadcasting Corp. (BBC) and West German television each have cameras in Los Angeles.

The BBC, which said there is "no danger" of its programming becoming "Americanized," was in turn ripped by Kenyan authorities for failing to cover African athletes.

Many U.S. TV viewers, and Juan Antonio Samaranch, president of the International Olympic Committee, have complained that ABC dwells excessively on Americans in its coverage.

The London Daily Mirror and Mexico's Televisa S.A., among others, admitted that ABC can hardly avoid a heavy American tilt because U.S. athletes have won about 40% of the gold medals.

"They have been covering first places," Televisa S.A.'s Guillermo Gonzalez said. "If the United States is in the first place, that's not their fault."

However, the Daily Mirror said, coverage is "creating ever-mounting criticism. They (ABC) are burying the Games beneath a Stars and Stripes flag."

Jarung Rakchati, news editor of TV-7 in India, praised the balance of the electronic coverage of events but said there should be more balance in featuring events and athletes. Indian coverage has focused heavily on field hockey, the country's surest shot for a medal, as well as weightlifting and gymnastics. But there have been complaints of too much swimming and cycling.

Australia, traditionally strong in swimming, has been mixing the ABC feed with footage from six Australian cameras.

Michael Thompson-Noel of Britain's Financial Times took on the American sports fan as well as ABC.

"The playing of the American anthem and hoisting of the American flag have become hackneyed in their repetitiveness—particularly when the victories they celebrate are accompanied by a howling and a hollering that would have made the mob in Nero's Colosseum seem fastidious in their restraint," Thompson-Noel wrote.

"A vision of loveliness the American sports fan is not. He pays to watch blood, arrives festooned in stars and stripes and sits belching in the sun."

He also railed against the "nonsensical frenzy of some of the commentators of the ABC, who psych and flagellate themselves into such a lather of overkill at the merest scent of an American victory that the distinction between programming and puffery became so finely etched as to be rendered invisible."

□

This may be the first case in Olympic track history of a 400-meter runner having to deal with being boxed in during a race.

When the starter's gun went off for the third heat of the men's 400 meters qualifying Saturday morning, Secundino Borabota from Equatorial Guinea in Lane 2 veered into Lane 1 and blocked Nigeria's Innocent Egbunike.

As the runners headed for the first turn, Egbunike, who competes for Azusa-Pacific, pointed to Borabota and tried to wave him off. Finally, the mixed-up Borabota returned to his designated lane. Egbunike won the heat in 46.63, while Borabota finished the race last but was disqualified anyway.

Asked why he went into Lane 1, Borabota said in broken English: "It was a small problem. I knew what lane I had, but I had a problem (injury?) with my foot that made me switch . . . When I get foot better, I was all right and come back to my lane."

Egbunike said he was relieved that Borabota's error didn't slow him down. "I hope this doesn't happen again," he said, smiling.

"I just saw him there, cutting in front of me at the gun. I kept telling him to please leave. Yes, I said please. He was still in my lane, but he gave me a little space on the inside, and I went by him."

—SAM McMANIS

□

If it is possible to duck-hook a javelin out of bounds, Norway's Reidar Lorentzen did it in his qualifying round Saturday morning.

The throw, far short of the automatic qualifying distance of 272 feet 4 inches, sailed 12 or 15 feet to the left of the left boundary line and almost speared one of a gaggle of orange-coated officials who weren't paying attention.

Spectators gasped as the javelin sent officials scattering.

—BILL SHIRLEY

□

Canadian 400-meter Bryan Saunders placed fifth in his heat Friday morning and failed to qualify for his next round. But Saunders said afterward he was satisfied with his performance and has enjoyed his stay in Los Angeles.

Anything had to be better than Saunders' last visit to Los Angeles. He came here in the spring to train and said he was stabbed in the stomach early one morning while trying to break up a robbery attempt.

"It happened on Feb. 18," Saunders said. "I'll never forget the date. I was driving my car down Hoover, and I saw this middle-aged man hassling a woman. I found out later they were boyfriend and girlfriend. Anyway, I got out of my car and kindly told the guy to give her a break. I turned to go back to my car and felt a little pain in my stomach. I opened the car door and realized I'd been stabbed."

Saunders, who was in the hospital for eight days and has a scar about six inches long, said the knife "nicked my spleen," and doctors were worried that he might have back problems."

But he returned to training a month later and made the Canadian Olympic team. "It was a comeback just to get here," Saunders said.

—SAM McMANIS

□

Indians and Pakistanis take their field hockey seriously, and so do their media. When either team fails to win, a handful of reporters grill the coaches unmercifully, often telling the coach—instead of asking—what went wrong.

The coaches seem to accept this with equanimity. When they disagree, they answer with gentle chiding, at worst. Still, it's hard to imagine American reporters asking Bobby Knight or Billy Martin the same questions—without getting punched out.

Questions directed at Indian officials Saturday after a loss to Australia included the likes of:

—"Don't you think your line is playing too far back?"

—"It doesn't seem like (star player) is doing his job." (The coach said he was.)

—"Didn't it seem like (opponent) shouldn't have scored that goal?" (The coach agreed.)

One reporter asked an Indian player, "Why did you boys let down in the second half?"

Through it all, one reporter will always ask, "Were you pleased with the team's performance?"

—ALAN DROOZ

□

Ruth Owens, widow of legendary Jesse Owens, was given the torch that her granddaughter, Gina Hemphill, carried into Memorial Coliseum for last week's opening of the Olympic Games.

"I will put this torch in Jesse's trophy room," Owens said Saturday. "I have all his trophies, pictures from the Berlin Games and countless other awards. My husband is never out of my mind."

□

Winning an Olympic gold medal can bring financial security to some athletes, but the prize itself is worth far less at the bank.

The much-coveted first prize is actually a silver medal coated with 6.5 grams of 24-karat gold, or 5.2% of the medal's weight. The cost of the medal came to about $130 and its value will fluctuate according to gold prices.

The specifications of the medals are regulated by the Olympic charter. The first-place medal must be gilded with at least 6 grams of gold, and the silver must be at least 92.5% pure.

A spokesman for the Los Angeles Olympic Organizing Committee said this year's second- and third-place prizes are 100% silver and bronze. He did not know the value of the silver and bronze medals.

A total of 1,454 Olympic sport medals will be awarded during the two-week Games. Boxing and judo award two bronze medals in all events. Medallions are also awarded to the top finishers in the demonstration and exhibition sports.

□

After winning the gold medal in the 400-meter medley relay Friday, backstroker Theresa Andrews and butterflier Mary T. Meagher were asked to name the members of their families that were on hand to cheer them on.

Andrews has eight brothers and three sisters. Meagher has nine sisters and one brother.

Freestyler Nancy Hogshead grabbed the mike from Meagher before she could answer and said, "Hey, we only got an hour before we have to report to doping control for our blood test."

—JOHN WEYLER

□

Apparently Dancing Barry doesn't do the Olympics.

Barry, a fixture at Laker games, has yet to be seen shaking, jiving and exciting crowds at the Forum, site of the Olympic basketball tournament.

A replacement has been found, though. A South Korean man, waving a huge flag behind his country's bench, awoke the Forum fans watching the South Korean women play Yugoslavia Friday morning. Even the American fans in attendance took part in the orchestrated applause that moved from one section of the arena to the next.

□

Nancy Hogshead, who won three golds and a silver in swimming, is 5-10 and weighs 158 pounds, but it's almost all muscle. During the Olympic team's training camp, Hogshead was tested at 13% body fat, by far the lowest figure for any female on the team.

"That's the first time I've ever taken a fat test," the 22-year-old Hogshead said. "It makes me so mad, too. All my life coaches have been telling me, 'Lose weight, lose weight, lose weight.'

"If I'd have taken one of these things years ago, I could have told those guys to shut up."

—JOHN WEYLER

□

Can any other sport match yacht racing for living nostalgia in the 1984 Olympics?

Owen Churchill, 88, of Los Angeles has been out watching the races on Angelita, the same 8-meter he sailed to a gold medal in '32. But Churchill is concerned about what will become of the boat after the Games.

Angelita was found rotting in a Santa Cruz boatyard a couple of years ago, and Peter Ueberroth, president of the Los Angeles Olympic Organizing Committee and a part-time sailor, restored her at a cost of $115,000.

"She cost only $22,000 new," Churchill noted.

But Ueberroth will be moving East after the Olympics to become baseball commissioner and has two offers to sell Angelita to private parties.

"I'd rather they put her in the (L.A. County) museum," Churchill said. "Somebody said there are only two things left from the '32 Olympics—the Coliseum and Angelita. That way she'd stay in good shape forever. I could go over and polish the brass twice a week."

—RICH ROBERTS

□

That's easy for you to say: Egyptian goalkeeper Adel El Maahour was knocked unconscious and lost a front tooth in a bone-rattling collision late in the first half of Egypt's soccer 1-1 tie with the United States. The goalie still looked shaky at the postgame press conference, but Egyptian Coach Abdou Selah took it all in stride.

"He is used to being hit by other players," the coach said. "And fortunately, one of our players is a dentist."

—TERRY SHEPARD

□

American three-day rider Bruce Davidson should get a cheer from feminists everywhere.

After the U.S. team won the gold medal in the three-day event, Davidson was asked to comment on the increasing influence and ability of women in his sport over the past few years.

The interviewer pointed out that Davidson's teammates, Karen Stives, who had just won the individual silver at Santa Anita, and Torrance Watkins Fleischmann, who won the bronze in the three-day at the Alternate Games in 1980, are the first American women ever to win individual medals in Olympic-level equestrian competition, in three-day, dressage or show jumping.

Unruffled, Davidson said, "Women competing at this level generally are better than the men."

—LYNN SIMROSS

□

The U.S. judo team, with affection, calls him "the Mouth That Roared." Referees and judges call him a gadfly. His landlord calls him, frequently, for the back rent.

What he is, really, is the Unsinkable Jimmy Martin.

Martin, of San Gabriel, is heavily in debt, burdened by a sore shoulder he can't afford to get fixed and still rankled by a questionable decision that kept him off the team.

So what does he do? Sue? Write nasty letters to the sports editor? Don a fake mustache a la Floyd Patterson and leave the country? Not Jimmy Martin.

He applied for—and got—a job as "locker room supervisor" at Cal State Los Angeles, site of the Olympic judo competition.

"Sure, I get a pang now and then," said the 143-pound six-time national champion, formerly captain of the squad, "but as far as I'm concerned, this is my team. I love 'em, each one of 'em. Anything I can do to help is a privilege."

—DICK RORABACK

□

Five drums of a flammable liquid, classified as a hazardous waste by Department of Environmental Health Services officials, were discovered about a half-mile from the Prado Regional Park shooting range, apparently dumped overnight Wednesday.

San Bernardino County health officials and Chino firefighters worked about three hours in transferring the industrial solvent to a safer location. Samples were sent to a Pasadena laboratory, where it was revealed that the substance was liquid waste with no acute danger to participants of the Olympic shooting championships.

Officials suspect the drums were dumped by a manufacturing firm such as a fiberglass producer.

During the cleanup operation, a chemist asked: "Does this make us the official emergency waste team of the 1984 Olympics?"

—ELLIOTT ALMOND

□

And you thought you'd heard all of the music of America at the opening ceremonies.

The music piped into the Stanford Stadium public address system before Olympic soccer games is vintage United States, too, but not exactly Gershwin. A country-western fan somewhere in central control treated the Germans, Saudis, Brazilians and other visitors to such American classics as "Ruby, Don't Take Your Love to Town" and "Yakety-Yak (Don't Talk Back)."

—TERRY SHEPARD

□

U.S. basketball player Jon Koncak, who has one season remaining at Southern Methodist University, thinks the exposure of the Olympics is carrying over to his school.

"Being on the Olympic team has meant a lot to me, and I hope to SMU, too," said Koncak, who is from Kansas City, Mo. "We're going to be on national television three times next year, and all of those games have fallen into place in the last three weeks or so."

"I think people know a little bit more about SMU now. It's no longer SM-Who in basketball. (Television basketball commentator) Al McGuire said we belong in the top 10. But he still can't pronounce my name."

□

California, the host of the Summer Games, has the largest representation on the U.S. Olympic team, while seven states share the title of smallest Olympic producer.

According to figures compiled by the U.S. Olympic Committee, 240 Californians are competing or serving as staff members for the U.S. Colorado is a distant second, with 55 athletes and staff members, while Pennsylvania is third with 47, New York fourth with 43 and New Jersey fifth with 41.

There is one athlete or staff member apiece from Alaska, Hawaii, Mississippi, Nevada, North Carolina, South Carolina and South Dakota, the USOC said. Three other states—Delaware, Idaho and Wyoming—have no representatives.

GRECO-ROMAN GOLD

LARRY BESSEL / Los Angeles Times

In Greco-Roman wrestling finals Friday at the Anaheim Convention Center, Ion Draica (1) and Vasile Andrei (4) won gold medals for Romania at 181 pounds and 220 pounds, respectively; West Germany's Pasquale Passarelli (3) spent the final 1:36 of the match arching his back to avoid a pin by Japan's Masaki Eto and win at 125.5 pounds, and Yugoslavia's Vlado Lisjak (2) pinned world champion Tapio Sipila of Finland to win the championship at 149.5 pounds.

United Press International

Hello Mary Lou, Goodby Heart

The first one to realize what she had accomplished was Mary Lou Retton herself. She had hardly landed, planting those little feet on the mat, when she threw back her arms and threw out her chest, less to salute the judges than her own achievement.

It was a perfect vault. She knew it, you knew it. Romania's Ecaterina Szabo, watching from a distant corner of the podium, knew it. You could tell she knew it the way she turned her head.

Her private coach, Bela Karolyi, of course, he knew it. Standing beyond the vermilion-draped rail, he had found footing even before her takeoff, anticipating his own vault. Do you remember the red-shirted man with the drooping mustache, leaping into the arena, hoisting "Little Body" aloft?

Mary Lou Retton, 16, certainly would be the women's gymnastics all-around champion. Had to be. Certainly, with that vault, she had come from behind Friday night to beat Szabo by the necessary five-hundredths of a point. Certainly she had just won the United States' first ever individual medal in women's gymnastics, and gold at that.

Who sails so far? So high? Who tumbles through space as effortlessly as she? Who lands so perfectly?

No one. And the judges' scores confirm the news. There was Retton's triumphant posture and there was Karolyi's theatrical exuberance. And there were four 10s, lit one by one in the judges' corners.

You may remember the roar that descended the stands Friday night, rolling downward into the pit, gathering an avalance of volume. You may remember thousands of people chanting "Mary Lou," waving little American flags. You may remember 9,023 fists, high in the air.

You may remember this: When it was final, a 16-year-old girl in brown bangs, dressed in an American flag, bounded back down the runway, her feet planted together. She was suddenly a human pogo stick. Having fun, you supposed.

—Richard Hoffer

United Press International

United Press International

United Press International

OLYMPICS '84

DAY 10

Benoit Follows 'Yellow Brick Road' to Gold

JOE KENNEDY / Los Angeles Times

Gold medalist Joan Benoit of the United States, carrying the cap she wore during most of the race, strides to victory in the first Olympic women's marathon.

She Says Win in Marathon Was a Breeze

By MARLENE CIMONS,
Times Staff Writer

The 26.2-mile footrace known as the marathon is a little like a compressed version of life. There is drama. There is joy. There is pain.

And there are always surprises, the uncertainty of never knowing what awaits down the road.

Joan Benoit came here prepared to suffer. She expected the drama and the pain, in exchange for the joy of winning the gold. She came ready to run this race, the first women's marathon in the history of the Olympic Games, like no other she had ever run before. She expected it to be like no other she had ever run before.

She was wrong.

She took the gold Sunday morning, running the third fastest women's marathon ever, 2 hours 24 minutes 52 seconds.

But it was a cinch.

"It was kind of like following the yellow brick road," she said. "I don't know how to say this without sounding cocky, but it was a very easy run for me today. I was surprised I wasn't challenged at all. Nobody came with me—and I didn't complain."

It was a dream come true for Benoit, but it was a nightmare for Switzerland's Gabriela Andersen-Schiess. Suffering from heat prostration, she slowed to a walk and staggered out of control on the final lap. Somehow she managed to finish, lurching across the line in 37th place. Fifty started the race, and 44 finished. Andersen-Schiess later recovered.

Benoit thought it would take more than a gifted athlete to win. She thought it would take the one with the strongest head. She has already proved over and over again how tough she is. She won the Olympic marathon trial only 17 days after knee surgery.

But this, after all, was to be the greatest showdown in the history of women's long-distance running. At long last, a confrontation between Benoit, America's favorite and holder of the world record (2:22:43), and Norway's Grete Waitz, world champion and Queen of the Roads, a woman who had never lost a marathon she had finished.

But the confrontation never took place.

For Waitz, the sentimental pick of many who have watched her run marathons in this country and who consider her a pioneer of women's running, it was a sad struggle for second. Running in pain with a back problem, she won the silver, being clocked in 2:26.18.

Unexpectedly, the bronze was won by Portugal's Rosa Mota, who has said many times she never thought she had a chance to win a medal. But in a dramatic move just after the 20-mile mark, she overtook and then outfinished a laboring Ingrid Kristiansen, of Norway. Breaking 2:30 for the first time,

Please see BENOIT, page 66

'I Always Thought the Finish Was Going to Be Right There'

By RICK REILLY, *Times Staff Writer*

When Runner No. 323 entered Memorial Coliseum Sunday, all was well with the Olympics. Marathon queen Joan Benoit was mugging with the American flag and ABC was beaming that smile from coast to coast.

For the millions watching, though, the next five minutes would not be such a pretty picture.

Runner No. 323 was Switzerland's Gabriela Andersen-Schiess, 39, a ski instructor from Sun Valley, Ida., run-walking in what looked like a drunken lurch, her right arm flailing, her left leg unbending at the knee. She dragged it along with her, weaving left, then right, going not so much forward as sideways, pulled by a weird gravity known only to her.

Such are the physical tortures of an athlete running in the throes of heat prostration.

"I didn't really know where I was," Andersen-Schiess said less than 12 hours later, nearly fully recovered. "The last two kilometers are mostly black. When I first came into the stadium, I thought the finish was right there. I didn't know I had a whole lap (around the track) to go. My mind wasn't working too good. I always thought (the finish) was going to be right there—right there. But it was always longer than I realized."

The terrifying part was that Andersen-Schiess did not realize that she had more than 400 meters to go.

Three times medics approached to see if she would accept help, and three times she literally ran from them. Had anybody touched her, helped her, given her water or sponge, she would have been disqualified.

"I didn't want them to help because I thought the finish was right there," she said.

Andersen-Schiess may not have been of whole mind at the time, but what she was operating on told her what she must do—finish history's first women's Olympic marathon—and so she did.

In five minutes and 400 meters of agony—for both the runner and the 70,000-plus spectators who cheered her on—she flopped one stiff leg in front of the other like a toddler until she at last crossed the finish line and collapsed into the arms of three medical officials.

The huge crowd that had hailed Benoit 20 minutes earlier as the best Olympic women's marathon runner, hailed Andersen-Schiess as the bravest. Despite her difficulties, she finished 37th with a time of 2 hours 48 minutes and 42 seconds.

"I guess I just kept walking and walking by instinct," she said Sunday night, having been proclaimed healthy by Swiss Olympic team doctors. "It was a little bit of will power or something. Your mind tries to dominate over your tired body. Your body may be screaming, 'No!', but your mind says, 'Well, yes, but it's so close.'"

After fainting into the technicians' arms, she was soaked in cool water, given water to drink, then taken from the track on a stretcher and given intravenous solutions, all to bring down her 101-degree temperature.

"It was like your body is on fire," she said. "I was really in pain for the next half-hour or hour. I was so hot until they cooled me down."

Olympians become Olympians because they teach the mind to fool the body and cheat the pain. Andersen-Schiess was living proof of that. But who

Please see RUNNER, page 66

JAY DICKMAN / Los Angeles Times

Gabriela Andersen-Schiess, suffering from heat prostration, staggers toward the finish of the marathon. She later recovered.

When Ashford Finally Realizes Dream, She Can't Stop the Tears

By MAL FLORENCE, *Times Staff Writer*

The realization of what Evelyn Ashford had accomplished didn't make an immediate impact on her. All of a sudden, the frustration of the United States' boycott of the 1980 Moscow Games and the injuries that clouded her future were gone.

She had just won the gold medal Sunday evening in the 100 meters at the Olympic Games. She also set an Olympic record of 10.97 seconds for good measure.

When the Coliseum public address announcer informed the crowd of her Olympic record, Ashford threw her arms into the air in jubilation. She then took a victory lap, but unlike Carl Lewis, she didn't take a flag from a spectator to accompany her.

Later, on the victory stand, Ashford couldn't hold back the tears. Then, when she was in an interview tent, she fondled her prize, the gold medal, that she

Please see ASHFORD, page 67

PATRICK DOWNS / Los Angeles Times

Demonstrating grace and power, Edwin Moses clears a hurdle en route to winning his 90th straight final in 400-meter hurdles.

The Victory Was Big, but Moses Admits the Pressure Was Bigger

By RANDY HARVEY, *Times Staff Writer*

Asked once about the pressure he feels because of his remarkable winning streak in the 400-meter intermediate hurdles, Edwin Moses said, "It's like going to your execution 15 times a year."

Eight years after he won his first Olympic gold medal, and almost seven years since he last lost a race, Moses still needs a blindfold and a smoke each time he settles into his starting blocks. It is never as easy as it looks.

If the tension was not apparent on his face before the Olympic final Sunday at the Coliseum, it was on the face of his wife, Myrella. She covered her eyes with her hands, then cried as his name was announced.

Moses came through. He dodged the bullets again. His time of 47.75 seconds did not challenge his world record of 47.02 or the Olympic record of 47.63 he set while winning the gold medal at Montreal in 1976.

But it was good enough for his 105th straight victory, his 90th straight in a final. It also was the 28th time he has run under 48 seconds.

If there were any doubts about whether he would continue in the race known as the mankiller, he dispelled them when he said he was looking to become the first man to run under 47 seconds before the end of this summer.

Only three others have ever run under 48 seconds. The only other man who has done it more than once, West German Harald

Please see MOSES, page 67

BENOIT

Continued from page 65

Mota clocked a personal best of 2:26:57.

It was a typical Joan Benoit race, almost from the start.

She took the lead by the third mile and never lost it. Even before the halfway point, her lead was commanding—more than 300 yards. She had at least 1½ minutes on the pack behind her, a pack that included Waitz and the two other favorites, Kristiansen and America's Julie Brown. Mota was also in the group, biding her time.

"I *did not* want to take the lead," Benoit said. "But I promised myself I'd run my race and nobody else's, and that's exactly what I did."

She said she hesitated at first. "I thought: 'This is the Olympic marathon—you'll look like a showboat falling off at the halfway point and watching everyone else pass you.' But I didn't have any second thoughts because I was in control. I said: 'You feel too good to blow this—so stay on top of your game.' "

But her pace was slow, hardly suicidal. Her time at 10 kilometers (6.2 miles), for example, was a leisurely 35 minutes 26 seconds.

It was surprising that the pack allowed her to escape. It was especially startling that Waitz did not follow her, a decision she would later regret. The Norwegian has dominated marathoning for the last six years and has never been intimidated by anyone. Kristiansen, in fact, said her teammate did not even wear a stopwatch, she was so confident that she would be close enough to the pace car to read its clock as she ran. But as the race progressed, Waitz had to ask Kristiansen for their elapsed time.

Waitz's husband, Jack, who always greets her at various points along the course as she races, knew it was over after the 13.2-mile halfway point.

"We have an expression in Norway: 'I knew the train had already left,' " he said.

Waitz, however, didn't seem to realize until it was too late that she would not be able to catch Benoit. She said later she held back initially to conserve herself for the final stages, when conditions were expected to be more difficult.

"I knew it was going to be very, very hot later," Waitz said of her decision not to follow Benoit. "She took a chance—and I didn't."

For all the concern about smog and heat, the weather was not as bad as it could have been. At the 8 a.m. start in Santa Monica, skies were overcast, with a temperature of 67 degrees and a high 95% humidity. As the runners moved inland, the sun broke through, temperatures rose into the mid-70s and the humidity began to drop. The pollution standard index was 92, meaning it was "not unhealthful."

"The air quality didn't seem to bother me today," Benoit said.

Hundreds of thousands lined the course, and Benoit called their support "uplifting." Benoit, who runs as if she sees nothing around her, broke her concentration only once, at about the halfway point, to smile at someone waving a black-and-white banner from Bowdoin College, her alma mater.

The rest of the American team did not fare as well as Benoit. Brown, one of the pre-race favorites, ran badly, finishing in 36th place at 2:47:33, far off her best of 2:26:26. Julie Isphording, who has been battling a sore foot, dropped out.

"When they started to pull away, I just couldn't go with them," Brown said, in tears. "I don't know what happened. I have no excuses. I tried to run from my heart, but I just didn't have it."

The most wrenching scene, however, was the struggle of Andersen-Schiess, who could barely stay on her feet and took nearly five minutes to complete the last lap.

"I did not see Gabriela finish, but I think it was a real honor for every woman in this race today," Benoit said. "It was a long time coming."

And of her own feelings, she said: "It was something very special. Something I've dreamed about. It still hasn't hit me. I can't believe I've won this marathon."

Around the Town With Joan Benoit

Joan Benoit (above left) raises her arms in victory and later kisses her parents in the stands (right) after winning the first Olympic women's marathon Sunday. At left, Benoit cools off on the course by squirting water on her face. Above right, she begins to pull away from the field early in the race on Wilshire Boulevard.

Photos: LARRY BESSEL, PAT DOWNS
Los Angeles Times
and United Press International

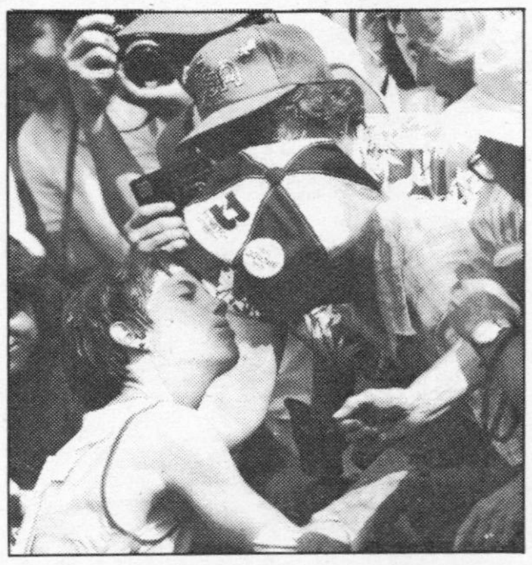

GOLD / JOAN BENOIT

This Time, the Celebration Involves Honest-to-Gosh People

By RANDY HARVEY, *Times Staff Writer*

Joan Benoit remembers when the celebration after a women's marathon was little different from training for one. The world was not interested in sharing either with her.

If she did not receive the acclaim she believed she deserved after her victory in the 1979 Boston Marathon, then she thought she might get it after breaking the American record in the fall of 1982. She should have known better.

"No one even seemed to know that she did it," said Lynn Petronella, a friend from Long Island. "Or if people did know, they didn't seem to care. Joan was tired and empty.

"She said: 'Don't leave me alone.' "

Less than two years later, Joan Benoit is left alone only when she escapes to the 19th-Century house she is renovating near her home in Freeport, Me.

She was attracting so much attention while training in Santa Monica a week before the opening of the Summer Games that she had to retreat to Eugene, Ore.

"It was very hot in Santa Monica, and I was wearing myself down," she said Sunday. "Not only that, but people recognized me. People wanted to race me down San Vicente Boulevard, and I was wearing myself out."

She did not sound the least bit annoyed.

One reason for her popularity no doubt is the television commercial she does for Nike.

□

It is the early morning after she won the 1983 Boston Marathon, in which she broke the world record. As she prepares to leave the house for another workout, a radio disc jockey is discussing Benoit's victory. She opens the front door, discovering a thunderstorm, sighs, then charges out into the rain.

As the door slams shut behind her, the disc jockey says: "If you're listening, way to go, Joanie."

□

That seemed to be the crowd's response Sunday morning, when Benoit, 27, was the first woman to emerge from the tunnel at the west end of the Coliseum in the first women's marathon in the history of the Olympics.

She is not known as one of the most outgoing of athletes, but she made the most of her moment. She had to run the final 500 meters of the 26.2-mile course around the track. On the backstretch, she waved to the crowd, then took off her cap and waved it above her head as she finished in 2:24:52

She was given a standing ovation that lasted through her victory lap. Everyone wanted to share these moments with Benoit.

"The cheers out of the crowd were very uplifting when I entered the stadium," she said. "I don't know how to express it. It's something very, very special, something I've dreamed about, something that hasn't hit me yet. I can't believe I've won the marathon."

It has been an unbelievable year for Benoit.

The world record she set last year certainly established her as one of the favorites, but it appeared that all might be lost when she injured her knee last spring.

Upon the counsel of doctors, she tried to train through the pain. That only made it worse. On April 25, she underwent arthroscopic surgery.

Only 17 days later, she won the U.S. marathon trials in one of the most courageous performances of this or any other Olympic year.

While preparing for the trials, she said she could not help but thinking about the wall mural of herself on Exposition Boulevard near the Coliseum.

"Somebody who I do not know in Los Angeles sent me a picture of the wall mural," she said Sunday. "I received it several days before my knee problems.

"My first thoughts when the knee started bothering me was, 'What about the wall mural? They put it up for nothing. I'm not even going to be there.' That was my inspiration for getting my rear in gear, so to speak."

Motivation never has been considered one of Benoit's weaknesses. Among the courses she runs while training near her home in Maine is one that is 16 miles long. Before she begins, she often tells herself that she will quit after 13 miles. She almost always runs the three extra miles.

"I don't know where my competitiveness comes from," she said. "I always ask myself that, and I haven't found the answer yet. I guess it's just one challenge after another.

"I grew up in a family with three brothers. It was survival of the fittest. I always played with boys. I had to hold my own from the start."

She talked about her youthful dreams of becoming an Olympic skier and how they ended with a broken leg. It was while rebuilding the strength in the leg that she discovered running.

"One thing led to another," she said.

On Sunday, it led to Exposition Boulevard, where she carefully avoided looking at the wall mural of herself as she ran past, and then to the Coliseum, where she won the gold medal in front of an adoring crowd.

This time, she did not celebrate alone.

IAN DRYDEN / Los Angeles Times

Running far ahead of the pack, Joan Benoit heads down Exposition Boulevard toward the Coliseum.

RUNNER

Continued from page 65

protects the athletes from themselves?

"If it had been a Canadian athlete, I wouldn't have let that happen," said Doug Clement, Canadian team doctor. "There were tears in my eyes. I was saying, 'My God, what a mess this is.' It was the dilemma of all time. Do you stop her or do you let her go and have blood on your hands?"

Second-place finisher Grete Waitz called the incident a tragedy. "What her body went through the last three or four miles will take a long time to recover from," she said. "I don't think she realized where she was. I don't like to watch."

Andersen-Schiess wasn't sure what should have been done. "I don't really know," she said. "I'd probably have been upset (if she had been helped before finishing). If you're that close, I don't think it makes much difference. They could have stopped me on the track and I still would have had the heatstroke."

Olympic medical officials said they had made the right choice in letting her stagger on. "It's our policy not to stop the athlete unless we feel her health is in danger," said Dr. Richard Greenspun, chief medical officer for track and field and one of the doctors on the scene. "None of us had the opinion that she was in danger and we had a dozen doctors on the (Coliseum) floor."

Among them were three medical officials who ran the last 400 meters with Andersen-Schiess, among them Red Hunter. "As long as we felt she was moving forward, looking around, we thought she should be allowed to continue," he said. "It had to be the most courageous thing I've ever seen."

Andersen-Schiess' husband, American citizen Dick Andersen, said he would have stopped his wife had he been in the infield.

"Because of personal attachment, I probably would have tried to take her off the course," he said. "But that doesn't mean that was right."

The irony is that Andersen-Schiess has made her mark in running with her stamina. She is the world masters champion of both the 10-kilometers and 25-kilometers and won the California International Marathon in Sacramento in December.

Still, she has a history of hot-weather trouble. She collapsed after three miles (about halfway) in the Continental Homes 10-kilometer race in Phoenix in March, and did not finish.

"I guess some people are more susceptible to it," she said. "In Phoenix, I was not acclimatized to the heat. I was hoping here that I would be more acclimatized." She trained for only two weeks in Southern California before the Olympics.

Still, she said it wasn't the temperatures that were her demons Sunday, ranging as they did between 66 at the 8 a.m. start and 76 at the finish, but the humidity—between 70% and 95% during the race.

Marathon director Bill Bedford said, however, that the overcast skies Sunday made for easy running conditions. "We couldn't ask for better conditions," he said.

What happened to Andersen-Schiess then? Dr. Gerald Finerman, head of the UCLA village medical center, said she may have underestimated how much fluid her body required to run 26-plus miles. "The smart runners will drink fluids, particularly before the race," he said.

Andersen-Schiess said she had done that. "I drank a lot the day before the race, on the morning of the race and during the race, too," she said.

Her mistake, if any, might have been missing the last aid station along the route. "I don't know where it was," she said. "I just missed it."

With two kilometers to go, she said she started to feel wobbly. "There was nobody there to watch."

From that point on, her mind was capricious. "I guess I just went on reflexes," she said.

But it was not just Andersen-Schiess who suffered from the heat Sunday. Runners who didn't finish were America's Julie Isphording, Japan's Akema Masuda, New Zealand's Anne Audain, Canada's Jacqueline Gareau, who won on this course at the L.A. International Marathon last winter, Honduras' Leda Diaz De Cano, and Nigeria's Ifeoma Mbanugo.

They did not make it. Andersen-Schiess did.

For all the talk, there remains that. She did finish and all the world watched her fight off the hallucinations and the fire in doing it.

"Yes," Gabriela Andersen-Schiess said, "but that's not the kind of publicity I was hoping to get."

ASHFORD

Continued from page 65

had dreamed of winning for so long.

"At first it didn't hit," Ashford said. "Then, when Bob Hersh (the announcer) said that I had set an Olympic record, it hit me. I had run faster than anyone in the Olympic Games. I was stunned. Then, when I was on the victory stand and I saw that gold medal . . ." Ashford was seemingly in control of the race all the way. She gradually accelerated and pulled away from the field to win by about 1½ meters. Her U.S. teammate, Alice Brown, was second in 11.13, with Jamaica's Merlene Ottey-Page third in 11.16. American Jeanette Bolden was fourth in 11.25.

There is, perhaps, no one on the American team who has hungered so for recognition and a gold medal. Or anyone who has worked so hard to earn it.

Ashford was the best sprinter in the world in 1979, when she won the 100 and 200 in the World Cup at Montreal. She beat the best, too, the East Germans—Marlies Gohr and Marita Koch.

She was ready for gold at Moscow, but the boycott dashed her hopes. Then, she pulled a muscle and didn't even try out for the team that was staying home. The boycott was a downer for her.

But she came back to set a world record of 10.79 at Colorado Springs last summer and was primed to meet the East Germans again and claim a gold medal at the World Championships at Helsinki, Finland.

It wasn't to be. She strained a muscle before the competition, got through the qualifying heats and then pulled up and pitched to the track in the final of the 100 with a pulled hamstring in her right leg.

She recovered from that injury and disappointment and trained carefully for the U.S. trials. She passed up the indoor season.

Things were going well for her in the trials when she pulled a muscle again in her right leg, but not the same place. She barely won the 100 final with her leg heavily taped. Then, she pulled up in a 200 heat, not wanting to risk further injury but taking away an opportunity of winning three gold medals in the Olympics—100, 200 and 400-meter relay.

Another rehabilitation period. And the question lingered, would Evelyn be ready for the Olympics? She proved Sunday that she was.

Ashford said that her leg doesn't bother her now and that she'd like to get three gold medals. But she'll have to settle for another gold in the sprint relay.

JOE KENNEDY / Los Angeles Times

Evelyn Ashford is a clear winner as she crosses the finish line in the women's 100 meters. Second was U.S. teammate Alice Brown (nearest camera). Ashford's time was 10.97.

"We're going to win. We set an American record on this track (United States-East Germany dual meet in 1983)," she said.

Ashford was beaten by Gohr in the 100 in that meet and couldn't get even for the defeat because of her injury at Helsinki.

She was asked if she had something to prove against the East Germans.

"I like competition, and the East Germans are good competition and a challenge," Ashford said. "But I don't feel I have anything to prove. I have the world record, and I'm the Olympic champion. I'd like to meet them. It would be fun.

"I have more races in me, and I look for some fast races in Europe."

Ashford, 27, had said that she hoped that fame and fortune awaited her after winning a gold medal.

It might. But right now, she was just relieved that it was over, that she had accomplished her dual goals—a world record and an Olympic gold medal.

She admitted that there was "fear in her heart" as she came back from her latest injury.

"I didn't want to start a trend of being injured," she said. "I didn't have a history of that."

Brown was skeptical that Ashford could come back so quickly from her leg injury.

"If she really pulled her hamstring, she couldn't come back and compete like she did today," Brown said.

Ashford said the injury was not as severe as the one she incurred in Helsinki, but she didn't want to take any unecessary risks.

Bolden and Ashford embraced after the 100, and Canada's Angela Bailey, who finished sixth, said:

"I'm happy for Evelyn. She finally got her gold."

Ashford broke the Olympic record of 11.01 set by West Germany's Annegret Richter in the 100 semifinals at Montreal. Ashford was fifth in the final. She was just coming on the world scene at that time.

Ashford looked sharp earlier in the day in the semifinals, winning her heat under control in 11.03. It was the fastest time in the semifinals and set the stage for the final.

"I wanted to get out of the blocks hard, and I got the impression I did," she said. "But I didn't feel in control. My legs were moving too fast for my body. It was nothing exciting."

Ashford was composed when she said that. On the victory stand, when the tears came, the emotion was obvious.

As for her future plans, she said: "I'm on a roll. I'll continue to compete as long as I have speed."

Ashford said that Wilma Rudolph, the famed American sprinter, was a role model for her and that she wanted to bring the gold medal in the 100 back to America.

An American woman sprinter hadn't previously won the 100 in the Olympics since Wyomia Tyus did it in 1968.

And now Ashford has reached the plateau she has always sought. Nobody can take that away from her now.

WOMEN'S

Track

■ 100 METERS

1. Evelyn Ashford (U.S.)
2. Alice Brown (U.S.)
3. Marlene Ottey-Page (Jamaica)

THE MEDALISTS

MOSES

Continued from page 65

Schmid, was in this final. He did it for the third time earlier this summer, but he admitted Sunday night that he was running for the silver medal in this final.

He is the only man to beat Moses since the 1976 Olympics, crossing the finish line first in a meet at Berlin in August 1977. But Moses since has beaten Schmid in nine finals.

The race Sunday found Schmid also chasing another American, Danny Harris of Perris, Calif. In only his 16th intermediate hurdles race, the 18-year-old Iowa State freshman defensive back held off Schmid at the finish line for the silver medal.

Harris ran 48.13, behind his world junior record of 48.02, to Schmid's 48.19. Sweden's Sven Nylander, who attended SMU, was fourth in 48.97. American Tranel Hawkins, who, like Moses was raised in Dayton, Ohio, finished sixth in 49.42.

Schmid later protested the result, claiming that Harris interfered with his progress when they were coming off the eighth of the 10 hurdles.

"I went over the hurdle I thought pretty well," Schmid said. "I was hindered . . .

"He hit me on the right side of my chest. I think I could have lost my balance for a few hundredths of a second. It was not made on purpose. It was in a normal movement of going over the hurdle."

Officials disallowed the protest but not before the awards ceremony was delayed for an hour.

Schmid did not appear disappointed in the decision, saying that he was grateful to place among the first three.

"I wasn't sure if I could win a medal because I saw the American trials, and the Americans were running so well," said Schmid, second to Moses in the world championships last summer.

"It could have been a silver, but the gold was impossible."

Harris also seemed to feel he had done the best he could considering that he has the misfortune of running the same event as Moses.

"I'm satisfied with the silver medal, and I'll be back in '88," he said.

There was a question in some minds whether the same could be said for Moses, 28. In a television interview following the final, he was asked whether he would be back on the track.

He said that he would not, probably thinking that the interviewer had been asking whether he would be back on the track before the end of the Olympics. There had been speculation at one time that he might run a leg for the U.S. 1,600-meter relay team.

THE MEDALISTS

MEN'S

Track

■ 400-METER HURDLES

1. Edwin Moses (U.S.)
2. Danny Harris (U.S.)
3. Harald Schmid (West Germany)

But rumors began circulating that he had announced his retirement.

Even before he could be asked a question at the post-race press conference, he shot that one down.

"First of all, I've been hearing rumors that this was my last race, and that's not true," he said. "That's absolutely not true. What more can I say?"

He should not have had to say anything following this race, which he ran conservatively over the final two hurdles and still won by more than three yards.

His only scare came before the gun. Even with all of his experience, he admitted he was nervous.

"I try to relax and not put pressure on myself," he said. "I'm not saying I don't feel pressure because I do, maybe more than anyone else."

He said he heard the photographers' cameras and started out of the blocks early. He had the same difficulty at the U.S. Olympic trials in June, when he was charged with a false start. It was not ruled a false start this time.

"Had I been pressed, I could have run a much faster race," he said. "At no time did I feel a threat."

The feeling that he did have when it was over was relief. The humidity had drained him, slowing his victory lap to little more than a trot before he found his wife, Myrella, and his mother and embraced them. He dedicated the race to his father, who died after a lengthy illness last December.

He had been waiting for this victory a long time. He would have been favored to win his second gold medal in Moscow in 1980, but the U.S. boycott deprived him of the opportunity. Nothing could stop him this time.

"After waiting eight years, and not being able to go in '80, this is a great relief," he said. "I'm very lucky to be here eight years later."

His fortune is the misfortune of his competitors. But he knows that as long as he remains in the sport he will face new challengers, such as Harris and Hawkins, and, of course, Schmid.

Asked if he believes he will ever beat Moses again, Schmid said: "The chance is always there. I don't think I'll ever give it up."

GABRIELA ANDERSEN-SCHIESS / A CLOSER LOOK

The Reaction

Could Happen to Anyone, Say Those Involved

By MARLENE CIMONS, *Times Staff Writer*

For those who fought long and hard to have the women's marathon included in the Olympic Games, the sight of Switzerland's Gabriela Andersen-Schiess struggling to finish was painful and frightening.

It was a sight they also said they hoped would not be distorted, or used to shut off further opportunities for women athletes.

They spoke of the 1928 Games, when most of the women who ran the 800 meters collapsed when it was over—and the "long" race was banished from the Games as a result. It has since been restored.

"I have faith, however, that people will see this as an isolated incident that could happen as likely to a man as to a woman," said Jacqueline Hansen, executive director of the International Runners Committee, a group whose goal it is to have a full slate of women's events included in the Olympics.

"I hate to think that this could hurt," she said. "This is no longer a testing ground. It could happen to any runner anywhere."

Julie Brown, who passed Andersen-Schiess during those final moments on the Coliseum track, agreed.

"She ran hard and obviously had problems in the heat," Brown said. "I had problems too. Other women had problems. But other women ran really well. People should focus on that. I think what people should see is that she didn't want to quit. She took it to the limit. It was the first women's Olympic marathon and it put a lot of determination into women."

America's premier middle-distance runner, Mary Decker, echoed Brown.

"We're fortunate we've only seen one incident like this up until now," she said. "Just because it happened in the women's marathon, and just because it happened to a woman, doesn't mean it can't happen to the men. And it doesn't mean they were wrong in putting the women's marathon into the Olympics."

Joe Henderson, former executive director of the International Runners Committee, said it was unfortunate that the incident was featured so prominently on television.

"That will be in people's minds because it was one of the last things they saw," he said. "But that kind of thing happens repeatedly in men's marathons. To indict women's marathoning would be unfair. Women's marathoning will not be permanently damaged by this. The important thing is that (Andersen-Schiess) not be permanently damaged by it."

Dr. Joan Ullyot, a sports medicine specialist and marathoner, said she thought that unlikely.

"She appeared to be suffering from heat exhaustion," said Ullyot, who watched it on television. "I think they were correct not to stop her. They tried to stop her, but she waved them off."

This, Ullyot said, was a clear sign that Andersen-Schiess was not disoriented and had not begun to lose her mental faculties—the danger point.

"Motor functions are the first to go," Ullyot said. "If she had gone in the wrong direction, or had fallen flat, that would be another thing. I thought she was more with it mentally than physically."

Ullyot added, "She didn't want to stop. And if somebody goes 26 miles in an Olympic marathon and is determined to finish, damn it, you let her do it."

United Press International

Struggling to stay on her feet, Gabriela Andersen-Schiess staggers toward the finish line.

Medical Analysis

Runner Is Lucky That It Was Only Heat Prostration

By HARRY NELSON, *Times Medical Writer*

If Swiss marathon runner Gabriela Andersen-Schiess had truly suffered heatstroke, rather than less serious heat prostration, during the women's marathon Sunday, she would have run the risk of brain damage or even death, medical authorities say.

Heatstroke is characterized by a substantial rise in body temperature. Temperatures as high as 110 degrees are not uncommon, a recent report by the Atlanta-based Center for Disease Control says. Such high temperatures can damage not only the brain, but nearly every other organ system in the body.

A heatstroke patient appears confused, and may go into a stupor and unconsciousness as the body temperature rises.

According to some authorities, heatstroke is second only to head and spinal injuries as the leading cause of death in athletes nationwide.

Dehydration is a key factor in causing heatstroke. Physiologists and sports medicine experts have reported that victims of dehydration may lose as much as 10% of bodyweight because of the body's attempt to counterbalance overheating by producing large amounts of sweat.

Such a massive loss of body fluid severely limits subsequent sweating and places dangerous demands on the circulation of blood.

According to a policy statement of the American College of Sports Medicine, even in weather conditions in which the temperatures and humidity are moderate but there is no cloud cover, the risk of overheating is "a serious threat to highly motivated distance runners."

The statement says that "organizational personnel should reserve the right to stop runners who exhibit clear signs of heatstroke or heat exhaustion."

The "mild dehydration" or heat prostration that Andersen-Schiess is said to have suffered resulted from the body's failure to adjust to the dilation of blood vessels in the skin to carry away the heat.

As with heatstroke, the patient is listless and may even become unconscious. The body temperature is normal, however, and the blood pressure is only slightly above normal. Unlike heatstroke, where the patient often has stopped sweating, persons with heat prostration sweat profusely.

The treatment for heatstroke is to immerse the person immediately in ice water. He or she must be watched continuously during two or three days of bed rest.

With the less serious heat prostration, the main treatment is to put the individual in a cool environment and administer intravenous salt solutions.

Gold Medal Goes Back to Finland

By JULIE CART,
Times Staff Writer

Just as Finnish citizens are waking up to a balmy midsummer's day, the news will be broadcast to that javelin-crazed nation that—for the first time in 20 years—Finland has won a gold medal in the javelin.

Arto Haerkoenen, who seemed as relieved as he was elated, beat a field thinned by upsets and Sunday night became the Olympic champion with a throw of 284 feet, 8 inches.

Somebody forgot to tell David Ottley of Britain that javelin throwing is only popular in countries that border the North Sea. The stevedore's son gave himself a silver medal for his 29th birthday, with 281-3. Kenth Eldebrink of Sweden won the bronze with 274-8.

Haerkoenen nearly caused heart failure to the sizable Finnish contingent in the Coliseum by starting slowly. His first throw was ruled flat, and he was seventh after the second round. Not until his third throw did he unleash a toss over 80 meters (262 feet). That throw went 276-8. He has thrown 303-2.

"I had difficulties with my first two throws," Haerkoenen said. "But when I did 84 meters, I relaxed."

Relaxation is something a Finnish javelin thrower has little chance to pursue. Like his countrywoman, women's javelin world record-holder Tiina Lillak, Haerkoenen gets his speed work in by dashing from reporters. His former playboy image added to his mystique, making the 25-year-old nearly irresistible to the Finnish public.

"It was very difficult to be in Finland because the Finnish people love sports so much," he said. "I hope everyone feels good because I feel great. I have been training six hours a day. I train in the winter by cross-country skiing. But no ski jumping."

The competition was subdued, with numerous throwers bombing out in the early rounds. Two casualties were former world record-holder Tom Petranoff of the United States and U.S. trials winner Duncan Atwood. Three other favorites, Raimo Manninen of Finland, Klaus Tafelmeir of West Germany and Einar Vilhjalmsson of Iceland failed to advance past Saturday's preliminary rounds.

Atwood had pulled a groin muscle in the qualifying round and aggravated the injury on his second throw. On that throw, he ran aggressively down the runway, but his leg crumpled under him at the release.

Petranoff had his own problems. His first two throws were flat, and his last throw was 257-3, exactly one foot farther than Atwood's best effort. With that throw, Petranoff knocked Atwood out of the final and moved into eighth place. On his next throw, Laslo Babits of Canada threw 264-8 to keep Petranoff out of the finals.

Ironically, it was Atwood who knocked Petranoff off the 1980 team. On his final throw, Atwood equaled Petranoff's effort and made the team because he had a better second-best throw.

Despite the fact that he already knew where he stood, Petranoff couldn't resist one quick peek at the judge's clipboard, just to be sure. At that moment, the "Star Spangled Banner" blared out for Evelyn Ashford's medal ceremony. With his hand over his heart and his eyes on the leader board, Petranoff saw the bad news.

"I don't really have any excuses, I felt pretty good," Petranoff said. "My first throw was a nervous throw, then my second throw was flat. That left me with only one. All I can say is thank God the Olympics are over. Life goes on. I'm looking forward to some rest. And good luck to the rest of the throwers."

For Atwood, his injury brought an end to a remarkable late-season improvement. He said he had thrown 285 last week, and was ready for a good throw here.

"Javelin is a complicated event," Atwood said. "If you're not totally glued together, you'll come unstuck. You have to learn to take the bitter with the rancid."

Ottley's surprise finish thrilled him, and may bring the event to the same prominence in England as it has in Finland.

"I've always admired the Finns, my heroes were Finnish throwers," the outgoing Ottley said. "The truth is, I'd like to be a Finn. Don't get me wrong—it's their attitude towards the javelin I like."

This relieved British journalists, who had chimed together for a rousing chorus of "Happy Birthday, Mate."

Petranoff appeared to handle his upset with equanimity, but perhaps his parting shot was a needed tension-reliever, and may well reflect the sentiments of other throwers—"At least I got out of the doping control!"

STEVE FONTANINI / Los Angeles Times

A member of Canada's eight-oared crew, which won the gold medal in an upset Sunday at Lake Casitas, shows the crowd who's No. 1.

U.S. Pair Wins Gold in Sculls

By BILL CHRISTINE,
Times Staff Writer

OJAI—In June, Brad Alan Lewis and Paul Enquist, who were trying to make the U.S. Olympic rowing team, weren't doing many things right at coach Harry Parker's sculling camp at Hanover, N.H.

"Every time I'd try to do something," Enquist said, "I'd tighten up. I just couldn't relax. It was frustrating."

Lewis, the 6-4, 29-year-old rower from Corona del Mar who made America's Olympic team in 1980 in the quadruple-oared sculls, was having the same problems. "I had a bad camp," Lewis said. "I deserved to get my walking papers."

Parker ranked Lewis eighth at the end of the camp, which was still good for a sculling berth, but was the equivalent of being a spare since there were only seven active spots—single, double and quadruple. Enquist's position was even bleaker. Parker ranked the 6-6, 28-year-old son of a Seattle salmon fisherman, ninth. He may as well have been ranked 99th.

A couple of days later, Lewis, who had decided to leave the camp, called Enquist. "Why don't we get together and still see if we can make the team in the doubles?" Lewis asked.

It was not an unreasonable proposition. The doubles boat that Parker picked would still have to win in open trials at the end of the month at Princeton, N.J., and Lewis and Enquist had finished sixth as a team in the 1983 world championships, even though they both thought they didn't row particularly well.

Lewis and Enquist won at Princeton. And Sunday, before 10,000 fans, they were victorious again at Lake Casitas as the United States won two gold medals, five silvers and a bronze in the two days of Olympic rowing finals.

The U.S. women, including the eight-oared crew that gave America its first rowing gold since 1964, started the weekend Saturday with a first and two seconds. Sunday, the men tacked on a gold, three silvers and a bronze. The five medals were the most by an American men's team since the United States won five at Amsterdam in 1928.

On a knoll on the outskirts of Lake Casitas, Parker, the esteemed coach from Harvard, appeared in the Lewis-Enquist boat tent to congratulate the scullers. "After a thousand (meters), I said to myself that it's going, it's working," Parker told them. Lewis and Enquist just grinned.

They didn't gloat, and no sheepishness was shown by Parker, who last week had said: "There's always hindsight, of course. If there was a mistake, it might have been taking the camp boat (Joe Bouscaren and Charlie Altekruse) to Europe before the trials. The fact that Lewis and Enquist are here shows what depth we had on the team this year."

Belgium's boat, with Pierre-Marie Deloof and Dirk Crois, led for most of the race, but Lewis and Enquist, rowing in the outside lane, caught them and won in a time of 6:36.87 for the 2,000-meter event. Belgium was ¼-length back.

"There was a slight headwind out there," Lewis said. "But that helps rowers who are bigger and who have worked on weights like we have to build up our strength. Give Harry (Parker) credit. This was a three-man effort."

Enquist knows his place in sculling. "As a single, I couldn't row my way out of a wet paper bag," he said.

THE MEDALISTS

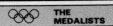

MEN'S

Rowing

SINGLE SCULLS
1. Pertti Karppinen (Finland)
2. Michael Kolbe (West Germany)
3. Robert Mills (Canada)

DOUBLE SCULLS
1. United States
2. Belgium
3. Yugoslavia

QUADRUPLE SCULLS
1. West Germany
2. Australia
3. Canada

PAIR OARS WITH COXSWAIN
1. Italy
2. Romania
3. United States

PAIR OARS WITHOUT COXSWAIN
1. Romania
2. Spain
3. Norway

FOUR OARS WITH COXSWAIN
1. Britain
2. United States
3. New Zealand

FOUR OARS WITHOUT COXSWAIN
1. New Zealand
2. United States
3. Denmark

EIGHT OARS WITH COXSWAIN
1. Canada
2. United States
3. Australia

NOTES

When Joan Benoit reached the peristyle end of the Coliseum on her victory lap in the marathon Sunday, a woman dressed in red running shirt and shorts leaped onto the track and began chasing the marathon champion.

The woman was immediately grabbed by security guards, who began ushering her back toward her seat. But when Benoit noticed the commotion, she interrupted her victory lap and took the woman by the hand. They embraced.

"I love you," Benoit said.

The woman was Lynn Petronella. A former marathon runner from Long Island, she said she has been one of Benoit's close friends for the last four years.

Petronella said she sent Benoit a pair of "Eye of the Tiger" earrings last week. "Eye of the Tiger" was the theme song from the movie "Rocky III."

"I was hoping she would wear them during the race because I wanted to be with her," Petronella said.

She was disappointed when Benoit told her Saturday she could not wear the earrings while running because they were too heavy.

But when they met after the race Sunday, Benoit pointed to her left earlobe. "I wore one," she said.

Petronella later discovered that her ticket was good only for the morning session at the Coliseum, which meant that she did not have a seat to see the awards ceremony for the marathon Sunday afternoon.

Benoit's mother, father and three brothers also were in the same predicament. Like Petronella, they had assumed that the awards ceremony would take place immediately after the race.

But Los Angeles Olympic Organizing Committee officials gave the Benoits special credentials that allowed them to see the ceremony. After Petronella explained her situation, she also was given a credential.

"Even though I'm not a Benoit," Petronella said, "I feel like one."

—RANDY HARVEY

□

The French, proud and even haughty over their judo prospects ever since the many-splendored Thierry Rey won the lightweight title in the '80 Games, have had no quarrel with Sports Illustrated's prediction of seven French medals in the eight weight divisions. If anything, SI's tally, they thought, was a little modest.

Wiry Guy Delvingt, in fact, was considered Rey's rightful heir. When asked for a thumbnail sketch of the 132-pounder, Jean-Francois Agogue of the national sports daily L'Equipe volunteered that Delvingt, one of six brothers from Orleans, was one of the most single-minded young men he'd ever encountered.

"All he *does* is judo," said Agogue. "With Guy, it's judo, judo, judo dodo (roughly: judo, judo, judo, beddie-bye)."

After New Yorker Ed Liddie smashed Delvingt to the mat in an improbable upset for the bronze medal, the French press delegation was momentarily stunned.

Finally, Agogue broke the silence.

"Dodo," he said.

—DICK RORABACK

□

Gold medal-winning gymnast Mary Lou Retton, when asked how she will handle all of the adulation and attention that will come her way with her gold medal, says with her typical enthusiasm: "I'm going to love it. I like all the exposure. I think it's neat."

Winning the gold was a "longtime dream. I think all athletes deserve it (the attention) for all the hard work they put in," she says.

Retton, who spends most of her time training, so much so that she stopped going to school and took mail correspondence courses, says of her lack of social life:

"Here I am Olympic champion—boys can wait, not too long, but they can wait."

Does she miss being a normal teen-ager? "I don't miss it at all. I'm lucky to have the opportunity and the talent (to compete in the Olympics)," she says.

Retton does take some time to relax between workouts in Houston, however. She watches "The Guiding Light" every day without fail on television. "That's my soap opera. I can't go a day without it," she says.

—ELLIOTT TEAFORD

□

U.S. light-heavyweight boxer Evander Holyfield said after a victory Saturday night that American boxers have more pressure on them to win than other boxing teams here, because so much more is expected of them by the loud, pro-American crowds.

Pressure?

How about the pressure on Swedish light-heavyweight Christer Corpi Saturday night? Corpi was boxing Jean Paul Nanga of Cameroon. Corpi lost, 4-1. But making defeat particularly painful for Corpi was the fact Sweden's King Carl Gustaf XVI and Queen Silvia were in the second row.

—EARL GUSTKEY

□

Like so many others, Tracy Caulkins watched the efforts of Joan Benoit Sunday, and she was gratified by what she saw.

"This has been a great Olympics for women," said Caulkins a few hours after Benoit won the first women's marathon. "You saw what Joan did, and we have (gymnastics star) Mary Lou Retton and (middle-distance runner) Mary Decker.

"I think we can all be role models for young athletes and help them compete."

Caulkins knows something about being a role model since she has been the most high-profile American female swimmer for years. Her swimming career ended with these Olympics.

In 1982, she passed Johnny Weissmuller as the most-honored individual in the history of United States swimming. She retires with 48 individual national titles to 36 for Weissmuller.

Caulkins won two individual gold medals during the weeklong swimming competition, a fitting conclusion to her career.

"Now I know I can get up in the morning and go to the beach," Caulkins said. "I can do anything I want. And I don't have to swim a stroke. It will be a different feeling."

□

Anyone still doubting that judo is one of the last strictly amateur sports in the U.S. wasn't at opening day Saturday.

Spotted moseying around the main entrance at Cal State LA was Frank Fullerton, president of U.S. Judo Inc., the No. 1 judo official in America.

Fullerton hovered about a souvenir stand, then popped for an official program.

Cost him $3, too.

—DICK RORABACK

□

When David Grylls had his toestrap come loose in the 4,000-meter team pursuit final—forcing the U.S. team to continue with only three riders—it wasn't the worst misfortune to occur to him this year.

Last February, the San Diego rider was pedaling alongside a team van when he fell. Grylls slid partway beneath the van, and it ran over his legs, slicing one and bruising the other. Surprisingly, neither was broken.

When Grylls returned to action, his teammates called him "Speed Bumps."

—SHAV GLICK

□

At least West German women's volleyball Coach Ryszard Niemczyk is a realist, if not a dreamer.

When West Germany was named to replace East Germany in the Olympic tournament, he took one look at the schedule and began pointing toward fifth place.

In their first two matches, the West Germans lost to China and the United States. On the day his team met China, Niemczyk got his players up at 5:30 a.m. and sent them out running.

"Our first two matches were practice matches," Niemczyk said. "We saw long ago that our best chance would be against Brazil."

The West Germans beat Brazil in their third match, and Sunday they beat Canada in the fifth-place semifinals. They'll meet South Korea Tuesday at noon for fifth place.

Just as Niemczyk planned it.

—JERRY CROWE

□

Mark Gorski and Nelson Vails, who finished 1-2 in cycling's match sprint at the Olympic velodrome, were talking about the future.

Both indicated that they would continue riding through 1986, when the World Championships will be held in the United States for the first time—in Colorado. Gorski said he probably would retire after that.

"Good, that means I'll win the gold medal in the 1988 Olympics," Vails said. "How can I lose; Mark will be my coach. Right, Mark?"

"If you say so, I'll be there," Gorski chuckled.

—SHAV GLICK

PATRICK DOWNS / Los Angeles Times

Ed Burke, at 44, gives it a whirl but fails to qualify for finals in the hammer throw.

Burke, 44, Smiling, but Dream Is Gone

By MIKE LITTWIN, *Times Staff Writer*

Somebody got the ending all wrong.

The comeback story of Ed Burke, the middle-aged hammer thrower, and his coach/wife Shirley had grabbed America by its collective heartstrings and threatened not to let go.

When Burke, at 44, made the Olympic team in June, 16 years after his last Olympic competition, we had found a hero. The Burkes suddenly were in demand, ready-made celebrities. Ed and Shirley were on TV more than Laverne and Shirley.

Then, in a tribute to middle-age America, Ed was chosen to carry the American flag at the Opening Ceremony.

And all for what? For Burke to bomb out in the qualifying round Sunday morning at the Coliseum. He couldn't even make the final 12, much less go for a medal.

But don't bother to break out the hankies. Ed was all smiles.

"We always have a little family meeting beforehand to discuss these crisis times," Burke said. "We figured if I come out of the final, great. If not, that's OK too."

Sure, he wanted to make the final. He even dreamed about getting a medal. However, his throw of 221-6 was well below par.

The dream was over.

The fans weren't letting go, however. As Burke left the stadium floor, fans were chanting his name. One gave him flowers.

"To make the final would have made me satisfied," Burke said. "To throw farther than I had thrown before, that gives you the crescendo—I'm happy, the family is happy."

United Press International

Evelyn Ashford flashes across the finish line, winning the gold medal in the 100-meter dash in an Olympic record time of 10.97. Second place went to Alice Brown, also of the U.S. After the race Ashford is hugged by teammate Jeanette Bolden.

JAYNE KAMIN / Los Angeles Times

Edwin Moses of the U.S. also strikes gold as he runs away with the men's 400-meter hurdles final in a time of 47.76 to make it his 105th consecutive win. Moses won the gold in the 1976 Montreal Olympics in the same event.

Designed By
Tom Trapnell

JAYNE KAMIN / Los Angeles Times

JAYNE KAMIN / Los Angeles Times

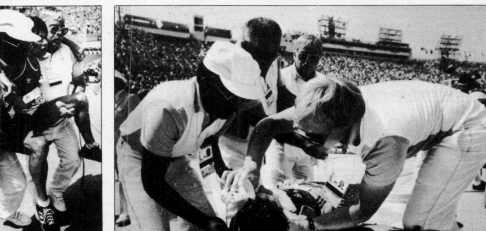

PATRICK DOWNS / Los Angeles Times

JAY DICKMAN / Los Angeles Times

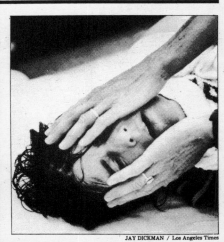

JAY DICKMAN / Los Angeles Times

Marathon runner Gabriele Andersen-Schiess of Switzerland is attended to by medical personnel after collapsing at the finish line in the Coliseum. She finished 37th in the race.

Los Angeles Times

Part VIII

OLYMPICS '84

DAY 11

Going flat out—Canada's Sylvie Bernier reaches for the gold in three-meter springboard event. She beat runner-up Kelly McCormick and Chris Seufert of the United States.

DAVE GATLEY / Los Angeles Times

Lewis Continues Gold Rush With Long Jump Win

By RANDY HARVEY, *Times Staff Writer*

Carl Lewis had another of his Olympic moments Monday night at the Coliseum. He did not make the most of this one, for which many among the crowd may never forgive him, but he has plenty more to go before the end of the week. So what the heck?

After winning the 100 meters by the largest margin in Olympic history Saturday, thus earning his first gold medal, Lewis grabbed an American flag, ran a victory lap or two and had the crowd in the palm of his hand through it all.

But when it was announced Monday night that Lewis had won his second gold medal, this one in the long jump, he was startled to hear that some of those cheers of two days earlier had turned to boos.

It was not difficult to determine the reason. Many people among the crowd of 85,870 had paid as much as $50 to see an evening session that had Lewis as the headliner. When

the world's best long jumper jumped only twice, one of them a foul, some of those people no doubt felt they had been robbed. It was like paying $50 to hear Frank Sinatra sing one song.

But Lewis does it his way.

Considering that only four people have ever cleared 28 feet in the long jump, Lewis' one and only legal jump of 28-0¼ was not so bad. Any of the other 11 competitors in the final, only one of whom has cleared 28, would have been ecstatic to have it.

The next best jumps Monday night were the two of 27-0½ by Australia's Gary Honey and Italy's Giovanni Evangelisti, neither of whom had ever had a legal jump of over 27 feet before.

Honey was awarded the silver medal because his second-best jump of 26-10 was better than Evangelisti's of 26-6½. American

Please see LEWIS, page 71

Brazil's Cruz Beats Coe, Jones in 800

By BILL SHIRLEY,
Times Staff Writer

Joaquim Cruz knew it was going to be a hard race—and it was. It was also a fast one, the third fastest 800 meters ever run by a human.

The young man from Taguatinga, Brazil, became the second-fastest 800-meter racer in history Monday at the Coliseum when he won the Olympic Games gold medal in 1 minute 43 seconds.

The time on a warm evening was an Olympic record, and only Sebastian Coe of Britain has run 800 meters faster than the slim, long-striding Brazilian. Coe, who has held the world record of 1:41.73 since 1981, finished second to gain his second straight silver medal. Coe also ran the second-fastest 800 of 1:42.33 in 1979.

Earl Jones, 20, of Inkster, Mich., and Eastern Michigan University, finished third, joining Coe in a futile chase down the stretch in pursuit of Cruz. Coe and Jones—and the other five runners—in fact, were racing for silver and bronze medals. Cruz had won the gold as soon as he slammed his foot on the accelerator coming into the stretch.

Please see CRUZ, page 71

Ovett in Hospital —Out of 1,500?

British star runner Steve Ovett was admitted to Orthopaedic Hospital Monday night with what Dr. David Archibald described as mild lung disease. The British team doctor said that Ovett, world record-holder in the 1,500 meters, was not expected to be able to compete in that event.

Ovett, defending Olympic champion in the 800 meters, finished last in the 800 Monday at the Coliseum and was then diagnosed as having broncho-spasms with hyperventilation. He was given intravenous feeding to increase his fluid supply.

Ovett is expected to be released from the hospital this morning. The 1,500-meter heats begin Thursday.

SKEETER HAGLER / Los Angeles Times

Carl Lewis is caught in mid-flight on first jump Monday night in long jump. His mark was 28-0¼, which turned out to be the winning jump, giving him his second gold medal of the Games.

Jim Murray

The Baryshnikov of the Barriers

I like to see Edwin Moses run the hurdles for the same reason I liked to see Rod Carew bat, Bing Crosby sing, Joe DiMaggio drift under a high fly, Joe Louis throw a left, Sammy Snead hit a drive, Swaps in the stretch. Palmer putt, Koufax with the hitter in a hole, Marcus Allen hit a line—or for that matter, a Swiss make a watch, an Arab sell a rug, a Manolete fight a bull or a Hemingway write about it, an Englishman do Shakespeare, or Roosevelt make a speech.

I love those guys who make it look easy. Who have that special combination of grace and talent that puts no strain at all on the viewer. They make it not a contest but a recital, a fugue for 10 hurdles by the artist. It's like watching Paderewski do the Moonlight Sonata or Heifetz do Bruch.

I'm getting so I don't like those guys whose hats fly off, whose faces look as if someone is holding lighted cigarettes to their feet, or who look as if they're going to die at the tape. I don't like those high-wire acts who pretend to slip, singers whose voices crack on the way to the high notes, and I hate it when they say, "And now, a stunt never before performed before a live audience anywhere!" I like to be able to say, "Watch this!" when Nolan Ryan breaks off a high hard one or Dempsey is measuring his man for the hook.

It's a principle called "empathy" and it has to do with identification. It's what makes "fans." That's not Sandy Koufax and Steve Garvey out there, that's you. The easier a performer makes it for you, the more you enjoy it. When he makes it hard, you go home exhausted, wrung out, emotionally drained. *You* are

the one who struggled through all those 3-and-2 counts, who had to foul seven off before you got the home run.

The great ones send you home relaxed and confident and with a new faith in yourself and a new outlook on life. The strainers put your teeth on edge, your nerves in a ball, and you want to go home and kick the cat and ask the world how anybody can drink this slop they call coffee nowadays?

Edwin Moses is one of the great virtuosos. You imagine Man o'War was like this. This modern Moses, this patriarch of the games Olympians play, comes on a track like Caesar inspecting the battlefield, a king trooping the guard. It's as if the other seven runners hadn't shown up. In a sense, they haven't.

Moses affably inspects the 10 hurdles, satisfies himself they are properly placed and heighted, like Paderewski checking the concert grand, Caruso testing the acoustics. He runs nonchalantly in place, strides out a few steps and then takes off over a hurdle or two.

The concert is ready. A little traveling music, maestro, the artist is on stage.

He could run the 400-meter hurdles in top hat and tails. It's like Muhammad Ali and George Chuvalo, a contest only if you consider the Johnstown Flood one. It's really just a complicated solo. When you see Baryshnikov dance, you're glad Tchaikowsky wrote.

Please see MURRAY, page 71

United Press International

Michael Jordan of the United States slams home 2 of his 14 points against West Germany.

Knight's Team Has Its Off Night, Wins by Only 11

By MARK HEISLER, *Times Staff Writer*

Like Uwes being led to the slaughter, the West Germans arrived for their appointment with the U.S. men's basketball team and trotted out a back door. The Americans led by 22 points early in the second half but by only 11 at the end. If there had been a spread, the Germans would have beaten it by at least 10 points.

The United States thus settled for a 78-67 victory Monday night over Uwe Blab, Uwe Brauer, Uwe Sauee and the rest of the Germans. The Germans became the first team to outscore the U.S. team in any half and the first to out-rebound them. What they won may have been only the battle of garbage time, but on the U.S. team, they pay off only on perfection.

In whatever style, the Americans advanced to the semifinals against the Canadians, whom they've already beaten by 21 points. Afterward, Canada's Jack Donohue said he believes that the only team here that could beat the United States is his. Wednesday, he gets his second chance.

The Germans go to the consolation round, a fate they accepted gracefully. They passed the ball around calmly for 20 seconds on their last possession before scoring, on a goal-tend against Michael Jordan.

Then they let Leon Wood dribble out the clock at the other end.

Coach Ralph Klein was asked later if this was going

Please see BASKETBALL, page 71

LEWIS

Continued from page 70

Larry Myricks, whose personal best of 28-1 would have won the gold medal, was nowhere close to his peak as he jumped 26-9¼ and finished fourth.

But Lewis has to live by a different standard than the others, his own. While no one else has cleared 28 feet more than once, Lewis has now done it 13 times.

His best is 28-10¼, close enough to Bob Beamon's 16-year-old Olympic and world record of 29-2½ to make him think that his next jump may be the one.

Lewis did not talk to reporters following his qualifying races in the 200 meters Monday morning, which he breezed through, but he did have a few words with one of his U.S. teammates, Thomas Jefferson.

"Carl said he felt a little sluggish this morning," Jefferson said. "But if he's feeling all right tonight, he said he'll go for Beamon's record on the first jump."

The first jump was the only legal one that Lewis took. He tried a second but fouled. He passed on his last four.

Afterward, in a radio interview, Lewis said: "This was probably the most difficult competition I've ever been in. Not because it's the Olympics but because we got going late because of the hammer throw."

The long jumpers could not begin their competition until the hammer throw was completed.

"It got cold very quickly," Lewis said. "It's a difficult thing. I was a little sore after the second jump, so I didn't want to risk it."

Even if one of his competitors had beaten Lewis' jump, he said he would not have returned to the competition.

"Maybe people don't realize how hard it is to run two 200s and then come back," he said.

But he promised to give a better, if not longer, show Wednesday in the semifinals and final of the 200 meters.

THE MEDALISTS

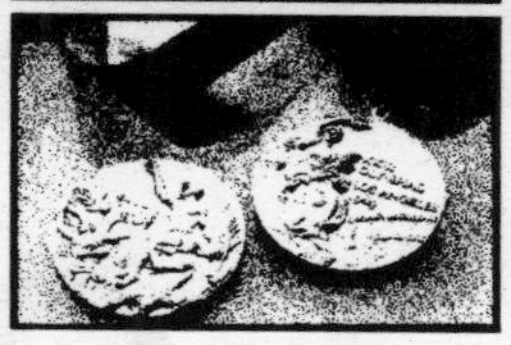

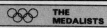

MEN'S

Track

■ LONG JUMP

1. Carl Lewis (U.S.)
2. Gary Honey (Australia)
3. Giovanni Evangelisti (Italy)

"I'm ready for one of the best races in my life," he said.

Asked if that meant he would challenge the world record of 19.72 seconds held by Italy's Pietro Mennea, Lewis said, "I think it's within me. If the opportunity is there, it's going to be here. The crowd has been very supportive, except for just a moment a few minutes ago."

A few minutes later, all was forgiven. As Lewis accepted his second gold medal during the awards ceremony, he was given a rousing ovation.

This might have been the easiest of the four gold medals Lewis is expected to win as he attempts to duplicate the performance of Jesse Owens at the 1936 Berlin Olympics.

In contrast, the long jump was the most difficult event for Owens in 1936. He fouled on his first two jumps, risking disqualification if he fouled on the third.

But a German long jumper, Luz Long, advised Owens to approach his third jump conservatively. He told Owens to move his mark back a few inches so that he would not come so close to the board on his takeoff. Owens accepted the advice, easily qualified for the final and won the gold medal. Long won the silver medal.

Lewis faced no such perils.

Even his competitors admitted that the competition for the gold medal was finished after Lewis' first jump. Continuing in the competition would have been just for show.

"I think Carl Lewis kills any other person's chances," Evangelisti said. "In fact, today's competition was nice from the second jump on for all the other competitors."

That sentiment was echoed by Honey, who injured his back in the qualifying Sunday and was satisfied just to be competing. "I couldn't care less if Carl wants to pass every time," he said. "It would give us a chance."

Honey and Evangelisti were the ones who provided the suspense, although it was silver medal suspense. Evangelisti was in second place until the third jump, when Honey passed him. On the fifth jump, Myricks also passed him.

But on his sixth and final jump, Evangelisti had the best jump of his life at 27-0½. He had visions of the silver medal in his head until the next man up, Honey, matched him.

The only other man who could have challenged them for a medal, Myricks, was the last man to jump. The crowd was solidly behind him as he began his approach, but his steps went awry and he fouled.

"I had a bad day at the wrong time," Myricks said.

Myricks has been critical of Lewis in the past, but he was not this time.

"He probably wouldn't have surpassed the record anyway," Myricks said. "He didn't look like he looks when he's jumping 28-10. It started to cool off.

"I don't blame him for not jumping. He's got a few more races to go, and he's had a few already.

"Of course, I can understand the crowd's viewpoint. They paid quite a bit of money to be here. So from that standpoint, maybe he should have jumped."

CRUZ

Continued from page 70

Coe was timed in 1:43.64, Jones in 1:43.83.

Steve Ovett, Coe's teammate and the 1980 Olympic champion, never got into the race and didn't beat anybody, finishing in 1:52.28. At 28, he appeared washed up only a year after breaking the 1,500-meter record.

After the race, Coe, who is 27, walked over to Ovett and said: "I guess we're a bit old to be playing with fire." It was only the fourth time the two splendid British distance runners had run against each other. The last time was at Moscow when Coe won the Olympic 1,500 meters.

The race, which Coe said was "obviously competitive," went just the way Cruz hoped it would. "I knew the pace was going to be hard," Cruz said. "I wanted to see if anyone would take the lead, and the Kenyan (Edwin Koech) did. He did just what I always want someone to do. I stayed behind him and saved a little for the finish."

He saved a bundle, actually. He blew by Koech & Co. at the last curve and ran the last 100 meters like a startled deer to win by about 10 feet.

Coe: "When I came onto the finishing straight, I felt I was in contention.

"I thought I had a good position. But he (Cruz) was a little bit stronger and a little bit faster. He is a supreme champion."

As Cruz crossed the finish line, he raised his right fist in celebration. On his victory lap, he was handed a green-and-yellow Brazilian flag, which he carried around the track.

Asked how he felt about winning Brazil's second gold medal in history, he said, "It is impossible to tell my feeling because my feeling is too strong. But it is important to see the flag of Brazil raised."

Brazil's last gold-medal winner was triple jumper Adhemar da Silva, who won his event in 1952 and 1956.

Cruz's hometown is a suburb of Brazil's capital, Brasilia. Population: About 40,000. "It is basically slums," a Brazilian sports writer said. Cruz came to the United States three years ago after his father, a carpenter, died. He first went to take a look at Brigham Young University but, reportedly, didn't like the cold weather in Provo, Utah. He then tried the climate in Eugene, Ore., and apparently thought it was an improvement. He stayed to run for the University of Oregon.

THE MEDALISTS

MEN'S

Track

■ 800 METERS

1. Joaquim Cruz (Brazil)
2. Sebastian Coe (Britain)
3. Earl Jones (U.S.)

"I came here to learn English—and I'm still learning," he said in pretty good English. Last June, he won both the 800 and 1,500 in the NCAA, a rare double. Running an impressive second to him in the 800 was Earl Jones.

Joaquim Cruz is 21. He has curly black hair, a nice smile and flashing white teeth. At 6-1½, 160 pounds, he also has the stride and strength of Alberto Juantorena of Cuba, who in 1976 set the Olympic record of 1:43.50. Cruz broke the record Monday.

The race, Coe said, was competitive but not rough. "It was as uncluttered a run as I've ever had in a major race."

In fact, Coe said, he had no real complaints. He ran badly in the 800 at Moscow and finished second to Ovett. But this time, he said, "I was beaten by a guy who was younger and stronger. I am not leaving dissatisfied."

But yes, he said, he was disappointed. "This was my last chance for a gold medal. But the silver medals, he said, "should match nicely."

MURRAY

Continued from page 70

When you see Moses hurdle, you're glad the Greeks invented. And De Coubertin revived.

A 400-meter hurdle race is as technical as grand opera. It requires a calculating skill as well as enormous raw talent. There are lots of Olympic races where you just get out there and do the same things lions do on the track of a zebra. There's nothing cerebral about a 100-yard dash. If God didn't take care of everything first, there's nothing you can do about it.

The hurdles appealed more to Edwin Moses. In the first place, he's a scientist. Physics is as uncomplicated to him as the infield fly rule to Tommy Lasorda. When other kids were making snowmen on the block, he was making rockets in the cellar.

He fell in love with the hurdles. He could run the 200 and the 400 on the flat. But there wasn't enough geometry in that. The 200 is for truck drivers. Cheetahs. The 400 intermediates is the thinking man's race.

They say that Edwin Moses' edge in the 400 hurdles is that he doesn't jump them, he just sort of ignores them. That is to say, he jumps the first hurdle—and then doesn't come down till the last. The joke is that Edwin doesn't really run the hurdles, he just breaks the long jump record three or more times during a round. They say it's just a rumor he takes steps between the sticks (13 of them, by the way, or two fewer than anybody else usually takes). His stride is just shorter than Man o'War's, but he could probably win the event in leg chains.

He's now won 90 straight races or 105, depending on whether you count heats or not. Only three other runners have ever broken 48 seconds in the event. Moses has done it 28 times. Of course, he holds the world record. He keeps setting it.

The thing is, Edwin Moses' 90th and probably most important race was not exactly vintage Moses—and yet he won it by daylight and was, as usual, the only one in the field to break 48. But he jump-started once, and his time—47.75—was hardly Mosaic. He appeared to go fractionally higher over the hurdles instead of shaving them on the way over as usual.

But what was Mosaic was that, typically, it was no strain on the viewer. For the Biblical seven years, this Moses has been undefeated. The Pharaoh of time cannot catch up with him either. He was his usual, affable congenial self before and after the event. It's not only no strain on the spectator, it's no strain on Edwin, either. ("The race went about as I expected," he said calmly after it. In other words, the piano was in tune and the scenery stayed up.) It was like Crosby singing, or Kelly dancing in the rain. Moses in the hurdles is one of the great soothing sights of all time. A great way to end your day. Beats even sunsets into the Pacific or springtime in the Rockies.

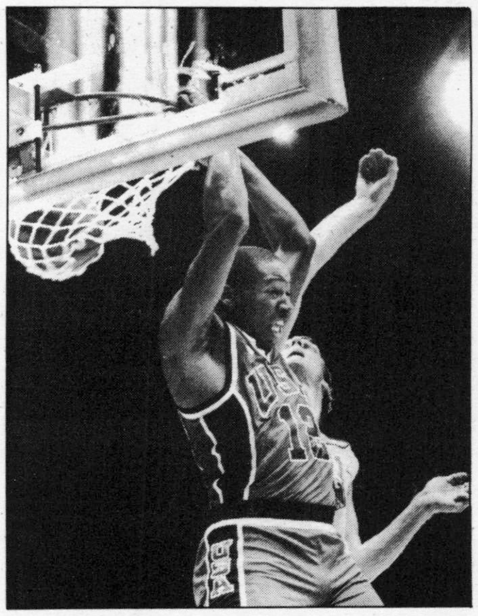

ROSEMARY KAUL / Los Angeles Times

Wayman Tisdale of the United States slams home a reverse dunk against West Germany in a 78-67 win.

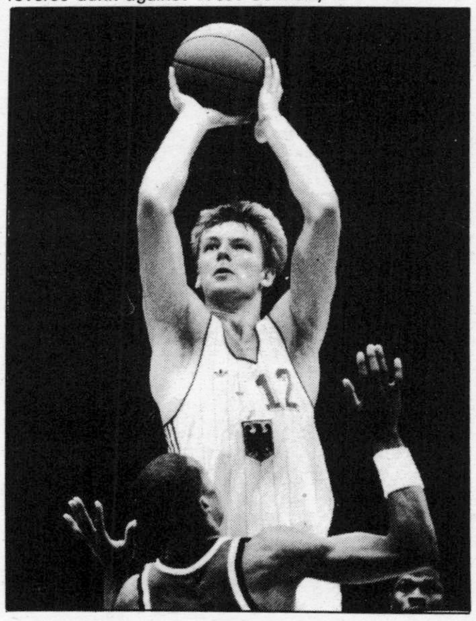

ROSEMARY KAUL / Los Angeles Times

West Germany's Detlef Schrempf fires a jump shot over Alvin Robertson of the United States. U.S. won, 78-67.

BASKETBALL

Continued from page 70

to be remembered as a loss in Germany.

"A loss is a loss," he said. "But it is funny, very funny. Against the Russian team in Paris, we had the best result. We were behind by two at the half (and 13 at the end of the game). But it's a loss. Sometimes you have a good loss. This is a good loss."

For Coach Bob Knight, it was the most animated night of the tournament. He was yelling at his players and instructing the referees, Constantino Rigas of Greece and Zolravko Kurilic of Yugoslavia, in their duties.

Afterward he appeared in the interview room, without any of his players for the first time, and calmly explained his various displeasures.

On his team: "I just didn't think we played with the kind of intelligence that's marked our performances. I just don't think I could go through the stats or look at it in any way and feel this was a good performance for us."

And on Kurilic and Rigas:

"I thought the officiating was incredibly bad for both teams. Teams at this level shouldn't be subjected to this."

Said Christian Welp, of the University of Washington and Germany:

"If our coach had yelled at the referees like Coach Bobby Knight, he would have been in the dressing room by halftime."

The Germans posed two problems for the Americans, who are used to dominating the boards and being able to run. The Germans have terrific size (7-1, three 6-11s and the 6-8 Detlef Schrempf, who sometimes plays guard). They play slowly on offense and exclusively zone defense and they can slow anyone down. Monday night, this team reduced a flag-waving crowd of 12,876 to yawning.

"The people were very quiet," Klein said later, not unhappily. "I have never seen the States play this kind of game in this tournament. There wasn't a lot of penetration. There was a lot of outside shooting. But that was what I wanted. No penetration, no dunks."

The great dunker, Michael Jordan, who came in shooting 64%, had his worst night of the Olympics. He missed 10 of his 14 shots, four of his 10 free throws and turned the ball over six times. Late in the second half, he tried to go baseline and put the ball down on the dribble a good two feet out of bounds.

From the bench came a yell loud enough to be heard upstairs:

"Michael, get in the game!"

And that wasn't from C.M. Newton, either.

Chris Mullin, one of the two outside shooters, went only 5 for 12, but that still left Steve Alford. He had 17 points, three assists and four steals and shot 7 for 12. The Indiana kid whose selection to the team was grumbled about by some is now shooting 66%.

Notes

Christian Welp: "For me, it's like a win. Before the game, nobody on our team thought we could win. We just didn't want to lose by 50 or 60 points." . . . **Ralph Klein** on the officiating: "I think as good a team like the American team doesn't need help from the referees."

Bernier Makes a Breakthrough, Winning Gold Medal for Canada

By SEYMOUR BEUBIS,
Times Staff Writer

Forget all that hype about the Olympic diving competition being strictly a showdown between the United States and China.

Canada's Sylvie Bernier, 20, destroyed that notion quickly Monday by winning the women's three-meter springboard—the first of four diving events.

Kelly McCormick, 24, and Chris Seufert, 27, both of the United States, took the silver and bronze medals, respectively, before an enthusiastic crowd of 12,418.

The two Chinese divers in the event—Li Yihua, 21, who was the leading qualifier in the preliminary round Sunday, and Li Qiaoxian, 17—finished a disappointing fourth and fifth.

Bernier, who qualified third in the preliminaries, won by doing what some believed she could not do well—hit dives under pressure.

She had ample opportunity to crack, but she didn't. She met every challenge, and there were many. She took the lead on the third dive and held it throughout.

Her final score was 530.70 points. McCormick finished with 527.46, and Seufert came from far behind in the early rounds to finish with 517.62.

McCormick had a shot at winning the competition on her final dive, a back 2½ somersault tuck. She needed scores of 8.5s from the judges, but she received straight 8s.

But it wasn't really the 10th dive that cost McCormick the gold, it was her eighth, a reverse 2½ somersault tuck with a 2.8 degree of difficulty.

"I was a little bit ahead of myself on the dive," she said. She laughed about the big splash she made, saying, "It looked like Hawaii Five-O."

She scored 6s on the dive and picked up only 51.24 points. Meanwhile, Bernier, doing the same dive on that round, hit for 7s and 60.48 points.

Usually, the seventh and eighth dives give Bernier the most trouble.

THE MEDALISTS

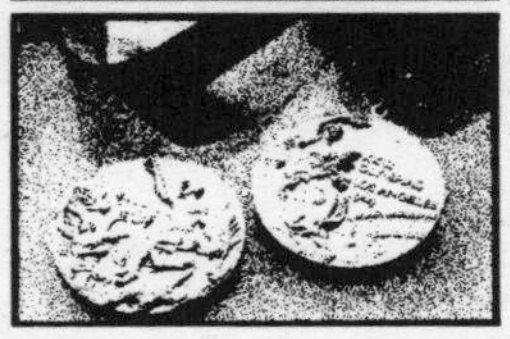

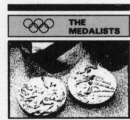

WOMEN'S

Diving

■ SPRINGBOARD

1. Sylvie Bernier (Canada)
2. Kelly McCormick (U.S.)
3. Christina Seufert (U.S.)

"I usually hit well on 8 of my 10 dives, but those 2 give me trouble."

Bernier said she didn't know that she was in first place until it was over. "I don't want to know where I am. I had an idea I was in the top three."

She said that she spent her time between dives listening to "Flashdance" on her Walkman.

"I have been diving for 12 years, and I know for me it is good not knowing what place I am in," Bernier said.

Until a few years ago, Bernier said she would watch the board—and not do well.

Now, she only watches her scores being posted on the board, no one else's.

McCormick was the sentimental favorite of the crowd. She is the daughter of Pat McCormick, who won four gold medals, two each in 1952 and 1956, and many were pulling for her to win one of her own.

But Kelly McCormick said she was not disappointed by her finish. "It's an honor to be able to dive here. . . . Sylvie did a great job. I'm really happy for her."

Seufert said: "This is the end of my career and my first Olympics, so getting the medal is the highlight of my career. I was very consistent, but a few of my dives could have been a bit sharper."

By virtue of her victory, Bernier became the first Canadian in history to win an Olympic gold medal in diving. The only other Canadian to win a diving medal of any kind was Irene McDonald, who gained a bronze in 1956.

She said she felt great about that. "I am very happy and proud," she said.

The 5-3, 110-pound Bernier said she came to Los Angeles with the intention of winning a medal, but she didn't know it was going to be the gold.

"I feel great," Bernier said. "But I am very tired."

Asked if there was a particular dive that won her the gold, she said: "I was consistent, that's it. There wasn't one dive that won it for me. I was consistent the whole way."

Bernier won the Can-Am-Mex gold medal last May, defeating Seufert among others.

Last year, she took the bronze in the Pan American Games (McCormick won it) and in the FINA Cup. She was seventh in the 1982 World Championships and was a silver medal winner in the Commonwealth Games later that year.

Even before the Olympic Games began, Bernier was tabbed by Ron O'Brien, the co-coach of the U.S. Olympic diving team, as one of five women who had a shot at winning the springboard competition.

But O'Brien thought the only way that could happen was if the four other highly skilled performers, the two women from the United States and two from China, did not turn in top-notch performances.

And that's exactly what happened.

Sanderson Takes Javelin, Injured Lillak Gets Silver

By JULIE CART, *Times Staff Writer*

Tessa Sanderson of Great Britan couldn't believe it. Neither could world record-holder Tiina Lillak.

Sanderson, on her first throw in the women's javelin Monday, beat one of the most sure bets in the Olympics. The fiesty Sanderson also doused the hopes of Finnish supporters, who had hoped Lillak would win that nation's second gold medal in the event.

Arto Haerkoenhen had thrilled a nation of javelin fans Sunday night with his win in the men's javelin.

Sanderson, 28, won with 228 feet, 2 inches, establishing an Olympic record. Lillak, limping on an injured right ankle, won the silver with 226-4, and Fatima Whitbread, to the delight of Union Jack-waving partisans, won the bronze with 220-3.

'I'm exhusted,' Sanderson said, although she didn't look it. What she did look was elated, but intent on establishing herself as the Olympic champion, not champion by default.

When asked if she felt she had won only because Lillak was injured, Sanderson said: "Tiina started the competition, so I have to believe she was fit."

Lillak and the Finnish team doctor, Pekka Peltokallio, thought she was fit, too. Reports of an injury to Lillak, who is the world champion and has thrown 245-3, began to circulate in the javelin world in June. But Lillak is a fierce competitor and she figured to compete well here.

She did, at first. Her first throw had potential, but the tail dragged during its flight, bringing the javelin down prematurely. On her second throw, Lillak had her characteristic aggressive approach run and got off what was to be her best throw. It was also her last.

She limped down the runway, slumped to a bench and disgustedly pulled off her shoes. Her swollen ankle, which she had broken in two places, had given her a sharp pain, she said.

She sat for a while, fighting tears, and passed her next throw. Then, after tentatively testing the ankle, Lillak sat on the Coliseum floor and methodically cut away the many layers of athletic tape that supported her ankle. She passed the remainder of her throws.

The hordes of Finns in the stands waved the white and blue national flag and chanted "Tiina, Tiina," as they had when Lillak became the heroine of the world championships in Helsinki.

There, Lillak was trailing Whitbread going into her last throw, and pulled out the winning toss to give the hosts their first gold medal of the competition.

Since then, Lillak has been hounded by reporters worldwide. Last spring, Lillak and other top Finnish athletes came to San Jose to train—and to escape the scrutiny of the media.

There was no escape Monday night. Even as Lillak was assisted off the field, she was followed by photographers trotting after her. On her way to doping control, the bright lights of television cameras snaped on as she was brought by, crying.

Later, in an emotional press conference, the 23 year-old Lillak broke down.

"In the back of my mind, I had the thought that this could happen," she said. "I am sure that without the injury I could have won. I think my first throw could have been a good one. I can't say I'm satisfied.

For Sanderson and Whitbread, it was a triumph they shared with their countrymen. As the athletes were preparing to leave the stadium after the competition, a man wearing a Union Jack t-shirt burst on the field and draped a much larger Union Jack over a bewildered Sanderson.

Sanderson and Whitbread, not known to be the best of friends, each grabbed an end and jogged an awkward victory lap. Javelin throwers don't have the running style of Carl Lewis, but the two British athletes—and the fans—didn't seem to mind.

When told by a British reporter that she had won the first individual gold medal by a British woman in 12 years, Sanderson exploded with a hearty laugh and a broad smile.

"I told myself that this was my last chance," Sanderson said. "I knew I had to go in there and hit like hell, and I did it.

"I hope Moscow is truly and finally buried. I did fail there (she failed to make the finals). But the fact is that that was the only time I have failed in my career.

"It took an awfully long time for me to come back. People gave up on me, but not my coach, Wilf Paish."

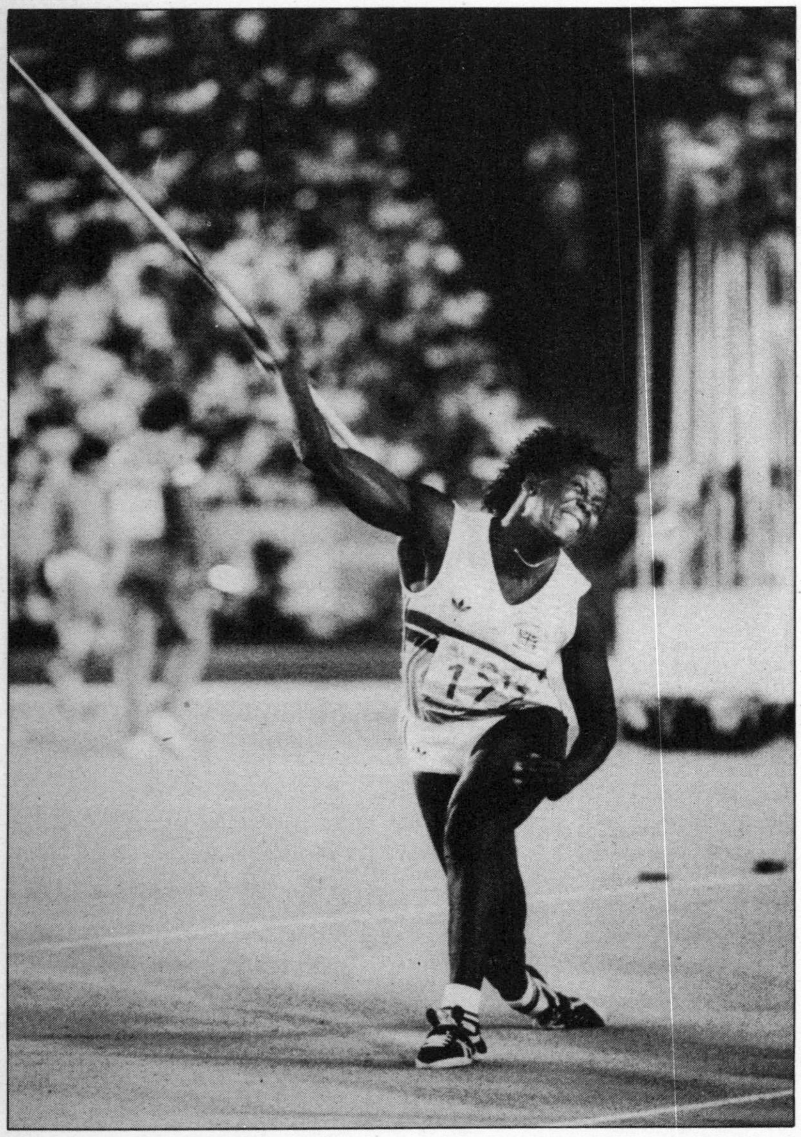

PATRICK DOWNS / Los Angeles Times

Tessa Sanderson of Britain shows the strain as she gets off throw in women's javelin. She won with mark of 228-2, upsetting world record holder Tiina Lillak of Finland, who threw 226-4.

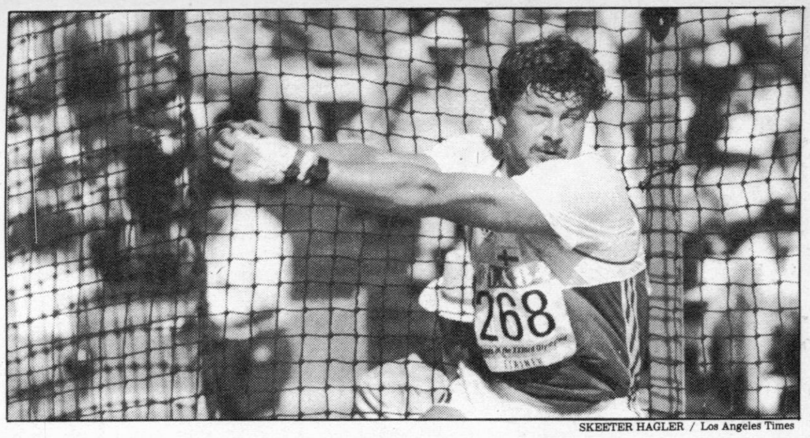

SKEETER HAGLER / Los Angeles Times

Gold medal winner Juha Tiainen of Finland builds momentum with the hammer . . .

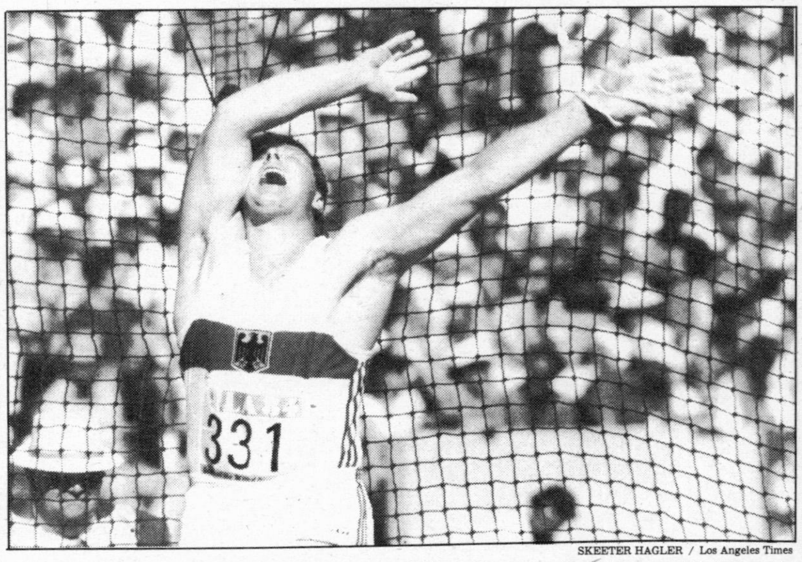

SKEETER HAGLER / Los Angeles Times

. . . and silver medalist Karl-Hans Riehm of West Germany launches it with 'oomph'.

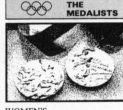

THE MEDALISTS

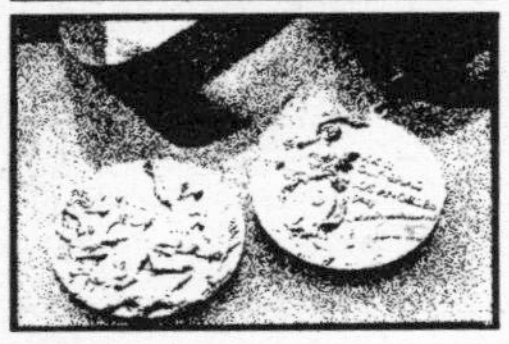

WOMEN'S

Track

JAVELIN

1. Tessa Sanderson (Britain)
2. Tiina Lillak (Finland)
3. Fatima Whitbread (Britain)

800 METERS

1. Doina Melinte (Romania)
2. Kim Gallagher (U.S.)
3. Fita Lovin (Romania)

Hammer Throw

Finland's Winner Isn't Especially Thrilled With Gold

By RICK REILLY, *Times Staff Writer*

Olympic spirit and international good will aside, the Soviet-led boycott made Monday's hammer throw an exercise in going in circles.

Finland's Juha Tiainen came into the Games ranked fourth behind three Eastern Bloc throwers. With them absent, he finished first. It figured, and Tiainen, the blond bear, knew it. He acted as though they had a hung a subpoena around his neck instead of a gold medal.

How you gonna' celebrate, Juha?

"Mmmm. Cake and coffee," he said.

And that, sports fans, was recorded as the only time a chuckle sneaked past his severe countenance.

His throw of 256 feet 2 inches was not his personal best and nowhere near either the Olympic or world record. Second and third went to two West Germans, Karl-Hans Riehm with a throw of 255-10, and Klaus Ploghaus, 251-7.

American Bill Green surprised Yankee doomsayers with a sixth-place finish at 248-0. He was the only U.S. thrower who advanced to the final.

"I'm happy to finish this high in the Olympic Games," said Green, who at only 24 considers himself still a rookie.

No such giddiness marked Tiainen's grim demeanor.

"I came to the Olympics knowing I should get the gold," said the 28-year-old Finn. "It's not the same thing without the Eastern Bloc countries here."

Tiainen, who asked to keep the interview to five minutes, chose to talk about a meet in East Berlin three weeks ago. There, he said, he finished second, beating Soviet star Sergei Litvinov, last year's world champion.

"I am glad for the gold, except it wasn't the same without them," he said of the absentees. "If they were here, I might have won a medal, but maybe not a gold medal."

Altogether, it has not been the most memorable of trips for Tiainen. He caught a virus training in San Jose, mecca for athletes who like to throw heavy metal objects. It gave him a head cold and constant headaches up until Sunday, he said.

"But I was afraid to take anything more than aspirin (because of doping tests)," he said. Because of that, he tired quickly this week in workouts and during the final.

There also was the heat on the field to sap the strength of the throwers. "The stadium was very hot," said Riehm. "It was a challenge to overcome it."

Tiainen overcame it after two miserable efforts that had him in sixth place, barely high enough to qualify for the final three throws. His third throw carried him all the way to the gold.

It was also enough to beat the Germans, who, in contrast to Tiainen, were actually excited about taking home some jewelry as souvenirs.

"I've waited 18 years for this medal," Riehm said. "And I don't care how long it took."

If that doesn't make a whole lot of sense, it may be because Riehm has been overly strained lately. In fact, he threw with a strained back and strained leg muscles. He said he was cramping a bit in his legs, too, just for good measure.

What *did* make an impression on Tiainen, as it did on all of the hammer types, was the enthusiasm of the American crowd at the Coliseum.

"It was better than in Moscow (in 1980)," he said. "At least here, they didn't whistle when it was your turn."

Said Green, "The crowd was great. All they were waiting for is someone to give it a long throw."

Unfortunately for these Olympics, that someone wasn't entered.

THE MEDALISTS

MEN'S

Track

HAMMER THROW

1. Juha Tiainen (Finland)
2. Karl-Hans Riehm (West Germany)
3. Klaus Ploghaus (West Germany)

Women's 800

Fast Pace Too Much for Gallagher

By MIKE LITTWIN, *Times Staff Writer*

Kim Gallagher expected the worst. Her coach, Chuck DeBus, had told her all about the bump-and-run tactics favored by Europeans. Maybe he had told her too much.

By the time Gallagher had brought home a silver medal in the 800 meters, the young woman from Amber, Pa., wasn't sure if her sport was running or tag-team wrestling.

Gallagher said she had been kicked. She said that the two Romanians in the race had been talking just before the contact. She thought they were talking about her.

"I heard them talking and that's just when I got kicked," she said. "I'm not complaining (but) it threw me off stride."

Were the Romanians ganging up on poor Kim? Maybe not. The way the Romanians tell it, they were going at one another.

Veteran Doina Melinte, 27, won the race Monday night in 1 minute 57.60 seconds. Her Romanian teammate, Fita Lovin, finished third in 1:58.83. Gallagher finished second in 1:58.63, a stride ahead of Lovin and several strides behind Melinte.

Absent, of course, was Czechoslovakia's mighty Jarmila Kratochvilova—Wonder Woman—who might have won the 800 meters, the 400 and maybe then the men's 10,000. The boycott robbed America of seeing the Czech star, who has the world record of 1:53.28. Instead, they got a pretty good race.

Gallagher, 20, wasn't going to win anyway, since the pace was much too fast for the hard-finishing runner. Nor did she have the experience necessary to win a race like this one. Almost unbelievably, the Olympics represented Gallagher's first international competition.

"They took my kick away from me with about 200 meters to go," Gallagher said.

Her American teammate, Ruth Wysocki, never got to kick either. In fact, she had to struggle to finish sixth, a place from which she could do little but watch the action.

Somewhere between 500 and 600 meters, the two Romanians began their conversation. But to hear Lovin tell it, Gallagher wasn't the subject of discussion.

"I had the inside lane," Lovin said. "I was ready to make my move. I need a long time to finish.

"At that point, the first-place finisher came in front of me and the second-place finisher as well . . . When someone is too close you always say something."

Lovin said something to Melinte in Romanian. She wouldn't say what. She did say there was some contact but that it was between the Romanians.

In any event, Gallagher, 20, got kicked. Welcome to the big leagues.

Gallagher couldn't be upset. She wanted the gold, of course, but the silver medal hanging from her neck felt very nice. It wouldn't have surprised Gallagher if she had finished face down on the Coliseum track.

"I expected to fall," she said. "I know how Europeans are when they want to win."

She had been told that Europeans can be rugged competitors and warned to watch out for elbows and knees.

With the race nearing the 600-meter mark, Gallagher was tiring. She was running in second place, but the pace was getting to her.

"I said to myself, 'Please don't let me get kicked now.' And that's just when I got kicked."

Soon after, she tried to go outside of Melinte, and the Romanian, who finished sixth in the world championships last year, simply blew her away. Twice, Gallagher tried to kick and twice she found she couldn't catch Melinte.

"I had planned to attack in the last 200 meters," said Melinte, a professor of physical education whose husband doubles as her coach. "I had some sensitivity, some fear, of Gallagher."

Said Lovin, "We were afraid that the pace was not fast enough for our plan. But it turned out not to be the case."

For her part, Gallagher knew she was in trouble when Gabriella Dorio of Italy went out hard, running the first 400 in 57.28. At about 600 meters, Melinte moved ahead and stayed there as Gallagher gave chase.

"I gave it to her at 150 (meters to go)," Gallagher said. "I gave it back to myself at 100. Then I gave it to her again at 70.

"Usually when I lose, I give up. But I said to myself, 'Hey, let's go for the silver.' "

She did hold on and felt a mixture of joy and relief.

"I was so nervous," she said. "After the race, I had the biggest headache of my life. I felt good, yet bad."

She has had a bad hip and woke up Monday morning with swollen glands. Sure, she was nervous. Now Gallagher can relax, though, and enjoy herself. She will head for Europe where she should meet up again with Melinte as well as the Eastern Europeans who weren't here.

First, though, Gallagher intends to go home to Amber, a suburb of Philadelphia.

"If I won the gold medal, they were going to have a parade for me," Gallagher said. "I don't know now. Maybe they'll call me a bum."

Foster Can't Rule Hurdle World, Much Less a Kingdom

Mixup at Start Gives Favorite Only a Silver

By ALAN GREENBERG,
Times Staff Writer

Add another ghost to Greg Foster's night gallery. And a display case. Don't call ghost-busters. Even for them, some jobs are just too big.

This one, the Olympic final of the 110-meter hurdles, proved to be too big for Foster. At least nobody will be bugging him any more about chasing the immortal ghost of world-record holder (12.93) Renaldo (Skeets) Nehemiah. Monday night, in the biggest race of his life, Foster couldn't even catch a relative upstart named Roger Kingdom.

And nobody was more surprised than the new Olympic champion himself, who ran down Foster in the race's last five meters to win in an Olympic record and personal best 13.20.

The dazed Kingdom, 21, a sometime student at the University of Pittsburgh, said later he thought he'd finished second.

He sure acted like it. After crossing the finish line, Kingdom coasted to a stop, and then stood alone on the track, gazing up at the replay on the Coliseum's big screen. Only after seeing the replay did he jubilantly raise his arms and run toward Foster, who had watched the replay up the track.

Together, they hugged and took a victory lap, waving to the crowd. Finland's Arto Bryggare, runner-up to Foster at the 1983 world championships at Helsinki, dashed hopes of a U.S. sweep, running 13.40 to win the bronze medal.

Former USC star Tonie Campbell, second to Foster at the trials, ran a poor race. Campbell, usually a superb technician, hit lots of hurdles and finished fifth in 13.55. His race over, he intentionally fell supine, on the track, covering his bespectacled eyes with his hands in grief.

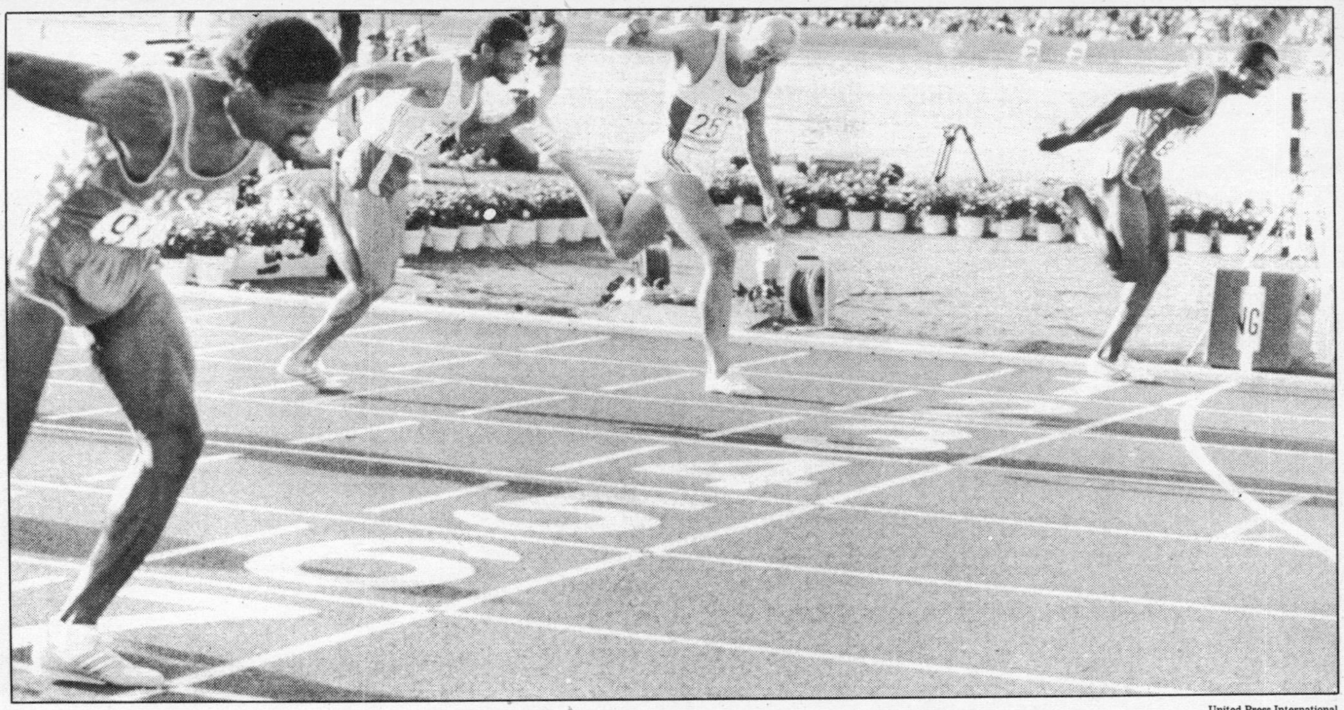

United Press International

Roger Kingdom (nearest camera) edges U.S. teammate Greg Foster (on inside) to win 110-meter high hurdles Monday. Finland's Arto Bryggare (Lane 2) was third.

If Foster was grieving over his loss, he didn't show it. Foster, who throughout his career has never been a gracious loser, was Monday.

"This might be the story that proves Greg Foster is not the guy he has been portrayed as," said Bob Kersee, Foster's coach. "He handled defeat very well. This might change his image."

What it won't change is the criticism, originally leveled by Nehemiah, now a San Francisco 49ers wide receiver, and Jim Bush, Foster's former coach at UCLA, that Foster can be rattled and psyched out in a race.

Foster drew lane one, the inside lane and a lane he doesn't like, for the final. Bryggare was in lane two, but Campbell and Kingdom, who were expected to be Foster's chief competition, were in the outside lanes, seven and eight, respectively. There's no way you can run your race and keep track of your opponent with a draw like that.

Foster got out of the blocks extremely well—both he and Bryggare said he false-started—and had a slight lead over Kingdom, his closest pursuer, by the fifth hurdle. Foster held that lead over the tenth and last hurdle, at that point glancing quickly to his right at Kingdom, who passed him a few steps from the finish, leaving Foster with the silver medal and a lot of explaining to do.

"Considering my start, it was a fair (average) race," Foster said. "I ran 13.23, which is lousy (Foster, whose personal best is 13.03 easily won both his heat and semifinal in 13.24). I thought I false started and the race should have been stopped. I jumped the gun, and I don't know why he (the starter) didn't call it back. But regardless, it was stupid of me to ease up at all. I hesitated, actually stopped dead in my tracks after the first two steps."

Replays showed that Foster never stopped, but he did seem to raise up, breaking his rhythm. Even so, the race seemed to be his until he looked over and Kingdom surged past him in the final meters.

"My start wasn't that good," Kingdom said. "I made my surge at the fourth hurdle, and I saw Greg vaguely out of the corner of my eye. I don't know at what point I had the lead. I thought I'd come in second. Then Tonie Campbell came over and told me, 'Man, you didn't come in second, you *won* it."

But Kingdom, the 1983 Pan Am and NCAA champion, whose personal best was a most unremarkable 14.07 in 1982, doesn't believe he deserves Foster's No. 1 world ranking just because he won Olympics gold. After all, he's new to such fast times. He won his semifinal earlier in the day in 13.24, a personal best until his time in the final.

"Right now, it (the gold medal) means I'm ranked second or third in the world," Kingdom said. "If you look at how Greg's been doing, if you look at his standard over the last few years, you can't judge a world ranking on one meet, even if it's the Olympics."

Foster said there won't be any more Olympics for him. He said he'll probably retire by 1986.

Asked how long he believes this loss will nag him, Foster said that "it'll probably nag you guys (the media) more than it'll nag me. As far as I'm concerned, it's over . . . For those of you who think I'm disappointed, I'm not. My mother's happy, my son's happy, I'm happy."

Asked if glancing at Kingdom might have cost him the race, Foster said, "Probably not, but who cares . . . If I hadn't eased up, I know I would have won the gold medal."

Maybe Greg Foster can live with that rationalization.

"When you're No. 1 in the world and you have to deal with the Nehemiah ghost-busters," Kersee said, "there's going to be an empty feeling when you don't win the gold."

But it looked as if Foster would win. Until Kingdom had come. For Greg Foster, it seems, it's always something.

THE MEDALISTS

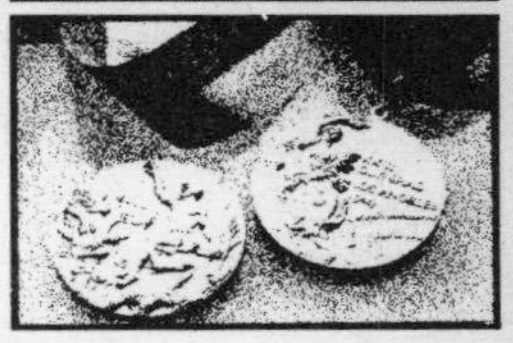

MEN'S

Track

110-METER HURDLES

1. Roger Kingdom (U.S.)
2. Greg Foster (U.S.)
3. Arto Bryggare (Finland)

Women's 400 Meters

Brisco-Hooks Has News for Eastern Bloc

By MAL FLORENCE,
Times Staff Writer

It has been written that the Olympic boycott by the Eastern Bloc countries has considerably diluted the quality of competition in women's track events.

That's a reasonable assessment, but American women, once outclassed by their European counterparts in the 400 meters, are coming on strong now.

Valerie Brisco-Hooks and Chandra Cheeseborough, who have traded the American 400 record this season, are now moving up in class—especially Brisco-Hooks.

She won the 400 Monday at the Olympic Games in the time of 48.83 seconds. She not only lowered the American record but broke the Olympic record of 48.88 set by East Germany's Marita Koch in the 1980 Moscow Games.

Brisco-Hooks became the fourth fastest performer of all time in the event, while Cheeseborough moved up to sixth on the all-time list with her 49.05 for the silver medal. Britain's Kathryn Cook got the bronze in 49.42.

Only five women have ever broken 49 seconds in the 400, and Brisco-Hooks is now in that select company.

Czechoslovakia's Jarmila Kratochvilova, the wonder woman, is the world record-holder at 47.99.

"We're not a step behind them anymore," Cheeseborough said. "They know it and we know it. It will be just us and the Europeans now. We look forward to competing against them."

Brisco-Hooks, who ran a strong race and wasn't vulnerable to Cheeseborough's kick as she was in the U.S. trials, was ecstatic after the race.

She knelt on the track in prayer, then ran a victory lap before making an early visit to the victory platform. It was there that she embraced her husband Alvin Hooks, who was holding their two-year-old son, Alvin Jr., and her coach, Bob Kersee. It was a scene that was jubilant and emotional.

Brisco-Hooks said that when she came across the line she realized that everything she had ever dreamed and worked for had come true.

Both Brisco-Hooks and Cheeseborough are converted sprinters. Brisco-Hooks, a quarter-miler at Locke High School, returned to the event because she wanted the opportunity of gaining a place on the Olympic 1,600-meter relay team.

She got more than that: A gold in the 400, a chance for one in the 200 and, most likely, another gold in the 1,600 relay. Cheeseborough plans to to run legs on the 400 and 1,600 relay teams, if possible. She faces a tight time schedule Saturday.

Brisco-Hooks said that she became dedicated to becoming an accomplished track performer in the aftermath of a tragedy.

"My brother, Robert, was killed by a stray bullet in 1974 while he was working out on the track," she said, adding that it strengthened her resolve to succeed.

She had her baby two years ago and was an undistinguished performer in 1983.

"When I didn't do well, I was encouraged by Bob Kersee," Brisco-Hooks said. "He told me that bigger things would happen for me."

And so they did.

If turnabout is fair play, then Brisco-Hooks and Cheeseborough are experts at the game.

Cheeseborough, 25, who competed in the 100 in the 1976 Olympics, broke the American 400 record May 13 in an invitational meet at UCLA. Brisco-Hooks then lowered it at The Athletics Congress meet in June at San Jose.

A few weeks later in the U.S. trials at the Coliseum, Brisco-Hooks and Cheeseborough met for the first time in a 400.

It was Cheeseborough's turn to set the record. She caught her rival on the last turn and then outkicked her in the final straightaway. Once again the American 400 record was broken—lowered to 49.28.

What a breakthrough. Rosalyn Bryant had held the record for eight years at 50.62 until Cheeseborough broke it for the first time.

Brisco-Hooks altered her strategy against Cheeseborough Monday. She wanted to negate Cheeseborough's kick, if possible.

Brisco-Hooks likes to go out fast and she did. She held her lead through the final turn, and Cheeseborough couldn't catch her in the stretch as she did in the U.S. trials.

"Instead of waiting for her like I did in the trials, I attacked the straightaway harder," Brisco-Hooks said.

Cheeseborough said that she got a "nice start" but added: "I'm not very fast in the first 200 because I'm not used to running the 400. I tried to come on hard, but I couldn't catch her."

Both Brisco-Hooks and Cheeseborough plan to run in Europe after the Olympics. Now, they're not quite in the same class with Koch and Kratochvilova, but they're getting closer.

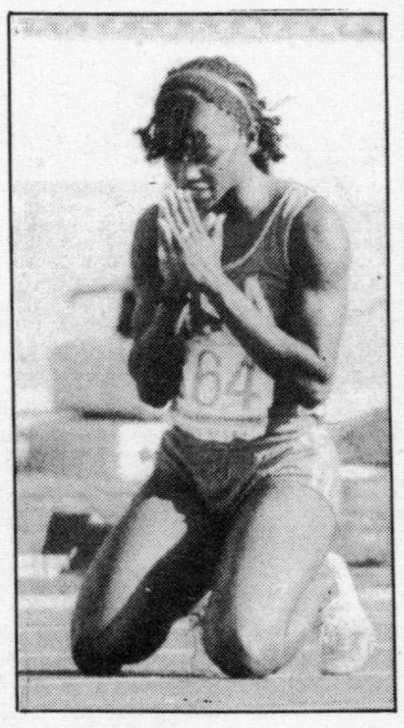

Valerie Brisco-Hooks

THE AGONY OF WEIGHTLIFTING

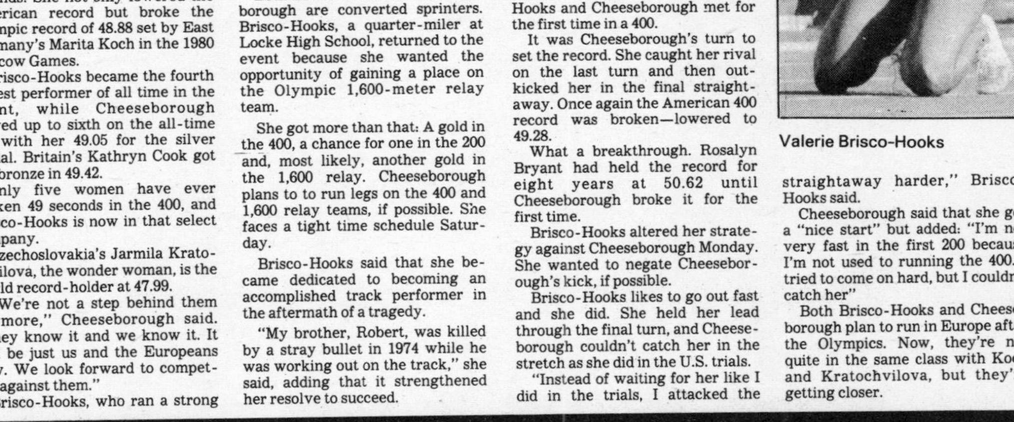

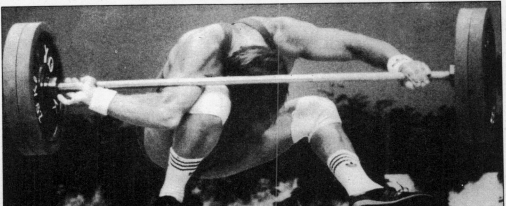

United Press International

Weightlifter Derrick Crass, a bartender from Colorado Springs, Colo., loses control of 286.5 pounds Sunday during competition in the 198-pound class. Crass, 24 on Monday, dislocated his right elbow and sprained his right knee.

NOTES

Ed Burke didn't make it to the finals in the hammer throw, but he thinks he may have another good throw or two left at age 44. He'll be going to Europe after the Olympics, first to Berlin and then to Budapest, Hungary, for a meet that most of the world's great hammer throwers, including those from the Eastern Bloc, will attend. It may be his last hurrah.

A man who knew when to come back, Burke also knows when to quit.

"There's a time to stop," he said. "A time to bring the fish in and the net, and take a picture of it while the sun is still shining. If you keep fishing and you catch the big one in the dark, nobody cares. They're already in the clubhouse.

"This could be my last year to compete, but I'm going to enjoy it."

—MIKE LITTWIN

□

When a petite gymnast, a strapping wrestler or an ace marksman steps into the winner's circle at the Olympics, each is given a bouquet that would rival a prom queen's.

Although many sports have traditionally awarded their winners flowers along with medals, the organizers of this year's Summer Games are giving out more bouquets than ever.

"Everybody loves them," said Patty Howard-Jones, spokeswoman for the Olympic awards and ceremonies division. "We are real proud of the flowers. We felt it was a nice touch."

The bouquets, the same for everybody, have the colors of the city's Olympic banners—a magenta-and-orange gerbera, an orange-and-purple bird of paradise, a lavender liatris and a yellow orchid.

□

The crowds at the Coliseum for the track portion of the Olympic Games have been enthusiastic but not always knowledgeable. Some examples:

Jimmy Carnes, president of The Athletics Congress, tells of the woman who asked an usher if the women's 3,000-meter race (first round) was scheduled Monday.

She was told it was canceled. Her reply: "I hope they give the gold medal to Mary Decker, anyway."

Another spectator wondered why there was a hurdle in front of the steeplechase water-jump pit. His companion said, "That's to keep people from falling in."

□

This item from the Roseville (Calif.) Press-Tribune:

Evelyn Ashford reportedly triggered an epidemic of leg cramps nine years ago among some of Roseville High's finest boy athletes.

"It was crazy," said former Roseville High track Coach Gary Genziinger. "All of the sixth-period classes would empty so they could see Evelyn take on the boys in the 100-yard dashes (which she won). There were a lot of guys who would suddenly grab their calves and feign leg cramps halfway through the race when she was leaving them in the dust."

—MAL FLORENCE

□

A Danish television newsman says his refusal to get involved in a dispute between an Olympic official and the Danish cycling coach got him ejected from the staging area of the Olympic bicycling time trials.

Frank With and his Denmark Radio crew were barred from the area after filming the confrontation Sunday in which With said venue official Jerry Ashley shouted obscenities at Danish Coach John Strove.

"I never expected this could happen in the United States," With said after the incident. "They told me I would be arrested if I tried to get back in. They won't even let us go back in and get our equipment or our documents. I would expect something like this to happen in the Eastern Bloc countries, but not here."

With, who was to broadcast the race for the Nordic Group—a news consortium from Denmark, Norway, Finland and the Netherlands—said he will lodge an official protest with the LAOOC. He said he also planned to edit his crew's film and air it so his Danish audience would know why he was unable to cover the race.

□

What is the secret to the ability of the U.S. women's volleyball team to come from behind, as it has several times during the Olympics?

The Americans are trained to do so.

In practice, the team is divided into two groups for scrimmages, with five players from the second team joined by assistant coach John Corbelli, a former member of the U.S. men's team.

The first team spots the second team 10 points a game, and Corbelli never leaves the front row. Practice doesn't end until the first team wins two out of three games.

"We've stayed sometimes until 9 o'clock at night," said setter Debbie Green, adding that the practices start at 1:30 p.m.

—JERRY CROWE

□

Long recognized for their innovative drafts in the National Football League, the Dallas Cowboys thought they had pulled another one when they selected Carl Lewis in the 12th round last spring.

So what if Lewis had never played football? At worst, it was a public relations coup. You can see the headlines now. "Lewis Goes From One America's Team to Another."

And if he did decide to give up his track and field career to play football, who is to say he would not become another Bob Hayes? During the U.S. Olympic trials, Lewis said: "I could be All-Pro if I wanted to."

But now the Cowboys have discovered that Lewis was ineligible for the draft. His class at the University of Houston graduated in 1983, which means he could have been drafted then but not in 1984. Technically, he is a free agent.

That also is bad news for the National Basketball Assn.'s Chicago Bulls, who made Lewis their 10th-round draft choice this summer.

—RANDY HARVEY

□

Javelin throwers Tom Petranoff and Duncan Atwood are not close friends, but they are close competitors.

After failing to advance to the final round in Sunday's finals, the two athletes from the United States tossed around low-level insults and generally made it clear that they wouldn't be taking any fishing trips together.

Atwood began the press conference by explaining to reporters the nature of a groin injury he sustained in the preliminary rounds and said he had misjudged his ability to overcome it. Petranoff then began by saying, "I have no excuses," to which Atwood shot back, "I don't have excuses, only reasons."

Then Petranoff, who was asked the bulk of the questions, took over the press conference. Atwood rolled his eyes and stared at the back of the press tent as Petranoff painstakingly explained the intricacies of javelin technique.

When Atwood was telling how he had hoped to get off a good throw early in the competition, Petranoff interrupted to explain the importance of that strategy. Atwood threw up his hands, shook his head and began a close inspection of the microphone.

In case anyone missed the message that he was bored, Atwood leaned forward and laid his head on his arms, pretending to nap on the table.

—JULIE CART

□

The tiny Himalayan kingdom of Bhutan has chosen the 1984 Summer Olympics to break out of its isolation and match its principal athletic skill with the world at large.

The sport is archery, and Bhutan's skilled archers—and women—are making their debut Wednesday. It is the first time the nation has ever sent a team abroad to compete.

"We are not going to be last. We will be respectable," predicts Bhutan coach Darwin Kyle, an American who is a member of the U.S. National Coaching Staff in archery.

King Jigme Singye Wangchuck, the British-educated sports enthusiast who has ruled Bhutan's 1.2 million people since 1974, lent his full support to the program.

Off the Record

At Times, It's Difficult to Compare East and West Swimmers

By JOHN WEYLER, *Times Staff Writer*

When it comes to deciding a winner, swimming is about as squeaky clean as sports get. There are no judges, no arbitrary decisions about style, just electronic devices that decide who finishes first and on down the line with the times measured to hundredths of a second.

So, it would seem, few sports are easier to handicap. Find out the best times of the field and pick the winner. Pretty simple, huh?

Well, not if you believe the swimmers and the coaches, who almost unanimously agree that once the gun sounds, you're talking about a race not a time trial. And close races—not the prospect of world records—bring out the best and sometimes even the worst in athletes.

Certainly, it's interesting to compare the times of those swimmers whose countries decided to boycott the 1984 Olympics with those who won medals here last week. But to draw any sort of absolute conclusions, they contend, is ludicrous.

Take, for example, the strange case of West Germany's Thomas Fahrner. Fahrner's time in the morning preliminaries of the men's 400-meter freestyle event was not fast enough to qualify for the final. Then, swimming in a meaningless consolation race—instituted for the first time in this Olympics to give the evening spectators a chance to see more countries represented—Fahrner went faster than gold medal winner George DiCarlo. Fahrner didn't get a medal, of course, but he did get the Olympic record.

Now if Fahrner had lived in East Germany and would have swum that time in the boycotting countries' upcoming alternative games, he could have said, "Ha. I would have won a medal in Los Angeles."

Since he had his chance at Olympic glory, however, all he could say was "I swam like bleep in the morning."

All of which lends credence to the contention that comparing times and drawing conclusions is, at best, assuming a great deal.

World record-holding backstroker Rick Carey easily won the gold medal in the 200-meter backstroke, for example, but he considered his time so slow that he pouted his way through the awards ceremony, snubbed the crowd and made a fool of himself before 2.5 billion television viewers.

East Germany's Dirk Richter has been faster than Carey's gold medal performance, but when Carey says, "I could beat him head-to-head any time and any place . . . in a three-foot deep pool with no gutters or anywhere he'd like to race," it's hard to doubt him. Carey may be arrogant, but he does not lose backstroke races.

"Shirley Babashoff (who won a gold and four silver medals in 1976) was a perfect example," said Olympic assistant coach Mark Schubert. "She was the ultimate racer. She *never* swam fast unless she was pushed."

There are, of course, two sides to this coin. Some swimmers fold in the big meets. Japanese breaststroker Hiroko Nagasaki was the fastest in the world in the 200-meter event last year and many considered her a favorite to win the gold medal. But most of her best times had come in low-pressure meets and she ended up fourth in the Olympics, more than a second and a half behind the bronze-medal winner and almost three-seconds slower than her own best time.

Mary T. Meagher, who owns both women's butterfly world records, just missed bettering her mark in the 200-meter event Saturday, but she wasn't sure that the presence of the powerful East Germans might have helped her reach that goal.

"If they were here," she said, "I could see myself feeling a lot more pressure. I could have been too nervous to swim my best. But then if there had been someone next to me, I probably wouldn't have zeroed in on the pain as much as I did tonight and I would have just raced.

"I guess it could go either way. I might have tensed up, too."

Still, the consensus of opinion is that competition makes for faster times.

"I'd say about 80% of the world records are set in races where there is stiff competition," Olympic Coach Don Gambril said. "And the ones that were set where there wasn't any pressure probably would have been faster if there was some.

"You try and compare times and you run into a lot of problems. In some cases, it's easy to pick a clear-cut winner. But anytime you look at an event where the swimmers are within a second or so of each other, you're talking about a race.

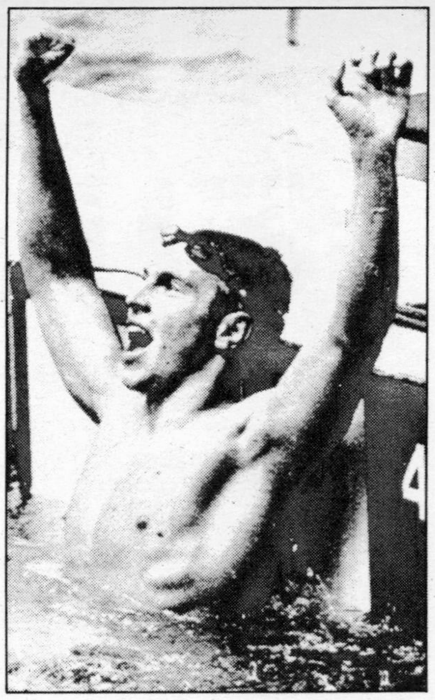

Associated Press

A faster time doesn't necessarily mean Vladimir Salnikov would have won in the Olympics.

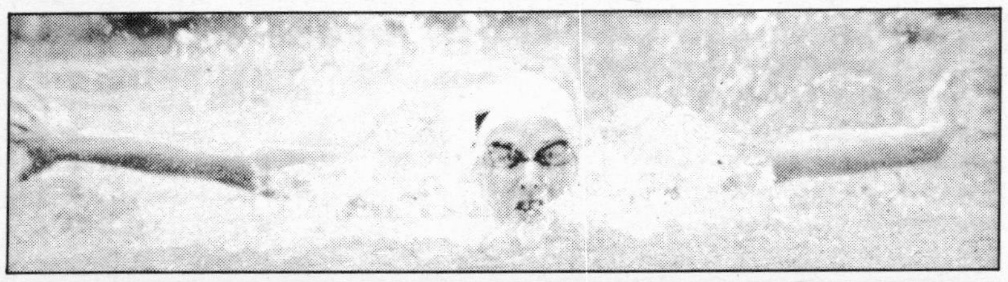

WOMEN

100-METER FREESTYLE	
Kristin Otto (East Germany)	54.94
Birgit Meineke (East Germany)	55.18
Gold—Carrie Steinseifer (U.S.)	55.92
Gold—Nancy Hogshead (U.S.)	55.92
Bronze—A. Verstappen (Nthrlnds)	56.08
Svetlana Koptchikova (USSR)	56.59

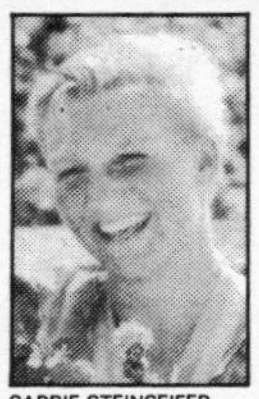

CARRIE STEINSEIFER U.S.

200-METER BREASTSTROKE	
Ute Geweniger (East Germany)	2:29.52
Elena Volkova (USSR)	2:29.74
Larisa Belokon (USSR)	2:30.31
Gold—Anne Ottenbrite (Canada)	2:30.38
Silver—Susan Rapp (U.S.)	2:31.15
Bronze—Ingrid Lempereur (Belgium)	2:31.40

200-METER FREESTYLE	
Kristin Otto (East Germany)	1:57.75
Birgit Meineke (East Germany)	1:58.75
Gold—Mary Wayte (U.S.)	1:59.23
Silver—Cynthia Woodhead (U.S.)	1:59.50
Bronze—A. Verstappen (Nthrlnds)	1:59.69
Karen Koenig (East Germany)	2:00.57

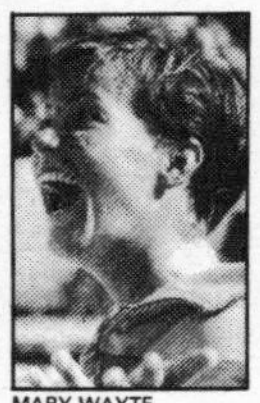

MARY WAYTE U.S.

100-METER BUTTERFLY	
Gold—Mary T. Meagher (U.S.)	59.26
Ines Geissler (East Germany)	59.88
Silver—Jenna Johnson (U.S.)	1:00.19
Bronze—Karin Seick (West Germany)	1:00.36
Tatiana Kurnikova (USSR)	1:00.60
Cornelia Polit (East Germany)	1:00.83

400-METER FREESTYLE	
Gold—Tiffany Cohen (U.S.)	4:07.10
Astrid Strauss (East Germany)	4:08.07
Silver—Sarah Hardcastle (Britain)	4:10.27
Anke Sonnenbrodt (East Germany)	4:10.37
Bronze—June Croft (Britain)	4:11.49
Irina Laritscheva (USSR)	4:12.90

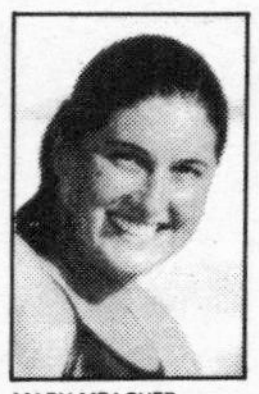

MARY MEAGHER U.S.

200-METER BUTTERFLY	
Gold—Mary T. Meagher (U.S.)	2:06.90
Cornelia Polit (East Germany)	2:07.82
Ines Geissler (East Germany)	2:08.03
Jacqueline Alex (East Germany)	2:10.55
Silver—Karen Phillips (Australia)	2:10.56
Bronze—Ina Beyermann (W. Germany)	2:11.91

800-METER FREESTYLE	
Gold—Tiffany Cohen (U.S.)	8:24.95
Astrid Strauss (East Germany)	8:28.36
Silver—Michele Richardson (U.S.)	8:30.73
Anke Sonnenbrodt (East Germany)	8:31.07
Bronze—Sarah Hardcastle (Britain)	8:32.60
Grit Richter (East Germany)	8:33.42

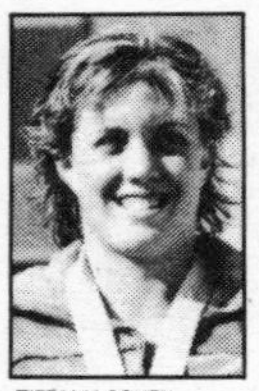

TIFFANY COHEN U.S.

200-METER INDIVIDUAL MEDLEY	
Ute Geweniger (East Germany)	2:12.60
Gold—Tracy Caulkins (U.S.)	2:12.64
Kathleen Nord (East Germany)	2:14.25
Silver—Nancy Hogshead (U.S.)	2:15.17
Bronze—Michele Pearson (Australia)	2:15.92
Irina Gerassimova (USSR)	2:16.72

100-METER BACKSTROKE	
Kristin Otto (East Germany)	1:01.13
Ina Kleber (East Germany)	1:01.32
Cornelia Sirch (East Germany)	1:01.48
Gold—Theresa Andrews (U.S.)	1:02.55
Silver—Betsy Mitchell (U.S.)	1:02.63
Bronze—Jolanda de Rover (Nthrlnds)	1:02.91

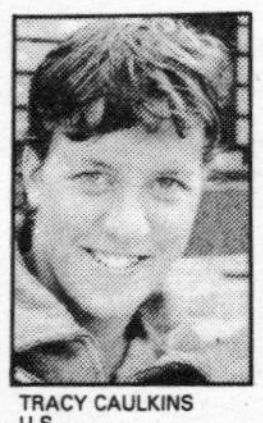

TRACY CAULKINS U.S.

400-METER INDIVIDUAL MEDLEY	
Gold—Tracy Caulkins (U.S.)	4:39.24
Petra Schneider (East Germany)	4:39.54
Kathleen Nord (East Germany)	4:39.95
Silver—Suzanne Landells (Australia)	4:48.30
Bronze—Petra Zindler (W. Germany)	4:48.57
Elena Dendeberova (USSR)	4:49.43

200-METER BACKSTROKE	
Kathrin Zimmermann (East Germany)	2:10.97
Kristin Otto (East Germany)	2:11.88
Birthe Weigang (East Germany)	2:11.90
Gold—Jolanda de Rover (Nthrlnds)	2:12.38
Silver—Amy White (U.S.)	2:13.04
Bronze—Anca Patrascoiu (Romania)	2:13.29

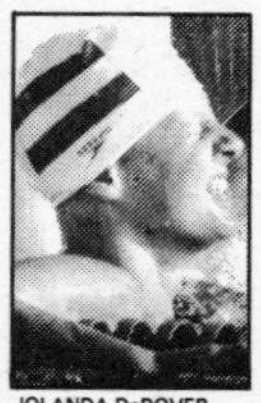

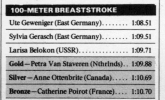

JOLANDA DeROVER HOLLAND

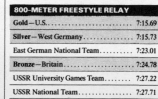

400-METER MEDLEY RELAY	
East German National Team	4:05.79
Gold—U.S.	4:08.34
SC Karl-Marx-Stadt (USSR)	4:10.48
Silver—West Germany	4:11.97
USSR National Team	4:12.69
Bronze—Canada	4:12.98

100-METER BREASTSTROKE	
Ute Geweniger (East Germany)	1:08.51
Sylvia Gerasch (East Germany)	1:09.51
Larisa Belokon (USSR)	1:09.71
Gold—Petra Van Staveren (Nthrlnds)	1:09.88
Silver—Anne Ottenbrite (Canada)	1:10.69
Bronze—Catherine Poirot (France)	1:10.70

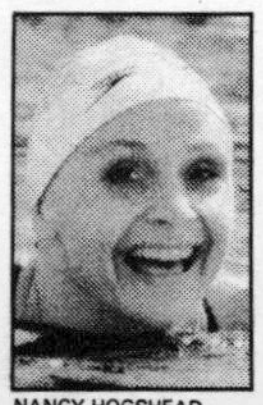

NANCY HOGSHEAD U.S.

100-METER FREESTYLE RELAY	
Gold—U.S.	3:43.43
East German National "A" Team	3:44.34
Silver—Netherlands	3:44.40
Bronze—West Germany	3:45.56
USSR University Games Team	3:49.64
USSR National Team	3:49.84

MEN

The chart compares the best times of athletes from boycotting countries in the last 1½ years against the time swum by the Olympic medalists. Obviously, incentives, such as competition, would also play a factor in determining the winners if all of the athletes would have participated. The shaded areas indicate this year's medal winners.

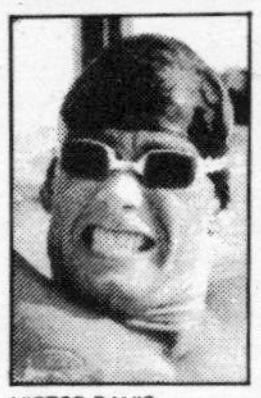

VICTOR DAVIS CANADA

200-METER BREASTSTROKE	
Gold—Victor Davis (Canada)	2:13.34
Silver—Glenn Beringen (Australia)	2:15.79
Robertas Zhulpa (USSR)	2:15.93
Dmitriy Volkov (USSR)	2:15.95
Dmitriy Kuzmin (USSR)	2:17.12
Bronze—Etienne Dagon (Switzerland)	2:17.41

100-METER FREESTYLE	
Joerg Woithe (East Germany)	49.58
Gold—Rowdy Gaines (U.S.)	49.80
Sergei Smiriagin (USSR)	50.13
Silver—Mark Stockwell (Australia)	50.24
Bronze—Per Johansson (Sweden)	50.31
Alexsei Markovskiy (USSR)	50.46

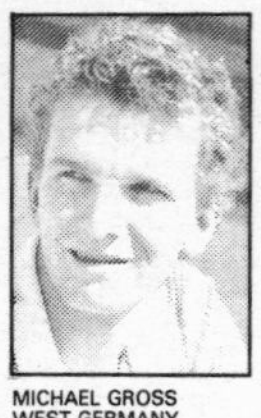

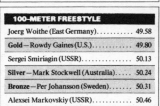

MICHAEL GROSS WEST GERMANY

100-METER BUTTERFLY	
Gold—Michael Gross (West Germany)	53.08
Silver—Pablo Morales (U.S.)	53.23
Thomas Dressler (East Germany)	53.84
Bronze—Glenn Buchanan (Australia)	53.85
Tino Ott (East Germany)	53.91
Karsten Drobny (East Germany)	54.06

200-METER FREESTYLE	
Gold—Michael Gross (West Germany)	1:47.44
Silver—Mike Heath (U.S.)	1:49.10
Sven Lodziewski (East Germany)	1:49.25
Bronze—T. Fahrner (W. Germany)	1:49.69
Lars Hinnenburg (East Germany)	1:50.73
Vladimir Shemetov (USSR)	1:50.96

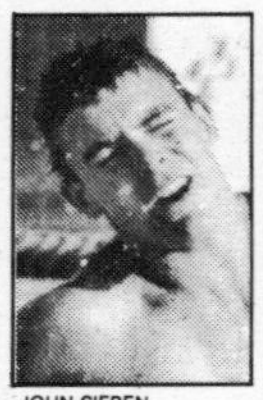

JOHN SIEBEN AUSTRAILIA

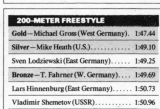

200-METER BUTTERFLY	
Gold—Jon Sieben (Australia)	1:57.04
Silver—Michael Gross (W. Germany)	1:57.40
Bronze—Rafael Vidal (Venezuela)	1:57.51
Sergei Fesenko (USSR)	1:59.74
Marcel Gery (Czechoslovakia)	2:00.44
Aleksandr Prigoda (USSR)	2:01.62

400-METER FREESTYLE	
Vladimir Salnikov (USSR)	3:48.32
Sven Lodziewski (East Germany)	3:49.27
Gold—George DiCarlo (U.S.)	3:51.23
Silver—John Mykkanen (U.S.)	3:51.49
Bronze—Justin Lemberg (Australia)	3:51.79
Sviastoslav Semenov (USSR)	3:52.25

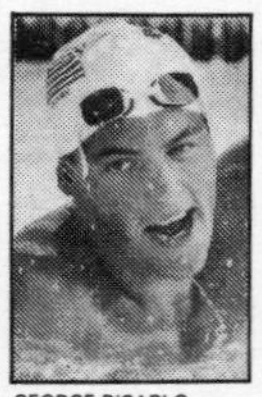

GEORGE DICARLO U.S.

200-METER INDIVIDUAL MEDLEY	
Gold—Alex Baumann (Canada)	2:01.42
Aleksandr Sidorenko (USSR)	2:02.93
Jens-Peter Berndt (East Germany)	2:02.95
Silver—Pablo Morales (U.S.)	2:03.05
Josef Hladky (Czechoslovakia)	2:03.55
Bronze—Neil Cochran (Britian)	2:04.38

1,500-METER FREESTYLE	
Vladimir Salnikov (USSR)	14:54.76
Gold—Mike O'Brien (U.S.)	15:05.20
Sviastoslav Semenov (USSR)	15:09.11
Silver—George DiCarlo (U.S.)	15:10.59
Bronze—Stefan Pfeiffer (W. Germany)	15:12.11
Sven Lodziewski (East Germany)	15:17.67

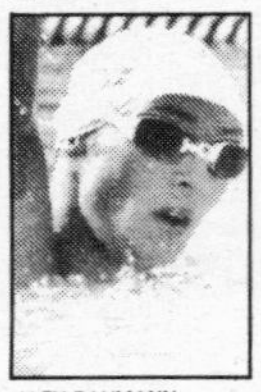

ALEX BAUMANN CANADA

400-METER INDIVIDUAL MEDLEY	
Gold—Alex Baumann (Canada)	4:17.41
Silver—Ricardo Prado (Brazil)	4:18.45
Jens-Peter Berndt (East Germany)	4:19.61
Bronze—R. Woodhouse (Australia)	4:20.50
Josef Hladky (Czechoslovakia)	4:23.52
Sandor Wladar (Hungary)	4:24.38

100-METER BACKSTROKE	
Gold—Rick Carey (U.S.)	55.79
Dirk Richter (East Germany)	56.10
Vladimir Shemetov (USSR)	56.24
Silver—David Wilson (U.S.)	56.35
Bronze—Mike West (Canada)	56.49
Frank Baltrusch (East Germany)	56.63

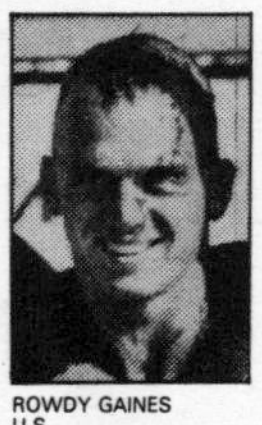

ROWDY GAINES U.S.

400-METER MEDLEY RELAY	
Gold—U.S.	3:39.30
Silver—Canada	3:43.23
Bronze—Australia	3:43.25
USSR National Team	3:43.99
USSR University Games Team	3:44.33
East German National Team	3:45.46

200-METER BACKSTROKE	
Dirk Richter (East Germany)	1:59.80
Gold—Rick Carey (U.S.)	2:00.23
Sergei Zabolotnov (USSR)	2:00.39
Vladimir Shemetov (USSR)	2:00.65
Silver—Frederic Delcourt (France)	2:01.75
Bronze—Cameron Henning (Canada)	2:02.37

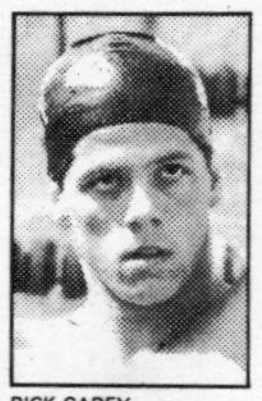

RICK CAREY U.S.

400-METER FREESTYLE RELAY	
Gold—U.S.	3:19.03
Silver—Australia	3:19.68
USSR National Team	3:20.88
USSR University Games Team	3:21.72
Bronze—Sweden	3:22.69
East German National Team	3:23.02

100-METER BREASTSTROKE	
Gold—Steve Lundquist (U.S.)	1:01.65
Silver—Victor Davis (Canada)	1:01.99
Dmitriy Volkov (USSR)	1:02.81
Bronze—Peter Evans (Australia)	1:02.97
Robertas Zhulpa (USSR)	1:03.32
Yuriy Kis (USSR)	1:04.04

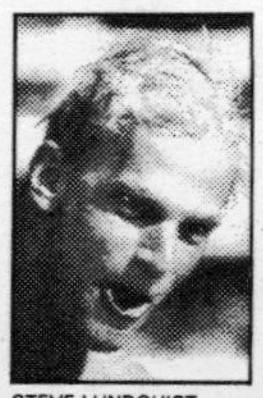

STEVE LUNDQUIST U.S.

800-METER FREESTYLE RELAY	
Gold—U.S.	7:15.69
Silver—West Germany	7:15.73
East German National Team	7:23.01
Bronze—Britain	7:24.78
USSR University Games Team	7:27.22
USSR National Team	7:27.71

Los Angeles Times

DAY 12 OLYMPICS '84

Jim Murray

Somebody Ought to Box the Ears Off Those Hats

For most sports fans, an Olympic Games is like being locked in a candy store overnight, marrying a girl with her own liquor store, getting washed ashore on a Pacific paradise with an entire company of chorus girls.

The track and field nuts have a cornucopia of fast fractions, non-winning times, Olympic records, personal bests. They think they've died and gone to Track and Field News heaven.

The chlorine set are ecstatic around the pool and the 10-meter platform, waving their flags, screaming for more world records, hugging themselves over negative splits in the backstroke.

The canoeists get their fill of repechages, the horsey set get to wear their jodhpurs and derby hats, the shootists get their jollies at the crack of the firearms and the splatter of the clay pigeons.

It's only that staple of the sports public, the ever-lovin' all-American fight fan that gets the short straw, the frustration of unfulfillment.

You would think a start list of some 300 fights in 10 days would set him to dreaming of a week in Valhalla, a happy hunting ground of split lips, cut eyes, torn ears, brain scans and sudden throat-catching cases of mid-ring unconsciousness, and would send him to new heights of euphoria.

Alas! it doesn't happen. Olympic fights are curiously unsatisfying exercises in futility for the bloodthirsty, the ringsider who wants to see the claret flow—or the ears swell. Or the eyes purple. There is no vent for "Looka that eye, Louie! Get the other one!" There are too few opportunities to jump to your feet and shout "Kill 'im!"

□

A fight fan raised in the eye-for-an-eye, hemorrhage-for-hemorrhage, smoke-filled galleries of St. Nick's Arena or the arnica puddles of the Hollywood Legion, any guy who ever implored his man, "Go to the liver, Tony!" is as curiously out of place at these polite pugilistics as a nun at a burlesque.

An old-time fight-handler was standing mournfully in a corner of the Sports Arena the other morning as two young hopefuls stood, plugging manfully, if ineptly, away in center ring. "They wear hats!" he spat contemptuously. "You ever think you'd live to see fighters wear hats outside a gym?" The "hats," of course, were headguards, mandatory, in this humane version of the manly art of self-defense. "What's next?" demanded our man from the past. "Goggles? Chest protectors? Facemasks? Call this boxing? This isn't boxing. This is a cotillion. A minuet. The Harvest Moon Ball. Synchronized dancing."

The confused crowd seems to agree with him. Boxing in America has always combined the strong features of a barroom homicide or a park mugging. In the Olympics, the referees stop the going if a shoelace comes undone. If a guy gets a nosebleed, they look around for a prosecutor. A light jab is almost the only punch that's legal, a knockdown is considered an unpardonable breach of manners, not to be encouraged and therefore rewarded only with the same score as a light touch of gloves or a slow clinch.

The "killer instinct," that dearly beloved homicidal urge of poem and song is frowned upon. If a referee sees one fighter in trouble or even breathing hard, the contest is stopped for a mandatory 8-count, no penalty. Any bleeding has to be wiped away at once and a doctor summoned if it persists or in any way stains clothing. Tony Galento would not have lasted through the introductions. The "Bayonne Bleeder" would have

Please see MURRAY, page 76

ANACLETO RAPPING / Los Angeles Times

Conrad Homfeld of Petersburg, Va., clears a jump on the way to clinching a gold medal for the United States in the team show jumping event at Santa Anita. (Story on page 77.)

Miller Conducts U.S. Symphony in Gold, 85-55

By CHRIS COBBS, *Times Staff Writer*

Cheryl Miller topped out somewhere near the flags and pastel banners suspended from the ceiling, elevating the U.S. women's basketball team to a long-anticipated gold medal Tuesday night at the Forum.

Miller was "outta sight" as the United States soared past South Korea, 85-55, before a crowd of 11,280.

If some fans had been anesthetized by the incessant buildup of American athletes, Miller's joyful play provided just the right touch for yet another American victory.

But if Miller touched the crowd with her individual artistry, it was her USC teammates, Pam and Paula McGee who provided perhaps the emotional high of the evening.

Pam presented Paula with her gold medal. Paula had just missed making the Olympic team.

"All our lives we wanted to be Olympians together," she said. "I was there physically, but my sister was there with me spiritually and emotionally."

Miller was here, there and everywhere, prompting South Korean Coach Cho Seung Youn to call her the best player in the history of women's basketball.

Miller, quite simply, is one plateau above everyone else in women's basketball and has been ever since she scored 105 points when she played for Riverside Poly High School. She is the female basketball equivalent of Carl Lewis, able to run faster and leap more nimbly than anyone else of her sex.

She seems most animated when the cameras are trained on her. Tuesday night, she gave a virtuoso performance that borrowed equally from Magic John-

Please see BASKETBALL, page 76

Mike Littwin

The Gold Is Great, but They Didn't Beat Soviets For It

The U.S. women's basketball team had just blown away the last and best of the competition with distressing ease.

Does it matter?

The American players received gold medals for their display cases, a deep sense of joy and perhaps little else. For there was something missing from the Forum floor Tuesday night—some much-needed drama.

In a more perfect world, it wouldn't have been the overmatched South Koreans struggling to keep pace with the United States before losing the gold-medal game, 85-55. No, it would have been the Soviet Union sharing the Forum court and helping to make a memory.

That's the rub, of course. The American team celebrated its victory, but this was hardly a celebration of women's basketball.

Who is going to remember this game? Will it produce a rush of support for women's basketball?

Will it make Cheryl Miller a star?

Please see LITTWIN, page 76

Rematch With China Is No Match; U.S. Women Left With the Silver

By JERRY CROWE, *Times Staff Writer*

One step short of fruition, the dreams of the U.S. women's volleyball came tumbling down and landed in a heap Tuesday night on the floor of the Long Beach Arena.

China soundly defeated the Americans, 16-14, 15-3, 15-9, to win the Olympic gold medal that some of the Americans had dedicated fully a third of their lives to attaining.

Although Coach Arie Selinger had said his mission was complete after the U.S. team beat Peru on Sunday night in the semifinals, it was clear he was just trying to relax his players for the final, which was played in front of another capacity crowd of 12,033.

When they lost, the tears flowed like the sweat of the eight-hour-a-day practices that had brought the Americans this far.

Obviously, the mission was not complete.

China, beaten by the Americans last Friday night in pool play, was clearly the better team when it mattered most, just as it was clearly the best team in the world throughout the quadrennial.

The Chinese won the World Cup in 1981 by beating Japan in the final in Japan, and won the quadrennial world championship in 1982 by beating Peru in the final in Peru.

They completed their sweep of major titles with a surprisingly easy win over a U.S. team that had been pointing toward this moment since 1978, making it perhaps the most experienced team in the history of American amateur athletics.

Please see VOLLEYBALL, page 76

JAYNE KAMIN and JOE KENNEDY / Los Angeles Times

Paula McGee (facing camera), who was cut from the U.S. team, shares emotional moment with sister Pam after gold medal victory. At right, tearful Paula wears Pam's gold medal.

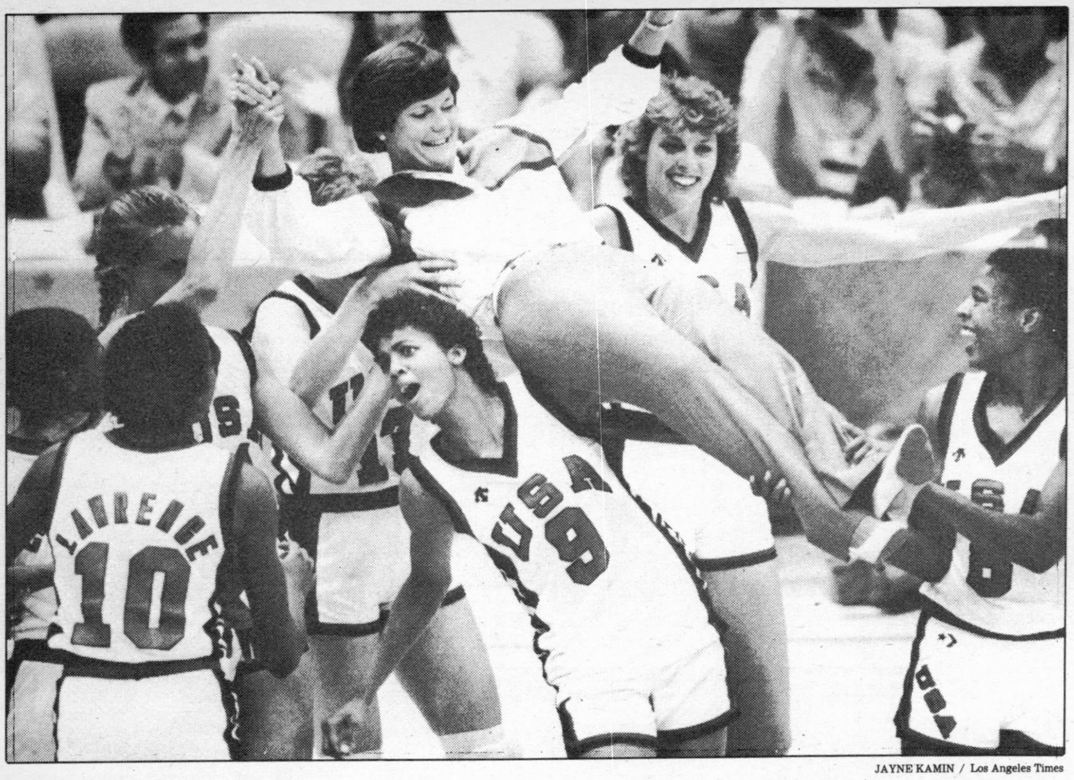

JAYNE KAMIN / Los Angeles Times

It is time for celebration as the U.S. women's basketball team whoops it up after its 85-55 win over South Korea in the gold medal game Tuesday night at the Forum. Coach Pat Head Summitt gets ride from Cheryl Miller and other team members.

BASKETBALL

Continued from page 75

son, Michael Jackson and Mary Lou Retton in its exuberance, passion and athleticism.

This was the first gold medal in women's basketball for the United States. The Soviet Union won in 1976 and 1980, the only times the sport had been contested at the Olympics.

Coach Pat Head Summitt thus added a gold medal to the silver she won as a player on the U.S. team in 1976.

China defeated Canada, 63-57, for the bronze medal.

Moments after the game ended, the South Koreans formed a circle and held Cho aloft.

The Americans responded in kind by giving Summitt the same treatment. The coach, in her red, white and blue ensemble, resembled a flag, of which there were hundreds being waved in the stands.

"It seems I've been second all my life," Summitt said, "so it was nice to finish on top for once."

Miller led the Americans with 16 points, 11 rebounds and 5 assists. Janice Lawrence had 14 points and 12 rebounds. Cindy Noble added 10 points.

Miller finished as the leading scorer in the tournament with 99 points.

She has nothing left to prove, as she admitted.

"I'm going to have to set some new goals because I've accomplished all my old ones," she said.

She modestly deflected Cho's praise.

"I don't think I'm the best," she said, "but I was playing with the best. I've been really blessed."

Miller's passing—maybe the least appreciated part of her game—produced a 42-27 halftime lead after the United States trailed briefly, 4-2, for the first time in the tournament.

After making a running interception, Miller heaved a 60-foot pass to Lawrence that got the offense moving after a sluggish start.

Later, she earned an unofficial gold medal in the floor exercise after tumbling in pursuit of a loose ball, and stomping the floor in exasperation when a pass eluded her.

Then she unleashed a one-hand, half-court outlet pass that led to a McGee layup.

Choi Aei Young's 6-for-9 shooting from long range accounted for much of South Korea's offense. Choi finished with 20 points.

In the second half, Miller, much like the rocket man at the opening ceremonies, electrified the crowd. She started the United States on a 14-point run, hitting a twisting layup, making a tap-in and arching another long pass to Curry.

She passed up a chance for a stuff when she went for a layup on a breakaway that put the game in the comfort zone, 56-38. With 4:13 left, she went to the bench, waving a towel and hugging Noble.

Later, when the medals were presented, Miller triumphantly held her arms aloft, sang the national anthem and embraced about half the team.

This was the evening of which Miller had dreamed while sitting in a rocking chair at home in Riverside. She would doze off and see her herself on the victory platform as a gold medal was draped around her neck.

"Everybody wants to be on top," Miller said in anticipation of the gold. "It was time for the Soviets to hand down the crown."

Miller had promised to unleash her whole game at the Olympics, and she did, leading the team in scoring, rebounding, floor burns and publicity.

It turned out to be almost sinfully easy. Miller's only fear had been not making the team, which prompted a teammate to throw a pillow at her in mock disgust. That might have been the only way for the world to stop her.

THE MEDALISTS

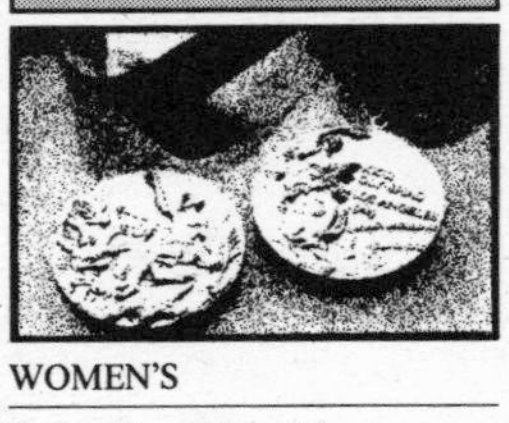

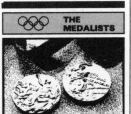

WOMEN'S

Basketball

HOW THEY FINISHED

1. United States
2. South Korea
3. China

LITTWIN

Continued from page 75

The answers probably are no, no and no. But if the Americans had beaten the Soviets in a game that they have come to dominate, maybe that would have made all the difference. Maybe women's basketball would have come into its own.

That has been the plan for U.S. women all along—to beat the Soviets. But the boycott robbed this tournament of any drama. Maybe the boycott beat the American team. Nothing else could.

Last year, American teams played the Soviets three times, winning once and then losing twice by a total of three points.

That's drama.

"Our first goal was to win a gold medal," said Kay Yow, the U.S. assistant coach. "The second thing we wanted to do was to play the Soviet Union.

"If my team (North Carolina State) was playing for the NCAA championship, I wouldn't mind if USC didn't show up. The Russians were invited. We didn't miss not having to play them.

"But beating them would have been good for our game."

It is a game that needs some help. If anyone can bring it to life, it is young Cheryl Miller. All she needs is a stage.

In leading USC to two NCAA championships in two seasons, the rising junior has done everything that can be done with a basketball, except dunk it. She didn't dunk it Tuesday either, but she played with a flair and excitement that transcends the women's game.

The women don't play above the rim, of course. And Miller is one of the few who even plays above the floor.

With the Americans leading, 50-38, Miller turned the game around in a flourish Magic Johnson would appreciate. She grabbed an offensive rebound and stuck it back in for a score. She grabbed a defensive rebound and drilled the ball upcourt to Denise Curry for a layup. Next, Miller was on the receiving end of a breakaway layup. Then, on a two-on-one fast break, she fed the ball to Curry for another basket.

Suddenly it was 58-38 and whatever hope the Koreans had at that point, Miller (16 points, 11 rebounds, 5 assists) had crushed.

But it's almost less what Miller does than how she does it. They should have judges when Miller plays.

She grabs rebounds with one hand. She passes the ball behind her back. She starts the fast break from wherever she gets the ball, often throwing it the length of the court against the Koreans. Once, she fell to the floor en route to a three-point play, tripping over nothing more than her own exuberance after the ball went into basket.

She's fun, but is she enough?

"I would love to (play the Russians)," Miller said. "There's no doubt in my mind it would have been a good game . . . I don't think anyone in the world could beat us right now."

That was the general consensus among the Americans, flush with victory.

South Korean Coach Seung-Youn Cho seemed to agree.

"Even if the Soviets had come the United States would still have a big advantage," he said. "Their level of pay and technique is the same, but the U.S. had the home-court advantage."

In this tournament, the United States had every advantage. No team came closer than 28 points. But more competition certainly couldn't have hurt.

"It would be difficult to evaluate whether a gold medal over Korea or the Soviet Union would have a greater impact," U.S. Coach Pat Head Summitt said. "I have to believe we have shown great players . . . and baseline-to-baseline intensity. I think we have exposed a great game to people around the world."

Maybe. But how many were watching?

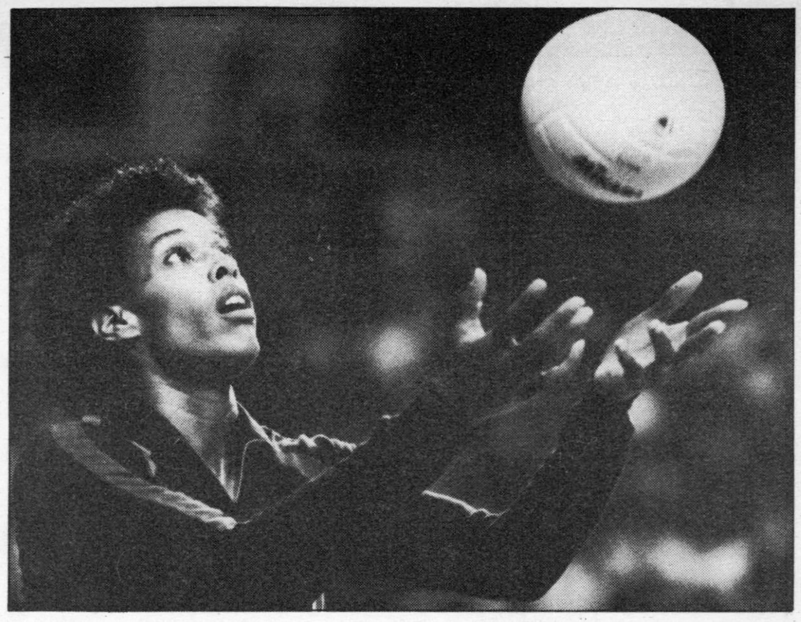

ROBERT LACHMAN / Los Angeles Times

America's Flo Hyman sets the ball against China. The U.S. won its first Olympic medal in volleyball.

VOLLEYBALL

Continued from page 75

The Chinese were much sharper and looked a lot quicker than they did last week.

Still, Selinger's team became the first U.S. team ever to win an Olympic volleyball medal.

"The team has nothing to be sad about," Selinger said.

The Americans, who came from behind in three of the four games to beat the Chinese last Friday, almost did it again in the first game Tuesday, rallying from a 14-9 deficit.

China had served for the game seven times before the United States tied it at 14-14.

That got the relatively subdued crowd a little more involved, but it quickly quieted down when China's Hou Yuzhu ended the game with two serves.

Paula Weishoff ducked under a floating Hou serve, thinking it was going out, only to have it land inside the baseline for an ace. Weishoff passed the next serve over the net to a leaping Lang Ping, who hit it down for the game-winner.

The Chinese romped in the second game as Selinger frantically searched for the right combination, substituting freely.

In the third, Selinger went back to his starting lineup, and the Americans opened a 4-1 lead. But China then scored eight straight points to take control.

China passed much better than it had last Friday, when the Americans had 13 service aces. On Tuesday, the Americans had only five aces.

"The key to the match was China's better service reception," Selinger said.

It was a tough road for the Americans just to reach this point.

Six of the women on the U.S. team—Flo Hyman, Rita Crockett, Carolyn Becker, Sue Woodstra, Debbie Green and Laurie Flachmeier—had been training together since 1978.

Those six, along with Julie Vollertsen, who joined the team in 1979, were veterans of the 1980 boycott.

THE MEDALISTS

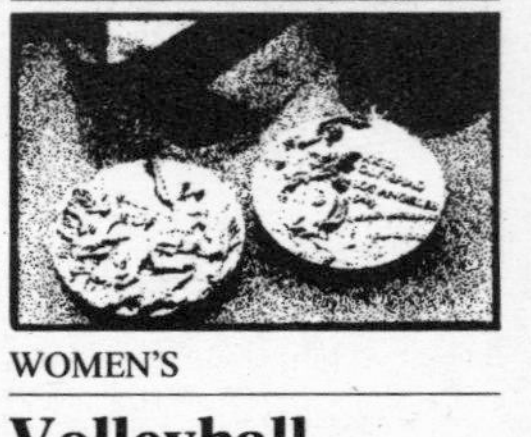

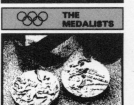

WOMEN'S

Volleyball

HOW THEY FINISHED

1. China
2. United States
3. Japan

After much soul-searching, they decided after the disappointment of 1980 to dedicate four more years to their dream; to continue, as Flachmeier put it, "to eat, drink and sleep volleyball."

Almost all of the players had to leave school and give up college scholarships to train with the team full-time in Selinger's regimented atmosphere.

None of the 12 players are married, none went to school while they trained (only one has a college degree) and none had jobs.

Unlike other programs, like China's, which allows Lang to work on a Ph.D while she trains, the Americans' involved nothing but volleyball.

They traveled the world, playing up to 100 matches a year.

All with a single-minded purpose: to win an Olympic gold medal.

Some called the program un-American.

But Selinger, hired by the U.S. Volleyball Assn. in 1975 to develop a competitive national team, defended his methods, saying he was only doing what had to be done for the Americans to catch up to the world's best teams.

"When I came, everybody said we can win everything, and I said, 'Why?' " Selinger said last year. "They said we have the talent. Well, Cuba has the talent. China has the talent. Everybody has the talent. The difference is the training."

They climbed the ladder in international volleyball, finishing fifth at the World Cup in 1981 and third at the world championships two years ago, but they weren't able to reach the top step.

Japan vs. Peru. Japan won the bronze medal, its worst Olympics finish, with a 13-15, 15-4, 15-7, 15-10 victory.

The two-time Olympic champions, who had never lost an Olympic match to anybody other than the Soviet Union before losing to China on Sunday night, didn't seem too disappointed with their showing.

Coach Shigeo Yamada said his current team is as talented as the Japanese team that won the gold medal in 1976, but that the level of competition in international women's volleyball had improved so much that the Japanese had fallen behind.

Emiko Odaka put down 21 of 37 kill attempts for the Japanese. Teammate Yoko Mitsuya was successful on 15 of 28 kill tries.

Peru's all-world hitter, Cecilia Tait, was 25 of 52 in kill tries.

South Korea vs. West Germany. The defense-minded South Koreans romped in the fifth-place match, winning in 52 minutes, 15-10, 15-10, 15-2.

Brazil vs. Canada. The Brazilians easily won the seventh-place match, 15-9, 15-3, 15-8, against an overmatched Canadian team that didn't win a game in five matches. The Canadians never scored more than 10 points in any one game during the tournament.

Volleyball Notes

The U.S. men's team, which lost for the first time in four matches Monday night to Brazil, plays Canada (3-1) at 6:30 p.m. tonight in the semifinals. The Americans had won 21 straight matches from the Canadians before losing to them twice last spring. Canada beat the world champion Soviet Union three times last month in Canada . . . In the other semifinal at 8:30 p.m., Brazil (3-1) meets Italy (3-1). Other matches today: Japan (3-1) vs. Argentina (1-3) and South Korea (3-1) vs. China (1-3) in the fifth-place semifinals; Egypt (0-4) vs. Tunisia (0-4) for ninth place.

MURRAY

Continued from page 75

had to wear gauze. Contests are stopped if one participant sneezes.

What the American fight fan finds totally insupportable is, the object is to score points, not fracture skulls. The matter is contested the way the Marquis of Queensberry intended you should. The whole tournament is conducted in such an atmosphere of suffocating politeness, it's even impossible to taunt your opponent in the ring. Talking deducts points. Ali would be unable to function. Imagine not being able to call your opponent a "washerwoman"!?

You can't really fight out of a crouch. Dempsey would be neutralized. You can't pull any backhands, eye gouges, rib laces, hit on the break, butt or elbow. Fritzie Zivic wouldn't win a round.

American boxing historically has treated the Olympic version of the sport as a kind of dandified, overcivilized corruption of the real thing, anyway. A sport for college boys, not real pugs. An occasional Fidel La Barba (Paris, 1924) came out of its ranks to campaign successfully in the pros (Fidel won the world flyweight title, fought for the featherweight championship against the Kid Chocolates, Bat Battalinos and Bushy Grahams). Norway's Otto von Porat fought the Jack Sharkey-Max Schmeling era heavyweights. Lou Salica went from the 1932 Los Angeles Olympics to the world bantam title.

But they were the exceptions, and it was not until Floyd Patterson and Ingemar Johansson came out of the '52 Helsinki Olympics to make millions on the U. S. circuit that the fight mob began to take to the international sport seriously as a breeding ground for meal tickets.

Muhammad Ali, then Cassius Clay, showed that it was the prime staging area for a career when he dazzled the Rome Olympics before taking the act on Broadway, and then, in 1976, Jacobs' Beach, the fight manager's Wall Street, hit the jackpot when a whole generation of moneymakers, TV champions and contenders came out of the Montreal Games. Sugar Ray Leonard was the most legit of them, but the Spinks brothers, the Howard Davises and Leo Randolphs all had their moments.

None of this conditions the red-combed, white-crested Americanus Fight Phanus for this white-blooded perversion of his once manly art. Even the postfight interviews gall him, where the interpreter translates a Romanian pugilist as saying of a loss, "I believe the majority of my blows with the left hand found their target, but I feel my opponent won the fight fairly and was superior in all phases of the contest." What kind of cop-out is that? Why doesn't he speak up like a man and say what the U.S. fan knows he means: "I outscored the bum 10-1 in left hooks, and I would've left him for dead if that kraut referee got outta my way. What fight do you think those judges were looking at?"

But the American fight fan is nothing if not resourceful. When the best American fighter, by common consensus, Mark Breland, merely won a 5-0 decision over a Romanian youngster the other night, the crowd had had quite enough of the *noblesse oblige*, compliment-swapping, flag-exchanging, being-a-brick-about-the-whole-thing and booed him lustily. The cry of the true fight fan was finally heard in the hall. "Breland, yer a bum! Mickey Walker would've handed you your head. Call yerself a fighter? Not in my old neighborhood."

Or, as the old-timer might scorn, "When they start fighting with their hats on, no wonder the whole country is going to the dogs!" I mean, whatever would John L. Sullivan say?

Equestrian

Only Show in Jumping: Spectacular U.S. Riders

By LYNN SIMROSS,
Times Staff Writer

U. S. show jumping Coach Frank Chapot had predicted all year that America's Olympic squad would win its first team gold medal ever and he was right. It was no contest.

Tuesday, at Santa Anita, the U.S. team of four riders was awesome, winning with an overall total of 12 points to 36.75 for Britain, the silver medalist. The British rallied to slip past West Germany, which finished with 39.25.

"The Americans made us look like fools," said West German anchor rider Paul Schockemohle, whose team was expected to provide the United States with its stiffest competition. "They were so good and unbeatable today. It was absolutely impossible to believe how they beat the competition."

Points for team jumping are scored on a cumulative basis for the two rounds, with the lowest total winning. Each of the team's four riders is scored, but the lowest scores of only three riders are counted.

Riders receive four faults for each rail down (there are 15 obstacles; 18 fences in all); three faults for a refusal and .25-second penalty for each second over the 119 seconds allowed to cover the course.

Joe Fargis of Petersburg, Va., was America's first rider and he set the tone for the day, scoring a clean round—no fences down and no time faults—aboard his 11-year-old mare, Touch of Class.

Touch of Class appeared to be bothered by the loud cheering of the partisan crowd of 31,046, but Fargis quickly got her under control. However, after the first round, he admitted that silence would have made the going a little easier.

"It (the noise) made my horse excited," Fargis said. "I'd like them to be quiet the next time."

Leslie Burr of Westport, Conn., was in the second spot, aboard Albany, and she completed her first round with one rail down for four faults. The third rider, Conrad Homfeld, aboard Abdullah, had an eight-fault total in round one, but America's anchor rider, Melanie Smith of Litchfield, Conn., was perfect, guiding Calypso through a clean round.

Discounting Homfeld's total, the Americans were leading the second-place West Germans by 16 points (4 to 20), after the first round. After the spectacular beginning, the fight was strictly for second place, especially when Fargis went clean again in the second round. Burr had eight faults in her second ride.

Homfeld, also of Petersburg, Va., clinched the gold medal when he rode Abdullah, a 13-year-old gray Trakehner stallion through a clean round. It was the first Olympic team show jumping gold medal for the United States since equestrian events became a permanent part of the Games in 1912.

Because of Homfeld's no-fault second round, Smith didn't even have to to ride again.

"This is really a special feeling because it's a team medal," Smith said afterward. "This is the most special feeling I've ever had."

Smith said the team had dedicated itself to winning the gold and had trained extremely hard.

"I didn't think it was that easy," she said. "I think our riders rode so beautifully and the horses went so well. We deserved it, whether we won by a lot or not."

With the Americans riding superbly, attention focused on the competition for the silver and bronze medals. It was a lot closer, and a lot more interesting.

After the first round, Spain was in third place, and Switzerland, Canada and Britain were tied for fourth. France was in seventh, only 1.75 points behind the trio of nations in fourth.

The West German four completed their round before the British riders and it appeared that they had a firm grip on second place. But Britain's brother act of John and Michael Whitaker came through with the silver medal on the line.

Riding third, Michael scored a clean round, one of only 10 all day. Then John, aboard 15-year-old Ryan's Son, knocked down only one fence and sustained one time fault to undercut the West Germans by 2.50 points.

"I knew I had to go with no more than one fence down to get the silver," John Whitaker said. "When the first one went down, I thought, that's it."

For the most part, riders praised the course, designed by Bertalan de Nemethy, former coach of America's show jumping squads.

Schockemohle called it "marvelous. An important course, more of a technical one, and very difficult."

U.S. Coach Chapot, a six-time Olympian, said he thought that it was the best Olympic course he'd ever seen, and that the other coaches he had spoken with agreed.

"Many times the course is very big, too big for the smaller horses," Chapot said. "This tested the rider's skill and the horses that were trained the best.

"And thank God we won."

Canada, Switzerland, and Spain all faltered during the second round, finishing fourth, fifth and seventh, respectively. France moved up to sixth.

"It is always an advantage to be at home," said Schockemohle, who had a fence down in each round. "But today, the Americans would have won anywhere."

On Sunday, three riders from each nation will compete for the individual show jumping medals, and if the U.S. riders sustain Tuesday's form, they will be difficult to stop.

"It will be tough to beat them," Schockemohle said. "but everything is possible in our kind of sport."

□

Officials of the Italian team suggested that there were "suspicious circumstances" surrounding the first-round ride of Filippo Moyersoen, who was unable to continue after a strap broke in two places along the girth of his horse, Adam II. Neither horse nor rider was injured in the resulting spill.

He was eliminated but came back to ride the second round. An inspection of the strap revealed a scrape running horizontally across the leather, clearly visible where the strap broke.

After saying it was "very strange" that the strap broke, Italian Coach Raimondo D'Inzeo said he would not protest or demand an investigation.

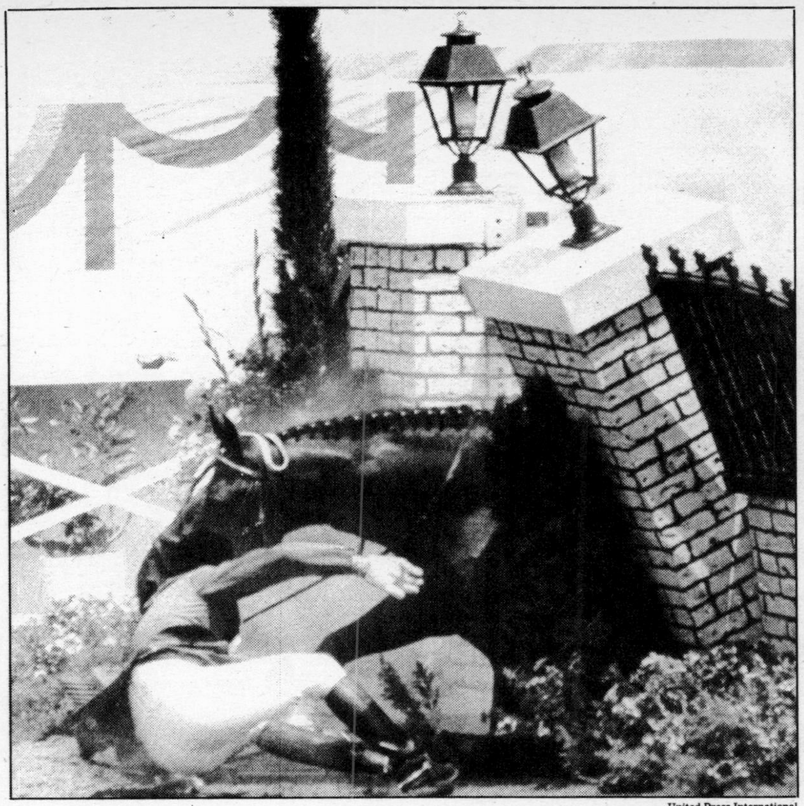

United Press International

Italy's Bruno Scolari, riding Joyau D'Or, tumbles to the ground after crashing through an obstacle during the Olympic team show jumping competition at Santa Anita on Tuesday.

THE MEDALISTS

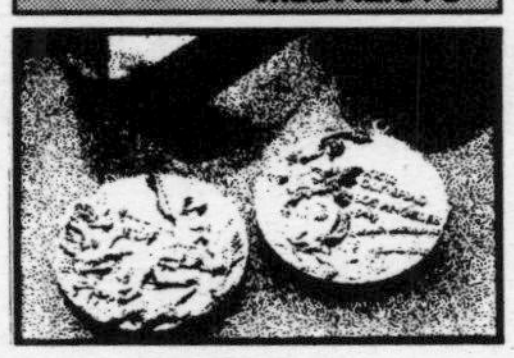

Equestrian

■ TEAM JUMPING

1. United States
2. Britain
3. West Germany

Women's Team Handball

There'll Be Gold for Yugoslavia, No U.S. Medals

By TOM HAMILTON, *Times Staff Writer*

They were turning somersaults for Yugoslavia, but there were tears in the eyes of some of the American women's team handball players Tuesday night at Cal State Fullerton.

Yugsolavia clinched its first gold medal in women's team handball competition with a 29-23 win over South Korea, whereas the United States lost any chance for a medal following an 18-17 loss to West Germany.

Both games played to capacity crowds of 3,300.

Yugoslavia's win was its fourth consecutive in the six-team tournament. Since the other five teams in the tournament have at least two losses, Yugoslavia is assured a gold medal when it plays China on Thursday because of its superior record.

The United States' loss to West Germany was its third in the round-robin tournament. West Germany and South Korea will meet for the silver medal on Thursday, with the loser earning the bronze. The United States closes out play against Austria on the same day.

Four years ago, Yugoslavia won the silver medal in Moscow, finishing second to the host country. The Soviet Union has never lost a game in Olympic competition, and Yugoslavia's coach, Josip Samarzija, was asked the obvious question: Did the Soviet-led boycott tarnish the gold?

"I think this time we were prepared to win the gold no matter who was here," he said. "We have been on top for a long time. The gold medal has been in the making for almost five years."

Still, Yugoslavia hardly looked like the team that had routed three previous opponents when it took the floor against South Korea. The Yugoslavs were tentative and sluggish, struggling to a 15-14 lead at halftime.

The quicker South Koreans gave Yugoslavia fits defensively, repeatedly scoring from the wing positions with some excellent one-on-one maneuvers. But South Korea's upset hopes were dealt a severe blow with 7:47 left in the first half when one of its top players, Yoon Byung Soon, broke her nose when she crashed hard on the taraflex surface while attempting to score.

The game was tied, 11-11, when the injured player was taken to the locker room on a stretcher, and South Korea never recovered. South Korea managed to stay close until Yugoslavia's Svetlana Dasic-Kitic put the game out of reach with three goals in a two-minute stretch.

Dasic-Kitic dazzled the crowd with a wrap-around-the-back shot that hit the mark with 5:48 left to play and then scored from the nine-meter line with 5:04 remaining to give her country a 27-21 lead.

"The shot (wraparound) was the beginning of the celebration," she said. "It's not something I normally do, that's for sure."

Teammate Ljubinka Jankovic completed the celebration by scoring a goal with three seconds left for the final score and then turning a somersault at midcourt.

"Believe me, we will party tonight," Jasna Kolar-Merdan said. Kolar-Merdan led all scorers with eight goals for a total of 41 in four games.

While Yugoslavia had something to celebrate, the U.S. women were trying their best not to show the hurt inside.

"We're hurting right now," said winger Sherry Winn. "We're frustrated, but at the same time we have to feel good knowing that we came within a goal of a team we'd never been closer to than 10 goals."

Continuing to follow a trend, the U.S. women fell behind, only to stage a furious comeback behind the scoring of Leora Sam Jones.

Fencing

West Germans Take Women's Team Foil Gold

By JOHN DART, *Times Staff Writer*

West Germany won its first-ever Olympic women's team foil title Tuesday night in Long Beach with a 9-5 victory over a similarly medal-hungry Romanian team.

Cornelia Hanisch, 32, the individual foil silver medalist, and Christiane Weber, 22, groomed as Hanisch's successor, both had 3-1 records to lead the West German squad. A near-capacity crowd of about 3,000 watched in the Terrace Theater.

Romania, like West Germany, had taken at least one bronze in previous Olympic women's team competition—but never the gold or silver medal.

Since the event was introduced in the 1960 Games, the Soviet women had won four times, Hungary once and France once. France won the gold in Moscow but was edged by Romania here in the semifinals, 8-7.

The French women gained the bronze, denying Italy a medal for the first time in five events. France defeated Dorina Vaccaroni—1983 world champion—and company, 9-7, in a 2½-hour match at Exhibition Hall.

Actually, Vaccaroni did poorly in team matches. She lost all three of her bouts against France (and was replaced in one bout) and was 1-3 against the West Germans. Temperamental and clashing with other team members, she has said she will retire for three years and study medicine, possibly returning to competition in 1988.

In the last bout for the bronze, Italy's Lucia Traversa received a painful cut on her right knee during the opening exchange with France's Veronique Brouquier, but took a 4-1 lead nevertheless. One more point and Italy would have won the match since its point total would have broken an 8-8 tie in bouts won and lost.

But Brouquier rallied for two more points and won the next two on fleches, or running attacks.

In Italy's earlier matches as well, it was always Traversa who had the final outcome tossed in her lap. Against West Germany, Italy was down 8-7 and Traversa (3-0) needed to win again, but this time by a good margin. When Zita Funkenhauser took a 4-2 lead, that was enough and Traversa's eventual 5-4 victory came to naught.

It was Traversa who won the decisive bout to give Italy an 8-7 win over upset-minded China. The Italian was down 4-1 but rallied to win 5-4 over Zhu Minzhu. Chinese coach Wen Kuquang immediately got up from his sideline seat and walked away, unable to look at his fencer or say anything for a prolonged period.

China later downed the U.S. women for fifth place, 9-5. Current U.S. champion Vinnie Bradford won three bouts and lost only to individual gold medalist Luan Jujie.

The American team placed sixth among 10 entries, a finish called respectable by team member Debra Waples. "We didn't get blown away," she said.

All three Americans in the men's individual epee preliminaries failed to advance to today's direct elimination round of 16 fencers headed by Angelo Mazzoni of Italy and Philippe Boisse of France.

U.S. coaches lodged a protest, however, after Robert Marx' last opponent, Volker Fischer of West Germany, was warned for unsportsmanlike conduct. Marx said Fischer hit the floor on the side of the fencing strip with his epee tip in a tactical manuever to cut into the time remaining in their bout.

U.S. officials claimed that such a warning is grounds for excluding the fencer from further play and have appealed the decision to permit Fischer to advance.

Judo

Wieneke of West Germany Upsets Britain's Adams for the Gold

By DICK RORABACK,
Times Staff Writer

In a stunning upset Tuesday night, young Frank Wieneke of West Germany brought Britain's supposedly indomitable Neil Adams to his knees to win an Olympic gold medal in the 172-pound division. It was the first time in Adams' long career that he had lost by *ippon* (judo equivalent of a knockout).

With all eyes on Adams, the methodical Wieneke, a 22-year-old German engineering student, inched up the ladder of opponents almost unnoticed, even after he had beaten Japan's Hiromitsu Takano in the first round. The Japanese, many felt, was not in top condition—an early tip-off being the sparcity of the usual crowd of Los Angeles' Asian community at the Cal State Los Angeles site.

Conversely, Adams, winner of the evening's silver medal, European champion and silver medalist in the 1980 Games, smiled frequently at the sea of Union Jacks virtually papering the walls of the gym.

The closest thing to a complete player in judo today, the popular Briton had pulled himself out of a working-class neighborhood in Coventry by his black belt to become not only a national hero, but one of his country's top sportswear models.

Wieneke, meanwhile, had dropped out of school only for a year, found himself a Korean trainer, and developed a self-discipline that obviously was a match for Adams' unmatched judo savvy.

Adams, in the opposite pool from Wieneke, had sliced through the best of his weight class, destroying the arm—and the medal chances—of America's Brett Barron in the process. Barron, who thrives on pressure perhaps more than any other American judoka, missed a throw in his rousing bout with Adams, his momentum landing him on his hands and knees.

Nobody would take such an awkward stance with Adams on purpose, and Barron knew it—too late. Adams was instantly on Barron's back. The Briton reached down, got Barron's right arm in a vise and the American was finished.

Barron had suffered a dislocated elbow, but even more important, a dislocated thumb as well. With a chance at the bronze later in the evening, the gutsy fighter from Millbrae, Calif., returned to the ring, his thumb taped tight to his fingers, but the famous Barron grip was obviously an impossibility.

Twin bronze medals were awarded to Romania's Mircea Fratica and Michel Nowak of France.

□

As far as the world's top judo players are concerned, the late sportswriter, Grantland Rice, was slightly off the mark. In judo, it's "not that you won or lost," but how you draw.

The random draw of opponents can be kind, virtually assuring a medal to a relatively mediocre player, or it can be cruel, pitting two champions in an early round and assuring the demise of one.

American draws to date have had mixed reviews. In Sunday night's draw, for example, Barron drew two of the world's top three judokas, Adams of England and Nowak of France, not only in his pool, but in his *quarter*.

In tonight's 189-pound division, American Bobby Berland has what has been termed a "cakewalk" to a medal. By contrast, Leo White, at 209 pounds, could not have pulled a worse—or better, depending on viewpoint—name out of the hat: In his first match, he squares off against Robert Van de Walle of Belgium, far and away the class of his division.

In the heavyweight division, American Doug Nelson, has a so-so draw, but in the open division, Dewey Mitchell has what appears to be a relatively safe passage to the final—a dubious advantage, since the other finalist is almost sure to be the spectacular Japanese giant, Yasuhiro Yamashita.

By now, of course, every player is psyched up over the draw, often in opposite directions.

"Cakewalk?" asks Berland, incredulously. "*Nothing* in judo is a cakewalk. In my pool, I have to play (Walter) Carmona of Brazil, a guy who beat me on a split decision the last time we fought. But even to *get* to Carmona, I have to get past either the Briton (Densign White, who is second in Britain only to the incomparable Adams) or the Italian (Mario Vecchio), neither of whom I've ever met.

"That Carmona fight is going to be a hell of a match—*if* I get that far. *Then* we start thinking medal."

As for White, his buddy, lightweight bronze-medalist Ed Liddie, radiates cautious optimism. "Leo's not down at all," says Liddie. "He's excited. Leo comes out strong—not like me. He doesn't have to warm up.

"If he catches Van de Walle even a little bit flat, he's in clover."

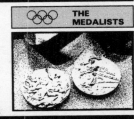

Judo

■ HALF-MIDDLEWEIGHT

1. Frank Wieneke (W. Germany)
2. Neil Adams (Britain)
3. (tie) Michel Nowak (France)
   Mircea Fratic (Romania)

THE MEDALISTS

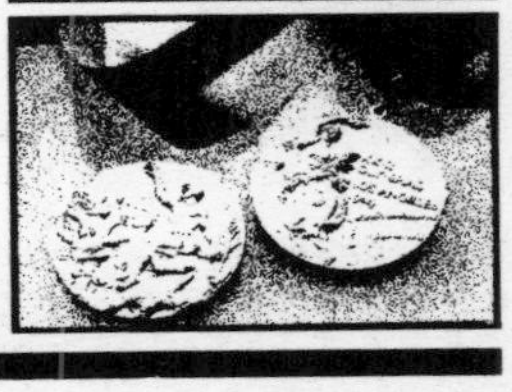

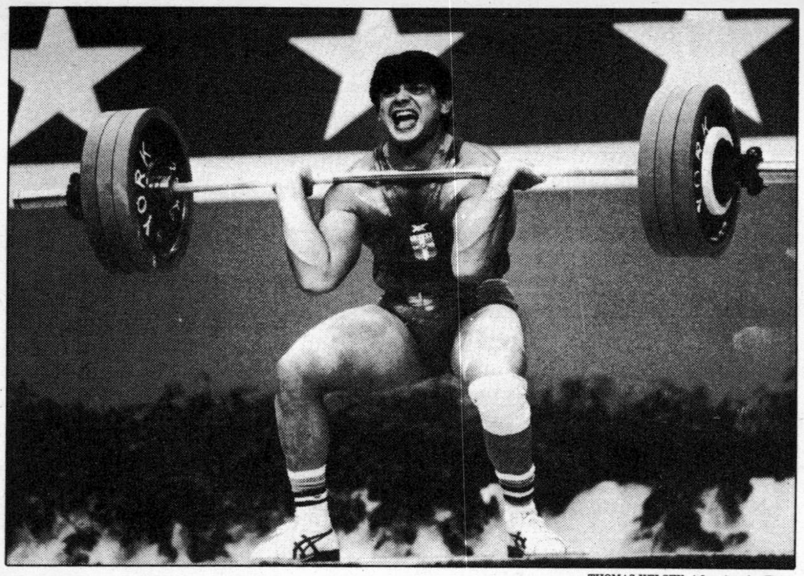

THOMAS KELSEY / Los Angeles Times

Weightlifter George Panayotakis of Greece strains under 413¼ pounds during the heavyweight competition Tuesday at Loyola-Marymount University. Panayotakis failed to complete the lift.

Weightlifting

Heavyweight Guy Carlton's Bronze Breaks a Medal Drought for U.S.

By CHRIS BAKER, *Times Staff Writer*

Guy Carlton became the first American weightlifter in eight years to win an Olympic medal when he earned the bronze in the heavyweight class (242 pounds) Tuesday night at Loyola-Marymount University.

"The only thing I can say is it's about time," said John Terpak, two-time Olympic weightlifter and now the general manager of the York Barbell Club.

Carlton, a 30-year-old construction worker from Colorado Springs, Colo., lifted a total of 832 pounds, finishing third behind Norberto Oberburger of Italy, who lifted 859.75 for the gold, and Stefan Tasnadi of Romania, who totaled 837.5 for the silver. Oberburger's gold medal was Italy's first in 60 years in the sport.

The last American to win an Olympic weightlifting medal was Lee James, who got the silver in the 198.25-pound class at Montreal. The last American to earn a gold medal was Chuck Vinci in the 123.25-pound class at the 1960 Games in Rome.

Carlton made a strong bid to win the gold medal on his last clean and jerk, trying to hoist 496 pounds, 16.5 pounds more than his previous best.

LMU's Albert Gersten Pavilion was a madhouse before Carlton's last lift, with many in the crowd of 3,087 waving American flags and chanting "USA! USA!" They fell silent, however, when Carlton strode onto the platform and pumped both fists into the air.

Carlton's wife, Jan, and their 9½-month-old baby daughter, Jeannie, were in the stands along with his parents, Guy and Betty. Carlton said that he almost never missed a lift when his daughter was watching, but he missed this one.

"All my life I had dreamed of having the opportunity to go for the gold medal," he said. "When I went out there for my last lift I was thinking of my wife, Jan, and little girl, Jeannie, and I was hoping to win it for both them and the USA."

Carlton went into his squat, but he couldn't get the bar to his chest, and that was that.

"My best clean and jerk ever was 217 kilos (479.5 pounds), so I was 7½ kilos (16.5 pounds) over my best clean and jerk."

Carlton might have been able to win the silver medal, but he made several strategic moves in the clean and jerk in an attempt to win the gold.

Carlton put down 468.25 pounds for his third attempt, but then called to the platform and requested an increase to 473.75. Carlton then asked for another increase to 496 pounds after Oberburger had lifted 473.75.

"The silver didn't really mean anything more to me than the bronze," Carlton said. "So I decided to go for the gold."

Carlton, the only member of the 1980 Olympic weightlifting team to compete here, almost gave up the sport after the U.S. boycotted the 1980 Games.

He changed his mind, though, and decided to continue training for 1984. He quit his job in a machine shop in Decatur, Ill., and moved his family to Colorado Springs to be near the Olympic training center. He works as a concrete finisher. His wife attends court reporter's school.

His wife said they had had to endure some hard times, financially, during the last four years, but added, "It's worth it because this is what he wanted to do and he wouldn't have been happy if he didn't lift weights. He was devastated (by the boycott). But we just kept going."

Carlton said he would like to keep lifting but that he might not be able to continue training for the 1988 Olympics unless he got a better job. He would like to become a weight training coach for a pro sports team.

Oberburger watched Carlton's final attempt on a TV backstage in the tent where the lifters warm up. "If he made it he was definitely stronger than me and he deserved it," Oberburger said.

Carlton missed the attempt, however, and Oberburger became Italy's first Olympic weightlifting gold medalist since 1924, when the Italians won the featherweight, middleweight and heavyweight classes at the Paris Games.

Oberburger, 24, has been lifting since he was 15. He finished third in the 242.5-pound class at the 1984 European championships and seventh in the 220.75-pound class at the 1983 world championships.

"I have been lifting for nine years," he said. "At one point this was very far away, but slowly and surely I have fought for it."

When Oberburger left his home town of Merano, Italy, to come to Los Angeles for the Games, his wife, Erna, was expecting their first child.

"I just got a call three days ago saying that the child (a girl) had been born," Oberburger said. "I still don't know what its name is yet, my wife hasn't told me."

Tasnadi, 29, a shoe factory worker from Cluj who finished fourth in the 242.5-pound class at the 1983 world championships, announced his retirement at a press conference after the competition.

"This was my last contest," he said. "The silver medal at the Olympics was the last one I needed to complete my collection."

Baseball

Japan Beats U.S. at Its Own Game for Championship Before 55,235

By BOB CUOMO, *Times Staff Writer*

The U.S. team picked to play in the Olympic baseball demonstration tournament at Dodger Stadium had been called the best American amateur squad ever.

The consensus was that the United States would easily finish first in the eight-team tournament.

But somebody forgot to tell Japan.

Tuesday night before a sellout crowd of 55,235, Japan defeated the United States, 6-3, to win the honorary gold medal.

Earlier Tuesday, Taiwan beat South Korea, 3-0, in 14 innings for third place.

Because baseball is a demonstration sport, the tournament results don't count in the official medal standings. The top three teams received special medals. International Olympic Committee President Juan Antonio Samaranch presided at the awards ceremony.

The United States was expected to win the tournament with a high-powered offense that produced 35 runs, a batting average of .322 and nine home runs while winning its first four tournament games.

Although they won Monday night's semifinal game against South Korea, 5-2, the Americans managed only six hits. Fortunately, one was a two-run homer by Oddibe McDowell and another was a two-run double by Cory Snyder.

Tuesday night the Americans were restricted to seven hits. Two were home runs, a solo shot to left in the third inning by Shane Mack and a two-run home run to left-center in the bottom of the ninth by Snyder.

Japan held a tenuous 3-1 lead after seven innings, but broke the game open in the eighth, scoring three runs on a home run by Katsumi Hirosawa, who drove John Hoover's 1-0 pitch high over the 370-foot sign in left-center.

For Hirosawa, the biggest player on the Japanese team at 6-1, 187, it was his third homer of the tournament. He finished with nine runs batted in.

Hirosawa 22, a student at Meiji University, is one of seven players from the collegiate all-star squad that lost six of seven games to the United States during a nationwide, pre-Olympic tour. He hit only .125 in the seven games, going 2 for 16 with no RBIs.

Hoover, who went the distance opening night last Tuesday to beat Taiwan, 2-1, allowing only four hits, wasn't nearly as sharp against Japan. During his 7⅔ innings of work, he allowed seven hits, all six runs and walked three.

Taiwan 3, South Korea 0 (14 innings)—Taiwan won third place when Lin Hua-Wei tripled home Li Chih-Chun and Yang Ching-Long followed with a line-drive home run to left to end the 3 hour 41-minute game.

Besides the clutch hitting of Lin and Yaang, Taiwan also received brilliant pitching from Chuang Sheng-Hsiung and Tu Fu-Ming, who combined for a three-hitter and 16 strikeouts.

Tu relieved Chuang with one out in the 11th inning with a runner on second base. He got out of that minor jam and blanked South Korea on one infield single the rest of the game.

Chuang had a no-hitter for 6⅓ innings, but Kang Ki Woong broke it up with a single to left. Kang had struck out his previous two at-bats and was hitting only .156 for the tournament.

Chuang, making his third appearance of the tournament—he beat Italy, 10-0, last Saturday—pitched 10⅓ innings. He allowed just two singles, walked three and struck out 13.

In 21⅓ innings, he has allowed 10 hits, no runs, walked four and struck out 20.

NOTES

From Times Staff Writers and Wire Services

Mary Decker, favored to win the 3,000 meters Friday, is just glad to be in the race.

"I think it's a miracle that I'm here and that I'll be able to compete," Decker said. "You can believe, coming down the homestretch Friday night, I'll be fighting."

Decker's chronic lower-leg problems cropped up again recently, and she feared she would have to undergo surgery on her right leg.

However, her doctor elected to give her an injection of cortisone and fluid in an attempt to free adhesions in the shin area. That was July 18.

"I could feel the adhesions ripping," Decker said. "It was the most painful injection I've ever had. The next day, I was really depressed. It was so sore I couldn't walk."

Said her coach, Dick Kopriva: "Three days after surgery she looked like Chester (the limping deputy) of 'Gunsmoke.' I don't mean the mustache, I mean the walk. But she was back on the track within four days of the injection."

The semifinals of the women's 3,000 meters will be held tonight.

—SCOTT OSTLER

□

Edwin Moses' wife, Myrella, said in an ABC television interview she did not want her husband to run in the 1988 Olympics because the pressure was too great. Not on him but on her.

Then Jim Lampley asked Moses if he wanted to compete in 1988. "Unfortunately, I might have to," said Moses, twice an Olympic gold medalist in the 400-meter intermediate hurdles.

Probably because of time constraints, Lampley failed to follow up on Moses' answer.

So the viewers were left to wonder why Moses, now 28, might have to run in the 1988 Games at Seoul, South Korea.

The answer has to do with the contracts that Moses has signed with apparel and shoe companies and other sponsors. The majority of his contracts, including his $2-million-plus deal with adidas, run through 1988.

He discovered early in negotiations that most companies were willing to make a more substantial financial commitment if it appeared they would benefit from their association with him for more than just this year.

Moses has confirmed that he earned $457,500 last year and could possibly double that figure this year.

—RANDY HARVEY

□

Gold medalist swimmer George DiCarlo said he sympathized with Swiss marathoner Gabriela Andersen-Schiess and could relate to what she was going through Sunday as she staggered around the Coliseum toward the finish line.

DiCarlo, who won the 400-meter freestyle last Thursday, ran a marathon four years ago after he failed to qualify to swim in the 1980 Olympic trials.

"I trained for four days, running five miles each day," he said. "On Friday, I tapered (rested), and on Saturday, I ran my first marathon."

Four and a half hours later, the 16-year-old DiCarlo said he looked about like Andersen-Schiess as he neared the finish.

"The last nine miles were pure torture. I crossed the finish line and fell into some lady's arms," DiCarlo said. "She asked if I needed a doctor. I said, 'No, just drag me over to that Coors truck.' "

—JOHN WEYLER

□

Sports Arena security people were startled when they spotted a metal box under the last row of the press section.

Police were summoned, the bomb-sniffing dog sent for, and the last row was cleared of newspeople. Police were about to evacuate the entire press section, when press steward Moon Mullins suddenly remembered something.

He found another press steward, Jesse Robinson, and asked: "Jesse, is that your metal box under the last press row?"

"Yes," Robinson said, "it's my lunch."

—EARL GUSTKEY

□

After an errant javelin sent orange-clad officials in the Coliseum infield running for cover Saturday, new rules were instituted to prevent this from happening again.

Starting Monday, inspectors lining the track were allowed to turn around and watch the field events when no races are in progress.

What if a race is in progress and they hear a roar from the crowd? Well, they are not supposed to move and hope that an errant javelin or hammer isn't heading their way.

—SAM McMANIS

□

Perhaps it was the excitement of having made the Olympic final in the women's javelin, or the emotional exhaustion of having the cumulative pressure of the Games behind her.

Whatever, Karin Smith of the United States mixed these metaphors when discussing the Soviet boycott's effect on the Games: "We didn't have the whole cake out there, only pieces of the pie. It just wasn't well seasoned. Maybe we needed more cinnamon." Should be interesting to be Smith's dinner guest.

—JULIE CART

□

Donna Murphy, the sports information director at Chicago State University, is handling reporters covering volleyball during the Olympics in Long Beach.

She told the Los Angeles Daily News that Italian journalists are arrogant, rude, pig-headed and refuse to stay off the court.

Murphy, who is half-Italian, has been able to understand only some of the "nasty, nasty" comments made to her and her student assistant by the Italian press corps.

But she called her 89-year-old Italian grandmother this week to learn a few colorful phrases, like "Please be quiet," "Please stay behind the barricade," and "Please wait your turn."

"I learned some other Italian phrases," she added, "but we can't start an international incident."

□

Swiss newspapers Tuesday debated the dramatic, heat-exhausted finish of Swiss Olympic marathon runner Gabriela Andersen-Schiess, generally expressing respect for her Herculean efforts and concern about her health.

Most newspapers carried pictures or stories about Andersen-Schiess on their front pages. Headlines included, "Oh Gaby, What Suffering" in the Tribune de Geneve, and "Now Gaby is the Heroine of America" in Zurich's German-language tabloid Blick.

Below the Blick headline was a picture of the Swiss runner being kissed by her American husband, Dick Andersen, and a color insert showing Andersen-Schiess stumbling toward the finish line.

This approach marked something of a turnaround for Blick, which had written in its late Monday editions of the "scandal" of the runner's stumbling finish before tens of thousands in the Olympic Coliseum and millions more on television.

□

The "Chariots of Fire" theme will be played at the wedding of Olympic women's marathon champion Joan Benoit.

Agreeing to fiance Scott Samuelson's wish, Benoit said Monday that her historic gold medal in Sunday's 26.2-mile race meant the music from the Oscar-winning Olympic movie would be OK.

"I'm getting married this fall, and I think the thing that motivated me the most up there was that Scott, my fiance, really wants to have them play 'Chariots of Fire' at the wedding," Benoit said, declining to reveal the wedding date. Her initial response to his request, she said, was, "No, only if I do well in the Olympics."

□

King Carl Gustaf XVI of Sweden was among the 3,300 fans at Cal State Fullerton for the team handball game between Sweden and Denmark. Denmark routed Sweden, 26-19, and later Swedish Coach Roger Carlsson was asked if his team was nervous with royalty in the house.

"We play for winning games, not the king," he said. So much for royalty in Sweden.

—TOM HAMILTON

□

For weightlifter Derrick Crass of Colorado Springs, Colo., the Games were short, and far from sweet.

Competing in the middle-heavyweight class, Crass failed to complete his first lift. His right knee collapsed while he was trying to snatch 286.5 pounds.

"It felt like the floor busted underneath my leg, like my foot went through the floor," Crass said.

When his knee gave way, the weight shifted and Crass dislocated his elbow trying to hold it up. He collapsed on the platform, and the weight hit him on the back of the head.

Fortunately, Crass was not seriously injured and said Monday that he could not recall being in pain at the time and did not know if he had lost consciousness. "It was so fast, I don't really know how I felt," he said. "I don't remember the pain at the time, but I'm sore today, that's for sure."

Crass said the knee had been giving him trouble for about a week and that he started his lift at a lighter weight than he had intended. "If I could have come in with what I was preparing to lift, I would have had a bronze, possibly a silver," he said.

□

American Jackie Joyner, after winning the silver medal in the heptathlon Saturday night—the same night on which her brother, Al, won the triple jump—was asked how the Joyners' feats might help the bad image of their hometown, East St. Louis, Ill.

Jackie tried to defend East St. Louis. Well, sort of.

"First of all," she said, "what you read about it in Life magazine (a recent article) isn't that bad, I think. The city itself isn't that bad a place to live, sort of. What we have done might help the city, maybe. If young people see what we did—I don't know—it might help them achieve something."

—SAM McMANIS

A FACE IN THE CROWD

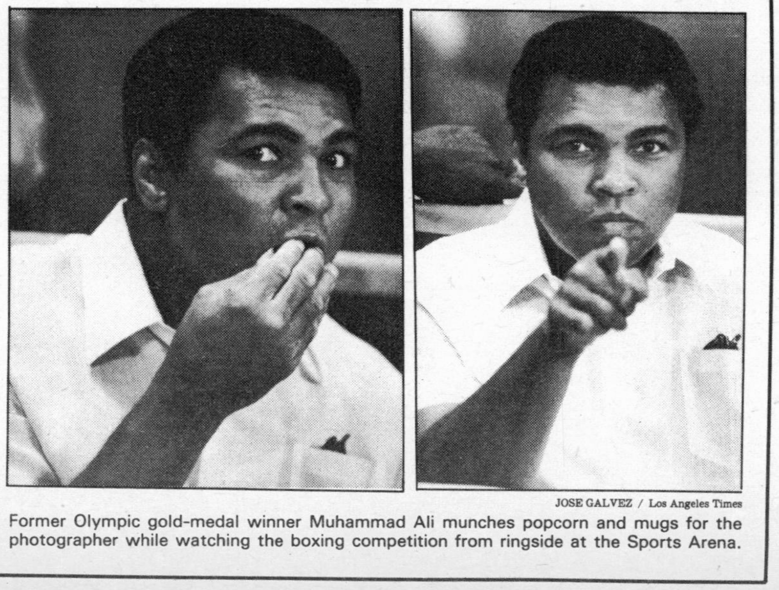

JOSE GALVEZ / Los Angeles Times

Former Olympic gold-medal winner Muhammad Ali munches popcorn and mugs for the photographer while watching the boxing competition from ringside at the Sports Arena.

American Janice Lawrence, left, goes for the ball against Julie Nykiel of Australia.

Anne Donovan of the U.S. hits the floor after taking an elbow in game against South Korea.

South Korea's Lee Mi Ja.

Cheryl Miller, U.S.

Kim Mulkey of the U.S. team gets ready to put her foot down against Canada's Debbie Huband.

On the Way to the Gold

South Korea's Sung Jung A, above, gets an elbow from Canada's Misty Thomas. U.S. player Cathy Boswell, above left, is fouled by China's Chen Yuefang.

Cheryl Miller of the U.S. makes it difficult for Patricia Mickan of Australia to get a pass off.

All photos by Times photographers, except where noted
Designed By Tom Trapnell

U.S.-South Korea game action.

GARY FRIEDMAN

DAY 13 OLYMPICS '84

Win or Lose, Citizen Budd Already Has Her Medal

Jim Murray

Soviet tanks rumble through Afghan villages, Middle East terrorists bomb busloads of schoolchildren, demagogues seize power in pivotal trouble spots, but to hear some people tell it, the principal threat to world harmony and stability in this Year of Our Lord was a little slip of a girl who wears glasses, carries dolls and hates to wear shoes.

Strong men frothed at the mouth at the sight of her. Editors who should know better wrote stern editorials condemning her. Councils of powerful politicians legislated against her.

If you ever wondered how they could have burned Joan of Arc at the stake, you had only to take a look at the life and times of Zola Budd and the time she ran a simple footrace in the rain one night at London's Crystal Palace. You had only to scan the pictures of the crowd at her event that night. Not since the Luftwaffe has any visitor evoked such contortions of hate on the faces of Londoners. Banners were unfurled, lips were curled, teeth were bared and the shout, "Go home, you South African white trash!" rent the night air. It was an extraordinary study in mob psychology. What they did to this Zola (Budd) called for another Zola (Emile) to properly express the outrage some men felt at this unconscionable abuse of a mere child, this unpretty form of child molestation, a rabble chastising a 5-foot 2-inch, 84-pound schoolgirl. It was enough to make Salem in 1692 perfectly understandable. Not

the Empire's finest hour. The Prime Minister herself decried it as "appalling."

Who are these people and why were they doing these terrible things to Zola Budd? Well, one of them was the Greater London City Council, others what one late gubernatorial candidate of the State of California called "the implacables of our civilization." People who would fire into lifeboats if someone told them it would advance it.

The cause, it so happens, is laudable enough. What it sets out to do is quarantine South Africa, remove it from the polite company of civilized societies and bring down its unacceptable policy of apartheid or racial superiority.

It's the methods that want examining.

Blaming Zola Budd for apartheid is like blaming Shirley Temple for the Johnstown Flood. First of all, she's 18 years old. She has a constituency of one. She's a farmgirl, not an activist; an athlete, not a provocateur.

She happens to be a great runner who chanced to be born in South Africa. So is a zebra. Do we hold it

responsible for the excesses of its government? Maybe Zola should grow stripes.

In a way, she did. At least, she shed her South African citizenship. She changed her spots. She gave up the land of her forbears, the comfort of her family, the solace of her friends, the things of her childhood and emigrated to a land many thousands of miles and a whole continent away—a child braving the unfamiliar, the hostile, the threatening.

She is as much a victim of apartheid as anyone else in her poor benighted country. A wise man once said, in dealing with the aspects of American apartheid, the then segregation in the South: "The white man in the South has the black man in a barrel and he's

sitting on it. As long as he's sitting there, the black man ain't going anywhere. But neither is the white man."

Zola wasn't going anywhere, sitting on the barrel. So, she got off it. In its way, that was as harsh an indictment of South African policy as a thousand "Zola, Go Home!" banners or a hundred thundering editorials or resolutions of a county council.

Athletes love to call attention to the sacrifices they make for their sport, the long hours they work, the aches and pains of practice, the time away from their loved ones or family, the pleasures forgone. Zola Budd's sacrifice gave new meaning to the term.

Her strange odyssey brought her

Please see MURRAY, page 81

JAYNE KAMIN / Los Angeles Times

Carl Lewis (center) throws arms around Kirk Baptiste (left) and Thomas Jefferson as they kneel on track after sweeping 200 meters. Lewis set Olympic record of 19.80.

Lewis Leads U.S. 200 Sweep, and It's One Gold to Go

By MAL FLORENCE, *Times Staff Writer*

The hard part is over. Carl Lewis won the 200 meters Wednesday night at the Coliseum and is only one gold medal away from emulating Jesse Owens' accomplishment of four gold medals in the 1936 Olympic Games at Berlin.

But Lewis may be wearing down. He said in a prepared statement that he has a sore leg and just "wanted to get the race over with."

He got it over in hurry. He was timed in an Olympic-record 19.80 seconds—breaking Tommie

Smith's record of 19.83 in 1968—as he led an American sweep. Fast-closing Kirk Baptiste gained the silver medal, while Thomas Jefferson got the bronze.

It was the first sweep in the 200 by any country since the United States did it in 1956 and only the fourth sweep in any track event since 1960.

Although Lewis' 19.80 was the third fastest 200 of all time, his coach, Tom Tellez, didn't believe that Lewis looked sharp.

"He looked a little bit tired and sluggish," Tellez said. "Kirk was coming after him at the end. It could be the fatigue he felt coming on in the long jump."

Lewis won the long jump Monday night. He had taken the gold medal in the 100 Saturday. Now, only the 400-meter relay remains for Lewis—and the Americans are heavily favored to get the gold.

These are the same events in which Owens established his mystique 48 years ago at Berlin.

Lewis has not consented to be interviewed by the general media. He said that he'll talk after the 400-meter relay final Saturday.

But he does talk to ABC television, and he said Wednesday night that he wwas "misquotd by the print media."

Lewis jumped only twice Monday night in the long jump—and the crowd booed him because they probably expected him to take all of his six jumps and, perhaps, break or threaten Bob Beamon's world re-

cord of 29-2½.

Later, in a tape-recorded interview, Lewis said that he wouldn't have taken any more jumps even if someone had surpassed his mark of 28-0¼.

Now, he says he was misquoted, despite the tape-recorded evidence to the contrary.

Lewis seemed to wobble a bit on the turn in the 200, and although he won by a fairly comfortable margin, Baptiste, a University of Hous-

Please see LEWIS, page 81

97,451 See the French Advance in Soccer

By GRAHAME L. JONES, *Times Staff Writer*

The largest crowd ever to attend a soccer game north of the Mexican border saw France defeat Yugoslavia, 4-2, in overtime Wednesday night to advance to the championship game of the Olympic soccer tournament.

A Rose Bowl crowd of 97,451—some of whom were still coming in at halftime—was treated to an incident-packed match in which:

—France took a 2-0 lead in the first half only to see Yugoslavia tie it up in the second 45 minutes while playing short-handed.

—Borislav Cvetkovic, the tournament's leading goal scorer, was ejected by Mexican referee A. Marquez Ramirez, thereby making him ineligible for Yugoslavia's bronze-medal game on Friday.

—Jovica Nikolic also was tossed out by Ramirez, meaning Yugoslavia will be without two of its leading offensive players.

—French defender Didier Senac suffered a skull fracture and was rushed to Arcadia Methodist Hospital.

The latter injury occured with only seconds left in the first half when Senac collided with a Yugoslav forward while leaping to head clear a corner kick.

He crumpled to the ground and had to be helped off the field. An Arcadia Methodist spokesman said Wednesday night that Senac had suffered a trimalar fracture and that French doctors would have to make the decision whether surgery would be performed here or in France. Senac was reported "resting comfortably."

The victory assures France its first-ever Olympic medal in soccer. In nine previous Olympic appearances, the best France had done was reach the semifinals in 1920.

For a while Wednesday, it seemed the French team would win with ease. They took an early lead on a goal in the seventh minute by Dominique Bijotat and increased that to 2-0 when Philippe Jeannol found the back of the net nine minutes later.

Please see SOCCER, page 81

Canadians Are Trampled Again as U.S. Gains Basketball Final

By MARK HEISLER, *Times Staff Writer*

Jack Donohue and his little band of would-be giant-killers got their rematch with the U.S. men's basketball team Wednesday night at the Forum, even if it wasn't quite all they'd hoped for. They got 14 of their shots blocked and managed to lose by only 19 points, which is a moral victory and all they were going to get in this matchup.

The United States beat Canada, 78-59. And now for the final everyone has been waiting for, the Americans vs. Spain, a team

they've already beaten by 33 points in this tournament.

"The game has to be played," Coach Antonio Diaz-Miguel told Spanish writers, laughing, in the wild celebration after his team's upset of Yugoslavia. "But some of the players are ready to give you their shirts so you can play in their place.

"Anyway, the Canadian coach has promised that his team is the only one that can defeat the Amer-

Please see BASKETBALL, page 82

Greg Louganis

It's a Golden Moment for Louganis

By SEYMOUR BEUBIS, *Times Staff Writer*

It was long overdue, at least four years late. But the ultimate diver, Greg Louganis, and the ultimate award, an Olympic gold medal, finally got together Wednesday.

The precise moment it happened, for the sake of history, was 6:57 p.m.—11 minutes after Louganis outclassed his 11 opponents in the men's three-meter diving competition.

So dominant was his performance that it was really Louganis, 24, of Mission Viejo, against himself, and the 11 others against each other.

The outcome was never really in doubt as Louganis took the lead on his first dive and added to it on his next 10, winning by an astounding 92.10 points.

A crowd of 12,871 basked in his magical performance, shouting "Greg, Greg," and waving American flags before each of his dives.

Louganis finished with his second-best point total ever, a 754.41. His best score was 755.49 points in the 1983 USA International at Fort Lauderdale, Fla.

The second-place finisher, Tan Liangde of China, 19, scored 662.31. Ron Merriott, 24, of Ann Arbor, Mich., put on a stirring stretch run to come from behind for the bronze medal. His score was 661.32.

After Louganis finished his final dive, he was

Please see LOUGANIS, page 81

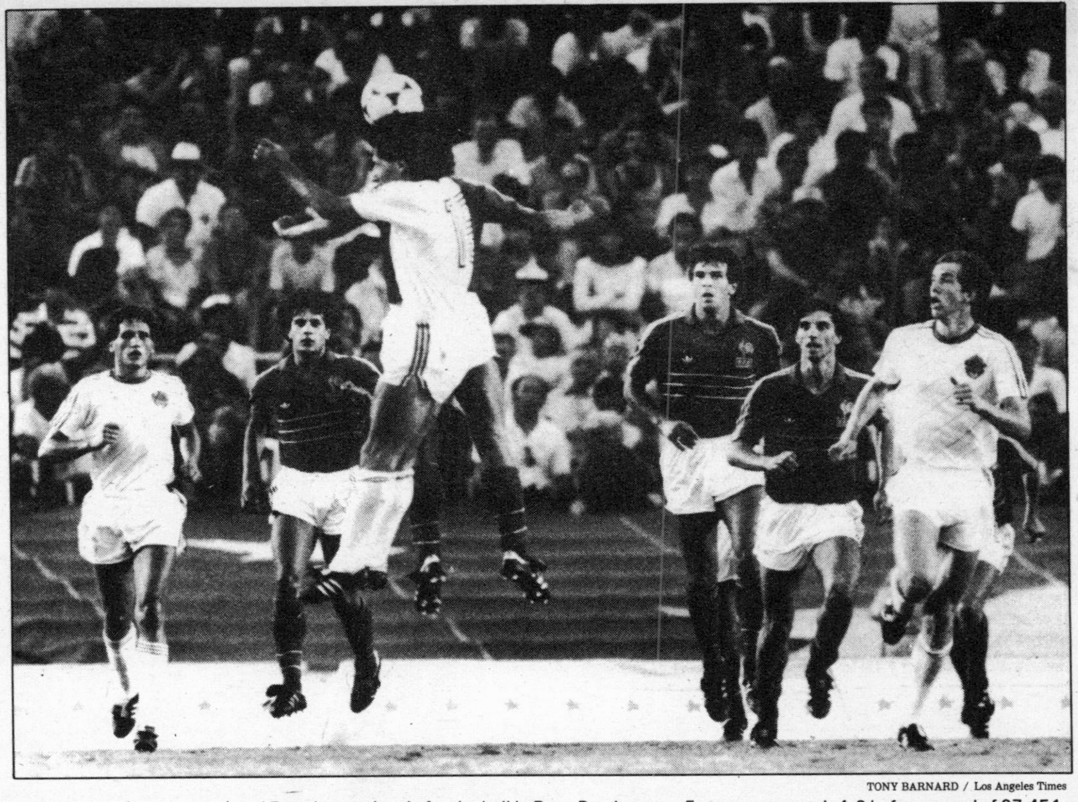

TONY BARNARD / Los Angeles Times

Yugoslavians (light jerseys) and French team battle for the ball in Rose Bowl soccer. France won match 4-2 before crowd of 97,451.

LOUGANIS

Continued from page 80

embraced by his coach, Ron O'Brien. "I told him that if anyone deserved to have a gold medal around his neck, it's you," O'Brien said.

O'Brien noted that Louganis had a smile "from ear to ear. It's the happiest I have ever seen him. He was a little tense before the start of competition, but the monkey is off his back now. He should be more relaxed when he competes in the platform."

Dr. Sammy Lee, an Olympic gold medalist in 1948 and 1952, who was Louganis' first coach when he started diving at 13, said: "Justice has finally been served, and how."

Lee was alluding to the fact that Louganis was probably deprived of two gold medals when the United States boycotted the 1980 Olympic Games at Moscow.

Louganis said he was ecstatic about his performance.

When asked if he was upset that he didn't exceed his all-time scoring record, Louganis said: "Records can be broken at any time, but Olympic gold medals are not easy to come by."

Louganis said the Olympic gold medal was indeed a missing link despite all his achievements.

"I was realizing that more and more as the contest came to an end . . . how much I wanted it."

About the only goal Louganis failed to accomplish Wednesday was breaking the 800 mark in scoring, something he wants to achieve before retiring.

Most of his scores in Wednesday's competition were in the 8.5 to 9.5 range. He received four scores of 10—one short of what he accomplished in the preliminary round.

His two top dives from a scoring standpoint were his 10th and 11th, a reverse 1½ somersault with 3½ twists, and a reverse 3½ somersault tuck.

He received 93.06 points on the 10th dive, getting a 9 and four 9.5s. His 11th dive, with a 3.5 degree of difficulty, the highest in the diving, earned him 92.40 points as he received two 8.5s and three 9s.

Merriott said he thought the critical round for him was the ninth. "My reverse 3½ was the critical point. I knew once I got by that I had a good chance for a medal." (He scored 82.95 points on that dive).

Asked if he was happy with the bronze medal, Merriott said that he wanted to be on the victory stand with Greg Louganis.

Tan said that he dived more to his potential Wednesday than in the preliminary round.

But he added that he didn't think he could beat Louganis now and that no other diver could either.

Louganis, of Samoan heritage, entered the Olympics the surest bet to win a gold medal this side of Carl Lewis.

If he had lost, it would have been the shocker of the Olympic Games.

Few men or women have ever dominated a sport as has Louganis.

His dominance started not long after he finished second on the 10-meter platform to Italian great Klaus Dibiasi in the 1976 Olympics.

But the U.S. Olympic boycott in 1980 kept him from winning the only gold medal that eluded him—the Olympic gold, at least until Wednesday.

He has won 26 U.S. national titles, more than any man. Cynthia Potter holds the record with 28. But Louganis will try to top her mark later this month at the Nationals in Santa Clara. He will be competing in three events.

The last time Louganis lost on the three-meter springboard was in 1981 at Fort Lauderdale, Fla., to Carlos Giron of Mexico.

Chances are he will never lose again. He will be heavily favored at the Nationals, and that could be his last meet, but he said that he has made no final decision.

But Louganis still has some more important Olympic business to take care of first. He will be going after a second gold medal—this time on the 10-meter platform—starting Saturday.

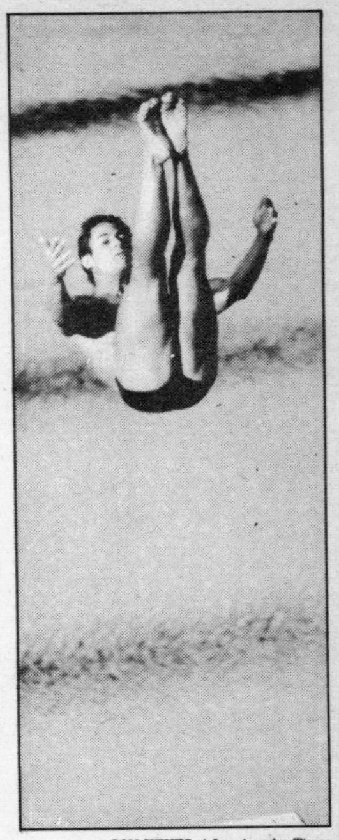

CON KEYES / Los Angeles Times

Greg Louganis does a back 2½ somersault in pike position.

SOCCER

Continued from page 80

On the first goal, Bijotat, a 23-year-old from the French club Monaco, accepted a pass at midfield, faked Yugoslav defender Marko Elsner, and stroked the ball past goalkeeper Tomislav Ivkovic.

The second French goal was described as "excellent" by Yugoslavia's coach, Ivan Toplak.

Awarded a direct free kick just outside the penalty area and to the right of the net, France gave the ball to Jeannol, who recently was traded from the French club Nancy to the more internationally famous Paris St. Germaine.

Jeannol, who turned 26 on Monday, fired a left-footed shot past a wall of five Yugoslav defenders and into the far corner of the net beyond the reach of Ivkovic.

That made it 2-0 and the French, who have not lost in Olympic qualifying competition or in the tournament proper, seemed to have things well under control.

Yugoslavia, which also was undefeated in the tournament and boasting the best offense with Cvetkovic, Nikolic and Stjepan Deveric, were not about to surrender, though. In four previous games, the Yugoslavs had scored 12 goals, including five in Monday's 5-2 quarter-final victory over West Germany.

Four minutes into the second half, the Yugoslav hopes took a blow when Ramirez, the referee, showed Nikolic the red card after linesman Jorge Romero of Argentina spotted him kicking France's Jean-Philippe Rohr.

That left Yugoslavia with just 10 men, but, in the 63rd minute, Cvetkovic cut France's lead to 2-1 with his fifth goal of the tournament. Cvetkovic started the move at midfield, passing to Deveric, who fed Mirsad Baljic on the left wing. Baljic crossed the ball into the goalmouth and Cvetkovic was there to side-foot it into the net.

With the largely pro-Yugoslav crowd brought back to life, Yugoslavia continued to press the attack. In the 75th minute, French goalkeeper Albert Rust threw himself to his left to punch out a header from Cvetkovic. The ball reached the on-rushing Deveric, who bundled it into the net to tie the score.

Shortly thereafter, Cvetkovic was ejected after a foul on Rohr—a controversial decision that was greeted by loud protests from the crowd—reducing Yugoslavia to nine players.

France failed to take advantage, however, and the game entered a 30-minute overtime.

Six minutes into the extra period, France's Guy Lacombe scored the goal that put his team in the gold-medal game on Saturday.

Yugoslav goalie Ivkovic made a superb save on a hard shot from Bijotat, punching the ball out to the wing. There, Jean-Claude Lemoult crossed it back into the goal area, Daniel Xuereb deflected it with a header and Lacombe scored from close range.

France made it 4-2 in the closing seconds when Xuereb hit an open-net goal after Yugoslav goalie Ivkovic came out to join the attack.

After the final whistle, several Yugoslav players had to be restrained from attacking the referee.

After the match, Toplak, Yugoslavia's coach, refused to criticize the officiating.

"I will not have any comment on the referee," he said.

Defender Mirsad Baljic, however, had no such hestitation.

"He was very weak and very bad," Baljic said.

Henri Michel, the French coach, agreed.

"Some of his whistles didn't improve our situation, especially when we began to play weaker in the second half," he said.

"There were times when we lost control of our game and it was only a matter of time before they (Yugoslavia) scored. A losing team has an advantage because it can come back, while a team ahead must worry.

"We congratulate Yugoslavia for pushing us and making us play our best."

Pasadena Soccer Notes

Wednesday's record crowd will be surpassed on Friday and Saturday. Both the bronze-medal game and the final have been sold out . . . LAOOC soccer commissioner **Alan Rothenberg** said Pasadena police have told him they are having more difficulty because of parking than they have for the January 1 Rose Bowl game or the Super Bowl. Police have asked that fans use the shuttle buses that leave from downtown Pasadena or car-pool . . . Dutch referee **Jan Keizer** has been selected to officiate the championship game on Saturday.

A Majestic Sight

When Louganis Dives, He Dances to His Own Music

By TRACY DODDS, *Times Staff Writer*

In Greg Louganis' Samoan heritage, there must be kings or tribal chiefs. He has that regal bearing. That majestic aura.

Louganis brings to his sport—his art—a dramatic beauty that comes from within, that cannot be imitated.

He won an Olympic gold medal Wednesday night diving from an ordinary three-meter springboard at the Olympic Swim Stadium. Picture him diving over waterfalls on an island paradise, surrounded by brilliant foliage, and he would seem to be more in his element.

There is nothing ordinary about Greg Louganis.

He is an athlete, yes, with a body that should be chiseled in marble. He has developed his muscular structure to perfection. But, then, a lot of athletes do that so that they can run faster or jump higher or hoist more iron. Louganis is also an artist. His years of ballet training show in his every graceful move. More than that, he is a performer. He studied drama at UC Irvine and he came away with a presence that is felt every time he makes an entrance onto the pool deck.

The combination of his strength, his grace and his flair, along with his intimidating reputation as the best in the world for at least the last three years, makes him untouchable.

And he doesn't just dominate when he gets to his final dives, those with a difficulty that only he will attempt. He's actually more impressive on the simpler dives. That's where his star quality shines through.

No one else scores in the 90s on a single dive the way he does. On his 10th dive, a reverse 1½ somersault with 3½ twists (difficulty 3.3) he had scores of 9, 9, 9.5, 9.5, 10, 9.5 and 9.5 for a score of 93.06. On his final dive, a reverse 3½ somersault in the tuck position (difficulty 3.5) he had scores of 9, 8.5, 9, 9, 8.5, 9 and 8.5 to score 92.40 points.

Those dives demonstrate his athletic ability, the strength he needs to get enough height off the board to do all that before meeting the water. It's his strength off the board that makes him so much more dominant off the springboard than he is off the platform. He's favored to win the gold off the platform, too, but at least the other divers start on more equal footing off the unmoving platform.

But Louganis is a champion, a joy to watch, more because of what he can do with the basic dives than what he can do with the dazzling dives. He makes the basics dazzle.

Take his third dive, a straight-forward dive, difficulty 1.6. He soars off the board. He spreads his arms and holds the pose, revels in it. Then he turns toward the water, bringing his arms over his head with dramatic poise, reaching for the water and then sliding in without so much as a ripple. Scores? He got a 9, 9.5, 9, 9, 10, 9 and 9.5. On his next dive, an inward dive pike (difficulty 1.4) he simply stands on the end of the board, hops backward, touches his toes in what most of us call a jackknife, and slides into the water. But it's breathtaking. A thing of beauty in its simple perfection. Incredibly, Louganis has managed to get his proud flamboyance into that simple move. His scores? He got a 9.5, 10, 9.5, 9.5, 10, 9.5 and 9.0.

Louganis has said that he doesn't approach his dives as mechanical, athletic moves. He thinks of them more as choreographed dance moves.

When he steps onto the board, he's visualizing the dive in his mind, hearing the music to which he'll perform that dive.

What kind of music? "That will vary from dive to dive," he said. "What works for one competition won't work for another. . . . I follow the rhythm of the day. It can be upbeat or it can be very melancholy."

In Olympic competition he was soaring to the sound of "Fame" and "Chariots of Fire."

Definitely upbeat.

"I started to realize, as the competition started coming to an end, how much I really wanted it," Louganis said. "I'm still very emotional. . . . Going into my last dive, my main thought was fear. A lot of emotions were coming to a head at that time."

Louganis said that he stayed calm between dives with the help of Gar, a little teddy bear who is his constant companion. Gar appeared with him at the press conference and kept him calm as he fielded questions on every possible subject.

He didn't want to say that the Olympic gold medal was a missing link. He said, "This was something that was missing, and it meant a lot to me. . . . But I don't think of myself as having any missing links in my life. If I attain it, or don't attain it, my life is full."

He is now 24, but he showed no signs of announcing his retirement after these Games. He said, "I don't know how much longer I'm going to dive. I'm definitely going to go to the outdoor nationals after this meet. But first things first. I've got platform coming up this weekend and so tomorrow I'm back at the pool working out. No rest for the weary."

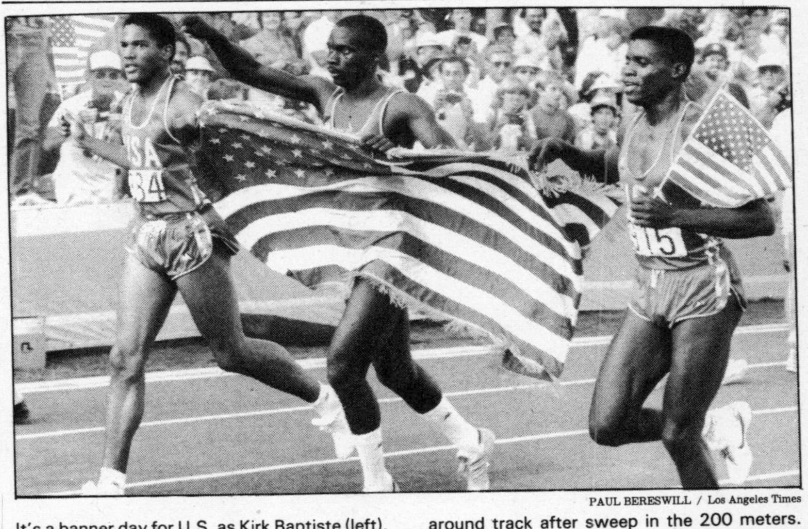

PAUL BERESWILL / Los Angeles Times

It's a banner day for U.S. as Kirk Baptiste (left), Thomas Jefferson and Carl Lewis carry flags around track after sweep in the 200 meters. Lewis won in 19.80 to earn third gold medal.

LEWIS

Continued from page 80

ton sophomore, was bearing down on Lewis.

Baptiste was timed in 19.96, breaking the collegiate record of 19.99 set by Calvin Smith last August at Zurich, Switzerland. It was also equal to the sixth-fastest 200 meters ever run.

When the race ended, the three Americans took a victory lap, which is becoming almost obligatory at the Olympics. Lewis and Baptiste carried small American flags, while Jefferson was given a large American flag from a fan in the stands.

Jefferson wrapped the flag around his two teammates as they slowly jogged around the track.

"Today was very special because I looked back at the finish and saw two other Americans right behind me," said Lewis in his prepared statement. "It was great to jog around holding the flag with two other guys and not just by myself.

"Going into the semifinals today, my leg was a little sore and it's still sore. So that's probably why I ran the turn harder than usual. I ran it hard and paid for it. There's nothing really wrong with the leg, my left. It's just a little sore all over. Jumping in the cold weather Monday night took a lot out of me."

Lewis then thanked the trainers and said he's looking forward to running the relay. "It's the easist event for me because I have three guys that are unparalleled in front of me."

Rules permit a substitution for a runner in earlier rounds preceding the final. But Tellez said that Lewis plans to run all three rounds of the relay starting Friday.

"Carl wants all the rounds in the relay," Tellez said. "If anyone drops the baton, he wants to be the one who drops it."

Imagine Lewis' chagrin if a teammate fumbled the baton and the U.S. didn't qualify for the final—with Lewis sitting out a round.

Lewis doesn't have any events today, and Tellez said he should benefit by the rest. Even though Lewis took only two long jumps Monday night, Tellez said that the event takes a lot out of athletes.

"Any long jumper that takes six jumps doesn't feel very good the next day," Tellez said. "No one knows what Carl is going through. I don't. The only one who could know is (the late) Jesse Owens."

To put Lewis' 19.80 in perspective, only world record-holder Pietro Mennea (19.72) and Lewis (19.75) have run faster.

Mennea set his record in the altitude of Mexico City in 1979. So Lewis is the fastest 200 sprinter at sea level.

The 32-year-old Mennea finished seventh in the time of 20.55. He was competing in his fourth Olympics. He was a bronze medalist in 1972, was fourth in 1976 and got the gold medal in 1980.

"Carl Lewis may break my world 200 record and he may do it tomorrow, or some day. But Carl Lewis will never break my record of four Olympic 200-meter finals," Mennea said.

Mennea said he injured his instep while training on a hard track in San Diego but added that he was proud of the way he ran Wednesday night. He also said that he knew he was no threat to Lewis.

Tellez said that Lewis didn't run the curve exceptionally well, but he had the lead coming out of it. He maintained it and drove to the finish. He didn't slow down and raise both arms in the air 10 meters from the finish as he did when he ran his 19.75 at Indianapolis last year.

Baptiste is known as a fast finisher.

"In the last 50 meters, I go for the extra gear," he said. "I put all of my energy into the last part of the race."

Writers persisted in asking Baptiste and Jefferson why Lewis is so great.

Baptiste: "He knows how to run the 200. It's only my second year of running it. But that's the closest I've ever been to Carl."

Baptiste won the NCAA 200 last June at Eugene, Ore., but Jefferson, of Kent State, didn't even make the finals. It was surprising that he made the U.S team in the trials and then he nailed down the sweep with a personal best time of 20.26, just getting to the line on a lean ahead of Joao Batista Silva of Brazil.

Jefferson said he wanted "all of the guys" wrapped in the flag and that he didn't care whether he won a gold, silver or bronze—he just wanted a sweep for the Americans.

Lewis is obviously dedicated to four gold medals, not world records, and he reaffirmed this Wednesday when he said on television:

"I think the most important thing is to win as many gold medals as I can and to be remembered as how many gold medals the American team has won. I've accepted challenges for years and years."

Three golds, one more to get—and he'll have some help.

MURRAY

Continued from page 80

to the Games of the XXIII Olympiad in Los Angeles' Coliseum Wednesday night and one of the great sport matchups of these or any Games. Zola was finally running for Queen, country and the London Daily Mail, which has bought the rights to her diary. The newest subject of the Queen was finally on a course she could handle—a race track. She didn't have to brave the flower of British home office politics, just Mary Decker.

Mary Decker is a case study in her own right. Mary has no trouble with her citizenship, her spectators generally are ruly, even sympathetic, but with Mary, you wish somehow, she looked more like she was enjoying herself. Mary approaches a race as if she were hoping for a call from the warden. Her eyes seem to be desperate, staring at something she doesn't really want to see. It's as if she fears the worst, or as if she just got the worst news she ever heard in her life.

It's not easy to tell what she's worried about. She usually wins her 3,000-meter races by zip codes, and she did again in the heat Wednesday night.

Citizen Budd, new of Her Majesty's loyal minions, was less fortunate. Running barefoot in a high fog, she faded to third in her heat. But a race she came through three continents, several time zones and a storm of jeering abuse to take part in Friday evening, was finally hers to win or lose—and not some politician's. You still get the feeling she didn't come this far through this much to settle for anything sub-gold or not to give Mary Decker finally something to look that unhappy about. Even if she loses, she won't.

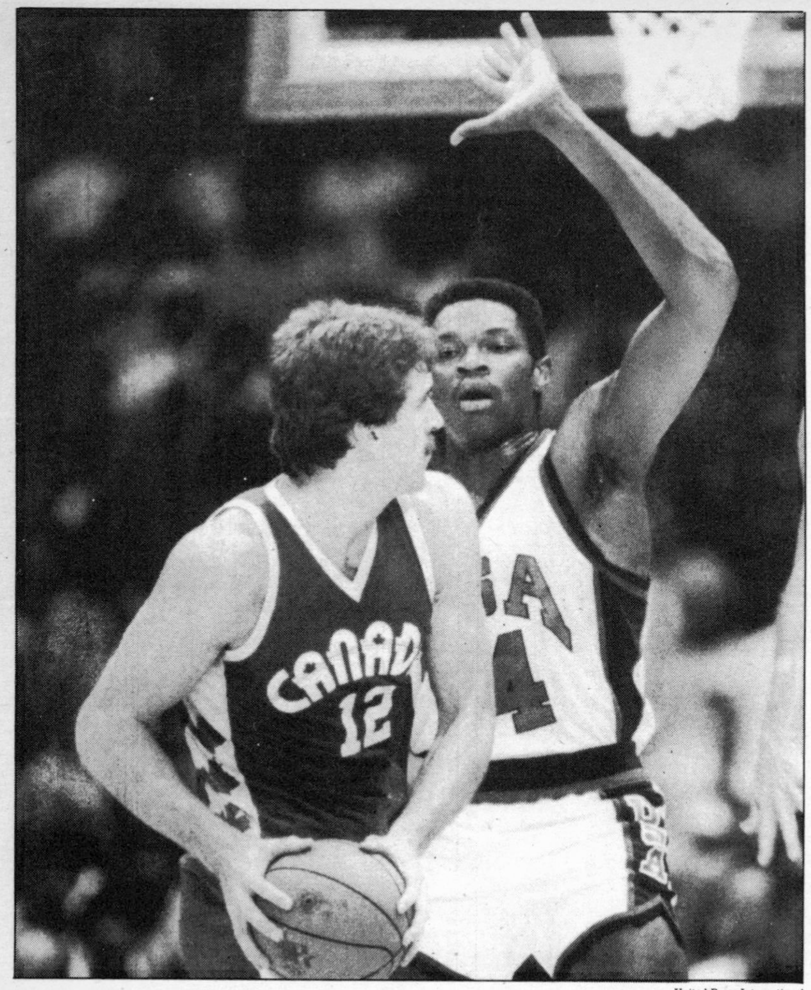

United Press International

Sam Perkins of the United States poses a tall problem for Canada's Bill Wennington (12). Perkins and teammates posed too many problems for Canadians and beat them, 78-59.

BASKETBALL

Continued from page 80

icans. So we're ready to play the Canadians."

No such luck. The Canadians started the game by falling 4-0 behind, grabbed a 6-4 lead, and that was it for Canadian bright spots.

They were still hanging in there, trailing, 16-12, when Patrick Ewing came in for the first time. Ewing went nine minutes of the first half, scored 10 points and blocked two shots. By halftime, the United States was 17 points up.

Ewing is a dominating player at Georgetown, but less so here in a different system. U.S. coaches were saying privately he seemed lost. Opponents noticed.

"I drove the lane twice, and Ewing didn't even try to stop me," West Germany's Christian Welp said Monday night. "I was so surprised the first time, I missed my shot by a mile."

Welp said Uwe Blab had been talking to his Indiana teammate, Steve Alford, and that Alford had told Blab that Ewing had been playing like this all along.

"I think, intimidating, if you people would drop that word from your vocabulary, you'd understand more about the game than you do now," said U.S. Coach Bob Knight. "I don't think players get intimidated. They take it in, get it blocked, bring it back out and shoot it again. Bad players get intimidated. Good players don't. I thought Patrick played very well. Intimidating, that's an overworked word."

Donohue, the noted after-dinner speaker—he calls his material "my Wheat Belt schtick"—was asked if *he* could say a few words about Ewing, too.

"No, I couldn't," he said. "Really, I couldn't. He's very big and very good. I didn't know which one he was. OK, he's the big guy, I know. The only difference I know between Ewing and (Chris) Mullin is Mullin's left-handed."

Mullin, the left-hander, led the Americans with 20 points. He got to start this game, with Steve Alford, the team's best outside shooters, in the sure knowledge that the Canadians were going to try to slow the game down, and that they'd play zone.

They did. It worked about as well as it ever has. Canada has now lost to the Americans by 21 and 19 points, which, in this tournament, passes for playing them tough. Only one other team, West Germany, which played zone and didn't run, has come closer. The Germans lost by 11. Everyone else has lost by 33 or more.

"All we can ask these guys is to spill their guts out," Donohue said. "They did that. Tonight we just didn't play well enough to win."

Donohue was asked if he could envision a scenario in which the United States would lose.

"Terrorist attack," he said. "No game. . . .

"Bobby Knight won't let 'em lose. There's not going to be any fat cats going into that game. They're a very good basketball team, they're very well coached. A scenario? I can't see them losing the game. Oh yeah, if the refs go bananas. . . ."

Moments later, the Canadians were led out. In came Knight, for the daily exchange of gifts with interpreter Marie Holgado. She gave him a set of those teeth that are wound up and chatter.

Knight was asked what he thought about Donohue's assessment. Knight wound up his new teeth and let them chatter.

Liberian Runner Shows Plenty of Heart

By ALAN GREENBERG, *Times Staff Writer*

When Basil Kilani of Jordan crossed the finish line 13th and next-to-last in Heat 1 of the men's 5,000 meters, Nimley Twegbe of Liberia still had more than two laps to go.

Twegbe was alone. But not really. As he plodded his final half-mile on tired legs late Wednesday afternoon, the Coliseum crowd of 80,909 began cheering his every step. He finished in 17 minutes 36.69 seconds, more than two minutes and 16 seconds behind the Jordanian—and nearly four minutes behind heat winner Canario Ezequiel of Portugal, who ran the distance in 13:43.28.

Twegbe is a shy 20-year-old from Monrovia, population 308,000, the capital of his West African nation. He was competing internationally for the first time.

Twegbe said the crowd's applause didn't frighten him. That's a wonder. The Liberian coach, James Davies, said that Twegbe had never before run in front of more than 1,500 people.

Not understanding that the crowd was applauding his effort, rather than mocking his finish, Twegbe felt humiliated.

"In my heart, I felt ashamed to be failing," he said. "I expected to be one of the winners."

As it was, Twegbe walked off the track with his head down, not even bothering to find out his time.

"Of course, I'm disappointed," Twegbe said.

Why? "Because I never finish on time."

Twegbe's pain wasn't just emotional. The son of a tax collector, he has only been running for three years, nearly always on dirt tracks. Until arriving at the Olympic Village at UCLA, Twegbe had never run on a synthetic track. He doesn't like them.

"After a few days at UCLA," he said, "I had much pain in my joints."

That was only half of it. Although Twegbe didn't mention it during an interview, Davies said that Twegbe had been running a fever for three or four days earlier this week.

Twegbe led his heat for the first lap, then faded badly. By his fifth lap on the synthetic Coliseum track, his joints ached. By the last lap, his heart did.

A 5-foot 4-inch, 140-pound engineering student, Twegbe trained alone until joining the Liberian national team, such as it is, earlier this year. He is the only distance runner on Liberia's seven-member Olympic team.

As such, he feels grave responsibility. Despite his aching joints, Twegbe said, he will run in the men's marathon Sunday, the final competition of what some people fear could be the final Olympic Games.

Nimley Twegbe says he has never run a marathon before. That doesn't much matter to him.

Pole Vault

Frenchman Quinon Beats Tully for Gold

By BILL SHIRLEY,
Times Staff Writer

Mike Tully was right. After pole vaulting 18 feet 11 inches for an American record at UCLA last May, he said that if he could clear that height again in the Olympics, he probably would win the gold medal.

Neither Tully, a former UCLA star from Encino, nor anyone else, however, could vault that high at the Coliseum Wednesday evening. Pierre Quinon of France came closest, clearing 18-10¼ on his first attempt. That won him the gold medal.

Tully, who passed all but four of the 12 heights in a competition that lasted 4 hours 10 minutes, won the silver medal at 18-6½ on his third—and final—attempt. Just last month, he had pushed his American record to 19-1 after winning the U. S. Olympic trials at 19-0¾.

Earl Bell of Jonesboro, Ark., and Thierry Vigneron of France, who also have vaulted over 19 feet, shared the bronze medal, each clearing 18-4½ without a miss at any height.

It was not a good evening for the best of American and French vaulters. In an era when the world's highest-paid amateurs are stronger and going faster and higher, their performance was mediocre at best. Even so, they did follow tradition. Vaulters, often erratic, seldom are at their best under Olympic pressure.

The event was expected to be a duel between the United States and France—and so it was. When Kimmo Pallonen of Finland was eliminated after clearing 17-10½, only Frenchmen and Americans were left.

Bell and Vigneron did not start vaulting until the bar was raised to 17-8½, and each made the height on his first attempt. Doug Lytle, the third American, also entered the competition at that height and cleared it on his first try. That, though, was as high as he went, missing at 18-0½. At the trials, Lytle cleared 18-8¾.

Quinon and Tully started vaulting at 17-10½, Tully making it on his first try and Quinon his second. Bell and Vigneron passed the height in the cat-and-mouse game vaulters play.

Bell vaulted again at 18-0½, clearing it easily on his first attempt. Vigneron, Tully and Quinon sat out that height. At 18-2½, Tully went over the bar on his first attempt. Bell, Quinon and Vigneron rested.

Bell and Vigneron went back to work at 18-4½, each making it on his first attempt. Tully and Quinon passed.

Bell and Vigneron would go no higher, however. They passed at 18-6½ but then neither could clear 18-8¼. Vigneron had two near misses, almost pushing the bar back onto its pegs with his left hand as he started his descent to the mat. Some vaulters have made that little maneuver an art. It's legal.

Meanwhile, at 18-6½, Quinon missed once, then passed the height. Tully missed his first two attempts, put on his warmup clothes, walked around the infield for a few minutes, then cleared the bar easily.

Quinon soared over 18-8¼ easily on his first try and it was clear that Tully was in trouble. After Quinon made the height, Tully passed. There was no point in his trying it.

There was also no point in Tully's trying 18-10¼ after Quinon had cleared that height—again on his first vault—pulling his right arm away from the bar at the last second. The silver was already his so Tully went for 19-0¼, and the gold.

He didn't come close, missing embarrassingly on his last two attempts. On his second try, he got to the top of his 16½-foot fiberglass pole and fell backward. On his last attempt, he dropped his pole, ran through the uprights and did a nice little flip. It might have been a 10 in gymnastics but it was a zero in pole vaulting.

So the United States, which dominated Olympic pole vaulting until 1972, drew another blank. The last four gold medals have been won by Europeans.

Quinon, 22, once held the world record at 19-1, but at the world championships at Helsinki last summer, he couldn't clear 17-8½. Vaulters go higher today with their long, limber poles, but they are about as inconsistent as the Dodgers' defense.

Tully did not seem disappointed that he had not won the gold medal. "I'm real happy with what I did tonight," he said. "The French vaulter did a great job. What can I say?"

Tully said his leg had cramped as he cleared 18-2½ the second time he vaulted. "I more or less had a flat tire on my last two jumps," he said. "I cramped up because I was out there for four hours."

Said Bell, "I'm in a pretty good mood. I'm a little bit disappointed but I'm glad to get a medal."

Quinon said the competition was too long and too tiring. The wind was in the vaulters' faces on their run and the atmospheric conditions were not very good, he said. The noise from the crowd also bothered him.

The wind got so bad, Quinon said, that he went to a stiffer pole halfway through the competition. It was a risk, he said, but because of the wind he thought it was worth a try.

Quinon hurt his thigh 10 days ago and has been taking daily treatments. He was seen rubbing his injured leg during the competition.

Vigneron also has a complaint about the conditions. "It was a very difficult competition due to the fact that Americans were rooting for Americans," he said.

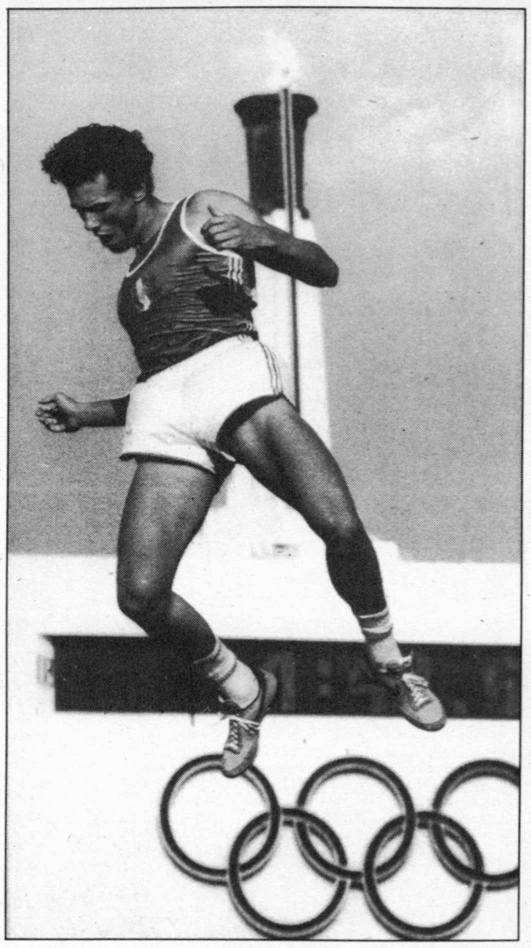

Associated Press

With the Olympic flame and rings prominent in the background, pole vaulter Pierre Quinon of France wins the gold medal.

THE MEDALISTS

MEN'S

Track

■ **POLE VAULT**

1. Pierre Quinon (France)
2. Mike Tully (U.S.)
3. (tie) Earl Bell (U.S.)
   Thierry Vigneron (France)

Women's 400 Hurdles

Moroccan Runner Surprises Field, Sets Olympic Record in the Process

By JULIE CART,
Times Staff Writer

The King of Morocco doesn't throw his money around.

Two years ago King Hassan II gave $30,000 dollars to three Moroccan athletes to enable them to support themselves while training for the Olympics.

Based on the result of the women's 400-meter hurdles race Wednesday, at least one-third of that was money well spent.

Nawal El Moutawakil established an Olympic record in winning the 400-meter hurdles, which was being run by women in the Olympics for the first time. Her time was 54.61 seconds.

Judi Brown of the United States, running from Lane 8, was second in 55.20, and Cristina Cojocaru of Romania was third in 55.41.

The normally stoic El Moutawakil, who last spring completed her freshman year at Iowa State, broke down after her race, then embraced Brown and Sandra Farmer of Jamaica. Looking dazed, the 22-year-old took a large red and green Moroccan flag and waved to the Coliseum crowd.

She became the first Moroccan athlete to win a gold medal in the Olympics and is only the second medalist ever from her country. She also became the first Moroccan woman to make an Olympic final.

Although El Moutawakil won the NCAA title in this event last spring, Ann-Louise Skoglund of Sweden had been picked to win. Skoglund made numerous technical errors, however, and finished fifth.

"All I wanted to do was to make it to the final," El Moutawakil said, still choked with emotion two hours after the race. "The people in my country had hoped this.

"As a woman, I think the gold medal for Africa and Arabia is something else. I don't know. I think it wasn't the problem for me to be a sportswoman in my country. I had a lot of encouragement from my father. He wanted me to be the best, in everything."

El Moutawakil's father died in November and she has dedicated her season to him.

"I wish he was here," she said. "He would be very proud."

El Moutawakil was born in Casablanca and began training in 1978, starting with sprints. She eventually moved to the 400, then the 400 hurdles, even though her size, 5 feet 2 inches, is a handicap in the hurdles.

El Moutawakil was not immediately available to the press, but a large contingent of Moroccan Olympic officials was happy to entertain questions from the press. The delegation was thrilled to be speaking to reporters, and jubilant over the win.

"I am, like all Moroccans, just ecstatic," said Abdellatif Semlali, minister of Moroccan sport. The race had been televised live to Morocco, where it was 2 a.m., and Semlali said he expected a call from King Hassan.

"We waited 24 years to have a medal, and it was gold," Semlali said. "Not only that, but it was by a Moroccan woman."

El Moutawakil's gold is only the fourth Olympic medal won by an African woman and is believed to be the first ever by an Arab woman. Three South African athletes won medals in 1932 and 1956.

In another surprising finish, P. T. Usha of India, the first Indian woman ever to make an Olympic final, missed the bronze medal by .01 of a second.

Brown ran well, but from the outside lane she had trouble seeing the rest of the field.

"If I ever get Lane 8 again, it will be a day too soon," she said. "I guess I'm my own worst critic. I didn't have as good a race as I wanted to. I didn't have any idea where anyone was. I came off the sixth or seventh hurdle, then I knew where everybody was—in front of me."

THE MEDALISTS

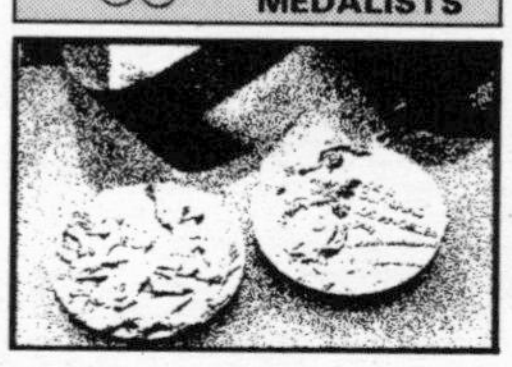

WOMEN'S

Track

■ **400-METER HURDLES**

1. Nawal El Moutawakil (Morocco)
2. Judi Brown (U.S.)
3. Cristina Cojocaru (Romania)

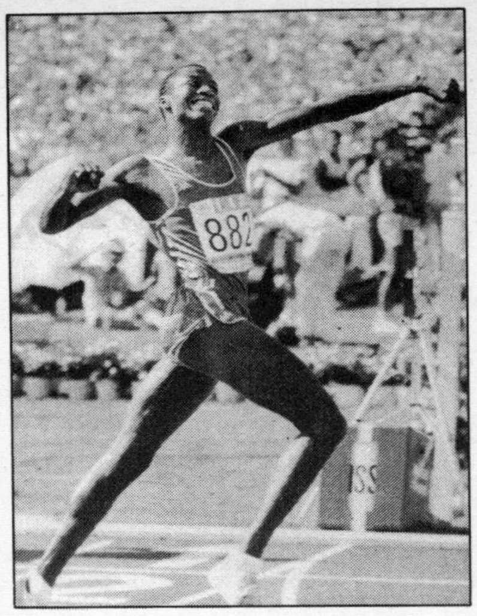

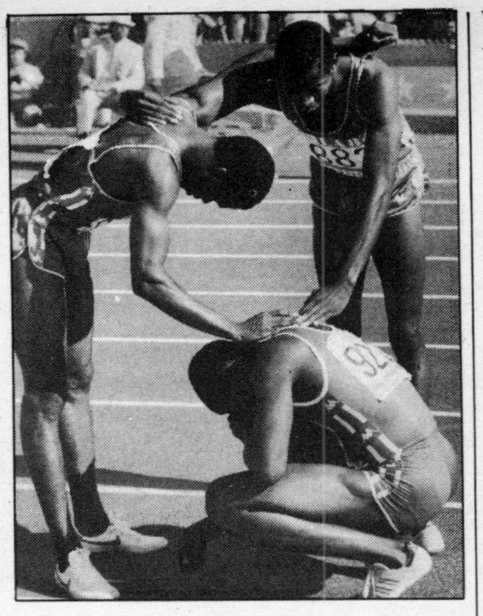

United Press International and PAUL BERESWILL / Los Angeles Times

Alonzo Babers of U.S. pumps right fist in triumph after winning men's 400 meters Wednesday. At right, Sunder Nix (left), who finished fifth, and Babers console U.S. teammate Antonio McKay, the favorite, who kneels on track and bows head after finishing third.

Yachting

It's All Gold or Silver for America's Fleet

By RICH ROBERTS, *Times Staff Writer*

American sailors claimed enough gold and silver in the 1984 Olympic yachting competition on the waters off Long Beach to almost sink the ghostship of the 1980 boycott.

The final tally when the yacht racing ended Wednesday was three gold medals and four silvers—an award in every class.

Four of the medalists were skippers who had won the deadend U.S. trials in 1980: Bill Buchan in Star and Robbie Haines in Soling, with gold medals; and John Bertrand in Finn and Steve Benjamin in 470 with silver medals.

Buchan's son Carl also won a gold crewing with Jonathan McKee in Flying Dutchman, while Scott Steele on a sailboard and Randy Smyth, with crew Jay Glaser on a Tornado catamaran, took silver medals.

But in a way, New Zealand's sailors were even more impressive. That nation of 3.2 million people produced two gold medalists: Rex Sellers in Tornado and Russell Coutts in Finn, plus a bronze for Bruce Kendall in boardsailing.

The other golds went to five-time world champion Stephan Van den Berg of the Netherlands in boardsailing and Luis Doreste of Spain in 470.

For a while late Wednesday afternoon it seemed Bertrand might even move up to a gold, at the expense of one of New Zealand.

Coutts placed fifth in the final race, one spot ahead of Canada's Terry Neilson and three ahead of Bertrand, to finish first in the standings, but then had trouble passing a weight check on his gear.

The sailors are allowed to wear only as many water-filled weight bottles, clothing and other gear that will not exceed 20 kilos (44.1 pounds) dripping weight. Every day one boat was drawn at random to be checked and Wednesday, by chance, it was Coutts' turn.

The first two times his gear was soaked and weighed, Coutts was over at 20.42 and 20.46 kilos. The last time, after re-arranging it on the bar that is lowered into the weighing tank, he passed at 19.06.

Bertrand said he was satisfied with his silver.

He said, "I'm pretty happy when you consider that a year ago I wasn't even sailing the boat, and two months of pure hell (his dispute with Russ Silvestri)."

He also said it was his last race in a Finn. "Thank God," he said.

Bertrand will get married Nov. 3 and then concentrate on another America's Cup campaign with John Kolius.

Wednesday he placed just well enough to edge Neilson by seventenths of a point, 37 to 37.7. Coutts had 34.7.

Coutts, a 22-year-old engineering student from Auckland, never finished first but sailed consistently well and won the first race on a protest against Bertrand, who fouled him on a port-starboard crossing.

But Bertrand said, "Coutts did a hell of a job sailing the boat."

Two nights earlier Coutts had some boils on his backside lanced without anesthetic rather than risk failing a drug test.

"I didn't get much sleep that night," he said.

The winds were up again Wednesday and Bertrand, standing by his boat, said, "I have a mast right here that might have done better in a breeze."

The mast was loaned by Silvestri but never used.

□

The U.S. performance is unmatched in Olympic yachting history. Americans had won two golds in three other Olympics and medaled in all five classes, with no golds, at Tokyo in '64. But even team manager Sam Merrick didn't expect to win at least a silver with every boat he entered, especially with a suspected weak link in boardsailing.

But Steele, a relative straw in the wind at 129 pounds, took advantage of light winds early in the series to post finishes of 1-2-1 and used his throwout Wednesday to stifle one rival, Klaus Maran of Italy, with some tactical sailing.

"I just sat on him," Steele said. "I didn't care where I finished."

His wife Kathy, the U.S. women's boardsailing champion, leaped into his arms on the beach, then sprayed him with champagne.

There also was some serious celebrating on Bill Buchan's dock. His daughters pushed him into the water.

Buchan, 49, of Seattle, said he wasn't counting on gold medals for both himself and son Carl, although "I felt very confident that Carl and Jonathan (McKee) would win a gold. I figured that one was in the bag."

McKee and Carl Buchan placed sixth—their worst finish but enough to edge Canada's Terry McLaughlin, who had to re-start after jumping the gun, spoiling a keenly anticipated two-boat contest in that class.

Bill Buchan, with crew Steve Erickson, started poorly and was as far back as seventh but wound up winning by 18 seconds.

"Honest to God, I don't know how we did it," he said. "I never sailed a Star boat that was that fast. In five minutes we went from no medal to a bronze to a silver to a gold."

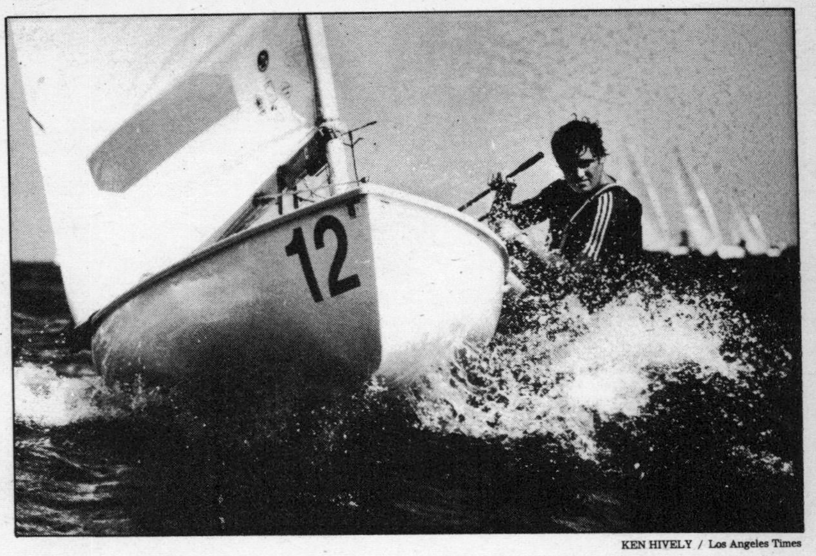

KEN HIVELY / Los Angeles Times

Russell Coutts of New Zealand splashes through rough seas on his way to a gold medal in Finn class in Olympic yacht racing at Long Beach. John Bertrand of U.S. was second.

Men's 400

After Others Did the Talking, Babers Does the Running and Grabs the Gold

By RANDY HARVEY, *Times Staff Writer*

In all the debate over whose name was on the gold medal for the 400 meters, one name that was almost never mentioned was Alonzo Babers.

But Babers, a second lieutenant in the U.S. Air Force, not only won the 400 at the Coliseum on Wednesday, he became the fourth-fastest man ever in the event with a time of 44.27. It is the fastest time in the world this year.

When it was over, he said he felt sorry for the six men who finished behind him.

The war of words had been won by a man who does not use them as weapons.

The same cannot be said for all of the world's best quarter-milers. Earlier this year, Jamaica's Bert Cameron, world champion in the 400 meters, said the Olympic gold medal had his name on it. The statement offended Antonio McKay, who, after winning the U.S. trials, vowed to "destroy Bert Cameron."

McKay never had the chance. Cameron pulled a muscle in his left leg in the semifinals Monday. While he bravely finished the race and qualified for the final, he was unable to make it to the starting blocks Wednesday.

He withdrew, leaving McKay the favorite. But even though he equaled his personal record, running a 44.71 from lane one, he never challenged for the lead and finished third.

McKay crossed the finish line only .04 ahead of Australia's Darren Clark and American Sunder Nix, who both were timed in 44.75.

Clark, 18, the only man in the final who does not attend a U.S. university, led for the first 300 meters after a quick start but had to settle for fourth place after fading in the stretch.

The first man to pass him was the Ivory Coast's Gabriel Tiacoh, who soon was passed by Babers.

"Babers came like a rocket," Tiacoh said.

"I knew I had to go get him," Babers said.

Tiacoh, who won the 400 at the Pacific-10 championships for Washington State, finished second in 44.54 and became the first person from the Ivory Coast ever to win an Olympic medal.

The only other person from the country to ever reach a final before Tiacoh was Gaoussou Kone, who finished sixth in the 100 at the 1964 Tokyo Olympics. Kone is now the coach of the Ivory Coast's track and field team.

The Ivory Coast is a nation on the West Coast of Africa with a population of about 6 million. Fourteen of them are Olympic athletes.

"Maybe the President will invite us all to visit him to celebrate," Tiacoh said.

In no mood to celebrate was McKay, the Georgia Tech freshman who said before the race he would not be satisfied with any medal other than a gold. He was true to his word.

Slumping to his knees after crossing the finish line, he could not be consoled by Babers, Nix or Judi Brown, who was on her way to the awards stand after finishing second in the women's 400-meter intermediate hurdles.

"This was the saddest day of my life because I ran my best and still got defeated," McKay said. "I went into the race thinking I could win. If I could run it again, I still think I could win.

"I had to drop to my knees and ask God to give me the strength to go on and not accept this defeat. I couldn't get up and walk away."

Asked what he said to McKay following the race, Babers said, "I told him he ran a great race. I felt really sorry for him, not only for him but for everybody else in the race. Everybody out there wanted to win the gold medal as much as I did."

Babers said his only regret was that Cameron was unable to run.

"Bert was jogging around at Cromwell Field (the practice track at USC) before the race, when he told me he was going to scratch out of the race," Babers said. "He told me he was behind me 100%."

Cameron might have been the only one who considered Babers a contender for the gold medal. When asked for his reaction earlier this month to McKay's comments about him, Cameron said the young American should not be worrying about him but Babers.

Babers was the only man to defeat Cameron last year, and he also beat him in a race this year.

Babers, 22, was born in Montgomery, Ala., but raised in Kaiserlautern, West Germany, the son of a career Air Force officer. Babers, who wants to become a pilot, has been ordered to report to Williams Air Force Base in Phoenix before Sept. 12.

When he was accepted into the Air Force Academy, he was a football player. But he broke his arm as a freshman and decided track was a safer way to get through college.

It was not until last year that he emerged as a world-class quarter-miler, running the first leg on the U.S. 1,600-meter relay team at the world championships and then beating Cameron at a meet in Zurich. He beat Cameron again this spring at the Bruce Jenner meet in San Jose.

Finishing second to McKay at the U.S. trials was a blessing, he said. "I didn't come into the Games with the pressure of being the favorite."

THE MEDALISTS

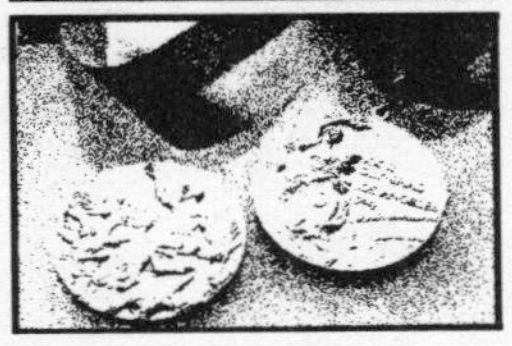

MEN'S

Track

■ 400 METERS

1. Alonzo Babers (U.S.)
2. Gabriel Tiacoh (Ivory Coast)
3. Antonio McKay (U.S.)

THE LOOK OF DETERMINATION

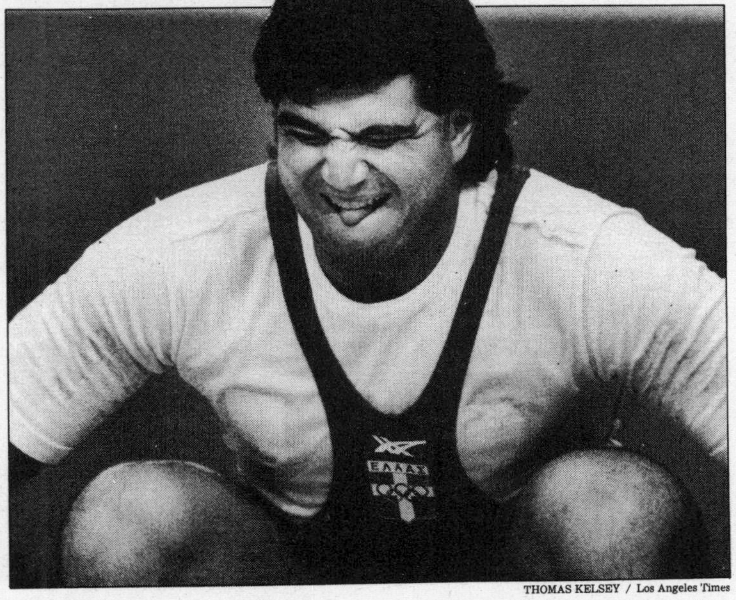

THOMAS KELSEY / Los Angeles Times

Weightlifting requires intense concentration, and if it means sticking out your tongue, then that's allowed. Heavyweight Ioannis Gerontas of Greece is a study in intense concentration while attempting to snatch 347 pounds Tuesday at Loyola Marymount University.

NOTES

Discus thrower Stefan Fernholm of Sweden, who qualified Wednesday with a throw of 206-2 for Friday's final, has his own technique for coping with nervousness in his first Olympic competition.

He pulled a small, crumpled piece of cardboard out of his pocket upon which he had written in Swedish his own three "clues" for staying calm while competing in his first Olympic Games:

(1) Keep cool.
(2) Relax.
(3) This is fun.

"The last is one thing I never want to lose sight of," Fernholm said. "This *is* fun for me."

—MARLENE CIMONS

□

Definition of a track nut by Steve Jacobson of Newsday: "These are the souls who time men's tries."

—BILL SHIRLEY

□

U.S. marathoner Julie Brown, who finished 36th in the women's marathon Sunday, is suffering from a virus, her manager said earlier this week. Brown, who said she "hit the wall" before Mile 14, couldn't understand why she had run so badly. She was examined Tuesday by a physician, who said she was suffering from a flu-like virus.

—MARLENE CIMONS

□

Has enthusiasm among volunteers at the boxing venue dipped a bit?

Apparently so, suggested a Sports Arena employee assigned to crowd control.

"The first day, it was great, and the second day it was great. After that, we started getting a 20% no-show factor."

Meanwhile, the "show" volunteers seem to be handling things just fine.

"We haven't had any dropoff in press relations," said Claudia J. Dinges, assistant sports information director at Ohio State and an enthusiastic volunteer at the Sports Arena.

"I am very glad I came. My motivation in coming was to have an association with journalists around the world. I hope doing this will make me better at my job at Ohio State."

Dinges, who paid her transportation expenses from Ohio, said she is housed by the LAOOC, is provided lunch and dinner when working and is furnished a uniform.

Her longest day on the job?

"Seven a.m. to 11:30 p.m.," she said. "But yesterday was my shortest—noon to 6."

And what does she miss most back home?

"I'm not married," she replied. "But I do have a cat. I miss my cat."

—JACK HAWN

□

Freestyle wrestler Randy Lewis thought he was going to die last winter when he became ill in Tbilisi, a city in Soviet Georgia.

At least, that's what the Soviet interpreters told Dan Gable, the U.S. Olympic freestyle coach, at the time.

"They said I had typhus," Lewis said, "and they wouldn't let me out of the hospital."

Lewis suspected his affliction was more likely caused by Soviet food. However, he had no trouble making the weigh-ins—once he got out of the hospital.

—DAVE DISTEL

□

Ellen Mueller-Preis, the Austrian fencer who won the 1932 gold medal in women's foil, is not enamored of the aggressive and less-than-classical styles of modern female foilists—with one exception.

The 1984 gold medalist, China's Luan Jujie, is "one class higher than the others," Mueller-Preis said while watching the fencing competition in Long Beach. Luan, who was coached in the more classical technique, also "thinks about how to change her style to accommodate to the situation," she said.

Mueller-Preis won three world championships and two Olympic bronze medals (1936 and 1948) besides her gold medal in fencing at the Downtown Armory in the Los Angeles Olympics.

"We were more friendly—more like gentlewomen—in those days too," said the Vienna resident.

In her gold-medal-deciding bout against J. Heather Guiness, she said the British woman acknowledged two touches which the bout director wanted to score against Mueller-Preis. That proved to be the margin of victory, 5-3.

—JOHN DART

□

Fred Lebow, director of the New York City Marathon, was pleased with the results of the first-ever Olympic women's marathon in spite of the fact much of the attention was focused on Gabriela Andersen-Schiess, who suffered heat prostration in the final 400 meters of the race.

"I think women are more tenacious than men," Lebow said. "A woman wouldn't quit, but a man would.

"You're going to see a boom in women's distance running because of this race . . . what Joan Benoit did (she won the gold medal running away from the field). Women will throw away their spiked heels and pick up jogging shoes in record numbers."

—ELLIOTT ALMOND

□

Kate Schmidt finished fourth in the U.S. track and field trials, barely missing a berth on her fourth Olympic team. She is a two-time bronze medalist in the javelin.

But when the women's javelin final began Monday, Schmidt was in the infield at the Coliseum.

Sitting on a stool near the javelin foul line, smoking a cigarette, Schmidt was taking notes for her job as a researcher for ABC. She certainly had better access to the athletes than any other member of the media. Several of the throwers came over to speak to her during the competition.

"It's a swell place to sit, isn't it?" Schmidt said. "I thought it would be hard for me to be at the track. But once I was here, it was great."

Schmidt's American record of 227-5, set in 1977, would have been good enough for a silver medal in the 1984 Olympics.

—RANDY HARVEY

Newspaper Claims It's Running New View of Decker

From Times Staff Writers and Wire Services

The naked truth, maybe: Zola Budd may want to show her bare heels to Mary Decker in the 3,000 meters, but one South African newspaper claims it has taken the idea a step further.

"What we're carrying on our front page this morning, would you believe, is a huge picture of Mary Decker with her back to us in the nude," Teddy Lofthouse, sports editor of the Rand Daily Mail, said recently.

"One of our big magazines called Fair Lady has been doing a series on Decker and Budd, and they got hold of it through Rapport, the Sunday newspaper. We ran it about 20 inches deep this morning on the front page. It was quite striking."

Probably not half as striking as Decker's response will be when she finds out, assuming, that is, that the photograph is for real.

Asked whether his newspaper would be following up with an equally revealing photograph of Budd, Lofthouse laughed. "I don't think it would be quite the same," he said. "The appeal's not there, somehow."

—GRAHAME L. JONES

☐

Human athletes aren't the only ones who don't always pass physicals. Three horses failed their veterinary tests for Wednesday's team dressage at Santa Anita.

Nittoku-Janbo and Nobunaga, both of Japan, and Abd al Rahman, of Mexico, failed their tests. Horses are treated better than humans, however, because the vets commission doesn't reveal why they failed. And the horses won't tell.

—SHAV GLICK

☐

There's a VIP tent located near the Sports Arena, and hostesses there say they've entertained Britain's Prince Philip and Princess Anne, Sweden's King Carl XVI Gustaf, and King Constantine, the exiled monarch of Greece.

But "King" Carl Lewis, the superman of track and field, caused the biggest stir, autographs and such, when he dropped by the other day.

"Royalty definitely took a back seat to Carl," a hostess said. "Everyone wanted to talk to him."

—MAL FLORENCE

☐

Observers have called the gold medal-winning U.S. team the best women's basketball team ever assembled. But just how good the U.S. team is no one is likely to find out because it missed a meeting with the Soviet Union, which was a no-show in Los Angeles.

U.S. Coach Pat Head Summitt wouldn't quite come right out and say the Americans could beat the Soviets, but she hinted at it during a Wednesday press conference.

"I think this is the best women's basketball team ever established in the U.S.," Summitt said. "The question is could this team beat the Soviet Union. I'm confident this is the best team in the world right now." About the possibility of a U.S.-Soviet showdown in the future, Summitt said: "I doubt if I can get this team to practice another time."

Pam McGee, who gave her medal to her sister, Paula, who didn't make the U.S. squad, added: "As far as playing the Soviet Union—I'm sorry. We have our gold medal."

—ELLIOTT TEAFORD

☐

Gold-medalist sprinter-jumper Carl Lewis autographed Bibles and explained the relationship between athletics and religion to a meeting at the First Baptist Church of Van Nuys Tuesday.

"When I compete, I enjoy it. When I stand on the victory stand, I enjoy it. But I always think of the Bible," Lewis told the audience of 2,000.

Lewis said he owes his career to Christ. "Of course, number one is Jesus Christ because without his support I wouldn't be here," he said.

Joining him at the podium was sprinter Valerie Brisco-Hooks, who won a gold medal in the women's 400 meters Monday.

Jess Moody, pastor of the church, said Lewis became a Christian in 1982 at the NCAA track and field championships in Houston.

☐

Zola Budd has gone from bum to heroine in Great Britain, with media coverage changing accordingly. Still, the ever-vigilant British press can't let a good story lie.

There remains lingering criticism among immigrant-rights groups protesting Budd's unprecedented 13-day citizenship approval, which they say was speeded up by her world-class running ability.

Accordingly, one Sunday paper recently ran a cartoon depicting two middle-aged Pakistani men huffing around a track—turbans unraveling—hoping for track and field stardom as a ticket to citizenship.

—JULIE CART

☐

John Whitaker of Great Britain was breezing along on Ryans Son-without a fault late in the team jumping at Santa Anita when the horse clipped barriers on the double jump at Gladestone Gate.

Ryans Son cleared the next and final jump, then kicked her hind legs in the air as if to say, "So much for you, Santa Anita!"

—SHAV GLICK

☐

Anaheim Convention Center officials were perplexed this week when Jim Kennedy, the chief of police, expressed interest in acquiring tickets for freestyle wrestling.

Once again, none are available at the box office.

However, a wrestling fan approached the ticket window and asked if he could get a refund on two tickets he did not need. In an Olympic twist worthy of Greg Louganis, the box office found itself buying tickets rather than selling them.

Obviously, the story would have been more delightful if the chief's tickets had been bought from a scalper.

—DAVE DISTEL

☐

Morley Myers of United Press International should get some sort of a medal for a sharp line describing Alexandru Siperco, Romania's elder statesmen of the Olympic movement.

Concerning Siperco's views on Romania's decision to come here despite the Soviet boycott, a very sensitive issue, Myers wrote:

"Siperco can dodge questions in French, English, Russian, German, Hungarian, and, of course, Romanian."

SILVER TEARS AMONG THE GOLD

As China's women's volleyball team (above) celebrates its gold-medal win Tuesday night at Long Beach Arena, Sue Woodstra (left) is consoled by a teammate as she cries into a towel. Paula Weishoff (right) isn't too pleased with the silver medal after the Americans lost three straight games to the Chinese.

Photos: ROBERT LACHMAN
Los Angeles Times
and United Press International

Siperco is also a writer, with novels, short stories, movie scripts and historical studies to his credit.

☐

It's sports trivia question time, fans. Who was Georgia's high school athlete of the year in 1980? No, it wasn't Herschel Walker, who went on to become a football star at the University of Georgia and sign a big contract with the New Jersey Generals of the USFL. It was Roger Kingdom, an upset winner in the 110-meter Olympic high hurdles, who beat out Walker for that honor. Kingdom, now at the University of Pittsburgh, also became the state's first two-time winner of the award in 1981.

☐

Most of the public in the U.S. and 18 other nations believe that the Olympic Games should be moved from country to country every four years as is done now, instead of adopting a permanent site in Greece as has been proposed, according to a Gallup Poll.

In the U.S., the poll showed 54% favor retaining the present system, while 37% prefer a permanent home in Greece, where the original Olympics were held.

The present system also was preferred by citizens of all but 2 of the 18 other countries participating in the international survey. But the Greeks voted 91% to 8% to have the Games returned to their country for good.

☐

Here are two candidates for the "Olympic Odd Couple" award:

Col. Harvey Schiller of the United States Air Force and Col. (ret.) Karl Heinz Wehr of the East German Army are running the boxing tournament at the Sports Arena. Schiller, 45, head of the chemistry department at the Air Force Academy, is the competition director. Wehr (pronounced: Vare), 57, is an International Amateur Boxing Assn. vice president and second in command here to Schiller.

"Karl and I have been putting in 12- to 18-hour days together here (at the Sports Arena) since he arrived July 5," Schiller said.

"It's struck me several times how well we've worked together in a sports endeavor—with both of us representing the military of opposing systems.

"Aside from needling him with a barb now and then, I haven't tried to convert him to capitalism, and he hasn't tried to convert me to communism. About the boycott, he uses the term 'non-participation,' I use the term 'boycott.' He feels strongly the boycott came down because of a (Soviet) fear of defections, not for the reasons stated.

"Karl's had some calls from European journalists who wanted his reaction to the crime-and-smog fears expressed in the East Bloc press, and he's told them neither has been a problem."

—EARL GUSTKEY

☐

The amount of security provided by the Los Angeles Olympic Organizing Committee has been well-publicized. But the "eyes and ears" of the committee were no match for a skunk who gained access into an unauthorized area (well, he wasn't wearing a badge) before the Olympic archery competition at El Dorado Park in Long Beach.

Officials quickly sprayed the area and were able to transfer the animal, but not before he left behind his scent.

"When I got in, you could smell it from the field," U.S. Coach John Williams said.

—ELLIOTT ALMOND

☐

Millions turned out to watch the torch. More millions have tuned in to see the sports events, and stadiums have been packed with cheering fans, but scratch any surface deep enough, and you'll find a fellow who's fed up with the Olympics.

"I'm sick of the Olympics," said Downey bartender Bill Mitchell. "I'm tired of hearing that song, for openers, and I miss 'Monday Night Baseball.'"

"The streets are messed up something fierce," said Dick Martin, who works in the liquor department of the 32nd Street Market near USC. " . . . The entire Japanese team is wiping us out of Scotch. That and Wild Turkey are the only American words they know."

The campus is in the heart of Olympic country, with the Coliseum and Sports Arena just next door. The swimming venue is also on the USC campus, as is one of three Olympic villages.

Mitchell suggests holding the Games each year on a platform "in the middle of the ocean."

"They can have it in a different ocean every time," he said, "and everyone would be happy."

THE LADY IS A CHAMP

American Cheryl Miller, perhaps the best female basketball player in the world, combines athletic grace with exuberance and flamboyance. She is also at ease behind a microphone, fielding questions with intelligence and wit.

Photos: ROSEMARY KAUL, Los Angeles Times
United Press International

Los Angeles Times

OLYMPICS '84

DAY 14

Jim Murray

You Won't See Equal of Owens

For almost 50 years, he towered over his sport like a skyscraper in a nest of shacks, a cathedral in a village. He was somehow larger than life, mythic in scope, celebrated in song and story.

No one could do what he could. He was the ultimate Olympian. All other performances were measured against his. He set records that were to endure for nearly a quarter of a century.

His name went into the language. His marks went on stone. Pretenders came and went, but no one could set the limits out where he did, break three records and tie a fourth on the same day, and later win four gold medals in a single Olympics.

No one, that is, until this year. This year, history finally caught up with James Cleveland (Jesse) Owens. There's a new name on the wall, a new kid on the pedestal.

An upstart named Carl Lewis has finally overtaken the legend. It says here.

□

But has he? Is he really "the new Jesse Owens"? Can there really be one?

Was anyone really "the new Babe Ruth"? The "new Joe Louis"? Did Tunney replace Dempsey?

Has Carl Lewis just done the easy part—matched Jesse's clockings? Is the hard part ahead? Does he get to take Jesse's rightful place in that higher order of human beings, world-class, all-time celebrities? Or is he just going to be the guy who replaced Ruth in right field, old What's-His-Name?

It's not going to be easy being "the new Jesse Owens."

To begin with, the original Jesse Owens was a superb athlete but a fairly uncomplicated man. He was made for the limelight, sunny, gregarious, generous. He wore the mantle of greatness easily on his broad shoulders.

He exited into a world where the Depression was on, the buck was short, life was cheap, and you had to pay the rent any way you could, even if you had a closet full of gold medals. Jesse did it in demeaning ways. He raced against cheap horses, campaigned on behalf of cheap politicians, wiped his feet and took off his hat when he needed a favor, which was often.

□

He became The-Man-Who-Licked-Hitler, somewhat to his surprise, to say nothing of Hitler's, but life was no 3-5 shot in 1936, and even Olympic heroes, even *the* Olympic hero had to settle for a $120-a-month job in a Cleveland playground, putting away the swings and locking up the basketballs. In those days, blacks couldn't play in organized baseball or go to college to get in organized football. The man-who-licked-Hitler couldn't lick Jim Crow.

Still, Americans love their stereotypes no matter how shabbily they treat them and no matter how broke and in hock. J. C. Owens became part of that pantheon of between-wars sports greats that everyone looked up to and included Ruth and DiMaggio in baseball, Jones in golf, Grange in football and Joe Louis in boxing. This was the real America's Team, and Jesse Owens became Our-Man-On-It-For-Track-And-Field.

Everyone knew Jesse Owens and Jim Thorpe. Wherever Jesse went in his later years, he was honored, deferred to, and in a real sense, loved. And if he was celebrated in America, he was downright revered in Europe. If he set records that were to last 24 years, he made friends that would last a lifetime.

He was a good guy to drink with, play cards with, play golf with. He liked the press, the public, travel and he fit easily into his role as good-will ambassador for track and field and American corporate life. If there were those who criticized his lack of militancy, and there were, Jesse shrugged. "I've been hun-

Please see MURRAY, page 86

JAYNE KAMIN / Los Angeles Times
Gold medalist Daley Thompson of Britain (center) displays power in 110-meter hurdles on second day of decathlon.

Daley Still Reigns in Decathlon

He Beats Hingsen, but Fails to Break Record

By MIKE LITTWIN, Times Staff Writer

There were the Mounties, FDR and the U.S. Olympic basketball team. Now, there's Daley Thompson.

Who says you can't win 'em all?

The Great Briton, who has won them all for six years, won his second consecutive Olympic decathlon—matching Bob Mathias' record—while falling just one point shy of Jurgen Hingsen's record.

Of course he beat Hingsen, who complained of a stomach upset he acquired just before bombing out in the pole vault. The West German Hercules, as the 6-7 Hingsen is known, seems always to have some physical problem when losing to Thompson.

Thompson beat him badly, 8,797 to 8,673. West Germany's Siegfried Wentz finished third at 8,412.

Was Thompson surprised to beat Hingsen so easily?

"No," Thompson said, "I always do."

Thompson does win them all. Get this: Under new decathlon scoring tables that will be recognized next April 1, Thompson becomes the record-holder. Thompson's Thursday total will be upgraded to 8,846 points, Hingsen's current world record to 8,831.

OK, it's confusing. But the thing to remember is that, somehow, Thompson always wins.

After beating Hingsen, pushing his record against the West German to 6-0, Thompson then took on the world. Yeah, the world took a beating.

He even gets the girl. Princess Anne, who is president of the British Olympic Assn., had come to watch Thompson compete. After the competition, she stepped down to the Coliseum floor to congratulate Britian's version of Muhammad Ali. If Thompson isn't the greatest, he'll do.

Thompson even took on ABC-TV.

In his victory lap after struggling to complete the 1,500 meters—the final event in the two-day, 10-event competition—Thompson pulled on a T-shirt just before grabbing a Union Jack.

On the front of the T-shirt: "Thanks America for a Good Games and a Great Time"

On the back: "But what about the TV coverage?"

He was referring to complaints about ABC's alleged bias toward American athletes. But ABC showed plenty of Daley Thompson. It showed him bearing down on the world record. He needed a pedestrian 4:34.8 to get it, but Thompson, struggling all the way after 10 hours of competition, came in at 4:35.

Thompson said the record was unimportant, that

Please see THOMPSON, page 86

Hyphenated Gold for Brisco-Hooks

She Follows 400 Win With Olympic and U.S. Records in 200 Meters

By MAL FLORENCE, Times Staff Writer

It isn't surprising that Carl Lewis is on his way to four gold medals, or that world champion Daley Thompson is the decathlon champion again. And everyone knows about queen Mary Decker, an international star.

But Valerie Brisco-Hooks, a virtually unknown athlete outside of the Los Angeles area until recently, is quietly stealing the show from some of the more-renowned athletes.

Brisco-Hooks got her second gold medal Thursday night by winning the 200 meters at the Coliseum in the Olympic and American-record time of 21.81 seconds.

She had previously won the 400, also setting American and Olympic records. And she'll be running on the 1,600-meter relay team that is favored to win.

So it's most likely three golds for Brisco-Hooks, the

mother of 2-year-old Alvin Hooks Jr. and wife of a former wide receiver with the Philadelphia Eagles.

The famed Wilma Rudolph is the only American woman to win three gold medals in one Olympics, and that was 24 years ago in Rome.

Brisco-Hooks also made Olympic history. She became the first athlete, man or woman, ever to win both the 200 and 400 in one Olympics, a most demanding double.

She simply exploded on the straightaway on her way to the gold medal. Florence Griffith, the former UCLA star, took the silver in the time of 22.04, and pre-race favorite Merlene Ottey-Page of Jamaica barely beat Britain's Kathy Cook, 22.09 to 22.10, for the bronze.

Please see HOOKS, page 86

Holyfield Stopped by 4-Letter Word

U.S. Light-Heavyweight Disqualified in a Match He Was Winning Easily

By EARL GUSTKEY, Times Staff Writer

The strangest thing happened to Evander Holyfield Friday night, on his uncontested way to not only the Olympic Games light-heavyweight boxing gold medal but the outstanding-boxer award as well.

A Yugoslavian referee threw him clear out of the Olympics with five seconds left in the second round.

And so the Americans, who may have received a couple of gift decisions on their way to putting 10 of their 12 boxers in Saturday's gold-medal finals, finally got a rotten break.

Rotten? That's not what most people in a near-riotous Sports Arena crowd of 11,729 were calling it. They chanted a popular American expletive with two syllables with the accent on the second. They threw stuff, too—paper cups, popcorn boxes and assorted trash, in the general direction of a hundred or so

referees and judges seated around the ring.

Holyfield, who was routinely beating up a tattooed New Zealander, Kevin Barry, was suddenly disqualified by referee Bligorije Novicic for hitting Barry in the second round with a crushing left hook after he'd been given the command, "Stop!"

Incredibly, it appeared Novicic was about to give Barry his fourth warning for holding Holyfield around the neck. In amateur boxing, the rulebook says, a third warning for a foul is supposed to result in disqualification of the offender.

Holyfield's left hook knocked Barry to the floor, and he got up shakily to take a standing-eight count.

USA Amateur Boxing Federation president Loring

Please see BOXING, page 86

DAVE GATLEY / Los Angeles Times
Breathtaking—Tracie Ruiz (front) and Candy Costie give United States the gold in synchronized swimming. (Story, page 87.)

BOXING

Continued from page 85

Baker immediately filed a protest with the International Amateur Boxing Assn. (AIBA).

AIBA president Col. Don Hull added to the confusion by announcing afterward that Barry would not be permitted to box in the final Saturday, since he was incapacitated by a head blow. Amateur rules prohibit a boxer from competing within 28 days after he's been knocked out.

It wasn't an official knockout, however, since Barry arose to take his standing-eight.

"We have a good case for overturning it, I think," said Rolly Schwartz, chief of officials for the USA/ABF, referring to Holyfield's disqualification. "The referee's mechanics were terrible. He (Barry) was grabbing Holyfield's neck enough in the first round to be disqualified in the first round. It gives us a good case."

Hull said the AIBA executive committee would rule on the U.S. protest today.

Shortly after the disqualfication was announced, Barry approached Holyfield in the ring, and said, according to Holyfield, "You won the fight fair and square." The stunning disqualification of Holyfield took the luster off a near-all-American semifinals show at Thursday's sessions.

Paul Gonzales, Meldrick Taylor, Pernell Whitaker and Mark Breland had all achieved relatively comfortable victories Thursday night before Novicic gave Holyfield the hook. Then, in the final bout, super-heavyweight Tyrell Biggs made it to the finals with a 5-0 decision.

Here are Saturday's gold medal bouts:

DAY SESSION

106 pounds—Paul Conzales (USA)-Salvatore Todisco (Italy).
119—Hector Lopez (Mexico)-Maurizio Stecca (Italy).
132—Pernell Whitaker (USA)-Luis Ortiz (Puerto Rico).
147—Mark Breland (USA)-An Young Su (South Korea).
165—Virgil Hill (USA)-Shin Joon Sup (South Korea).
201—Henry Tillman (USA)-Willie deWit (Canada).

NIGHT SESSION

112—Steve McCrory (USA)-Redzep Redzepovski (Yugoslavia).
125—Meldrick Taylor (USA)-Peter Konyegwachie (Nigeria).
139—Jerry Page (USA)-Dhawee Umponmaha (Thailand).
156—Frank Tate (USA)-Shawn O'Sullivan (Canada).
178—Anton Josipovic (Yugoslavia)-Opponent to be named.
201+—Francesco Damiani (Italy)-Tyrell Biggs (USA).

The Americans' protest will be heard at 2 p.m. today at the University Hilton Hotel.

Baker said the key points are whether or not Holyfield's blow was started before or after the referee issued the command to stop and whether Holyfield, through his headgear, was able to hear the command over the crowd noise.

The Americans might also raise the question of whether or not Novicic, a Yugoslavian, was aware that disqualifying Holyfield would pit a Yugoslavian boxer, Anton Josipovic, in the finals against a far weaker opponent than Holyfield, Barry.

Whitaker engaged Chun Chil Sung of Korea in a slow, dull battle of counter-punchers. Whitaker waited for Sung to miss, Sung waited for Whitaker to miss. It went on (and on, and on, and on . . .) like that for three rounds. Whitaker never once cut loose with the blazing combinations he'd showed in his first three bouts.

The only clue that something important was taking place was the "KO-REEA!" from upstairs, Section 17, where the South Korean cheering section chanted.

"I wanted to feel him out for a couple of rounds," Whitaker said. "He's strong—I didn't want to walk into anything. My plan was to give him a boxing lesson.

"I'm ready (for the final), I'm in the best shape of my life. I'm not even breathing hard between rounds. He never hurt me, I caught all his best shots with my gloves."

Breland started Luciano Bruno of Italy off with power jabs, just as had in setting up Mexico's Genaro Leon with a one-round knockout the night before. Bruno simply has a harder chin. The world champion banged his right off Bruno's skull a half dozen times but never put him down with hit. He did deck him with a left hook, however, in the Italian's corner with 40 seconds left in the bout.

Last April 13 in the same building, Breland decisioned Bruno in the world championships, 5-0, as Bruno rushed and bulled the Brooklyn welterweight unsuccessfully all over the ring.

This time, Bruno tried a standup boxer routine but this didn't work, either. He was tentative at the outset, flinching when Breland so much as wiggled his right.

Gonzales, who fought Jose Marcelino Bolivar of Venezuela, nearly keeled over from heart failure when the judges' scores were announced. Gonzales was in the blue corner, and the PA announcer began by saying: " . . . and the winner, in the *red* corner . . ." At that, anguish spread over Gonzales' face, but melted into a grin when the referee raised his hand.

"It shocked the bleep out of me," he said afterward. "I thought I was back in Venezuela for a second." He was referring to his controversial decision loss to Puerto Rico's Rafael Ramos at last summer's Pan Am Games.

Thursday night, it was a rout. The closest score on the cards was 60-57 for Gonzales.

Of his gold medal opponent Saturday, Italy's Salvatore Todisco, Gonzales said: "He keeps coming at you and he's very powerful. But I'm going to give him a boxing lesson. Then I'm going to hang the gold medal around my mother's neck, because she deserves it more than I do."

Taylor, after his runaway decision win over Venezuelan Omar Catari, was asked by a reporter who should be named the tournament's outstanding boxer.

"I'd vote for Meldrick Taylor," he said, grinning.

So would Catari.

'He's very good and will probably win the final," Catari said afterward.

If it looked easy, it was.

"I *made* it look easy," said Taylor, 17. "Everything was working tonight—my jab, my left hook, the overhand right. I put him down with the right because I'd hurt him with my left just before that and he was looking for it again."

Boxing Notes

The L.A. Olympic Organizing Committee announced months ago that the semifinals and finals for the boxing tournament are sold out. Tuesday, a memo was distributed to the press announcing that tickets were available for all remaining sessions. The Sports Arena was barely half-filled for Thursday's morning semifinals, 8,419. One LAOOC official blamed the foulup on "Our wonderful computerized ticket sales system." Said the boxing tournament's ticket manager, **Jayne Hancock:** "I have absolutely no idea what happened. But I do know we've had a lot of complaints from people who paid for $95 seats who are sitting up high and have lots of empty seats in front of them." . . . The U.S. team had set an Olympic medal record before the first semifinal bout Thursday. The previous total medal record was nine, set by Cuba in Moscow. The Americans had clinched 11 bronzes going into the semifinals. Cuba holds the gold-medal record of six.

THOMPSON

Continued from page 85

he'll get it some other time.

After setting a world record for the first five events Wednesday, Thompson did say he was going for the record Thursday. He was even thinking of 9,000 points.

But the record lost its importance during the second event of the day—the discus. Hingsen threw 166-9, a personal best. Thompson, meanwhile, was throwing terribly. After two throws, he had a best of 134-4 and was 176 points behind Hingsen in this one event. But on the third throw, Thompson threw 152-9, a personal best, and cut the 176-point deficit to 76 to keep his overall lead.

Then the pole vault. Hingsen said he became violently ill after the discus. Maybe Daley contributed to that. Whatever, Hingsen needed three tries to clear 14-9, and that was it for him. His pole broke in half at one point. His right hand kept slipping off the pole. Thompson, meanwhile, cleared 16-4¾ to end the race.

All that was left to see was if Thompson could break Hingsen's world record of 8,798.

He threw 214-0 in the javelin and then needed 4:34.8 in the 1,500 to get the record.

"The 1,500 is pretty emotional," said America's John Crist, Thompson's good friend and sixth-place finisher in the decathlon with 8,130 points. "Sometimes you're dead and you can't go any faster."

Thompson labored until he got to the finish line, then he grabbed a Union Jack and ran a victory lap. He had just that much left.

On the victory stand, he was mugging in Daley Thompson fashion. He can joke, but more than that, he can compete. Thompson has won two Olympic titles, a world title, a European title and a Commonwealth title since last losing in 1978. He has set the record three times, twice while competing against Hingsen.

At Helsinki, Finland, in the world championships, Hingsen fell behind after a bad high jump and then blamed his poor showing on sudden cramps in his legs.

His biggest problem, of course, is Thompson. Daley, 26, is the world's problem.

He intends to stick around for four more years and go for a record third decathlon at Seoul, South Korea, in 1988.

"I'll be 30, and it will be time to pass it along to someone else," Thompson said.

He's going to be a tough act to follow.

MURRAY

Continued from page 85

gry," he explained evenly. "Where were they when I needed a job?"

This is the legacy, then, that young Master Lewis inherits. This is where the man-who-ain't-Jesse-Owens starts when he wins his fourth gold medal, as he surely will, Saturday night.

The "new Jesse Owens" is a much more complex human being than the real one.

Carl Lewis is never going to work in a playground for $30 a week. He's never going to pick up anybody else's towels. He's never going to have to race horses or shine shoes or sweep floors or work a circus. He's going to be a corporation, not make speeches for one. He doesn't need Hitler to make him famous, ABC will take up the slack.

But he has already shown a lack of feel for history, a degree of aloofness that may blur his place in it. Jesse Owens set a long jump record that stood for 24 years in the Olympics. Carl Lewis had four jumps left in his event and a mark that was over a foot short of the Olympic record and, in fact, was only tied with the second-best Olympic jump ever. He had an arena full of fans imploring him to go for it. He declined. "Jesse would have gone over it on two broken ankles," sniffed a journalist. "He wouldn't be about to leave a world record laying there."

Carl Lewis has scrupulously avoided the press tent. Hustled off the field by a cordon of security types, he has stared stonily ahead as the quote-starved scriveners lean over the fence at him. He has saved his comments for worldwide television. But there is no way Jesse Owens would have passed up a concentration of 7,000 of the world's journalists, without giving them the benefit of his wisdom, maybe playing cards with them.

There's more to being Jesse Owens than just four gold medals, two new records. This may be the "Carl Lewis Olympics," but for it to be the "Carl Lewis Era" in the years ahead may require a whole new outlook. You make America's Team *after* you make the medals. Otherwise, two guys will be standing at a bar some day and one will wonder, "Say, what's the name of that guy who tied all of Jesse Owens' records in the Olympics that time? 'Earl' Something, wasn't it?"

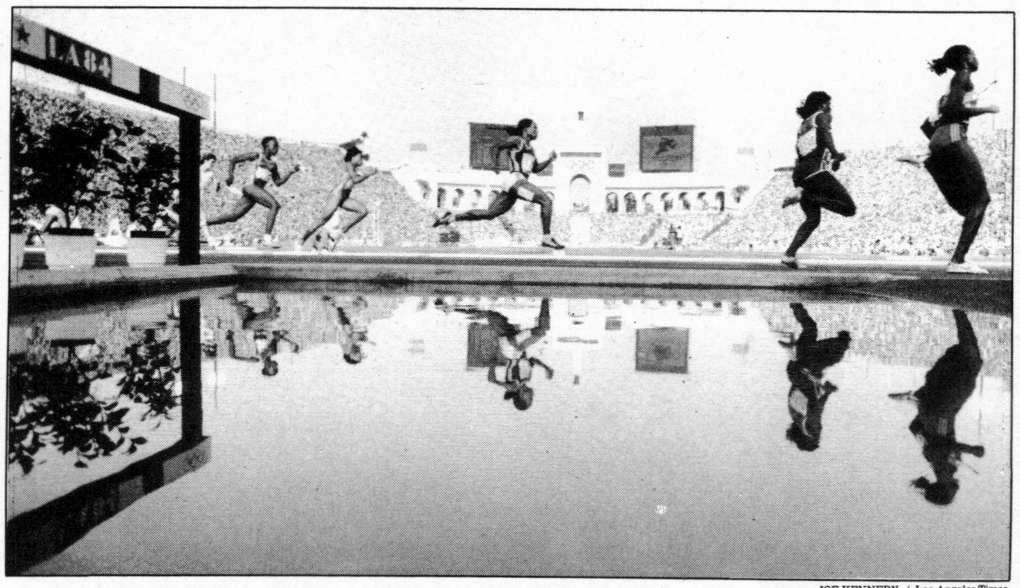

JOE KENNEDY / Los Angeles Times

Women running in the 200-meter final Thursday are mirrored in a water jump on the adjacent steeplechase course.

Ugh! No More 'Americans Going for Gold,' Please

Skip Bayless, Dallas Times Herald: "At the risk of being shipped to Leningrad, I must say I've had enough of America. Oh, not our country, whose L.A. is staging a Games for the ages. But if I see another American team or athlete go for another gold, I may go berserk.

"If I hear 'American' and 'gold' and 'record' in the same breathless breath again, I may forever roller-skate up and down Venice Beach listening to Jim McKay's greatest hits on my Walkman. I may join the 'Ban Diana Nyad Coalition' in Santa Monica. I may even try out for the Lithuanian water polo team.

"I mean, how much apple pie can we eat? The real broken record is our national anthem, which has been played so many times at Olympic medal ceremonies that it is No. 1 in Kasey Kassem's Top 40 this week. Is all that glitters American gold?"

□

Neil Allen, London Daily Standard: "IOC President Juan Antonio Samaranch's complaint about ABC coverage underlines something that those of us who have visited the States before take for granted—that American television is terrible.

"Over dinner the other night the British actress Susan Hampshire was marveling at how wooden and unexpressive are the TV presenters, all dressed up and nothing of value to say. One sample quote to savor was the comment on the entry of Iceland to the stadium at the Opening Ceremony.

" 'Here's Iceland, now, Bob. Now you've been there.' 'Yes, indeed, Tom, and while I was there I visited their national library. A very literary people are the Icelanders.' "

□

London Daily Mail: "What Los Angeles is transparently in love with is the limelight generated by staging an Olympic Games. . . . Los Angeles, birthplace of a thing called hype, undisputed world capital of unbridled materialism, a city where the meek inherit duodenal ulcers and the modest crawl away to die, wishes it to be known that the boring old Olympics are at last to be staged with style."

□

From AP, on Olympic Village life: "The Chinese are the biggest mystery (due to the language barrier). UCLA village guide Charles Finn III says: 'Everyone wants to talk to them and hardly anyone can. There's a lot of bowing going on.' "

□

From UPI, Vienna: "A report from Los Angeles in Bulgaria's Communist Party daily Rabotnichesko Delo said: 'Television, the sports industry and the sports magnates are increasingly domineering sport in the West. . . . (ABC) is now determining to the highest degree the content, meaning, setup of the sports competitions. They are becoming a *sui generis* missile carrier and a means for psychological brainwashing at the same time. The television is becoming a huge manipulative force, a sharp-pointed imperialistic and chauvinistic tool.' "

HOOKS

Continued from page 85

From obscurity to world class, that's Brisco-Hooks' story. She wasn't even ranked among the top 10 in the U.S. in the 200 or 400 in 1983. She only ran the 400 this year hoping to get a place on the U.S. relay team.

Her time of 21.81 broke the U.S. record of 21.83 held by Evelyn Ashford. She becomes the No. 3 performer of all time behind East Germany's Marita Koch, the world record-holder at 21.71, and Marlies Gohr at 21.74.

Tears streamed down Brisco-Hooks' cheeks on the victory stand, and later in the interview tent there was a family reunion. Young Alvin was blowing into the microphone, and mother was trying to hold him on her lap but he escaped.

Then Valerie, who attended Locke High and Cal State Northridge, introduced her family—her husband, Alvin; her mother; her three brothers, Charles, Terry and Gus along with Gus' wife, Nancy.

This was the real version of "All in the Family."

Asked what motivated her to do what no other Olympic athlete has done, golds in the 200 and 400, Brisco-Hooks said:

"I didn't have anything to prove. But lots of people believed in me and I didn't want to disappoint them. Also, my brother was coming in from Arizona to watch me run."

After Brisco-Hooks gave birth to her son, it only strengthened her resolve to become a world-class performer, according to her husband.

"She didn't need much encouragement," said Hooks, who played football at Cal State Northridge, "and I gave her all the support I could."

That meant taking care of young Alvin, doing household chores and putting his own career on hold.

Of Thursday's race, she said: "I didn't have that good of a start and I really had to run a strong curve. When I came out of it, I was looking for Florence. If I was going to be beaten by anyone, I wanted it to be her."

Brisco-Hooks and Griffith are teammates and friends on the Tiger World Class team and are both coached by Bob Kersee, who was recently named the UCLA women's track coach.

Griffith ran a very strong turn and held the lead until Brisco-Hooks took command in the straightaway.

Someone asked Griffith when she thought she was going to medal?

"When I got in the blocks," she said coolly, eliciting laughter among the press corps. "I was determined not to let anyone inside of me catch me. I was determined to go after her (Brisco-Hooks) and catch her before the straight."

Griffith, in Lane 4, caught Brisco-Hooks, in Lane 7, but gave way to her on the straightaway.

Ottey-Page, who is married to high jumper Nat Page, got her second consecutive bronze medal in the Olympics. But she was unhappy with her lane assignments.

"I drew Lane 8 and Lane 1 (heats) and then I got Lane 2," she said. "I have long legs and I don't run the turn that well from Lane 2. Before the race I was so weak, I didn't know if I could go through with it."

There had been some conjecture that Brisco-Hooks might run a leg on the 400-meter relay team and try for an unprecedented four gold medals for an American woman. But she said the Saturday final for the two relays are only an hour apart and after all her previous work, she said "it would be too much for me."

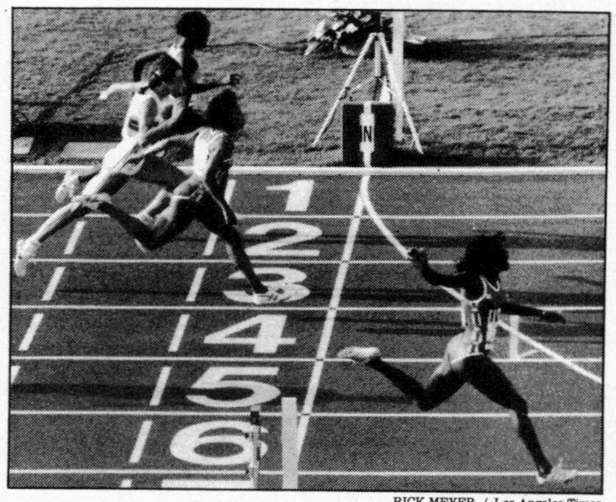

RICK MEYER / Los Angeles Times

Valerie Brisco-Hooks of U.S. is runaway winner of women's 200 meters Thursday, her second gold medal. Florence Griffith of U.S., in Lane 4, is second, and Merlene Ottey-Page of Jamaica, Lane 1, is third. Brisco-Hooks' time of 21.81 set a U.S. record.

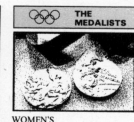

THE MEDALISTS

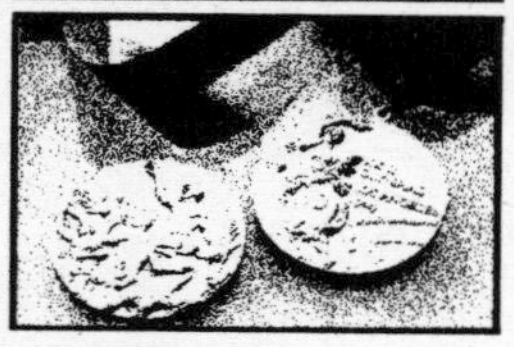

WOMEN'S

Track

■ **200 METERS**

1. Valerie Brisco-Hooks (U.S.)
2. Florence Griffith (U.S.)
3. Merlene Ottey-Page (Jamaica)

Synchronized Swimming

Ruiz and Costie Make Winning Performance Out of Their Last Duet

By JOHN WEYLER, *Times Staff Writer*

There's nothing unusual about gold medalists with tears in their eyes. We've seen it so often these last two weeks that the reasons these athletes are crying have become as clouded as their vision on the victory stand.

But Tracie Ruiz knew why she was crying as she bent over to accept her gold medal Thursday afternoon. And when she tried to explain it more than an hour later, she started crying again.

Ruiz and Candy Costie culminated a 10-year partnership and two years of dedication unparalleled in their sport as they won the first-ever synchronized swimming Olympic gold medal in the duet competition. Canadians Sharon Hambrook and Kelly Kryczka took the silver and Japan's Saeko Kimura and Miwako Motoyoshi won the bronze.

Ruiz will attempt to make it a U.S. sweep Sunday in the solo event, but Thursday all she could think about was 4 a.m. giggling sessions when she and Costie were too tired to even complain about the seven hours of swimming, running, weightlifting and practice that were ahead. And about childhood arguments that evolved into the compromises that talented 21-year-olds with considerable egos must make to stay together.

Thursday marked the end of a dream. But it also marked the end of a team.

"I don't know whether I'm happy or sad," Ruiz said, softly. "I mean I do know . . . I'm both. All the years we've spent together. . . ."

Ruiz bowed her head, put her hands over her eyes and tried to suppress the sobs. "We're like sisters, I know we'll always stay in contact," she said. "It's just I have such mixed emotions. Our sport finally made it to the Olympics and we are representing the U.S. and we won the gold medal.

"Everything will be different from this moment on, though. I guess that's how life goes."

The effervescent Costie wasn't nearly as introspective. She paraded around the swim facility arm-in-arm with her fiance, U.S. water polo player Doug Burke (who scored the winning goal in an 8-7 victory over West Germany on Thursday), and she was smiling and laughing.

"How do I feel?" she said, repeating the question incredulously. "It feels absolutely incredible. And the fact that we worked so hard for so long . . . knowing that we couldn't have worked any harder . . . makes it extra special. And winning it with Tracie makes it extra, extra special."

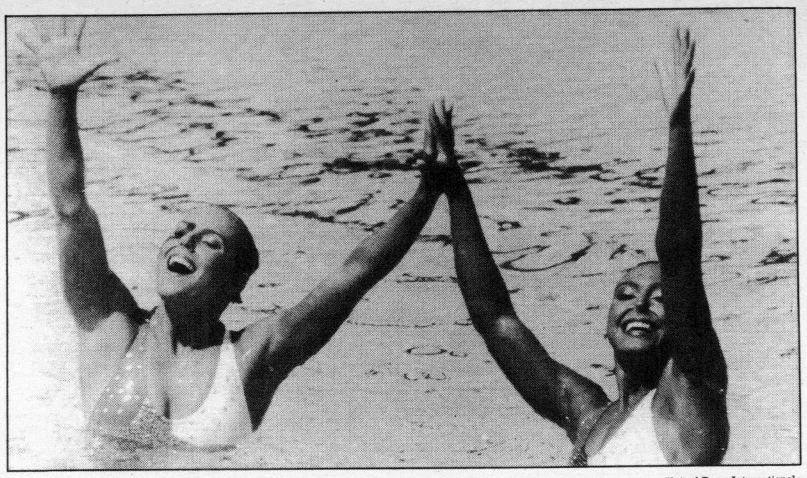

United Press International

Candy Costie (left) and Tracie Ruiz were winners of duet competition in synchronized swimming.

There wasn't much doubt that Ruiz and Costie would be wearing new golden necklaces Thursday. They had a comfortable lead after the figures competition (which counts 50% of the total score), and the routine portion is by far their strongest area in the event.

Swimming last, the U.S. team had the sold-out Olympic Swim Stadium crowd on its feet, clapping along with their final piece of music, "Yankee Doodle Dandy," a bit of showmanship they added to their routine specifically for the Olympics. The partisan spectators weren't the only ones impressed with the routine—which begins with the duet performing the first 50 seconds underwater. Ruiz and Costie received a 10 (from the U.S. judge) and the rest 9.9s for a routine score of 99.0 and a total of 195.584.

Canadians Hambrook and Kryczka, who also had one 10 (from the Canadian judge) got a 98.2 routine score and finished with a total of 194.234. The Japanese team was well back at 187.992.

Hambrook and Kryczka were obviously unhappy with the judging. "I think we swam the best we've ever swam," Hambrook said. "Our coach (Debbie Muir) told us she didn't see one mistake."

Japanese Coach Masayo Imura was more tactful, but she also questioned the judging. "The U.S. team is very powerful, and I'm not trying to say the judges are fair or not fair," Imura said, "but I would like to know at what point they rate the other teams above us . . . for our self-improvement."

Ruiz and Costie didn't really need to outscore the Canadians, anyway. In fact, they would have won the gold with a 97.7.

"I felt better going into today's competition than I've ever felt," said U.S. Coach Charlotte Davis, who brought the girls together 10 years ago and has been a key figure in their progress ever since.

"They've been swimming this routine so consistently for the past two months, I really wasn't nervous."

Ruiz and Costie must not have been anxious, either. They performed another near-flawless exhibition of the strength and variety that made them the gold medal favorites. The routine also included the unique "thread the needle" leg maneuver they unveiled in Monday's preliminaries.

"Our goal has always been to create a routine that had a lot of variations," Ruiz said. "We want to elicit a response from the crowd whether it's chills or just a smile."

Costie was beaming. Davis was grinning, too. And even Ruiz was smiling through the tears.

"It's not sad, really," Davis said. "This is what we've worked for. I feel a great amount of pride in what they've done here today and how far we've come. No, it's not sad. I wouldn't trade this day for anything."

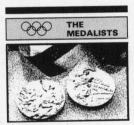

THE MEDALISTS

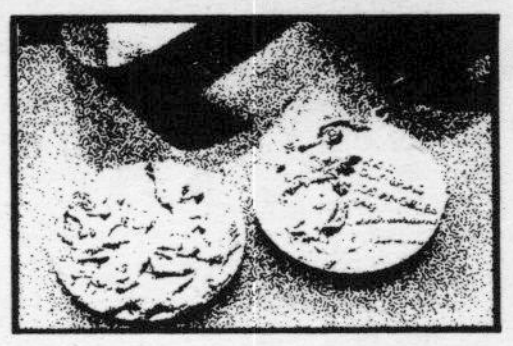

Synchronized Swimming

DUET

1. United States
2. Canada
3. Japan

On the way to winning the first silver medal and highest ranking ever for the United States, Bobby Berland (below, left) beats Walter Carmona of Brazil in the 189-pound class, and afterward (below, right) raises his fist emotionally to the crowd. However, in the battle for the gold, he was pinned (right) by Austria's Peter Seisenbacher.

Photos: LORI SHEPLER Los Angeles Times

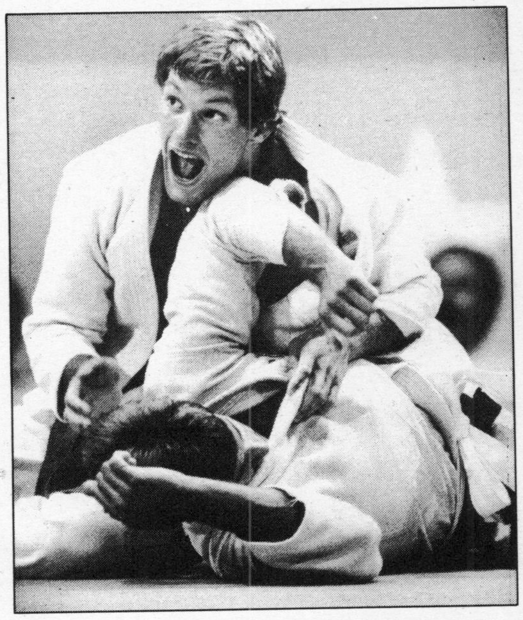

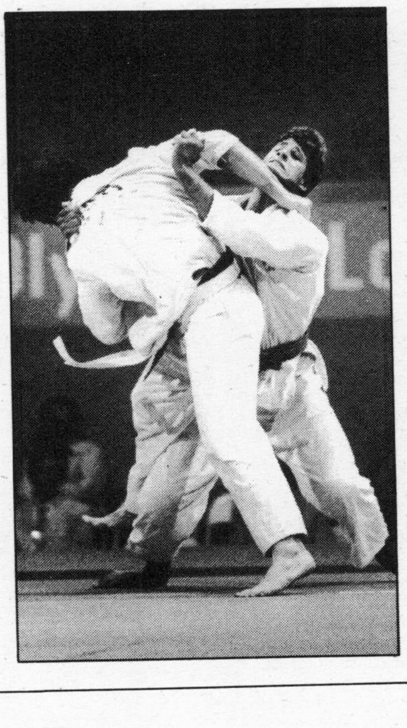

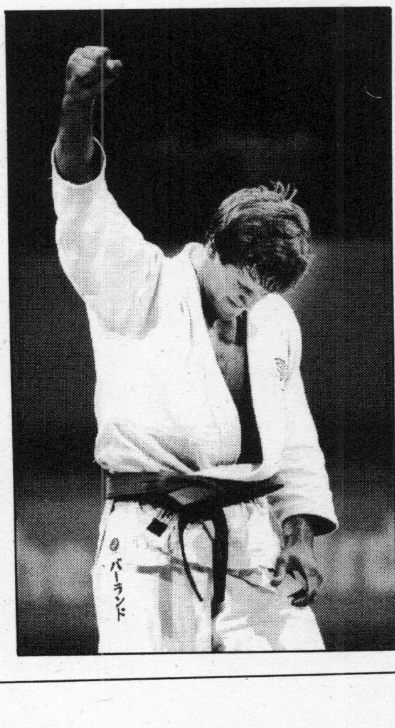

South Korea Tops Brazil to Win Second Gold in Night of Upsets

By DICK RORABACK, *Times Staff Writer*

Ha Hyoung Zoo defeated Douglas Vieira of Brazil in the 209-pound class Thursday and gave South Korea its second gold medal in Olympic judo competition. Vieira won the silver, and bronze medals went to Gunter Neureuther of West Germany and Bjarni Fridriksson of Iceland.

However, the evening's matches in Eagles' Nest Arena at Cal State Los Angeles proved to be an unending procession of startling upsets as America's Leo White managed to accomplish the near impossible—twice.

First, White, a 26-year-old captain in the Army, walloped Belgium's Robert Van de Walle, defending Olympic champion, everybody's favorite and the class of the 209-pound weight division.

With American flags whipping in the Cal State gym, and with a berth in the final virtually assured, White, two matches later, was stunned by Fridriksson, a crew-cut book salesman whose country boasts only 350 judo players.

Neureuther, second-ranked in the world, also crumbled early, a second-round victim of unheralded Britain's Nicholas Kokotaylo.

No. 3, France's Roger Vachon, was bounced by Austria's Robert Koestenberger in his first bout. Koestenberger fell to unheralded Yuri Fazi of Italy, and Fazi was literally pushed out of contention by Vieira.

Neureuther and the ecstatic Fridriksson, however, survived to nail down bronze medals. (For Iceland, it was only the second medal ever in Olympic competition. Vilhjalmur Einarsson placed third in the triple jump in 1956.)

By the final match, not even the most rapid followers of the martial art were entirely sure who was going to fight whom.

Emerging from the flak was Vieira, rugged, moon-faced and sporting a three-day growth of Brazilian beard, and Ha, a 23-year-old with a knee brace, a bandage over an injured shoulder, and a permanent smile.

Both men were admittedly bemused by their eminent position. Ha said later he expected to meet Van de Walle or White in the final, and was not at all prepared for the Brazilian. Vieira, for his part, was simply dumbfounded—and fought that way.

Vieira, as they say, ran, but he couldn't hide. The powerful South Korean caught up with him, lifted him twice like a half-sack of rice, and won an easy decision for the Olympic title.

South Korea's Ahn Byeong Keun won in the 156-pound division earlier in the week.

White, for his part, was beyond communication after his fall. Having slammed Van de Walle with a two-fisted throw—one hand on the Belgian's sleeve, the other on his shoulder, he was, by the account of his teammates, still three feet off the ground when he faced the crew-cut Icelander.

Fridriksson took advantage of White's figurative levitation. After a White throw was disallowed (a splendid toss, but from a kneeling position, which is a judo no-no), he pursued the Icelander, tried one of his patented foot sweeps, missed by 12 inches, and found himself rudely upended in a beautiful counter-throw.

For the Icelandic salesman, it was truly one for the books.

THE MEDALISTS

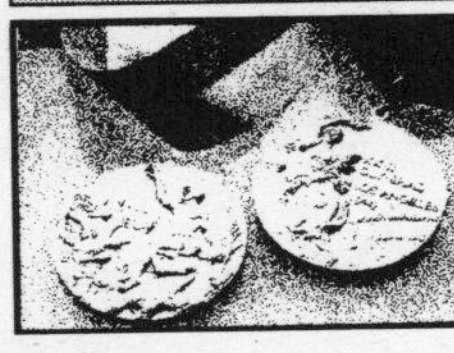

Judo

HALF HEAVYWEIGHTS

1. Ha Hyoung Zoo (South Korea)
2. Douglas Vieira (Brazil)
3. (tie). Bjarni Fridriksson (Iceland) Gunter Neureuther (West Germany)

NOTES

Hot Stuff Department: There was about a half-minute left in India's field hockey game Thursday when smoke started rising from behind the scoreboard at East Los Angeles College. Were Sikhs burning an Indian flag? Was the scoreboard on fire? Had a bomb exploded in the parking lot?

It turned out to be a fire in ABC's mobile food trailer and was easily tamed.

Everybody can use a hot meal now and then.

—ALAN DROOZ

□

Bubbly goalie Gwen Cheeseman of the U.S. women's field hockey team was beginning to realize the Olympics were over for her team after their last game Thursday. "I can't believe that it happened and it's all over," the diminutive 32-year-old said.

"Every day in practice I used to complain about the 100 pounds of equipment I had to carry. I loved carrying that 100 pounds of equipment today."

The U.S. team tied its last game but can still win the bronze medal if the Netherlands beats Australia today by three goals. "No problem," Cheeseman said. "We root for Holland all the time. Really."

—ALAN DROOZ

□

West German tennis player Steffi Graf had taken her seat behind the press conference microphone Thursday when venue press chief Steve Rourke asked if she needed an interpreter.

"Huh?" Graf said.

"Do you want an interpreter?"

"What?"

Rourke rephrased the question. "Do you speak English?" he asked.

"Oh yes," Graf said with a smile. And then she proceeded, quite clearly, to discuss her career highlights, her strengths as a tennis player and what playing in the Olympics means to her.

Now, if she can learn what the term *interpreter* means . . .

—MIKE PENNER

□

The Golden Knights will be dropping in on Saturday's soccer final at the Rose Bowl—from about two miles up.

The Knights are the U.S. Army's demonstration parachute team, which has performed at such various places as Super Bowl XVII, the 1983 Gator Bowl and the 1980 Winter Olympics at Lake Placid.

They serve as the U.S. Army's good-will ambassadors as well as an impressive recruiting tool with their precise landings.

For the Rose Bowl drop, the Knights plan on entering the stadium with an Olympic flag, the LAOOC stars-in-motion flag and the game ball.

—GERALD SCOTT

□

Through the first 11 days of the 1984 Olympic Games, former, current and future UCLA athletes had won a total of 21 medals, including eight gold, eight silver and five bronze, according to the Bruin sports information service.

Gymnast Mitch Gaylord leads all Bruins with four medals, including a gold for the U.S. team victory, a silver on the vault and bronze medals on the rings and the parallel bars. Peter Vidmar finished the gymnastic competition with two gold medals—one for the team championship and the other on the pommel horse—and added a silver in all-around competition.

Overall, 48 former, current and future Bruins are competing in the Games, representing the U.S. and 12 other countries. This is believed to be the largest group ever from a single university to compete in the Olympics.

OLYMPICS '84/NOTES

Compiled By JERRY GILLAM

U.S. Boxing Judge Says Jurors Cause of Controversy

From Times Staff Writers and Wire Services

An American boxing official blasted the scoring by jurors at the Olympic boxing tournament Thursday, following two unpopular jury decisions at the morning session that put Shawn O'Sullivan of Canada and Henry Tillman of the United States into Saturday's finals.

"The problem is the judges for the most part are doing a fine job, it's the jury members who aren't," said the U.S. official, who said he did not want to be identified.

"The judges are the front-line guys, the best we have. But many of the jurors are political hacks, generally much older guys, who just aren't sharp. And two of the five for every bout are seated at the competition table, not right at the ring apron.

"Take a look at them, they're smoking cigarettes, talking on the telephone; people are walking back and forth in front of them . . . they're just not studying the bouts like they should be.

"So it's not a question of jurors consciously favoring one country over another, it's a simple matter of incompetence.

"The O'Sullivan and Tillman decisions were bleep."

The juror system, being used for the first time in the Olympics, calls for five jurors to back up the five judges. All 10 score a bout. If the judges call a bout 3-2, the jurors' cards are picked up. If they vote the other way by 4-1 or 5-0 margins, the judges are overruled.

—EARL GUSTKEY

□

As South African Zola Budd was leaving the Coliseum following her 3,000-meter qualifying heat, a fan with a heavy British accent called to her: "Hey, why do you run without shoes?"

Responding too softly for anyone but her coach and a Los Angeles Olympic Organizing Committee press aide to hear her, Budd said: "I always run without shoes."

In case the press aide had not heard Budd, her coach, Pieter Labuschagne, said: "She always runs without shoes."

"Well," the press aide said, "you should have a card printed up that says you always run without shoes."

Budd giggled.

□

Considering that she has been in Britain for only six months after leaving her home in South Africa, Zola Budd is as much a curiosity item to the British athletes as to everyone else.

None of them have gotten to know Budd, 18, because she is so quiet. "The most anyone has heard her say is, 'Would you like a cup of tea?'" one British athlete says.

Labuschagne told several British athletes not to be offended by Budd's personality. He said she is not attempting to be aloof but is very shy. He told them she was just as quiet around her friends in South Africa.

—RANDY HARVEY

□

The winner of the silver medal in epee fencing, unheralded Bjorne Vaggo of Sweden, was the 1978 NCAA epee champion from Notre Dame. Did the United States let a future Olympic medalist get away?

Not really. Vaggo left Notre Dame after only one semester.

The 28-year-old Swede, now an industrial engineer with Volvo, said he wanted to improve his English at Notre Dame. "I loved it," he said, but he left the Fighting Irish campus because "I couldn't improve my fencing (in this country)."

—JOHN DART

□

France's Pierre Quinon is one of the world's most erratic pole vaulters. He set a world record of 19-1 last year, since broken several times, after failing to clear any height at the world championships only two weeks earlier.

But after winning the gold medal Wednesday, Quinon said he has been working with a "relaxation specialist" to achieve consistency.

He said he tried group therapy, but it did not work.

"You must be totally alone in therapy," he said, "because when you are competing, you are out there alone."

A FISHEYE LENS

United Press International

ABC is giving you those underwater shots during the diving by submerging cameraman Tim Cothern up to 1 hour 20 minutes at a time. He uses an Ikegami camera with a zoom lens.

United States pole vaulter Earl Bell, who tied for the bronze medal with France's Thierry Vigneron, was the winner of the good loser award Wednesday at the Coliseum.

During the press conference for Quinon and Vigneron following the pole vault competition, Bell popped his head into the media tent and, in his Jonesboro, Ark., drawl, said: "*Vive la France.*"

—RANDY HARVEY

The letdown was only temporary.

Bobby Berland, American winner of the silver medal in the 189-pound division of the judo tournament, fingered his shiny new bauble, wished aloud that he could change the color to gold—then turned his sights to Seoul, South Korea.

The 1988 Olympics? Berland is only 22 but plans to go for his MBA, has a working interest in the computer industry and already holds a seat on the Chicago Mercantile Exchange. Still, he's hardly a man to settle for second-best.

"Remember the dream?" he asked.

A week before his match, in a lighter moment on the lawn at the USC Olympic Village, Berland had told The Times:

"It's been kind of hard to sleep. I dozed off last night and dreamt I was on top of a victory podium, hand over my heart, listening to the national anthem.

"Half an hour later, a friend called from Chicago to say there was a picture of me in Time magazine.

"There I was, at the opening ceremonies, looking at the flag—with my hand over my heart. It was weird."

Seven days later, Berland looked down at his silver medal again and brightened perceptibly.

"You know," he mused, "the dream never said what year!"

—DICK RORABACK

□

Synchronized swimming may have made it into the Olympics, but some of the sport's top officials aren't sure whether or not they've made it into the 20th Century.

Within ten minutes after the completion of the first two rounds of the figures competition, the media received computer printouts of the current standings. Final results of all three rounds did not come out until more than two hours after the competition ended, however.

The problem was Jan Armbrust, the technical delegate for Synchronized Swimming to FINA (swimming's governing body), who demanded that all the scores be manually verified before he would declare them "official."

So much for the computer age.

—JOHN WEYLER

□

The Greek government invited Gabriela Andersen-Schiess, the Swiss distance runner who staggered around the Coliseum track to finish 37th in the women's marathon at the Olympics, to visit Greece.

Government Sport Secretary Kimon Koulouris said Andersen-Schiess had been asked to make a 10-day visit to Greece, the birthplace of the Olympic Games, in recognition of her courage and "athletic effort in the Olympic spirit."

The Swiss runner received a standing ovation from the crowd as she collapsed at the finish line of the marathon race Sunday. She recovered several hours later, after medical treatment.

□

Don Rabska and his Los Angeles Olympic Organizing Committee staff who run the archery venue at El Dorado Park in Long Beach have a special daily duty called "DP," which stands for Duck Patrol.

Because the facility is fenced in, one duck family has been fenced out from an elderly couple who have fed the ducks for years. So Rabska's staff has become the ducks' surrogate feeder for the duration of the Olympics.

—ELLIOTT ALMOND

□

Tessa Sanderson of Britain, who set an Olympic record in winning the women's javelin Monday, spent some time in a press conference defending her win in light of the absence of the boycotting East Europeans.

What she didn't know was that she would have to defend herself from an official of her own British Amateur Athletic Board.

Marea Hartman, treasurer of the BAAB and long-time staff member of the British national team, has sold her story to a weekly tabloid in England.

One of the juicier bits to reach Los Angeles was the tale of Sanderson's alleged propensity for nakedness. Hartman tells of one training camp where the team was housed in a monastery. Hartman says Sanderson ran naked through the grounds of the retreat and once startled a meditating monk.

In a press conference, Sanderson denied the report, but one member of the British team reported Sanderson as saying, "I never saw any bleedin' monk!"

Another notorious prankster, British decathlete Daley Thompson, posted this sign on teammate Sanderson's door in the Olympic village: "Tessa Sanderson Wins Olympic Gold Medal . . . In the Nude."

—JULIE CART

GREG LOUGANIS

RISING TO THE OCCASION

Photos:

DAVID GATLEY and CON KEYES

Los Angeles Times

It is a solemn, but happy Greg Louganis who has, at last, realized his dream of winning an Olympic gold medal. The 24-year-old diver from Mission Viejo, who performed in brilliant fashion Wednesday night in winning the three-meter springboard competition, will be the odds-on favorite to win his second gold medal Sunday in the 10-meter platform. "He's the best there has ever been," said Louganis' coach, Ron O'Brien. "Greg has brought a new dimension to diving."

China's Tan Liangde is somersaulting to silver medal . . .

. . . Ron Merriott of the United States wins bronze . . .

. . . but Greg Louganis, shown in midst of performing a back 2½ somersault in pike position, remains in a class all by himself.

OLYMPICS '84/STOP ACTION

110-Meter Hurdles 14.34 (922 pts.)

United Press International

JAYNE KAMIN / Los Angeles Times

Discus 152'9'' (810 pts.)

A Daley Double

JOE KENNEDY / Los Angeles Times

Daley Thompson of Britain became only the second winner of back-to-back Olympic decathlons Thursday night, putting away Jurgen Hingsen of West Germany but missing Hingsen's world record by one point. Thompson's total for the two-day, 10-event test: 8,797 points.

Before Thompson, only Bob Mathias (1948-1952) of the United States had won consecutive gold medals in the decathlon.

Pole Vault
16'4¾''
(1,052 pts.)

Javelin
214'0''
(824 pts.)

JAYNE KAMIN / Los Angeles Times

1,500 Meters
4:35.0 (556 pts.)

OLYMPICS '84
DAY 15

Decker's Fall Stirs the Great Debate

Copyright, 1984, HIRAM CLAWSON / Los Angeles Times

Mary Decker of U.S. falls (above) after tangling with leader Zola Budd of Britain in women's 3,000, then cries in pain (below) as trainers attend to her. She injured her hip.

She Blames Budd After 3,000 Loss

By RANDY HARVEY,
Times Staff Writer

Mary Decker was on top of the world for a year, but Friday night came the fall. It was swift and decisive and painful, although her tears were for soothing emotional instead of physical wounds.

Just into the second half of the 3,000 meters at the Coliseum, Decker and South African Zola Budd, the two central characters in this continuing saga, got their feet tangled.

While Budd, who runs for Britain, retained her balance and extended her lead, Decker, who was in second place, grasped at the early-evening air, looking for something, anything, to hold on to.

All she got was the number off Budd's back.

Decker tumbled into the infield, struggling for a moment to regain her footing and continue the fight, then collapsing, in tears, onto her back.

"It was like I was tied to the ground," said Decker, whose injury later was diagnosed as a pulled left hip muscle. The chief medical officer of the Los Angeles Olympic Organizing Committee, Dr. Tony Daly, said Decker could begin running again today.

Today is too late for Decker, who won the world championship last year in the 1,500 and the 3,000 but chose to compete at the longer distance in the Olympics because she felt a gold medal would be waiting for her at the end of it.

Instead, it belonged to Romania's Maricica Puica, who had a time of 8:35.96. Even if Decker had not met her untimely finish, she was no cinch to beat Puica, who has the best time in the world this year in the 3,000.

Britain's Wendy Sly, who overcame a hamstring injury to be here, finished second in 8:39.47, while Canada's Lynn Williams was third in 8:42.14. Cindy Bremser of Madison, Wis., was fourth in 8:42.78.

Budd faded badly on the final lap, finishing seventh in 8:48.80. That is more than 11 seconds behind her best time, her poor result coming perhaps as a result of the cut she received on her left heel when spiked by Decker just prior to her fall. As usual, Budd did not wear shoes.

An umpire for the International Amateur Athletic Federation, which governs track and field and supplies the officials for most major international competitions, disqualified Budd for obstructing Decker's path.

British officials protested the decision. After viewing films of the incident from six different angles, the IAAF appeals jury ruled that Budd was not at fault and reinstated her to seventh place.

As for whether the contact was caused by Budd or Decker or by both, the debate is likely to continue for years. Track and field experts are still arguing over the cause of American Jim Ryun's fall during the qualifying for the 1,500 meters in the 1972 Munich Olympics.

Decker had the lead for the first three laps, running at a world-record pace for the first two before slowing to allow someone else to take charge. She will be second-guessing that decision for some time to come.

Coming off the final turn on the fourth lap, about 1,300 meters from the finish, Budd moved around Decker and into the lead. They appeared to trade elbows as Budd went past. No harm, no foul. Then, as Budd moved to the inside lane,

Please see 3,000, page 91

ZOLA

Post-Race Rebuke by Decker, Her Idol, Bewilders Youngster

By BETTY CUNIBERTI,
Times Staff Writer

A tearful Zola Budd was "very upset emotionally," British Team Manager Dick Whitehead said, after Budd's feet tangled with those of runner Mary Decker, sending the American to the ground and out of the Olympic 3,000-meter race Friday night.

Budd tried to approach Decker in a Coliseum tunnel after the race, as Decker was being helped out. But Decker waved her off, saying: "Don't bother." With a bewildered look on her face, Budd made her way past reporters, had first-aid administered to a bruised Achilles heel, apparently scraped in the accident, and got on the bus to return to the Olympic Village. As Budd sat outside the Coliseum, talking with a small group of people, Whitehead said he told her that it was her first Olympics, and she ought to be proud.

"All she said was, 'How's Mary?,'" Whitehead said.

Back in South Africa, Budd would run barefoot through the countryside, come home and, as she went to bed, look at the picture on her wall. It wasn't a picture of her mom or dad, or one of her cherished pets, or her class in school, or a rock star.

It was a picture of Mary Decker.

In those days it seemed impossi-

Please see ZOLA, page 91

PATRICK DOWNS / Los Angeles Times

MARY

The Queen of Track Suddenly Becomes Frightened Child

By ALAN GREENBERG,
Times Staff Writer

Mary Decker, America's sweetheart, broke her date with destiny and a lot of hearts, including her own, Friday night.

At the bitter end, her throne was not the Olympic medal stand but a portable medical rescue unit. No victory lap, just X-rays. Her beautiful smile never blazed across world television, it was buried—first in the infield grass, then in the massive neck of her fiance, hulking British discus thrower Richard Slaney.

As befits a queen, Decker's feet never touched the ground once she left the track. But this was no conquering hero, this was a crying, distraught womanchild of 26 being carried off in her lover's arms, brown eyes liquid with tears as she peeked over his shoulder, curled up like a frightened child.

And so concludes another gut-wrenching episode in the scintillating but star-crossed career of Mary Decker, Mary Decker. But this was no scripted soap opera. These tears, these traumas are real. The only residuals Decker will get from these re-runs is mental anguish. Unlike her, we can change the channel on Mary Decker, and search the TV listings in four years for her next Olympic command performance.

Please see MARY, page 91

Knight's Team Hauls the Gold Out of Forum

By MARK HEISLER, Times Staff Writer

Knight fell for the final time on the men's basketball competition at the Forum, and it was suddenly way past bedtime for the Spaniards. They got blown apart, collected their silver medals and left laughing. For them, Friday night's result was not the surprise of the ages.

The Americans, who'd beaten them by 33 points earlier, beat them by 31 this time, 96-65. They thus won the gold medal everyone had earmarked for them and came about as close as is humanly possible to pleasing Coach Bob Knight.

Afterward, Knight proclaimed this the best amateur team anywhere, including the Union of Soviet Socialist Republics, whose representative wasn't here for rebuttal.

"I have one word to say about the Russians," he said, in a farewell interview-room special. "You people have never seen the Russians play, and I've been watching them for two years. The Russians wouldn't have won here. They can't play defense. They couldn't have beaten some of the teams in this tournament, and if you guys don't know that, you're not as smart as I think . . . And I don't think you're too smart, anyway.

"We'll beat their butt anywhere they want to play."

In this, his moment of triumph, could he get a witness?

Nope. This was his close personal friend, Antonio Diaz-Miguel:

"I believe that would be a very good game to watch because the Soviet Union has players such as (7-4 Viktor) Tkatchenko, (7-1 Arvidas) Sabonis, (6-11 Alexander) Belostenny who can equalize rebounding of the United States. It has perhaps some more experience than the American players. And it has very good shooters."

Please see BASKETBALL, page 92

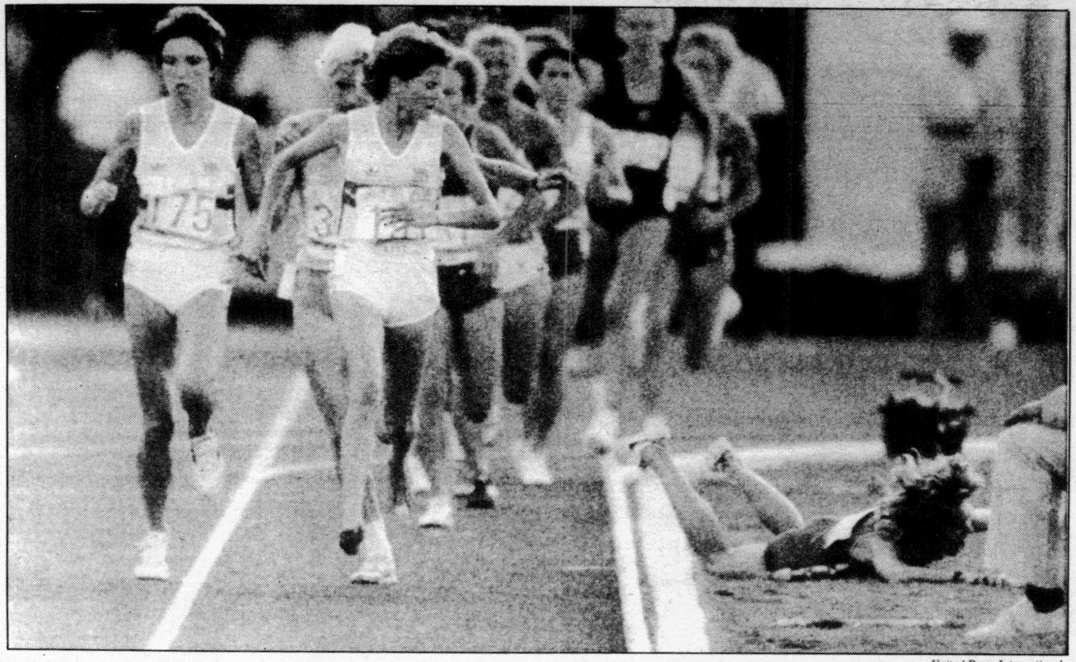

United Press International

Britain's Zola Budd looks over her shoulder to see Mary Decker sprawled on the infield after the American fell in 3,000-meter race.

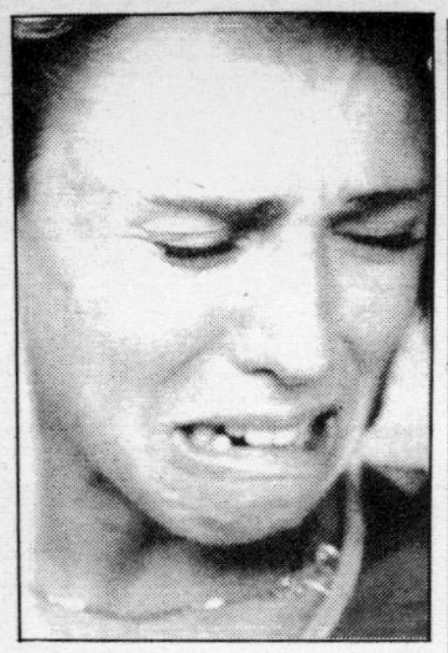

MARY DECKER

THE MEDALISTS

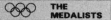

WOMEN'S

Track

■ 3,000 METERS

1. Maricica Puica (Romania)
2. Wendy Sly (Britain)
3. Lynn Williams (Canada)

ZOLA

Continued from page 90

ble that they might ever meet, due to the international ban on South African runners. But Budd, realizing her marvelous gift, left her home country, her friends, all that was familiar to her, to apply for British citizenship and run in the 1984 Olympics.

There, in her first international track meet, she would meet Decker, the woman on the wall, America's queen of running.

It was to be Budd's coming-out ball. But instead, it was more like a gangland rumble.

In an incident that will be argued for years, Budd made an attempt to pass Decker on the fourth lap of their 3,000-meter race. Their legs tangled, and Decker plunged to the ground, out of the race.

Budd was booed by the crowd thoughout the rest of the race, the jeers swelling out from each successive section as she passed.

Welcome to the Big Girls' race, Zola.

Afterward, Budd was disqualified, then reinstated in seventh place after an eight-member jury of officials reviewed films from six angles for about 20 minutes.

Some say it was Budd's inexperience that led her to close in on Decker too soon. Although Decker, who had already tired of hearing about Budd before the race, felt Budd was clearly to blame, not everyone agreed.

Swiss runner Cornelia Buerki, who also is South African-born, said she had a clear view of the incident from her position back in the pack, and she thought Budd was not to blame.

"I would say it was Mary's fault," said Buerki. "She was trying to pass Budd on the inside, and she spiked Zola's Achilles. She tripped on Zola's foot, and then she fell. Zola couldn't help anything because she can't see in the back of her head."

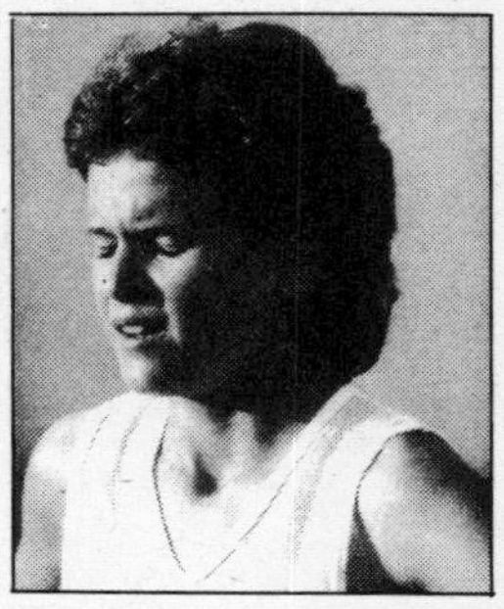

Zola Budd

Buerki also said that Budd's seventh-place finish in 8 minutes 48.80 seconds, some 13 seconds behind winner Maricica Puica, was understandable under the circumstances, and not an indication of what to expect from Budd in the future.

"Zola's season started in September, so that's a long season," said Buerki. "Plus this was her first international competition, and that might have been part of it, too. I'm sure in four years time no one will be able to beat her."

Budd had had more than her share of hard knocks before her first international race. She has been called "white trash" by anti-apartheid demonstrators and told, in a front-page headline in a British newspaper to "GO HOME."

One of those willing to drive her to the airport had been British 3,000-meter runner Wendy Sly, Friday night's surprise silver medalist.

Friday night, Sly said she felt sorry for Budd.

"She's been under a lot of pressure and had a lot of attention," Sly said. "But she's come through."

3,000

Continued from page 90

she cut off Decker, forcing her to shorten her stride.

About 10 meters later, Decker seemed to be ready to pass Budd on the inside. Budd, running on the outside of Lane 1, swayed ever so slightly to her left.

Decker spiked her on the left heel. Budd's left leg shot out from under her, leaving her almost bowlegged for a split second. It was that quick. Decker's right foot and Budd's left crossed. Decker's left foot went over the curb and onto the infield. The rest of her soon followed.

The other runners said Decker screamed something at Budd, although no one could make out exactly what it was.

"I didn't see Mary fall, but I heard her fall," Sly said.

As Dr. Daly and Decker's fiance, British discus thrower Richard Slaney, ran to her side, the race continued. But at every turn, the crowd booed Budd. As a South African whose move to Britain six months ago so that she could compete in the Olympics was not unanimously approved by the British, the sound was not unfamiliar to her.

Obviously distraught, Budd ran the rest of the race in tears.

Afterward, Budd, her eyes red, approached Decker in the tunnel leading away from the track and tried to apologize.

"Don't bother," Decker said. "I don't want to talk to you."

Budd was whisked away by British officials before she could give her explanation to the media. But after returning from the hospital, Decker appeared at a press conference and left no doubt that she blames the bare feet of Budd for her catastrophe.

"Well, Zola Budd tried to cut in without being, basically, ahead," Decker said. "Her foot upset me. To avoid pushing her, I fell.

"Looking back, I should have pushed her. But the headlines tomorrow would have read, 'Mary Decker Pushes Zola.'

"I don't think there's any question she was in the wrong. Maybe it was inexperience on her part, but she was not in front. You have to be a full stride ahead in front before you cut in on anyone. I do hold her responsible."

The interview ended moments later, when Decker broke into tears and was carried away from the media tent by Slaney.

As soon as Decker hit the ground, the U.S. women's coach, Brooks Johnson, was off and running from his seat in the Coliseum to find an official. "Where do I go to protest?" he said.

Not everyone thought a protest was in order. Switzerland's Cornelia Buerki, who finished fifth in the race, did not think Decker was being fair in blaming Budd.

"If it was anybody's fault, it was Mary's" said Buerki, who, like Budd, was born in South Africa. "She tried to get inside of Zola. She hit Zola in the Achilles tendon. It was not Zola's fault. She was in front.

"I wouldn't say it was anybody's fault. But if you had to give somebody blame, it was Mary. She tried to get around Zola, and she hit her."

Detached observers felt that the incident occurred as a result of the inexperience of both runners.

Running for most of her 18 years in South Africa, whose track and field athletes are not allowed to compete internationally because of the government's apartheid policies, Budd did not have experience against world-class fields until she moved to Britain in March.

She ran a road race in May against Norwegians Grete Waitz and Ingrid Kristiansen but had not faced international competition on the track until she ran here.

Her strategy always has been to charge into the lead from the gun and run alone, perhaps because so few of her competitors have been able to stay with her. But there were questions about how she would react when running with a pack.

"She looked like she didn't know how to run with a lead," said American middle-distance runner Craig Masback, who now works for the International Olympic Committee. He meant that she did not know how to run with a small lead.

As soon as Budd took the lead coming off the curve, Masback said, she should have moved over as far as she could in Lane 1, not tempting Decker with the sliver of daylight to the inside.

At the same time, Decker, even though she is eight years older than Budd, also is unaccustomed to running in traffic. Like Budd, Decker prefers to set a fast pace and dare everyone else to follow.

"Mary seemed indecisive," Masback said. "She made a halfhearted attempt to take back the lead. If this had been a men's race, a man would have given the leader a little push to let him know that he was coming through. Steve Ovett would have shoved somebody. But the women aren't as experienced at this kind of distance."

This was the first women's 3,000 in the history of the Olympics.

In tears, her left heel bleeding, the crowd booing her, Budd remained in the lead for another lap and a half. But with 600 meters remaining, Sly took over. With one lap remaining, Budd began to fade.

One hundred meters into the final lap, Puica started her kick. Sly tried to stay with her, but she did not have the strength.

Canada's Williams passed Budd, then Bremser, then Buerki, then Portugal's Aurora Cunha.

"I hope nobody blames Zola," British Team Manager Nick Whitehead said. "She's emotionally drained after her first big race."

Almost overlooked in all of the discussion of Decker and Budd was Puica, but that is the way it has been since it became apparent that the American and the South African would meet for the first time here. Even though Puica had a better time than both of them entering the Olympics, the pre-race headlines were reserved for Decker and Budd.

The last laugh could have been Puica's, but like everyone else, she was not in the mood. "I regret what happened," she said. "I feel sorry for Mary."

MARY

Continued from page 90

Chances are, the screen will be blank.

As befits tragic heroes, Decker will be remembered for what she hasn't done, rather than what she did.

She was 14 and a running prodigy, but not yet world class when the 1972 Olympics arrived. She was injured and couldn't even jog without pain when the 1976 Olympics hit. In 1980, President Carter knocked her—and the rest of America's athletes—out of the Moscow Games by announcing a U.S. boycott.

And Friday night, in the 3,000-meter Olympic final, Mary Decker, America's queen, was done in by a barefoot 92-pound South African sprite who only four months ago became a British subject—Zola Budd. Budd probably doesn't even know how to curtsy.

But Budd, however inadvertantly, did something no other competitor has ever done—strip Decker of her dignity. With one misstep on Budd's heel, Mary Decker was suddenly Humpty-Dumpty, falling like some sort of overweight clod out for a weekend jog. Only this time, the whole world was watching.

It happened 80 meters from the finish line on the fourth lap of a 7½-lap race. It'll be argued and replayed forever, but it seemed like Budd, leading the pack, stepped to the inside, cutting in front of Decker. Decker then tripped on Budd's left foot, clawing the air as she lost her balance, ripping Budd's number off her back as Decker tumbled.

As she fell, she twisted her hip and fell on the infield grass, Budd's number next to her.

"The first thing that went through my mind was 'I have to get up,'" Decker said. "When I did that, it felt like I was tied to the ground. All I could do was watch them run off. It was very frustrating. There have been lots of years of frustration . . . Obviously, me and the Olympics don't have a good relationship, because something always seems to happen."

Decker managed a weak smile. This was at a 10-minute press conference more than one hour after the race. The ever-present Slaney and LAOOC head physician Tony Daly at her side.

Press liaison Don Steffens, who was in the infield as Daly and Dr. Eugene Osher and Slaney huddled over Decker, said the first thing Decker said to Slaney was, "I'm going to protest this."

But to what end? In the biggest race of her life, Mary Decker didn't even rank as an also-ran. First, you have to finish the race.

The race over, flanked by Daly and Slaney, she gingerly crossed the track under her own power, tears streaming down her face. As they neared the tunnel, Slaney picked her up to carry her across the threshold.

He set her down on the tunnel steps and kneeled at her side.

"Zola Budd did this to me," Steffens recalled her telling Slaney.

The 3,000-meter runners began to pass by, hunkering down to slip by Slaney. Each, in turn, offered condolences.

Then came Budd. She extended her hand to within inches of Decker's face. Decker waved her away.

"I didn't say (to her) 'Leave me alone,'" Decker said. "I said, 'Don't bother.' I don't think there's any question that she was in the wrong."

After 15 minutes in the tunnel, Slaney carried Decker out to the waiting medical unit, where she was embraced by her mother. From there, she was taken to nearby Orthopaedic Hospital.

Slaney was carrying her when she reappeared—smiling.

"I've got either a muscle strain, tear or pull, which is good news, if you can call falling good news," Decker said.

A few minutes later, a British reporter thanked Decker for "having the courage to come here."

She started crying again, practically in torrents. The press conference—and Mary Decker's Olympic dream—was over. Slaney carried her out.

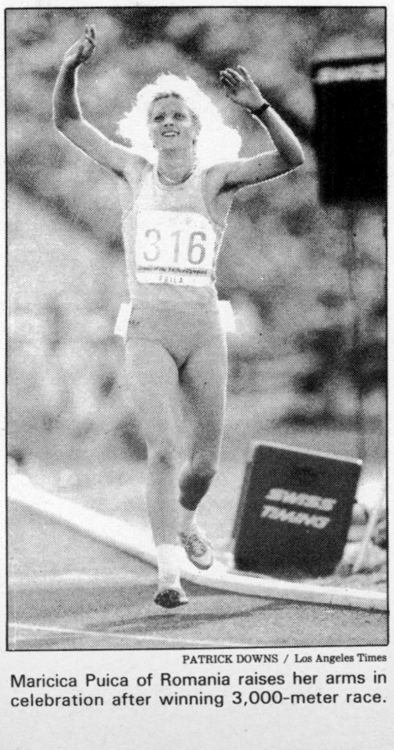

PATRICK DOWNS / Los Angeles Times

Maricica Puica of Romania raises her arms in celebration after winning 3,000-meter race.

Although No One Noticed, Puica Raced Home a Winner

By SAM McMANIS, *Times Staff Writer*

Lost in all the controversy surrounding Mary Decker's fall and Zola Budd's disqualification and subsequent reinstatement in the eventful first Olympic women's 3,000 meters Friday night was the gold-medal-winning performance of Romania's running machine, Maricica Puica.

After Decker's fall, which occurred after the final turn on the fourth lap, hardly anyone noticed that Puica took control of the race and used a strong kick to blow away Budd and the rest of the field in a time of 8:35.96.

But despite her efforts, Puica may end up being the answer to a trivia question: Who won the race in which Mary tripped?

Someday, when the controversy dies, Puica's name will be in the record book and she will still have the gold medal. They can't take the trappings of victory away from her. Friday night, she seemed content to settle for that, because she certainly wasn't getting much attention from the Coliseum crowd or the world press.

Maybe people will notice tonight when Puica goes for her second gold medal in the 1,500 meters against countrywoman Doina Melinte, the 800-meter winner, and America's Ruth Wysocki.

When Decker fell 80 meters up the track, the crowd booed Budd. The fans weren't exactly cheering when Puica crossed the finish line, either. Afterward, all the press wanted to know was her opinion of the collision and subsequent fall.

So today, not many know that the first 3,000 winner is a 34-year-old Romanian housewife who missed most of last year with an injured left ankle incurred while playing basketball. Puica (pronounced "Pwee-ka") also broke Decker's world mile record with a 4:17.44 in 1982.

More biographical data:

Puica, who has been competing since 1969, is a muscular 5-6, 121 pounds and has blonde hair and an engaging smile. Her husband and coach, Ion Puica, is the former principal of the high school at which Puica learned to run.

Although absent from last year's world championships in Helsinki because of the basketball injury, she recorded the best 3,000-meter time this year with an 8:33.57 in July. She also won the world cross-country championships this spring at the Meadowlands.

So, it's safe to assume that Puica is by no means an unknown. It only seemed that way Friday night. Some experts were even picking Puica to beat Decker, Budd and the rest—fair and square.

"I thought this was a tough competition," said a composed Puica through an interpreter. "But, no matter what happened, I still thought I could win. I feel very sorry for Mary. I couldn't tell what happened."

Puica was in third place at the time of the incident, but she quickly overtook Budd and then opened up a comfortable lead on the straggling pack of runners. With her finishing kick, she beat Britain's Wendy Sly by almost four seconds.

It was an impressive victory for Puica, who probably would have run faster than 8:35.96 if she had been pushed.

Almost an hour later, Puica sat before two dozen reporters for 10 minutes, clutching flowers and answering questions about Decker and Budd and—oh, yes—even some about herself.

"It was tough for me to decide (who was at fault)," Puica said. "I was just paying attention to what I was doing, how I was running my race. I really didn't need to go that fast the last 400 meters. Anything close to that would've been sufficient. In any case, I'm sorry for what happened to Mary. She is a fine competitor."

Puica seemed truly sorry Decker had tripped. She said she was ready for the challenge of meeting Decker and had peaked for both the 3,000 and today's 1,500.

That training, however, did not include any more basketball. Puica said she gave that up after the ankle injury that left her hobbling for a long time.

"All I was doing was playing basketball one day and I stepped between two mattresses," said Puica, puzzling American reporters. "You see, we play basketball in the wrestling room at the high school and there was a gap in the mats."

Perhaps such unusual training techniques are needed for a world-class runner who is 34, an age when many athletes settle for fun runs. But Puica and her husband-coach take running very seriously.

Ion Puica has said Maricica "lives a healthy life." That means she goes to bed every night at 8:30, except for Christmas and New Year's. Then, she reportedly stays up until 12:05.

At 10 p.m. Friday, Puica was not asleep. She had just left doping control at the Coliseum and was talking to friends.

With a tough 1,500-meters ahead of her today, Puica probably should have been back in bed at the village. But she wanted to savor her 3,000-meter victory, even if there were only a handful of people who joined in the celebration.

"I think I'm prepared for the 1,500," she said. "I'm in shape. I've worked a long time for these Olympic games, just like Mary Decker."

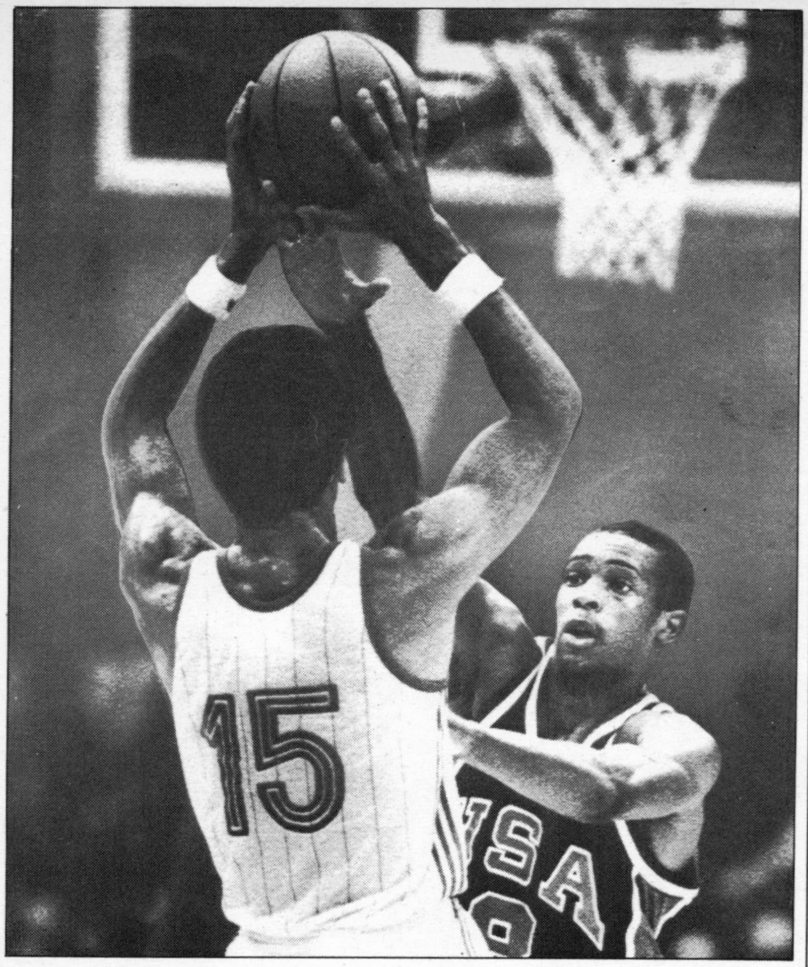

Associated Press

Defensive pressure was a key to the United States' gold medal victory in men's basketball as Spain's Juan Antonio San Epifanio finds out as he is hounded by guard Alvin Robertson.

BASKETBALL

Continued from page 90

The United States has a lot of things, including the defense the Spaniards call *hombre-hombre*, man-to-man. In Friday night's first half, they saw some serious *hombre-hombre*.

The Americans forced 15 turnovers and held the Spaniards to 22 field goal attempts, of which they made nine. They went without a field goal for 9:12, in which time the United States went from a three-point lead to a 27. Once again, garbage time was proclaimed before halftime.

Diaz-Miguel made a little pass at Knight's domination of the referees:"I think they were afraid of my friend, Bobby. After his technical foul, no more problem."

And he noted the rough play: "I only want to ask the question to officials of FIBA (Federation International du Basketball Amateur), if you are going to charge those as fouls? If not, I will train my players that way."

Then he fell back on his best defense: "Yes, I know about that defense. I tell him (Knight), we exchange Patrick Ewing and Michael Jordan for two of my players. He didn't want my players."

The tournament ended as it had begun. Knight went out screaming. Jordan went out flying. The crowds were out somewhere else.

In the last seconds of the first half, with the United States ahead, 52-29, guard Leon Wood had the ball tipped away from him and Knight kicked a tray holding cups of water. The waterboys, by now veterans of such situations, wiped up the spillage. When the half ended, Knight made a beeline for Wood and yelled at him as they walked off. Then, for emphasis, he blasted his right fist into his left palm.

Jordan scored 20 points and tried to pull the super-jam he'd been saving all tournament, a windmilling, double-pumping, fly-by, etc. But he was interrupted during his taxi by a small Spanish guard named Jose Luis Llorente, who bumped him off balance. Jordan settled for carrying the ball on his hip for a moment and laying it in.

Said Rick Brewer, the North Carolina publicist sitting in the press box: "He was going to do the dunk he did at Maryland."

That would have brought the capacity house down, except that, once again, there was no capacity house. Attendance in the Forum Friday night was announced at 15,067.

The U.S. team was haunted by its own superiority. The team that played to 99% of capacity in exhibitions across the country, which drew almost 70,000 in the Hoosier-dome, averaged 13,300 until Friday night. The Lakers averaged 2,000 more than that last season and they played 41 home games.

It went farther than that. An American team trying to prove itself the finest amateur basketball team of all time, found itself sharing the plight of Thai kayakers and Senegalese shooters. It couldn't get on TV.

The games were so one-sided that ABC kept cutting away. In the semifinals, it hung in for five minutes before departing, with the Americans ahead, 8-6. An ABC official said that basketball announcer Keith Jackson was complaining about the lack of air time.

But, if the Americans never really happened as a news story, they were still one hell of a basketball team. In the end, they got on the victory stand and the crowd chanted, for them, for "Bobby! Bobby! Bobby!" No one heard a discouraging word all night, except for Leon Wood.

Notes

Just for the record, the Soviet Union beat the Spaniards three times, twice in Spain in exhibitions this spring, and by 27 points in the Olympic qualifying tournament in Paris. It also beat the West Germans and the French handily in Paris. The Russians also lost an exhibition in Belgrade to the Yugoslavs . . . How distraught was **Antonio Diaz-Miguel**? "I'm very happy," he said. "This is a historic moment for Spain because we never won a medal. It's the greatest victory in the history of Spain. We all cried when we defeated Yugoslavia (in the semifinals) because we had won a medal." . . . **Robert Kleine** of Slater Mo., the father of U.S. center **Joe Kleine**, said he and the parents of **Steve Alford** got in an angry argument before the game with ABA-USA officials, who wouldn't let them move to seats reserved for athletes behind one basket. Kleine said parents of the players had seats near the ceiling. "We don't want the best seats in the house," he said. "We aren't selfish. We just don't want to be up top."

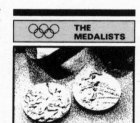

THE MEDALISTS

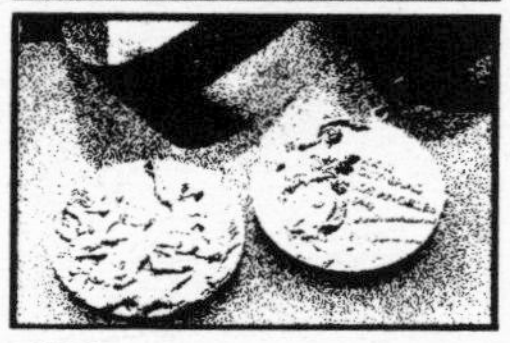

MEN'S

Basketball

■ HOW THEY FINISHED

1. United States
2. Spain
3. Yugoslavia

China's Zhou Takes a Step Into Spotlight

By SEYMOUR BEUBIS,
Times Staff Writer

Zhou Jihong isn't considered the best woman diver in China. That honor goes to Chen Xiaoxia, perhaps because the Chinese place a premium on age and experience.

But they may have to do some quick rethinking after Friday. After all, how can you be only the second best diver in China, and the *best* in the world?

Zhou, 19, earned the latter honor in the women's 10-meter platform by beating 11 others, including Chen, 21, the "Queen of Diving" in China, who finished fourth.

The two U.S. divers, Michele Mitchell, 22, and Wendy Wyland, 19, both of Mission Viejo, finished strongly—taking the silver and bronze medals—but they just ran out of dives before an excited crowd of 10,062.

"It was one of the fiercest struggles I have ever seen," said Ron O'Brien, co-coach of the U.S. Olympic team and also the coach at Mission Viejo.

"It was a gallant effort by our girls. We had a chance of going 1-2, but it depended on what the Chinese girl did. I've seen them (Chinese divers) miss in just that type of situation before," O'Brien said.

It almost happened again, but not quite.

Zhou, a petite 5-1, 97-pounder who looks 14 rather than 19, did not do a good eighth and final dive, but it was just good enough to give China its first-ever Olympic diving gold medal.

Her forward 3½ somersault pike earned her two 6s and three 6.5s for a total of 56.70 points. But she had entered the final round with a big enough lead—slightly more than 11 points—to hold off the fast-closing Mitchell.

The final point totals showed Zhou with 435.51, Mitchell with 431.19 and Wyland at 422.07. Chen was fourth with 419.76.

Zhou, who started as a gymnast but switched to diving, said she was "very happy to win a gold medal."

"When I was doing my last dive I was very nervous. I decided to do my best and not worry about the scoring," she said.

Asked how her victory will be received in China, she laughed. "I believe back in China people will all know my name."

She said she dived to her potential, but that her teammate Chen did not. Actually, Zhou scored about 27 fewer points in the finals than she did in the preliminary round. Of course, the pressure was not nearly so great.

"The people in China will be very surprised with her (Zhou's) victory," said Zhou Zongxin of the New China News Agency. "Everyone thinks of Chen as being our best diver."

The victory by Zhou Friday was no major surprise to the people in the United States, however, particularly to those who had seen her perform in the preliminary round Thursday. She was the top qualifier then by about 28 points.

She has outperformed her more renowned teammate in international meets during the last two years, although Chinese Olympic Coach Liang Boxi said that Chen has done better in competition in China.

Zhou won the FINA World Cup last year, beating both Wyland and Alla Lobankina of the Soviet Union. Two years ago. she was third at the world championships (Wyland won).

O'Brien said he felt the first four rounds were the key to the competition and that the U.S. divers just fell too far behind.

At the end of the fourth round, Zhou had a 13-point lead over Mitchell and about a 23-point lead over Wyland. Chen was in third place at the time, nine points behind.

"That was the key," O'Brien. "Our girls just didn't get off to a good start. I'm pleased with the way things turned out. Sure we could have gone 1-2, but we could have also gone 3-4. Our goal here is for each of our divers to win a medal."

The dive that probably sealed the win for Zhou was her sixth, a back 2½ somersault pike with a 2.9 degree of difficulty. It earned her five 8.5s for a total of 73.95 points, the top total for a dive.

Mitchell's sixth dive, which put the pressure on Zhou, who was diving last (12th) in the order, was her best one.

The forward 3½ somersault tuck with a 2.7 degree of difficulty received three 8.5s and two 9s.

Wyland, who was fifth after four dives, started her comeback in the fifth round. But she would not have been able to get third unless Chen faltered.

That's exactly what happened. Chen did not score well on either her sixth or seventh dives. She totalled 52.20 and and 58.80 compared to Wyland's 65.61 and 67.86.

Wyland said she was pleased with how she came back on her optional, starting with her fifth dive.

"I had kind of a slow start on the required dives. I would like to have seen those go a little better. But I came back really strong and I'm pleased with that. I think that shows what kind of a person I am."

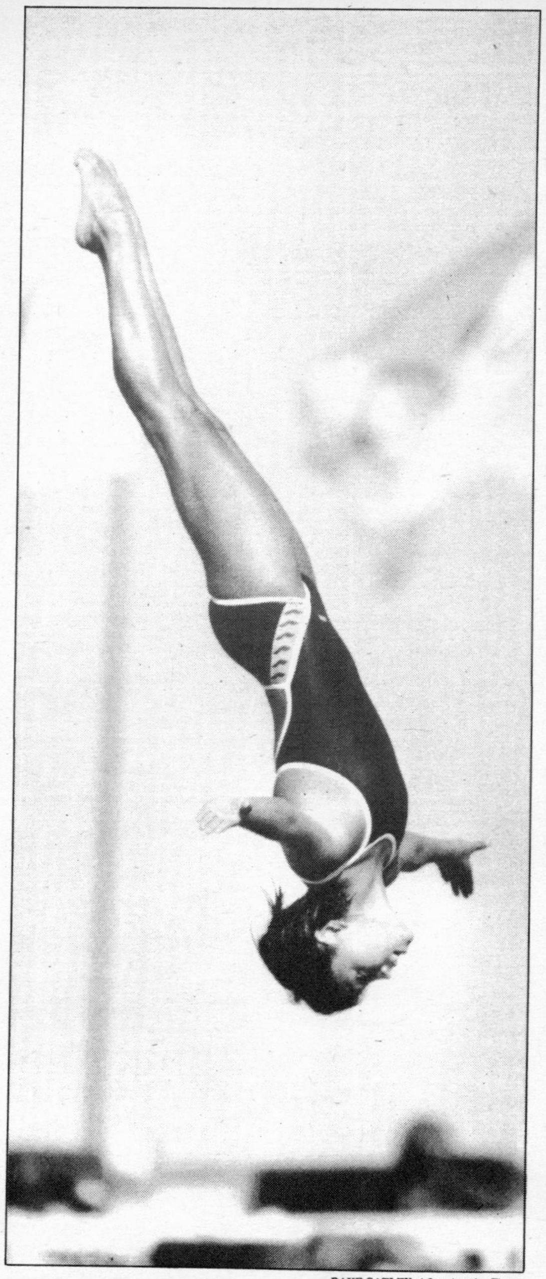

DAVE GATLEY / Los Angeles Times

Zhou Jihong is the winner of the 10-meter platform finals Friday, giving China its first-ever Olympic Games diving gold medal.

WOMEN'S

Diving

■ PLATFORM

1. Zhou Jihong (China)
2. Michele Mitchell (U.S.)
3. Wendy Wyland (U.S.)

THE MEDALISTS

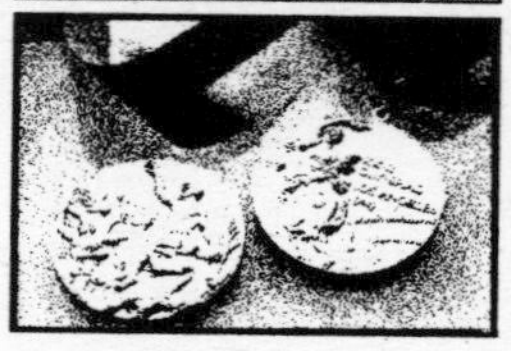

Diving / Women's Platform

Mitchell, Wyland Take Everything but the Gold

By TRACY DODDS, *Times Staff Writer*

Wendy Wyland left Rochester, N.Y., when she was 14 to train with Coach Ron O'Brien at Mission Viejo. Michele Mitchell left Tucson at the end of her college career to join them.

They came west in search of an Olympic gold medal.

Friday night, Mitchell won the silver medal and Wyland took the bronze in women's platform diving.

"That's good," O'Brien said. "When you're taking on the whole world with a club, a silver and a bronze is not bad."

Mitchell, who was one big tickled-pink bundle of joy after the competition, said: "We had a team meeting before the Games began, and we decided that everyone should go home with a medal." So far, so good. Every American diver has won a medal, with Greg Louganis and Bruce Kimball still to go in the men's platform event. O'Brien was holding out hope for a gold-and-silver sweep Friday, even as the winner, Zhou Jihong of China, took her last dive.

"The Chinese girl has missed that last dive badly in other meets for ones and twos," O'Brien said. "It's her hardest dive, and she saves it for last, which puts a lot of pressure on her."

But pressure is what diving is all about. That's why none of the divers ever want to know where they stand during a meet. They look at their own scores, but they don't look at the standings. They retreat to their Walkman headphones so that they don't hear the other scores.

As Mitchell put it, "It's bad enough when you're three stories up, all by yourself, with 20,000 people or two billion people (with televisions) watching you. That's when you really don't want a circuit overload."

Zhou didn't overload or short out. She hit the dive just well enough to win.

For Mitchell, who is 22, the silver medal was an unexpected pleasure. Mitchell, a graduate of the University of Arizona, has come on strong in the last year or so but certainly has not been counted as one of the top U.S. Olympic bets. She had surgery on her shoulder in February 1983, which set her back. And until the second semester of '83, she was training with no other competition on the platform in Tucson.

For Wyland, the bronze medal fell a little short of her hopes. Wyland, 19, is the defending world champion on the platform and won the Pan-Am title last year. Wyland will be a freshman this fall at USC. She'll continue to dive throughout her college career, which will make her quite a veteran for the 1988 Games.

Wyland claims that her sobbing when the final standings were posted reflected excitement, not disappointment. Asked how an Olympic bronze medal compared to the gold in the world championships and the Pan American games, she said: "Right now, I'd put it probably about equal with them."

Mitchell was considered a surprise winner when she set the U.S. record with a score of 477.09 points to win the U.S. Olympic trials. Wyland was expected to win.

But neither wanted to call it an upset that Mitchell finished ahead of Wyland in Olympic competition.

"We train every day together," Mitchell said. "But it's only what happens in the meet that counts. I'm not really surprised. We both had the capability of diving well. We both have proved that."

Mitchell even downplayed the fact that she was making a comeback from surgery so recently—although she did admit that hitting the water at more than 30 m.p.h. on a possibly tender shoulder is a ridiculous prospect.

"When I got back up on the 10-meter platform, I thought that there was a good chance that I would be physically ready for the Olympics," Mitchell said. "But this sport is head games, it's mind games. You can talk yourself into or out of a meet at any time."

Women's 100 Hurdles

Fitzgerald-Brown Proves a Point in Upset Win

By CHRIS BAKER, *Times Staff Writer*

THE MEDALISTS

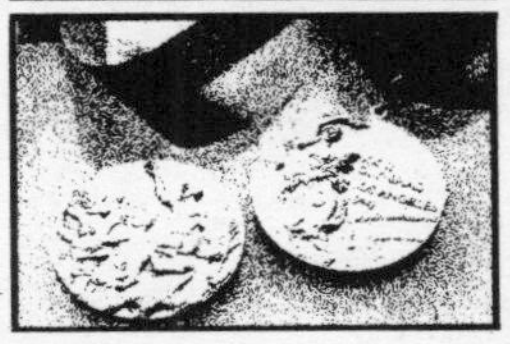

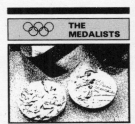

WOMEN'S

Track

■ 100-METER HURDLES

1. Benita Fitzgerald-Brown (U.S.)
2. Shirley Strong (Britain)
3. Kim Turner (U.S.)

Benita Fitzgerald-Brown ran the race of her life to win the Olympic gold medal in the women's 100-meter hurdles Friday night at the Coliseum.

Fitzgerald-Brown, who finished second to Kim Turner in a memorable four-way photo finish at the U.S. Olympic trials last month, upset Shirley Strong of Britain in the Olympic final. Fitzgerald-Brown was timed in 12.84 seconds, Strong in 12.88.

Fitzgerald-Brown moved into the lead by the fourth hurdle and managed to out-lean Strong at the finish.

Said Fitzgerald-Brown: "My number one goal going into the meet was to establish myself as one of the best hurdlers in the world. Even though the Eastern Bloc countries weren't here, I feel I am one of the best hurdlers in the Western world. I wanted to garner a little respect. We wanted to prove that Americans are good hurdlers."

Strong: "I don't remember a thing about the race. The only thing I remember about the race is the finish and charging for the tape."

Fitzgerald-Brown didn't act as if she'd won the race until after viewing a replay on the Coliseum's giant video board. She then ran over to where her family was seated, grabbed a large American flag from a fan and took a victory lap around the track.

"My start was half decent," Fitzgerald-Brown said. "It must have been fairly good because I faded in the middle part of the race. I remember seeing Shirley Strong out of the corner of my eye about mid-race. I had nicked a hurdle, I think it was the second. Once I saw her I sort of shifted into another gear. When she started catching me, I didn't panic. I just kept going."

Turner and Michele Chardonnet of France leaned together at the tape. Both runners were timed in 13.06.

At first the officials called it a dead heat for third, but Turner was given the bronze after the jury of appeals reviewed photos and video tapes of the race for 50 minutes.

Chardonnet ran off the track crying after she was moved from third to fourth.

Jean Poczoubt, the French track coach said, "I think it was a dead heat. It was very disappointing. We have filed a protest to the IAAF and they will rule on it by Sunday."

Said Mort Tenner, the Olympic competition director for track and field: "The case involving the French runner was reviewed for 50 minutes. The photos of the race were enlarged and there was a very long discussion."

Protests are nothing new for Turner, who was involved in the four-way finish at the trials.

"This was a replay of the Olympic trials," she said. "But I've been working on my lean at the finish line since then. There was no tie, I got the bronze."

There was some booing during the medal ceremony when it was announced that Chardonnet had been moved to fourth.

"That was poor sportsmanship," Turner said. "I was really afraid for my life up there with all the crazy things going on in the world."

Turner said she injured her left hamstring last Monday and had to take acupuncture treatments.

"I went for acupuncture twice a day for the last four days," she said.

Fitzgerald-Brown and Turner said they were motivated by comments made by Stephanie Hightower.

After being shut out of the Olympics in the four-way photo finish in the trials, Hightower said that no American hurdler would win a medal in the Games.

"Stephanie Hightower said that the American hurdlers were sub par," Fitzgerald-Brown said. "I wanted to prove to her that we are very good hurdlers, too."

Said Turner: "She (Hightower) can go on being vindictive. It's history now. But I don't appreciate a lot of what she said."

Pam Page, the other American in the race, finished eighth with a time of 13.40.

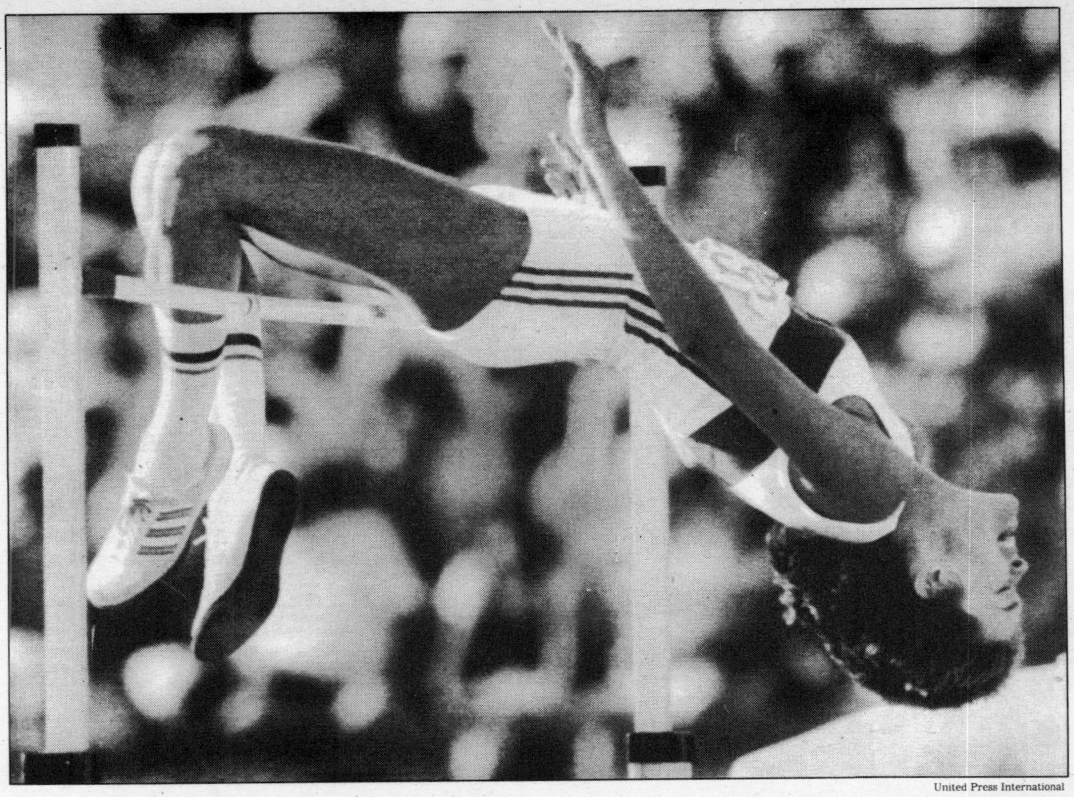

United Press International

Ulrike Meyfarth, a gold medal winner in 1972, clears an Olympic record 6-7½ to win another gold Saturday at the Coliseum.

Women's High Jump

Meyfarth Shakes Pressure, Wins the Gold

By JULIE CART, *Times Staff Writer*

The long road back for two veteran high jumpers ended successfully on the sun-baked Coliseum floor Friday afternoon.

Ulrike Meyfarth, the West German who won the gold in 1972, but faced bitter defeat in ensuing years, won the gold with an Olympic record of 6 feet 7½ inches. Sara Simeoni of Italy, the 1980 Olympic champion, came out of retirement to win the silver at 6-6¾, then quickly went back in.

Yet another veteran, Joni Huntley of the United States, astonished the experts—and herself—to win a bronze at 6-5½.

The 28-year old Meyfarth's Olympic odyssey began 12 years ago in Munich. There, as a 16-year-old, she won the gold, tied the world record and became the youngest person ever to win an individual gold medal in track and field.

She became an instant sensation in West Germany. She also developed instant headaches. Because of the time spent in training, Meyfarth was unable to pass her university exams in 1975. That frustration set back her training for the Montreal games.

In Montreal, Meyfarth bombed. Her fortunes with the West German media and public plummeted.

"What happened in 1976 was a problem in my head, I think," Meyfarth said, speaking in both English and German during a press conference. "The pressure before Montreal was a lot. It was four years after my Olympic gold."

Meyfarth intended to redeem herself in Moscow, but the West Germans joined the boycotting nations and Meyfarth had to wait four more years. Until now.

Over the years, the 6-2 Meyfarth has had numerous offers for modeling and commercial endorsements. But in this Olympic year, Meyfarth said she was trying to shield herself from the intense media pressure.

"I blocked all the offers and endorsements," she said. "The pressure was great, but otherwise, I tried to block it out. I must have my own life. I have made it in another way, like the Americans. I did it my way."

Simeoni's way has been pressure-filled, as well. The effervescent Italian is beloved in her homeland. She, like Meyfarth, felt an obligation to continue in her sport.

But Friday night, the 31-year-old Simeoni announced she was retiring from the high jump.

"I had suffered before this meet and because of my age, I don't think I have the strength to go on like this," she said. "At this moment, I just want to enjoy this for a while."

Huntley, who wasn't even expected to make the U.S. Olympic team, jumped well over her previous outdoor best of 6-2¾. American record-holder Louise Ritter finished 8th.

In the end, only Huntley, Meyfarth and Simeoni were left jumping.

At 6-6¾, Simeoni made it with good clearance, then stayed motionless in the pit, only her back heaving up and down with her laughter.

Finally she got up, only to plop down again. When she eventually left the pit, she jubilantly shook her arms to the crowd and kissed a startled photographer as she dashed around the infield.

But Meyfarth had come too far to let this slip by. She steeled herself, ran her usual charging approach and made it, popping out of the pit with a joyful fist shake.

Huntley, smiling all the while, missed her three attempts, but still finished with the bronze.

At 6-7½, Meyfarth cleared on her first attempt, donned sunglasses, and patiently watched as Simeoni missed her first two attempts.

After Simeoni missed on her final try, Meyfarth thrust her fist in the air and ran to embrace her two West German teammates. Then Meyfarth asked the bar be moved to 6-9½, which would tie Bulgarian Lyudmilla Andonova's world record. She missed all three attempts, but had, as a nice consolation, an Olympic gold medal.

Water Polo

Trailing, 5-2, Yugoslavs Rally to Tie U.S. and Win the Gold

By MILES CORWIN,
Times Staff Writer

The U.S. water polo team has suffered through a boycott. The team has struggled to obtain funding. The team has fought to keep its sport alive.

During the past eight years the players have endured adversity many times. They endured once again Friday night.

The United States blew a 5-2 third-quarter lead and lost the gold medal to Yugoslavia.

The game ended in a 5-5 tie, and the Yugoslavs were awarded the gold on the basis of a goal differential. Yugoslavia defeated its Olympic opponents by 14 goals. The U.S. margin was nine. It was the best U.S. water polo finish since 1904, when the Americans won the gold in an exhibition tournament not entered by foreign nations.

The nucleus of the U.S. team has spent eight years enduring 6 a.m. workouts, lost weekends, marathon evening practices and financial sacrifices. The U.S. played seven games against some of the world's best water polo teams.

And the U.S. players did not lose a game.

"I'd rather of lost this game by a goal and have it decided," U.S. Coach Monte Nitzkowski said. "The disappointment is great because I thought we played well."

Inconsistency beat the United States. While Yugoslavia was a force in the Olympics, overpowering every team it faced, the United States was an up-and-down team.

In many games, the Americans played superbly one quarter and sloppily the next. They often just played well enough to win.

But for the first three quarters Friday night the U.S. played superb defense and continually forced the Yugoslavs to rush their shots right before the 35-second shot clock ran out.

In the first quarter the Yugoslavs shot 1 for 8 and the score was tied, 1-1.

The Americans kept hounding the man with the ball and dropping off to help out the hole guard. The United States had a 3-2 lead an the end of the first half, and Yugoslavia was thoroughly frustrated. It shot 2 for 13.

Joe Vargas put the Americans ahead, 4-2, at the beginning of the third quarter. He took advantage of a 6-on-5 opportunity and placed the ball in the upper right-hand corner. The Yugoslavs turned the ball over and Vargas scored again off a drive.

The United States had a 5-2 lead with about three minutes left in the third quarter and appeared to be in control. The vocal crowd of about 6,000 at Pepperdine University—in the stands and lining the hill above the pool—gave the United States a boost. The Americans had the lead, the crowd and the momentum.

But with time running out in the third quarter Milovoj Bebic scored on a drive, while the Unites States' Doug Burke had his head in the water.

Yugoslavia scored again with four minutes left in the game on a surprise outside shot. A minute later Bebic tied the score on a layout.

The United States had the ball with a minute left and a chance to win, but an American player was whistled for an offensive foul with 40 seconds left, and that was the game.

The United States appeared tentative on offense when it went ahead by three goals. Although Yugoslavia is a young team—average age 23—it kept its cool and stormed back.

"We were tentative in our shooting, but not in the rest of our game—we countered hard and swam well," Nitzkowski said. "We didn't shoot the ball enough in the game."

□

Water polo in the United States has come a long way. In 1976 the American team failed to qualify for the Olympics. The method of hastily assembling club team players every four years was abandoned.

Money was raised, a national team was formed, and Nitzkowski was appointed coach. The approach soon paid dividends. The United States placed second in the major international tournament in 1979 and was one of the favorites to win the gold medal at the Moscow Olympics.

When the U.S. boycott was announced, the team was devastated. But Nitzkowski, assistant coach Ken Lindgren and eight players, the nucleus of the team, put their lives on hold for another four years.

The average age of the team is 27. For almost eight years they have been practicing every weekend and before and after work. Some turned down job offers. Others had to delay going to graduate school.

"This isn't a sport like track where you can make money after the Olympics," Nitzkowski said. "They're not going to sign any big contracts or get paid to play somewhere. They all worked for one thing. They wanted a gold medal."

Holyfield Disqualification Stands, but He Gets to Keep Bronze Medal

By EARL GUSTKEY,
Times Staff Writer

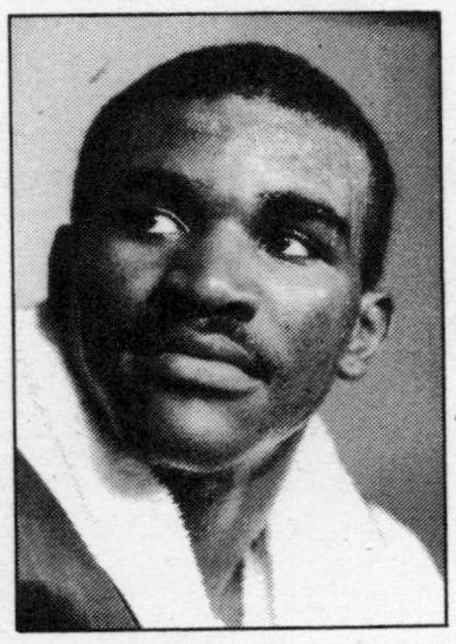

Evander Holyfield

A U.S. protest over the disqualification of light-heavyweight Evander Holyfield in the Olympic boxing tournament semifinals Thursday night was rejected Friday.

At a Sports Arena news conference, a five-member International Amateur Boxing Assn. (AIBA) protest committee announced that it had unanimously upheld the action of Yugoslav referee Bligorije Novicic, who disqualified Holyfield late in the second round of his bout with New Zealand's Kevin Barry.

Holyfield knocked Barry down with a left hook less than one second after Novicic gave a "stop" command. At the time, it appeared Novicic was about to disqualify Barry for holding Holyfield's neck. Barry had been reprimanded several times before. Instead, Novicic disqualified Holyfield, who was easily winning the bout and appeared headed for a gold-medal win in today's finals. Holyfield, the committee ruled, will not lose the bronze medal, awarded to both semifinalists.

There was bedlam in the Sports Arena when Novicic disqualified Holyfield. U.S. head coach Pat Nappi rushed the referee along the apron, shouting at him, then quickly left the ring area.

"I was afraid if I didn't get out of there, I'd have hit the guy," Nappi said Friday.

Novicic left the floor area under police escort, in a chorus of thundering boos and a shower of paper trash.

Said USA Amateur Boxing Federation president Loring Baker: "The decision was unanimous, we're not happy with it, but we accept it. We contended that the New Zealand boxer had his arm wrapped around Holyfield's head, squeezing his headgear against his ear, and couldn't hear the 'stop' command.

"In reviewing the video with the protest committee, we found the incident in question was the ninth such incident of the bout—hitting after the 'stop' command. Both boxers hit the other four times each after 'stop' commands."

A Laguna Beach neurologist, Dr. Ted Nolan Thompson, said Friday it was neurologically impossible for Holyfield to have stopped the punch following the referee's command.

"I taped the bout and played it back many times," he said. "Sound waves are processed by the brain at a speed of about 120 meters per second, or about 10 times faster than Carl Lewis can run. But in a situation where a person's concentration is fixed on a hand-eye activity, like boxing, that process is much slower. It would be like walking up behind Reggie Jackson while he's watching a fast ball come right over the plate and saying: 'Don't swing.!' In my opinion, it was neurologically impossible for Holyfield to have stopped that punch in that short a time frame. To disqualify him is a terrible mistake."

The official statement by the protest committee, chaired by Prof. Anwar Chowdhry of Pakistan:

"The protest committee discussed at length the protest of the USA in bout No. 331 (USA vs. NZL). We heard Mr. Loring Baker, president of USA boxing and also Mr. Ashton, chairman of the R/J (referee-judge) Commission. We also viewed over and over again the video . . . my committee is unanimously of the view that the decision of the referee is according to the rules of AIBA and stands.

"But they have also taken notice of the fact that infringements of the rules were also being made by the New Zealand boxer. In view of this the committee recommends that the U.S. boxer, although being disqualified, should be awarded the medal due to him."

In addition to Chowdhry, members of the committee include: Len Mills, Great Britain; Stanley Moore, Ghana; Karl-Heinz Wehr, East Germany, and Taid Houichi, Tunisia.

Compiled By JERRY GILLAM

I Say, Daley Old Chap, What Will the Queen Think?

From Times Staff Writers and Wire Services

The outrageous Daley Thompson, world's greatest decathlete and one of the world's greatest talkers, may be in some hot water back home in Britain.

After winning the Olympic decathlon for the second time Thursday night, Thompson was congratulated by Princess Anne, who is here as president of the British Olympic Assn.

Asked what she said to him, Thompson, who resembles a muscular Richard Pryor, said: "She said I was a damn good-looking guy."

Some British writers thought it was pretty unusual that royalty would deign to come down on the Coliseum floor to speak to a mere athlete. Not Thompson.

"Not when you're as close as we are," he said.

Thompson also said some other things involving the Princess that may not be suitable for a family newspaper.

Wonder what the Royal Family thinks?

—MIKE LITTWIN

□

William Simon, president of the U.S Olympic Committee, on these Games:

"For all their warts, they're still a time of peace in a troubled world. These Olympics reminded me of ancient Greece when they called all the wars off for two weeks and competed for the spirit of it. So the wars will all start up again Monday, so what? At least we had this."

—RICK REILLY

□

Carl Lewis has his bodyguards as he breezes past the interview area that he won't visit, presumably until after his final event today, the 400-meter relay.

His burly bodyguards are press officers, not security personnel, and they call themselves The Flying Eggs.

"We adopted that name because we've put a shell around Lewis," said one Flying Egger.

—JULIE CART

□

High jumper Dwight Stones has an Olympic heritage, and it's not because he is competing in his third Olympics. His grandfather, Hal Roberts, arranged all the music for the 1932 Games in Los Angeles.

"He was the USC bandleader and the band was known as Hal Roberts and his Trojans before it was called the Trojan Marching Band," Stones said.

Stones, however, went to UCLA, much to the dismay of his family. "USC was late in trying to recruit me, although I always wanted to go there," he said.

—MAL FLORENCE

□

You never know what nuggets of information you will find in a media guide.

According to a media packet put together by the Canadian Volleyball Assn., the favorite pastime of Canadian men's volleyball Coach Ken Maeda is "frequenting Calgary's Japanese restaurants, especially when his wife is out of town."

—JERRY CROWE

□

Missy Kane of Knoxville, Tenn., did not advance to tonight's final of the women's 1,500, but at least she did not lose by a knockout.

"I was just praying I'd keep my feet underneath me," she said after finishing seventh in her heat during Thursday's qualifying.

"A couple of girls fell. Eight of us had blood on our bodies. It was like a fight out there."

The other American in the heat, Diana Richburg, also failed to qualify for the final. "I was getting pushed and bumped and everything," she said.

Another American, Ruth Wysocki, ran in the other semifinal heat and experienced no problems. She does not expect to be so fortunate tonight.

Asked if she expected a physical final, she said: "Yes, I do, to a degree. I was watching the 3,000 semifinal Wednesday night. Some of the girls threw a lot of elbows at the start. They want you to know they're there and that they mean business."

Asked what she would do if she were shoved, she said: "I'll shove back."

Wysocki, who lives in El Toro, Calif., beat Mary Decker in the 1,500 at the U.S. Olympic trials. But Wysocki said that does not mean she should replace Decker as the favorite in tonight's final. Decker chose not to run in the 1,500, preferring to concentrate on Friday night's 3,000 meters.

"I think that's asking a little bit much," Wysocki said.

Wysocki said, however, that she was aware of the great expectations for her.

"When I went onto the track before the 1,500 qualifying, I heard people shouting, 'Go Ruth, Go Ruth,' " she said. "I thought, 'Boy, they'll hate me if I don't make the final.'

"I keep telling myself I'm just here for the experience of being in the Olympics. I keep telling myself I don't care what anybody else thinks, or what anybody else expects, I can only do what I can.

"The people who matter most to me are going to take me back no matter what happens."

—RANDY HARVEY

□

Pietro Mennea, the only runner who has made the men's 200-meter finals in four straight Olympic Games, was holding court for Italian reporters in the interview area. They all wanted to know if Mennea, who holds the world record of 19.72 seconds, set in 1979 at Mexico City, was ready for retirement.

"Competition gives me motivation for living," said the slightly-built sprinter from Barletta, a village on the Adriatic Sea. "I try to do my best, and when I do that, that is my motivation. I was satisfied with my performance here. I could not retire now. How many runners in the world can get in the Olympic finals? Why should I retire. Maybe I cannot beat Carl Lewis, but I can beat a lot of people. Perhaps someday in the future, I will retire. Everyone must, sometime. But for me, not now."

Mennea finished seventh here. In 1972, he won a bronze medal; in 1976, he finished fourth, and in 1980, he won the gold medal.

—SHAV GLICK

□

John Kauke, a Pacific Palisades ham radio operator, said he talked to a ham who said he had figured out what happened during the controversial Evander Holyfield-Kevin Barry Olympic boxing bout Thursday night.

Kauke said: "This guy came on the air saying he wanted to talk to someone in L.A. So I talked to him. He said he'd studied the videotape numerous times and concluded that Barry was holding Holyfield in such a way around his neck that his glove was covering up the earhole in (Holyfield's) headgear and he could not hear the referee give the 'Stop' command."

Holyfield was disqualified by a Yugoslav referee for decking his New Zealand foe less than a second after the referee had told him to stop.

—EARL GUSTKEY

□

Synchronized swimming is an all-female sport, and it looks as if it will stay that way, even though many of the girls competing in the Olympics would like to see it change.

The problem is basically physical and has more to do with buoyancy than anything else.

U.S. duet gold-medalist Candy Costie was asked if she could envision the day when there would be coed synchronized swimming.

"We're ready for it," she said eagerly. "Now all you've got to do is find a man who can float."

—JOHN WEYLER

□

Angle of the week: LOS ANGELES (UPI)—The United States, which had done so well in the yachting and rowing competition, failed to live up to the heritage of its American Indian ancestors and got completely shut out of medals in six 500-meter canoeing events today at the Olympic Games.

□

How do you know when you're in a disoriented state From long venue hours and souvenir mania?

A memo to a select few venue volunteers sent on the internal Olympics computer terminals offered a chance to win yet another memento of the Games . . . from doping control, thanks to cooperation on the athletes' part.

"As you know these (urine) samples come in an official 1984 Los Angeles Olympiad vial featuring the moving stars logo . . . hermetically sealed to avoid duplication," said the tongue-in-cheek message.

Judge, I move for a change of venue . .

—JOHN DART

□

Archers like to wear something over their heads to protect themselves from the glaring sun. U.S. archer Ruth Rowe is known for wearing unusual hats during competition. She fashioned a tall, droopy white hat with a big red stripe for the Olympics.

So, when New Zealand's paraplegic archer, Neroli Fairhall, was in the market for a hat, Rowe simply whipped up another just like her own for Fairhall.

Remember, archers sat at the Olympic villages for a week and a half without much to do before their competition began.

—ELLIOTT ALMOND

□

Every day during the Olympic equestrian events at Santa Anita, Larry Bortstein, assistant director of publicity, has been asked to get an official weather forecast, including temperature, humidity and smog readings, for the press.

One day, Bortstein decided to put up his own thermometer on a bulletin board in the press center. Above it, a hand lettered sign read: "Bortstein's Official Olympic Weather Station."

Next to the thermometer, which read 90 degrees in the shade by 3 p.m., Bortstein listed his own moods from top to bottom—High, Affable, Mean, Cranky and Low. Below the thermometer, a Coke cup reading "Relative Humidity" was pinned on the board to catch moisture from the air.

When last seen, several journalists were pitching pennies at Bortstein's humidity cup.

They missed.

—LYNN SIMROSS

□

Olympic gold medalist Joan Benoit was back in Maine Friday, looking forward to a weekend of solitude after her victory last Sunday in the Games' first marathon for women.

"Joan has a cold," said her father, Andre Benoit, a Portland department store executive. "She wants to be alone for the weekend. I won't even be seeing her."

Municipalities hoping to organize welcoming celebrations for the 27-year-old distance runner are still trying to arrange a format she would find acceptable.

Officials in Cape Elizabeth, where Benoit grew up, and in Freeport, where she now has her home, said they were aware that she was uncomfortable with splashy festivities and would make their plans accordingly.

□

To qualify for the 1988 Olympics, U.S. field hockey Coach Gavin Featherstone is already thinking about the 1987 Pan American qualifier—and not fondly. The Americans will have to win the Pan-Am title in Ecuador, a country that doesn't play hockey.

"They don't play, they don't have a field. It is a farce to have to go to the Pan-Am Games to qualify," Featherstone, a former British player, said. "It's not a real international tournament, more like backyard games. We will have to play on grass in Ecuador while the international tournaments are on Astroturf. I don't even know the capital. We didn't learn that in school."

For the record, it's Quito.

The coach, who expected to win several games in the Olympics but ended up 0-7, was asked if he would stay on through 1988.

"Of course I'm committed to '88," he said. "It would be a bit daft now to say to someone, 'C'mon buddy, this Englishman's done all the hard work, come in and grab the glory.' "

—ALAN DROOZ

□

An Olympic jury "robbed" Italy's Angelo Musone of victory in the super-heavyweight boxing semifinals against American Henry Tillman in the Olympics, Italian newspapers said Friday.

Both Rome's Corriere dello Sport and Milan's La Gazetta dello Sport called the 5-0 jury decision scandalous.

"Musone was victimized and truly robbed by the jury," La Gazetta dello Sport said of the controversial bout, where an appeals jury reversed the ringside judges' decision in the Italian's favor.

The decision was greeted by boos and whistles from many of the 11,000 spectators watching the bout. Musone burst into tears and refused to shake hands with Tillman.

Corriere dello Sport called the jury's decision hallucinatory, saying, "It shows that in these Olympics, the United States can't be allowed to lose. It is written in the books."

Mayor Piero Squeglia of Marcianese, hometown of the Italian boxer, called Musone the real champion. He said the jury was "under psychological pressure from the United States" to rule in Tillman's favor.

The mayor said the residents of Marcianese, near the southern port city of Naples, were devastated and that the town planned to pull down the giant television screen it had erected to watch the final bout.

□

Mark Breland and his boxing teammates spent a week in Las Vegas about a month ago, then got

MEDALSOME ADMIRERS

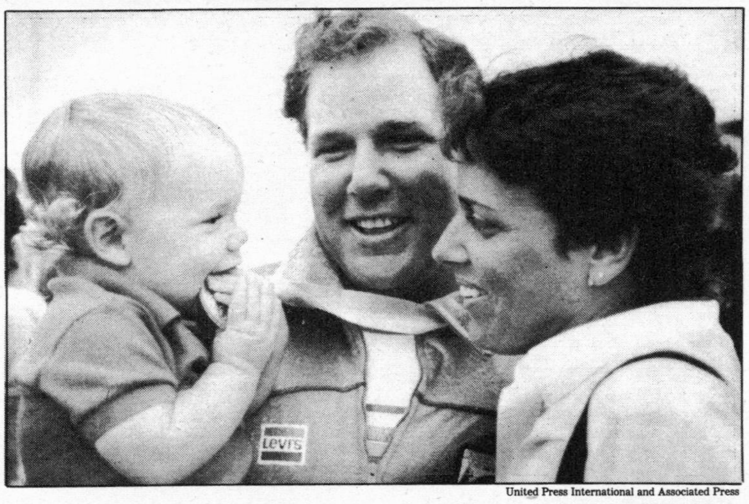

United Press International and Associated Press

If you'd like to get somebody's attention, try wearing an Olympic medal. Young Brian Haines of Coronado, Calif., gives the old taste test to his dad's gold (above), much to the amusement of dad, Robbie Haines, and the yachtsman's sister, Caroline. And entertainer Joan Rivers (below) takes a closer look at gymnast Peter Vidmar's awards on "The Tonight Show."

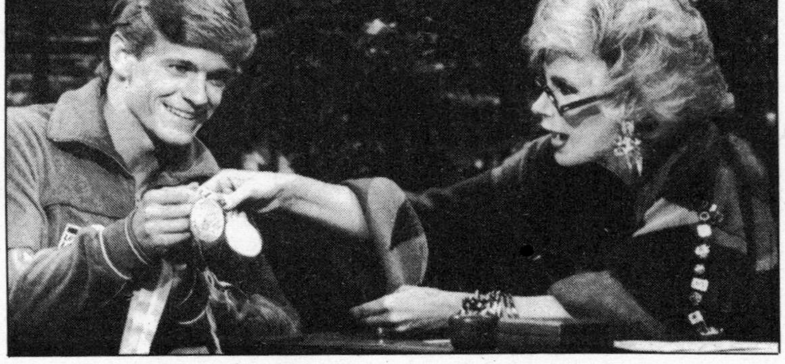

DON'T POUND THESE NAILS

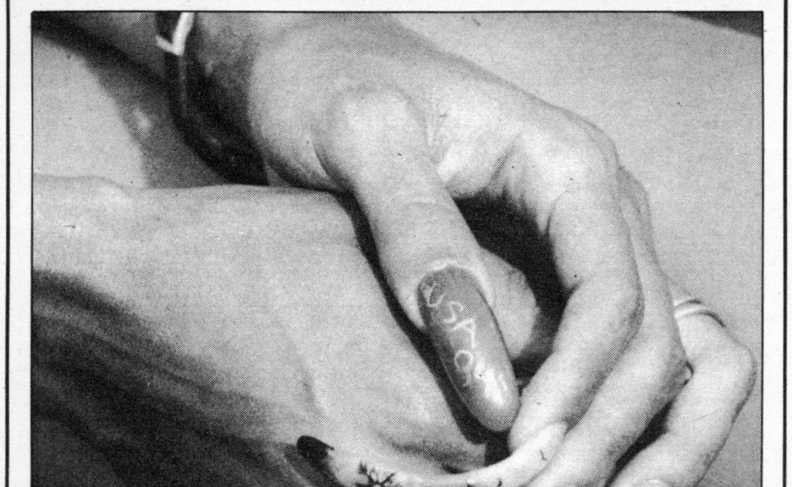

JAYNE KAMIN / Los Angeles Times

Sprinter Florence Griffith of the United States, a silver medalist in the women's 200 meters, displays her long and decorative fingernails. She only has to be careful when she starts.

SAILING, SAILING . . .

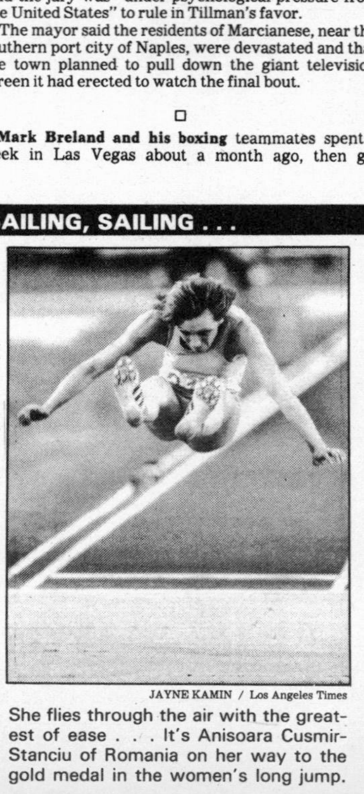

JAYNE KAMIN / Los Angeles Times

She flies through the air with the greatest of ease . . . It's Anisoara Cusmir-Stanciu of Romania on her way to the gold medal in the women's long jump.

NOTES

Continued from page 94

together at a big ranch in Texas for another week or so.

That's living, right?

Not quite. It wasn't party time on either occasion. It was the usual sweat-it-out training and boxing routine en route to the Olympics.

So what's on tap after the Games?

"Well, a lot of guys drink beer," said Breland, the unofficial leader of the U.S. squad. "We might have a beer party.

"I have a *big* radio," he added with a wide smile, "95 watts, and we're going to party."

—JACK HAWN

□

Indian guru Sri Chinmoy, who has led the peace meditation at the United Nations since 1970, gave a cello concert for peace Thursday night at Eddie West Stadium in Santa Ana, and 5,000 people showed up—among them Olympian Carl Lewis.

Lewis, winner of gold medals in the 100- and 200-meter dashes and the long jump, appeared onstage, and Chinmoy played a special song to congratulate him. The American track star is a born-again Christian who also appeared at a Baptist church in Van Nuys earlier in the week.

Chinmoy, who left India 20 years ago to come to the United States, is a marathon runner, a watercolor artist and the author of more than 600 books. He released seven doves symbolizing peace during the concert

The audience included Chinmoy's followers, the curious and people for peace.

□

Bela Karolyi, the Romanian immigrant who coached U.S. gymnasts Mary Lou Retton and Julianne McNamara to eight Olympic medals, says he's been besieged by prospective students since his proteges showed the world what he taught them.

"The phone has been ringing off the wall this week," Karolyi said Thursday, shortly after returning to his North Houston gymnasium from Los Angeles. "The calls are coming in continuously.

"Parents are calling from all over the country, wanting to get their daughters started in the program. I couldn't begin to tell you how many calls we've had in the past few days."

Despite the crush, Karolyi said he was accepting everyone who applied.

"How can I refuse people who come to me with an open heart?" he said. "You just never know which one might grow up and be another Mary Lou Retton."

Karolyi came to the United States three years ago, five years after another of his students, Nadia Comaneci, had become a gold medalist at the 1976 Olympics. He opened his gym two years ago.

□

Mary Lou Retton cannot escape the admiring eyes of fans since her Olympic victories—even in a crowded shopping mall. Now, thanks to a car dealer and the governor of West Virginia, she will find it still harder.

After the gymnastics star of the Games had greeted thousands of admirers in a six-block parade in Charleston, W.Va., Thursday, she was given a shiny, red Corvette by auto dealer Tag Galyean.

Two hours later at the Capitol, Gov. Jay Rockefeller announced he would bend a State rule a bit to allow "Mary Lou" to be imprinted on a vanity license plate. Some West Virginian's cars have special tags bearing a name or slogan instead of a number, but the rule limits them to six digits.

"Was I going to go to jail on behalf of Mary Lou?" kidded Rockefeller, who is running for the Senate. "I'm going . . . She's getting a license plate."

□

Vendors inside the Coliseum are selling soft drinks for $1.25, but outside the site of the Olympic track and field events, Eugene Hendrick will sell you a drink, of water, for a mere 50 cents.

"Water, ice water here," Hendrick shouts at the crowd though a Styrofoam cup fashioned into a megaphone.

The overhead is low. Ice, the foam cups and jugs of bottled spring water are the tools of his two-week trade. He sells 50 gallons of water a day and has potential daily profits of up to $500 a day, he said.

"I see potential in this, and I've got a few ideas if I can talk to the big guys," he said, speaking of the executives at the bottled water companies

□

Richard Aggiss, Australian field hockey coach, was waiting for the question. No one had thought twice about the number of players 30 and older when the team went undefeated in pool play. When the Aussies were upset by Pakistan, 1-0, in the semifinal, however, age became a topic at a postgame press conference.

"I knew if we lost, the team would be (portrayed as) too old," Aggiss said. "The average age is 28. It had nothing to do with our performance. There's no point in saying we're too old. We just didn't hit a goal."

If it wasn't age, then did Pakistan, perhaps, have a "hoodoo" on Australia, one Pakistani reporter asked.

Aggiss gave him an odd look and said: "At the moment, I don't feel like talking much more."

—ALAN DROOZ

□

Gymnast Peter Vidmar, finished with his Olympic competition, reflected Friday on how he hasn't been able to dodge autograph seekers wherever he and his wife, Donna, go.

They thought they could avoid the limelight by driving up to Solvang earlier in the week for a quiet dinner. "The whole restaurant started applauding when they realized we were in there," he said. And when he walked into a 7-Eleven store for some milk and cereal at 11:30 the other night, "Flashbulbs starting going off everywhere."

Vidmar did find some peace during a huge family reunion at an El Segundo park Monday. The park was practically empty, and nobody intruded on the family fun. "I set up a sort of mini-Olympics for all the little kids, and it was great," he said. "I was even able to go all-out and play soccer for an hour and a half without having to worry about getting hurt. I was finally able to let loose. I even cut my eye. It was great!"

—TOM GORMAN

□

They didn't get to call themselves the official wines of the Olympics, but a vintner said he was thrilled that his and 21 other wineries were able to donate 2,000 cases of wine to the sports venues.

Brooks Firestone was responsible for pairing the wineries with the hospitality coordinators of the different sports.

His Firestone Vineyards of Santa Barbara was matched with the canoeing and rowing venue, Mondavi with boxing and track and field, and Parducci with wrestling.

The wines, used for banquets and receptions, were selected according to the type of food served. Cabernet was used for banquets, table wines for barbeques, Firestone said.

The Los Angeles Olympic Organizing Committee asked the Wine Institute, the industry's trade organization, to solicit the donations.

□

Discus throwers Meg Ritchie of Britain and Ria Stalman of the Netherlands are close friends, in and out of competition.

After both women had advanced in Friday's qualifying round, Ritchie was asked how the friendship would stand up through the final.

In her heavy Scottish brogue, the jovial Ritchie replied, "Well, Ria and I are good friends. It doesn't really matter if I finish first and Ria is 10th and I'm first. Saturday night we'll sit down with a jar of beer. Oh, maybe I meant that last bit the other way around."

A wee bit of a Freudian slip, eh Meg?

—JULIE CART

PARDON MY REACH

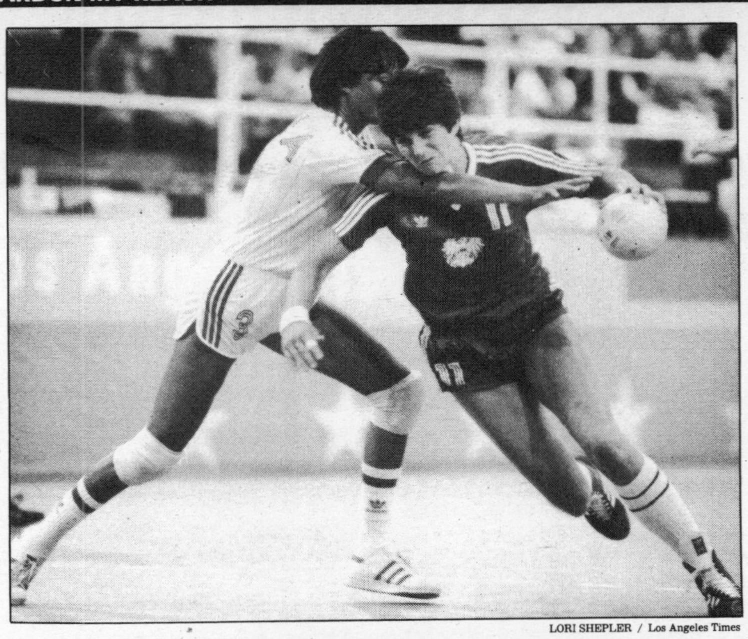

LORI SHEPLER / Los Angeles Times

Apparently on her way to getting clotheslined, Gabriele Gebauer of Austria tries to escape from American Reita Clanton Thursday night during U.S. women's 25-21 team handball win.

Women's Field Hockey

U.S. Gets an Assist and a Medal

By ALAN DROOZ, *Times Staff Writer*

The improbable sequence the U.S. women's hockey team needed not only to win a medal but to decide their own fate came through and, with a big assist from the Netherlands, the U.S. women won the bronze medal Friday, coming out of the stands for a dramatic shootout with Australia before 7,693 fans.

It was the Americans' first appearance in the Olympics, which added women's hockey in 1980, when none of the top teams appeared in Moscow. Hence, it was Holland's first gold and the first silver for West Germany (2-1-2). The loss knocked out Australia, which went into the game with a chance at the gold.

Briefly, the U.S. women, having completed round robin play Thursday, needed the Netherlands to beat Australia by the score of 2-0.

Lo and behold, Holland got second-half goals from Sophie von Weiler and Fieke Boekhorst and the U.S. women got their wish. They and Australia had identical 2-2-1 records and identical goal totals.

Out of the East Los Angeles College stands they came to blow Australia away, 10-5, in the 10-stroke showdown. U.S. goalie Gwen Cheeseman stopped four of the first six shots. Fittingly, the top U.S. shooter and tournament's top scorer, Beth Anders, clinched the medal with her second shot and the team's seventh straight.

"We got a chance and I'm proud of the team that they took advantage of it," U.S. Coach Vonnie Gros said. "That's a sign of a real champion."

Gros had earlier criticized the round-robin format and said, "I understand how Australia feels. If I had to vote, I wouldn't vote for this system."

But she wasn't giving back the medal. "It feels super," she said.

Dutch Coach Gijsbertus van Heumen saw his favored team go 4-0-1 and said, "We played defense very easily—we made no mistakes—and I think they (Australia) were in the circle only three times. I think we played very strong."

The spectacular von Weiler led the tournament with five field goals while Boekhorst had five penalty corners.

Anders, Sheryl Johnson, Judy Strong, Chris Larson-Mason and Julie Staver all hit 2 of 2 in the penalty stroke contest.

When the shootout was over, the crowd chanted a combination of "USA-Holland, USA-Holland."

Canada 4, New Zealand 1—Canada may have been the tournament's best team over the last three games but made its move a game too late.

Coming off a victory over Australia and a tie with the Netherlands, Canada needed eight goals to qualify for the bronze. The Canadians (2-2-1) got halfway there, Sheila Forshaw scoring 47 seconds into the game and Darlene Stoyka, Terry Wheatley and Laura Branchaud adding goals.

Mary Clinton scored for New Zealand (0-5), which scored only two goals in the tournament.

THE MEDALISTS

WOMEN'S

Field Hockey

HOW THEY FINISHED

1. Netherlands
2. West Germany
3. United States

Men's Field Hockey

Last-Place U.S. Team Falls Again

By ALAN DROOZ, *Times Staff Writer*

The U.S. men's field hockey team failed in its last chance for an Olympic victory Friday, but it went out shooting.

The U.S. team lost for the second straight time on a penalty stroke shootoff after regulation ended, 2-2, and overtime ended, 3-3, before a morning crowd of 4,616 at East Los Angeles College.

This time Malaysia was the winner, taking 11th place in the Olympics by hitting 9 of 10 penalty strokes to the U.S. team's eight.

The United States took a 2-1 second half lead on two goals by Brian Spencer, but Malaysia's Ow Soon Kooi scored his second goal with 3:19 left to force overtime.

Malaysia scored first and appeared to be on the way to a victory when the United States, playing a man short, scored a penalty corner goal with 2:47 remaining. Gary Newton scored on a pass from Drew Stone.

The game came down to penalty strokes and Malaysia's only miss was wide. All shots on goal got past goalie Bob Stiles. A diving stop on one U.S. shot and a hand save on another by Malaysia's Zulkifli Abbas were the difference.

The United States lost its previous game to Kenya on a similar shootout to leave the Americans 12th in a 12-team field, but Coach Gavin Featherstone and players were upbeat about the future.

"The players did a good job here. They forced themselves into world reckoning," Featherstone said. "We have not just 18 months now but four years to go for a medal. We think it's realistic to talk about a medal in 1988."

Mike Newton said, "I'm sure some teams expected to come in here and kick us around and found it wasn't that easy. We had the fitness, we just didn't generate our own luck."

Kenya 1, Canada 0—In a game punctuated by by several near-fights, Kenya put a shot in the net in the 93rd minute that was first disallowed, then after consultation between the officials, counted. Lucas Alubaha scored the goal on a deflection. Canada protested the game.

Kenya (3-4) placed ninth, Canada (1-5-1) was 10th.

New Zealand 1, Spain 0—Arthur Parkin's rebound of his own shot a minute into the second half clinched seventh place for New Zealand (3-2-2).

Spain (3-4) had eight penalty corner chances and five shots on goal but couldn't find the net despite a determined charge in the final minute.

Field Hockey Notes

Today's gold medal game between Pakistan and West Germany highlights a men's triple-header starting at 9:15 a.m. In the opening fifth-place game, India faces the Netherlands. The bronze medal game at 11:15 matches Australia and Britain . . . Today's session is sold out . . . Spain's **Carlos Roca** received the tournament's first red card expulsion with 34 seconds left when he shoved an official and had to be restrained . . . The U.S-Malaysia game was the first playoff in which more than one goal was scored . . . Canadians **Sheila Forshaw** and **Darlene Stoyka** scored seven of their team's nine goals.

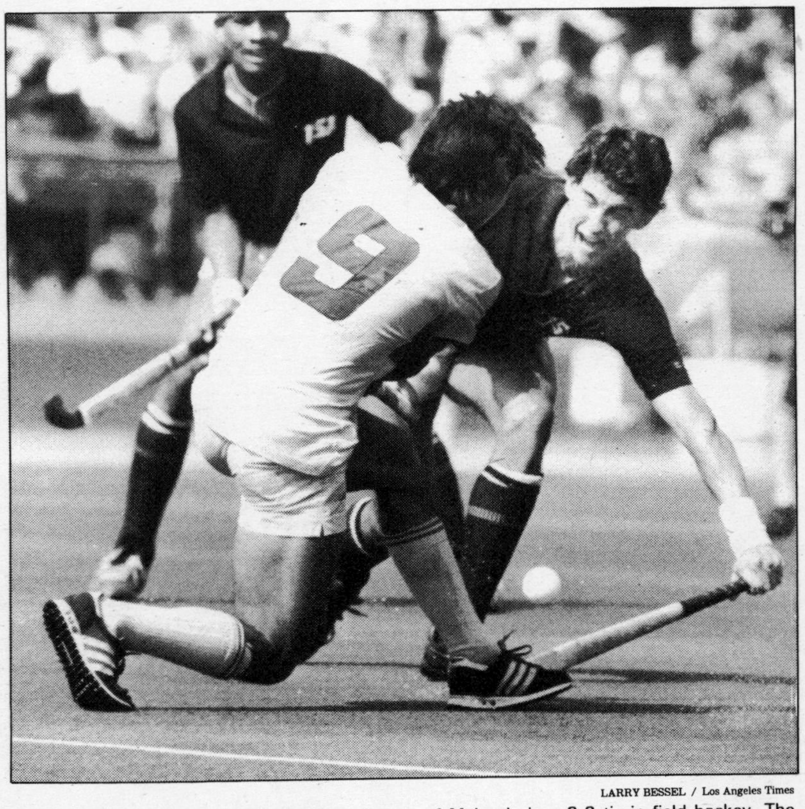

LARRY BESSEL / Los Angeles Times

David McMichael of the United States winces as he blocks a shot by Soon Mustafa Bin-Krim of Malaysia in a 3-3 tie in field hockey. The Americans lost the match on penalty strokes.

OLYMPICS '84

DAY 16

Lewis Makes Fourth a Gold Record

By MIKE LITTWIN, *Times Staff Writer*

It just got a little more crowded on Mt. Olympus, or wherever it is that heroes gather these days. King Carl Lewis—love him or not—made these Olympics his own, stamping them for all time with his collection of four gold medals.

Running the anchor leg of the men's 400-meter relay late Saturday afternoon before a Coliseum crowd of 90,861, Lewis won his final gold with a flourish, completing the final 100 meters in 8.94 seconds as the U.S. team collected both a gold medal and a world record of 37.83 seconds.

But even as he evoked the memory of his childhood idol, Jesse Owens, Lewis also evoked angry comments from a relay teammate who thought Lewis was receiving too much of the credit.

So it goes for Lewis. If the fans love him—and they

seem to, despite the boos he received Monday after winning the long jump—many of his fellow athletes do not.

The first two questions in the post-race press conference were directed to Lewis' teammates, asking them their opinion of Lewis' performance.

After the second question, Sam Graddy, an emotional man of 20 years, got up from behind the microphones and calmly walked out of the room.

"I left the table because I'm tired of being made to feel less than Carl," said Graddy, who ran the opening leg. "I've got my reasons, but I don't want to talk about them."

Many athletes have been critical of Lewis, the track star with the designer clothes and Grace Jones haircut whom some see as a showboat. In these Olympics, he

was never a showboat—but all show. He came here to win four golds and duplicate Jesse Owens' 1936 Berlin Olympics. And he did it.

He won the 100 in 9.99 seconds, the long jump at 28 feet ½ inch and the 200 in 19.80—all world-class performances. Jesse Owens had won the same three events and then led off the winning relay 48 years ago.

When will we next see their kind?

And yet, there was something of anticlimax about Lewis' gold chase. He was heavily favored in every event he entered and routinely blew away the competition in each.

This last flourish—a world record, the first world record in track and field at the 1984 Olympics—was a nice touch, however.

"I have kind of the dirty work in the relay," Lewis

said. "All I have to do is run against the clock. It's like, 'We did our job, now you go get the world record.'"

That's just what he did, taking the handoff from Calvin Smith, who had run brilliantly on the curve to give Lewis a large lead, and bringing the baton home for the record. Lewis' finish will be compared to Bob Hayes' anchor leg in 1964, which was timed in 8.9 seconds.

Jamaica finished second in 38.62 seconds and Canada third in 38.70.

Lewis burst onto the scene in 1979 as a long jumper, and a year later, at 19, was the best in the world. For the last three years, he has been No. 1 in the 100, and last year, he began to run the 200 in earnest and made that event his own.

Please see LEWIS, page 97

Jim Murray

The Loser Was Left Standing

The first thing they teach you in boxing, right after "Never lead with your right," is "Protect yourself at all times." The referee says it before all fights. "When I say break, break. Protect yourself at all times, shake hands now, and come out fighting."

If Kevin Barry of New Zealand had learned this simple fundamental of the prize ring, if he had learned how to duck, he would not today be the light-heavyweight boxing silver medalist of the 1984 Olympics. He'd be just another palooka saying, "I coulda been a contendah." He won a fight with his face.

One punch puts lots of guys in the championship finals of a fight tournament. But usually, they're delivering it, not taking it. Kevin was taking all the way. Not since Max Schmeling in 1930 has anyone won a boxing title lying on the floor. Kevin Barry did not exactly have to be awakened to be told he'd won. But he had to be helped up.

When a referee stops a contest, normal procedure is to award it to the guy who's still standing up. In this case, that would have been Evander Holyfield, an old-fashioned pugilist who thought this was still the sport of Dempsey, Tunney and John L. Sullivan, where when you spotted an opening, you threw a punch at it, and Evander had just thrown the best left hook he ever threw in his life. It caught Kevin Barry flush on the chin and immediately put Evander Holyfield out of the tournament.

□

It wasn't a low blow, it wasn't a rabbit punch, an eye gouge. He didn't knee him in the groin, bite him, choke him, call his mother names, impugn his ancestry or take out a blackjack. He did what he had been trained to do from the age of 8. When he saw an exposed chin, he hit it. He did what you're supposed to do when an opponent drops his guard. Knock him down.

But if there's anything they hate in an Olympic Games, it's a knockdown. The only thing they hate worse is a knockout. They hate to have to revive a guy to raise his hand. They prefer their medal winners conscious. And alive, if possible.

Evander Holyfield, who has the right name for it, now becomes a classic figure of historic injustice like that doctor who fixed John Wilkes Booth's leg, or the Count of Monte Cristo. Or the Long Count at Chicago. He now becomes the official martyr of the 1984 Olympics. Mary Decker doesn't quite make it because she, like Kevin Barry, ignored the first law of infighting, protect yourself at all times, and participated in her own collapse.

The irony of the sad story of Evander is that the referee who threw him out of the tournament appeared at the time of the incident to be moving in to disqualify the *other* fighter. In case you've been wondering about that thumbs-up

Please see MURRAY, page 97

Halfway home—Chandra Cheeseborough takes the baton from Jeanette Bolden and turns on the afterburners as the U.S. team wins the women's 400-meter relay.

JAY DICKMAN / Los Angeles Times

PATRICK DOWNS / Los Angeles Times

Calvin Smith (right) passes off to Carl Lewis on the anchor leg of men's 400-meter relay

Saturday. U.S. won in 37.83, setting a world record and giving Lewis his fourth gold medal.

Coe Wins in Race of Attrition

He Becomes First to Take Olympic 1,500 Gold Twice

By RICK REILLY, *Times Staff Writer*

All around him they fell, but Sebastian Coe would not.

First fell the favorite, Brazilian Joaquim Cruz, scratched from the starting list because of sickness.

Second fell unlucky Steve Ovett, clutching his chest with one lap to go, leaving the Coliseum via a stretcher for the second time in as many finals.

Third fell the American, Steve Scott, who had run with a bizarre abandon, only to dissolve into the pack and finish 10th.

Fourth fell the Spaniard, Jose Abascal, a gallant and doomed leader through the final turn.

And fifth and finally fell the only man between Sebastian Coe and his gold—fellow Brit Steve Cram. So stubborn was Cram that Coe would have to kick on him not once, not twice, but thrice.

And when he had, and Cram had finally given way, Coe was alone with 90,861 fans and his Olympic 1,500 meter gold—a match for his 1,500 gold from Moscow in 1980. He is the only man in the history of the Games to win it twice.

He finished in an Olympic-record time of 3:32.53 (about a 3:50 mile pace). Cram was next in 3:33.40, followed by Abascal in

3:34.30. American Jim Spivey was fifth in 3:36.07.

It was Coe's second medal of these Olympics—he won a silver in the 800—and his first gold. But more than gold, Coe will hold next to his heart a delirious sense of accomplishment.

One year ago, he lay in a hospital bed, his life threatened by a rare viral infection.

Who could've seen him then and known what fires burned within?

Who could've known he would rise and run again? Who could've known he would make the British

Please see 1,500, page 97

U.S. Boxers Pound Out a Record Nine Gold Medals

Decisions for Americans Tate, Biggs Provoke Boos at the Sports Arena

By EARL GUSTKEY, *Times Staff Writer*

American fighters won nine gold medals Saturday in Olympic finals. The only loser was Virgil Hill (left), beaten in the 165-pound class by Korea's Shin Joon Sup.

SKEETER HAGLER / Los Angeles Times

It happened as nearly everyone expected it would, with a record number of American gold medals—nine—in the finals of the Olympic Games boxing tournament Saturday.

Certainly, the Sports Arena public address announcer wasn't caught unprepared. In the four-hour break between the day and night sessions Saturday, he practiced saying into the microphone: "Ladies and gentlemen, would you please rise for the playing of the national anthem of the United States of America."

He said the line nine times Saturday, five times in the evening, for flyweight Steve McCrory, featherweight Meldrick Taylor, light-welterweight Jerry Page, light-middleweight Frank Tate and super-heavyweight Tyrell Biggs.

The final United States tally, a box score for the Olympic record book: Nine golds, one silver, a bronze and one shutout. For the tournament, make it 52 victories in 55 bouts for the Americans in the 345-bout, 359-boxer, 13-day tournament.

The 1984 U.S. Olympic boxing team said it would set a new standard, and it did. The previous record five-gold medal U.S. teams of 1952 and 1976 were easily outdistanced Saturday. Even Cuba's six golds at the 1980 Moscow Olympics went under.

Would this have happened had the Eastern Bloc countries been present? Of course not. But on a night when five grinning, laughing, crying and flag-waving Americans paraded to the top rung of the medal platform, no one wanted to talk about the unhappy boxers in Cuba and the Soviet Union who must have cried a little, listening for or watching results from Los Angeles.

The Americans were here, and they weren't. As flyweight champion Steve McCrory put it, after he'd decisioned Yugoslavia's Redzep Redzepovski: "To hell with the Russians and the Cubans. I got my gold medal. I'm still the hardest-

Please see BOXING, page 97

LEWIS

Continued from page 96

"Two years ago, nobody thought I could do it," Lewis said of winning four medals. "A year ago, I didn't know if I could do it."

Now, all Lewis has to do is rest up for a week back home in Houston, begin his triumphant tour of Europe and rake in the money.

Asked how he saw his image translating into dollars and cents, Lewis said the payoff—which could amount to millions—was secondary.

"Right now, I don't care," he said. "My job is over. If I make 50 cents or $50,000, it doesn't matter. I have four gold medals, and that's one thing no one can take away."

No one is taking anything from Lewis, who is in position to do all the taking. His only concern was in the relay, where someone else's mistake could cost him his fourth gold. There were no mistakes, only clean handoffs and flying feet.

Graddy went out in 10.29, followed by Ron Brown's 9.19 on the curve and Smith's 8.94 down the stretch. Smith and Lewis were on the team that set the previous record of 37.86 last year in the world championships at Helsinki, Finland.

The relay is Lewis' only record. And the guys who helped him get it have some pretty good stories of their own.

Smith, the world record-holder in the 100 and world champion in the 200, missed making the Olympic team in each event because of an injury. The relay was his only chance for a medal.

"I don't know if it was worth it," he said of the gold, "but I feel better because of it."

Brown, who will be joining the Rams as a wide receiver as soon as he can sign a contract, had finished fourth in the 100 on a bad leg.

"Our team is only as strong as our weakest link, and I didn't want to be the weakest link," Brown said. "(Getting the record) was just a matter of whether we could get the stick aound and if I could stay healthy."

Brown and Smith are two sprinters who pass as Lewis' friends. But they, too, were taken aback by all the questions about Lewis. All other sprinters are destined to remain in Lewis' shadow.

Graddy, the silver medalist in the 100, took the lack of spotlight the hardest. "I enjoyed it. I'm happy for him . . . As we came around that final turn, I didn't think Seb had it in his legs. But he did. I didn't think I had it in my legs, either, and I didn't."

Scott: "Sebastian definitely

1,500

Continued from page 96

Olympic team again? And who could've known he would stand on the highest victory platform less than eight months after jogging his first steps again?

Not even Sebastian Coe himself.

"This whole year has been as much a mental battle as physical," Coe said later. "To make a comeback within a year is something, but to do it in an Olympic year—with all the jitters that go with it—I am elated."

Sweeter still, Coe had won a race of integrity. There was no tripping, no protests, no venom, no thousandth-run replays. Even the men he beat were proud to have fallen to him.

"I was beaten by a better athlete on this day," Cram said. "I enjoyed it. I'm happy for him . . . As we came around that final turn, I didn't think Seb had it in his legs. But he did. I didn't think I had it in my legs, either, and I didn't."

Scott: "Sebastian definitely

proved himself to be the greatest 1,500-meter runner this year. I wanted a great miler to win it, and if it wasn't going to be me, I'm glad it was him."

In effect, Scott had sacrificed his name for the glory of the event.

He took the race out early and insanely fast. After a medium-slow first lap, Scott jumped to the fore and picked up the pace to nearly absurd speeds for the next two laps. Said Cram: "I figured we'd hit the bell lap at about 2:41. Instead, we hit it at about 2:38 (actually 2:39.04)."

For Scott, it was calculated craziness. He had been beaten by Cram's kick in the 1,500 at the world championships last year in Helsinki and vowed he would not let it happen again.

This time, "I wanted a miler's race." The idea was to take the lead and hope only he would have the strength left to keep it up. Instead, "I was the one who ended up dead on my feet."

Scott began to fade at the end of three laps, and the lead was taken up by the young Spaniard, Abascal, with the moisture of Coe and

Cram's breath on his neck. "I was surprised how much Coe had left," Abascal would say.

On the final turn, Coe and Cram swallowed Abascal up and took the duel out between themselves.

"My strategy was to get to the front sometime on that last lap," Cram said. "But Seb was just too much in control. He wouldn't let me past him on the bend. When I couldn't get by him, I knew that unless Seb's legs finally gave out, I wouldn't win it."

Coe had come too far now to give out. Coming down the glory stretch, Coe was feeling, "the best I've felt for two years. And that's the best I've felt in the 1,500 meters since 1981."

As he crossed the line, he stopped in his steps, spun around and into the line of sight with the Union Jack and "a persistent bunch of fans" from Chelsea. He pointed to them in elation—and not to the British press seated above them in vengeance, as ABC broadcaster Marty Liquori told the nation.

No, Sebastian Coe's triumph was too delicious for pettiness. This was of larger stuff.

But where does it fit in Coe's elegant trophy case? He has set world records and won international races. "This is probably a little more satisfying than Moscow (the 1980 gold in the 1,500), just because I've been fighting for a long time with a lot of problems. I know it sounds like a cliche, but this is a dream come true for me. This time last year, I was lying in a hospital bed . . . I was just worrying about getting healthy again. I mean, I didn't run from July until Christmas . . . Right now, I'm just pleased to be sitting at an Olympic Games, even if I hadn't won a medal."

But is it tainted without Cruz, who scratched with the flu after winning the 800, and without Ovett, who has suffered respiratory problems throughout these Games? "I'm sorry he (Cruz) wasn't in the race," said Coe. "It's very unfortunate. We both tackled two events, and I just lasted a little better. I don't think he would have been battling for first or second, anyway."

MURRAY

Continued from page 96

signal refs have been giving in this tournament, it signifies a warning to the fighter to stop doing whatever it is he's been doing wrong. In Kevin Barry's case, he had been holding Holyfield by the back of the neck while he punched him at the front. Kevin had collected more thumbs than Fritzie Zivic's last 10 fights. As the Yugoslav ref seemed about fed up when, suddenly, he noticed that Holyfield had committed a social blunder. He struck his opponent.

Holyfield thought that's what he was in there for, but in this game, that's a little like using somebody else's toothbrush. They would almost prefer this be a timed sport with opponents competing against a wired punching bag rather than each other. This sport is about as far removed from Dempsey-Firpo as checkers in the firehouse.

The notion that Evander Holyfield would have to sucker-punch anybody to win a medal is preposterous, least of all, Kevin Barry. He was so far ahead at the time he would have won 5-0 if he hadn't shown up for the last two rounds or dropped dead.

The decision was so flagrant, they didn't have the nerve to take a medal away from him, although a bronze medal is about as impressive here as a certificate of attendance. But a disqualified fighter is supposed to be a non-person in this tournament.

The best fighter in his weight class sat quietly in the boxing arena Saturday while they made ready to give his medal to some ponderous Yugoslav. Evander Holyfield took his persecution with glacial calm. Why, someone had wanted to know, hadn't he kicked the water bucket, attacked the ring posts, charged the referee, or threatened to take the thing clear to the Supreme Court? Said Evander: "I figured if I didn't conduct myself like a gentleman, the protest would

not go in my favor. Besides, it's not my nature."

But what about now, the next day, when the protest had already been refused? "Oh, it's too late," smiled the man without the gold medal. "Now, I'm wishing I hadn't thrown that punch. If I hadn't been so hungry, so greedy . . . Well, you see, I didn't need that punch. I didn't need to knock him out. It was a reflexive thing. I have been fighting since I was 8 years old in amateur tournaments, and it's hard to call back a punch. It isn't like taking back something you said. I never heard the referee call, 'Stop,' till the other fighter was already knocked down, but if I had, I don't know that I could have stopped the punch. It was in the mailbox. Judges with a pencil can do more than a guy with fists. I didn't need the punch.''

As it happened, Kevin Barry did. It was one of the most devastating punches in ring history. When one punch can win three medals in one swoop, it should go immediately to the punchers' Hall of Fame.

It won for Barry the silver and Evander the bronze. And because it knocked Barry out, it guaranteed the Yugoslav the gold because the rules provide a knocked-out fighter cannot fight again for 28 days. This, then, won the Yugoslav the gold because Barry could not compete. It may be the most devastating single punch in history or at least since Marciano, behind on points, kayoed Joe Walcott in Philadelphia in 1952. They should bronze the punch, too, call Evander henceforth "One Punch" Holyfield.

There were 345 bouts in the XXIIIrd Olympics. You get the feeling Bout No. 331 will be remembered like the Dempsey-Tunney Long Count long after most of them have been forgotten. The U.S. won nine gold medals. But the bronze-medal winner got the greatest cheer any bronze-medal winner ever got in history. And maybe the greatest any gold got either. The only guy who ever knocked himself out of an Olympic Games.

BOXING

Continued from page 96

hitting flyweight in the world.''

The less-than-capacity crowd, announced at 16,353, couldn't have been called a homer. Many of those present booed when Page and Biggs were given narrow decision victories. And in a no-class exhibition in the light-heavyweight medal ceremony, there were boos for the gold medalist Yugoslav, Anton Josipovic, because he happened to have reached the finals before American Evander Holyfield was disqualified in the semifinals Thursday.

And for Holyfield, of course, came the loudest cheers of all the medal ceremonies. He waved his flag and smiled appreciatively at those according him a standing ovation. And in a touching gesture, Josipovic, the man who'd just been booed, pulled Holyfield up to the top of the platform with him, and raised his hand in token victory.

"I believe in the Olympic spirit of friendship and goodwill," Josipovic said, "I don't think Holyfield was responsible for me being up there. I believe we should share it at least. I have been a fair man in sports and I'm sorry it turned out the way it did."

The final five winners:

—McCrory decisioned Redzepovski, 4-1.

—Taylor decisioned Nigerian Peter Konyegwachie, 5-0.

—Page decisioned Thailand's rugged, unyielding Dhawee Umponmaha, 5-0.

—Tate, in the most unpopular

decision of the night, decisioned Canada's Shawn O'Sullivan, 5-0.

—Biggs decisioned Italian Francesco Damiani, 4-1, a verdict also greeted with boos.

McCrory said he'd won the most difficult fight of his life in a gold medal bout.

"He (Redzepovski) was the toughest, yes. I'm in part dedicating this gold medal to Holyfield, it was the worst thing that ever happened in the history of boxing."

Taylor, 17, after what he said was one of the toughest bouts, said he wanted to cry on the victory stand but couldn't.

"I was emotional," he said. "I wanted to have a little joy crying, but I couldn't get it out. I was a little shy, I guess."

Last February, in Reno at the USA-Cuba dual, USA Amateur Boxing Federation executive director Jim Fox watched Taylor walk across a hotel lobby and said: "Don't quote me until he does it, but there goes your 1984 Olympic Games gold medalist."

He was right, but Taylor had the fight of his life. For the first time in his career, Taylor was getting consistently rocked by lefts and rights to the head by the powerful Nigerian.

But his jab and body punches found the mark just enough to get a three-point edge on four of the five scorecards.

Page was facing perhaps the strongest boxer in his weight class in the tournament. Umponmaha is an athlete who walks right through left jabs. In the best bout of the night, both slugged away until midway through the final round, when, finally, neither had much

left and both seemed a punch away from being knocked out.

They fought as if in slow motion, right down to their last gasps, flailing away at each other like sleepwalkers. The crowd booed the 5-0 judges' vote (the PA announcer incorrectly announced it as a jury overturn).

Tate and O'Sullivan went at each other like two cavemen in animal skins. O'Sullivan seemed to have Tate tottering on the brink of being KO'd several times, but Tate's jab and an occasional scoring flurry of his own, was the difference.

For a breathtaking second at the end of the first round, there was a flashback to the Holyfield disqualification of Thursday night. Tate hit O'Sullivan hard after the bell, but referee Constantin Kiriac of Romania only waggled a finger at Tate, who bowed deeply from the waist in apology.

The boos rolled down in deafening waves from the red seats when it was announced Tate won on every card. O'Sullivan got a standing, roaring ovation when he left.

Biggs decisioned Damiani for the third straight time after Damiani made the token ring appearance to get his walkover win for the light-heavyweight gold. Damiani tried something new this time. In his previous two losses to Biggs, he mauled, shoved, wrestled and leaned on the taller Philadelphian.

But Saturday night, Damiani himself used a jab frequently and stayed just close enough to employ power combinations, hoping to take out Biggs with a hook. It never happened. And Biggs himself in the third round went out of his customary jab-and-move game plan

JOSE GALVEZ / Los Angeles Times

Shin Joon Sup of South Korea tearfully celebrates after victory over Virgil Hill of the U.S.

when he waged a furious slugging match with the Italian in centering.

When it was over, the longest face at ringside belonged to Raul Villanueva, president of Cuba's amateur boxing federation.

"It is very sad," he said. "I feel certain our boxers would have made the finals in seven weight classes today."

Boxing Finals / Early Session

Tillman Beats DeWit; Breland, Whitaker Win

By JACK HAWN, *Times Staff Writer*

Middleweight Virgil Hill's defeat in the boxing finals Saturday afternoon at the Sports Arena may have put a damper on the American team's celebration, but for Los Angeles, at least, it was a gold-medal sweep.

Paul Gonzales and Henry Tillman not only fulfilled their longtime dreams, but also capped two notable turnarounds.

Both are former troublemakers who seemed destined for the worst. Gonzales left the East Los Angeles gangs years ago to enter a ring, and only three years ago, Tillman climbed from one behind bars.

Today, both are Olympic champions, apparently headed for bright careers in the pro ranks.

For Gonzales, it was effortless.

The 20-year-old light-flyweight merely went through the motions in being declared a winner after Friday's announcement that his opponent, Italy's Salvatore Todisco, had suffered a broken thumb on his right hand.

For months, Gonzales has been talking about being only "an inch away," and he finally mounted the victory stand without having thrown a punch.

Tillman, however, threw plenty.

Providing the day's biggest surprise, the 24-year-old heavyweight upset the Canadian Golden Boy, Willie deWit, after having lost to him twice in pre-Games competition.

Two other Americans won gold medals in the afternoon session—lightweight Pernell Whitaker and welterweight Mark Breland. South Korea finally won its first gold medal ever when Shin Joon Sup edged Hill, 3-2, and Italy's Maurizio Stecca took the gold with a 4-1 win over Hector Lopez, a 17-year-old Glendale Hoover High student who represented Mexico.

But it was Tillman's upset that stole the show.

Winning all three rounds on The Times' card, he outmaneuvered the Canadian, scoring more clean blows from inside, where they boxed almost exclusively.

Asked if he ever was hit solidly, Tillman replied, "No, not really flush solid. They were glancing blows. . . . I sidestepped him and let him go by me."

Although the decision was unanimous, the margins varied considerably, two judges favoring Tillman by four points, one by three points, one by two points and

one card was even, 59-59.

DeWit, whose defeat may have cost him a few zeroes before the decimal point on a professional contract, at least at the outset of his pro career, called the decision "very close. I can't complain."

He said he "would love to" get a rematch with Tillman as a pro, predicting the outcome would be different, because in a 10-round bout, his strength and punching power would prove to his advantage. Also, he would not be hindered by amateur rules, which limited his effectiveness Saturday.

Tillman, who served 300 days at the California Youth Authority facility at Chino for an armed-robbery conviction, praised his coach, Mercer Smith, for helping him turn his life around.

Smith, employed by the youth authority as a physical education instructor, plucked Tillman from the ranks while he was incarcerated and taught him to box.

"There's a saying in the California criminal justice system," Smith said, "that one-third will come back, one-third will never come back and one-third you can turn around. Henry Tillman is in that (the latter) category."

Smith said he is working on a deal for Paul Gonzales and Tillman to make their professional debuts on the same Los Angeles card in November.

Gonzales, meanwhile, plans a vacation, "so I can enjoy this gold medal."

There will be a family celebration, he said, "but I don't know what's planned. But I know I'm going to indulge myself in a big pizza tonight.

"I never had a doubt I'd win a gold medal. Pro people say there is no money in the lighter weights, but I'm going to change all that."

Gonzales was the first to climb the victory platform Saturday afternoon, and in both hands he held flags—Old Glory and one from Mexico.

"I carried two flags because I am a Mexican-American," he said, "and part of my Olympic dream was to walk to the gold-medal ceremony with the American and Mexican flags. My (10-year) dream is no longer a dream; it's reality."

For Mark Breland and Pernell Whitaker, it was reality, too—also relatively easy.

Breland, finishing his amateur career with a record of 110-1 after his six Olympic victories, totally outclassed South Korean An Young Su, 5-0.

One judge had a seven-point spread, two gave it to Breland by six points and two by five points.

Breland, a 6-3, 21-year-old New Yorker who has impressed fans here in his last three matches after disappointing them, perhaps, in his first three, finished with a flourish.

Whitaker's fight against Luis Ortiz also was a mismatch, ending at 2:57 of the second round when the Puerto Rican's coach called it quits.

Ortiz, circling, jabbing and staying out of range in the first round, couldn't avoid serious trouble in the second, when Whitaker, a southpaw, began finding his target with solid lefts to the head.

Whitaker would not comment on reports that he might sign a professional contract with Atlantic City manager Lou Duva.

"This is the Olympics and has nothing to do with professionalism," he said.

Also uncertain about his immediate future, Virgil Hill, barely able to contain his disappointment, preferred to dwell on his immediate past.

Asked how he felt long after losing to Shin, he said, "I feel terrible, rotten. I worked 12 years for this moment . . ."

Winning a silver medal didn't pacify him.

"Who remembers second place?" he asked. "I remember Sugar Ray Leonard, Howard Davis, the Spinks brothers (1976 Olympic winners); I don't remember who they beat.

"I know I won that fight. I lost the second round big but won the first and third."

The Times card disagreed, calling the first, virtually actionless round, even, and giving Shin the second, Hill the third for a 59-59 total. South Koreans were ecstatic, and in tears, after Shin's hand was raised.

It was a close one on the official cards: 59-58, 59-59 and 59-58 for Shin, 59-59 and 60-58 for Hill.

Perhaps the most thrilling fight of the day was the bantamweight match won by Stecca.

It, too, was close: 59-59, 59-58, 59-58, 60-56, for Stecca; 59-59 for Lopez.

Jorge Maisonet of Puerto Rico takes punches from Charles Nwokolo of Nigeria in their 139-pound fight. Maisonet won the match.

MARK BOSTER

LORI SHEPLER / Los Angeles Times

Pat Powers (No. 13), Dusty Dvorak (No. 1) and Steve Timmons exult after gold medal victory.

Brazilians See Plenty of Red; U.S. Gets Gold

By JERRY CROWE, *Times Staff Writer*

In the absence of the world champion Soviet Union, the United States provided the Olympic men's volleyball tournament with its own Big Red Machine Saturday night at the Long Beach Arena.

The red-clad Americans crushed Brazil, 15-6, 15-6, 15-7, to finally bring a gold medal to the country where the sport was invented in 1895.

So what if the Soviets weren't here?

They were invited, weren't they? And, besides, they were beaten by the Americans four times in the Soviet Union two months ago.

Actor Tom Selleck, the team's honorary captain, made it a point to come into the interview room afterward to remind the media that the Americans had, indeed, beaten all the teams that weren't here.

"It's their gold medal," he said of the Americans.

And then U.S. Coach Doug Beal, who played for three U.S. teams that couldn't even qualify for the Games, had his say.

"We've felt for a long time that we had the best team in the world," he said. "And we felt that tonight we played certainly the best match of the tournament, but (also) the first match representative of the way this team can perform."

The lettering on the T-shirt held aloft by captain Chris Marlowe afterward said it all for the Americans: "We Did It."

The crowd of 12,033, which had roared its approval throughout the match, ate it up.

The Americans, 13th two years ago at the world championships and unable to even qualify for the Games since 1968, had finally won a medal.

They did it against a team that had finished second to the vaunted Soviets at the world championships and had easily defeated the U.S. team in straight games last Monday night.

There will be considerable debate, of course, about whether the Americans' medals are tainted in light of the Soviet-led boycott.

Four of the world's top 10 teams were not here, including, of course, the Soviets, who have not lost in a major international competition since losing the Olympic final to Poland in 1976.

But there was nothing tainted about the Americans' performance in the final.

In marked contrast to their lopsided loss to the Brazilians last Monday, when Brazil put down 55% of its kill attempts compared to the Americans' 40%, the Americans romped this time.

Led by Steve Timmons (17 of 26) and Pat Powers (22 of 37), the North American champions were successful on 57% of their kill tries.

And Brazil put down only 48%.

"They made us feel uncomfortable," said Brazilian Coach Paulo Freitas. "We never had the opportunity to break the momentum. And the States had the better transition game. They just dominated the game."

MEN'S

Volleyball

■ HOW THEY FINISHED

1. United States

2. Brazil

3. Italy

THE MEDALISTS

What was the difference between Monday's match and Saturday night's?

"This game mattered and that one didn't," said the Americans' Karch Kiraly, who won a sportsmanship award from the International Volleyball Federation.

When last they met, the Brazilians had to win to reach the semifinals and the Americans didn't, having already qualified for the medal round.

Not that the Americans didn't try last time, but they definitely didn't show all they had.

In the first match, Paul Sunderland and Steve Salmons started for the Americans. In the final, neither played a minute.

Beal went back to his regular starting lineup—Timmons, Powers, Kiraly, Aldis Berzins, Craig Buck and setter Dusty Dvorak—and kept them on the floor for all but a few points.

Dvorak's setting was superb, as usual, and so was the passing of Kiraly and Berzins. The 6-8 Buck was strong in the middle, and Timmons and Powers pounded away from the outside.

The Americans went up, 10-3, in the first game and scored the game-winner when a pass went through the hands of Brazil's usually steady setter, William da Silva.

Everything was going right for the United States. In the second game, a spike bounced high off Powers' head and was eventually put down for a winner.

The match finally ended, appropriately enough considering the dramatic turn of events from their first meeting, with Dvorak stuffing a spike by Bernard Rajzman back onto Brazil's side of the court.

Rajzman put down 65% of his kill attempts last Monday. This time, he put down only 48%.

And Beal, who has been criticized by his detractors for everything from his selection of the players to his aloof manner with his team and the media, had finally been vindicated.

"This justifies the work, the program and who's on the team," Beal said.

But later he said: "I feel happy. My job isn't to be vindicated or not vindicated. It's (my job) to put a good team on the floor."

No one can deny he did that. Including the Soviets.

Italy vs. Canada. The Italians, who got into the Games only because of the boycott, won the bronze-medal match, 15-11, 15-12, 15-8.

When Italy beat Canada last week in the preliminary round, the Canadians blamed their own overconfidence for the loss.

This time, they were just plain outplayed by a team that finished fourth last fall in the European championships and had been training together for less than two months before the Olympics.

Franco Bertoli put down 21 of 33 kill attempts for Italy, which put down 50% overall.

101,799 Show Up to Watch France Win Its First Medal—a Gold One

By GRAHAME L. JONES, *Times Staff Writer*

With a full moon rising over the rim of the Rose Bowl and the strains of the Marseillaise soaring into the warm evening air, France was crowned Olympic soccer champion.

A 2-0 victory over Brazil in front of a U.S.-record crowd of 101,799 Saturday night gave the French the gold medal, their first medal of any kind in Olympic soccer.

How does it feel?

"Superb," French Coach Henri Michel said.

"We don't really realize what has happened. We're in a dream world," said Daniel Xuereb, the man whose fifth goal of the tournament had clinched the victory in the second half.

It took more than half an hour after the match had ended for the medal award ceremony to begin, but very few in the crowd left.

As the French players climbed the victory stand, followed by Brazil, the silver medalists, and Yugoslavia, which won the bronze, a huge roar went up. The reception for the Yugoslavs was especially warm.

After International Olympic Committee president Juan Antonio Samaranch and FIFA president Joao Havelange had presented the medals and bouquets of flowers to each of the 51 players on the three teams, the crowd rose for the French national anthem.

Thousands of flash bulbs erupted in the stands as the flags of the three nations were brought to full staff. Afterward, the French and Brazilian players ran to their supporters in the crowd, tossing them the bouquets they had just received.

After a victory lap by the French, the Rose Bowl darkened for a fireworks display that followed. By 9:40, it was all over, the first Olympic soccer tournament to be held in the United States had ended.

Why had the French succeeded where 15 other teams had failed?

"Solidarity," said the 25-year-old Xuereb. "From the beginning to the end there were no stars but team play. We cut down on many mistakes. Our win is due to a total team effort."

Both of France's goals were scored in the second half. And both, as Xuereb said, were due, in part, to unselfish play.

The first came in the 55th minute when midfielder Guy Lacombe won the ball and passed to Jean-Philippe Rohr on the right wing. Rohr sent a perfect cross into the goal area, where Francois Brisson met it

MEN'S

Soccer

■ HOW THEY FINISHED

1. France

2. Brazil

3. Yugoslavia

THE MEDALISTS

squarely with his head and sent the ball arcing over the outstretched arms of Gilmar, the Brazilian goalkeeper, and just beneath the crossbar.

The second goal—the one that ended Brazilian hopes—came seven minutes later. This time, it was Xuereb and Dominique Bijotat who combined to beat the Brazilian defense.

Bijotat, who worked tirelessly throughout the game on offense and defense, fired a shot that Gilmar had to fling himself to his right to palm away. Xuereb, sprinting in from the left, reached the ball seconds before a Brazilian defender and sent it spinning into the back of the net.

There were still some 28 minutes left to play, but the Brazilians seemed to loose their fire. In fact, Brazil's attacking moves had misfired most of the game when confronted by the strong French back four. Philippe Jeannol and Michel Bibard played strong defensive games for the French while goalkeeper Albert Rust was seldom troubled.

"I thought that Brazil was a much superior team in the first half," Brazilian Coach Jair Picerni said, "but the French deserved to win because they played a much better offensive game in the second half.

"We're not going to hide the facts. We made a few mistakes. In the first half, we played well. However, after their first goal, the team lost a little of its hope. So much so that we lost the game."

Despite losing, the Brazilians will be taking home the first medal the country has won in Olympic soccer.

"This was very important for us," Brazilian striker

ROSEMARY KAUL/ Los Angeles Times

In a tightly marked game, it was rare when either France or Brazil could find running room.

Augilmar Oliveira said. "We left Brazil thinking we could win. We showed the world some excellent football and we met an excellent football team in France."

The win was France's second international success this year. In June, France, which had never won an international honor, captured the European Championship.

The question being asked now is whether France can extend its run of success when the stars of international soccer gather again—in the World Cup in Mexico in 1986.

Soccer Notes

Total attendance for the 32 games of the Olympic soccer tournament came to 1,421,627, or an average of 44,426 per game. The 11 matches at the Rose Bowl drew a total of 691,699 fans, an average of 62,881 per game. Stanford Stadium in Palo Alto attracted 465,423 to nine games, an average of 51,714.

Men's High Jump

Mogenburg Hits Gold; Zhu Settles for Bronze

By ALAN GREENBERG,
Times Staff Writer

Surely, there must be an ancient Chinese proverb to ease mental anguish, but, whatever it is, it obviously hadn't yet dawned on Zhu Jianhua.

This much had. The world record-holder in the high jump (7-10), the sheltered man-child on whose slender shoulders weighed the hopes of one billion Chinese, had just managed only a bronze medal in the Olympic final Saturday. Good enough for a lot of other athletes. But not nearly good enough for Zhu Jianhua.

As Zhu walked off the Coliseum field, head down, Carlo Thranhardt of West Germany, another medal contender who'd bombed out even worse, threw his arm around Zhu's shoulders as if to say, "it's not the end of the world."

Zhu, 20, acted like maybe it was. Once he'd fulfilled his obligations on the medal stand and in doping control, Zhu left the Coliseum without talking to the Chinese press, let alone the world's.

"Zhu was really upset and hardly spoke to anyone. He was almost in a daze," said Justin Rudelson, an interpreter who had accompanied Zhu after the event. "He was completely confused. He didn't even speak in doping control, he just nodded his head."

The most dramatic thing Zhu did was smash his palms against the high jump pit after failing in his final attempt at 7-8½. A few minutes later, when Sweden's Patrik Sjoberg also failed in his final attempt at 7-8½, West Germany's Dietmar Mogenburg, who'd cleared it like he'd cleared every other height—on his first try—clasped his hands to his head and then raised them skyward. The gold medal was his.

American record-holder (7-8) Dwight Stones, whose goal was to add a third Olympic bronze medal to his collection—he was third at Munich in 1972 and at Montreal in 1976—cleared 7-7 and finished fourth. U.S. teammate Doug Nordquist cleared 7-6 and finished fifth.

THE MEDALISTS

MEN'S

Track

■ HIGH JUMP

1. Dietmar Mogenburg
   (West Germany)

2. Patrik Sjoberg (Sweden)

3. Zhu Jianhua (China)

The gold medal wasn't just vindication for Mogenburg, who was only 18 in 1979 when he was ranked No. 1 in the world, it was also vindication for Stones, in his new role as TV commentator. All along, Stones had predicted a Mogenburg victory, citing his ability to, yes, *rise* to the occasion in big meets.

And Mogenburg, whose winning jump equaled his personal best, was never better than Saturday. He made each of his six jumps with plenty to spare. With the gold medal assured, he attempted but failed thrice at what would have been a world record 7-10 1/2.

"I was luckier this time, better mentally prepared for the noise," said the 6-7 Mogenburg, who was the 1982 European champion but tied for fourth at the 1983 world championships at Helsinki. "I just tried to concentrate and block everything out."

There was a lot to block. The high jump pit is set at the peristyle end of the Coliseum, where there was all manner of commotion. The peristyle end is where the medal ceremonies take place, and every time the winning anthem was to be played, the high jump competition had to stop.

"It was a zoo out there, a three-ring circus," Nordquist said.

But the jumpers knew to be ready for the interruptions of blaring music and medal ceremonies.

What they weren't ready for was exhausted 1,500-meter competitor Steve Ovett quitting his race and easing himself down directly behind the high jump pit, where he was immediately surrounded by doctors and officials.

Suddenly, it was a four-ring circus.

And Zhu's turn to jump.

It was to be Zhu's second attempt at 7-7¾. He'd failed in his first attempt—his first miss of the meet.

Stones said that Zhu wanted to jump, was ready, but the officials, noting the mess Ovett had inadvertently caused at the back of the pit, insisted that he wait.

So Zhu passed.

"He (Zhu) had smoked (easily cleared) 7-7," Stones said. "At that point, I thought, 'Wow, we're really going to have jump high today (Saturday). When he had to wait for Ovett, that broke his (Zhu's) concentration, it would have broken mine. If I'm Zhu, I've got to hope he (Ovett) collapses somewhere else. I don't care who you are, that's going to break your concentration."

And it seemed to break Zhu's. Nordquist said Zhu seemed quite rattled, even started planting his foot halfway down the bar, rather than at the standard, as he had on his earlier jumps. He'd looked so flawless at the lower heights, clearing 7-0½, 7-3, 7-5¼ and 7-7 with seemingly the greatest of ease.

"He was oozing confidence, the way he was going over at the lower heights," Nordquist said. "After that, I think he was a little afraid."

Stones: "I was very surprised by the Chinese jumper's inability to jump higher. I shook hands with him afterward and said, 'at least you have four years from now.'"

For Zhu, who also finished third at the 1983 world championships in Helsinki, there is plenty of time.

For Stones, 30, who's winding down a brilliant 12-year international career, there isn't.

"I could be very upset with my fourth-place finish, but I jumped 2.31 (meters) and performed very well," Stones said. "I cleared 7-7, it's a respectable height, four inches higher than I've ever jumped at an Olympics before."

Other performers, were, by their own standards, even more than respectable. Like silver medalist Sjoberg, a 19-year old prodigy who trains six hours a day and calls himself "a professional high jumper." His 7-7¾ equalled his personal best.

JAYNE KAMIN / Los Angeles Times
Dietmar Mogenburg of West Germany fails in world-record attempt after winning the gold medal.

ANACLETO RAPPING / Los Angeles Times
Bronze-medalist Zhu Jianhua of China and silver-medalist Patrik Sjoeberg of Sweden miss jumps.

Women's 1,500

Italy's Dorio Finds the Right Tactic

By RANDY HARVEY,
Times Staff Writer

Italy's Gabriella Dorio had just won the women's 1,500 meters at the Coliseum Saturday, but an Italian journalist still felt she needed advice.

"When you receive your medal, do something different," he told her. "Do not laugh or cry."

To which Dorio replied, "Oh, let me cry just a little bit."

Dorio, 27, had been waiting eight years to have an Olympic gold medal, or, for that matter, any medal, hanging around her neck.

She was sixth in the 1,500 at the 1976 Montreal Olympics. In the 1980 Moscow Olympics, she was eighth in the 800 and fourth in the 1,500. Last Monday, she was fourth in the 800.

But the kick that betrayed her in that race won this one for her, as she ran past Romania's Doina Melinte, the 800 champion, in the final 100 meters.

Dorio finished in 4:03.25 to Melinte's 4:03.76. Romanian Maricica Puica, who won the 3,000 meters less than 24 hours earlier, came from far behind on the final lap to finish third in 4:04.15.

American Ruth Wysocki, who upset Mary Decker in the 1,500 at the U.S. Olympic trials, was never a factor, finishing eighth in 4:08.92.

"I feel like I let everybody down," Wysocki said. "I don't want anybody saying I'm a fluke because I don't think I am.

"At least I made the finals. At least I stayed on my feet. I'm trying to think of all the positive things here."

Never having faced international competition before last week, Wysocki, 27, might have been too inexperienced to contend with the tactics of the European runners.

All of the other runners expected Dorio to set the pace, as she had in the 1,500 qualifying Thursday and in the 800 final. But Dorio learned her lesson from the 800 Monday, when she had the lead going into the final turn, only to be passed by Melinte, American Kim Gallagher and Romanian Fita Lovin.

Dorio let Great Britain's Christina Boxer have the early lead in this one, staying on her heels for the first two laps. When Dorio took the lead with 600 meters to go, only Melinte went with her.

"I went to make my move, and they were gone," Wysocki said.

At least one person in the race missed Decker, who qualified for this event by finishing second in the U.S. trials but chose to concentrate only on the 3,000 here. She failed to finish in the final Friday night after getting her feet tangled with Zola Budd and falling.

"When Mary is in the race, you know the pace is going to be good from the start," said Canadian Brit McRoberts, who finished seventh.

"Without her, this became a real tactical race. There was a lot of jostling, the same kind of thing you saw in the 3,000.

"We were all running in a pack, and then, all of a sudden, Dorio and Melinte were opening up a gap. They just got the jump on us. That's the experience of the Europeans."

With 300 meters remaining, Dorio again dropped back and allowed Melinte to have the lead. But coming off the final turn, Dorio's superior strength proved to be the difference. Melinte, who is better in the 800 because of her speed, could not respond.

The most impressive final lap was run by Puica, who was sixth going into the last turn but passed three runners to win the bronze medal.

"I would have liked to win the gold, but, from a tactical point of view, I made a mistake," said Puica, 34, who was running for the fourth

time in four days. "I attacked too late."

Puica easily beat Dorio in the 3,000 earlier this year, but this was the Italian's night.

"I was afraid because I took the lead in the 800 and lost it," Dorio said. "I said to myself, 'Stay back and try to go on the last lap.'

"I started to go when I felt good with 600 meters to go. Then I felt Melinte coming. So I let her go and waited until I could pass her.

"This is the third Olympic Games I have been trying to win. I've been

training for this race ever since I finished sixth in Montreal. I felt I could do something good. It's fun to talk now but, in the past, there have been crises when I've thought of quitting."

Dorio said she was inspired by Italian teammate Sara Simeoni's second-place finish Friday in the high jump.

"The flowers she got for winning the silver medal, she gave them to her friends," Dorio said. "I took one, and I promised her I would get a medal, too."

JAYNE KAMIN / Los Angeles Times
After missing a medal at two previous Olympics, Gabriella Dorio of Italy beats field Saturday and celebrates her 1,500 win.

JAYNE KAMIN / Los Angeles Times
Sebastian Coe of Britain turns to the stands and flashes a big smile as he wins the Olympic 1,500 meters Saturday in 3:32.53.

100

U.S. silver medalist Andy Rein locks up the legs of Finland's Jukka Rauhala (upper left) in a 149.5-pound freestyle semifinal match. And India's 125.5-pound Rohtas Sing finds double trouble, getting pinned by gold medalist Hideaki Tomiyama of Japan (above) and falling victim to a spectacular move by Puerto Rico's Orlando Caceres (left) while losing, 12-4.

PHOTOS:
Mark Boster,
Los Angeles Times

It's a Family Affair for U.S. as Mark Schultz and Lou Banach Win Golds

By DAVE DISTEL,
Times Staff Writer

Meathead and Archie weren't there, but "All in the Family" enjoyed a revival at the Anaheim Convention Center Saturday night.

Mark Schultz and Lou Banach both won and joined their brothers, Dave Schultz and Ed Banach, as freestyle wrestling gold medalists for the United States.

Mark Schultz stopped Japan's Hideyuki Nagashima, 13-0, in 1:59 to win at 180.5, and Lou Banach pinned Syria's Joseph Atiyeh in 1:01 to win at 220.

Ed Banach, Lou's twin, started the show with a gold at 198 pounds Thursday, and Dave Schultz kept it going with a gold Friday at 163.

Toss in Randy Lewis, Bobby Weaver and Bruce Baumgartner, and Dan Gable's U.S. wrestlers totaled seven golds. That equalled the Soviet Union's Olympic record, set in Moscow in 1980 during the U.S.-led boycott.

Two other U.S. wrestlers won silver medals. Japan's Hideaki Tomiyama beat Barry Davis, 8-3, at 125.5, and South Korea's You In Tak won a 5-5 criteria decision over Andy Rein at 149.5. The nine U.S. medals broke the previous record of six.

American wrestlers' finished with a combined record of 40-5.

After Lou Banach's win concluded the tournament, he and his brother took turns carrying each other around the arena.

The Schultz brothers were a bit more restrained, possibly to keep anyone from saying they were acting like animals. The International Wrestling Federation had accused them of using excessive brutality in their techniques. Mark broke the elbow of one opponent with an illegal hold and Dave wrenched another's knee.

In the aftermath of his win Saturday night, Mark Schultz expressed surprise that a controversy had been swirling around him and his brother.

"I guess it's because I broke the Turk's arm," Mark said. "I just threw a hold and I heard his elbow crack and I thought, 'Oh no, they're going to disqualify me.' My brother didn't help when he broke some guy's knee off."

Schultz said he thought about apologizing to Turkey's Resit Karabacak, but didn't.

"I was afraid he'd tell me to go to hell," Schultz said. "And what I did wasn't intentional."

Both Schultzes were closely watched in the aftermath. In the championship match Saturday night, Mark stayed with rather basic moves and piled up points so quickly it was over almost before it started.

In the aftermath, Schultz laughed at his reputation for brute strength.

"People think because I have this build that it's all brawn and no brains," he said. "They think that I can go right out and beat the hell out of 'em with no techniques. My brother's built completely differently, so he's all brains and no brawn—like a Texas Instruments calculator."

And the Banachs were not exactly shorted when it came to brawn. One opponent went the distance against each of them, and Lou won four of his five matches by pins.

Banach's quickest match was the one for the gold medal against Syria's Atiyeh, an All-American from LSU with dual citizenship. Regardless, Atiyeh's silver was Syria's first medal.

"The gold medal stands for persistence," Banach said. "There's a lot of hard work. And the mental part is probably the toughest."

But he said he felt no pressure to match his brother's gold.

"Eddie stands alone," Lou said, "and I'm the same way. I just had to do my best."

South Korea's You had to do a little beyond his best. He had to overcome back spasms that caused him to be a portrait in pain as he stood atop the victory stand with a bouquet of flowers and his gold medal.

He had shoved the pain to the back of his mind during the match—and during a victory lap around the three mats.

"I was so excited about the gold medal," he said, "that I forgot about the pain."

He also had to overcome a protest by the U.S. coaches on the scoring of a three-point move by You that provided the tie-breaking criteria.

"The freestyle rules seem to change every tournament," Rein said. "It can be disappointed and frustrating. I didn't come all this way for a silver medal."

Tomiyama's win was a bit more routine as he took charge with a gut wrench that broke a tie at the end of the first period. His 85-year-old grandfather had come from South Korea to watch him.

"When he appears," Tomiyama said, "I win. He's my good-luck charm."

However, Tomiyama wants more than merely luck in his corner. He wants to retire as a competitor and become a wrestling coach.

"I will learn and practice coaching for a year or so with Dan Gable," Tomiyama said. "I want to learn his skills and I want to learn the Yankee spirit. We've seen the Americans winning the gold medals and we can learn a few things from them."

When he gets to the University of Iowa to learn at the master's knee, he will be in the same wrestling room with the silver medalist. Davis will be a senior.

"No doubt we'll work out together," Davis said. "Maybe he can help me. He's the Olympic champion."

Tomiyama's plans represented one final delicious twist to what had really been Dan Gable's week.

When it was over, the crowd chanted his name—and demanded his presence on the mats. Ed Banach carried him into the arena to a thunderous ovation.

Wrestling Notes

All four Americans had to win afternoon matches to get to the gold medal showdowns. **Barry Davis** had the toughest struggle, rallying to win, 6-4, over Yugoslavia's **Zoran Sorov. Lou Banach** and **Mark Schultz** both overwhelmed their opponents, Banach pinning Japan's **Tamon Honda** in 1:56 and Schultz pinning Italy's **Luciano Ortelli** in 1.36. It was a prelude of things to come. **Andy Rein** went the distance to beat Finland's **Jukka Rauhala**, 14-4 . . . The gold medals by the brother teams were not firsts. **Sergei** and **Anatole Belaglazov** of the Soviet Union won golds in 1980 .

Archery

Pace Puts the Gold Under His Thumb

By ELLIOTT ALMOND,
Times Staff Writer

In 1973, when Darrell Pace was a budding archer at age 17, he almost severed a thumb while cleaning a motorcycle. Pace was wiping off the machine with a rag while it was running and got his thumb caught in the rotating chain.

His thumb was sewn together, leaving a scarred reminder of an accident that almost ended the career of the world's greatest archer before it really got going. The injured thumb is the same one that Pace uses to help pull a bowstring to full draw. Without it, he would have difficulty stabilizing a bow.

But it says something about Pace's ethos that shortly after the accident he tried shooting with a cast. Pace is determined, and that characteristic has never left him.

Pace eventually forgot about the accident, graduated from Cincinnati archery leagues and within three years became the 1976 Olympic champion. Still, something seemed to be missing. Pace wasn't accepted by fellow archers because, they claimed, he didn't always act like a gentlemen. And heck, archers have an image to keep up.

But today, Darrell Pace has embraced the world of archery as his own. He is this quiet sport's champion of champions, a man on a path as direct as the arrows he shoots.

He was elevated to a higher status Saturday after winning his second Olympic gold medal by obliterating all challengers. Silver medalist Rick McKinney, the marksman who defeated Pace last October at the world championships, was a whopping 52 points behind the winner. Bronze medalist Hiroshi Yamamoto was 53 points back.

In the women's competition—one that proved to be much closer than the men's—South Korean teen-ager Seo Hyang Soon was an upset victor over Li Lingjuan of

THE MEDALISTS

Archery

■ MEN

1. Darrell Pace (U.S.)

2. Rick McKinney (U.S.)

3. Hiroshi Yamamoto (Japan)

■ WOMEN

1. Seo Hyang Soon (South Korea)

2. Li Lingjuan (China)

3. Kim Jin Ho (South Korea)

China and South Korea's Kim Jin Ho. Seo, who has been a member of Korea's national team for only four months, totaled 2,568 points over four days. Li scored 2,559 and Kim had 2,555.

Pace, one of the world's best archers for a decade, won with the nonchalance of a card dealer. He openly rooted for his longtime rival McKinney to earn the silver, and chatted with the audience at the El Dorado Park range in Long Beach—some 9,000 strong that included about 20 members of his family.

His lead was such that there was time to take a lunch break midway through Saturday's match to meet the press. Can you imagine Michael Jordan taking time out at halftime of the gold-medal basketball game to talk with reporters?

But let the archer beware. Pace, who failed to win an Olympic gold medal in 1980 because of the U.S. boycott (the only time the United States' has not won the men's archery competition since the sport was reinstated in the 1972 Games), is thinking of competing in 1988. And 1992. And 1996. And then we'll see.

"He is the Cassius Clay of archery," said Steve Lieberman, a for-

mer world champion. "He is one of the best of all time. It's not just equipment—he's a better athlete."

Pace, who had to leave a job as an electrical technician in Cincinnati to remain a competitive archer because he needed time off to attend tournaments, doesn't go in for all the comparisons.

"I'm just another archer," he said. He took this attitude into the day's final round of 72 arrows. Though Pace was leading by 35 points, he didn't feel the win was secure. "Even when I was up by that much, it seemed like two,"

Pace said. "I kept thinking, what if something happens. What if Rick has one of those incredible days and makes up 25 points? You never know what will happen."

But with Pace on the line, you can guess.

Last June, sitting in his mobile home in Hamilton, Ohio, Pace told his wife Beth to prepare for a week-long cross-country tour for all American medal winners. "I'm sure we'll be going on that," Pace said as he marked off the dates on his calendar.

The way he's shooting, he'll be

going on many more. Thumbs up.

Archery Notes

Li, who completely missed a target Wednesday because she had to change equipment the week prior to the tournament, ended up nine points away from a gold medal. Had she not missed the target chances are she would have challenged for the gold. . . Fame often is fleeting. After **Darrell Pace** won the gold medal, he was waiting to participate in archery's closing ceremonies—the athletes' march. A L.A. Olympic Organizing Committee official approached him and asked, "Are you a medal winner?" . . . Pace's four-day total of 2,616 broke his old Olympic record of 2,571 set in 1976.

LORI SHEPLER / Los Angeles Times

Gold-medal winner Darrell Pace has a bird's-eye view of the bull's-eye during archery competition at El Dorado Park in Long Beach.

OLYMPICS '84/NOTES

Compiled By JERRY GILLAM

The Dash for Cash: Athletes Turning Gold to Green

From Times Staff Writers and Wire Services

For the stars of the Olympics, the gold medals are only the icing on the cake, which is filled with riches in commercial endorsements.

And there is a well-defined pecking order for Olympic athletes seeking to cash in on their physical prowess, said Nina Blanchard, whose agency specializes in glamorous models like Cheryl Tiegs and Ken Norton, the former world heavyweight champion.

"If someone is good-looking and a medal winner, the combination is virtually unbeatable," Blanchard said. "If they aren't good-looking but a big medal winner, they still make money.

"Then there are those who are very attractive but were also-rans and nobody knows their name. They still have a chance of making money."

A flood of advertising contracts is expected to be signed immediately after the Games end today, since in most sports, athletes aren't permitted to sign commercial contracts and retain their amateur standing.

Estimates of how much money an athlete could command for commercial endorsements vary widely.

Swimmer Mark Spitz is estimated to have parlayed his seven gold medals from the 1972 Games into more than $5 million.

□

It's listed innocently enough as Dive 307C in the Olympics, but competitors know it as the "Dive of Death."

Russia's Sergei Shalibashvili was killed when he tried it. America's Greg Louganis' hopes for a gold medal in platform diving rest on it.

The diver stands on a platform 33 feet above the water, jumps up and begins doing 3½ reverse somersaults. As he comes down, his head must clear the edge of the platform. There is no margin for error.

Shalibashvili lost his balance slightly just before trying Dive 307C in the World University Games at Edmonton, Canada, last July. His head hit the top of the platform, crushing his skull. He later died.

Louganis had to watch in horror as that happened; he then followed the unfortunate Soviet diver off the platform.

Ron O'Brien, the coach of the U.S. diving team, said: "It's the meanest dive of them all, no doubt. But Greg had never had any problems with it."

In fact, O'Brien said Louganis needs to start getting a little closer to the platform.

"He's never been close to the platform on that dive," O'Brien said. "His problem has been that he's too far away from it. That's understandable considering it's the hardest dive being done."

Louganis' Dive 307C is scheduled to come shortly after 1 p.m. today—his final effort in a 10-dive program.

He will try the dive whether he's ahead or behind in a go-for-broke shot at becoming the first male in Olympic history to win both diving gold medals. He won the gold medal in the springboard last Wednesday.

"Once you get to a meet you can't change your program, and the dive is in our program," O'Brien said. "Greg has been working on it since Dec. 1, 1982. He's ready."

Some strains of international harmony were sounded Friday night during the preliminary competition of the rhythmic gymnastics at Pauley Pavilion. While Switzerland's Grazia Verzasloni was performing her routine, the tape playing her music broke. Verzasloni, unsure of the rules, continued to perform, *a cappella,* a difficult feat at best.

Meanwhile, Eugen Filipsecu, the piano player for the gymnasts from West Germany, sensing her desperation, quickly sat down at the piano on the far end of the floor and began improvising on the keyboard, trying to capture her rhythm. Did he know Verzasloni?

"No, I did not."

Was he familiar with her routine, her music?

"No, I wasn't."

Nobody in Pauley Pavilion could have guessed either.

Play it again, Eugen.

—RICHARD HOFFER

□

American 1,500-meter runner Jim Spivey looks like he has spent more time across the way at the Sports

MASS MEDIA

JOE KENNEDY / Los Angeles Times

A large section of the Coliseum stands was converted into an oversized press row for the worldwide media during track and field competition.

Arena boxing venue than at the Coliseum track this week.

Spivey met the press after Thursday night's 1,500-meter semifinal with a left eye so red and swollen it was almost closed. No, Spivey didn't get into a fight. He said he awoke one morning last week with what was diagnosed as a sty in his eye. He said doctors gave him clearance to race.

"It's a viral infection," Spivey said. "I don't know how or why it happened. There's also a lump (at his left temple) where the gland is puffed up. It hasn't bothered my running. They (doctors) almost thought I'd have to wear an eye patch."

The thought of wearing an eye patch sort of appealed to the good-natured Spivey. He said it might bring him some attention.

"Everybody looks at (Sebastian) Coe, (Steve) Scott, (Steve) Ovett, but I might even get on TV if I walked out there for the final with an eye patch."

—SAM McMANIS

□

The Colombian fighter who boxed without his contact lens is the athlete best remembered by Carole Baker, coordinator of the 24-hour clinics at the three Olympic villages.

"He just walked into the UCLA clinic one day by accident and found out he could get a free pair of lens," Baker said. "Suddenly, he could see again. He told us he lost the lens three months ago and had been boxing with one lens."

□

It took about 10 minutes after Mary Decker's tragic collision with Zola Budd in the 3,000 meters for the jokes to start circulating through the Main Press Center—official Olympic headquarters for black humor.

The first one-liner: Mary Decker lost the 3,000-meter race by a bare foot—Zola Budd's.

□

At the Rose Bowl Friday night, the nonpartisan crowd treated the European soccer players to a distinctly American phenomenon at halftime when it performed a "human wave," featuring spectators in successive sections of the bowl standing in turn with arms raised to create a wave effect.

The stadium announcer said the ripple went around the oval 14 times to set a world record.

□

Some former Olympians living in the San Francisco Bay Area are disturbed by the patriotic and commercial excesses they believe are ruining the spirit of the Olympic Games in Los Angeles.

"Not much thought was given to what nationality you were, at least not among the athletes," said Alex Tarics, a gold medalist with the Hungarian water polo team in the 1936 Berlin Olympics.

"We were all friendly with each other," he said. "We just wanted to excel among ourselves."

Roxanne Anderson, a member of Canada's 400-meter relay team that won a bronze medal in the 1936 Games, said: "It's all right to advertise the USA, but quite another thing to advertise somebody's sweatshirt."

"We didn't dare, in my day, wear anything that smacked of advertising," said Anderson, a former Amateur Athletic Union official who fought for the rights of women athletes during the 1950s.

□

American judo Coach Paul Maruyama hopes Bobby Berland's silver medal—America's first in the event—will help change the public perception of the sport.

"In America, at least, judo is still considered a martial art sport—a variation of kung fu or something like that, violence prone . . . not fit for any athlete," Maruyama said. "We've been suffering from a serious identity crisis."

□

A great deal of ink has been expended on judo's infamous "chokehold,'" most of it without full understanding of the maneuver.

American Team Manager Dr. Jim Wooley, himself a former Olympic competitor, explained the mechanics of the diabolic grip.

"You grab your opponent by the lapels of his *gi* (the judo uniform) and apply pressure to the sides of the neck—more precisely, to the carotid sinuses.

"You're decreasing the flow of blood to the brain, causing a physiological state of sleep, which isn't all that unpleasant.

"Ordinarily, you tap out (surrender) when you're in a chokehold, but you can pass out first without knowing it.

"The referees are alert to what's happening, though, and if they see the feet go limp, they stop the match."

Has Wooley ever been choked out?

"Oh, sure. Most of us have. You begin to snore, then to dream. Colorful dreams. It's amazing!"

—DICK RORABACK

□

The sport of fencing arose from, and gradually replaced, duels of honor. But there was some anticipation at Long Beach last week that two saber medal winners might meet again in the team finals and "settle" a little argument.

After the saber final won by Jean Francois Lamour, runner-up Marco Marin told a news conference that he lost because of the bout judging.

"I think I won the gold medal. I think he (Lamour) thinks the same thing," Marin said.

When the Italian's remarks were translated, Lamour responded: "I think I won the gold medal. I think his answer is strange."

The Frenchman, obviously miffed by the brash 21-year-old, left the news conference. But Christian D'Oriola, a widely respected fencing master, insisted that the two make up in the hallway and shake hands.

Nevertheless, when Italy and France met in the saber team finals a few nights later, those aware of the offstage spat waited for some fireworks. Marin won his first three bouts, but before his bout with Lamour came up, Italy had clinched victory with a 9-3 record, and the grudge match never took place.

—JOHN DART

□

Post-mortem on the U.S. women's field hockey bronze, the result of a shootoff that they came out of the stands to win:

—Coach Vonnie Gros said: "The team was at a party—more like a wake—the night before when our goalie, Gwen Cheeseman, figured out the math and said, 'Hey, we have a chance. We've gotta go home.' I was up at five in the morning going over my figures and figuring out my lineup."

—Beth Anders, who went rushing from the stands to suit up with three minutes left in the Australia-Holland game: "We were all running in different directions. First, I couldn't get out to my car, then I couldn't get out of the gate to get dressed. I was afraid I was going to miss it."

—Anders on the team's 10-for-10 shooting: "We've never done that. Not even in practice."

ON THE PASS LINE

PATRICK DOWNS / Los Angeles Times

Runners form a mass of humanity as batons are passed during a qualifying heat in the men's 400-meter relay race Friday at the Coliseum.

OLYMPICS '84

FINAL CURTAIN

Jim Murray

The World Came and Conquered All Our Hearts

Goodby, world. It was so nice to know you. Good of you to come.

Arrivederci, Italia. *Vaya con Dios,* Mexico. *Adios,* Espana. *Sayonara. Auf Wiedersehen. Adieu. Shalom.*

Turn out the lights. The party's over. Pack up the costumes. Put away the paper hats. Turn off the loudspeaker. Pay the band. We'll take one more cup of kindness yet for days of Auld Lang Syne, then pick up all the glasses and put them in the sink. Never mind the dishes. We'll take care of those tomorrow. Drive carefully. We don't want to lose anybody.

It's been a ball. Don't cry. Go out the way we came in, singing and dancing. A toast to absent friends, to loved ones who couldn't be here. Promise to write. Keep in touch. Thanks for the memories.

Thanks, Carl Lewis. You might have been a headache but you never were a bore, and you made it a benchmark Olympics.

Thanks, Rowdy Gaines and Rick Carey, and Tracy Caulkins and Tiffany Cohen, America's Sea World, for making the Olympic pool more fun than a school of dolphins around the Love Boat.

Thanks, Mary Lou Retton and Ecaterina Szabo for making us all 16 years old again and bringing to life a doll-shop window.

Thanks, China, for doing more to restore a historic friendship and affection between two peoples who have always loved each other than any Presidential mission could

ever have done.

Thanks, Romania, for showing us our struggles are with regimes not people and for not letting a bunch of pot-bellied generals deprive their kids of their golden moment in life. Wear your medals in health. Better yet, wear them in Russia.

Thank you, Comrade Chernenko for winning more gold medals for the United States than any athlete in history.

Thank you, Peter Ueberroth and Paul Ziffren and Harry Usher for showing Americans they didn't know their own strength and that their own politicians had too little faith in them.

Thanks, Mary Decker and Zola Budd, I'm sorry it had to come to this, but candidly, an Olympics without its raging controversy is no Olympics at all, is like a meal without wine. Thanks for the wine. It was a very good year.

Thanks to Paul Gonzales and for all the lovely little guys who bled and scarred for their medals and showed the kids of the world there's a better way out of the barrios and projects than a gun or knife or powder.

Thanks to Evander Holyfield for showing the world Americans are not all spoiled brats who curse officials, break rackets, abuse audiences and sulk and rant, by accepting a rank injustice with grace and courteousness and a nobility of spirit.

Thanks, Bobby Knight, for making a bunch of young men, no matter how gifted, realize it

Please see MURRAY, page 103

Olympics Go Out With a Big Bang —and Even More

By RICHARD HOFFER, *Times Staff Writer*

The Olympic flag was lowered and marched up the peristyle, suddenly bathed in a pink light. The Coliseum lights were dimmed. And the Olympic torch, which had blazed above the Coliseum like a refinery fire for 16 days and nights, was extinguished. Then four bombs exploded above, small white clouds left hanging in the night sky.

Some 100,000 people sitting in the ensuing silence did as told and pointed blue-lensed flashlights into the sky, producing a compacted bowl of city lights, a sparkling field, a carpet strewn with emeralds. It was a nearly extra-terrestrial sight, certainly one challenging to the senses; the heavens inverted in a concrete bowl.

The party was on, the biggest of its kind, a celebration of and for the athletes who had distinguished these 1984 Olympics with their achievement and their striving. A world was invited to watch, to enjoy their party, too. But Sunday night's Closing Ceremony, everybody's match for the gloriously excessive and

extravagant Opening Ceremony, belonged to the athletes, winners and losers, all clustered in the infield, their eyes, as usual, to the skies.

This all followed some pomp and circumstance, after medals were awarded in the marathon, which had finished inside the Coliseum, to the crowd's roar, and to the equestrians. They picked up the orange pylons after 78 had finished, declared the marathon over and marched in flags, banners and, of course, the athletes.

Peter Ueberroth, president of the Los Angeles Olympic Organizing Committee, assumed the huge stage, a structure that, with pools on two sides, resembled nothing so much as the parking lot of a Las Vegas casino. He thanked the athletes, then charged them with the responsibility of "a true victory lap," in which they would "go forth as ambassadors of peace and good will."

Juan Antonio Samaranch, president of the International Olympic Committee, assumed the stage.

Please see CLOSING, page 103

Lopes, 37, Wills a Marathon Win

JAYNE KAMIN / Los Angeles Times

With the rest of the field nowhere in sight, Portugal's Carlos Lopes wins the men's marathon.

Portuguese Runner Sets Olympic Mark

By MARLENE CIMONS,
Times Staff Writer

In the lifespan of marathoners, 37 is old. Very old. You just don't go out and win 26.2-mile races against young guys at that age.

What about experience, though? That's supposed to count for something, too, especially in the marathon. There are lessons in the marathon. Novices at such grueling events are usually not among the proven competitors.

Obviously, nobody told Carlos Lopes any of these things.

Lopes believes that a runner can stay tough and strong in middle age and has said so. All it takes, he has said, is the will to do so.

He proved it Sunday, winning the gold medal in an astonishing upset that nobody could have predicted.

"The keys are endurance and happiness," he said when it was over. "I bet on my youthfulness."

In a dramatic finale to the 1984 Olympic Games, Portugal's Lopes—in only the second marathon he has ever finished—outran everyone else who was favored. The field was an unusually strong and talented one that included world champion Rob de Castella of Australia, Toshihiko Seko of Japan, and world record-holder Alberto Salazar of the United States.

Lopes broke the old Olympic marathon record by 34 seconds, clocking 2 hours 9 minutes and 21 seconds.

The silver and bronze medal winners were as much a surprise as Lopes.

Ireland's John Treacy, running in his first marathon ever, was second in 2:09:56 for the silver, and Britain's Charlie Spedding, running in his third marathon, won the bronze in 2:09:58.

"When I got to 20 miles, I said, 'I'm feeling great—where's the wall?' " Treacy said.

Salazar, who holds the world record of 2:08:13, tried a new stategy that failed him badly. He planned to run an even, 5-minutes-per-mile pace, expecting to catch up to the fading leaders if he fell behind. It didn't happen. He just

Please see MARATHON, page 103

Louganis Overwhelms His Competition and Outdoes Even Himself

By SEYMOUR BEUBIS, *Times Staff Writer*

Call him the Baryshnikov of diving, the Superman of his sport, or the diver from another planet. For once, in the case of Greg Louganis, all the hyperbole accompanying a sports great might just be justified.

Yes, he did it again Sunday, winning his second Olympic gold medal in four days, this time in the men's 10-meter platform event.

He might have won more. But the one-meter springboard, at which Louganis also excels, is not an Olympic event.

Louganis, 24, of Mission Viejo, did it his way, fashioning a performance of grace and strength that overwhelmed his 11 opponents—and the judges.

He became the first diver in history to break 700 on the platform, one of his dreams, by scoring 710.91 points. The previous best score was a 688.05, which he established Saturday in the preliminary round.

His score beat second-place Bruce Kimball, 21, of Ann Arbor, Mich., by a staggering 67.41 points. And as is often his style, he led from the first dive through the 10th and last.

Louganis received five scores of 10 from the judges, but 9s and 9.5 flowed like champagne at a wedding.

A star-spangled, sun-drenched crowd of 10,278 loved it.

"You've just watched the greatest diver ever," said Ron O'Brien, Louganis' coach at Mission Viejo and co-coach of the U.S. diving team along with Dick Kimball.

"We won't see another like him in our lifetime," O'Brien added.

O'Brien staked a claim for Louganis as the best athlete in the Olympic event.

"His two gold medals are equal to Carl Lewis' four or maybe more," O'Brien said. "Greg only had two events, but you have to take into consideration just how dominant he was in them."

This is how dominant Louganis was. He won the platform by 67.41 points and the springboard by 92.10—and this against world-class competition in the Olympic Games, an unheard-of feat.

O'Brien equated Louganis' performance with someone running a 9.5-second 100-meter dash.

Dick Kimball likened it to a major league baseball player hitting .450.

In finishing second with 643.50 points, Kimball, 21, called "The Comeback Kid," because of his quick and successful return to diving after being seriously injured in an auto accident in 1981, staged

Please see LOUGANIS, page 103

CON KEYES / Los Angeles Times

Greg Louganis performs an inward 1½ somersault as he wins the 10-meter platform diving Sunday for his second gold medal.

TUESDAY: OLYMPICS '84 TAKES A LOOK BACK AT THE L.A. GAMES

MARATHON

Continued from page 102

fell more and more behind.

"I stayed through 17 miles, but after that I slowed down and they picked it up in the end," he said.

Despite several intensive weeks of heat training in Gainesville, Fla. and Houston, Salazar said "I've just never run a good race in the heat. Even with heat training, I didn't today. I'm disappointed, but I felt I did everything I could. Looking back 20 years from now, I'll never be able to say I didn't do everything I could."

Salazar finished 15th, running 2:14:19, his slowest marathon ever. He even placed behind teammate Pete Pfitzinger, who beat him last May in the U.S. trial. Pfitzinger was 11th in 2:13:53.

"I didn't feel all that good at the start, but I started feeling good later, at the freeway," Pfitzinger said. "But I guess if you only run the second half fast, that doesn't do much in the Olympics."

The third American, John Tuttle, dropped out at about the 12 mile mark.

"I was surprised that Lopes went so fast," Tuttle said. "The heat affected all of us."

Unlike the women's marathon a week ago—where gold medalist Joan Benoit took the lead after the third mile and never lost it—the men's marathon did not become a race until after the 22nd mile. There, Lopes, Treacy and Spedding broke away and made it a three-man battle. Between the 23rd and the 24th mile, Lopes was ahead and building his lead.

By the time he had reached the coliseum, his lead was nearly half a minute. Lopes, who has more experience on the track than on the roads, did not even need his well-known finishing kick. "At 35 kilometers, Lopes just took off," Treacy said. "Charlie and I tried to go with him, but we just didn't have it. At that point I knew I was just going for the silver."

It was a typical race for the first 20 miles. A huge pack of about 15, including de Castella, Seko, Lopes, Treacy, Spedding, Juma Ikangaa of Tanzania, Joseph Nzau of Kenya, Rod Dixon of New Zealand, Djama Robleh of Djibouti and Takeshi Soh of Japan, stayed together at a comfortable pace that translated into a 2:11 finishing time. But the leaders picked it up during the last six miles.

Everyone expected de Castella to begin surging at the 20th mile in an attempt to put some distance between himself and Seko—the man with the deadly kick. De Castella did make a move—but it was backward.

"I stopped to get a leading drink and when I looked up, the leading guys had 50 meters on me," de Castella said. "Before I knew it, it was 100. It was very hot, but I can't put it down to one or two things. I just on this day didn't have it. The other guys just ran better.In a marathon, I've learned not to be surprised by anything." He eventually finished fifth, in 2:11:09.

"He ran well," said his coach, Pat Clohessy. "He beat Ikangaa. He beat Salazar. He beat Seko and he beat Dixon. He fought it out--that's to his credit."

A mile after de Castella began to fade, Seko was the next casualty. Dropping back, he finished 14th in 2:14:13 and said after the race that he had been experiencing stomach problems since his arrival in Los Angeles.

Conditions for the race were not extreme. Temperatures ranged from 78 to 74, and the air quality was good.

This was Portugal's first gold medl of the games. A week ago in the women's marathon, Portugal's Rosa Mota was the surprise bronze medal winner.

Lopes, a loan officer in a Lisbon bank, has started four marathons and finished two, including Sunday's. He dropped out of the 1982 New York City Marathon after 20 miles. In that race, he stopped to avoid bumping into a woman crossing the street and his legs cramped. He also dropped out of the Rotterdam Marathon this past April.

In 1983, however, he ran a stunning 2:08:39, only 2 seconds behind de Castella, who finished first.

Lopes, who also won the world cross country championships in New York in March, said Sunday that he wants to compete for another year and then retire.

The 1976 Olympic silver medalist in the 10,000 meters, Lopes alsorecently ran a personal best at that distance, 27 minutes 17.48 seconds, second only to the world record of his countryman, Fernando Mamede.

Lopes said he was convinced he was going to win after about 37 kilometers.

"It was very difficult, because in a marathon you can feel very good or very bad at 40 kilometers," Lopes said. "I came prepared to win--and to lose.

"When I entered the stadium, I felt very happy,"he said. "I felt compensated for all the hard work."

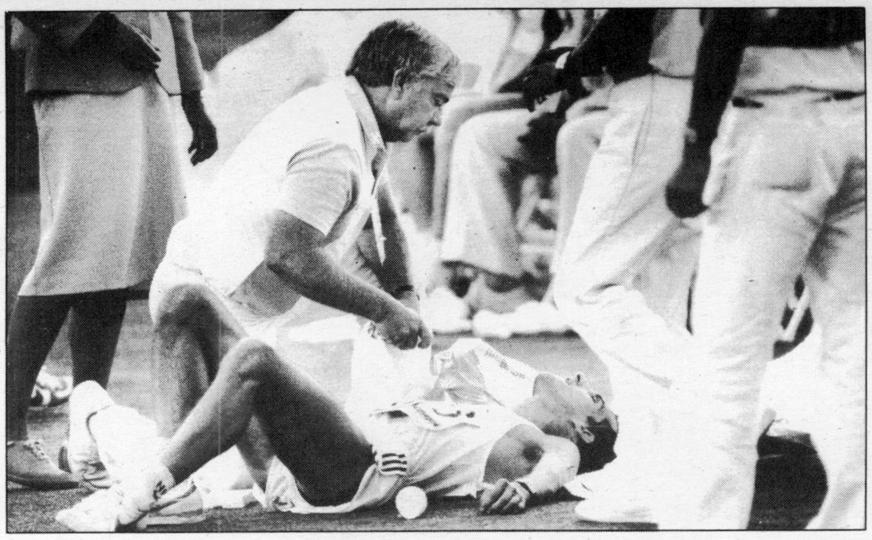

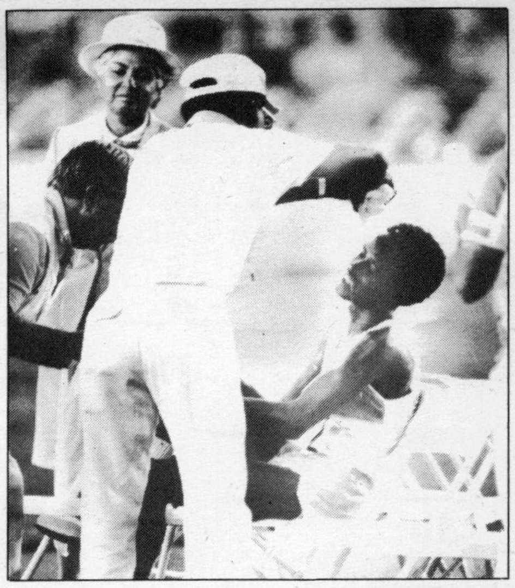

JAYNE KAMIN / Los Angeles Times

Medical assistance is sometimes required by marathon runners. Lee Hong Yul of South Korea (left) and Abdullahij Ahmed of Somalia receive attention in Sunday's event.

MURRAY

Continued from page 102

was a privilege to play for your country that is not to be lightly taken or cheaply earned, and for showing that our young people are not cynical or jaded but yearning for leadership, for how else do men become leaders?

Thanks to Daley Thompson and Sebastian Coe, the Great Brits. They beat one-half of the world in their specialties in the Moscow Olympics and now have done exactly the same to the other half of the world. They have certified an Olympics is an Olympics.

Thanks, soccer fans. You've been yelling you'd support first rate foreign football if it came attached with nationalistic trappings. Damned if you didn't.

Thanks, ABC, for one of the greatest stories ever told. So, you waved the flag a little bit. Who did it hurt? Take a tip: Never apologize.

Thanks to security for keeping the story on the track, the pool, the lake and the pitch and not the hospitals, the morgues and the chancelleries and making the only "tragedies" of the Games runners falling down.

Thanks to Baron de Coubertin. What a lovely idea he had! Thanks to the Juan Samaranches, Madame Berlioux and Lord Killanins who persevered through boycotts, revolutions, wars, hijackings, terrorism and murder to keep the Baron's ideals going, like riding three horses going in opposite directions at once.

Thanks, Hollywood and David Wolper and Tommy Walker and C.B. DeMille and Flo Ziegfeld and Victor Herbert and Irving Berlin and Beethoven and Deanna Durbin and Guiseppe Verdi, the All-American marching band, 76 trombones, and whoever else had anything to do with the non-athletic portions of the opening and closing extravaganzas.

Thanks to every guy and girl who never won a medal, thanks to every marathoner who finished 78th, every sprinter who missed out in the heats, every jumper who missed the finals.

Thanks to the gallant horses who jumped the bridges, thanks to the men who held the stopwatches, measured the hurdles, raised the crossbars, refereed the contests, took the tickets, moved the traffic or just answered the phones.

Thanks to Robbie Burns for "Auld Lang Syne." Without it, we wouldn't have known how to say goodby. Nobody wanted to anyway.

They doused the L. A. Olympic flame at 9:30. But where it glows, in a nation's heart, it can never go out. The Games went out as they had come in—on a note of joy, and hope and promise. America gave a party and the world came. The ones you want at your party anyway. The world's Olympians. Victors all.

We'll miss them. May they come back soon.

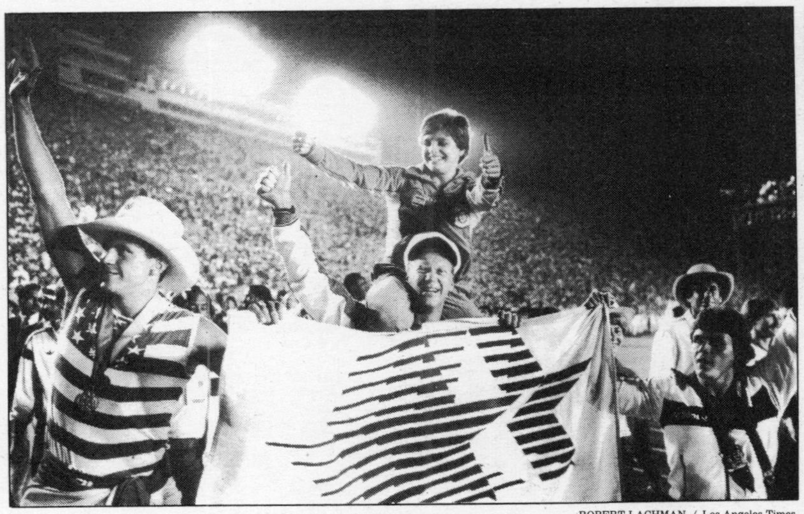

ROBERT LACHMAN / Los Angeles Times

Among those with a huge reason to celebrate the closing of the '84 Olympic Games in Los Angeles Sunday night is Mary Lou Retton, women's all-around gymnastics champion.

CLOSING

Continued from page 102

"I now declare," he said, "the Games of the XXIII Olympiad closed."

But the party was on. David Wolper's production, a down-home effort during the Opening Ceremony, moved the crowd a century ahead in time Sunday, achieving a futuristic effect of happy proportions.

A "saucer" suddenly emerged out of the darkness, a great ring of strobing lights, that hovered above the peristyle. Suspended—presumably—from a helicopter, the saucer lingered, finally achieving communication. As the Olympic trumpets sounded the notes to the theme from "2001;" the saucer tentatively answered, in the synthesized voice we ascribe to aliens. First the trumpets. Then the saucer. Slow, at first. Then faster, the core of the saucer turning a molten red, then strobing out in a flare of neon before it drifted out of sight, back to the stars.

Out of the darkness, green lasers laced the sky, fanning out to light the seats, accompanied by great stings of sound.

And then, and then . . . it just kept happening. A man hooded in metal, a strange man, was lit, standing under the torch, way above the Coliseum. With light focused on him, he said, "I have come a long way because I like what I am seeing . . . I salute you."

Fireworks lit the eastern skies, great firebombs, for nearly half an hour. And at their conclusion, pop singer Lionel Richie took the strange stage and sang a 12-minute, Olympic version of his hit "All Night Long." Smoke flooded the stage, sparks erupted. And 200 break dancers, kids right off the Los Angeles streets, ringed it, breakin' and poppin', all night long.

Though the show seemed to belong to the backstage wizards, with their wonderful special effects, their cages full of doves, their dancing waters, their huge balloons, their laser lights, it was not really their party.

If there was any doubt as to who these games belonged to, it established earlier, midway through the ceremonies when the athletes were finally admitted to the Coliseum. The International Olympic Committee had lifted its "six athletes per country" rule earlier in the day, acknowledging the unusual demand for athlete participation, and had allowed all interested athletes to march onto the Coliseum floor.

And there they were, thronging the entrance to the Coliseum, threatening to overrun the stately procession of flag bearers, 400 in all, and the sober march of each nation's representative, carrying the 140 identifying placards.

Great clots of athletes trailed the dignified parade, carrying flags, banners—"L.A., We Love it!"—and even other athletes. Little Mary Lou Retton, the gymnast who flew through the air to a nation's unqualified delight, rode through it this night, atop another athlete's shoulders.

It was as spontaneous as anything that has happened in these 16 days, demonstrating not so much the Olympic spirit as, well, just spirit. U.S. gymnast James Hartung marched shirtless, tucked inside a baffled formation of white-flag bearers. He waved to the crowd. Australians marched around the track, carrying square yards of their flag. They bounced a girl with a knapsack up and down in it.

Then it got out of control. Meant to mass in the infield, protected from the stage by a ring of white-uniformed flag bearers, the athletes instead broke back onto the track. First the Australians, hauling their huge flag onto the track for one more lap. Then the athletes from Great Britain sailed the Union Jack into the race.

The public address announcer said, above the roar of the crowd, "Please leave the track and return to the center." He said it twice and more nations flooded the track, some going one on one in collision courses. The athletes, presumably tired of their game, were finally collected in the infield.

Many pronouncements, many little effects that tested imagination and challenged our more normal conceptions of what a party should or could be.

In the end, it came to the traditional singing of "Auld Lang Syne." Huge balloons floated into the sky as "76 Trombones" was played. Then "If My Friends Could See Me Now." The athletes danced, waved flags and refused to leave the field.

It must have been a sight indeed, as the Olympic gods looked down, smiling on the hurly-burly of youth, athletes joined hand in hand, ringed along the track, celebrating an achievement of joy as much as of athletics.

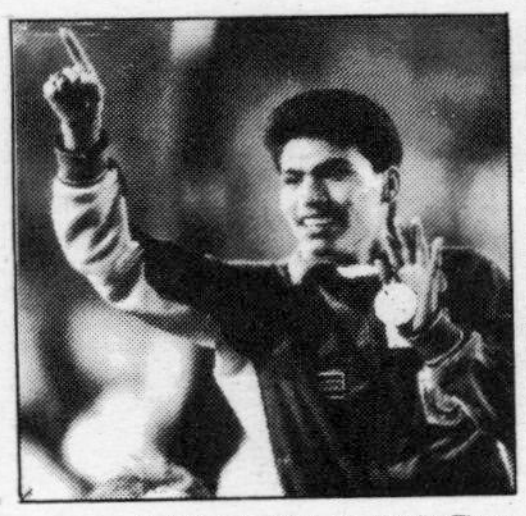

JAYNE KAMIN / Los Angeles Times

Boxer Paul Gonzales of Los Angeles proudly displays gold medal during Closing Ceremony Sunday at the Coliseum.

LOUGANIS

Continued from page 102

another comeback.

He was fourth after seven dives, but his last three were things of beauty, and they, combined with some poor late dives by the two Chinese competitors, Li Kongzheng, 25, and Tong Hui, 21, won Kimball the silver medal.

Li took the bronze with a score of 638.28.

The victory by Louganis gave him a place in the record book. He became only the third person in Olympic history to win both the three-meter springboard and the platform.

Peter Desjardins of the United States did it in 1928 and Albert White, also of the United States, accomplished it in 1924.

Louganis said he felt great about his accomplishments. He admitted being scared just before doing his last dive, even though the victory was virtually certain unless he completely blew the dive. (He was 52 points ahead of Li at the time).

"But then I thought whatever I do my mother is going to love me and I went for it," Louganis said.

He nailed his final dive, a reverse 3½ somersault tuck, with a 3.4 degree of difficulty, the highest in the book in platform, for four 9s and a 9.5 for a total of 92.82 points.

But his best dive of the day was his ninth, a back 3½ somersault tuck, 3.3 degree of difficulty. He drilled it for five 9.5s and 94.05 points.

Louganis said that breaking the 700-point barrier has always been a dream.

"I feel good because I finally put it together. I knew that I was on the verge of doing that and it felt good. This was like a dream come true. You want your best performance to be at the Olympic Games."

O'Brien said he has never seen Louganis dive any better from the platform then he did on Sunday. "He couldn't have done it at a better time."

Bruce Kimball said he regarded the 710.91 score by Louganis "as a great one. Probably no one will come close to it for a long time with the exception of Greg."

Louganis' win also gave the United States the most gold medals in the eight days of diving competition.

Of the four gold medals available, Louganis won two, in both men's events; Sylvie Bernier, 20, of Canada, won the women's three-meter springboard, and Zhou Jihong, 19, of China reigned in the women's 10-meter platform.

Each of the seven U.S. diving Olympians won a medal.

Besides Louganis and Kimball, Kelly McCormick, 24, of Columbus, Ohio, and Chris Seufert, 27, of Ann Arbor, Mich., took the silver and bronze in the springboard behind Bernier. Michele Mitchell, 22, and Wendy Wyland, 19, both of Mission Viejo, went 2-3 behind Zhou in the women's platform, and Ron Merriott, 24, of Ann Arbor, won the bronze in the men's springboard.

Out of the 12 medals available in the competition, only Bernier was able to crack the U.S.-China dominance of the sport.

The United States finished with two gold, three silver and three bronze medals. China won one gold, one silver and one bronze.

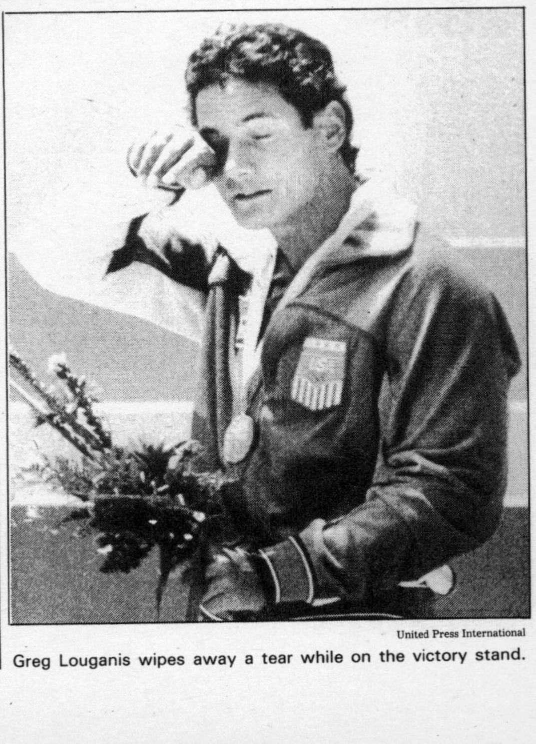

United Press International

Greg Louganis wipes away a tear while on the victory stand.

Perfect Finish by Fargis Has a Touch of Class

By LYNN SIMROSS, *Times Staff Writer*

It was a first class day for American rider Joe Fargis on this last day of Olympic equestrian competition at Santa Anita.

Fargis and his little bay mare, Touch of Class, outjumped teammate Conrad Homfeld and Abdullah for the individual gold medal, with a no-fault round in a tension-packed jumpoff for the gold.

The gold-silver finish for Fargis and Homfeld, who run a horse farm in Petersburg, Va., gave the United States its first one-two individual Olympic show jumping medalists since equestrian sports became a permanent part of the Games in 1912. The only other show jumping gold for the United States was won by Bill Steinkraus at Mexico City in 1968.

"This is the greatest moment by far in my life," Fargis said after winning before a crowd of 32,904. "But I don't think I'll be a celebrity. I don't feel like a celebrity.

"I hope this finish for Conrad and me helps glamorize and promote our sport, but Moses Malone (of basketball's Philadelphia 76ers) is still the most famous person in Petersburg."

Taking the bronze medal was Switzerland's Heidi Robbiani, 33, a relative newcomer to this level of competition. She rode in her first international Grand Prix in Rome in May, 1982.

Robbiani, aboard Jessica V, scored a clean round in the separate jumpoff for the bronze medal. She beat out Canada's Mario Deslauriers, who had four faults,

and her Swiss teammate Bruno Candrian, with eight faults. Four faults are assessed for each rail down on the course.

In the first round, the riders were faced with 12 obstacles, 15 fences in all, and in the second, 10 obstacles (13 fences). The jumpoffs were contested over six obstacles (7 fences).

All three medalists said the course, designed by former U.S. show jumping coach, Bertalan de Nemethy, was a challenge.

"This is the biggest, dimension-wise, I ever jumped with her," Fargis said, referring to his 16 hand, 11-year-old mare.

"And with the word Olympics wrapped around it, and being the home team, it made it even tougher."

But Sunday, Fargis' horse, a race track reject, showed her class, just as she did in the team competition last Tuesday, when the pair had two clean rounds in leading the United States to the team gold medal, this country's first.

Fargis said that in becoming such an outstanding jumper, Touch of Class finally found something she liked to do.

"She's a former racehorse," Fargis said of his horse which raced six times at Eastern tracks, with a top finish of seventh. "And she wasn't successful at that. She was a hunter. And she wasn't successful at that. Then she became a jumper. She's done well at that."

Until Sunday, though, Touch of Class, had not convinced everyone in the equestrian community. Horsemen felt that Touch of Class was too small to make it around such a huge course. Fences in the first

ANACLETO RAPPING / Los Angeles Times
Joe Fargis salutes Santa Anita crowd after winning gold medal.

ANACLETO RAPPING / Los Angeles Times
Joe Fargis of Petersburg, Va., urges Touch of Class over a 10-rail fence en route to a gold medal.

Equestrian

THE MEDALISTS

■ INDIVIDUAL JUMPING

1. Joe Fargis (U.S.)

2. Conrad Homfeld (U.S.)

3. Heidi Robbiani (Switzerland)

round ranged up to 5 feet, 10 inches in height. The water jump, used in both the first and second rounds, but not the jumpoffs, was a chasm of 15-6.

Fifty-one riders from 18 nations competed in the first round, with the top 25 advancing. However, after one round, three riders were tied for 25th, so 27 riders saddled up for round two.

At the end of the first round, only two pairs had clean rounds—Fargis and Touch of Class, and Britain's Michael Whitaker, with his mare Overton Amanda. Homfeld had four faults after the first round as did his teammate Melanie Smith aboard Calypso.

In the second round, Homfeld and Abdullah went without a miss. That put the pressure on Fargis and Touch of Class. Only a perfect round would take the gold outright. The pair went through smoothly and effortlessly, but rolled the last rail, setting up the jumpoff for the gold.

Whitaker, riding last, fell out of the running for the top prize when he sustained 28.5 penalty points in the triple-combination. He dropped to 24th.

In the jumpoff, Homfeld and Abdullah performed well but knocked down two fences.

"I just wanted to be neat and quick," said Homfeld, 32. "At least see that I didn't give it away, that he had to come after me."

Fargis had watched Homfeld's ride and then he and Touch of Class came through with the perfect ride when they needed it.

Surprisingly, he said the second round was actually tougher than the jumpoff because the course was the "biggest course I've jumped on her." Fargis said he "didn't know for sure" she could jump that well,

but "I didn't have a big doubt."

The second round was troublesome for most riders, especially the No. 3 obstacle, a high oxer called the Beverly Hills. Coming out of a sharp turn after No. 2, the competitors could not determine how many strides their mounts would need to get to and over the fence at No. 3.

No. 3 undid Smith and Calypso, her Dutch-bred gelding. The pair knocked down the No. 3, and then rolled off the top bar at the last fence for a two-round total of 12. Had the pair cleared the last fence, they would have gotten to the jumpoff for the bronze. As it was, Smith, who collected a team gold Tuesday, finished in seventh place.

Since Touch of Class and Homfeld's stallion Abdullah emerged as the class of the field, Fargis was asked if the two horses might be mated soon. Fargis smiled and said: "It's not up to us, but certainly not tomorrow. Maybe in five or six years."

Fargis explained that the owners of both horses would decide that question. Sandron Inc. owns Touch of Class; Sue B. Williams, Abdullah.

As the two American medalists completed their press conference before heading to the Coliseum for the closing ceremonies, a grinning Frank Chapot, the U.S. show jumping coach, sat nearby.

"It feels very good that we were so successful," Chapot said.

All in all, the American equestrian team ended up with three golds and two silvers, its best showing ever in the Olympics.

Both the show jumping and three-day event squads took gold team medals. Fargis and Homfeld, gold and silver individual in show jumping, and Karen Stives, of Dover, Mass., individual three-day silver.

OK, Wave the Flag, but for the Right Reasons

The Olympic Games were a roaring success. Nobody died. Pins were traded. No terrorists struck. Traffic moved. The LAOOC made a bundle of money. More pins were traded. Athletes tried their hardest. The best of them won gold medals. Even more pins were traded. And Los Angeles survived with its reputation and its streets mostly intact—no small feat.

The Opening Ceremony was a critical success. The Closing Ceremony was performed with all the flash and schmaltz any Hollywood production could hope to muster. They didn't have any flying saucers visiting Moscow.

So why did I leave the Coliseum Sunday night feeling vaguely dissatisfied with the whole affair?

It hit me sometime during the Closing Ceremony when a hundred nations' athletes broke out of long months of training to join in a mass tribute to themselves. They formed a wonderfully disorganized parade, everyone marching to his or her individual drummer. There was a lot of embracing and mugging, climbing on shoulders, kisses blown to the crowd, and,

most of all, an overriding sense of group accomplishment.

You could feel the joy on the stadium floor clear up to the cheap seats (which went for $50 each.)

It was no less than a breakout. The stadium announcer pleaded for athletes to return to the center of the field and many of them plain refused, running around the track instead. *Having fun.*

Yes, it was wonderful. Except that it gave the lie to this Olympic movement. And to this Olympic fortnight.

These Olympics were less a celebration of the athletes than they were a celebration of America. ABC-TV knew from the beginning it would be that way, and they unashamedly played to the Sunday patriots.

What is patriotism? That's too deep a question for this space in the newspaper, but I'm sure that waving flags at American athletes has nothing whatever to do with it.

Two weeks ago, little American flags outside the various venues were going for three bucks. On Sunday afternoon, the

Mike Littwin

vendors outside the Coliseum were unloading their remaining flags for a buck, in a kind of patriotic closeout sale.

I was disappointed four years ago in the orgy of self-congratulation that followed America's miracle upset of the nasty Soviets in ice hockey. I wondered why so many in this nation felt it necessary to identify so closely with victory in a sports arena. Did it prove somehow that our way of life was better? If so, what would it have meant if the U.S. team had lost?

But, at least, at Lake Placid there was sports drama. Everyone likes it when the little guys beat the big guys.

So how do you account for what happened here?

The Soviets decided to pay us back for boycotting their Olympics by boycotting ours. The East Germans reluctantly joined them, thus reducing the world's sports giants from three to one.

And the remaining giant beat up on the rest of the world.

The giant was us and we cheered him to the very end. You wouldn't pay to see the Raiders playing Cal State Northridge. You wouldn't cheer when Lyle Alzado ran over some 180-pound lineman.

But that's what we did these two weeks. It was OK to cheer and it was OK to root. But was it OK to feel that we accomplished something? Individual athletes accomplished something, many against inferior competition. But, in any case, you and I did no more than watch.

Joe Fargis won a medal in equestrian individual jumping, a sport so obscure that most people have no idea what it entails except that there is a rider and a horse. But he was an American, and he got a roar of approval from the huge Coliseum crowd. It didn't matter what he won. It mattered only where he came from.

There are some Olympic ideals that make little or no sense—say amateurism. The rich old men set amateurism as an Olympic standard only to exclude the working class. Well, in more egalitarian

times, we've found a way to make a sham of amateurism. Athletes can make money and still compete. Jim Thorpe would be proud.

But the idea that athletes and not countries are competing has been lost long ago. But I wonder if it was ever so obscured as it has been here.

My favorite Olympian was Britain's Daley Thompson, so enchanting in a roguish sort of way. The world's greatest athlete loves to compete and he loves to have fun, poking fun at himself, at princesses, at the world.

He is my Olympic ideal. He is someone to root for. Carl Lewis and Mary Lou Retton, root for them, too.

But if Americans want to wave flags, wave them for the right reasons. Wave them because the United States put on an impressive Games, because the locals were helpful and friendly, because athletes can compete in this country to please only themselves, because most people here have plenty of food in their bellies.

That's why I'm proud. Carl Lewis and the rest have nothing to do with it.

PATRICK DOWNS / Los Angeles Times

A capacity Coliseum crowd, gathered for the Closing Ceremony, watch marathon runners circling the stadium track. Portugal's Carlos Lopes won the gold medal in the last competition of L.A. Games.

Long Race Ends in Living Room Venue

It's Sunday evening and you've been glued to your television for 16 days and nights now.

It hasn't been easy, but you're tough. You prepared for this by watching the full slate of USFL games and videotapes of the Winter Olympics.

There were times you could have given up, when the going got tough.

I was walking down the street the other day and through an open front door I heard, honest, a man in genuine anguish: "Every time I turn on the TV it's that stupid Howard Cosell."

You've made a lot of sacrifices to achieve your goal of watching the entire Olympics, wire to wire. You have a lot of people you'd like to thank. Your mother and father, who bought you your first television. The pizza delivery man . . .

There were times you thought of giving up. Times when you grew weary, when it seemed like equestrian events would never end, times when you found yourself trying to carry on conversations with Jim McKay.

I was out at the events a lot, but I think I know how you feel. My wife and I happened to be in a department store Friday evening and we hurried to the TV section to watch the women's 3,000-meter race.

We watched the rows and rows of TV sets, watched in shock as 42 Zola Budds collided with 42 Mary Deckers, sending the 42 Deckers crashing to 42 Coliseum infields.

By now you're on a first-name basis with "our kids"—Carl, Evelyn, Evander, Peter, Rowdy, Mary, Mary Lou, Mary T. They became like family. You got up close and personal with Jurgen Hingsen's wife as she ironed Jurgen's underwear and with Greg Louganis as he bodysurfed.

Scott Ostler

By Day 5, it was becoming difficult to tell where the regular coverage left off and the commercials began. You found yourself rooting for airport luggage handlers who were going for the gold.

You became proficient at scoring springboard dives and epee lunges and pommel-horse routines. You learned to critique the pace of the marathoners and the stride of the steeplechasers. Someday, you are confident, that knowledge will come in handy.

They tried to spoil it for you. Halfway through the Games, the media tried to tell you the TV coverage was too pro-American, the TV announcers were cheerleading our kids and ignoring the athletes from, say, Trinidad and Tobago, which you thought were brand names for RV motor homes.

You liked the coverage. What did these people think you wanted to hear more than the Star Spangled Banner? Volga Boatman?

But red, white and blue or otherwise, you couldn't get enough. You read somewhere that as recently as 1960, they televised one hour per day of Olympic coverage. One hour! Hell, you were logging one hour a day of up close and personal features on Olympic pin trading; more than an hour a day of candy commercials.

You felt a pang of loneliness when old Jim signed off every night, and you kept the TV on just in case they came back with a bulletin, or another short feature on pin trading.

Then the critics tried to nitpick your Games to death. They called it the overkill Olympics, and the

overpriced Games. They said it was too Hollywood and too L.A. They were expecting what? A Wyoming-style ambiance? If they wanted a bland Olympics, they should have lobbied to hold the thing in Des Moines.

From your venue, your living room, it was a grand show. And now you're watching the Closing Ceremony, where people have paid $500 apiece to watch the show in person, the highlight of the first two hours of which was the awarding of some equestrian medals.

But you weren't going to tune out now. You've paid an even bigger price. You've come too far to throw in the towel this close to the finish line. The spirit of Gabriella.

Now here's a flying saucer hovering over the Coliseum, and laser beams piercing the night air. Will Kathleen Sullivan interview the alien? Will Jim Lampley give us UFO stats?

Now there are fireworks and 100,000 colored flashlights and happy music, or are you hallucinating?

Bring on the break dancers, the chorus lines and orchestras and Lionel Ritchie. You're hot. You're ready to watch "All Night Long." They're not going to stop you now.

And now, finally, it's over.

You've done it, pal. You turn off the TV. It's still smoking, like a pistol.

You've gone the distance. You're tired but happy. How can you ever go back to "Dallas" and "Love Boat" and real TV?

You know the Olympic people aren't going to knock on your door, shake your hand and place a gold medal around your neck.

But you're a competitor and *you* know when you've turned in a gold medal performance. You feel good. You smile at the blank TV screen.

SPORT	GOLD	SILVER	BRONZE	TOTAL
Archery (2)	1	1	0	2
Basketball (2)	2	0	0	2
Boxing (12)	9	1	1	11
Canoeing (12)	0	0	1	1
Cycling (8)	4	3	2	9
Diving (4)	2	3	3	8
Equestrian (6)	3	2	0	5
Fencing (8)	0	0	1	1
Field Hockey (2)	0	0	1	1
Gymnastics (14)	5	5	6	16
Judo (8)	0	1	1	2
Modern Pentathlon (2)	0	1	0	1
Rowing (14)	2	5	1	8
Rhythmic Gymnastics (1)	0	0	0	0
Shooting (11)	3	1	2	6
Soccer (1)	0	0	0	0
Swimming (29)	21	13	0	34
Synchronized Swimming (2)	2	0	0	2
Team Handball (2)	0	0	0	0
Track and Field (41)	16	15	9	40
Volleyball (2)	1	1	0	2
Water Polo (1)	0	1	0	1
Weightlifting (10)	0	1	1	2
Wrestling/Greco-Roman (10)	2	1	1	4
Wrestling/Freestyle (10)	7	2	0	9
Yachting (7)	3	4	0	7
Total Medals (221)	83	61	30	174

MEDALS WON BY THE U.S. IN THE 1984 SUMMER GAMES

Number of gold medals U.S. could have won in parenthesis.

Yasuhiro Yamashita of Japan, gold medalist in Olympic judo open division, celebrates victory with teammates.

CELEBRATION!

Yugoslavia team handball players wave from victory stand after winning gold medal.

Gabriella Dorio of Italy won 1500 meters.

High jumper Patrik Sjoberg of Sweden takes silver medal.

Great Britain's Sebastian Coe lets out a yell, above, as he crosses finish line for gold medal and Olympic record in 1,500-meters.

Left, Tyrell Biggs of the U.S. wins super-heavyweight title in boxing.

All photos by Times photographers except where noted. Designed by Tom Trapnell

Top: American Mark Schultz does flip after winning gold medal in 180.5-pound freestyle wrestling division. **Middle:** Lou Banach rides on shoulders of his brother Ed after winning gold medal in 220-pound freestyle wrestling. Ed won gold in 198-pound division. **Bottom:** South Korean freestyle wrestler You In Tak needs help getting onto stand to receive gold medal in 149.5-pound division.

Raul Gonzalez of Mexico, winner of 50-kilometer walk.

Salute to Medalists, Well Known and Unknown

After six Olympics, it's only natural, I expect, for them to run together in the mind.

Let's see. It was the 10,000 at Munich where Lasse Viren fell down, then got up to win and set the world record, wasn't it? Or was it the 5,000 at Montreal?

It was at Tokyo, wasn't it, that the Tunisian Gammoudi crashed into the field on the last lap and knocked the Australian Ron Clarke out of all chance. Or did the pictures show he knocked Billy Mills out of it, but Mills won, anyway?

Did you actually say to a Canadian journalist in the midst of the first heat of the 1,500 at Munich: "What's Jim Ryun doing running back there in the pack with all those rinky-dinks, he's liable to be knocked down!" or do you now only think you did?

You looked up just in time to see Bob Beamon's record jump at Mexico City, even though you were across the track chatting with

Jim Murray

Jesse Robinson at the time, didn't you? Of course, you did. Who would be buying a Coke at a time like that?

But medals do not always go to the swift or victories to the brave. We have today, accordingly, updated our own honors list, medals going to individuals whom you might not otherwise be celebrating today. The medal is in the form of a bottle cap held together by two pieces of Kleenex and bearing the Latin words for "Lower, Slower and Fatter." America leads in this medal count, too. They go to:

(1) Any journalist who could write one complete story on women's gymnastics without using the word *pixie*.

(2) Any country that had a national anthem you could leave the stadium humming.

(3) Any journalist, print or electronic, who could open an interview with something other than, "Slug, your feelings, if you can tell us, on winning the (gold, silver, bronze, last place)? Your thoughts right now."

(4) Any competitor who has just won a gold medal and doesn't say, "It hasn't hit me yet."

(5) Any spectator who just paid $200 a seat and happened to be bending down getting a tuna fish sandwich during a race and looked up and said, "What's Mary Decker doing lying down on the ground like that for? Is the race over?"

(6) Any homeowner who bought a new stereo, refrigerator, bedroom set or RV on time plan figuring he would get the payments from $50-a-day parking fees on his Exposition Park area lawn.

Please see MURRAY, page 108

Joan Benoit

Carl Lewis

Mary Lou Retton

Greg Louganis

Peter Vidmar

Li Ning

Daley Thompson

Carlos Lopes

Valerie Brisco-Hooks

Faces Above the Crowd

Just as in every Olympics, the Games of the XXIII Olympiad produced a new group of heroes, some of whom on a future day will be remembered as Olympic legends. From the surrounding gallery of gold medal winners, the future legends will perhaps include Carl Lewis, the winner of four gold medals in track; Joan Benoit, the winner of the first women's marathon, and Daley Thompson, only the second man to win consecutive decathlons. For all of those who took part, it was a memorable 16 days.

Contributing to this page were Los Angeles Times photographers Tony Barnard, Larry Bessel, Patrick Downs, Dave Gatley, Skeeter Hagler, Jayne Kamin and Ken Lubas.

Cheryl Miller

MURRAY

Continued from page 107

(7) Any ticket broker who promised to take his wife to the Greek Isles on the proceeds from scalping track and field tickets who passed on a chance to buy soccer tickets because, "These are Raider fans; they don't like any game you play only with the feet."

(8) To Gabriela Andersen-Schiess, the Swiss marathoner, for getting more publicity out of the event than the winner. For instance, did you know who won the 1908 marathon, the one where Dorando Pietri collapsed in the stretch? It was Johnny Hayes, an American department store clerk and now a trivia answer. Dorando got songs written about him, including one by Irving Berlin. For the record, Joan Benoit won the 1984 marathon, but Gabriela will be a song title.

(9) To a young runner who ran up on the heels of a British competitor and tumbled to the ground and lost all chance for a medal. Mary Decker? Hardly. No, it was Pierre Deleze, who tumbled over Steve Ovett at the very finish line of his heat in the 1,500, a race that would have put him in the semifinals. His fall aroused no international controversy, no "Is Ovett Guilty?" headlines. No discus thrower carried him off the track. Ovett didn't apologize to him. All that happened was that some official came up to him and said: "Get up, you're holding up traffic," and someone else said crankily: "Can't you watch where you're going? You could've cost Steve the race!"

(10) To the Soviet track and field team for outstanding sportsmanship in leaving all those gold and silver medals lying around to be picked up by the American athletes. The Americans did the same thing for them in 1980, and I'm sure they just wanted to return the favor.

(11) To that 11-year-old mare that got claimed out of some county fair races in West Virginia, where she went off at boxcars and never won but who became a combination of Black Beauty and Trigger for one night in the Coliseum, the most famous since the one who fanned Roy Rogers with his hat.

(12) To Seoul, Korea. Don't worry, the Russians will come. Will they ever!

THE FINAL MEDAL COUNT

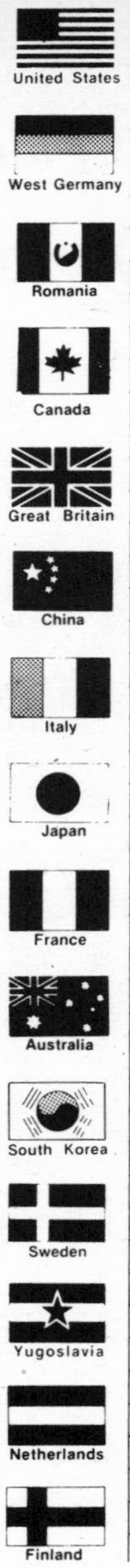

COUNTRY	GOLD	SILVER	BRONZE	TOTAL
United States	83	61	30	174
West Germany	17	19	23	59
Romania	20	16	17	53
Canada	10	18	16	44
Britain	5	10	22	37
China	15	8	9	32
Italy	14	6	12	32
Japan	10	8	14	32
France	5	7	15	27
Australia	4	8	12	24
South Korea	6	6	7	19
Sweden	2	11	6	19
Yugoslavia	7	4	7	18
Netherlands	5	2	6	13
Finland	4	3	6	13
New Zealand	8	1	2	11
Brazil	1	5	2	8
Switzerland		4	4	8
Mexico	2	3	1	6
Denmark		3	3	6
Spain	1	2	2	5
Belgium	1	1	2	4
Austria	1	1	1	3
Portugal	1		2	3
Jamaica		1	2	3
Norway		1	2	3
Turkey			3	3
Venezuela			3	3
Morocco	2			2
Kenya	1		1	2
Greece		1	1	2
Nigeria		1	1	2
Puerto Rico		1	1	2
Algeria			2	2
Pakistan	1			1
Colombia		1		1
Egypt		1		1
Ireland		1		1
Ivory Coast		1		1
Peru		1		1
Syria		1		1
Thailand		1		1
Cameroon			1	1
Dom. Republic			1	1
Iceland			1	1
Taiwan			1	1
Zambia			1	1

Rick Reilly / Impressions

Moments That Last a Lifetime

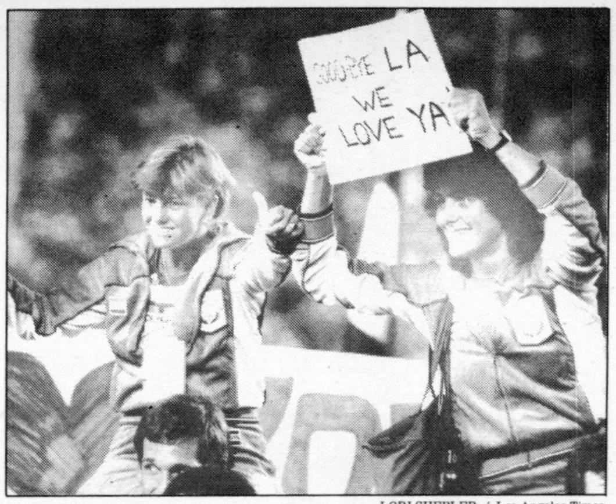

LORI SHEPLER / Los Angeles Times

There were many moments to celebrate during L.A. Olympics, and these two athletes did just that during closing ceremonies.

It is not so easy to find the real Olympics, so you take them where you can get them. For me:

—They were in the sneeze of Chinese gymnast Li Ning, who unleashed an Olympic-size ahchoo one day and said, "Thank you." Li howled with laughter right along with the rest of us, though he knew not why.

—They were not in the wallet of American volleyball player Craig (Fast) Buck, who opened himself up for business on the last day outside the Coliseum and slapped a price tag on memories.

Big sale! Everything must go! And did go, including Buck's team warm-ups ($110), jerseys, practice T-shirts, team pins, even the bags he carried them in. "Figure I'll make a few hundred dollars," said Buck, whose American team won the gold medal.

Hey, by the way, where's the medal, Craig?

Craig . . . ?

—They were in the fickle knees and unforgettable face of Swiss marathoner Gabriela Andersen-Schiess, who deserved to ride out on the shoulders of athletes—not medics—after running the longest lap of her, and our, lives.

—They were not in the heart of Mary Decker, whose Olympic Experience consisted of checking into not one but two swank hotels, leaving spike marks on the calf and heel of 18-year-old Zola Budd, spreading blame like fertilizer on everybody from Budd to Kathleen Sullivan, and then flying home on bitter wings.

—They were in the eyes of American sprinter Evelyn Ashford, who crossed the finish line first in the 100-meter dash, jogged 10 more paces, then had victory physically slap her in the face, spin her in a circle, double her over. So long had Ashford had a vise to her temples—the sum of fret and fear that comes from chasing something for eight years—that when it was finally loosened, it hurt.

—They were not in the capital-gains brain of Carl Lewis, who insulted us with his Olympic dash for cash, a business proposition that held within it all the spontaneity of a mortgage foreclosure.

Lewis deserved golds not only for his speed and talent for sustaining long chunks of time without touching the ground, but for his marketing strategy. Here was Lewis winning the 100-meter dash, then searching the stands for an American flag. One was not simply handed to him—as one was to American figure skater Scott Hamilton as Hamilton celebrated his Winter Olympic victory at Sarajevo, Yugoslavia. No, Lewis went seven rows up for one. And not a $5 flag, either. A huge, American Legion convention job. Does this guy know a magazine cover shot when he sees one?

He does. Although he had no time to talk to America through the print media during the two weeks of athletics, he had time to arrange his own Time magazine cover halfway through. Three golds to go, Carl winked to us from magazine stands. And open the first page, and it reads: "Copyright, Carl Lewis." Next, Carl Lewis, Inc., corners the market on sincerity.

—They were in the coast-to-coast teeth of Mary Lou Retton as she turned a double-twisting double Tsukahara into the arms of her coach, the lovable Transylvanian, Bela Karolyi, both of them awash in the glory of a vaulted 10 when anything less just would not do.

"Little Body!" Karolyi screamed, and Retton, half his size, hugged him and hung there from his neck, drunk with that most wondrous of all things—unexpected glory.

—They were not in the sad answer of Edwin Moses to ABC's Jim Lampley, when asked if now, after 105 straight wins, he could finally retire in peace and satisfaction. "Afraid not," Moses said. He explained that, unfortunately, he has too many years left on endorsement contracts, and although he would prefer to retire at this most fitting moment, well, the lawyers just won't let him and . . . Sigh.

—And, most of all, they were in bursts of emotion that maybe only athletes can understand, to wit:

STEVE LUNDQUIST, 100-meter breaststroke gold-medalist, reaching down to the pool to hug loser John Moffet and try to heal Moffet's injuries to both leg and heart.

—PAM McGEE, conducting an elegant ceremony with her sister, Paula, in which no anthem was played, no flags raised, but the purest of gold medals was awarded.

—MOHAMED RASHWAN, explaining why he hadn't tried to attack the injured leg of gold-medalist Yashuro Yamashita. "That would be against my principles," the Egyptian judo player said. "I don't want to win that way."

And the happiest thing of all is that, thanks to the Rashwans and Rettons of the world, when you do find your Olympics, you get to lock them away forever.

OLYMPIC LASER SHOW

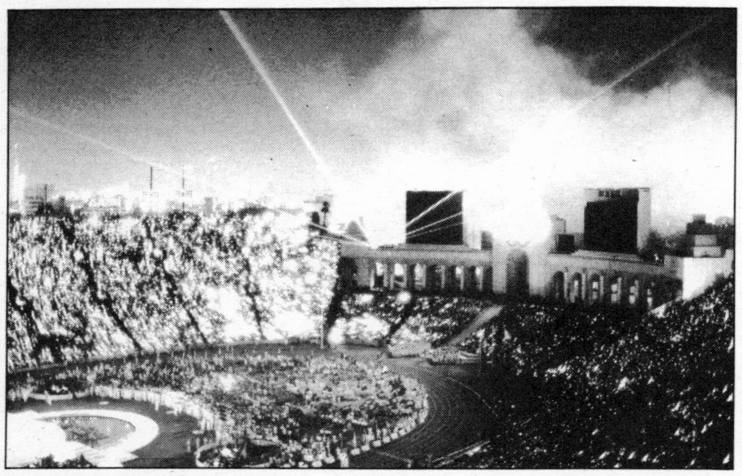

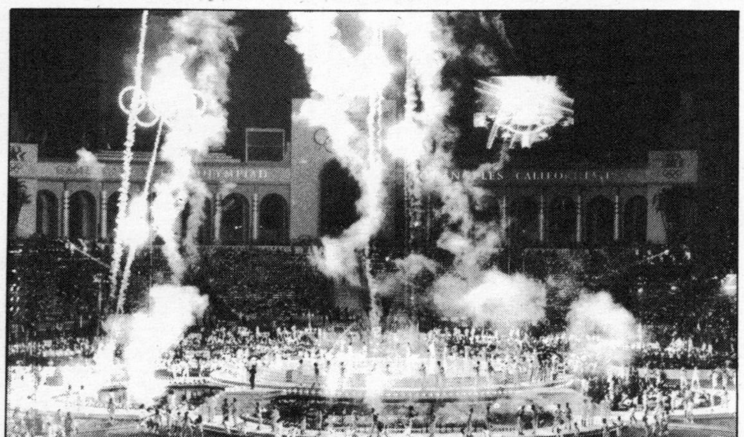

BOB CHAMBERLIN and RICK MEYER / Los Angeles Times

Laser lights (top), a spaceship (middle) and fireworks help close the Olympic Games.

Alan Greenberg / Impressions

U.S. Won; Deck Was Stacked

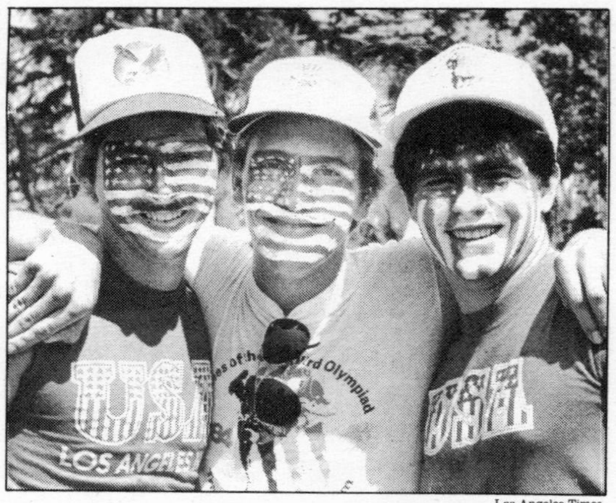

Los Angeles Times

U.S. fans quickly took up the spirit of the Games, painted faces and all, and seemed to love all the gold medals by the U.S.

Covering the Olympics enriched me in many ways, but it also robbed me of something precious, something I hope I'll recapture in time:

Taking pleasure in hearing "The Star-Spangled Banner."

No more chills. No more goose bumps. Just bleeecch. Enough already.

No, I'm not a Commie pinko, although I would have loved hearing the Soviet anthem—a bunch of times, in fact—at the medal ceremonies these last two weeks.

Please don't tell me to go live in Russia. I've seen a bit of the world, and I think our slice of it is the best.

I thought so when I was a college freshman at Syracuse University in 1970, even after four of my peers at Kent State were killed by national guardsmen. I thought so when I was building barricades in freezing weather to keep ROTC supplies off campus.

I thought so through Vietnam, and Watergate, and every other mess we've gotten ourselves into. To me, you love your country like you love your children. You criticize it when you think it does wrong, because you want it to be better, stronger.

Our country is not necessarily any stronger with the end of these Olympics. But it is smugger.

For that, we can thank ABC-TV and the Eastern Bloc boycott. ABC paid $225 million to televise this shindig, and it never promised to be objective, although that responsibility is implicit in journalism. At the 1984 Olympics, the network ballyhooed every U.S. medal-winner, while burying the achievements of many a foreigner.

ABC's jingoistic approach exacerbated an already lopsided situation caused by the absence of the boycotting nations. West Germany's Michael Gross aside, from the moment the swimming competition kicked off the Games, I felt as though we were invading Grenada over and over again. It was overkill that might have even given Dirty Harry pause. Who says Americans like a fair fight?

Not that some good, from the U.S. viewpoint, didn't come out of the boycott. Without the Soviets and friends, the United States won a lot of medals it wouldn't have had a chance at otherwise. That windfall translates into more American heroes. More publicity. More incentive for U.S. corporations to sponsor grass-roots programs. And therefore, a greater spur to thousands of American kids, tomorrow's Olympians.

Another good thing: If the boycotters had shown up, the United States might well have gotten its butt kicked. All of which, incidentally, matters a lot more to the spectators, who live vicariously, than to the athletes.

Times reporters interviewed hundreds of Olympians before and after their competition. They probably didn't find five who didn't have deep respect for the skills and sacrifices made by their rivals to reach the Olympics, whatever their nation. Within their select fraternity, athletes—like surgeons, like stone masons, and yes, like sports-writers—know the price you pay.

Perhaps you, as a U.S. fan and citizen, are repulsed at the thought of hugging or honoring a Soviet. No U.S. athlete is. Under the skin, you are not the U.S. athlete's brother; his rival is.

As you read this, many top American track and field athletes are leaving to compete in Europe. There, some will lose to Soviet Bloc competitors. They know this, but still they go.

Sure, they go because there is appearance money to be made. But they go for love of competition, competition that hasn't been arbitrarily muted or destroyed by international politics.

And they also go, Olympic gold medals safely tucked away, because they know there is no feeling more hollow than to be called great by those incapable of distinguishing greatness from mediocrity.

They go because they know, as we all should, that the greatest sin in life is not failing, but failing to try.

In four years, the Olympic world will try again, at Seoul, South Korea, a nation whose existence the Soviet Union doesn't recognize.

Will there ever be another Olympics unstained by boycott? Who knows? All I know is that the most disappointed I've been, after 11 years in newspapering, was when a colleague awakened me on the morning of May 8 and said, "The Russians aren't coming, the Russians aren't coming."

I like a fair fight, but all too often, the Games of the 23rd Olympiad, while a wonderful show, were rarely that. I am thankful for what we had.

But, oh, what might have been.

THE CHAMPIONS

One More Look at the 1984 Medal Winners

SEO HYANG SOON

ARCHERY

Men's
GOLD—Darrell Pace, Hamilton, Ohio
SILVER—Richard McKinney, Glendale, Ariz.
BRONZE—Hiroshi Yamamoto, Japan

Women's
GOLD—Seo Hyang Soon, South Korea
SILVER—Li Lingjuan, China
BRONZE—Kim Jin Ho, South Korea

BOXING

Light-Flyweights
GOLD—Paul Gonzales, Los Angeles
SILVER—Salvatore Todisco, Italy
BRONZE—Keith Mwila, Zambia, and Jose Bolivar, Venezuela

Flyweights
GOLD—Steve McCrory, Detroit
SILVER—Redzep Redzepovski, Yugoslavia
BRONZE—Eyup Can, Turkey, and Ibrahim Bilali, Kenya

Bantamweights
GOLD—Maurizio Stecca, Italy
SILVER—Hector Lopez, Mexico
BRONZE—Dale Walters, Canada, and Pedro Nolasco, Dominican Republic

Featherweights
GOLD—Meldrick Taylor, Philadelphia
SILVER—Peter Konyegwachie, Nigeria
BRONZE—Omar Catari Peraza, Venezuela, and Turgut Aykac, Turkey

Lightweights
GOLD—Pernell Whitaker, Norfolk, Va.
SILVER—Luis Ortiz, Puerto Rico
BRONZE—Martin Ndongo Ebanga, Cameroon, and Chun Chil Sung, South Korea

Light-Welterweights
GOLD—Jerry Page, Columbus, Ohio
SILVER—Dhawee Umponmaha, Thailand
BRONZE—Mirk Puzovic, Yugoslavia, and Mircea Fulger, Romania

Welterweights
GOLD—Mark Breland, Brooklyn, N.Y.
SILVER—An Young Su, South Korea
BRONZE—Joni Nyman, Finland, and Luciano Bruno, Italy

Light-Middleweights
GOLD—Frank Tate, Detroit
SILVER—Shawn O'Sullivan, Canada
BRONZE—Manfred Zielonka, West Germany, and Christophe Tiozzo, France

Middleweights
GOLD—Shin Joon Sup, South Korea
SILVER—Virgil Hill, Williston, N.D.
BRONZE—Mohamed Zaoui, Algeria, and Aristides Gonzalez, Puerto Rico

Light-Heavyweight
GOLD—Anton Josipovic, Yugoslavia
SILVER—Kevin Barry, New Zealand
BRONZE—Mustapha Moussa, Algeria, and Evander Holyfield, Atlanta

Heavyweights
GOLD—Henry Tillman, Los Angeles
SILVER—Willie deWit, Canada
BRONZE—Arnold Vanderlijde, Netherlands, and Angelo Musone, Italy

Super-Heavyweight
GOLD—Tyrell Biggs, Philadelphia
SILVER—Francesco Damiani, Italy
BRONZE—Robert Wells, Great Britain, and Salihu Azis, Yugoslavia

STEVEN McCRORY

CYCLING

Men

4,000-meter Individual Pursuit
GOLD—Steve Hegg, Dana Point
SILVER—Rolf Golz, West Germany
BRONZE—Leonard Harvey Nitz, Sacramento

Individual Road Race
GOLD—Alexi Grewal, Aspen, Colo.
SILVER—Steve Bauer, Canada
BRONZE—Dag Otto Lauritzen, Norway

1,000-Meter Time Trials
GOLD—Fredy Schmidtke, West Germany
SILVER—Curtis Harnett, Canada
BRONZE—Fabrice Colas, France

4,000-meter Team Pursuit
GOLD—Australia
SILVER—United States
BRONZE—West Germany

Sprint
GOLD—Mark Gorski, La Jolla
SILVER—Nelson Vails, New York
BRONZE—Tsutomu Sakamoto, Japan

Points Race
GOLD—Roger Ilegems, Belgium
SILVER—Uwe Messerschmidt, West Germany
BRONZE—Jose Manuel Youshimatz, Mexico

100-Kilometer Road Team Trials
GOLD—Italy
SILVER—Switzerland
BRONZE—United States

Women

Individual Road Race
GOLD—Connie Carpenter-Phinney, Boulder, Colo.
SILVER—Rebecca Twigg, Seattle
BRONZE—Sandra Schumacher, West Germany

ALEXI GREWAL

FENCING

Men

Individual Epee
GOLD—Philippe Boisse, France
SILVER—Bjorne Vaggo, Sweden
BRONZE—Philippe Riboud, France

Individual Foil
GOLD—Mauro Numa, Italy
SILVER—Matthias Behr, West Germany
BRONZE—Stefano Cerioni, Italy

Individual Saber
GOLD—Jean-Francois Lamour, France
SILVER—Marco Marin, Italy
BRONZE—Peter Westbrook, New York

Team Foil
GOLD—Italy
SILVER—West Germany
BRONZE—France

Team Sabre
GOLD—Italy
SILVER—France
BRONZE—Romania

Team Epee
GOLD—West Germany
SILVER—France
BRONZE—Italy

Women

Individual Foil
GOLD—Luan Jujie, China
SILVER—Cornelia Hanisch, West Germany
BRONZE—Dorina Vaccaroni, Italy

Team Foil
GOLD—West Germany
SILVER—Romania
BRONZE—France

U.S. WOMEN

BASKETBALL

Men's
GOLD—United States
SILVER—Spain
BRONZE—Yugoslavia

Women's
GOLD—United States
SILVER—South Korea
BRONZE—China

CANOEING AND KAYAKING

Men's

500-meter Kayak Singles
GOLD—Ian Ferguson, New Zealand
SILVER—Lars-Erik Moberg, Sweden
BRONZE—Bernard Bregeon, France

500-meter Canoeing Singles
GOLD—Larry Cain, Canada
SILVER—Henning Jakobsen, Denmark
BRONZE—Costica Olaru, Romania

500-meter Kayak Doubles
GOLD—New Zealand
SILVER—Sweden
BRONZE—Canada

500-meter Canoeing Doubles
GOLD—Yugoslavia
SILVER—Romania
BRONZE—Spain

1,000-meter Kayak Singles
GOLD—Alan Thompson, New Zealand
SILVER—Milan Janic, Yugoslavia
BRONZE—Greg Barton, Homer, Mich.

1,000-meter Canoeing Singles
GOLD—Ulrich Eicke, West Germany
SILVER—Larry Cain, Canada
BRONZE—Henning Jakobsen, Denmark

1,000-meter Kayak Doubles
GOLD—Canada
SILVER—France
BRONZE—Australia

1,000-meter Canoeing Doubles
GOLD—Romania
SILVER—Yugoslavia
BRONZE—France

1,000-meter Kayak Fours
GOLD—New Zealand
SILVER—Sweden
BRONZE—France

Women's

500-meters Kayak Singles
GOLD—Agneta Andersson, Sweden
SILVER—Barbara Schuttpelz, West Germany
BRONZE—Annemiek Derckx, Netherlands

500-meter Kayak Doubles
GOLD—Sweden
SILVER—Canada
BRONZE—West Germany

500-meter Kayak Fours
GOLD—Romania
SILVER—Sweden
BRONZE—Canada

EQUESTRIAN

Three-Day Event
Individual
GOLD—Mark Todd, New Zealand
SILVER—Karen Stives, Dover, Mass.
BRONZE—Virginia Holgate, Britain

Team
GOLD—United States
SILVER—Britain
BRONZE—West Germany

Team Jumping
GOLD—United States
SILVER—Britain
BRONZE—West Germany

Individual Dressage
GOLD—Dr. Reiner Klimke, West Germany
SILVER—Anne Jensen, Denmark
BRONZE—Otto Hofer, Switzerland

Team Dressage
GOLD—West Germany
SILVER—Switzerland
BRONZE—Sweden

Individual Jumping
GOLD—Joe Fargis, Petersburg, Va.
SILVER—Conrad Homfeld, Petersburg, Va.
BRONZE—Heidi Robbiani, Switzerland

GYMNASTICS

GREG LOUGANIS

Men
All-Around
GOLD—Koji Gushiken, Japan
SILVER—Peter Vidmar, Los Angeles
BRONZE—Li Ning, China

Team
GOLD—United States
SILVER—China
BRONZE—Japan

Floor Exercises
GOLD—Li Ning, China
SILVER—Lou Yun, China
BRONZE—Koji Sotomura, Japan, and Philippe Vatuone, France

Horizontal Bar
GOLD—Shinji Morisue, Japan
SILVER—Tong Fei, China
BRONZE—Koji Gushiken, Japan

Parallel Bars
GOLD—Bart Conner, Morton Grove, Ill.
SILVER—Nobuyuki Kajitani, Japan
BRONZE—Mitch Gaylord, Van Nuys

Side Horse
GOLD—Li Ning, China, and Peter Vidmar, Los Angeles
BRONZE—Tim Daggett, West Springfield, Mass.

Rings
GOLD—Koji Gushiken, Japan, and Li Ning, China
BRONZE—Mitch Gaylord, Van Nuys

Vault
GOLD—Lou Yun, China
SILVER—Koji Gushiken, Japan; Shinji Morisue, Japan; Li Ning, Japan; Mitch Gaylord, Van Nuys

Women
Floor Exercises
GOLD—Ecaterina Szabo, Romania
SILVER—Julie McNamara, San Ramon, Calif.
BRONZE—Mary Lou Retton, Fairmont, W.Va.

Balance Beam
GOLD—Simona Pauca, Romania and Ecaterina Szabo, Romania
BRONZE-Kathy Johnson, Huntington Beach

Vault
GOLD—Ecaterina Szabo, Romania
SILVER—Mary Lou Retton, Fairmont, W.Va.
BRONZE—Lavinia Agache, Romania

Uneven Parallel Bars
GOLD—Ma Yanhong, China and Julianne McNamara, San Ramon, Calif.
BRONZE—Mary Lou Retton, Fairmont, W.Va.

All-Around
GOLD—Mary Lou Retton, Fairmont, W.Va.
SILVER—Ecaterina Szabo, Romania
BRONZE—Simona Pauca, Romania

Team
GOLD—Romania
SILVER—United States
BRONZE—China

Rhythmic
GOLD—Lori Fung, Canada
SILVER—Doina Staiculescu, Romania
BRONZE—Regina Weber, West Germany

JULIANNE McNAMARA

DIVING

Men's
Platform
GOLD—Greg Louganis, Mission Viejo
SILVER—Bruce Kimball, Ann Arbor, Mich.
BRONZE—Li Kongzheng, China

Springboard
GOLD—Greg Louganis, Mission Viejo
SILVER—Tan Liangde, China
BRONZE—Ron Merriott, Ann Arbor, Mich.

Women's
Platform
GOLD—Zhou Jihong, China
SILVER—Michele Mitchell, Mission Viejo
BRONZE—Wendy Wyland, Mission Viejo

Springboard
GOLD—Sylvie Bernier, Canada
SILVER—Kelly McCormick, Columbus, Ohio
BRONZE—Chris Seufert, Ann Arbor, Mich.

HITOSHI SAITO, LEFT, THROWS ANGELO PARISI

MODERN PENTATHLON

Team
GOLD—Italy
SILVER—United States
BRONZE—France

Individual
GOLD—Daniele Masala, Italy
SILVER—Svante Rasmuson, Sweden
BRONZE—Carlos Massullo, Italy

SOCCER

GOLD—France
SILVER—Brazil
BRONZE—Yugoslavia

WATER POLO

GOLD—Yugoslavia
SILVER—United States
BRONZE—West Germany

FIELD HOCKEY

Men's
GOLD—Pakistan
SILVER—West Germany
BRONZE—Great Britain

Women's
GOLD—Netherlands
SILVER—West Germany
BRONZE—United States

JUDO

Lightweights
GOLD—Ahn Byeong Keun, South Korea
SILVER—Ezio Gamba, Italy
BRONZE—Kerrith Brown, Britain and Luis Onmura, Brazil

Extra-Lightweight
GOLD—Shinji Hosokawa, Japan
SILVER—Kim Jae Yup, South Korea
BRONZE—Eddie Liddie, Colorado Springs, Colo. and Neil Eckersley, Britain.

Half-Lightweights
GOLD—Yoshiyuki Matsuoka, Japan
SILVER—Hwang Jung Oh, South Korea
BRONZE—Marc Alexandre, France and Josef Reiter, Austria

Half-Middleweights
GOLD—Frank Wieneke, West Germany
SILVER—Neil Adams, Britain
BRONZE—Michel Nowak, France and Mircea Fratica, Romania

Middleweights
GOLD—Peter Seisenbacher, Austria
SILVER—Robert Berland, Wilmette, Ill.
BRONZE—Seiki Nose, Japan, and Walter Carmona, Brazil

Half-Heavyweights
GOLD—Ha Hyoung Zoo, South Korea
SILVER—Douglas Vieira, Brazil
BRONZE—Bjarni Fridriksson, Iceland and Gunter Neureuther, West Germany

Heavyweights
GOLD—Hitoshi Saito, Japan
SILVER—Angelo Parisi, France
BRONZE—Cho Yong Chul, South Korea and Mark Berger, Canada

Open Category
GOLD—Yasuhiro Yamashita, Japan
SILVER—Mohamed Rashwan, Egypt
BRONZE—Mihai Cioc, Romania, and Arthur Schnabel, West Germany

TEAM HANDBALL

Men's
GOLD—Yugoslavia
SILVER—West Germany
BRONZE—Romania

Women's
GOLD—Yugoslavia
SILVER—South Korea
BRONZE—China

ROWING

MEN

Single Sculls
GOLD—Pertti Karppinen, Finland
SILVER—Peter-Michael Kolbe, West Germany
BRONZE—Robert Mills, Canada

Double Sculls
GOLD—United States
SILVER—Belgium
BRONZE—Yugoslavia

Quadruple Sculls
GOLD—West Germany
SILVER—Australia
BRONZE—Canada

Pairs With Coxswain
GOLD—Italy
SILVER—Romania
BRONZE—United States

Pairs Without Coxswain
GOLD—Romania
SILVER—Spain
BRONZE—Norway

Fours With Coxswain
GOLD—Britain
SILVER—United States
BRONZE—New Zealand

Fours Without Coxswain
GOLD—New Zealand
SILVER—United States
BRONZE—Denmark

Eights With Coxswain
GOLD—Canada
SILVER—United States
BRONZE—Australia

WOMEN

Single Sculls
GOLD—Valerie Racila, Romania
SILVER—Charlotte Geer, West Fairlee, Vt.
BRONZE—Ann Haesebrouck, Belgium

Double Sculls
GOLD—Romania
SILVER—Netherlands
BRONZE—Canada

Quadruple Sculls With Coxswain
GOLD—Romania
SILVER—United States
BRONZE—Denmark

Pairs Without Coxswain
GOLD—Romania
SILVER—Canada
BRONZE—West Germany

Fours With Coxswain
GOLD—Romania
SILVER—Canada
BRONZE—Australia

Eights
GOLD—United States
SILVER—Romania
BRONZE—Netherlands

TRACK AND FIELD / MEN

Men's
100 Meters
GOLD—Carl Lewis, Houston
SILVER—Sam Graddy, Atlanta
BRONZE—Ben Johnson, Canada

200 Meters
GOLD—Carl Lewis, Houston
SILVER—Kirk Baptiste, Beaumont, Texas
BRONZE—Thomas Jefferson, Cleveland

400 Meters
GOLD—Alonzo Babers, Montgomery, Ala.
SILVER—Gabriel Tiacoh, Ivory Coast
BRONZE—Antonio McKay, Atlanta

800 Meters
GOLD—Joaquim Cruz, Brazil
SILVER—Sebastian Coe, Great Britain
BRONZE—Earl Jones, Inkster, Mich.

1,500 Meters
GOLD—Sebastian Coe, Great Britain
SILVER—Steve Cram, Great Britain
BRONZE—Jose Abascal, Spain

3,000-Meter Steeplechase
GOLD—Julius Korir, Kenya
SILVER—Joseph Mahmoud, France
BRONZE—Brian Diemer, Grand Rapids, Mich.

5,000 Meters
GOLD—Said Aouita, Morocco
SILVER—Markus Ryffel, Switzerland
BRONZE—Antonio Leitao, Portugal

10,000 Meters
GOLD—Alberto Cova, Italy
SILVER—Martti Vainio, Finland
BRONZE—Michael McLeod, Britain

Marathon
GOLD—Carlos Lopes, Portugal
SILVER—John Treacy, Ireland
BRONZE—Charlie Spedding, Britain

110-Meter Hurdles
GOLD—Roger Kingdom, Pittsburgh
SILVER—Greg Foster, Los Angeles
BRONZE—Arto Bryggare, Finland

400-Meter Hurdles
GOLD—Edwin Moses, Laguna Hills
SILVER—Danny Harris, Perris, Calif.
BRONZE—Harald Schmid, West Germany

400-Meter Relay
GOLD—United States
SILVER—Jamaica
BRONZE—Canada

1,600-Meter Relay
GOLD—United States
SILVER—Britain
BRONZE—Nigeria

20-Kilometer Walk
GOLD—Ernesto Canto, Mexico
SILVER—Raul Gonzalez, Mexico
BRONZE—Maurizio Damilano, Italy

CARL LEWIS TIMES FOUR GOLD MEDALS

50-Kilometer Walk
GOLD—Raul Gonzalez, Mexico
SILVER—Bo Gustafsson, Sweden
BRONZE—Sandro Bellucci, Italy

High Jump
GOLD—Dietmar Mogenburg, West Germany
SILVER—Patrik Sjoberg, Sweden
BRONZE—Zhu Jianhua, China

Pole Vault
GOLD—Pierre Quinon, France
SILVER—Mike Tully, Encino
BRONZE—Thierry Vigneron, France, and Earl Bell, Jonesboro, Ark.

Long Jump
GOLD—Carl Lewis, Houston
SILVER—Gary Honey, Australia
BRONZE—Giovanni Evangelisti, Italy

Triple Jump
GOLD—Al Joyner, East St. Louis, Ill.
SILVER—Mike Conley, Chicago
BRONZE—Keith Conner, Britain

Decathlon
GOLD—Daley Thompson, Britain
SILVER—Juergen Hingsen, West Germany
BRONZE—Siegfried Wentz, West Germany

Discus
GOLD—Rolf Danneberg, West Germany
SILVER—Mac Wilkins, San Jose
BRONZE—John Powell, Cupertino, Calif.

Hammer Throw
GOLD—Juha Tiainen, Finland
SILVER—Karl-Hans Riehm, West Germany
BRONZE—Klaus Ploghaus, West Germany

High Jump
GOLD—Dietmar Mogenburg, West Germany
SILVER—Patrik Sjoberg, Sweden
BRONZE—Zhu Jianhua, China

Javelin
GOLD—Arto Haerkoenen, Finland
SILVER—David Ottley, Britain
BRONZE—Kenth Eldebrink, Sweden

TRACK AND FIELD / WOMEN

Women's
100 Meters
GOLD—Evelyn Ashford, Los Angeles
SILVER—Alice Brown, Altadena
BRONZE—Merlene Ottey-Page, Jamaica

200 Meters
GOLD—Valerie Brisco-Hooks, Los Angeles
SILVER—Florence Griffith, Los Angeles
BRONZE—Merlene Ottey-Page, Jamaica

400 Meters
GOLD—Valerie Brisco-Hooks, Los Angeles
SILVER—Chandra Cheeseborough, Jacksonville, Fla.
BRONZE—Kathryn Cook, Britain

800 Meters
GOLD—Doina Melinte, Romania
SILVER—Kim Gallagher, Santa Monica
BRONZE—Fita Lovin, Romania

1,500 meters
GOLD—Gabriella Dorio, Italy
SILVER—Doina Melinte, Romania
BRONZE—Maricica Puica, Romania

3,000 Meters
GOLD—Maricica Puica, Romania
SILVER—Wendy Sly, Britain
BRONZE—Lynn Williams, Canada

Marathon
GOLD—Joan Benoit, Freeport, Maine
SILVER—Grete Waitz, Norway
BRONZE—Rosa Mota, Portugal

100-Meter Hurdles
GOLD—Benita Fitzgerald-Brown, Dale City, Va.
SILVER—Shirley Strong, Britain
BRONZE—Kim Turner, Detroit

400-Meter Hurdles
GOLD—Nawal El Moutawakil, Morocco
SILVER—Judi Brown, East Lansing, Mich.
BRONZE—Cristina Cojocaru, Romania

400-Meter Relay
GOLD—United States
SILVER—Canada
BRONZE—Britain

1,600-Meter Relay
GOLD—United States
SILVER—Canada
BRONZE—West Germany

High Jump
GOLD—Ulrike Meyfarth, West Germany
SILVER—Sara Simeoni, Italy
BRONZE—Joni Huntley, Portland, Ore.

Long Jump
GOLD—Anisoara Stanciu, Romania
SILVER—Vali Ionescu, Romania
BRONZE—Susan Hearnshaw, Britain

Shotput
GOLD—Claudia Loch, West Germany
SILVER—Mihaela Loghin, Romania
BRONZE—Gael Martin, Australia

Discus
GOLD—Ria Stalman, Netherlands
SILVER—Leslie Deniz, Gridley, Ariz.
BRONZE—Florenta Craciunescu, Romania

Javelin
GOLD—Tessa Sanderson, Britain
SILVER—Tiina Lillak, Finland
BRONZE—Fatima Whitbread, Britain

Heptathlon
GOLD—Glynis Nunn, Australia
SILVER—Jackie Joyner, East St. Louis, Ill.
BRONZE—Sabine Everts, West Germany

VALERIE BRISCO-HOOKS

SWIMMING

MEN

100-Meter Freestyle
GOLD—Rowdy Gaines, Winter Haven, Fla.
SILVER—Mark Stockwell, Australia
BRONZE—Per Johansson, Sweden

200-Meter Freestyle
GOLD—Michael Gross, West Germany
SILVER—Mike Heath, Dallas
BRONZE—Thomas Fahrner, W. Germany

400-Meter Freestyle
GOLD—George DiCarlo, Denver
SILVER—John Mykkanen, Placentia, Calif.
BRONZE—Justin Lemberg, Australia

1,500-meter Freestyle
GOLD—Mike O'Brien, Mission Viejo
SILVER—George DiCarlo, Denver
BRONZE—Stefan Pfeiffer, W. Germany

100-Meter Backstroke
GOLD—Rick Carey, Mount Kisco, N.Y.
SILVER—David Wilson, Cincinnati
BRONZE—Mike West, Canada

200-Meter Backstroke
GOLD—Rick Carey, Mount Kisco, N.Y.
SILVER—Frederic Delcourt, France
BRONZE—Cameron Henning, Canada

100-Meter Breaststroke
GOLD—Steve Lundquist, Jonesboro, Ga.
SILVER—Victor Davis, Canada
BRONZE—Peter Evans, Australia

200-Meter Breaststroke
GOLD—Victor Davis, Canada
SILVER—Glenn Beringen, Australia
BRONZE—Etienne Dagon, Switzerland

100-Meter Butterfly
GOLD—Michael Gross, West Germany
SILVER—Pablo Morales, Santa Clara
BRONZE—Glenn Buchanan, Australia

200-Meter Butterfly
GOLD—Jon Sieben, Australia
SILVER—Michael Gross, West Germany
BRONZE—Rafael Vidal, Venezuela

200-Meter Individual Medley
GOLD—Alex Baumann, Canada
SILVER—Pablo Morales, Santa Clara
BRONZE—Neil Cochran, Britain

400-Meter Individual Medley
GOLD—Alex Baumann, Canada
SILVER—Ricardo Prado, Brazil
BRONZE—Rob Woodhouse, Australia

800-Meter Freestyle Relay
GOLD—United States
SILVER—West Germany
BRONZE—Britain

1,600-Meter Freestyle Relay
GOLD—United States
SILVER—Australia
BRONZE—Sweden

400-Meter Medley Relay
GOLD—United States
SILVER—Canada
BRONZE—Australia

WOMEN

100-Meter Freestyle
GOLD—Carrie Steinseifer, Saratoga, Calif. and Nancy Hogshead, Jacksonville, Fla.
BRONZE—Annemarie Verstappen, Netherlands

200-Meter Freestyle
GOLD—Mary Wayte, Mercer Is., Wash.
SILVER—Cynthia Woodhead, Riverside
BRONZE—Annemarie Verstappen, Netherlands

800-Meter Freestyle
GOLD—Tiffany Cohen, Mission Viejo
SILVER—Michele Richardson, Miami
BRONZE—Sarah Hardcastle, Britain

400-Meter Freestyle
GOLD—Tiffany Cohen, Mission Viejo
SILVER—Sarah Hardcastle, Britain
BRONZE—June Croft, Britain

100-Meter Backstroke
GOLD—Theresa Andrews, Annapolis, Md.
SILVER—Betsy Mitchell, Marietta, Ohio
BRONZE—Jolanda De Rover, Netherlands

200-Meter Backstroke
GOLD—Jolanda De Rover, Netherlands
SILVER—Amy White, Mission Viejo
BRONZE—Anca Patrascoiu, Romania

100-Meter Breaststroke
GOLD—Petra Van Staveren, Netherlands
SILVER—Anne Ottenbrite, Canada
BRONZE—Catherine Poirot, France

200-Meter Breaststroke
GOLD—Anne Ottenbrite, Canada
SILVER—Susan Rapp, Eden Prairie, Minn.
BRONZE—Ingrid Lempereur, Belgium

100-Meter Butterfly
GOLD—Mary T. Meagher, Louisville, Ky.
SILVER—Jenna Johnson, La Habra
BRONZE—Karin Seick, West Germany

200-Meter Butterfly
GOLD—Mary T. Meagher, Louisville, Ky.
SILVER—Karen Phillips, Australia
BRONZE—Ina Bayermann, West Germany

200-Meter Individual Medley
GOLD—Tracy Caulkins, Nashville, Tenn.
SILVER—Nancy Hogshead, Jacksonville, Fla.
BRONZE—Michele Pearson, Australia

400-Meter Individual Medley
GOLD—Tracy Caulkins, Nashville, Tenn.
SILVER—Suzanne Landells, Australia
BRONZE—Petra Zindler, West Germany

400-Meter Freestyle Relay
GOLD—United States
SILVER—Netherlands
BRONZE—West Germany

400-Meter Medley Relay
GOLD—United States
SILVER—West Germany
BRONZE—Canada